The Stalin Cult in East Germany and the Making of the Postwar Soviet Empire, 1945–1961

THE HARVARD COLD WAR STUDIES BOOK SERIES

Series Editor: Mark Kramer, Harvard University

Recent Titles in the Series

The Stalin Cult in East Germany and the Making of the Postwar Soviet Empire, 1945–1961
Alexey Tikhomirov

Mao and the Sino-Soviet Partnership, 1945–1959: A New History
Zhihua Shen and Yafeng Xia

The Soviet Union and the Horn of Africa during the Cold War: Between Ideology and Pragmatism
Radoslav A. Yordanov

The Power of Dynamic Détente Policies: U.S. Diplomacy between the Military Status Quo and the Transformation of Europe, 1964–1975
Stephan Kieninger

The Tito–Stalin Split and Yugoslavia's Military Opening toward the West, 1950–1954: In NATO's Backyard
Ivan Laković and Dmitar Tasić

Bridging the Baltic Sea: Networks of Resistance and Opposition during the Cold War Era
Lars Fredrik Stöcker

US–Spanish Relations after Franco, 1975–1989: The Will of the Weak
Morten Heiberg

Stalin's Legacy in Romania: The Hungarian Autonomous Region, 1952–1960
Stefano Bottoni

Mao and the Sino-Soviet Split, 1959–1973: A New History
Danhui Li and Yafeng Xia

A Cold War over Austria: The Struggle for the State Treaty, Neutrality, and the End of East-West Occupation, 1945–1955
Gerald Stourzh and Wolfgang Mueller

The Soviet Invasion of Czechoslovakia in 1968: The Russian Perspective
Edited by Josef Pazderka

Stalin's Double-Edged Game: Soviet Bureaucracy and the Raoul Wallenberg Case, 1945–1952
Johan Matz

The Red Army in Austria: The Soviet Occupation, 1945–1955
Edited by Stefan Karner and Barbara Stelzl-Marx

The Hungarian Agricultural Miracle?: Sovietization and Americanization in a Communist Country
Zsuzsanna Varga

Soviet Policy in Xinjiang: Stalin and the National Movement in Eastern Turkistan
Jamil Hasanli

The Soviet Union and Cold War Neutrality and Nonalignment in Europe
Edited by Mark Kramer, Aryo Makko, and Peter Ruggenthaler

The Stalin Cult in East Germany and the Making of the Postwar Soviet Empire, 1945–1961

Alexey Tikhomirov
Translated by Jacqueline Friedlander

LEXINGTON BOOKS
Lanham • Boulder • New York • London

Published by Lexington Books
An imprint of The Rowman & Littlefield Publishing Group, Inc.
4501 Forbes Boulevard, Suite 200, Lanham, Maryland 20706
www.rowman.com

86-90 Paul Street, London EC2A 4NE

British Library Cataloguing in Publication Information Available

Library of Congress Cataloging-in-Publication Data

Names: Tikhomirov, Alexey, author.
Title: The Stalin cult in East Germany and the making of the postwar Soviet empire, 1945–1961 / Alexey Tikhomirov.
Description: Lanham : Lexington Books, [2022] | Series: The Harvard Cold War studies book series | Includes bibliographical references and index.
Identifiers: LCCN 2021060793 (print) | LCCN 2021060794 (ebook) | ISBN 9781666911893 (cloth) | ISBN 9781666911909 (ebook)
Subjects: LCSH: Germany (East)—Politics and government. | Stalin, Joseph, 1878–1953—Influence. | Political leadership—Germany (East)—History. | Communism—Germany (East)—History. | Political culture—Germany (East)—History. | Political rehabilitation—Germany (East) | Post-communism—Germany (East)
Classification: LCC DD283 .T55 2022 (print) | LCC DD283 (ebook) | DDC 943/.1087—dc23/eng/20220105
LC record available at https://lccn.loc.gov/2021060793
LC ebook record available at https://lccn.loc.gov/2021060794

For Cecilia

Contents

List of Figures   ix

Acknowledgments   xi

Abbreviations   xiii

Introduction   1

1   Father of the People, Face of the Nation: The Premodern and Modern Foundations of Personality Cults   29

2   The Empire of Stalinism: The USSR and East Germany after 1945   47

3   From the "Red Tyrant" to the "Liberator": The Image of Stalin in the Soviet Occupation Zone of Germany   73

4   "The Best Friend of the German People": The Making of the Cult Community in the GDR   141

5   "The Fierce Enemy of the German People": The Personality Cult and Iconoclasm in East Germany   241

6   "We Wanted to Make a God but He Turned Out to Be the Devil": The Politics and Practices of De-Stalinization in the GDR   269

Conclusion   307

Bibliography   317

Index   361

About the Author   369

List of Figures

Figure I.1 Nazi propaganda poster showing Stalin as the embodiment of the Jewish-Bolshevik threat, 1941–1944. 3

Figure I.2 "Stalin—This Is Peace!": socialist propaganda of "the best friend of the German people" in the GDR, 1952. 4

Figure I.3 GDR poster: "Working day of two worlds. Two ways, two worlds—we have decided, German-Soviet friendship means prosperity and peace." Ca. 1950. 6

Figure 3.1 Red Army soldiers celebrating the victory. Early May 1945. 76

Figure 3.2 "Generalissimo I. V Stalin": Unter den Linden, East Berlin. 1945. 79

Figure 3.3 GDR poster: "Our path to peace and prosperity: German-Soviet friendship ruins all the arsonist's plans to start a war." 1950. 81

Figure 3.4 Including Ernst Thälmann's cult in the Stalin cult: a meeting about renaming the Krupp Factory in Magdeburg as the Ernst-Thälmann-Werk. April 30, 1951. 83

Figure 3.5 Wilhelm Pieck, the president of the GDR, with a birthday present—a bust of Stalin. January 3, 1950. 92

Figure 3.6 Anti-Nazi banner in the US sector of Berlin (Neukölln) declaring "That was the reorganization of Europe. 4.5 million antifascists were brutally murdered in Auschwitz alone! Eradicate Nazism, root and branch." Summer 1945. 109

Figure 3.7 A column of marchers in a May First parade holding portraits of the classics of Marxism-Leninism. May 1, 1953. 110

Figure 3.8 Walter Ulbricht, Wilhelm Pieck, and Otto Grotewohl on the reviewing stand at the SED's Fourth Congress, held April 30–May 6, 1954. 113

Figure 4.1   An exhibit about Stalin at a conference of SED state
            delegates held in the House of Workers in Halle/Saale.
            December 1949.   151
Figure 4.2   An FDJ member looks at an item in an exhibition of
            gifts for Stalin held in the House of German-Soviet
            Friendship. December 1950.   158
Figure 4.3   Erich Honecker surrounded by FDJ members at a
            regional conference in Chemnitz. July 6, 1951.   174
Figure 4.4   A demonstration in East Berlin during the Third World
            Youth and Student Games. August 9, 1951.   176
Figure 4.5   GDR leaders at the unveiling of a monument to the
            Soviet leader on the Stalinallee in East Berlin. August
            3, 1951.   190
Figure 4.6   Unveiling a monument to Stalin in Riesa. March 4, 1954.   191
Figure 4.7   Contrasting socialist leaders with their Western
            counterparts: a column marching in a May First
            demonstration in East Berlin, 1951.   193
Figure 4.8   Stigmatizing, deriding, and disgracing the enemies
            of socialism: a demonstration of Young Fighters for
            Peace during the Third Youth and Student World
            Games in East Berlin. August 12, 1951.   194
Figure 4.9   The subjection of public space to the Stalin cult:
            preparations for the Third Youth and Student World
            Games on the Alexanderplatz, East Berlin. July 1951.   195
Figure 4.10 The dramaturgy of the Stalin cult: mourning Stalin's
            death with a funeral march in Leipzig. March 9, 1953.   196
Figure 4.11 GDR poster: "Workers! Be vigilant, seize your
            enemies!" April 1949.   205
Figure 4.12 *Richtfest* at the new high-rise building on Weberwiese.
            January 19, 1952.   213
Figure 5.1   The grande finale of a demonstration celebrating
            the Soviet leader's birthday and the renaming of the
            Frankfurter Allee as the Stalinallee. December 21, 1949.   250
Figure 5.2   Closing ceremonies of the World Youth and Student
            Games in East Berlin. August 19, 1951.   250
Figure 5.3   An incident taking place during the uprising of June
            17, 1953 on Brunnenstrasse in East Berlin.   256
Figure 5.4   An incident taking place during the uprising of June
            17, 1953 on Brunnenstrasse in East Berlin.   257
Figure 6.1   Reviewing stand at the SED's Fifth Congress, held in
            East Berlin, July 10–16, 1958.   292

Acknowledgments

This book is a revised and expanded version of the Russian edition of *"Best Friend of the German People": Stalin's Cult in East Germany (1945–1961)*, which was published in the ROSSPEN series History of Stalinism in 2014. The opportunity to further develop and deepen my monograph for an English-speaking readership became possible at Bielefeld University. I sincerely thank Frank Grüner for his comprehensive support and for a stimulating working environment.

This book is based on my dissertation, "The Image of Stalin in East German Public Opinion (1945–1956)," which I wrote under the supervision of Professor Alexander S. Khodnev at the Iaroslavl' K. D. Ushinskii State Pedagogical University. There I had the great fortune to work and study with Anna Afanas'eva, Lubov' M. Arkhipova, Iulia Barlova, Alexander Eremin, Alexander M. Ermakov, Alexei Khmel'tsov, Natalia Kolgushova, Andrei B. Sokolov, Anna Tikhomirova, and Alexander S. Khodnev. I would like to thank them for their cordiality and support.

Several European academic centers and research-funding bodies provided support for my project. A grant from the Robert Bosch Foundation allowed me to spend a year teaching courses on Russian history and culture at the University of Karlsruhe and to begin collecting primary source materials for my dissertation. Grants from the Institute of European History in Mainz and the German Historical Institute Moscow, the Office of the Minister-President of Thuringia at the University of Jena, the Gerda Henkel Foundation at the Institute for Eastern European History and Area Studies of the University of Tübingen, and the Hertie Foundation at the University of Chemnitz allowed me to continue my research in German archives. I completed the book at the School of Slavonic and East European Studies, University College London. To the heads of these institutions and their researchers, as well as the staffs of the archives I worked in, I would like to express my deep gratitude for their generous support.

The book would not have been possible without the expert advice and collegial support of many scholars whom I had the privilege of meeting on my academic path. At various stages while writing this book, I had important and stimulating conversations with Simone Barck, Christine Bartlitz, Dietrich Beyrau, Victor Dönninghaus, Andrei Doronin, Heinz Duchhardt, Benno Ennker, Alexei Filitov, Jan Foitzik, Monika Gibas, Rainer Gries, Thomas Lindenberger, Rósa Magnúsdóttir, Eva Maurer, Ralph Melville, Stephan Merl, Beate Neuss, Christian Noack, Jan Plamper, Silke Satjukow, Claus Scharf, Susanne Schattenberg, Ingrid Schierle, Annette Schuhmann, Walter Sperling, Alexander Vatlin, and Elena Zubkova.

Having a careful and friendly translator like Kim Friedlander was a real pleasure. I would like to thank her for her fine work.

I would like to thank my parents and relatives for doing everything possible to open up the "big world" that reached far beyond my "small motherland."

Cecilia's love, support, and help—and her confidence in me, without any doubts—have been invaluable. This book is dedicated to her.

Abbreviations

CDU	Christlich Demokratische Union (Christian Democratic Union)
DSF	Gesellschaft für Deutsch-Sowjetische Freundschaft (German-Soviet Friendship Society)
FDJ	Freie Deutsche Jugend (Union of Free German Youth)
GDR	German Democratic Republic (Deutsche Demokratische Republik)
Glavlit	Glavnoe upravlenie po delam literatury i izdatel'stv (General Directorate of Literature and Publishing)
KPD	Kommunistische Partei Deutschlands
KPSS	Kommunisticheskaia partiia Sovetskogo Soiuza (Communist Party of the Soviet Union)
MGB	Ministerstvo gosudarstvennoi bezopasnosti (Ministry of State Security)
MID	Ministerstvo inostrannykh del (Ministry of Foreign Affairs)
MK	Mezhdunarodnaia Kniga (International Book)
NKVD	Narodnyi komissariat vnutrennykh del (People's Commissariat for Internal Affairs)
NSDAP	Nationalsozialistische Deutsche Arbeiterpartei (National Socialist German Workers Party)
OVP	Otdel vneshnei politiki (the Soviet Central Committee's Department of Foreign Policy)
RIAS	Rundfunk im amerikanischen Sektor (Radio in the American Sector)
SED	Sozialistische Einheitspartei Deutschland (Socialist Unity Party)
SIB	Sovinformbiuro (Soviet Information Bureau)
SKK	Sowjetische Kontrollkommission (Soviet Control Commission)

SPD   Sozialdemokratische Partei Deutschlands (German
            Social Democratic Party)
SVAG   Sovetskaia voennaia administratsiia v Germanii (Soviet
            Military Administration in Germany)
TASS   Telegrafnoe agentstvo Sovetskogo Soiuza (Telegraph
            Agency of the Soviet Union)
TsK   Tsentral'nyi komitet (Central Committee)
VKP(b)   Vsesoiuznaia kommunisticheskaia partiia (bol'sheviki)
            (All-Union Communist Party of Bolsheviks)
VOKS   Vsesoiuznoe obshchestvo kul'turnykh sviazei s
            zagranitsei (All-Union Society for Cultural Relations
            with Foreign Countries)

Introduction

On February 18, 1943, the auditorium of the Berlin Sports Palace was filled to capacity. Joseph Goebbels, the Nazi minister of propaganda, stood at the microphone. His task was anything but simple. He had to raise the Nazis' spirits after their shattering defeat at Stalingrad and inspire the masses to continue the war. To mobilize all available resources and strengthen declining faith in the Führer, Goebbels presented the complicated situation at the front as a question of life and death, not just for the German nation but for European civilization as a whole. Goebbels called on the country to engage in total war against the "barbaric, Jewish-Bolshevik threat" embodied by Joseph Stalin:

> Bolshevism has always proclaimed its goal openly: to bring revolution not only to Europe, but also to the entire world, and plunge it into Bolshevist chaos. This goal has been evident from the beginning of the Bolshevist Soviet Union, and has been the ideological and practical goal of the Kremlin's policies. . . . This is a direct threat to every European power. No one should believe that Bolshevism would stop at the borders of the Reich, were it to be victorious, because of a treaty on paper. The goal of its aggressive policies and wars is the Bolshevization of every land and people in the world.... The German people, in any event, are unwilling to bow to this danger. Behind the oncoming Soviet divisions we see the Jewish liquidation commandos and behind them terror, the specter of mass starvation and complete anarchy in Europe. International Jewry is the devilish ferment of decomposition that finds cynical satisfaction in plunging the world into the deepest chaos and destroying ancient cultures that it played no role in building. . . . With burning hearts and cool heads we will overcome the major problems of this phase of the war. We are on the way to eventual victory. That victory rests on our faith in the Führer. He expects us to

1

do that which will throw all we have done before into the shadows. We do not
want to fail him. As we are proud of him, he should be proud of us.[1]

On December 1, 1949, an article titled "Friendship with Stalin Forever"
was published in the newspaper *Neues Deutschland*, the SED's main print
organ. This text kick-started the official campaign to celebrate the Soviet
leader's seventieth birthday in East Germany. At the same time, the leaders of
the GDR, a propaganda state created on the Soviet model, were trying to get
rid of the Nazi stereotypes that had shaped perceptions of Stalin, while also
making efforts to affirm a new image of the Soviet leader as a "friend, teacher
and guarantor of peace."[2] After Germany's defeat in World War II, a *foreign*
state leader, not *the Germans' own* Führer, was proclaimed the champion of
national pride:

> On December 21, 1949, Generalissimo Stalin, the leader of the peoples of the
> Soviet Union, the most powerful state figure of our time, turns seventy. All
> peace-loving and nationally conscious Germans are taking part in this festive
> day with especially warm feelings. No other foreign political figure in the past
> and the present has had the interests of the German people so close to his heart
> and defended them the way Generalissimo Stalin has. . . . After many errors,
> which we paid for with our blood, may the German people realize what Stalin's
> friendship and likewise the friendship of the Soviet Union means in all its exclu-
> sivity! For Stalin embodies those powerful, progressive social forces which
> today already define the fate of numerous states and, on an ever-increasing
> scale, [the fate] of the entire world. Friendship with Stalin means friendship
> with the mighty Soviet Union, with the people's democracy of China, the
> people's democratic republics of Europe, with the entire large camp of peace
> and progress. . . . Friendship with Stalin is a guarantee of victory, peace and the
> future. . . . In this spirit, on December 21 the thoughts and hopes of countless
> Germans turn to Stalin, who is helping us build up a life of freedom and happi-
> ness in a united, democratic, and peace-loving Germany![3]

In East Germany, in the heart of Europe, exactly twenty years after the Stalin
cult was established in the Soviet Union in 1929, the Soviet leader's seventieth birthday marked the heyday of his cult. Who would have thought that
Germans would bow down to their "sworn enemy" on the former territory of
the Third Reich? During the four years after the end of the war, Stalin's image
changed radically. National socialist visual images of Stalin as a "devil," the
"red tsar," and a "bloodthirsty tyrant" were replaced by representations of
the Generalissimo, the guarantor of peace in Europe who became the "best
friend of the German people." In official public discourse, Stalin evolved
from an "enemy" into the "Führer," occupying the same symbolic position

of national leader that Hitler held until the moment Germany surrendered on May 8, 1945, merely a few months earlier. The appearance of a new expression in the postwar East German political lexicon—"Führer Stalin"—was an indicator of a deep semantic reworking of the sphere of symbolic politics and representations of power (Figure I.1; Figure I.2).

These two quotations, one from Nazi, one from Soviet propaganda, allude to an intriguing situation. On one hand, after 1945 East Germany was considered a representative example of the Sovietization of the Central and East European countries and a typical member of the bloc of socialist states.[4] A political system based on the Soviet model took shape in the GDR and the other socialist countries: a single-party dictatorship established by using terror and repressing those who did not conform while also energetically propagandizing the happy future communism promised and the ideals the New Person embodied. On the other hand, East Germany is a special case among the socialist states. The GDR is unique because of its exceptional situation in postwar European politics. The Germans and the Soviets were former enemies. Germany lost the war, the USSR won it. And immediately after the peace, each side perceived the other in terms of negative stereotypes and images of enemies which exposed the radical incompatibility of the Soviet and German worlds. The Red Army troops in the Soviet Occupation Zone

Figure I.1   Nazi propaganda poster showing Stalin as the embodiment of the Jewish-Bolshevik threat, 1941–1944. *Source:* Bildarchiv im Bundesarchiv (Koblenz). Signature: Plak 003-039-010.

Figure I.2 "Stalin—This is Peace!": socialist propaganda of "the best friend of the German people" in the GDR, 1952. *Source:* Bildarchiv im Deutschen Historischen Museum (Berlin). Signature: P94/1706. Artists: Harald Hellmich and Klaus Weber.

also reinforced formal agreements between the allies, who saw the presence of Soviet soldiers as a guarantee that reeducating the Germans would go forward and Nazi ideology would thus be decisively eradicated from the population's conscience. Moreover, as the Cold War took hold, the GDR found itself on the boundary separating the competing capitalist and socialist systems. In the Eastern bloc, its position was symbolically an ideological frontline between the *good world* (the "people's democracies") and the *evil world* (the capitalist countries) (Figure I.3). The Soviet side lent its support to representations of the GDR as a "showcase for socialism" and "the citadel, sentry and frontier of peace" which would avert the new war that the Western—Americanized—parts of the globe were supposedly threatening to start. These factors made the establishment of the Stalin cult in East Germany a singular case. Treating East Germany as both a representative and a special case of the Sovietization of Central and Eastern Europe after World War II makes it possible to examine how the process of Sovietization played out: the strategies and mechanisms through which Soviet influence took root as well as the logic and the failures, the planned and the unexpected aspects of the cultural accommodation, and transfer of the Stalin cult from the USSR to the territory of its former enemy.[5] As a result, this book is an *entangled history* of the Stalin cult in the Eastern bloc taking East Germany as a case study.[6]

GOALS AND OBJECTIVES OF THIS STUDY

This is a multifaceted study of the emergence, evolution, and dismantling of the Stalin cult in East Germany between 1945 and 1961. To analyze the complexities of the cult over its lifespan, the book follows three broad avenues of investigation: (1) it reconstructs political, social, and emotional life in the Soviet Occupation Zone after the defeat, asking how the postwar situation influenced the ways in which Soviet propaganda of Stalin was transferred and adapted to German conditions; (2) it studies the agents, mechanisms, and content of the propaganda of the cult during the wave of Sovietization while also tracking the specifics of the process of forgetting the Soviet leader in the GDR as de-Stalinization unfolded across the Eastern bloc after 1956; (3) it analyzes how the Stalin cult was perceived across a wide range of social groups and generations and examines the ways the cult was interpreted in the public and private spaces of the East German subject's life.

Each avenue of investigation includes three sets of questions. The first set focuses on German society's postwar experiences and responses to the emergence of the Stalin cult. How did German society survive the defeat, which, for a significant sector of the population, meant their worldview collapsed, they lost a sense of orientation in the present, and they had to renounce their

WERKTAG ZWEIER WELTEN

Zwel Welten, zwei Wege – wir haben entschieden,
Deutsch-Sowjetische Freundschaft heißt Wohlstand und Frieden

Figure I.3   GDR poster: "Working day of two worlds. Two ways, two worlds—we have decided, German-Soviet friendship means prosperity and peace." Ca. 1950. *Source:* Bildarchiv im Bundesarchiv (Koblenz). Signature: Plak 100-041-026.

plans for the future? How did lived experience of the capitulation and the memory of life in the Third Reich influence the reception of propaganda of Stalin? Which aspects of postwar daily life conditioned opinions about Stalin, contributing to the rejection or acceptance of the Soviet leader? What was the Stalin cult's appeal for a society that had lost the war? How effective was Soviet propaganda that invoked the morality of German society and guilt feelings about unleashing a worldwide catastrophe? Was the Hitler cult a serious competitor and a symbolic barrier to Bolshevik propaganda? How did the Stalin cult contribute to a total overhaul of the system of public symbolism— public space and official spheres; ideas about time; interpretations of the past, present, and future; obliteration of the old symbols of imperial Germany and the Third Reich—in a context where new representations of power were being affirmed? Did the SED regime succeed in politicizing the private spaces of the individual's life, subjugating the private zone to state and party goals? And finally, how did the Stalin cult's Bolshevik project shape the political scenario of development in East Germany, the territory that became the periphery of the postwar Soviet empire and the front line in the systemic Cold War conflict?

The second group of questions involves reconstructing the mechanisms whereby the Stalin cult was transferred from the USSR and propagandized in East German society. How was the Soviet cult of Stalin disseminated and adapted to German postwar conditions? What was the content of the rituals, myths, and practices of the personality cult in the GDR? In terms of planning, organization, and administrative procedures, what did it take to establish the Stalin cult in an environment that was culturally different from its Soviet homeland? What types of roles and meanings dominated the propaganda of Stalin's image? Which power techniques did the propaganda state use to penetrate the subject's consciousness and program it with ideas about morality? More specifically, in what ways did propaganda's attempts to program the subject's consciousness address two key questions: How could Germans rid themselves of guilt feelings about participating in the Nazis' war crimes? How might they create a *normal* life by joining the side of the "victors"? How did the East German political elite use transfer of the leader cult to create a postwar political order, secure the Kremlin's patronage, and gain access to the center's political, economic, military, and symbolic resources to stabilize its own power? How did the Soviet occupying forces, in cooperation with the SED, attempt to construct the sense that the postwar political order was legitimate, despite its obvious lack of popularity? What role did the transfer of cult knowledge and practices to East Germany play in Stalinizing the SED? How were Soviet representations of the leader incorporated into East Germany's system of public symbolism in the immediate postwar period and how were they removed after 1956? In which ways did the mass media help to involve the population in the Stalin cult, and what kinds of media were most successful in the propaganda apparatus's work?

The third set of questions addresses the perception of the Stalin cult in East Germany. How did the cult influence the GDR's social structure, reinforce class identity, and shape the postwar generations? Which social actors negotiated with the "workers' and peasants' state" about the foundations of existence—and who was excluded from the field of political communication? Did the Germans see their defeat as a "national catastrophe" or as a "liberation from fascism"? Divided and depressed by the defeat, how did German society perceive Sovietization and how did it respond to the image of Stalin as a "liberator" and "friend"? How did the official rhetoric about German guilt for unleashing World War II define both official discourses and the social practices of the subject's everyday behavior? What role did the Stalin cult play in politically mobilizing the population, indoctrinating it, and producing the loyalty and subordination that ensured the stability of the postwar Sovietized order? How did the population interpret propaganda campaigns through the prism of the "brown" past and their acute need to normalize the present? Which spaces and possibilities did ordinary citizens have for expressing popular and alternative opinions about Stalin? How did the power institutions monitor, control, and punish those who held other attitudes? How did the Stalin cult make its way into the spaces of daily life and include the private in the discourse of power? The answers to these questions show how the Stalin cult drove the formation and legitimation of Soviet-style, subaltern postwar societies which were dependent on Moscow. Crucially, they shed light on the ways the Stalin cult strengthened the imperial hierarchy of power relationships, determined how these dictatorships functioned, and promoted the vitality of closed societies.

SOURCES AND LEVELS OF ANALYSIS

Archival materials from Russian and German archives are the source base for this study. These sources can be divided into two main categories. The first is composed of documents generated by the Soviet Military Administration in Germany (SVAG), the KPD, and the SED—the power institutions that created the discursive reality of the SED regime's legitimacy and stability. They dramatized the regime's popularity and support across a broad spectrum of the population. In these sources, Stalin is the "best friend, teacher and father of the German people." On the other hand, the same sources present actions intended to thwart the establishment of the Sovietized order in East Germany as "criminal acts" (*kriminal'nye prestupleniia*), "enemy activity" (*vrazheskaia deiatel'nost'*), and "fascist reaction" (*fashistkaia reaktsiia*). The East German and Soviet power structures called on the population to fight energetically against "foreign and domestic enemies" in order to maintain the discursive purity of the society of social consensus they were staging. As these sources show, in order to subordinate private interests to the party's goals and tasks, propaganda presented the state and people's harmonious coexistence as a key element of this consensus.

The sources that belong to the first category show how, after its transformation into the periphery of the Soviet empire, East Germany tried to forget the language of the Third Reich, learned to "speak Bolshevik," and demonstrated its own subordination to the center by reproducing Soviet rhetorical templates about "class struggle" against "enemies of the people" in official public spheres.[7] The language policy of modern dictatorships was an integral part of the social engineering that attempted to enter into the minds of individuals to change what they thought and to inculcate loyalty to the ideals of the state's propaganda. Language was a way to realize power and an instrument for forming a one-dimensional social reality to which the individual had to adapt and accommodate him/herself—and which s/he had to use to make sense of life in a dictatorship. The language of the dictatorship represented power relationships and reproduced power because it was transformed into public ritual. It became social practice, offering citizens the opportunity to participate in state- and nation-building.[8] By signaling citizens' political loyalty, language became an indicator of belonging, showing membership of the collective "we." Sources from the first category describe the totalitarian subject, someone with no autonomy who was completely controlled by the state and party, a person who took part in official rituals and was the bearer of socialist morality. However, the sources comprising the second category reveal a different picture.

The reports produced by the SED's Eastern Bureau make up this group of sources. They show what the propaganda of Stalin in the GDR looked like to Western observers.[9] In comparison with the first group, these sources used an alternative language to narrate social reality, one which reflected the SED's unpopularity and, as a result, a high level of oppositional activity and resistance to the dictatorship, especially among workers at industrial enterprises and in the GDR's industrial centers. Describing its invalidity in the eyes of ordinary citizens, the reports of the SPD's Eastern Bureau created a discourse of the SED regime's illegitimacy in East Germany. These sources create the impression that there was a liberal subject who—despite the dictatorship's violence and coercion—was brave enough to resist and viewed the totalitarian regime's norms and ideals with sober reason.

Integrating these two groups of sources makes it possible to avoid mutually exclusive viewpoints and bipolar assessments of the subject's life under the conditions of a dictatorship. Using sources of both "Western" and "Soviet" provenance allows us to understand the *hybrid* nature of the subject's behavior in Soviet-style societies. Under a dictatorship, this was someone who was able to obey and adapt, negotiate and resist the regime *simultaneously*, depending on the situation, place, and time, or whether s/he was in a public or a private sphere, each with its own perceived discursive, behavioral, and emotional norms.[10]

The sources are analyzed on two levels.[11] The first level of analysis is the sphere of party-state messages and representations. Here, the focus is on the state and party's monopoly on defining, distributing, and controlling the narrative about the Soviet leader and his image. This is where idealized representations of the "best friend of the German people" were transmitted by the propaganda organs and educational institutions, the mass organizations, and the mass media. This is the level of the party-state discourse about Stalin in which, by definition, official sources must be used. The minutes of SED Politburo meetings let us reconstruct the decision-making mechanisms which demonstrate the emergence of the Stalin cult in the GDR. These minutes also shed light on how the East German political elite helped to establish the cult by developing clientelistic relationships with representatives of SVAG and its structures, the Soviet Central Committee, and, not least, by building personal relationships with Stalin himself. Documents from VOKS, the All-Union Society for Cultural Relations with Foreign Countries (held in GARF), materials from the Central Committee's Department of Propaganda and Agitation (held at RGASPI), and documents from the German desk at the archive of the Ministry of Foreign Affairs of the Russian Federation enabled me to analyze both the institutional and informal channels through which the image of the "leader" was imported to East Germany. Documents about work with regional cells in the provinces and *Länder* of the GDR generated by local SED representatives and those from the SED Central Committee's department of party organs made it possible to recreate the mechanisms and content of regional-level propaganda. Materials from the German-Soviet Friendship Society (Gesellschaft für Deutsch-Sowjetische Freundschaft or DSF) and the Free German Youth (Freie Deutsche Jugend or FDJ), which are held in the Bundesarchiv (Federal Archives of Germany), made it possible to reconstruct propaganda campaigns, which, in turn, shed light on how the Stalin cult was used to mobilize, indoctrinate, and subjugate East German society. The archival materials were supplemented with published sources: literature put out by the propaganda organs; materials from the socialist press; memoirs written by both former SVAG staff members and people who worked for the SED's party-state apparatus; and the reports about their trips to the USSR composed by representatives of the mass organizations. Acoustic and visual sources are a separate subgroup. These materials give insight into the regime's iconography and allow the historian to penetrate the "official mood" of East German society between the end of the 1940s and the beginning of the 1950s.

The second level of analysis deals with the sphere of interpretations and reactions to the propagandized image of Stalin across a broad spectrum of social actors and generations. This is the space of East Germans' daily life as consumers and recipients of the propaganda of Stalin. It is the realm of the everyday life of the historical subject who was drawn into a web of communications with the state and the party, official rituals, and strictly organized public spaces. This level of analysis is intended to show how the population interpreted propaganda narratives, ideas about socialist morality, and the key concepts of friendship with Stalin and love for him. It also demonstrates the ways in which Bolshevik propaganda was integrated, reworked, or sloughed off in postwar daily life. To understand the East Germans' emotional attitudes toward Stalin, I have used memoirs written by contemporaries and reports from various institutions, including SVAG's political dispatches, Communist Party international information reports about Germany, and reports generated by the Stasi as well as those from the SPD's Eastern Bureau. These documents describe a broad range of practices around the reception and adaptation of images of the Soviet leader and the emotions, and reactions to those images which grew out of the memory and experience of representatives of different generations and from various professional and social groups. These sources can certainly be tendentious, and they tell us much more about the political order the regime constructed than about citizens' actual sentiments or public opinion in a dictatorship.[12] Nonetheless, these sources make it possible to reconstruct public opinion at least partially and to draw conclusions about the shifting boundaries of the SED regime's tolerance for the population's rhetoric and behavior in a Soviet-style society.

TERMINOLOGY: "PERSONALITY CULT" OR "STALIN CULT"?

This book uses the terms "cult of the leader" (or "leader cult"), "personality cult," and "Stalin's personality cult" as synonyms. Nonetheless, it is also important to look at their differences. After Khrushchev's Secret Speech at the Soviet Communist Party's Twentieth Congress, the term "personality cult" was identified with Stalin. Not long after the Soviet leader's death in March 1953, his successors were already beginning to talk about the "personality cult," connecting this term with Stalin's absolute power, which rested on terror and repression. Mikhail Odesskii and David Fel'dman point out that after Khrushchev's speech, "personality cult" began to mean "individualism in its most extreme manifestation, leading to absolute *proizvol* [despotism or abuse of power]."[13] Thus, "personality cult" turned into a metaphor characterizing the Stalinist period and a personal style of rule.

However, studying the history of the concept of the "personality cult" has shown that the term was used until 1956 in the Marxist tradition and the social-democratic movement as well as in the Communist Party's rhetoric.[14] Scholars focus on the traditionally negative connotations of the notion of excessive glorification of political figures, which does not correspond to the true state of affairs, that is, what actually happened. As a rule, this concept was used to discredit someone, and it was instrumentalized in the practice of denunciation. Balázs Apor concludes that in Stalinist political culture the "term 'cult of personality' functioned as a general term of condemnation" which was used to stigmatize people who fell out of favor with the regime and were classified as *enemies of the people*.[15] In using this term as part of the political lexicon of the era of de-Stalinization, Stalin's successors were well aware that it denigrated the leader's authority. They invoked the concept's "negative" capital, blaming the terror on Stalin personally as opposed to attributing it to "collective leadership," the category that absorbed the principles of party democracy and a return to Leninist norms of party life, symbolizing the renunciation of terror and the need to rehabilitate the victims of political repression. The term was used until the breakup of the Eastern bloc to discredit leading state and party figures. The term has recently become extremely politicized, notably in accusations that the Russian authorities are establishing personality cults of state leaders.[16] This makes using the concept as a category of historical analysis more complicated. It is no accident that current scholars prefer more neutral terms like "leader cult," "ruler cult," or "the cult of number one."[17] The less emotionally loaded concept of the "Stalin cult" appears in this book's title.

The concept of the "leader's cult" is understood here as a way to personify power and sacralize the political by putting the figure of the leader at the center of the social and political order. Ideology, institutions, and the rule of law have both enabled and circumscribed the potential for generating solidarity and mobilizing the population, but the image of the ruler has the power to give the abstract ideas of the state and the nation a human face and body. This "human" connection between the ruler and the ruled was crucial for generating an emotional attachment to the paternalistic order and it contributed decisively to the emergence of the cult community, with its sacred boundaries, which were defined through symbols, narratives, and rituals.[18] Proclaiming that some people were the leader's "friends" and others his "enemies," the state and the nation enhanced the sacrality of the cult community's borders by defining modes of belonging or being excluded from it. This approach treats the ruler cult as a complex web of meanings and a symbolic space of empowering interactions within which negotiations between the state and the individual took place.[19]

By providing a fundamental source of identity and security, leader cults played a key role in making imagined communities with a shared understanding of the past, present, and future.[20] Reconfiguring time and space in cultic rituals and everyday practices shaped collective memory by reducing complexity; such reconfigurations presented the charismatic leader as a repository for power, authority, and, most importantly, trust. The use of new types of mass media (photography, print media, radio, film, and television) was essential in constructing the ruler's charisma.[21] Followers of all ages were mobilized to participate in charismatic communication with the ruler. This reinforced the scale of social engineering, which set in motion the (self-)fashioning of modern subjecthood and offered a space for participation in political projects.[22] The rise of new media made cults one of the cornerstones of everyday experience by putting into circulation information, images, and performances involving political figures which were designed to appeal to everyone: men, women, and even children.[23] Understanding this allows us to develop a productive analytical approach that integrates state- and nation-building *from below* with the well-studied mechanisms of power *from above*.

HISTORIOGRAPHICAL OVERVIEW

In recent decades, the historiography of twentieth-century dictatorships has focused on three key questions: How did these dictatorships really function? In what ways was the vitality of a closed society ensured? How were totalitarian subjectivities formed and publicly manifested?[24] In the 1950s, Hannah Arendt, Carl J. Friedrich, and Zbigniew Brzezinski, the founders of the totalitarian paradigm, stressed the limited individual autonomy and personal freedom available to the subject under national socialism and Stalinism.[25] Their liberal critique of totalitarianism was a political result of Cold War competition that aimed to demonstrate capitalism's superiority to the system reigning in the socialist bloc. In the 1970s and 1980s, as the history of everyday life and cultural history developed, innovative analytical approaches for understanding totalitarian orders appeared. *Alltagsgeschichte* opened up a way to explore everyday practices of the self-empowerment, self-improvement, and self-politicization of ordinary people, who demonstrated, especially in ego documents, their ability to create spaces of agency and invent practices for participation in mass dictatorships.[26] This perspective on power—viewing it *from below*—showed that in modern dictatorships the private and the public were not opposed to each other, but in fact were both important resources for creating identities and generating social solidarity. Moreover, cultural history revealed semantic shifts in concepts and imaginations, the structures of regimes and communities, and the meanings of symbolic communication and ritual orders.[27] As scholars demonstrated, the dynamic process of drawing semantic boundary lines between politicization and depoliticization produced mass conformism and generated spaces of individual autonomy—and in doing so ensured a dictatorship's stability. By accepting the rules of public rhetoric and behavior prescribed for party-state spheres, actors helped turn the dictatorship into a form of everyday life. Society grew into the regime's structures, reproduced them, and used them to normalize socialist daily life. The state needed the support of its citizens and their trust to stabilize its order, but individuals (as well as groups of various kinds and society as a whole) used the state's requisites to optimize their own plans and negotiate "normalcy" with the state. The ritualization of the public and private life led to mutual dependence: the dictatorship could not exist without society and vice versa. Analysis of this symbiosis is the key to further understanding the stability, viability, and reproduction of authoritarian regimes.

New scholarship has shown that by no means did twentieth-century dictatorships, supported by the secret police, rely *solely* on state-sponsored violence and terror to create a climate of fear and suspicion. To a much greater extent, these were dictatorships of complicity, collaboration, and belonging. Using the concept of citizenship, they were sustained by drawing broad sectors of the population into the sphere of the political and foisting on the individual a set of official meanings which allowed them to integrate themselves into authoritarian systems of living and generate spaces for self-optimizing and attaining individual happiness as a useful member of society.[28] Moreover, recent scholarship reveals the fact that power and ideology were translated into the social practices of daily life and it shows how they mirrored the embodiment of power and reflected power relations.[29] At the same time, this tendency contributed to the study of the pluralization of lifestyles, experiences, and memories from the perspective of history *from below*.[30] Research on individualizing strategies for adapting, negotiating, and resisting power shows the abundant capacity of ordinary people to endow ideology with their own meanings (their *Eigen-Sinn*) of life in a dictatorship.[31] In other words, as individuals, people turned the dictatorship into social practice and a form of everyday normality, translating the macro process of building a new social order into the micro level of each person's daily life. Analysis of the complex relationship between the state and the population, as well as the multiple forms, channels, and media of their communication, led to a critique of totalitarian theory and the emergence of the revisionist "beyond totalitarianism" paradigm.[32] In the context of this historiographic trend, historians' attention is increasingly focused on the daily life of power—the space where state and citizen met every day, a space in which power repeatedly manifested itself and was reaffirmed, accepted and doubted, rejected and renegotiated.

The scholarship on ruler cults has come out in full bloom.[33] Political leaders' personality cults have traditionally been treated as classic signs of the totalitarian nature of Soviet-style societies.[34] Nonetheless, scholarly interest in the phenomenon of personality cults as a way to personify power and politically mobilize the masses has recently been increasing. Scholars are no longer confined exclusively to the classic dictatorships of the twentieth century—the Mussolini cult in fascist Italy, the Hitler cult in Nazi Germany, and the Lenin and Stalin cults in Soviet Russia.[35] The study of leader cults is currently expanding, both geographically and temporally, and has become a significant part of the global history of communism.[36] This includes work on cults devoted to Ho Chi Minh, the first president of North Vietnam, the general secretary of the Brazilian Communist Party Luiz Carlos Prestes, Mao Zedong in China, and Fidel Castro in Cuba.[37] This expansion of research on leader cults indicates that there is a global paradigm of the anthropomorphization of the political which is rooted in cults of monarchs and those that developed around heroes as the formation of states and nations crested in the nineteenth and early twentieth centuries.[38] As shown in studies of the role played by the production and reception of images of power in legitimating dominance during the Early Modern period, the personality cult was not the product of secularization and modernity alone. Its origins can be traced at the very least to the late Middle Ages, stemming from several interconnected processes whereby mass politics and the mass media emerged: the nationalization of the masses; the heyday of monarchical courts with their branching administrative apparatus; the growth of informal patron-client networks; and the manifestation of the signs and practices of symbolic politics.[39]

With the fall of the Iron Curtain and the end of the Cold War, previously closed archives in the former USSR and Eastern European countries became accessible. A detailed study of how postwar Sovietization unfolded in Central and Eastern Europe was the first important achievement of the archival revolution in the 1990s. As a result, the Stalin cult in Soviet-style European societies, along with the cults of regional party and state leaders (whom people nicknamed "Stalin's pupils" and "little Stalins") became firmly established as an area of scholarly inquiry.[40] Those working in this field are writing cultural histories of Soviet-style societies based on studying the role leader cults played in producing, stabilizing, and legitimizing authoritarian regimes. As a result, historians have focused on questions about ideological transfer from the USSR to socialist bloc countries, strategies for adapting Soviet norms to the local realities of societies on the peripheries, and reactions in these places to Sovietized daily life.[41] Scholars are increasingly studying symbolic politics as a crucial way to analyze processes of social integration and disintegration and mechanisms for creating inclusion and exclusion, and to better comprehend how social consensus and tolerance for socialist regimes were forged, despite the weak legitimacy of these regimes and their obvious unpopularity among the population. To explain the phenomenon of social consensus and to understand why the population tolerated authoritarian regimes, we need to do more research on how the spaces of private life and the individual's personal niches—for example, work and free time, tourism and recreational activities, consumption and gender relations—were politicized.[42] These were places where the regime and the individual met, the spaces where the subject was controlled, mobilized, and indoctrinated. At the same time, these spaces became a platform for negotiations during which the participants sought compromises, conflicts and rivalries played out, differences were reestablished, and agreements about the fundamentals of coexistence were "concluded."[43]

Until perestroika, the Stalin cult was not part of the Russian scholarly literature. In the immediate aftermath of Khrushchev's Secret Speech in 1956, the Soviet dictator's image was initially depoliticized, that is, it became accessible to a certain amount of popular criticism. But then, having become a forbidden topic for public debate, it was once again intensely politicized.[44] During the second half of the 1960s and throughout the 1970s, the Soviet state became a "dictatorship of memories" (*Erinnerungsdiktatur*), using remembrance of the great achievements of the Stalin era—victory in World War II and laying the foundations for socialist construction—as its main strategy for regenerating the masses' trust in Soviet power.[45] Against the backdrop of this glorification of the Stalinist past, the desecration of Stalin's name became an unspoken taboo, since it amounted to a criminal act and a public sign of casting doubt on the legitimacy of the Soviet order. The prerogative of defining the extent of knowledge about Stalin and the borders of permissible rhetoric was allocated exclusively to the KPSS Central Committee. At a Politburo meeting about the publication of an article to mark the ninetieth anniversary of Stalin's birth, B. N. Ponomarev, one of the Central Committee's secretaries, noted that "This is a very complex figure—Stalin in history, and one has to be careful with him."[46] Soviet historiography adhered to this principle. As a result, official information about the Soviet leader was limited to dry, concise descriptions in encyclopedia entries, enumerating his positions, titles, and awards.[47]

The beginning of perestroika and the 1990s saw an opening up of public discussion about the nature of Stalinism and the policy of using state-sponsored violence and terror against ordinary citizens.[48] The revisionist work of D. A. Volkogonov, Roy Medvedev, A. V. Antonov-Ovseenko, and F. D. Volkov highlighted the criminal side of the Soviet leader's activities, about which the general public had previously known little.[49] These works, which were based on declassified archival materials, presented for the first time documentary evidence about several very significant things: Stalin's role in political repression; how struggles within the intra-party leadership and against the opposition were carried out; Lenin's and Stalin's conflictual relationship; and the Red Army command's strategic mistakes during World War II. In unmasking Stalin, scholars initially focused on the tragic influence of the Soviet leader's personality on the course of Russian history and they raised questions about his moral responsibility for the crimes committed.[50] Recently Jörg Baberowski's work dramatically foregrounded the impact of Stalin's paranoid personality on the escalation of violence while he was establishing his personal dictatorship and leader cult.[51] Benno Ennker discovered that in Stalin's inner circle the interactional dynamics around the leader's trust and distrust became a driving force that strengthened the dictator's personal power and his cult.[52] Jan Plamper drew attention to the importance of studying the intellectual and creative elites who produced the leader cult and the roles their cultural products played, both in the work of the propaganda organs and in validating regimes based on personal power.[53]

Another important result of the opening of Russian archives and those of former Eastern bloc states was that historians began to use previously inaccessible reports and summaries of the population's sentiments which were put together to give the government a window into public opinion.[54] More broadly, this scholarship laid the foundation for research on the image of power and studies of the image of political leaders in the "mass consciousness."[55] British historian Sarah Davies's 1997 book initiated a discussion about the expediency of using official reports to reconstruct public opinion in closed societies. Davies was the first to point out Stalin's central place in party and state documents about the sentiments of the population.[56] In the Russian historiography, Elena Zubkova, Mariia Zezina, and Olga Velikanova pioneered the use of these sources.[57] Elena Zubkova was one of the first historians to raise questions about the existence of public opinion in totalitarian societies. Analyzing reports and summaries of the sentiments of the population, Zubkova looked at Soviet public opinion after World War II, where the person of the Soviet leader was simultaneously both the bearer of hopes and expectations and the object onto which public grievances and discontent were projected. She argued that propaganda and terror were the main instruments of social control, that is, they were both fundamental for disciplining society's sentiments; they were designed to enhance the regime's authority and to create the impression that it was one with the population.[58] On one hand, the Soviet image of the "leader" was an anti-crisis instrument for the regime, creating a feeling of trust and predictability. On the other hand, analysis of the summaries revealed the wide range of perceptions of Stalin among different social, national, and age groups in Soviet society.[59] Since then, historians have never stopped arguing about the extent to which propaganda could—and could not—shape the language and behavioral patterns of ordinary citizens.[60]

A micro-historical approach to studying personality cults allowed us to take a new look at the old question of propaganda's impact on the individual psyche. This perspective makes it possible to show how the political is reflected in the individual and how the individual is expressed in the social. Along these lines, Greg Eghigian has analyzed a case study of a mentally ill woman in the Soviet Occupation Zone in Germany.[61] He reached the conclusion that medical sources like clinical records and illness narratives can tell historians much more than traditional party-state documents. Such sources reflect the norms of public culture and their social context, which were defined by the collapse of the national socialist worldview, the propaganda of German-Soviet friendship, and the intensification of the Cold War. The case Eghigian studied, a female schizophrenia patient who conversed with Stalin's ghost during periods of paranoid delusions, shows how deeply the experience of defeat and symbolic propaganda figures could penetrate into the subject's mental structures and destroy them. By analyzing mental pathology, he reconstructs both the norms of Sovietized reality in which the patient and many other Germans were living and a particular individual's experience of trauma from the Soviet occupation. This perspective leads to the discovery of original sources and methodological approaches from the history of medicine, the history of science, and the history of emotions which give us insight into the Stalin cult's impact on the consciousness, morality, and conscience of individuals in the postwar, traumatized society.[62]

Until now there has not been a comprehensive study of the Stalin cult as a powerful tool in the making of the postwar Soviet empire. In recent years, a series of new books about certain aspects of the Soviet leader's cult in East Germany have come out. Maoz Azaryahu and Katharina Klotz independently developed the concept of a pantheon of the socialist "gods" and national heroes of the East German state in which Stalin was given a major place from 1945 to 1956.[63] While Klotz pointed out how important the tradition of the leader cult was in the German communist and proletarian movement in the 1920s, Azaryahu drew attention to the instrumentalization of the propaganda of Stalin in reshaping the ideological landscape and the role of symbolic politics in the political topography of the GDR. Jan Plamper sees the roots of the East German Stalin cult in the pan-European tradition of the personality cult, which was reinforced by ideas about the leader prevalent in the German communist milieu.[64] Jan Behrends reconstructs the general dynamics of German-Soviet friendship, which the Soviet leader personified, embodied, and guaranteed.[65] For Behrends, the main source of the Stalin cult was localized in Moscow. It became an indicator of the German communists' dependence on the Kremlin and was only established as a result of the forced Sovietization of East Germany.

Researchers agree that the mass media played a central role in constructing Sovietized reality.[66] German historian Jörg-Uwe Fischer has shed light on how Stalin's image was represented on East German radio and television and in illustrated magazines.[67] In analyzing the official discourse about the Soviet leader, he differentiated channels for broadcasting the propagandistic myth which targeted various types of addressees and therefore was tailored to a given audience's age, gender, professional, and social characteristics. More extensive research on staging the Stalin cult in the media was done using Soviet material. This work has examined the dramatization of Stalin's image in films, the press, literature, the mass Soviet festival, folklore, and traveling exhibitions and museum shows.[68] Stalin cult representations in public space are an integral part of several works on public symbolism and the monumentalization of political leaders and national heroes in monuments, memorials, and the creation of special sites of memory.[69]

In assessing the Soviet leader's image, historians have concentrated primarily on two topics: celebrations of Stalin's seventieth birthday and the mourning that took place after his death in March 1953. This is a weak point in the existing scholarship on the Stalin cult in East Germany. Such a limited focus creates a static picture of perceptions of the Soviet leader's image in the GDR and fails to include the dynamics of its establishment, development, and dismantling. Questions about the deconstruction of the myth of the leader and the tabooing of collective memories of him are especially poorly understood aspects of de-Stalinization, but ones that can shed light on the phenomenon of cultural forgetting as a social practice for getting rid of the traumatic experience of defeat and the subsequent Soviet occupation.[70] Therefore, further work on the Stalin cult's impact on postwar German society and how ordinary citizens perceived the cult is needed. The way, on one hand, the personality cult's official rhetoric influenced the Sovietized subject's identity and, on the other hand, how s/he instrumentalized the language of the personality cult in searching for personal meanings of life under a dictatorship remains little studied.[71] Historians' engagement with only the most striking aspects of this topic, while ignoring the cult's day-to-day operations in the GDR, their focus on the production of official knowledge about Stalin, and consistent under-use of both Russian and German sources in the scholarly literature all call for a comprehensive analysis of the Stalin cult in East Germany. A study of this kind will give us a deeper understanding of the resources and mechanisms used to mobilize the population politically in subaltern regimes in the context of the postwar Soviet empire. The present book undertakes to carry out this project. My analysis is also a contribution to the study of the complicated relationship of Germans and Russians during the "short twentieth century," treating the hitherto understudied aspect of the transfer and adaptation of the Soviet Stalin cult to postwar East Germany's daily life as an integral part of German-Russian entangled history.[72]

RESEARCH METHODOLOGY

The boom in social, gender, and cultural history, and the history of daily life and mentalities cast doubt on the very idea that political history should exist. In 1981, Jacques Le Goff declared that "[t]raditional political history is a corpse" and called on historians to write a "new political history."[73] Le Goff criticized historians' one-sided focus on reconstructing the chronology of political events, describing the functioning of party-state structures, producing biographies of great men and chronicling their deeds, and writing histories of political thought. It is no secret that the international historiographies of the Soviet past have long been dominated by "strong" history—traditional political history—which has produced biographies of leading state figures and detailed accounts of repressions and terror carried out in the framework of state-sponsored violence. This important scholarship is widely acknowledged and respected, and, in the eyes of most historians (especially male historians), is considered a "serious" area of research. This contrasts with "weak" history—gender and cultural history, the history of emotions and subjectivity. These are far less widely acknowledged and are seen as less authoritative fields of exploration. They are more marginal and are usually subject to gender discrimination because these are "unmasculine" ways of doing history and are often undertaken by women.[74]

Nonetheless, our ideas about political history and the ways to write it have changed profoundly in recent decades.[75] Historians now speak more often about the *cultural history of the political*, which is the methodological basis for this book.[76] The "cultural turn" in the humanities made political history an integral part of cultural history.[77] This book is about the history of the political; to a lesser extent, it is a history of politics. Two key features distinguish the political from politics. One is the fact that the political is not only anchored in formal institutions of power but is also rooted to a much greater degree in spaces where the justification, rejection, and protection of unequal social relations can be identified. The other is that working out a social solidarity that guarantees the stability of daily life and gives people a sense of the legitimacy of the political order is a key feature of the political.[78] As Mikhail Krom puts it, the new political history is concerned with "the regime's daily routines and the secret of its success (or lack thereof) with the population."[79] Thus, political history now includes the sphere of daily life (which was previously alien to it) in trying to answer the key question of *"how* a regime functioned in a specific sociocultural contexts."[80] As a result, historians are increasingly interested, on one hand, in the specific ways in which the political makes its way into the microworlds, social practices, and rhetoric of particular groups, generations, and individuals, and, on the other hand, they want to understand how these actors influence the content and dynamics of the political, and the ways it is (re-)defined.

Studying the political means exploring power and power relationships. Under this rubric, analyzing the phenomenon of power and treating it as a way to carry out "legitimate violence" provides a method for examining power as social practice.[81] The central thesis of this trend is that domination is not only based on violence—the logic of giving orders and obeying them—but also depends to a much greater degree on the interconnections between and interdependence of the rulers and the ruled. Thus, power and the symbolic boundaries of the political should be understood as the results of the bargaining, negotiating, and compromising which happen in the effort to find consensus. Power is the continuous process of negotiating a social contract between "above" and "below" about the shared foundations of coexistence. These negotiations are the result of a credit of trust and the establishment of a radius of tolerance beyond whose boundaries lies the sphere of violence and the arbitrary exercise of power. Boundaries between the political and the nonpolitical, the private and the public, the moral and the amoral, between power and anarchy, are created when a multitude of actors communicate in the field of the political. The construction of these boundaries transforms the political into "an arena of social, economic, and cultural conflicts" comprising the essence and the content of the political.[82] Analysis of the processes, mechanisms, and agents which establish, define, and revise the aforementioned boundaries of power and the power of boundaries must become the subject of research as well as the force driving the modernization of political history.[83]

In the new political history, power is treated as a semantic system encoded in the regime's symbols, myths, and rituals.[84] To analyze personality cults, historians reconstruct the web of meanings transmitted through these symbols, myths, and rituals.[85] This system of public symbolism makes appeals to the public, indoctrinates and mobilizes the masses, and establishes rules about what can and cannot be said, done, and felt. Symbols, myths, and rituals are transformed into the organizing structures of the social order, defining the standards of public rhetoric and social behavior so that the right kinds of public rhetoric and behavior become indicators of membership in the cult community.[86] Thus, the symbols of the leader's cult—its portraits and posters, busts and monuments—were visual artifacts of power that occupied the dictatorship's public space. The myth of the leader contained within itself a cosmological narrative about the imagined cult community's origins, the tasks it needed to complete in the present, and its future mission.[87] It reflected collective ideas about time and space and defined the matrix of collective memory, reprogramming old traditions and creating new ones.[88] Rituals helped translate myths into social practice, using the symbols of power to construct public space. Thus, an analysis of the Stalin cult tells us about the symbolic nature of the regime's legitimacy by showing how the dictatorship and the Soviet-style society in East Germany functioned between 1945 and 1961 as the periphery of the postwar Soviet empire.

By analyzing the population's reception of these myths, symbols, and rituals, I reconstruct the representations of power which made it possible for actors to interpret their environment, make sense of life, and take in an array of information about the boundaries of permissible rhetoric and forbidden behavior.[89] "Silent" in traditional political history, the "masses" do not appear as a passive, faceless population, obediently reconciling themselves to their fate. Instead, they become social agents "with their own faces and history."[90] As a result, actors' social practices and daily life, their experience and memory, the constellation of their ideas about the past, present, and future become the focus.[91] At this level of analysis, the historian's task is to reconstruct the connections between the state and the individual, the system of signs and social reality, the macro and micro levels of the organization of daily life which at first glance are often not so obvious.[92] In other words, we are talking about reconstructing the emotional ties between the population and the state, trust and distrust, citizens' rights and obligations, all of which are established and articulated, realized and disputed in the field of the political.

A productive way to analyze the propaganda of the Stalin cult and the reception of the cult in East Germany is to look at postwar German sensibilities through the prism of generational history.[93] Different generations and cohorts were the carriers of specific values, ideas, and identifying signs, which were recorded in time and space. A collective sense of "us" unites people into a generation. This is a feeling based on the special spiritual cohesion of its representatives. It comes from a single vision of the world, a single set of expectations and hopes, a single way to resolve conflicts, and shared algorithms for communicating with a regime. At the same time, belonging to a given generation implies the existence of certain opportunities and possibilities, taboos and restrictions, feelings and emotions, mechanisms of inclusion and exclusion, ways of remembering, forgetting, and maintaining silence about the past. In creating portraits of generations, it is impossible to forget that they are made up of single individuals. The question of how the regime's official scenario was interpreted in the life of a particular person, on one hand, and, on the other hand, which resources ordinary people generated and applied to influence the world of big politics ought to become an established subject in the new political history. In this light, political history has a new opportunity: it can exchange its status as the "backbone" of history for the return of authority to its "real core."[94]

STRUCTURE OF THE BOOK

The book has six chapters and is organized both chronologically and thematically. The first chapter develops the analytic framework for the book by giving an overview of the premodern and modern foundations of personality cults of the ruler. The second chapter examines the reasons, methods, and actors involved in designing the postwar Soviet empire, a sphere of influence that expanded into the territory of East Germany as a result of the fall of the Third Reich. The third chapter discusses the arenas in which Stalin's image evolved in the Soviet Occupation Zone and the factors responsible for this move from the negative image of the "red tyrant," which prevailed under national socialism, to the positive image of the "best friend of the German people," which came to the fore in the period when the GDR was established. Chapter four focuses on the rhetorical, ritual, and emotional structures of the leader cult, which were directed toward making an imagined cult community and were intended to create representations of cohesion with Moscow and to politicize postwar daily life. By analyzing iconoclastic gestures, their meanings, and forms in the context of public symbolism, the fifth chapter presents a new way to approach the reception of the cult and its influence on the population. Chapter six examines the politics and practices of de-Stalinization, which provoked a crisis of the symbolic politics of Stalinism in the GDR. In doing so, this chapter chronicles the process whereby the state and the party consigned memories of the Soviet leader to oblivion—indeed, made them taboo—while they simultaneously searched for anti-crisis representations of the regime. The final section presents the study's main conclusions.

NOTES

1. Goebbels, "People, Rise Up," 117, 118, 138. This translation is from a collection of Goebbels's speeches translated and edited by Randall Bytwerk. Bytwerk based his translation on "the speech as delivered," noting that "although copies were distributed to the press, Goebbels made several points more strongly in his oral presentation than in the printed version," "People, Rise Up," 113. Bytwerk's source is a recording of the speech, "Kundgebung der NSDAP, Gau Berlin, im Berliner Sportpalast: Proklamation des totalen Kriegs," Deutsches Rundfunkarchiv (Wiesbaden), No. 260052.

2. Kenez, *Birth of the Propaganda State*.

3. "Freundschaft für immer mit Stalin! Aufruf der provisorischen Regierung der Deutschen Demokratischen Republik zum 21. Dezember," *Neues Deutschland*, December 1, 1949, 1–2.

4. On Sovietization in Central and Eastern Europe, see Volokitina et al., *Moskva i Vostochnaia Evropa*; Petrov, "Formirovanie organov nemetskogo samoupravleniia"; Bairau, "Vykhodtsy iz sovetskogo inkubatora"; Bonwetsch, "Die Sowjetisierung Osteuropas"; Jarausch and Siegrist, *Amerikanisierung und Sowjetisierung*; Naimark and Gibianskii, *Establishment of Communist Regimes*; Lemke, *Sowjetisierung und Eigenständigkeit*; Connelly, *Captive University*; Creuzberger, *Gleichschaltung unter Stalin?*; B. Apor, P. Apor, and Rees, *Sovietization of Eastern Europe*; Applebaum, *Iron Curtain*.

5. Passeron and Revel, "Penser par cas."

6. Werner and Zimmermann, "Vergleich, Transfer, Verflechtung."

7. Klemperer, *LTI*; Kotkin, *Magnetic Mountain*.

8. Jessen, "Diktatorische Herrschaft als kommunikative Praxis." On the interdependence of language and the twentieth-century political order, see Steinmetz, *Political Languages*.

9. The SPD's Eastern Bureau was established in 1946 after the forced merger of the KPD and the SPD. It was tasked with organizing the SPD's illegal work in East Germany and supporting the population's anti-SED activities. Two of the bureau's most important jobs were to collect information about politics, economics, and society in the Soviet Occupation Zone/GDR and compile reports about the population's oppositional sentiments. The bureau's headquarters were initially in West Berlin but in June 1951 they were transferred to Bonn, where the archive of the SPD's Eastern Bureau is currently held by the Friedrich Ebert Foundation. See Bärwald, *Das Ostbüro der SPD*.

10. Tikhomirov, "Prisposablivat'sia, dogovarivat'sia, soprotivliat'sia."

11. My analysis of the Stalin cult in East Germany is based on the model of communication developed by Silke Satjukow and Rainer Gries in their work on socialist heroes, "Zur Konstruktion des 'sozialistischen Helden.'"

12. On the possibilities inherent in reports and political dispatches as well as the limitations of these sources for analyzing the Stalin cult in the GDR, see chapter 2, especially the section on "The Boundaries of the Dictatorship of Discourse: Creating A Unified Discursive Space of Socialism."

13. Odesskii and Fel'dman, "Poetika 'ottepeli.'"

14. Plekhanov, "Individual in History." See also Plamper, "Modern Personality Cults"; Cohen, "Cult of Number One."

15. B. Apor, "Leader Cults in Eastern Europe," 51.

16. See Cassiday and Johnson, "Post-Soviet Cult of Personality."

17. For example, see Cohen, "Cult of Number One"; Postoutenko and Stephanov, *Ruler Personality Cults from Empires to Nation-States and Beyond.*

18. Hein-Kircher, "Führerkult und Führermythos."

19. Blockmans, Holenstein, and Mathieu, *Empowering Interactions.*

20. Anderson, *Imagined Communities.*

21. For examples, see Falasca-Zamponi, "'Culture' of Personality"; Möller, *Charismatische Führer*; Häusermann, *Inszeniertes Charisma.*

22. Mosse, *Nationalization of the Masses.*

23. Loiperdinger, Herz, and Pohlmann, *Führerbilder*; Leese, *Mao Cult*, 256.

24. For the GDR, see Meuschel, *Legitimation und Parteiherrschaft*; F. Mühlberg, *Bürger, Bitten und Behörden*; Fulbrook, *People's State.* For the USSR, see Inkeles and Bauer, *Soviet Citizen*; Fainsod, *How Russia is Ruled*; Yurchak, *Everything Was Forever.* For a comparative analysis of dictatorships, see Kershaw and Lewin, *Stalinism and Nazism*; Russo, *History and Memory Compared*; Corner, *Popular Opinion*; Postoutenko, *Totalitarian Communication*; Merl, *Politische Kommunikation*; Lim and Petrone, *Gender Politics and Mass Dictatorship.*

25. Arendt, *Origins of Totalitarianism*; Friedrich, *Pathology of Politics.*

26. Halfin, *From Darkness to Light*; Hellbeck, *Revolution on My Mind.*

27. Edelman, *Politik als Ritual*; Glebkin, *Ritual v sovetskoi kul'ture*; Kraa and Rytlewski, "Politische Rituale"; Rolf, *Das sowjetische Massenfest*; Danyel, "Politische Rituale als Sowjetimporte"; Gries, "Dramaturgie der Utopie."

28. For example, Fulbrook, *People's State*; Von Klimó and Rolf, *Rausch und Diktatur*; Palmowski and Eley, *Citizenship and National Identity.*

29. Sabrow, "Herrschaft und Alltag," 14.

30. Lüdtke, *Everyday Life in Mass Dictatorships*; Arthurs, Ebner, and Ferris, *Politics of Everyday Life*; Harvey et al., *Private Life and Privacy.*

31. Lüdtke, "Herrschaft als soziale Praxis"; Lindenberger, "Alltagsgeschichte und ihr möglicher Beitrag." See also Krylova, "Tenacious Liberal Subject."

32. Geyer and Fitzpatrick, *Beyond Totalitarianism.* For a critique of totalitarian theory in relation to scholarship on the SED dictatorship, see Ross, "Politischer Gestaltung und sozialer Komplexität."

33. For an example, see Postoutenko and Stephanov, *Ruler Personality Cults.*

34. Friedrich and Brzezinski, *Totalitarian Dictatorship.*

35. On Italy, see, for example, Falasca-Zamponi, *Fascist Spectacle*; for Germany, see Bühmann, "Der Hitlerkult"; on the Lenin cult in the Soviet Union, see Velikanova, "Obraz Lenina"; Ennker, "Leninkult und mythisches Denken"; Ennker, *Die Anfänge des Leninkults*. On the Stalin cult, see Khlevniuk, *Khoziain*; Plamper, *Stalin Cult*; Gill, *Symbols and Legitimacy*; Ashirova, *Stalin-Kult in Zentralasien*; Löhmann, *Der Stalinmythos*.

36. Morgan, *International Communism and the Cult of the Individual*.

37. See Santana, "Cavalier of Hope"; Quinn Judge, "Ho Chi Minh"; Dror, "Establishing Ho Chi Minh's Cult"; Hung, "Cult of the Red Martyr"; Leese, *Mao Cult*; Gonzalez, *Secret Fidel Castro*.

38. For example, Asch and Freist, *Staatsbildung als kultureller Prozess*. For work on the period spanning the second half of the nineteenth century to the early twentieth century, see Eriksonas, *National Heroes*; Wolf, "Monarchen als religiöse Repräsentanten"; Gerwarth, *Bismarck Myth*; Riall, *Garibaldi*; Gerwarth and Riall, "Fathers of the Nation?"; Todorova, *Bones of Contention*.

39. See Mosse, *Nationalization of the Masses*; Wilentz, *Rites of Power*; Kantorowicz, *Zwei Körper des Königs*; Wortman, *Scenarios of Power*, vols. 1 and 2; Paulmann, *Pomp und Politik*. On patron-client relationships in Russian political culture, see Afanas'ev, *Klientelizm*; Orlovsky, "Political Clientelism in Russia"; Ransel, "Character and Style"; Hosking, "Patronage and the Russian State."

40. B. Apor et al., *Leader Cult in Communist Dictatorship*; "Communism and the Leader Cult"; Halmesvirta, "Cultic Revelations"; Ennker and Hein-Kircher, *Der Führer im Europa*.

41. For example, Jarausch, *Amerikanisierung und Sowjetisierung*; B. Apor, P. Apor, and Rees, *Sovietization of Eastern Europe;* Leach, *Architecture and Revolution*.

42. See Merkel, *Utopie und Bedürfnis*; Badstübner, *Befremdlich anders*; Crowley and Reid, *Socialist Spaces*; Gorsuch and Koenker, *Turizm*; Pence and Betts, *Socialist Modern*; Siegelbaum, *Cars for Comrades*; Crowley and Reid, *Pleasures in Socialism*; Giustino, Plum, and Vari, *Socialist Escapes*.

43. Koleva, *Negotiating Normality*.

44. Jones, *Dilemmas of De-Stalinization*.

45. Merl, *Politische Kommunikation*, 53, 114–20. One sees a similar logic of analysis in Jones, *Myth, Memory, Trauma*.

46. "V spokoinom tone," 149.

47. For example, see the entry for "Stalin" in the following encyclopedias: *Bol'shaia sovetskaia entsiklopediia*, vol. 40 (1957), 419–24; *Entsiklopedicheskii slovar'*, vol. 2 (1964), 422; *Sovetskaia istoricheskaia entsiklopediia*, vol. 13 (1971), 780–85.

48. See Mark von Hagen's detailed analysis of discussions about Stalinism during perestroika and in the post-Soviet period in "Politics of Post-Soviet History."

49. Volkogonov, *Triumf i tragediia*; R. A. Medvedev, *O Staline i stalinizme*; Volkov, *Vzlet i padenie Stalina*; Antonov-Ovseenko, *Stalin bez maski* and *Teatr Iosifa Stalina*.

50. Razumikhin, *Vozhd': Khozian: Diktator*; Mudragei and Usanov, *Kvintessentsiia: Filsofskii al'manakh*; Mertsalov, *Istoriia i stalinizm*.

51. Baberowski, *Verbrannte Erde.*

52. Ennker, "Stalin Cult, Bolshevik Rule and Kremlin Interaction."

53. Plamper, *Stalin Cult.* See also Hollander, *From Benito to Hugo Chavez.*

54. For a detailed analysis of information gathering and the preparation of reports and political dispatches on the population's moods in which Stalin was given a central place, see the third paragraph of chapter 2.

55. In recent years, a number of books examining the representation and reception of the regime in various historical periods have come out. For example, Lobacheva, *Samoderzhets i Rossii*; Lukin, *Narodnye predstavleniia*; Kolonitskii, *Simvoly vlasti*; Uortman, *Stsenarii vlasti*, vol. 1.

56. Davies, *Popular Opinion.*

57. Zubkova, "'Dvuklikii Ianus'"; Zubkova, "Öffentliche Meinung und Macht"; Zezina, "Shokovaia terapiia"; Zezina, "Iz istorii obshchestvennogo soznaniia"; Velikanova, *Public Perception of the Cult of Lenin.*

58. Zubkova, "Mir mnenii sovetskogo cheloveka"; Zubkova, "Obshchestvo vyshedshee iz voiny"; Zubkova, *Obshchestvo i reformy*; Zubkova, *Poslevoennoe sovetskoe obshchestvo.*

59. Zubkova, *Russia after the War.*

60. See Velikanova, *Popular Perceptions of Soviet Politics.*

61. Eghigian, "Der Kalte Krieg im Kopf."

62. See Jensen and Morat, *Rationalisierungen des Gefühls*; Frevert, *Emotions in History*; Steinberg and Sobol, *Interpreting Emotions*; Plamper, *Geschichte und Gefühl*; Brückweh et al., *Engineering Society* as well as Black, *A Demon-Haunted Land.*

63. Azaryahu, *Von Wilhelmplatz zu Thälmannplatz*; Klotz, "Personenkult in der Ära Ulbricht."

64. Plamper, "The Hitlers Come and Go . . ."

65. Behrends, *Exporting the Leader*; Behrends, *Die erfundene Freundschaft.*

66. For example, Holzweißig, *"Die schärfste Waffe der Partei"*; Führer and Ross, *Mass Media, Culture and Society*; Lindenberger, *Massenmedien im Kalten Krieg*; Münkel and Seegers, *Medien und Imagepolitik im 20. Jahrhundert.*

67. Fischer, "Stalins Geburtstag"; Fischer, "Illustrierte Trauer–staatliche Totenfeiern."

68. On film, see Bulgakowa, "Herr der Bilder" and "Der Mann mit der Pfeife"; Hülbusch, *Im Spiegelkabinett des Diktators.* For the press, see Brooks, *Thank You Comrade Stalin!* The image of Stalin in literature has been examined by Evgeny Dobrenko in *Metafora vlasti.* For literature, see also Dobrenko, "Mezhdu istoriei i proshlim"; Giunter, "Totalitarnoe gosudarstvo kak sintez iskusstv" and "Arkhetipy sovetskoi kul'tury"; Klark, "Polozhitel'nyi geroi." On the Soviet mass holiday, see Rolf, *Sovetskii massovyi prazdnik*; Petrone, *Life Has Become More Joyous*; Rolf, "Leader's Many Bodies." Folklore is examined in Borev, *Staliniada*; Miller, *Folklore for Stalin.* On traveling exhibitions and museum shows, see, for example, Devlin, "Visualizing Political Language"; Kivelitz, *Die Propagandaausstellung in europäischen Diktaturen.*

69. For example, Koselleck and Jeismann, *Kriegerdenkmäler in der Moderne*; Tacke, *Denkmal im sozialen Raum*; Fowkes, "Monumental Sculpture"; Rausch, *Kultfigur und Nation*; Tikhomirov, "Symbols of Power."

70. See Halbwachs, *Das Gedächtnis*; Butzer and Günter, *Kulturelles Vergessen*; Esposito, *Soziales Vergessen*.

71. For example, Kotkin, *Magnetic Mountain*, 198–237; Halfin, *Terror in My Soul*; Hellbeck, *Revolution on My Mind*; Kämper, "Telling the Truth."

72. For example, see Koenen, *Der Russland-Komplex*; Zarusky, *Stalin und die Deutschen*; Satjukow, *"Die Russen" in Deutschland*; Beyrau, "Mortal Embrace"; Satjukow, *Befreiung?*; David-Fox, Holquist, and Martin, *Fascination and Enmity*.

73. Le Gof, "Politicheskaia istoriia," 190.

74. Silvana Seidel Menchi's article examining the dichotomy in historical writing on the family and marriage in the Early Modern period helped me to formulate these ideas about "strong" and "weak" history. See Seidel Menchi, "Storia alta, storia sommessa."

75. Ute Frevert has analyzed the evolution of traditional political history toward the direction of cultural history in "Neue Politikgeschichte." See also Bessmertnyi, "Nekotorye soobrazheniia"; Barlova, "'Novaia politicheskaia istoriia' v sovremennoi istoriografii"; Krom, "Novaia politicheskaia istoriia," 13.

76. See Mergel, "Überlegungen zu einer Kulturgeschichte der Politik"; Landwehr, "Diskurs-Macht-Wissen"; Nicklas, "Macht-Politik-Diskurs."

77. Bachmann-Medick, *Cultural Turns*.

78. "Das Politische als Kommunikationsraum," 26; Steinmetz, "Neue Wege."

79. Krom, "Novaia politicheskaia istoriia," 13.

80. Krom, "Novaia politicheskaia istoriia," 13. Italics in the text.

81. See Lüdtke, "Einleitung"; Lindenberger, "Die Diktatur der Grenzen," 21–23; Fitzpatrick, "Politics as Practice."

82. Stoun, "Budushchee istorii," 173.

83. Frevert, "Neue Politikgeschichte," 164.

84. See, for example, Feinstein, *State Symbols*; Sherlock, *Historical Narratives*; Gill, *Symbols and Legitimacy*.

85. Hein, *Der Pilsudski-Kult*.

86. Anderson, *Imagined Communities*. On the construction of an imagined cult community in the postwar Soviet empire, see Tikhomirov, "Stalin Cult."

87. See Anderson, *Imagined Communities* as well as Eliade, *Myth and Reality*; Cassirer, *Der Mythos des Staates*; Dörner, *Politischer Mythos und symbolische Politik*; Voigt, *Des Staates neue Kleider*; Bizeul, *Politische Mythen und Rituale*; Hein-Kircher and Hahn, *Politische Mythen*.

88. Hobsbawm, "Inventing Traditions."

89. Baberowski, "Repräsentationen sozialer Ordnungen."

90. Gries, "Propagandageschichte als Kulturgeschichte," 567.

91. See De Certeau, *Practice of Everyday Life*; B. Davis, Lindenberger, and Wildt, *Alltag, Erfahrung, Eigensinn*.

92. Schlumbohm, "Mikrogeschichte—Makrogeschichte."

93. For example, Mannheim, "Das Problem der Generationen"; Schüle, Ahbe, and Gries, *Die DDR aus generationengeschichtlicher Perspektive*.

94. Le Gof, "Politicheskaia istoriia," 190.

Chapter 1

Father of the People,
Face of the Nation

The Premodern and Modern Foundations of Personality Cults

A great man is great not because his personal qualities give individual features to great historical events, but because he possesses qualities that make him most capable of serving the great social needs of his time, needs which arose as a result of general and particular causes. Carlyle, in his well-known book on heroes and hero-worship, calls great men beginners. This is a very apt description. A great man is a beginner precisely because he sees further than others and desires things more strongly than others. He solves the scientific problems brought up by the preceding process of intellectual development of society; he points to the new social needs created by the preceding development of social relationships; he takes the initiative in satisfying these needs. He is a hero. But he is not a hero in the sense that he can stop, or change, the natural course of things, but in the sense that his activities are the conscious and free expression of this inevitable and unconscious course. Herein lies all his significance; herein lies his whole power. But this significance is colossal, and the power is terrible.

> Georgii Plekhanov, "On the Role of the
> Individual in History"

In conceptualizing a dialectic of the birth of the hero in his 1898 essay "On the Role of the Individual in History," Georgii Plekhanov (1856–1918), the first Russian Marxist, was well aware of Marx and Engel's antipathy to the "cult of personality" and Western social democrats' hostility to it.[1] Nonetheless, he formulated the guiding principle of the birth of the hero by defining the leader as a messiah who could recognize the past's cause-and-effect relationship with the present. More importantly, he identified the leader as someone who could also organize the masses and draw them to his side as he strove to resolve pressing social and political problems. The ideological movements of fascism in Italy, Nazism in Germany, and Bolshevism in Russia adopted the topos of the "charismatic situation"—the collective expectation of a savior who would appear in the midst of a crisis and resolve it.[2] Plekhanov left no room for doubt in asserting that by taking the monopoly on state violence into their hands, not collectives but heroes would make history.

In 1919, before the rise of totalitarian states in the early part of the twentieth century, German sociologist Max Weber described the charisma of the leader not as a person's "divine grace and exceptional qualities," but as a set of social relationships between the ruler and his flock which was based on identity-building, emotional engagement, and trust in the leader. In fact, around 1900, intellectuals captured the *Zeitgeist*, the spirit of the times, reflecting the legitimation of modern personality cults on a wave of modern state- and nation-building. An age of masses turned into an age of leaders.[3] After decades, at the Communist Party's Twentieth Congress in February 1956, Soviet leader Nikita Khrushchev stigmatized the term "personality cult" (*kul't lichnosti*) in his Secret Speech, which laid out Stalin's crimes: immediately after this speech, the personality cult became a negative feature of communism which was not only used as a weapon by critics of the Soviet Union and the "people's democracies" but has also been reproduced in popular culture and academia alike to the present day.[4] Despite this stereotype of Eastern Europe as the only place where the ruler's personality cult determined the shape of politics, culture, and society, the phenomenon examined here goes far beyond the framework in which authoritarian and totalitarian political orders are usually analyzed.[5] In recent years, research on rulers' personality cults has gained currency as a heuristic analytical tool for explaining the legitimacy of authoritarian regimes, their ability to mobilize people, and the power they exert in various contexts around the globe.

Ruler or leader cults have been usually identified as a manifestation of modernity. Jan Plamper described five features that separate modern personality cults from their premodern forerunners.[6] First, for modern ruler cults, the source of ruler's legitimacy is support from the people, rather than the divine right of kings to rule. In addition, modern cults are the products of mass society. They are not the province of small elite but instead draw in society as a whole through educational institutions (schools) and state service (the army). Moreover, they arise only in closed societies as a result of such societies' standardized information fields, which circulate narratives and images of leaders in the mass media at the expense of a more pluralistic flow of information. Crucially, violence facilitates harsh control over which images of the leader are permissible in the public sphere and which are taboo. Finally, the modern personality cult is an "exclusively patricentric phenomenon," unlike traditional, gender-mixed cults, which included queens, tsaritsas, and princesses.

Instead of drawing a sharp dividing line between the premodern and modern worlds, a more fruitful approach is to search for continuities between the two epochs which can explain more deeply the reproduction and perhaps the radicalization of leader cults in modern times. In fact, the modern ruler's cult was often rooted in premodern narratives, rituals, images, and symbols that were reinvented, dynamized, and integrated into the process of modern state-, society-, and subjectivity-building.

This chapter gives an overview of the premodern and modern foundations of personality cults of the ruler. Their intersections have transformed the leader cult into a powerful tool for making modern politics, managing a mass society, and creating modern subjectivities. It presents evidence that ruler cults were vital for many political and social orders, going far beyond the socialist/communist regimes and modern dictatorships of the twentieth century. The concept of the ruler personality cult has moved beyond the framework created by totalitarian theory and has gained currency in research on state-, empire-, and society-building. Rather than focusing on differences, I am looking above all for the similarities and shared structures that united many personality cults, without neglecting their particularities.

THE PATRIARCHAL AND FAMILIAL
FOUNDATIONS OF THE RULER CULT

Ruler cults have been and continue to be part of the political landscape. To understand how they emerged, it is necessary to look at the most basic structural element of such cults: the shared image of the ruler as the father of the state and nation. For centuries, emotional and moral bonds uniting the ruler and the people were conceptualized as the ties of spiritual kinship joining the members of a harmonious and happy family headed by a caring patriarch.[7] In fact, these bonds were considered as binding as blood ties. Lynn Hunt's pioneering research has shown how important metaphors and images of kinship are in explaining how political orders function:

> If kinship is the basis of most if not all organized social relations, then it is also an essential category for understanding political power. Traditionalists in European history had long pointed to the family as the first experience of power and consequently as a sure model of its working; just as the father was "naturally" the head of the family, so too the king was naturally the head of the body politic.[8]

The tradition of seeing the ruler as a paternal authority has its roots in ancient Rome. Roman emperors received the honorific title "Pater Patriae," which represented the ruler as the father of the country. In Roman thought, however, this title was imbued with deeper meaning because it implied that the ruler was the spiritual leader of his subjects.[9] The paternalistic model of the state did not vanish with the fall of Rome. In the Middle Ages, the political and religious doctrine undergirding the European monarchies reinforced the state's patriarchal essence by invoking the king's divine right to rule: because the ruler's right to govern issued directly from God's will, his power was not only claimed as legitimate but received that approval from the highest possible authority. As God's representative on earth, the monarch was understood as the most important moral and judicial authority in his realm. The genealogy of this sacred right to govern reveals the source of later representations of secular political leaders as the "Father of the Fatherland" or the "Father of the Nation." For example, Russian emperor Peter I (1672–1725), Victor Emmanuel II (1820–1878), the first king of a united Italy, and the first president of Czechoslovakia, Tomáš Garrigue Masaryk (1850–1937), were all called the "Father of the Fatherland." Don Stephen Senanayake (1883–1952), who was the first prime minister of Sri Lanka, Julius Kambarage Nyerere (1922–1999), the first president of Tanzania, and Nelson Mandela (1918–2013), the first president of post-apartheid South Africa were also honored with the title "Father of the Nation." While it is a crucial foundation for the emergence and flourishing of leader cults, a narrative about founding fathers is also at the heart of the history of the United States and the European Union.[10]

The leader cult was a buttress of the symbolism of the paternalistic state. On the one hand, it stipulated that as the paternal authority the ruler was morally obligated to care for his family's dependents. On the other hand, the population's expectation of care gave subjects the moral right to demand protection, defense, and justice from the ruler. The discourse of the ruler loving his subjects as he loved his own children set out a moral obligation to which his followers were obliged to respond by expressing gratitude, trust, and love for the "father" in the everyday practices of letter writing, presenting gifts, and participating in state-sponsored events.[11] Consequently, imagining the state as a family, the ruler as the father, and his subjects as children gave everyone who was part of this symbolic system a fundamental sense of belonging that defined the entire grammar of inclusion and exclusion within the cult community. Attempts to challenge the legitimacy of this sacred authority were equated with sin and were often criminalized: crimes against the ruler were seen as a direct threat to the symbolism of the unity, loyalty, and harmony of the family and were depicted as a bacillus that endangered the healthy body of the nation as a whole.

A key element of the image of the "family," one that was shared around the globe, was the powerful call for consolidation around the ruler. The

paternal image of the ruler aiming to unify people of different faiths, ethnicities, and social origins into one political body was particularly visible in
the context of empires. The fact that religious and ethnic differences could
be surmounted because subjects identified with the ruler has often been a
crucial component of the viability of empires and multinational states.[12] In
the British Empire, King George III (1738–1820) enjoyed the title "father
of his people" while Queen Victoria (1819–1901) was called the "mother
of her people" because of royal acts of empathy—letters, visits, and phil-
anthropic donations—directed toward their subjects.[13] In the Late Ottoman
Empire, the sultan, "who watches equally over all of his subjects and cares
for all of them as a human and good-natured father," had an integrating function.[14] Likewise, Stalin was the "father of peoples" who urged many different
nationalities and ethnicities to refashion themselves into a single "Soviet
people."[15] Even the visual images of Stalin that were distributed in countries
on the peripheries fit national stereotypes and had stylistic features drawn
from numerous indigenous folk arts.[16] These examples point to the semantics
of the idea of the family associated with feelings of closeness, solidarity, and
unity. Such perceptions are connected with the absolute power ascribed to
the head of the family; they prescribe the entire family's subordination to the
familial patriarch. "The family," as Michael Herzfeld pointed out, "provides
an easily understood model for the loyalty and collective responsibility that
citizens must feel toward the state."[17] Consequently, imagining the leader as a
"father" and the state as a "family" was crucial in forging a politically united,
imagined cult community.[18]

The image of the state as a family was not only an ideological, political,
and theological concept, it was also the lived experience of everyday life.
In the course of secularization and the formation of modern states, these
religion-based practices of daily life did not disappear. Instead, losing their
religious connotations, they moved into the sphere of the political and put
down roots in official discourses and institutions, informing civic rituals and
communicative practices. I would like to mention just one example. Spiritual
kinship in the form of godparenthood was a Christian tradition used by both
the ruler and the folk for creating an empathic power relationship based on
the concepts of reciprocity and moral obligation.[19] The ruler was often asked
to be a godparent for his subjects' children. Across the Eastern bloc, the leadership in the Soviet Union, Yugoslavia, and Romania adapted the premodern
religious institution of the godparent.[20] Naming children after rulers allowed
people to create an emotional bond with state leaders.[21] Spiritual kinship
with the ruler usually implied an expectation of financial support given in
exchange for political loyalty—a tradition that survived in modern times as
the perception of the state taking the patriarchal role of the caring father who
looks after everyone who needs help.[22] These practices show that modern

states were not formed exclusively by the institutional, ideological, and normative transformation of the state and society. In fact, the resources for legitimizing the state that drew on the elementary structures of kinship played a very significant role in creating modern political orders and forming modern subjectivities. Metaphors of family and kinship connected the population emotionally with the regime (and vice versa) since such imagined bonds conveyed fundamental ideas about the social order in ways that were accessible and understandable to a broad public. By privatizing the ruler's image and integrating it into individual lifestyles, ordinary people became active consumers as well as producers of the cult's languages, rituals, and artifacts.

THE SPATIAL AND RITUAL ORDERS
OF THE CULT COMMUNITY

As a stabilizing and ordering entity, the ruler cult occupied the very center of the symbolic universe. In the workings of the cult community, the leader was the cornerstone of the spatial and ritual order, thereby involving the entire society in "working towards the ruler."[23] Thus, the population built and renamed cities, wrote letters, and sent gifts to the leader, sought personal audiences with him, and participated in festivities of veneration, which became integral parts of building authority and even sacrality toward the leader. Constructing the capitals of nation-states on the wave of urbanization and industrialization in the modern age, along with the acceleration of the media-technological revolution, heightened the ruler's representations and, in staging the leader as the very center of the state and nation, strengthened the significance of this visibility.[24] New media made it possible to reach large swathes of territory at a single point in time and, in that way, to create a cultic space through the press, radio, and television. The emergence of this medial public sphere produced the impression of both synchronicity and the nation's unity. The formation of a single discursive, spatial, and ritual order preserved the cult community's homogeneity. In what follows, first I analyze the spatial and then the ritual structures of the cult community.

Spatialization of the Ruler Cult and Unification of
the Cult Community

The ruler's cult has always had the semantic connotations of spatial consolidation, ideological standardization, and the desire for unity around the leader as the sacral center of power. Mapping leaders through public representations—monuments, posters, and other media—was an integral part of the spatial design of the cult community as was a division of the territory into sacred precincts and profane areas. Changing city landscapes and renaming squares, streets, and parks with the rulers' names, as well as putting monuments, posters, and busts of them in central places, was reinforced by the introduction of public representations, festivals, ceremonies, and rituals in which members of the cult community venerated the leader.[25] As a result, the sacred spaces were highly politicized: they were organized, controlled, and subjected to monitoring as part of daily life in order to embed the individual in a web of ideological meanings.[26] On one hand, the cult became lived experience in such spaces and these places were "training grounds" where people learned how to belong to the nation and the state. On the other hand, these politically saturated spaces had a significant potential for conflict: the population used iconoclastic practices to contest and renegotiate them.[27]

The ruler's travels through his/her realm were an important ritual of knitting disparate territories into a state or an empire. Elizabeth I (1533–1603) resided in London but, by traveling throughout England, she increased her personal charisma among the inhabitants of many parts of the country, including the members of different denominations.[28] The high visibility of Russian emperors in St. Petersburg impacted the spatial organization of the empire by representing the capital as the sacral center of power. "For all of us," a Guards officer living in the provinces wrote, "Petersburg was the enchanting residence of the Tsar. And everyone who traveled to Petersburg was considered one of the elect, who could expect the happiness of being close to the Tsar."[29] Late Ottoman sultans toured their empire to make themselves visible in public, that is, to offer their subjects a physical space for having direct visual and emotional access to the ruler's body.[30] Until the middle of the eighteenth century, when monarchs of the German-speaking lands traveled through their realms, their subjects showed their closeness to the ruler with a potent symbolic act: they unharnessed his horses and drew the carriages by themselves.[31] Masses of people greeted Napoleon III (1808–1873), when he journeyed through the outlying parts of the empire. In doing so, he enacted the symbolic unity of the periphery and the center as his subjects addressed their greetings to his person.[32]

The monarch's travels became a space that integrated regional traditions into the ruler's cult, and they provided a time for doing this. On these occasions, subjects honored their rulers in accordance with local customs. Songs and poems of praise in which elements of the local mythology and topography were interspersed with language and imagery shared across the realm were written in local dialects and adopted to regional circumstances, images, and narratives.[33] Oral traditions passed from generation to generation and ever more rapidly spreading printed materials taught the population how to express their love for the ruler, how to honor him/her, and what was forbidden in displays of love and deference.[34]

The ruler's meetings with delegates who traveled from the regions to the capital were another way to create representations of unity around the cult. These usually took place in the capital—in the ruler's residence and in direct contact with his/her body. For example, in the premodern world, the practice of giving audiences opened up direct access to the sacral center of power and buttressed the reproduction of the myth undergirding the ruler cult. Audiences not only allowed leaders to appear in the role of the caring father-leader but also let subordinates affirm their personal loyalty to the leader. The functions that audiences performed for monarchs and the princes of the church show up again in Mussolini's Italy and Stalinist Russia, Tito's Yugoslavia and Mao Zedong's China.[35] The networks of railroads and air routes which made it easier to travel in the twentieth century, as well as improvements in telecommunications, increased the importance of the diplomacy leaders practiced and their trips to other countries. These visits reinforced the leader's authority in the eyes of the population and burnished their image as major players in world affairs.[36]

The cult community's collective memory, which took the form of museums and exhibitions dedicated to the rulers, reinforced the cult's spatialization. Museums and exhibitions became tourist attractions and spaces for experiencing closeness to power.[37] To celebrate sovereigns' birthdays, exhibitions featuring the installations about the leader's biography, and displays of gifts sent to him were organized and museums were founded. Exhibits of gifts sent to Stalin in 1949 for his seventieth birthday staged the unity of the entire communist world, displaying declarations of the people's love for the Soviet leader expressed on a global scale. For Tito's seventieth birthday, in Belgrade, at that time the capital of Yugoslavia, an entire museum was opened in which gifts for the leader from every corner of the country and foreign countries were exhibited.[38] The many versions of the badge produced in honor of Mao Zedong were collected in the Museum of the Chinese Revolution in Beijing: every badge-producing unit was required to submit several examples as expressions of revolutionary art and the creativity of the masses, and as a symbol of Chinese unity around the leader.[39] In general, places where leaders were born, lived, and died became sites of national memory and were objectified by being turned into museums or tourist attractions. Even today Mussolini's birthplace (Predappio, Italy) and Tito's (Kumrovec, Croatia) are places of pilgrimage for their supporters, drawing the curious as well.[40]

Cultic space was a medial space, and consequently a space of vibrant communication from which steady streams of information, rumors, scandals, and emotions went out. Certainly, modern media—photographs, posters, telegrams, radio, and television programs—helped to popularize leaders and create the medial sphere of the personality cult.[41] Technological and media developments put the ruler at the center of public attention: the king, the leader, or the president became the icon, the personification of the imagined cult community, be it the nation, state, or empire. Expanded opportunities for replicating images and reaching a broad audience transformed rulers into communicative figures. This gave the public the impression that they themselves were participating in high politics and had a front-row seat for the political and private life of leaders, becoming privy to their passions and the state of their health.

In particular, the quick and cheap distribution of photographs and the public's interest in this medium turned leaders into political icons. That allowed ordinary people to privatize public figures for individual use and personal purposes in private spaces.[42] Citizens' requests for autographed photographs of their rulers became a mass phenomenon in the second half of the nineteenth century. In Germany, a fad for seeking the monarch's autograph was a sign of an increasing public interest in politics and the need of ordinary people to take part in producing the cult as well as their desire to manipulate the power structures to achieve personal goals.[43] By staging global sorrow at Queen Victoria's death and likewise Joseph Stalin's, the press, the telegraph, and the postal services played a central role in motivating millions of people to mourn these dead leaders.[44] The dead bodies of both the British monarch and Soviet dictators symbolized the unity of their cult communities and made the events commemorating their deaths a starting point from which the ruler's posthumous cult emerged. The funeral became a decisive moment when the emotional experience of cohesion around the figure of the ruler was dramatized and expressed in ritual laments.[45] Posthumous cults around former leaders, including Lenin in the Soviet Union, Kaysone Phomvihane in Laos, Ho Chi Minh in Vietnam, and Mao Zedong in China, were seen as a stabilizing, integrative element in establishing new governments and overcoming the crisis situation resulting from the leader's death.[46] Aiming to promote national/imperial memory and continuing the sacralization of power, the posthumous cults were manifested by building mausoleums, museums, and monuments to remember dead leaders.[47]

Ritual Unification of the Cult Community

The rituals of the ruler cult were an important instrument for generating the cult community. More specifically, they offered people a way to participate in power. By affirming the unity of the cult community, these rituals showed that citizens belonged to the state and enabled them to display their loyalty to the leader as his subjects. These rites helped the regime construct its political order, fill public space with its symbols, and explain to cult participants how the world was organized; of equal importance, they also indoctrinated the population and mobilized it to serve the state's interests. In Durkheimian terms, it could be said that personality cult rituals created, reproduced, and revitalized collectively held ideas that help people understand and interpret their surroundings.[48] These rites translated myth into collective action: narratives were enacted—indeed, they came to life—in public space and they aroused (as was intended) positive emotions: love, pride, and gratitude. These feelings were the "digestive enzymes" that allowed the state's ideology to penetrate citizens' bodies and be assimilated into the consciousness of millions of individuals.[49] Sharing the emotional experience and behavioral actions of the rituals made it possible for people to identify personally with the ruler, who was the incarnation of the nation, the state, or the empire.[50]

By providing a space for both sociopolitical integration and the crucial experience of affective identification with the ruler, rituals allowed people to participate in leader cults emotionally but also to encounter them as visual, acoustic, and whole-body sensory experience. In addition, they created communicative spaces, offering many channels through which the population could interact with the rulers. Entering into spiritual (indirect) or physical (direct) contact with the leader was a way to get closer to the sacral center and enjoy its advantages. However, contact with the ruler also created moral expectations and became a way for participants to make moral demands. By ascribing power, legitimacy, and authority to the leader, engaging in cult practices was also a way to share the construction of the sacral center.

Since the second half of the eighteenth century, celebrating the ruler's birthday has been an important moment for the symbolic production of unity and for generating the emotional experience of solidarity between the leader and his/her followers. This tradition became especially widespread in modern states. For example, in Yugoslavia, every year, in the weeks before Tito's birthday, "Tito's baton" was carried across the country by a relay of young people before it was presented to him on May 25.[51] The way Stalin's seventieth birthday was celebrated across the Eastern bloc in 1949 is another example of the power of symbolic politics in securing the ruler's cult. Creating a shared experience of solidarity with Moscow and evoking the feeling of the "we" for the imagined cult community became a constitutive ritual that centralized and synchronized the postwar Soviet empire. The entire periphery used the leader's birthday to carry forward two types of centralization: the promotion of social integration around local communist regimes and the production of symbolic subjection to their patron, Stalin.[52]

Gift-giving is another common element of power relationships with roots in the Early Modern period.[53] That is, giving gifts to rulers became another ritual for establishing a direct connection between the leader and the individual. Georg Simmel argued that gifts create social relationships and strengthen or challenge these relationships by circumventing officially established hierarchies and the lack of direct access to the ruler.[54] With increasing urbanization, greater anonymity in daily life, and the growing complexity of social reality, gifts to leaders were a key way to create emotional ties between the donor and recipient, going, figuratively speaking, from hand to hand, and from person to person. Gifts given to monarchs to mark a coronation, a royal couple's wedding, or the christening of their children poured in from all corners of the empire. Thus, the topography of gift-giving was defined as the territory within which subordination to the ruler took place, with possibilities for limitless symbolic colonization and expansion to new territories. These semantics of gathering together of the empire by giving gifts was already evident in the Gospels of Otto III. This illuminated manuscript was written around 1000 CE for Emperor Otto III. One of the illustrations shows gifts being presented to the emperor by four women, who personify the four provinces of the Holy Roman Empire: Rome, Gallia, Germania, and Sclavinia. This practice and this semantics of gift-giving can be traced through the centuries and has persisted to the present day. Thus, the Marble Hall in the Ethnographic Museum in St. Petersburg was the impressive site used to stage the public display of gifts from various peoples in the empire and from friendly countries that demonstrated Alexander III's might and magnificence.[55]

Marcel Mauss emphasized the emotional power of gifts, arguing that they created reciprocal relationships and the expectation of exchange.[56] Subjects not only presented gifts to the leader, but they also expected something from him in return.[57] They asked for a letter with a photograph, just a few lines that would be a memento, and they promised to preserve the leader's letter as a family heirloom that would be handed down from generation to generation. German monarchs gave presents to their subjects for their weddings and on becoming a godfather to their children.[58] To reinforce the giver's moral influence, letters with speeches, poems, songs, and drawings praising the ruler frequently accompanied gifts. In these works, rulers were often called "father" and "mother," which reflected the popular perception of the state as a family and the rulers as close relatives.[59] Some donors thought that handmade gifts would make the giver's connection with the ruler even more personal and would lend that bond a more individual character. Authors often vowed to accomplish particular goals and complete various acts which would help the ruler and the state. Thus, the practice of giving gifts to leaders indicates that there was a way to produce the leader cult from below; this opened up the possibility that broad social strata, even those far from politics, could be included in the political project.[60] For subjects, it was a way of making sense of belonging to the sacred center due to the (self-)staging of bonds of trust and participation in festivals, holidays, and celebrations of the ruler's birthday.

Mass celebrations and public rituals of honoring rulers became a constituent element in the functioning of leader cults. From the turn of the eighteenth century, leaders' birthdays became national and state holidays. This gave the population a chance to become acquainted with the biographies of leaders and to develop the sense of belonging to a nation by identifying with the leader. With the establishment of a cult's ritual order, the cult's artifacts and commodities were introduced into the economic system and the prevailing cultures of consumption. For example, during the Cultural Revolution in China over 2.5 billion Mao badges were produced.[61] The production of items bearing the leader's image sometimes touched off a struggle, in particular, when different producers of consumer goods competed for the right to use the leader's name and image as a marketing tool.[62] The expanding commercialization and politicization of European societies consolidated the sacralization of national leaders and its increasing visibility in both the public and private spheres.[63]

The upsurge of nationalism at the end of the nineteenth century and the beginning of the twentieth was intertwined with the militarization of society and representations of leaders as military heroes, skilled tacticians who courageously led their men into battle. In early twentieth-century Poland, the cult of Marshall Pilsudski, which revered him as the savior who would preserve the Polish state in the face of the Soviet military threat, fed already strong nationalistic feelings.[64] "Fathers of the nation"—Garibaldi in Italy and Bismarck in Germany—lived on in public memory as military statesmen who led successful struggles for national unification and were guarantors of stability in times of rapid historical change.[65] Military language and dress were significant in staging the cult of Mustafa Kemal Atatürk (1881–1938) as the founder of the Republic of Turkey.[66] Remembering military victories became important for creating collective memory and strengthening feelings of patriotism, invincibility, and nationalism. For that reason, the cults of Alexander Nevsky and Ivan the Terrible flourished in the Soviet Union during the total mobilization of the population during World War II. These historical figures were invoked not only to arouse a military spirit in the population and to inspire feelings of patriotism but also to create historical models for identification with the military feats of past centuries.[67] As leaders and heroes, they became figures around whom the nation's historical narrative coalesced because they provided a shared sense of belonging, unity, and power.

PERSONALITY CULTS AND HISTORICAL CHANGE

Ruler cults were not exclusively an invention of modernity. They have always relied on tradition and reinvented it.[68] Thus, the Chinese practice of honoring communist leaders had its roots in the cult of emperors and kings.[69] The Kim cult in North Korea incorporated elements of Japanese emperor worship.[70] In Stalinist Hungary, the Rákosi cult drew legitimacy from a tradition of popular veneration of the founder of the state, Saint Stephen, and the first royal family, the House of Árpád.[71] Despite their revolutionary radicalism, Bolshevik leaders inherited scenarios of power that developed during the Tsarist period.[72] With their logics of patron-client networks and politics of pomp based on the theological concept of the divine right of kings, the cults of European monarchs became the preconditions for the emergence of modern—secular, medial, and masculine—leader cults. The mixture of tradition and innovation, the religious and the secular, the political and the everyday in the realization of symbolic politics had its roots in practices of worshiping monarchs and national leaders which emerged in the middle of the eighteenth century and this mélange became evident in what Eric Hobsbawm called "the age of extremes," especially in totalitarian states and communist countries.[73] Even today, the image of the "great man," the "strong head of state," the "father of the nation" continues to influence international politics and define nationalist projects in many parts of the world.[74]

Historical change from premodern to modern times has been marked by three major, interconnected shifts that impacted the emergence of modern personality cults as the sacred center of a particular social order. First of all, the image of the ruler went from being an *invisible* to a *visible* entity. Hidden from the eyes of society in earlier times, concealed behind palace walls and blocked from direct view by their courtiers, rulers gradually began to appear in public more frequently, started to take part in ceremonies open to the populace, and began to arrange times when the people could have contact with them, directly and through various types of media.[75] Since antiquity, the common perception that what is visible constitutes authentic facts—or *truths*—and the idea that power is so powerful due to public representations of it has suggested a very close connection between visuality and both realizing power and (de)legitimizing political orders.[76] The ruler's increasing visibility was further reinforced by the Enlightenment idea of popular sovereignty, which forced European monarchs and modern dictators alike to make the issue of legitimacy central to systems of public symbolism created to gain their subjects' support.[77]

In addition, the ruler's image changed radically. No longer represented as *cold*—in other words, emotionless and remote—his image underwent a transformation and he was displayed as a *warm*—empathic, emotional, and, not least, human—leader. When the state was personified in the body of the ruler, the abstract idea of the state became visible, tangible, and accessible.[78] Emotions became a resource for creating emotional bonds with the state by virtue of (in)direct communication with the ruler. The ruler's former emotional coldness and passivity on ceremonial occasions, when he was often accompanied by intermediaries, was replaced by his active role, openness, and indeed high visibility at the center of public discourses, iconography, and rituals. Moreover, by showing empathy, making exceptions from the rules, and offering the possibility of a direct response to the needs, fears, and hopes of a single individual, the ruler's warmth could compensate for the bureaucratic indifference of the state apparatus. Likewise, over the long span of European history, the sovereign's power to grant pardons fostered the perception that the ruler was an empathic institution for administering justice.[79] Technical and technological progress, improvements in the channels of communication and the means of mobility, the expansion of literacy, the availability of an inexpensive popular press, the emergence of radio, and later television, in a rapidly changing world of increasing urbanization and ever more politicized big cities all helped to create a vibrant public sphere full of emotions, preoccupations, contradictions, hopes, and illusions about the ruler. At the same time, this public sphere offered spaces and times for participation, belonging, and making sense of life through emotional identification with the ruler.

Finally, the image of the ruler made a transition from *uniformity* to *multiplicity*, moving toward a plurality of meanings and representations, producers and recipients, appropriations and opportunities for consumption. As scholarship on leader cults shows, the history of ruler cults is the history of a dichotomy between uniformity (the production of a single perception of a leader) and multiplicity (the coexistence of multiple perceptions of a leader). In reality, the ruler cult united both cultural production and social reception in everyday life by offering such integrating structures as language, ritual, time, and space to increase communal solidarity.[80] Even in modern dictatorships, the complexity of the social actors involved and the variety of unique, individual experiences at play challenged and changed the message which the uniformity of ruler cults transmitted.[81] Since the mid-twentieth century, nostalgia and consumption have become two driving forces that created (and continue to create) a variety of individualizing discourses and practices which ordinary citizens used to develop a personal identity through the process of imagining the ruler.[82] Improvisation, creativity, the manipulation of artifacts, symbols, and communicative strategies which built spaces of agency for diverse individuals allowed large sectors of the population to produce, participate, interpret, and use these tools as part of the life of the state, the nation, the country, the city, and, last but not least, one's self. Linking an individual "I" with the leader became a way of self-fashioning that included not only buying and using goods bearing the leader's image, for example, clothing, watches, and dishes, but also creating one's own homemade pictures, postcards, collages, playing cards, and other things featuring portraits of leading state figures. A person's choice to be tattooed with the image of the leader marks the point of confluence of an individual body with the leader's political body: in this way many bodies of the ruler are multiplied on the physical bodies of individuals.[83] Unpacking the regime's standardized messages in the fates of millions of individual citizens and filling these messages with personal meanings is the driving force behind the regeneration of ruler cults in the contemporary world.

NOTES

1. Plekhanov's essay was first published in 1898 in the Russian journal *Nauchnoe obozrenie*. The English translation of the essay from which the epigraph at the beginning of this chapter is taken was published in 1940 as part of a collection of Plekhanov's writings. See Plekhanov, "On the Role of the Individual," 59–60.

2. Lepsius, "Das Modell der charismatischen Herrschaft"; Ennker, "Der Führer im Europa."

3. Cohen, "Cult of Number One," 611.

4. Jones, *Dilemmas of De-Stalinization*.

5. For examples, see Gill, "Personality Cult"; Thompson, "Reassessing Personality Cults"; Apor et al., *Leader Cult in Communist Dictatorships*; Luckey, *Personifizierte Ideologie*; Morgan, "Communism and the Leader Cult" and *Leaders, Tribunes and Martyrs*; Apor, "Communist Leader Cults in Eastern Europe."

6. Plamper, "Introduction: Modern Personality Cults."

7. On the *Begriffsgeschichte* of "family" over the *longue durée*, see Schwab, "Familie."

8. Hunt, *Family Romance*, 196.

9. Alföldi, *Der Vater des Vaterlandes*; Gradel, *Emperor Worship*.

10. Bernstein, *Founding Fathers Reconsidered*; Directorate-General for Communication (European Commission), *Founding Fathers of the EU*.

11. Stephanov, *Ruler Visibility*, 265.

12. On the late Ottoman Empire, see Stephanov, *Ruler Visibility*.

13. See Plunkett, *Queen Victoria*.

14. Stephanov, *Ruler Visibility*, 265.

15. Martin, *Affirmative Action Empire*.

16. Stites, "Utopian or Antiutopian?"

17. Herzfeld, *Social Production of Indifference*, 12.

18. For the Soviet Union, see Clark, *Soviet Novel*, 134–35.

19. On the *Sattelzeit*, see Büschel, *Untertanenliebe*, 314.

20. On state leaders as godparents, see Tikhomirov, "State as a Family"; Grigorov, "Could a Communist Leader be a Godfather?" In Yugoslavia approximately 45,000 people (godchildren and their families) were involved in spiritual kinship with Tito. See Halder, *Der Titokult*, 170–76.

21. Tikhomirov, "State as a Family," 412.

22. For example, Halder, *Der Titokult*, 158–59; Ironside, "Late Stalinist Welfare State."

23. The idea of working toward the sacred center or a leader has been outlined in several works, including Kershaw, "Working Towards the Führer"; Ennker, "Stalin Cult, Bolshevik Rule"; Rolf, "Working Towards the Centre"; Leese, *Mao Cult*, 128–47; Apor, *Invisible Shining*, 147–74. On the "process of mental centralization" in the Russian empire, see Stephanov, "Publichnye chestvovaniia."

24. Clark, *Moscow, the Fourth Rome*; Bernhard, "Metropolen auf Achse"; Bodenschatz, *Städtebau für Mussolini*.

25. Azaryahu, *Von Wilhelmplatz zu Thälmannplatz*; Crowley and Reid, *Socialist Spaces*; Dobrenko, *Landscape of Stalinism*.

26. For an example, see Cummings, "Leaving Lenin."

27. On the variety of forms and meanings of iconoclasm in premodern and modern political cultures, see Tikhomirov, "Symbols of Power."

28. Geertz, "Centers, Kings, and Charisma," especially 16–20.

29. Quoted in Wortman, "Moscow and Petersburg," 245. The increasing social demand for the ruler's visibility in capital cities became so strong during the nineteenth century that in absolutist Austria there was much criticism of Empress Elisabeth for her "prolonged absences from Vienna and her refusal to participate in imperial ceremonies." See Giloi, *Monarchy, Myth, and Material Culture*, 97.

30. Stephanov, *Ruler Visibility*, 261.

31. Büschel, *Untertanenliebe*, 310.

32. Truesdell, *Spectacular Politics*, 164.

33. Stephanov, *Ruler Visibility*, 262; Plamper, "Georgian Koba."

34. Stephanov, *Ruler Visibility*, 264.

35. See Schieder, *Mythos Mussolini*; Kershaw, *Hitler: 1889–1936*. From 1943 to 1980, Tito visited 1,677 Yugoslavian towns and villages, as discussed in Halder, *Der Titokult*, 98–99, 157 and Schmidt-Glintzer, "Mao Zedong die Inkarnation Chinas," 269.

36. Paulmann, *Pomp und Politik*; Derix, *Bebilderte Politik*.

37. On royal tourism in Germany, see Giloi, *Monarchy, Myth, and Material Culture*, 94–103.

38. Halder, *Der Titokult*, 108.

39. Leese, "Cult of Personality," 215.

40. Duggan, *Fascist Voices*, 429–35; Halder, *Der Titokult*, 278–79; Belaj, "I'm Not Religious."

41. Berenson and Giloi, *Constructing Charisma*.

42. Duggan, *Fascist Voices*, 73–74.

43. Giloi, "Autograph Hunting."

44. Plunkett, *Queen Victoria*.

45. Historians have identified some elements of the public funeral rituals of fourteenth-century rulers. These included displaying the ruler's military insignia, which was accompanied by the tears of the crowd, as described in Boytsov, "Ghostly Knights." On the funerals of modern leaders, see Riall, *Garibaldi*, 376–77; Stephanov, "Publichnye chestvovaniia," 102.

46. Ennker, *Die Anfänge des Leninkults*; Tumarkin, *Lenin Lives!*; Leese, "Cult of Personality," 341; Barmé, *Shades of Mao*; Großbolting, *Der Tod des Diktators;* Dror, "Establishing Ho Chi Minh's Cult".

47. Gentile, *Politics as Religion.*

48. Durkheim, *Die elementaren Formen*, 498.

49. Hein, *Der Pilsudski-Kult*, 11.

50. Dörner, *Politischer Mythos*, 54.

51. Halder, *Der Titokult*, 193–214; Leese, *Mao Cult*, 345.

52. For a detailed discussion, see chapter 4.

53. This has been a growing area of historical research in recent years. See, for example, N. Z. Davis, *Gift in Sixteenth-Century France*; Heal, *Power of Gifts.*

54. Simmel, *Untersuchungen*, 667.

55. Sosnina and Ssorin-Chaikov, "Archaelogy of Power," 13.

56. Mauss, *Die Gabe*, 4.

57. Algazi, Groebner, and Jussen, *Negotiating the Gift.*

58. Büschel, *Untertanenliebe*, 313–24.

59. Büschel, *Untertanenliebe*, 321.

60. Ssorin-Chaikov and Sosnina, "Faculty of Useless Things."

61. Leese, *Mao Cult*, 215.

62. For examples of this, see Behrenbeck, "'Der Führer'"; Schrift, *Biography of a Chairman Mao Badge*; Gaudenzi, "Dictators for Sale."

63. On the commodification of political symbols, see Moor, *Selling God*; Daunton and Hilton, *Politics of Consumption*; Lamla and Neckel, *Politisierter Konsum*; Casey, *Che's Afterlife*; Scarpellini, *Material Nation*; Swett, *Selling Under the Swastika.*

64. Hein, *Der Pilsudski-Kult.*

65. Gerwarth and Riall, "Fathers of the Nation?"; Gerwarth, *Bismarck Myth.*

66. Navaro-Yashin, *Faces of the State*; Hanioğlu, *Atatürk.*

67. Schenk, *Aleksandr Nevskij*; Perrie, "Nationalism and History."

68. Hobsbawm and Ranger, *Invention of Tradition*. For medieval Europe, see Klaniczay, *Holy Rulers*. For an example of Stalin in the German Democratic Republic, see Abusch, *Stalin und die Schicksalsfragen*. On the role of the book *Ruhnama* in nation-building in Turkmenistan, see Turkmenbashi, *Ruhnama.*

69. Leese, *Mao Cult*, 4–5.

70. Armstrong, *North Korean Revolution*, 223.

71. Apor, *Invisible Shining*, 39.

72. For examples, see Getty, *Practicing Stalinism* and Brandenberger and Dubrovsky, "The People Need a Tsar."

73. Hobsbawm, *Age of Extremes*. See also Dikötter, *How to Be a Dictator.*

74. For some examples, see Goscilo, *Putin as Celebrity*; Denison, "Art of the Impossible"; Polese and Horák, "Tale of Two Presidents."

75. On the medieval legitimization of the invisibility of the ruler's physical body because it can damage the sovereign's political body, see Kantorowicz, *King's Two Bodies*, 7. On the growing visibility of the ruler with the onset of modernity, see Stephanov, *Ruler Visibility* as well as Plamper, *Stalin Cult.*

76. On the primacy of seeing in the hierarchy of senses, see Jütte, *Geschichte der Sinne*, 75–77.

77. Barclay, "'Invention' of a Monarchical Tradition"; Büschel, *Untertanenliebe*; Frevert, *Gefühlspolitik*; Giloi, *Monarchy, Myth, and Material Culture*. On legitimacy

and popular support in twentieth-century mass dictatorships, see Kershaw, *'Hitler Myth'*; Corner, *Popular Opinion in Totalitarian Regimes*; Postoutenko, *Totalitarian Communication*; Merl, *Politische Kommunikation in der Diktatur*.

78. Walzer, "Role of Symbolism," 194.

79. Prosperi, *Justice Blindfolded*, especially chap. 5, "Justice and Grace"; N. Z. Davis, *Fiction in the Archives*; Härter and Nubola, *Grazia e giustizia*.

80. For examples, see Glyptis, "Living Up to the Father"; Cassiday and Johnson, "Post-Soviet Cult of Personality."

81. For a comparative and communicative approach to analyzing socialist heroes, see Satjukow and Gries, *Sozialistische Helden*.

82. For examples of different cultural meanings of nostalgia, see Boym, *Future of Nostalgia*; Todorova and Gille, *Post-Communist Nostalgia*; Maertz, *Nostalgia for the Future*.

83. Irina Paperno analyzed the fusion of the bodies of physical subjects with the real (mortal) and political (symbolic) body of the leader in the shared tears shed over Stalin's death in March 1953 in "Intimacy with Power." See also Postoutenko, "Stalin's Two Bodies?" On multiple aspects of body politics, see Waylen et al., *Oxford Handbook of Gender and Politics*.

Chapter 2

The Empire of Stalinism

The USSR and East Germany after 1945

THE STALIN CULT BETWEEN THE CENTER AND THE PERIPHERY: SOVIETIZATION AS SYMBOLIC POLITICS

The gala premiere of the Soviet epic film *The Fall of Berlin* took place in June 1950 in East Berlin. The invited guests included the East German political establishment and an official Soviet delegation. In the closing scene, a plane lands in Berlin, in front of the Reichstag during the May 1945 Victory Day celebration. The door of the plane opens and Stalin—garbed as the generalissimo, in a white dress uniform with epaulets and decorations—appears before the jubilant masses. With numerous portraits of Stalin amid rippling flags, the crowd greets the victor who liberated the world from fascism with wild ovations.[1] In this scene, the words of Stalin's biographer, Henri Barbusse, seem to be realized on the screen: "He [Stalin] is the very center, the heart of all that radiates from Moscow through the entire world."[2] The film presents the viewer with a new sacral center of power and a new leader. More broadly, the scene of Stalin arriving in Berlin from Moscow symbolizes the coming of the Stalin cult from the center to the periphery as a result of the Sovietization of the countries of Central and Eastern Europe after World War II.

The export of the Stalin cult to the Eastern bloc became the symbolic instrument by which the center expanded to the periphery.[3] Moscow's global "civilizing mission" justified this extension of the boundaries of the postwar Soviet empire: the USSR promised help in building socialism and communism in order to achieve the "bright future," to strengthen peace throughout the world, and, in the eschatological sense, to save Western European civilization.[4] The propagems of "the friendship of the peoples" and "one brotherly family" crossed the borders of the Soviet Union, legitimizing the gathering of states loyal to the socialist idea into a single empire—a cult community with an integrated center around Stalin.[5] Propaganda presented Moscow as the exemplar for imitation, in effect telling those on the periphery: "Here is where the leader works. Here is where world politics happen, and the most important decisions are made, decisions that shape the fates of millions of people. This is where the future is being built." In the metanarrative of empire, the center was a treasure chest of symbolic capital: it was the repository of experience and knowledge, and the code of honor and morality, the source of material resources and power.

On the periphery, Sovietization was based on symbolic politics—the propaganda of integrating narratives, symbols, and images of empire—instead of fear and coercion.[6] When yesterday's Bolshevik revolutionaries encountered European political cultures, new tactics were needed to establish communist rule in Europe. In May 1945, Marshal Zhukov declared in Berlin that "We have stormed Berlin, but we will first have to fight for the souls of the Germans. It will be a difficult battle and now our front line runs right here."[7] Henceforth the task became "to win the [population's] hearts and minds, love and trust" for the USSR while working toward the main goal—to build Soviet-style societies that Moscow could unify and control. Designing a single discursive space of socialism, introducing a new cycle of party-state rituals and holidays, and creating new national myths and histories infused with Marxist-Leninist theory, the concept of class struggle, and Stalin's life story drove the homogenization of the ideological landscape and the synchronization of the empire's political life. Personality cults of communist leaders, especially the Stalin cult, were the core of both the symbolic politics of Stalinism and modern mass politics in state- and society-building. By 1949, in conjunction with the transnational campaign to celebrate Stalin's seventieth birthday, the countries of the Eastern bloc had definitively nationalized Soviet representations of the personality cult. These representations were reproduced in official ceremonies, in the public spaces of cities and villages, and in the mass media. The Bolshevik propaganda state became the propaganda empire of Stalinism.[8]

Despite the formal sovereignty of the "people's democracies," imperial representations propagandizing the cult of the Soviet leader were constructed to create the impression of unity, stability, and an indestructible bond joining the center—Moscow—and the periphery—in this case, East Germany. However, a more detailed, decentralized approach to analyzing the Stalin cult shows that it was not identical across the Eastern bloc. Moscow offered the periphery only one scenario for the Stalin cult. On the outskirts of the empire, it was translated into each state's language and incorporated into national symbolic systems; it was superimposed on regional traditions and representations of the past, took account of local models of collective memory, and allowed for continuity with already existing forms of shared memory and the structures organizing daily life. The center developed many different strategies for communicating with the outskirts. As a result, the national polyphonies of the Stalin cult rang out in unison. In East Germany, propaganda of the cult of the Soviet leader under the rubric of "Stalin, the best friend of the German people" was the outcome of this policy.

The process of annexing the periphery to the center was similar to the medieval commendation ceremony, which created a bond linking a lord and his vassal. This relationship was based on the principle of mutual obligations: the patron offered protection in exchange for the client's promise of loyalty.[9] The imperial hierarchy governing Stalin's relationship with the East German leadership was constructed on this paternalistic principle.[10] To strengthen this masculine union, the rhetoric of the "blood tie" was employed along with arguments for using a single code of honor and invocations of the shared experience of revolutionary struggle and political persecution.[11] All of these arguments were used to create representations of "political kinship" which offered European societies the Soviet metaphor of the "big family of peoples" as a model for postwar solidarity: the image of the USSR as the "older brother" legitimated the need for supporting the inexperienced "younger brothers" from whom obedience and loyalty were required.[12] This symbolic politics of Stalinism had advantages for both sides. It allowed the East German leadership to receive economic, military, and political aid from the Soviet Union. The GDR could not have existed without these resources. For the Kremlin, symbolic politics justified intervention in European politics and gave it leverage in the affairs of the states of Central, Eastern, and Southern Europe.

Although Moscow's economic, military, and administrative resources were important in cementing the postwar Soviet empire, ideology was its central nexus.[13] Ideology had the potential to transform space, society, and the individual by regulating the dynamics of several processes that were crucial for the common project of building a communist future: differentiation and homogenization; inclusion and exclusion; and social engineering. It defined communist rule by reshaping identities, moralities, values, tastes, and sentiments and, more generally, by establishing socialism as a way of life. Ideology promised that communist modernity could be achieved by legitimizing violence and terror, and eliminating the "weeds," thereby bringing purity and order to the "new man" living in the "gardening state."[14] In asserting Soviet hegemony in Eastern Europe in the early postwar years, the Kremlin invoked the right of nations to self-determination, which was well known to the Bolsheviks. At the Allied Conference in Potsdam (July 17–August 2, 1945), Stalin repeated this principle:

> We do not have and cannot have such goals . . . as to impose our will and our regime . . . on the peoples of Europe waiting for our help. Our goal is to support

these peoples in their liberation struggle . . . and then to give them the freedom
to settle on their land as they wish.[15]

Promoting national particularism and ethnic diversity made it possible
to include different peoples, territories, and cultures in the cult community.[16] The principle of the "friendship of peoples" justified the policy of
Sovietization and was effectively used to strengthen the empire by creating
societies closely bonded with the Soviet Union and sharply increasing the
export of cultural products about the "first socialist country."[17]

The Stalin cult became an indicator of the extent to which the East German
political leadership depended on the Kremlin and a sign of the Soviet Union's
postwar imperial ambitions. This symbiosis appears especially vividly in
"Giving Thanks" ("Danksagung"), the poem that Johannes Becher, one of
East Germany's best-known politicians and intellectuals, wrote on Stalin's
death in March 1953.[18] It describes what the Stalin cult meant in producing
the postwar Soviet empire's symbolic universe: for the GDR it promised to
resolve the "German question" by reuniting the state and nation under the
aegis of the Soviet leader, while for the USSR, the cult ensured the expansion
of the Soviet sphere of influence in East Germany and beyond its western borders.[19] Thus, East German cultural production about the Stalin cult shows that
the periphery itself thrived on and was sympathetic to the center's imperial
sentiments. For East Germany, the cult of the Soviet leader was an instrument
for legitimating its totalitarian rule. For the Soviets, the Stalin cult became a
global project of symbolic politics with the potential for the limitless export
of Stalinism to new territories.

THE BOUNDARIES OF THE "DICTATORSHIP
OF DISCOURSE": CREATING A UNIFIED
DISCURSIVE SPACE OF SOCIALISM

When the Red Army arrived in Germany, Moscow began to export Soviet
narratives, symbols, and rituals to a defeated society. The victors transferred
Bolshevik imaginations of how the "new world" should be constructed to
former enemy territories and attempted to make them work on German soil.
More decisive was the establishment of the apparatus of surveillance and
institutions of oversight which aimed to transform the negative picture of
the Soviet Union as an "enemy" into the positive image of the "first socialist
country in the world." In so doing, the liberators brought a set of representations that crucially reshaped the organization of knowledge, experience, and
collective identity, above all through the emergence of official discourse and
ways of controlling it.[20] According to Michel Foucault, language constructs

the world and objectifies reality.[21] By establishing a framework for seeing, living in, and interpreting the postwar situation under Soviet occupation, the leadership of the USSR imposed strict discursive and behavioral rules on East Germans, directing them to perceive Sovietization in a positive way. Therefore, reconstructing the official discourse, or, more precisely, the mechanisms whereby it was produced and protected from damage, is to expose a "fundamental code of culture," which removes the veil of inaccessibility to uncover the register of public language and rules of conduct.[22] This reconstruction moreover reveals both the areas of subordination and the spaces of belonging in which citizens become not only "prisoners" of the discourse of power but also its consumers, beneficiaries, and producers.

On June 9, 1945, Marshal Georgy Zhukov announced the creation of the Soviet Military Administration in Germany (SVAG).[23] It was the highest executive, legislative, and judicial body in the Soviet Occupation Zone to implement the provisions of the Potsdam Agreement in East Germany.[24] The Red Army was given the official status of the Group of Soviet Occupation Forces in Germany. According to the documents, the new power structures were supposed to help democratize postwar Germany but, in fact, they facilitated the gradual Sovietization of every aspect of life and made it possible to establish the "dictatorship of discourse" by defining the boundaries of permitted rhetoric, topics, sentiments, and behavioral patterns in public spaces.[25]

In liberated Germany, 50,000 Soviet citizens employed by SVAG implemented Stalinist orders. In an internal political report of September 7, 1946, Lieutenant Colonel Staroselskii described them as "random people who are unable to write correctly and have very limited horizons [who are assigned to] perform complex tasks and study problems which they do not understand but which are also alien [to them]."[26] Although they risked being sent back to the USSR for inappropriate or criminal behavior, SVAG employees were not infrequently accused of abuse of office and financial misconduct. Murder, responsibility for car accidents, and drunkenness, with a resulting arbitrariness toward the local population, were added to the "blacklist" cataloging a Soviet citizen's immoral behavior when abroad. But these accusations mainly concerned lower- and middle-level SVAG employees. A political report about the emotional health of Soviet employees abroad described their mixed feelings—engagement and passivity as well as homesickness and excitement about being in the West. And, although many of them could not speak the language and did not know much about German history or local traditions, their common ideological goal was unequivocal: to build a new social order by reeducating the Germans.

In contrast, the highest administrative posts were occupied by well-educated military men who spoke German fluently and had the skills to orient themselves to the postwar situation.[27] In spite of the strong impulse toward unification from Moscow, the postwar Soviet empire was a cult community that balanced the search for ideological consistency with practical flexibility, getting rid of differences and establishing homogeneity, thereby combining pragmatic solutions with utopian visions. Without a doubt, SVAG officials were limited by the Bolshevik experience and their knowledge of Soviet administration, but at the same time, they were forced to take into account local memories and the subaltern society's mood. Those in the higher echelons were sensitive to the challenges of the times and were aware of the need to adapt Soviet propaganda to German conditions. G. M. Bespalov, the head of SVAG's Information Bureau, criticized an excessive Soviet coloration in the work of the propaganda agencies and proposed a move to "a more delicate and clever promotion that introduces the audience to the advantages of the Soviet social order in a subtle way."[28] To achieve this, he suggested creating a single focal point for propaganda in Moscow, in order to unite the efforts of VOKS, the TASS news agency, the Sovinformbiuro, and enlisting other organizations in promoting the USSR's achievements in East Germany. In a conversation with Jürgen Kuczynski, the chairman of the Society for the Study of Culture of the Soviet Union, Bespalov made specific suggestions about how to discuss socialist development with an audience with a Western mentality: give considerable space to cartoons, humor, and photographs of such scenes as intermissions at theaters with buffets supplied with snacks; tidy and uncrowded tram carriages; full shops with well-dressed, smiling customers; and nightlife in Moscow and other capitals of the "people's democracies." Socialism was supposed to show off its style and present an appealing face in reports on fashion, holidays, sports, and "great personalities" (*velikie lichnosti*).[29]

A typical feature of the Soviet style of rule—which manifested itself in East Germany in full measure—was the effort to control every kind of information issued from every possible source.[30] The all-encompassing system of surveillance established the practical and symbolic boundaries of the "dictatorship of discourse" which helped to clamp the subject in a rhetorical and behavioral vise of unfreedom. SVAG's Propaganda Department played a key role in creating the mechanisms for subordinating the East German population to the rules of life, Soviet style. The new department, which was headed by Sergei I. Tiul'panov, was created by Order No. 29 of August 18, 1945, and belonged to SVAG's Political Section.[31] In January 1947, the Central Committee of the VKP(b) recommended that the name of this organ be changed to the "Information Department" since reports from various places indicated that for Germans the term "propaganda" had negative associations with Goebbels and his ministry.[32] Historians argue that as the largest structure to be introduced, the Propaganda Department was able to construct a single ideological line and pursue an independent political course in the Soviet zone.[33] However, we note that from the very beginning of the Propaganda Department's operations, this approach assumed that the department would work closely with the Central Committee's Department of Propaganda and Agitation. The sources show that the secretaries of the Central Committee approved, coordinated, and directed every step that the German division took. Moscow approved lists of literature, films, lectures, and exhibitions for the Soviet zone.[34] The ideological goal of all of these measures was to give the German people a positive picture of the Soviet Union.

In fact, the Soviet occupation was supposed to be an ideological occupation. To achieve the goal of making the ideological landscape uniform, SVAG's efforts to gain complete control of all information sources began early on. These included confiscating fascist literature, registering all printing presses and other means of replicating print materials, and creating a system for censoring print production.[35] Order No. 1 of April 30, 1945, issued by the head of the garrison and military commandant of Berlin, required that all owners of printing presses, typewriters, and other apparatus for replication of printed materials register with military commandants, whose consent was required to print, store, and distribute materials of every kind whatsoever.[36] "Nazi and militaristic literature," which threatened to distort the positive image of the Soviet Union and the Soviet leaders, was removed from libraries and bookstores.[37] SVAG also set up collection sites where private individuals could bring their Nazi literature. The materials that were collected and seized were locked in closed repositories.[38] Against this backdrop, I. S. Kolesnichenko, the head of SVAG in Thuringia, recommended that the Central Committee of the VKP(b) make the kinds of strategic decisions that would fill the book market in Germany with Soviet Marxist political literature and fiction, so the Germans would have nothing else to read but Soviet publications.[39] According to a report from August 1948, by that time SVAG's press had already published more than 2.5 million Russian-language textbooks. These included many articles about the Soviet Union, poetry by Russian authors, and materials about Soviet leaders, the structure of the state, and the history of the USSR. Russian was introduced as the first foreign language pupils would study in all schools in the Soviet zone, reaching over 700,000 children.[40]

From August 18, 1945, onward, censorship was concentrated in the sector for propaganda and censorship in SVAG's political department.[41] Even the smallest note could not be published unless it had the Soviet censor's stamp. All print production was controlled as were presses, cinemas, German information agencies, theaters, and cabarets as well as channels for distributing information, including telephone and telegraph lines and radio.[42] The censorship honed the discursive register—the set of metaphors, images, rules of rhetoric, assumptions, and prohibitions—that both the media and the population of the entire Soviet zone had to use. A variety of topics could not be discussed in the press and on the radio: criticism of SVAG's orders, inordinate praise of the Red Army, the topic of "refugees from the east," and any comparisons of the postwar development of East Germany with the western zones mentioning the dismantling of industry and reparations. SVAG insistently recommended monitoring the way the surnames and titles of Soviet leaders and SVAG officials were written to make sure they were correct. Every month reports on consultations with German newspapers were sent to SVAG's Information Department. These internal documents identified "mistakes" that had appeared in newspapers and made recommendations for improving the way propaganda influenced the population.[43] For example, reports about organizations for women and young people were allowed only in the context of coverage of antifascist activities. On the other hand, it was recommended that letters from former prisoners of war with descriptions of positive experiences during Soviet captivity should be published. Likewise, SVAG sought to reassure the population while being vague about the timeline for releasing German POWs.[44]

The harsh rules governing the use of public rhetoric helped to criminalize violations of the dictatorship's discursive order. Surprisingly, even members of SVAG's staff became victims of the policy of "learning to speak Soviet." For example, after a slip-up passed the censor, one which included "distortions of quotations from Comrade Stalin's statements [that twisted them] into an anti-Soviet form," L. I. Novik lost his position as the head of the Propaganda Department's censorship section in the provinces of Mecklenburg and Western Pomerania.[45] In addition, ordinary people who violated the rules of rhetoric and behavior were declared, using Bolshevik language, to be "fascist elements" and "enemies of the people," and they were excluded from the rest of the population in several ways.[46] Having become objects of intimidation and violence, they were arrested, or expelled, or subjected to administrative punishments, and there were cases where people disappeared without a trace.[47] For the regime, censorship of public space was just a first step. The larger goal was to use it to introduce internal self-regulation of individual behavior, which would reduce to the minimum deviations from the dictatorship's discursive register.

On November 27, 1946, the newspaper *Tägliche Rundschau* published a notice about the abolition of preliminary censorship in the Soviet zone. However, Soviet control of the media continued as before. Sergei Tiul'panov explained that "the only change was in the forms of control over the press," not a complete end to Soviet monitoring.[48] From now on, during personal conversations with Soviet censors, the editors of East German newspapers and radio made a commitment to use only preapproved materials from SVAG's Information Bureau and TASS. The Allgemeine Deutsche Nachrichtendienst (General German News Service), which was created in October 1946, had the same goal: to unify the regime's political discourse in the Soviet zone by excluding all alternative opinions.[49] Censorship was also maintained in the work of the publishing houses: publication of materials was permitted only if they were licensed by SVAG authorities. By using and replicating unified information, the "dictatorship of discourse" sought to monopolize the right to interpret reality in order to construct a monolithic political space and its own regime of "truth."

Censorship became a key element of the Soviet occupation forces' media policy.[50] In August 1946, Sergei Tiul'panov announced that

> along with the decisive struggle against each individual anti-Soviet sortie, it is necessary to systematically propagandize the Soviet Union, to show the German people and inculcate into its consciousness the fact that the USSR is the mightiest power in the world, that only in it does [the German people] have a reliable defender and a guarantee against a possible repeat of the catastrophe into which Germany was plunged as a result of both world wars.[51]

He called on the regional heads of the Propaganda Department to "force the editorial boards of German newspapers and radio to carry out systemic propaganda of the Soviet Union."[52] As a result, the Propaganda Department was put in charge of supervising work done by the Information Bureau, SVAG's publishing house, the Berlin department of Soiuzintorgkino (the foreign trade organization that dealt with films), and the editorial boards of *Tägliche Rundschau*, the radio stations, and the House of German-Soviet Friendship in Berlin.[53] Censorship of radio programs and newspapers, as well as the theater and cinema, fell within the Propaganda Department's remit.[54]

According to a statement made by Moscow, as of December 1946, the Propaganda Department controlled thirty-seven newspapers, five radio stations, and fifty-two magazines.[55] As the cultural adviser reported, no Soviet film could be released in German cinemas without special permission from the Department of Propaganda.[56] Trying to exclude alternative information sources from East Germany's discursive field, SVAG installed silencers for Western radio stations.[57] A local initiative in the fight against nonconformist opinions was devised in Erfurt. There, the FDJ set up "detective brigades" at the post office and the railway. They aimed to find out which radio programs the population was listening to and identify people who frequently visited the western zones to bring "capitalist" newspapers back to East Germany.[58] The effort to exert ubiquitous control over the circulation of information led to an order issued by SVAG on June 12, 1946, in Mecklenburg Province to monitor all pigeon breeding and postal pigeon stations. This was a result of Soviet bureaucrats' anxiety that some people in different occupation zones were using airmail to exchange letters.[59] The "dictatorship of discourse" had to have securely guarded boundaries—on earth and in the skies.

Nonetheless, the territory bordering West Germany was particularly problematic in terms of maintaining informational homogeneity in East Germany because of the direct discursive competition of the capitalist and socialist systems. Although the Control Council adopted Directive No. 55 "On the Interzonal Exchange of Printed Materials and Films" on June 25, 1947, SVAG used all available channels of influence to close the Soviet zone's external borders, through which Western newspapers, magazines, and films could pass.[60] Because Soviet officials feared their negative influence on the population, it pressured the major wholesalers, who, in turn, blocked retail trade and sent large shipments of newspapers back to the West, explaining that they were doing this due to low demand.[61] Discouraged by the lack of agreement about how to implement interzonal payments, SVAG forbade East Germans to subscribe to Western periodicals. The Western magazines, newspapers, and other periodicals were ordered to stop the subscriptions and return the money subscribers had paid or suggest that they subscribe to newspapers produced in the Soviet zone.[62] From the autumn of 1948 on, SVAG moved to a more explicit policy of banning print materials produced in the West or even those published in East Germany without a Soviet license.[63] Efforts to remove all sources of alternative knowledge led to a purge of public space that included regularly checking bookstores, kiosks, beauty salons, and public libraries, putting kiosks, buffets, and restaurants in and near train stations under observation, and creating squads of criminal police whose job was to monitor the post offices, train stations, and riverboat stations to check automobiles and trucks going between the zones. Guarding border territories and places of potential contact with the western zones reflected SVAG's determination to unify discursive space by strengthening and closing the external borders of the "dictatorship of discourse."

However, the fact that the two German states were side by side inevitably led to disruptions of official attempts to create a consolidated East German information space. For example, one day in the summer of 1952, leaflets with anti-SED slogans were found strewn around in one of the border areas. The local authorities brought in soldiers, the police, and workers to collect them. The workers were told that if they concealed the leaflets in order to distribute them elsewhere they would be fined heavily. On the way back, a police observer was in each car and the people who had been sent to gather the leaflets were searched when they got out.[64] People living in areas bordering on West Germany were especially able to form their own ideas about the positive trends in the neighboring zone. In one instance, an SED member in the border town of Harz attempted to block the locals' Western contacts. At a meeting, this SED member talked about successes in building socialism and described the increasing hunger, shortages, and unemployment in the western zones. But his audience responded to this propagandistic tale with angry cries of displeasure. As had happened earlier, proximity to West Germany enabled everyone living in border areas to cross the border more than once to buy food and other goods to avoid starvation.[65]

The practice of compiling reports and political dispatches on the moods of the population was in itself an important tool used to create the "dictatorship of discourse." On November 30, 1945, Tiul'panov signed an order about composing political reports for all the *Länder* and regions which were supposed to reflect prevailing German public opinion on current issues.[66] On April 8, 1946, a decree about the preparation of monthly, quarterly, and annual reports for the civilian structures followed. In order to control compliance with this order in the provincial and district administrations, "information departments" were created. KPD members were the only ones who could be in charge of these.[67] These organs usually processed the initial reports from the regional and district representatives of the political parties, the mass organizations and organs of local government, the security organs, and mayors.[68] Then the information went to the regional departments of the information departments attached to the military commandants, and only after that did it reach the central bureau in Karlshorst.[69] It was obligatory to send a copy of each report to the operations sector of the Soviet Ministry of Internal Affairs and the NKVD for investigation of "particularly dangerous issues" in the population.[70] In this way, the reports were not only a tool for collecting public opinion but were also an effective way to control and take action against nonconformist behavior.

Questions about the East German population's relationship to Stalin generally occupied a central place in informational and political reports produced by Soviet and administrative authorities.[71] However, there were also several situations in which the regime took a special interest in the Germans' attitudes toward the "leader." Among these were propaganda campaigns organized to celebrate Stalin's birthday, the popularization of his works, and an interview that he gave to foreign journalists. In those cases, SVAG (or, from October 1949, the Soviet Control Commission [Sowjetische Kontrollkommission or SKK]) gave special orders about studying public opinion. As a rule, such "commissioned" opinion polls offered the "expected" results, which were supposed to confirm the success of propaganda work with the population. In 1950, trade union officials at enterprises in Jena were ordered to fill out questions from the German-Soviet Friendship Society with the following questions: "Were events for celebrating Stalin's birthday organized?"; "Did individuals and groups make commitments [that they would fulfill in honor

of the leader]?"; "Were congratulatory telegrams sent to the Soviet Union?";
"How successfully were enterprises and workplaces decorated [with banners,
posters, and the like]?"[72]

The reports were supposed to be presented to the mayor's secretariat with
"strict punctuality" on December 22, that is, on the day after the celebrations were over. A year later, reports noted that throughout the country the
Germans had gained more familiarity with carrying out campaigns and these
had become more of a routine matter but the list of questions in which the
regime was interested became broader: "How many events were there and
with how many participants?" "How many collective and individual letters
were sent to Stalin?" "How many collective and individual commitments
were made in conjunction with Stalin's seventy-second birthday?" "How
many Stalin corners and exhibitions were organized?" "How many discussions about the Soviet leader's works took place?"[73] The officials made a
point of mentioning examples of the best letters, congratulatory telegrams,
drawings, and presents for Stalin.

When previously secret archives in Russia and Germany became accessible in the 1990s, scholars were able to begin talking about the reliability
and expediency of using reports and dispatches as historical sources.[74]
Taking a social constructivist approach, I read such sources as a mirror of
power relationships and as an ideological way to frame reality rather than
using them as an opportunity to delve into the world of actual public opinion.[75] Thus, the discussion that follows centers on the representations of the
regime reproduced by those who wrote the dispatches. In other words, it is
concerned with the official understanding of how to construct the state and
society, classes and social hierarchies, "friends" and "enemies," and ideas
"from above" about how to construct interpretations of the past, present, and
future in a progressive narrative of development leading toward the "bright
future." In the reports and dispatches, the state and the party constructed a
world of public opinion which would lend legitimacy to the political order
that they created.[76] On one hand, the reports staged a society of consensus,
a harmonious unity of the opinions of the SED and the population. On the
other hand, the reports simultaneously established the discursive boundaries
of the rhetoric the population was allowed to use and the behavior they could
engage in. If they went beyond the borders of the permissible, they could be
branded as "enemies of the new social order" and "enemies of Stalin," and
consequently punished.

Notes made by the censor in the margins of the reports give the historian
a unique opportunity to catch a glimpse of the attitudes of SVAG's staff and
to understand the categories that guided them in their day-to-day routines.
Thus, in a dispatch about the moods of the population in the province of
Mecklenburg and Western Pomerania, the word "terrorist" was written next

to the opinion of someone in the village of Waltersdorf who was in favor of future retaliation against all the Russians' accomplices. The negative comments made by a former KPD member who lived in Greifswald and was critical of German communists and the Soviet regime's reparations policy, while expressing sympathy for life in the western zones, were characterized as "treason," and he was described as a "bastard."[77] The sentiments a priest in Pasewalk expressed in a conversation with a KPD member, which conveyed some doubts about whether the Communist Party's course was popular or appropriate, were called a "provocation."[78] And the owner of a printing shop in the town of Gadebusch, who complained about exporting grain to the Soviet Union, was called a "lying bastard."[79]

However, words like "good" and "correct" were written next to affirmative comments about the KPD's and SVAG's activities. The censor noted the positive effect produced when a German who had been in British captivity refuted provocative rumors in a conversation with the population of the village of Zittow in the Schwerin region:

> I was going to go home in the summer, but I was afraid because in England a rumor started that the Russian army was robbing everyone and raping women and anyone who protested was shot [and] all the healthy people were being sent to Siberia. I came home anyway and became convinced that this was a pack of lies.[80]

The comments in the margins confirm SVAG's intention to create its own regime of "truth," which was a mix of official knowledge and representations of reality which legitimized the Red Army's presence and Soviet policies in postwar East Germany. A zone of "untruth" was simultaneously established. Alternative opinions that the regime would not tolerate, ideas that were seen as violations of the Soviet order, fell into this zone, and those holding such views were labeled "reactionaries," "fascists," "enemies," "scum," "imperialists," and "militarists."[81]

In East Germany, the structure of the reports reflected the Soviet practice of using the principles of class struggle and a bipolar division of the world as the basis for compiling political dispatches.[82] Their main goal was to represent "nationwide support" for the political order, which would confirm the legitimacy of the occupying powers and, after October 1949, the SED dictatorship. The first part of every report always included expressions of enthusiasm, approval, and support for the occupying regime's actions. The authors of the reports usually attributed positive feelings about the regime to workers and peasants. In the framework of Marxist-Leninist ideology, they were supposed to provide social support for the "worker-peasant state." These were precisely the social groups (along with members of the party and the mass organizations) who were designated as "friends of Stalin." The second part of the report gave examples of antigovernment sentiments. Here intellectuals, housewives, and pensioners were much likelier to show up as the sources of negative or "hostile" sentiments. These ranged from making critical comments and asking provocative questions at meetings to shouting out antigovernment opinions and passing on rumors. At the farthest end of this spectrum were notes describing actual acts of iconoclasm and vandalism of the regime's official iconography.

In the political dispatches, former members of the NSDAP were a social group that posed particular dangers for the "new antifascist democratic order." Because of their "dark past" (*temnoe proshloe*), they were automatically labeled as "instigators" and "wreckers," "saboteurs," and "warmongers"—covert accomplices linked to the major threat, which was attributed to the "imperialist, capitalist West."[83] The state strove to exclude people expressing anti-Soviet or pro-Nazi opinions from social mobility and political activity, resorting to limiting their rights as citizens, criminalizing, and repressing this segment of the population. It was not a coincidence that starting in 1946 SVAG demanded that reports include personal information about the people whose views were recorded: name, gender, age, place of residence, party membership, profession, and social status. With this information in hand, SVAG was able to project the discursive constructs of the regime's "friends" and "enemies" onto real persons by legitimating social mobility for its supporters and repression for "other-minded people."[84]

Despite the predetermined and tendentious nature of the reports and dispatches, working with negative opinions enabled the regime to learn about spaces of agency and negotiations involving discursive borders where the population was allowed or forbidden to articulate different opinions. In beer halls and cafeterias, while standing in line and at bus stops, on the platforms and in the waiting halls of train stations, that is, in spaces which were more anonymous and impersonal, the population sensed that control was weaker, which meant they could speak more candidly.[85]

Often important information was communicated in informal spaces via rumors, including those about Stalin. Rumors comprised a field of information parallel to and in competition with the regime's official discourse. They signaled a lack of public confidence in one-sided, party-state information. On one hand, the constant circulation of rumors indicated an attempt to form an alternative collective identity in order to create some distance from the SED's rhetoric and rituals. On the other hand, rumors grew out of the population's desire to get used to postwar realities in order to find models for interpreting reality and for telling the new regime about their disappointments, anxieties, and hopes. The fact that rumors were rife shows how much people longed for a normal daily life that would allow them to fill the gaping holes in the available information, which were creating anxiety and a sense of instability. Thus, on the eve of the regional elections in Saxony, rumors went around about the consequences of not voting for the SED. People were saying if you did not vote for the SED, the authorities would reduce the already meager food rations and curtail the production norms, and POWs would remain in Soviet captivity even longer.[86]

In addition, rumors about taxes on bicycles, pianos, radios, furniture, and even windows facing onto the street stirred up anxieties. To stop them, SVAG regularly organized lectures with titles like "Rumors and Reality" and published information in the press refuting this kind of hearsay.[87] One such publication reprinted excerpts from Stalin's interview with US journalist Harold Stassen on April 9, 1947. During the foreign ministers' meeting in Moscow (March 10–April 24, 1947), there was no progress on the "German issue." Instead, a transition to the "doctrine of deterrence" was recorded: the recognition of a divided Germany and the Western powers' refusal to explore further compromises with the USSR as the Marshall Plan, which provided American economic aid for Western Europe after World War II, was taking shape. To prevent "panic-inciting rumors" that war was coming, the German newspaper reprinted Stalin's statements about how the prospects for cooperation between the socialist and capitalist systems would rule out a new global confrontation.[88]

Rumors have an enormous potential for mobilizing people by provoking social anxieties and even panic as soon as they begin to make the rounds. Unsurprisingly, the regime was afraid of rumors and attributed them to "Nazi elements who spread propaganda."[89] Thus, rumors that Soviet soldiers were concealing and then reselling food caused the wave of "hunger riots" that rolled across East Germany in the first postwar years.[90] In another case, in May 1951 the residents of a small town received anonymous telephone calls urging them to flee to the West if they wanted to save their lives and avoid sudden arrest. The source of the calls was never discovered but the information instantly flew around the city and sowed panic.[91] The spontaneous way that rumors spread, the impossibility of controlling them, and the difficulties involved in identifying their sources were extremely worrying for the authorities. However, the propaganda bodies, in cooperation with the Soviet security authorities, made efforts to identify and arrest people pushing gossip.[92]

Censoring private letters was another way to gain access to the population's thoughts and feelings.[93] In East Germany, this was carried out by the NKVD's military censors, who aimed to unmask "hidden enemies" among civilians. SVAG arbitrarily put an end to military commandants' attempts to examine private correspondence and punished them.[94] In particular, mail sent to the western zones was subject to mandatory censorship. SVAG's department of military censorship compiled thematic reports documenting anti-regime sentiments, based on letters that had been examined. According to a report compiled by the Social Democrats, the main post office in Potsdam was outfitted with a secret office for censoring letters. There, every day of the week, including Sunday, from 8 a.m. until 10 p.m., people (mostly women) worked under the supervision of a Russian officer. Reports described the content of the letters, and criticism of the SED, the Red Army, the Communist Party, and SVAG received special attention. As a result, mail delivery could take up to eight days.[95]

Party meetings were another way for the party and society to communicate. These gave the SED opportunities to become familiar with the population's opinions but also enabled them to shape those views by explaining the official discourse. Meetings enabled different actors and authorities to take each other's measure, engage in dialogue, compete, and negotiate with each other. They were spaces of agency where the population could discuss problems, bring up negative experiences, ask uncomfortable questions, and articulate their own visions of Germany's development.[96] Consequently, after every meeting the organizers had to fill out an obligatory questionnaire that asked about the number of participants, the questions people asked, and "anything special that happened."[97] For example, at one meeting, a worker asked how talks about recovery and progress in the GDR were actually going if his grandchildren did not have shoes and his family did not have enough to eat. An agitator immediately responded in the spirit of antifascist rhetoric: "Comrade, you did not formulate the question correctly! The question should sound different: Why did Hitler start a war in 1939 and [why did he] attack the peace-loving Soviet Union in 1941?"[98] As we will see, SVAG invoked Germans' collective guilt for unleashing World War II, using this idea to block critical perceptions of postwar realities and to shame them for the Nazi past. Despite the frequent lack of consensus about the issues discussed, meetings invariably ended with the ritualistic gesture of approving a resolution that expressed trust in the regime.

A special role in protecting the discursive borders of the Soviet zone was assigned to the NKVD, which was led by Ivan A. Serov. Formally, this security body was subordinate to Marshal Zhukov, the head of SVAG, but in reality, it reported directly to the USSR MGB and had the power to act independently in occupied territory. Its task was to eliminate political opponents of the USSR and the SED, former "nationalist elements," "spies," and "war criminals." By October 1945, the NKVD had already eliminated 359 cells of the clandestine Nazi Werewolf organization. In the first half of 1946, 3,300 people were arrested and another 213 "terrorist groups," with 1,350 members, were exposed.[99] At times, NKVD officers organized operations to identify "enemy elements" and arrest all suspicious persons. One of these "mopping up operations" was carried out on April 27–30, 1948, with unexpected raids and continuous sweeps of train stations, restaurants, hotels, and so on, carried out by the NKVD. Despite the fact that most of those arrested (19,717 people) were soon released, the purpose of such operations was to intimidate the local population and self-legitimize NKVD activities in order to objectify the hidden "enemy."[100] In general, on the territory of East Germany, former Nazis were arrested and sent to the USSR for forced labor or were imprisoned in former Nazi camps, which, after the peace offensive, were turned into special NKVD camps.[101] As of November 1947, more than 60,000 Germans were being held there.[102] Between May 1945 and May 1949, 41,907 German citizens died in these camps, which held 35 percent of the total number of German prisoners in the Soviet zone.[103]

To penetrate the world of opinion, the NKVD created a network of agents. As of January 1, 1946, more than 2,300 people worked for the Soviet "system of resistance to spying" (*sistema soprotivleniia shpionazhu*) in Germany. They observed the opposition parties and monitored the expression of anti-Soviet sentiments among the population. The SED also recruited "informers."[104] In the Soviet zone, the Socialist Unity Party became one of the first authorities to demand communication from the party about "the distribution of suspicious and provocative information." As a low-level East German bureaucrat at one of the party schools put it, "each [party] member must know that . . . you are speaking to the Party and you must tell the Party everything."[105] Party members were advised to pass on "dangerous" information stated by family members, relatives, friends, or acquaintances. They were also enjoined to report on what they heard on public transport, while standing in lines, and in hotels, in restaurants, and at train stations.[106] In an article in *Neues Deutschland* that appeared in early January 1950, Kurt Hager, the head of the party training division of the party's executive committee, called for the principle of "heightened vigilance" on the part of every party member.[107] Reacting to signals from the center, the district assembly of SED party functionaries adopted a resolution about creating "party groups of 20–25 people who can observe the population and quickly report on negative sentiments about the SED regime" in every village in the Börde district.[108]

With the establishment of the East German Ministry of State Security (the Stasi) in February 1950, a finely tuned mechanism for surveillance and combating opposition was created. Following the Soviet model, the Stasi created its own network of agents: their job was to report on every deviation from the official party line and to denounce everybody who doubted legitimacy of the "second German state." As the "eyes and ears" of the regime, they were supposed to observe, unmask, and take measures against "enemies of the people." In its first year alone, the Stasi arrested 2,625 "spies, diversionists, terrorists, and saboteurs."[109] Between 1950 and 1952, 30,000 people were recruited to be "secret informants" and "secret collaborators."[110] The network of informers had to include members of every social group and all the generations, even children. Thus, a primary school pupil who broke a window and had been late to school several times was called to the secretariat of the Union of Free German Youth for a "serious talk about immoral behavior": in exchange for weekly reports about discussions among his classmates, he would be given an official pardon for his shameful misdeeds.[111] Members of the mass organizations and the police also had to report on violations of discursive purity in the ideological space of the GDR. For example, during Carnival in Leipzig, the police dressed in costumes and wore masks so that they could join processions anonymously and mingle with the throngs of people enjoying the festivities in order to eavesdrop on antistate jokes.[112]

In parallel and in cooperation with the Stasi, the functions of prosecuting and condemning the "enemies" of the SED continued to be carried out by the Soviet authorities of the MGB (Ministry of State Security, the NKVD's successor). After the introduction of the death penalty in the USSR, more than 1,100 Germans were executed in Moscow between 1950 and 1953.[113] More than 22,000 Germans were convicted by Soviet military tribunals in East Germany as "spies," "saboteurs," and "enemies of the socialist system" and sentenced to long prison terms.[114] According to historian Nikita Petrov, some years earlier, in the period from 1945 to 1947, as a result of verdicts handed down by Soviet military tribunals in Germany, at least 5,000 Germans were shot.[115] The fundamentally different feature of a new wave of shootings of Germans after January 1950 became their removal to the USSR for the sentence to be carried out: as a rule, they were executed in the Butyrskaia prison in Moscow, and their bodies were burned in that city, in the Donskoe Cemetery's crematorium. In one such case, a twenty-year-old German was transported to Arkhangel'sk and shot on March 3, 1953. He had been charged with hooliganism: a terrorist group that he had supposedly organized allegedly destroyed a "peace corner." The decisive arguments for criminalizing the defendant were summarized by the fact that he had thrown knives at a portrait of a GDR leader.[116]

To summarize, it should be said that from the very beginning, SVAG set the boundaries of the "dictatorship of discourse," an ever-expanding web of rules and norms, prohibitions and taboos, mechanisms of control and subordination which intersected, amplified, and duplicated each other to achieve one and only one goal: to maintain the discursive purity and ideological homogeneity of East German political space. The GDR was transformed into a propaganda state analogous to the Soviet Union in its use of Bolshevik methods of censorship and media politics, agitation work, and opinion gathering. The regime's totalizing propaganda discourse was necessary to draw in and mobilize all of society: from children to elders, from workers and housewives to pregnant women and sick people.[117] It was recommended that agitators politicize the private spheres of the everyday life by placing posters with propaganda slogans on the landings in apartment blocks and encouraging people to set up "red corners" with socialist literature and newspapers at home. The party advised them to visit families in private and to have conversations with housewives and pregnant women in order to persuade them of the correctness of the SED's politics.[118] The only way the new regime showed any caution was to warn agitators that they should not try to propagandize at people's homes early in the morning because "the population does not like to let people into an apartment that has not been straightened up."[119]

The Bolshevik concept of "unified public opinion," which flowed from the principle of the unity of state, party, and private interests, guided propaganda activities.[120] This idea legitimized the creation of a "dictatorship of discourse" in which the SED, as the largest "party of workers and peasants," was given a monopoly on producing official narratives, images, and rituals that were aimed at reshaping the way to interpret reality. The fact that the West was nearby, however, contributed to the pluralization of public opinion in East Germany. Here, people were constantly reading Western books, magazines, and newspapers, and RIAS radio programs stoutly refuted claims made by Soviet propaganda. The constant presence of alternative, Western discourses turned the Bolshevik project of building a socialist society of unity and agreement into nothing less than undertaking to create a utopia.

Western media did not singlehandedly disrupt the homogeneity of East Germany's information space. Letters from friends and relatives, trips, and chance of meetings with people who lived in the western zones were much more reliable sources of information for East Germans. In March 1953, while propaganda was attempting to create the sense that the entire country was mourning Stalin's death, 58,000 people fled from East Germany to the West.[121] Even efforts to "immure" society by building the Berlin Wall in August 1961 did not bring the desired outcome. Only as a result of the web of control, surveillance, and prohibitions in which the entire society was enmeshed did the SED state succeed in maintaining the fragile boundaries of the "dictatorship of discourse." The following chapters will examine how important the Stalin cult was in stabilizing and decentering the East German political order.

NOTES

1. Hülbusch, "Dzugasvili der Zweite," 232–33.

2. Barbius, *Stalin*, 5.

3. On the Soviet Stalin cult, see Plamper, *Stalin Cult*; B. Apor et al., *Leader Cult in Communist Dictatorships*; Ennker, "Führerdiktatur—Sozialdynamik und

Ideologie"; Ennker, "Politische Herrschaft und Stalinkult 1929–1939." On exporting the cult to Central and Eastern Europe, see Tikhomirov, "Eksport kul'ta Stalina"; Behrends, "Exporting the Leader."

4. Alexander Abusch, "Ein neuer 'Retter' der abendländischen Kultur," *Neues Deutschland*, December 3, 1948, 3. See also Behrends, "Vom Panslavismus zum 'Friedenskampf.'"

5. The term "propagem" refers to the official narratives, visual images, and symbols that are in constant circulation in mass communication environments. These transmit ideological information to social actors in order to indoctrinate and mobilize the population on the regime's behalf. For a more detailed discussion of this concept, see Gries, "Zur Ästhetik und Architektur." On the key propagems of the Soviet empire, see Clark, *Soviet Novel*; Dobrenko and Naiman, *Landscape of Stalinism*; and Dobrenko, *Political Economy of Socialist Realism*.

6. See Rees, "Sovietization of Eastern Europe." On the USSR as a civilization of violence, see Baberowski, "Zivilisation der Gewalt" and *Der rote Terror*.

7. Hartmann, *Die Gesellschaft für Deutsch-Sowjetische Freundschaft*, 40.

8. Gaßner, Schleier, and Stengel, *Agitation zum Glück*; Behrends, "Freundschaft zur Sowjetunion"; Plamper, "Georgian Koba." For the concept of the "postwar Soviet empire," I draw on Michael W. Doyle's *Empires* and Stefan Plaggenborg's *Experiment Moderne*, 245–49.

9. Muir, *Ritual in Early Modern Europe*, 29–31.

10. Applebaum, *Iron Curtain*; Paczkowski, "Polish-Soviet Relations."

11. On the masculine nature of power in general, see Bourdieu, *Die männliche Herrschaft*; Baberowski, *Der rote Terror*, 15; Easter, *Reconstructing the State*.

12. Clark, *Soviet Novel*, 114–15.

13. On empires in history, see Eisenstadt, *Political System of Empires*; Lieven, *Empire*. For a discussion of the cultural and ethnic diversity of empires, see Barkey, *Empire of Difference*; Gerasimov et al., "New Imperial History."

14. Bauman, *Moderne und Ambivalenz*.

15. Quoted in Stykalin, "Ideologiia i kul'turnaia ekspansiia," 15.

16. See Slezkine, "USSR as a Communal Apartment"; Martin, *Affirmative Action Empire*; Plamper, "Georgian Koba"; Hirsch, *Empire of Nations*.

17. Stykalin, "Politika SSSR po formirovanii obshchestvennogo mneniia."

18. For example, "Es wird ganz Deutschland einstmals Stalin danken. / In jeder Stadt steht Stalins Monument. / Dort wird er sein, wo sich die Reben ranken, / Und dort in Kiel erkennt ihn ein Student. // . . . Dort wirst du, Stalin, stehn, in voller Blüte / Der Apfelbäume an dem Bodensee, / Und durch den Schwarzwald wandert seine Güte, / Und winkt zu sich heran ein scheues Reh." "Danksagung" can be found in Caspar, *Du Welt im Licht*, 219–23. See also Rybakow, "Johannes R. Bechers, Stalin-Oden."

19. On the fascination with Stalin in the West, see von Busse, *Faszination und Desillusionierung*.

20. Baberowski, "Selbstbilder und Fremdbilder"; Chartier, "Die Welt als Repräsentation."

21. Foucault, *Die Ordnung der Dinge*.

22. Foucault, *Die Ordnung der Dinge*, 23.

23. The decree creating the Soviet Military Administration in Germany was published on June 6, 1945, by the Council of People's Commissars of the USSR (Sovet Narodnykh Komissarov SSSR). See Broszat and Weber, *SBZ-Handbuch*, 49.

24. SVAG's main office was in the Berlin suburb of Karlshorst. Its Order No. 5 of July 9, 1945, made provisions for establishing five regional branches of the Soviet Military Administration. These would be located in Brandenburg, Mecklenburg, Saxony, Saxony-Anhalt, and Thuringia. The commanders of the troops stationed there were appointed heads of the regional administrations. There were representatives of SVAG or military commandants on all regional levels: on the administrative boards of districts, regions, and cities. See Fait, "Landesregierungen und Verwaltungen," 73.

25. I have borrowed the term the "dictatorship of discourse" from Martin Sabrow, "Einleitung: Geschichtsdiskurs und Doktringesellschaft."

26. RGASPI, f. 17, op. 128, d. 157, l. 82–83.

27. Hartmann, *Die Gesellschaft für Deutsch-Sowjetische Freundschaft*, 39–40.

28. On our propaganda in Germany, 15.07.1946, RGASPI, f. 17, op. 128, d. 157, l. 72.

29. From the diary of G. M. Bespalov, "Zapis' besedy s professorom Kuchinskim," 27.04.1948, RGASPI, f. 17, op. 128, d. 573, l. 71–73.

30. Cf. Zubkova, "Mir mnenii"; Izmozik, *Glaza i ushi rezhima*.

31. Foitzik, *Inventar*, 68. In addition, the resolution about creating a propaganda department was adopted by the Council of People's Commissars of the USSR on October 5, 1945. See Zakharov, Filippovykh, and Khainemann, *Politicheskie struktury SVAG*, 72.

32. "Proekt zapiski komissii TsK VKP(b) I. V. Stalinu o rabote Upravleniia propagandy SVAG (ranee 25 dekabria 1946 g.)," in Bonvech, Bordiugov, and Neimark, *SVAG: Upravlenie propagandy*, 197.

33. According to Norman Naimark's data, in late 1945 and early 1946 the Propaganda Department expanded to include ten sections with 1,500 Soviet staff members. See Bonvech, Bordiugov, and Neimark, *SVAG: Upravlenie propagandy*, 11. See also "Stenogramm der Bemerkungen des ZK-Sekretärs A. Kuznecov zur Arbeit der Propagandaverwaltung der SMAD auf der Sitzung des Sekretariats des ZK der KPdSU vom 9. Dezember 1946," in Bonwetsch, Bordjugov, and Neimark, *Sowjetische Politik in der SBZ*, 252–55.

34. For a list of appropriate literature, see RGASPI, f. 17, op. 132, d. 225, l. 1–2. On films, see, for example, "Spisok fil'mov, rekomendovannykh Predstavitel'stvu 'Soveksportfil'm' v Germanii dlia vkliucheniia v repertuar festivalia, posviashchennogo 30-letiiu sovetskoi kinematografii," RGASPI, f. 17, op. 132, d. 250, l. 103. An example of a list of lectures and talks is "Tematika lektsii, chtenie kotorykh zhelatel'no organizovat' v Dome Kul'tury SSSR v Berline i klubakh Obshchestva po izucheniiu kul'tury SSSR silami lektorov, prislannykh iz SSSR," RGASPI, f. 17, op. 132, d. 108, l. 11; and for exhibitions, see "Tematika vystavok, kotorye zhelatel'no poluchit' ot VOKS'a dlia klubov Obshchestva po izucheniiu kul'tury SSSR," RGASPI, f. 17, op. 132, d. 108, l. 12.

35. In West Germany, copies of *Mein Kampf*, which US soldiers were especially eager to acquire, flooded the black market. Up to 2,000 German marks or even American dollars were paid for Hitler's book. See Biulleten' 93/192 ot 26 avgusta 1947 g., RGASPI, f. 17, op. 128, d. 369, l. 100.

36. "Prikaz nachal'nika garnizona i voennogo komendanta g. Berlina No. 1 o regulirovanii politicheskoi i sotsial'no-ekonomicheskoi zhizni goroda ot 30 aprelia 1945 g.," in Timofeeva and Foittsik, *Politika SVAG*, 85–87. Order No. 19 of August 2, 1945, issued by the head of SVAG, G. K. Zhukov, continued Soviet control over the press. See GARF, f. R-7184, op. 1, d. 49, l. 4.

37. "Prikaz SVAG No. 39 ob iz"iatii natsistskoi i militaristskoi literatury ot 8 sentiabria 1945 g.," in Timofeeva and Foittsik, *Politika SVAG*, 92–93.

38. GARF, f. R-7077, op. 2, d. 52, l. 5; GARF, f. R-7133, op. 1, d. 271, l. 3.

39. Zamestitel'iu nachal'nika Upravleniia propagandy i agitatsii TsK VKP(b) tov. Ponomarevu ot nachal'nika Upravleniia SVA zemli Tiuringiia Kolesnichenko "Ob ideologicheskoi okkupatsii," RGASPI, f. 17, op. 128, d. 572, l. 84.

40. Spravka o propagande dostizhenii Sovetskogo Soiuza, avgust 1948 g., GARF, f. R-7317, op. 10, d. 37, l. 215–218.

41. "Prikaz SVAG No. 92 o rabote sektora propagandy i tsenzury Politicheskogo otdela SVAG, 18 avgusta 1945 g.," in Timofeeva and Foittsik, *Politika SVAG*, 90–91.

42. For example, see "Pis'mo nachal'nika USVA federal'noi zemli Tiuringiia I. S. Kolesnichenko prezidentu zemli doktoru R. Pauliu o poriadke ispol'zovaniia nemetskimi organami samoupravleniia telefonno-telegrafnoi sviazi," in Petrov, Lavrinskaia, and Nokhotovich, *SVAG i nemetskie organi samoupravleniia*, 279–80. On censorship of Soviet films, see GARF, f. R-7077, op. 1, d. 172, l. 12, 17.

43. GARF, f. R-7133, op. 1, d. 282, l. 99.

44. "Ukazanie ispolniaiushchego obiazannosti nachal'nika Otdela propagandy USVA federal'noi zemli Tiuringiia V. S. Babenko nachal'nikam otdelenii propagandy o pravilakh tsenzury gazet ot 28 noiabria 1945 g.," in Timofeeva and Foittsik, *Politika SVAG*, 103–105.

45. Timofeeva and Foittsik, *Politika SVAG*, 132–33.

46. Tikhomirov, "Feinde des Volkes."

47. For example, see Archiv der sozialen Demokratie der Friedrich-Ebert-Stiftung (hereafter AdsD), SPD-PV-Ostbüro 0349 A/B, unpag.; 0383 H-K, unpag.; 0362 I, unpag.

48. "Ukazanie nachal'nika Upravleniia propagandy SVAG S. I. Tiul'panova nachal'niku Otdela propagandy USVA federal'noi zemli Saksonii A. P. Vatniku i nachal'nikam otdelenii propagandy okrugov ob izmenenii form kontrolia pressy ot 27 fevralia 1947 g.," in Timofeeva and Foittsik, *Politika SVAG*, 157–61, here 158.

49. See Holzweißig, *"Die schärfste Waffe der Partei,"* 33–35.

50. Cf. Kenez, *Birth*; Brooks, *Thank You, Comrade Stalin!*; Lenoe, *Closer to the Masses*; Pike, "Censorship in Soviet-Occupied Germany."

51. "O propagande Sovetskogo Soiuza v nemetskoi pechati i radio, 28 avgusta 1946 g.," GARF, f. R-7077, op. 1, d. 194, l. 21–22.

52. "O propagande Sovetskogo Soiuza v nemetskoi pechati i radio, 28 avgusta 1946 g.," GARF, f. R-7077, op. 1, d. 194, l. 21–22.

53. In 1947, SVAG's press put out a book series titled *The Soviet Union*. Each volume was supposed to reflect different aspects of success in building socialism under Stalin's leadership. These materials were used to teach Russian which, according to Soviet data, over 700,000 children were studying in schools in the Soviet zone. See Kaprinskij, *Die Gesellschafts- und Staatsordnung der UdSSR*; Minz, Rasgon, and Sidorov, *Der große vaterländische Krieg*; Michajlow, *Die Weiten und Reichtümer des Sowjetlandes*; see also GARF, f. R-7317, op. 10, d. 37, l. 217.

54. Bonvech, Bordiugov, and Neimark, *SVAG: Upravlenie propagandy*, 137–42. On censorship in East Germany, see Barck, Langermann, and Lokatis, *"Jedes Buch ein Abenteuer"*; Holzweißig, *Zensur ohne Zensor*; Strunk, *Zensur und Zensoren*; Barck, "Fettered Media."

55. Bonvech, Bordiugov, and Neimark, *SVAG: Upravlenie propagandy*, 195.

56. GARF, f. R-7077, op. 1, d. 172, l. 12.

57. For example, see "Ukazanie nachal'nika Upravleniia propagandy SVAG S. I. Tiul'panova nachal'niku Otdela propagandy USVA provintsii Brandenburg Ia. I. Mil'khikeru o razvitii transliatsionnoi radioseti i obespechenii tshchatel'nogo kontrolia radioperedach," in Timofeeva and Foittsik, *Politika SVAG*, 108.

58. AdsD, SPD-PV-Ostbüro 0362/I, unpag.

59. GARF, f. R-7103, op. 1, d. 21, l. 292.

60. For example, "Donesenie o politicheskikh nastroeniiakh naseleniia Berlinskogo okruga, 28 dekabria 1945 g.," GARF, f. R-7077, op. 1, d. 181, l. 82–83.

61. "Dokladnaia zapiska nachal'nika Otdela informatsii USVA zemli Saksoniia-Angal't N. S. Rodionova nachal'niku Upravleniia informatsii SVAG S. I. Tiul'panovu o rasprostranenii gazet zapadnykh zon ot 29 dekabria 1947 g.," in Timofeeva and Foittsik, *Politika SVAG*, 224–25.

62. "Pis'mo nachal'nika Upravleniia sviazi SVAG N. A. Borzova prezidentu Glavnogo upravleniia pocht i sviazi NEK V. Shrederu o podpiske na periodicheskie izdaniia, vykhodiashchie v zapadnykh zonakh okkupatsii Germanii, i o predlozhenii naseleniiu podpisat'sia na izdaniia, vykhodiashchie v Sovetskoi zone ot 29 aprelia 1948 g.," in Timofeeva and Foittsik, *Politika SVAG*, 240–41; see also GARF, f. R-7077, op. 1, d. 192, l. 210.

63. "Dokladnaia zapiska zamestitelia Glavnonachal'stvuiushchego SVAG po politicheskim voprosam A. G. Russkikh sekretariu TsK VKP(b) M. A. Suslovu i nachal'niku Glavnogo politicheskogo upravleniia VS SSSR I. V. Shikinu o meropriiatiiakh po iz"iatiiu iz prodazhi pechatnoi produktsii zapadnykh zon Germanii, 20 oktiabria 1948 g.," in Timofeeva and Foittsik, *Politika SVAG*, 271–73.

64. AdsD, SPD-PV-Ostbüro 0361 I, unpag.

65. "Reiseeindrücke aus der russischer Zone, 26.06.1949," AdsD, SPD-PV-Ostbüro 0361 I, unpag.

66. Kynin and Laufer, comps., *9 maia 1945 g.–3 oktiabria 1946 g.*, 24.

67. Broszat and Weber, *SBZ-Handbuch*, 216.

68. For example, see GARF, f. R-7317, op. 10, d. 31, l. 63.

69. Kolesnichenko, *Bitva posle voiny*, 11.

70. However, the procedures developed to collect and analyze the population's opinions were not always carried out smoothly. A revealing example is the

competition between the NKVD's operational group and the military commandant in the town of Coswig for the right to gather popular opinions in Germany. See "Raport voennogo komendanta g. Kosvig V. N. Gordienko nachal'niku komendatskoi sluzhby SVA provintsii Saksoniia G. D. Mukhinu o protivozakonnykh deistviiakh rabotnikov mestnoi opergruppy NKVD v otnoshenii rabotnikov voennoi komendatury i apparata burgomistra, 31 oktiabria 1945 g.," in Petrov, Lavrinskaia, and Nokhotovich, *SVAG i nemetskie organi*, 290–95, especially 294.

71. Informational reports (*Informationsberichte*) were usually compiled by the regime's civil organs, but political reports (*politdoneseniia*) were put together by the organs of the Soviet Military Administration in Germany (SVAG).

72. Stadtarchiv Jena. B III IIh Nr. 5, unpag.

73. Richtlinien für die Berichterstattung des 72. Geburtstages J. W. Stalin, Dresden, den 14.12.1951, Staatsarchiv Dresden, LRS. Ministerium für Volksbildung Nr. 195, unpag.; see also Thüringisches Hauptstaatsarchiv Weimar, Land Thüringen--Ministerium für Volksbildung Nr. 1485, Bl. 72.

74. For more on the use of reports and overviews of the public's sentiments in historical research, see Davies, *Popular Opinion*; Holquist, "'Information is the Alpha and Omega'"; Velikanova, "Berichte zur Stimmungslage"; Vihavainen, *Sovetskaia vlast'—narodnaia vlast'?*; Plamper, "Beyond Binaries."

75. See Berger and Luckmann, *Die gesellschaftliche Konstruktion der Wirklichkeit*.

76. For example, see Stimmen zum Stalin-Interview vom 21.12.52. Sonderbericht, BStU (Der Bundesbeauftragte für die Unterlagen des Staatssicherheitsdienstes der ehemaligen Deutschen Demokratischen Republik), AST Erfurt, AS 42.

77. "Dokladnaia zapiska o nastroenii nemetskogo naseleniia po provintsii Meklenburg i Zapadnoi Pomeranii ot 22 noiabria 1945 g.," GARF, f. R-7103, op. 1, d. 10, l. 96.

78. "Dokladnaia zapiska o nastroenii nemetskogo naseleniia po provintsii Meklenburg i Zapadnoi Pomeranii ot 22 noiabria 1945 g.," GARF, f. R-7103, op. 1, d. 10, l. 96–97.

79. "Dokladnaia zapiska o nastroenii nemetskogo naseleniia po provintsii Meklenburg i Zapadnoi Pomeranii ot 22 noiabria 1945 g.," GARF, f. R-7103, op. 1, d. 10, l. 99.

80. "Dokladnaia zapiska o nastroenii nemetskogo naseleniia po provintsii Meklenburg i Zapadnoi Pomeranii ot 22 noiabria 1945 g.," GARF, f. R-7103, op. 1, d. 10, l. 97.

81. Dealing with complaints about the insulting, abusive way the Soviet administrative cadres spoke to Germans was a standard feature of the Soviet military commandants' everyday activities. See, for example, "Donesenie nachal'nika otdeleniia propaganda UKV Berlinskogo okruga L. L. Kolossa nachal'niku Otdela propagandy USVA provintsii Brandenburg Ia. I. Mil'khikeru 'Ob otnoshenii voennogo komendanta goroda i uchastka Oranienburg maiora Khamidova k rukovoditeliam mestnykh organov samoupravleniia i partiinykh organizatsii,' December 6, 1945," in Petrov, Lavrinskaia, and Nokhotovich, *SVAG i nemetskie organi*, 308–10.

82. Cf. Zubkova, "Mir mnenii," 28; Behrends, *Die erfundene Freundschaft*, 238–40.

83. Gibas, "'Bonner Ultras.'"

84. On practices of repressive persecution in East Germany, see Gieseke, *Der Mielke-Konzern*, 28–39.

85. See, for example, AdsD, SPD-PV-Ostbüro 0287 A I, unpag.; and Jan Plamper, "'Die Hitler kommen und gehen . . . ,'" 440–41; Rossman, *Worker Resistance under Stalin*; Zubkova, *Obshchestvo i reformy*.

86. AdsD, SPD-PV-Ostbüro 0350, unpag.

87. GARF, f. R-7077, op. 1, d. 192, l. 199, 201, 229; f. R-7212, op.1, d. 188, l. 39–40.

88. Politicheskoe polozhenie v Khemnitskom okruge za vtoroi kvartal 1947 g., GARF, f. R-7212, op. 1, d. 205, l. 1947. See also *New York Times*, May 4, 1947, 10; *Pravda*, May 8, 1947, 1.

89. GARF, f. R-7077, op. 1, d. 181, l. 83.

90. For example, "Spetsdonesenie nachal'nika Otdela propagandy USVA federal'noi zemli Saksoniia A. P. Vatnika nachal'niku Upravleniia propagandy SVAG S. I. Tiul'panovu o provokatsiiakh v g. Drezdene i ego prigorodakh vo vremia pervomaiskikh prazdnikov," in Timofeeva and Foittsik, *Politika SVAG*, 170.

91. AdsD, SPD-PV-Ostbüro 0349 A/B, unpag.

92. For an example, see Gerüchte im Kreis Bautzen, Dresden, in Sächsisches Hauptstaatsarchiv in Dresden (SächsHstAD), 11376 Landesregierung Sachsen (LRS), 4609, unpag.

93. On the practice of censorship in Soviet Russia, see Izmozik, "Perliustratsiia."

94. GARF, f. R-7212, op. 1, d. 13, l. 374.

95. Potsdam—Geheime Postzensur, den 17.02.51, in AdsD, SPD-PV-Ostbüro 0362 I, unpag.; see also Spetssoobshchenie "Po pis'mam s otritsatel'nymi vyskazyvaniiami nemetskogo naseleniia o povedenii otdel'nykh voennosluzhashchikh Krasnoi Armii na territorii Meklenburgskoi provintsii" ot 30.11.1045 g., GARF, f. R-7103, op. 1, d. 10, l. 120–122; "Pis'mo nachal'nika Opersektora NKVD SSSR po provintsii Meklenburg D. M. Nikitina nachal'niku USVA provintsii M. A. Skosyrevu o nedopustimosti privlecheniia nemtsev-antifashistov k tsenzurirovaniiu nemetskoi pochtovoi korrespondentsii, 6 marta 1946 g.," in Petrov, Lavrinskaia, and Nokhotovich, *SVAG i nemetskie organi*, 321–22.

96. For example, GARF, f. R-7077, op. 1, d. 194, l. 20.

97. For example, see Berichtsbogen für Versammlungen und Veranstaltungen; GARF, f. R-7077, op. 1, d. 192, l. 123; and Thüringisches Hauptstaatsarchiv Weimar. Ministerium des Inneren. Nr. 124. Bl. 2.

98. AdsD, SPD-PV-Ostbüro 0322 I, unpag.

99. Uhl, "Repressionen als Instrument," 77.

100. Petrov, *Po stsenariiu Stalina*, 105.

101. Petrov, *Po stsenariiu Stalina*, 21; Mironenko, Niethammer, and von Plato, *Sowjetische Speziallager in Deutschland*, vol. 2.

102. Petrov, *Po stsenariiu Stalina*, 106.

103. Petrov, *Po stsenariiu Stalina*, 77.

104. See Lüdtke and Fürmetz, "Denunziation und Denunzianten"; Altendorf, "Denunziation im Hochschulbereich"; Fitzpatrick and Gellately, "Introduction."

105. "Jedes Mitglied muss wissen, . . . du sprichst zur Partei und der Partei muss man alles sagen." Quoted in Stieglitz and Thonfeld, "Denunziation als Medium," 83.

106. For example, see AdsD, SPD-PV-Ostbüro 0287 AI, unpag.; SAPMO-BARch (Stiftung Archiv der Parteien und Massenorganisationen der DDR im Bundesarchiv). DY 30/IV 2/9.02/44, unpag.

107. Kurt Hager, "Die Aufgaben der Partei im Kampf um erhöhte Wachsamkeit," *Neues Deutschland*, January 8, 1950, 4.

108. AdsD, SPD-PV-Ostbüro 0361 I, unpag.

109. Petrov, *Po stsenariiu Stalina*, 160.

110. Gieseke, *Der Mielke-Konzern*, 58. According to researchers' data, in October 1989 there were 91,000 official Stasi employees but 174,000 unofficial collaborators. See Müller-Enbergs, "Zum Verhältnis von Norm," 56.

111. AdsD, SPD-PV-Ostbüro 0383 H-K, unpag.

112. AdsD, SPD-PV-Ostbüro 0361 III, unpag.

113. In the Soviet Union, the death penalty was abolished by the Decree of the Presidium of the USSR Supreme Soviet of May 26, 1947, and reintroduced by the Decree of January 12, 1950.

114. Schmeitzner et al., *Todesurteile sowjetischer Militärtribunale*.

115. Petrov, *Po stsenariiu Stalina*.

116. Petrov, *Po stsenariiu Stalina*, 157.

117. Über unsere Haus- und Hofarbeit. Der Agitator Nr. 2. Hrsg. vom Parteivorstand der SED, Abt. Agitation, 1951, AdsD, SPD-PV-Ostbüro 0322 I.

118. GARF, f. R-7133, op. 1, d. 55, l. 200.

119. Über unsere Haus- und Hofarbeit.

120. Gibas, "Die 'einheitliche öffentliche Meinung'"; Zagatta, *Informationspolitik und Öffentlichkeit*, 11–35.

121. Gieseke, *Der Mielke-Konzern*, 61. According to Nikita Petrov, in the first half of 1952, 52,234 people fled to the FRG from the GDR, in the second half of the year 78,831, and in January–March 1953 the number of refugees reached 84,034, including 1,836 members of the SED and 1,781 members of the FDJ. See Petrov, *Po stsenariiu Stalina*, 73.

Chapter 3

From the "Red Tyrant" to the "Liberator"

The Image of Stalin in the Soviet Occupation Zone of Germany

THE POLITICS OF HATE: TOWARD AN EMOTIONAL ECONOMY OF VICTOR AND VANQUISHED

In the German Empire, the East had long been associated with disorder, backwardness, and barbarism.[1] As Gregor Thum observed, Germany saw the "east" as the antithesis of the "civilized" West, a "mythical landscape" onto which Germans could project their anti-Western and antimodern fantasies.[2] Caricatures depicting Russians with Asiatic features and wearing Cossack hats had been part of German visual memory since World War I. Verbally, in Nazi propaganda they were "Asiatic hordes," "bloodthirsty murderers," "death" itself, or the "Devil," barely human creatures who threatened the security of the "national community" and the well-being of Western civilization as a whole.[3] The visual norms mentioned above were reinforced by anti-Semitic images; in the Third Reich, they were combined to create the topos of the "Jewish-Bolshevik menace" to Europe. This amplified the crucial binary, which was highly charged in visual and verbal content, pitting the "master race" (*Herrenmenschen*), that is, the German "Aryan race," against the "sub-humans" (*Untermenschen*), Slavs, Jews, Sinti, and Roma in a life-or-death struggle.[4] Ritualistic humiliation of Jews and other members of local populations displayed the hierarchy and differences between the "higher" and the "lower races," which were integral to realizing the German project of conquest in the East. The Nazi image of intellectually backward, uncultured, physically underdeveloped Slavs justified violence on the Eastern front. As a result, Stalin himself came to embody the "dangerous and wild, culturally backward and Asiatic country," and anxiety about pan-Slavism, global proletarian revolution, and a worldwide Jewish conspiracy surged.[5] By describing him as a "bloodthirsty and soulless tyrant," "the incarnation of the Judeo-Bolshevik threat," "the embodiment of death, famine, and destruction," and "a fiend from hell and the devil himself," Nazi propaganda turned Stalin into the personification of several stereotypes of the abhorred communist enemy.[6]

On the Soviet side, long before the war ended, the leadership began to define the normative emotions, rituals, and practices needed to emotionally manage its army. In the fight against Nazi Germany, the Red Army constituted an *emotional community* mobilized by hatred of the Germans.[7] The Soviet leadership pursued a deliberate, carefully constructed policy of revenge and retribution with roots in the decade preceding the war. As Soviet society became increasingly militarized in the 1930s, representations of "fascist agents" were integrated into the narrative legitimating the Great Purges of 1937–1938.[8] During the Great Fatherland War, the well-known novelist and journalist Ilya Ehrenburg's reports of Nazi atrocities appeared in the army newspaper *Krasnaia Zvezda* (Red Star). His soldier-readers took his precepts, such as "The best Germans are dead Germans," as a guide to action.[9] At the front, Soviet propagandists demanded retaliation and informed the troops about the Wehrmacht's brutal crimes.[10] Frontline newspapers reported on how cruelly the Nazis treated civilians and published instructions about which emotions the troops should express to the enemy and how a real soldier should conduct himself in war.[11] In parallel, the print media celebrated instances of soldiers' heroism and bravery.[12] Even the Red Army intelligentsia showed a marked readiness to take revenge.[13] Jewish soldiers at the front spoke of a "double hatred": the desire to avenge both their ravaged Soviet homeland and the annihilation of the Jewish people.[14] Likewise, the dominant feeling of hostility toward Germans was certainly a factor in the positive way local populations received Soviet soldiers during the liberation of Poland and Czechoslovakia.[15] The national camp's program in postwar Poland demanded that at least three Germans be killed to avenge the death of each Pole, calling for "German soldiers [to] fertilize our soil *en masse*."[16] As witnesses to (and often victims of) Nazi arbitrariness, local communities were "powder kegs" of hate for the occupiers. In Warsaw, the "civic code of morality" made the rounds in the underground press and leaflets with the slogan "A nation's greatest defeat is its humiliation."[17] Because the urge for revenge drove the patriotic national powers, the Red Army was partly seen as a liberating force in the fight against a common enemy.

Soldiers were emotionally mobilized before the battle on a daily basis to boost their morale. To activate the desire for retaliation, reports were presented to the troops as well as discussions about what the enemy was doing to the Soviet homeland: the plundering and the damage they caused, not to mention the unprecedented scale of human casualties.[18] At one of these meetings, each member of the Komsomol was told to write down in a shared notebook what his own family had suffered at the hands of the Germans.[19] With their officers standing by, soldiers pledged to take revenge on the enemy.[20] *Listovki*—sheets of paper—reprinted the oath soldiers took to fight against the enemy and distributed information about enemy atrocities against civilians and POWs.[21] Official reports from the front made it clear that the politics of hatred was justified. However, in the spring of 1945, Soviet commanders tried to reduce the hate propaganda in an attempt to curtail the violence accompanying the Red Army's advance on European territory. On February 9, 1945, appealing to Red Army soldiers, *Krasnaia Zvezda* proclaimed, "We aren't Germans, we don't kill women and children."[22] Moscow's directives ordered soldiers to renounce retribution and treat German civilians more humanely.[23] However, establishing order in the army remained beyond Moscow's reach, and the troops' desire for vengeance intensified as the Red Army drew closer to Berlin. The escalating violence was largely the result of war propaganda which incited Soviet citizens to hate the Germans and taught soldiers that it was their "moral duty" to avenge the suffering of their families and the destruction of their motherland. This propaganda was grounded in the collective memory of the well-known Russian saying, with its biblical roots, "He who raises the sword will die by the sword" (Figure 3.1).[24]

The Soviets depicted the war as a sacred struggle of "good" against "evil." After the capture of Berlin, in their letters home, Red Army soldiers called themselves "victors" who had killed the "beast" in the "fascist predator's lair."[25] Comparing Nazi crimes to the monstrous acts of nonhuman creatures gave the soldiers of the liberating army a completely free hand to take revenge, because the sacred mission of protecting their own families, their communities, and the state justified violence.[26] Revenge also became a permissible motive for retaliating against the Germans. "Death for death, blood for blood. I don't feel sorry for these people-haters, these animals," as Russian officer Vladimir Gelfand noted in his diary when he crossed the border into Germany in the spring of 1945.[27] As a result, on German soil Red Army soldiers described themselves as "masters of the situation" who held the fate of the German people and the German state in their hands.[28] They saw their arbitrary use of power as the workings of "the court of the victor" and "the court of history" or as "compensation."[29] From a military perspective, acts of vengeance were valid as the lawful exercise of justice.

Soviet soldiers' written communication with their families and relatives on the home front played a crucial role in legitimating revenge.[30] They interpreted vengeance as a moral duty and, in their letters to friends and family members at home, they felt obliged to report on how they were carrying out this imperative.[31] They described what they observed about the defeated people from this perspective. As a soldier wrote on May 9, 1945, "I ran and looked at the Berliners. Overcome with shame, they couldn't look you right in the eye. The

Figure 3.1　Red Army soldiers celebrating the victory. Early May 1945. *Source:* Bildarchiv im Bundesarchiv. Signature: Bild 183-E0406-0022-018.

ones who wanted to defeat us in 2 months are now lying at our feet."[32] Letters from the home front were also intended to maintain Red Army morale through personal reports of enemy atrocities and the scale of human suffering under Nazi occupation. In collective letters from working collectives, people thanked Red Army soldiers for their heroism and for defending them against the enemy.[33] For both sides, empathy and compassion for the enemy were taboo. Under the moral mandate to exact vengeance, these were signs of unmanly, unpatriotic weakness. A Red Army soldier confirmed the mood among his comrades as they invaded German territory: "We are taking revenge for everything, for our wounds, for Leningrad, for Moscow, for the children and the old people, for our girls."[34] Thus, hate took on the emotional force of moral duty, linking the front lines with the home front through the civic duty enjoined on both realms to participate in the shared struggle against the enemy.[35]

"LIBERATOR," NOT "VICTOR": MYTHS OF
THE BEGINNING IN POSTWAR GERMANY

On May 13, 1945, a German translation of Stalin's radio broadcast to the Soviet people was read out to Germans to mark the end of the Great Patriotic War:[36]

The great day of victory over Germany has come. Fascist Germany, forced to its knees by the Red Army and the troops of our allies, has acknowledged itself defeated and declared its unconditional surrender . . . The great sacrifices we made in the name of the freedom and independence of our Motherland, the innumerable privations and sufferings our people endured during the war, the hard work in the rear and at the front laid on the altar of our fatherland were not in vain and have been crowned by our complete victory over the enemy . . . Three years ago, Hitler publicly announced that his mission was to dismember the Soviet Union and wrest the Caucasus, the Ukraine, Belorussia, the Baltic lands, and other regions from it. He openly announced that "We will destroy Russia so that it can never rise again." That was three years ago. But Hitler's wild ideas were fated never to come to pass. The course of the war scattered them like dust. In fact, what happened was the exact opposite of what the Hitlerites raved about. Germany was smashed to pieces. The German troops are surrendering. The Soviet Union is celebrating its victory, although it does not intend to dismember or destroy Germany.

Comrades! The Great Patriotic War has ended with our complete victory. The war in Europe has ended. An era of peaceful development has begun.[37]

The Soviet leader signified that the war had ended with the long-awaited word: "Victory!"

The triumphant victory of the Soviet people was the Germans' traumatic defeat. The figure of speech Stalin used—"Germany on its knees"—emphasized that the enemy had been humiliated and dishonored. After the war ended, Stalin demanded repentance and shame for Nazi crimes from the Germans. As a result, the population, crushed by the defeat, met the victors with red armbands and white ones and hung out red and white flags. These were the visible symbols of capitulation; they acknowledged the Red Army's role as the victor.[38] At the Potsdam Conference, answering Truman's question about how the "concept of Germany" should be defined, Stalin continued to use the rhetoric of the winner of the war. He said,

This is a country without a government [and] without borders because the borders have not been determined by our troops. Germany does not have troops, including border troops, it is divided into zones of occupation. It is a defeated and broken country.[39]

On the level of symbolic politics, this statement depreciated the country's sovereignty, the source of the state's national honor and dignity. Rhetoric of this kind, emphasizing the former enemy's humiliation and its greatly diminished status in the international arena, intensified the Soviet people's pride in their triumph.

In Germany, during the first postwar months of 1945, visual markers of the Red Army's victory appeared in public spaces throughout the Soviet zone. These signs publicly proclaimed the hierarchy that would prevail in the conquerors' communication to the defeated. Posters with the caption "What Comrade Stalin Says about Germany and the German People" were put up all over East Germany.[40] These posters listed the decisions made at the Potsdam Conference. They were produced in print runs of 210,000 and sent to every military commandant's office in the Soviet zone.[41] At the same time, the population became familiar with a new image of Stalin as the victor on whose will and words the fate of the German people would henceforth depend (Figure 3.2). A middle-school mathematics teacher in Bernau reacted to the postwar Soviet representations of power with the observation that "The victors are not judged for what they have done. Those who are defeated are always to blame and have to answer for everything."[42]

The image of Stalin as the victor was promoted against a backdrop of mass disillusionment with Hitler, whose cult had been the mainstay of the Third Reich's political system.[43] For German society, the only way to defend itself and rationalize the defeat was to distance itself from the crimes of national socialism by ascribing all sins to Hitler. With the loss of the former sacral center of power, which had been the source of social integration for the "racial community" or *Volksgemeinschaft*, apathy, despair, and feelings of alienation and depression washed over the population.[44] An ordinary citizen named Klaus Gerber wrote that

> The great disappointment in what we so blindly believed, that national social-
> ism was the only possible form of rule, has depressed us. Little by little we
> have begun to realize that this is not so! This was a shock: suddenly everything
> changed, it was no [longer] majestic and absolute but became a criminal politi-
> cal system.[45]

The "old" values had collapsed, but the "new" ones created more fear and distrust than hope and optimism about the future.

Humiliated and dishonored, the German "society of the catastrophe" needed new narratives and visions which they could believe in—ones offering a fresh strategy for development and liberation from the "dark past," narratives and imaginations which would justify the difficulties of postwar reality and open a perspective on a successful future. A society in ruins needed a different system of coordinates: new goals, tasks, values, different points of reference and fresh tactics, strategies, emotions, and moral norms. This system might not only lead it out of the crisis of defeat but could also reunite diverse segments of the German population divided by their traumatic experiences, and give them a revitalized, positive way of seeing themselves.

Figure 3.2   "Generalissimo I. V Stalin": Unter den Linden, East Berlin. 1945. *Source:* Bildarchiv im Deutschen Historischen Museum (Berlin). Signature: 04/466. Photographer: Heinz Röhnert.

To a certain degree, the Soviet occupation authorities were able to respond to this challenge quickly. In close cooperation with the SED, they set about constructing political "myths of a beginning," official narratives about the new start which would legitimate the political order of the occupation, create a new sense of "we," and lay the foundations for the population's loyalty to the postwar order.[46] Narratives about how the Red Army had freed the German people from fascism and the myth of German antifascism played key roles in defining East Germans' new self-understanding. These narratives soon became personified, incorporating the Soviet leader's image, which merged with the myths, symbols, and rituals of the Stalin cult. In fact, plans for East Germany's development along Soviet lines were essentially a search for a new *Führer*, that is, another leader-messiah who would enable the nation to achieve its desired goals. The way forward would be to work side by side with the Soviet Union, to build socialism together as brothers and friends, not sworn enemies. Examining each of the propaganda narratives mentioned above in more detail will make this clearer.

During the final period of the war, the population viewed, and had been primed to view, Soviet soldiers as rapists, marauders, thieves, and murderers, not liberators. To replace these negative impressions with a positive image of Red Army soldiers, narratives about how these soldiers had freed Germany from Nazi rule had to be created and popularized.[47] As occurred in the Soviet Union, the concepts of "Stalin" and "victory" merged, and in East German official discourse too, "leader" and "liberation" became synonymous.[48] Propaganda presented the Red Army and Stalin as rescuers of the German people and saviors who freed them from the "yoke of fascism." The narrative of liberation included not only the break with the "fascist past" but also a simultaneous rescue from the "cabal of capitalism." West Germany was proclaimed enemy number one of the "new, antifascist, democratic Germany" and was presented as an "outpost of American imperialism," a "base for remilitarizing and preparing for a new war," and the "site for restoring German imperialism."[49] In socialist propaganda, West Germany was the Third Reich's political stepchild. Representations of the new enemy were an ideal way to create a stark contrast with East Germany. This opposition was crucial for staging the SED's political regime as the *best* Germany, the state that was morally purer than the FRG, because all remnants of Nazism had been decisively rooted out there (Figure 3.3).

In the myth of antifascism, the advent of the Red Army was described as the long-awaited moment of liberation. All the fascists, militarists, and warmongers fled to the West, transforming East Germany into a territory that was free of fascism. After the fall of the Third Reich, this narrative made it possible to restart nation-state building with a clean slate. As a result, the postwar phase of "antifascist-democratic rebuilding" (*Erneuerung*) of Germany acquired

Figure 3.3   GDR poster: "Our path to peace and prosperity: German-Soviet friendship ruins all the arsonist's plans to start a war." 1950. *Source:* Bildarchiv im Bundesarchiv (Koblenz). Signature: Plak 100-041-027.

historical legitimacy in the communist antifascist tradition, whose roots went back to the Weimar Republic.[50] In 1935, an antifascist popular front was created at the Seventh International Congress of the Communist International, and Stalin was publicly declared to be its leader. Wilhelm Pieck, the future president of the GDR, was among the first to introduce the Stalin cult to the congress's international audience, ending his speech at a session by saying, "We are going to fight for freedom, for peace, for bread, for Soviet power, for socialism. Our motto is fight for Soviet power. Our banner is the banner of Marx-Engels-Lenin-Stalin. Our leader is Stalin."[51]

The myth of antifascism had several important implications which helped shape East Germany's political culture. It highlighted a shared German-Soviet tradition of struggle with a common "enemy"—the Hitler state. This shared tradition automatically justified the postwar ties between German communists and the Soviet Union, and legitimated German communists who drew closer to Stalin as the "leader of the antifascist movement." In addition, the myth of antifascism became an important precondition for creating an SED political regime that modeled itself on the Soviet Union. Condemning former Nazis was an integral part of the antifascist idea about what de-Nazification entailed, but it also meant fighting against "other-thinking" people by criminalizing oppositional sentiments and using terror against people whom the regime found displeasing.[52] Moreover, propagandizing the myth of antifascism offered the East German population deliverance from guilt about wartime crimes and encouraged them to undergo a political conversion, which would turn "enemies" into "Stalin's friends." This myth offered the individual ready-made models of behavior; by adopting these models, the subject turned defeat into victory. Being able to identify oneself as an antifascist also gave people an alibi for charges of complicity in Nazi crimes. Antifascism became a key part of the GDR's ideology, which paved the way for the later radicalization of the Stalin cult.

To popularize the myth of antifascism, SVAG set about developing the cultural memory of German communist antifascist heroes. Honoring opposition fighters who had sacrificed their lives to bring liberation closer was a key component of this effort. The most vivid example is the cult of Ernst Thälmann.[53] Representations of him as the "leader of the working class" and the "best friend of the Soviet Union" allowed the German political elite to construct Soviet-style historical traditions and symbols of German-Soviet friendship. Within the ranks of the SED, Thälmann was presented as the "leader of the party," "a true seeker of Germany's national unity and independence," and a "friend of Lenin and Stalin." The fact that the Nazis murdered Thälmann in Buchenwald allowed the SED to canonize him as a hero of the resistance and a great martyr. The symbolic capital that accrued to the figure of Thälmann, who personified the myth of antifascism in the GDR, was integrated into the Stalin cult and used to increase the Soviet leader's popularity in the role of the "the world's chief antifascist" (Figure 3.4).

The discourse of gratitude to the Soviet leader emerged from previous uses of Stalin's image to personify political myths. In the Soviet Union, the entire society had already been enjoined to express gratitude to the "leader" and the party from the 1930s.[54] Acknowledging liberation from Nazi rule became a positive, emotionally saturated strategy for rapprochement with Moscow and a way to win the Soviet leader's trust. This tendency was particularly apparent in late 1947 and in the first months of 1948 in conjunction with the rejection of a "national German path to building socialism" and the transition to the Sovietization of East Germany. The first East German rituals of gratitude to Stalin took place on February 23, 1948, in conjunction with the thirtieth anniversary of the creation of the Soviet Army in 1918. In towns in the Templin area, speeches about the Red Army's mission of liberation emphasized "Comrade Stalin's outstanding role in the leadership of the armed forces of the Soviet Union." Mass organizations and educational institutions sent telegrams with congratulations and expressions of gratitude to the military command posts. For example, a certain Herr Wiegelmann, a member of a local Kulturbund, wrote that "I am very grateful to the Soviet

Figure 3.4 Including Ernst Thälmann's cult in the Stalin cult: a meeting about renaming the Krupp Factory in Magdeburg as the Ernst-Thälmann-Werk. April 30, 1951. *Source:* Bildarchiv im Bundesarchiv (Koblenz). Signature: Bild 183-10511-0002.Photographer: Wilhelm Biscan.

Army because it freed the German people and other peoples from Hitler's oppression and because it helped us lay claim to a new democratic order." In another instance, a Herr Berndt asked representatives of SVAG to convey his warm wishes for "successes and good health to Generalissimo Stalin."[55]

Thus, the "myth of the beginning" and the "myth of antifascism" offered a new scenario of the postwar social order in which the person of the Soviet leader had the central role. For a defeated society, the positive image of Stalin pointed toward a strategy of national and state development. Such representations of Stalin promised resources and new ways to resolve political, economic, and national issues quickly by offering the possibility of joining a history of successes, suddenly on the side of the victors, not the vanquished. In conversation with colleagues, someone on the staff of the administration of the federal state (*Land*) of Brandenburg reflected that

> Now I want one thing: to use the defeat and make it a victory in the sense of creating a strong and indestructible union with Russia. Under those conditions,

Germany's defeat would become a loss for fascism alone and a win for the
German people.[56]

Postwar destabilization, a sense of disorientation, and the feeling that they
were in a hopeless situation all helped make Stalin's image attractive to part
of the population in the Soviet zone. Appealing to people who felt so over-
whelmed, the profoundly symbolic image of the "best friend of the German
people" offered a choice between progress and regression, the future and the
past, the resolution of current problems and continuing chaos. Because of
the defeat and the framework of international law, German society had no
choice but to quietly accommodate themselves to postwar reality and learn
"to be friends" with Stalin. Thus, the subsequent alignment with the Stalin
cult was a postwar survival strategy: it was not the result of fanatic faith in a
new *Führer* but rather a rational choice, granting access to the basic political,
economic, and ideological resources which would ensure a normal daily life,
provide a sense of stability, and strengthen the SED regime as the dominant
political force in a divided country.

STALIN AS GUARANTOR OF PEACE,
SPIRITUAL FATHER, AND TEACHER:
REPRESENTATIONS OF GUILT AND THE
QUESTION OF GERMAN NATIONAL HONOR

The German population was well informed about the postwar heyday of the
Stalin cult in the Soviet Union. *Tägliche Rundschau*, the newspaper published
by SVAG, regularly reprinted material from *Pravda*—photographs of Stalin
in his Generalissimo's uniform, his personal decrees and directives as the
leader of the victorious state, press releases about the Soviet leader's meetings with the other Allied leaders, telegrams sent to him by leaders around the
world, receptions in the Kremlin, and parades on Red Square. The socialist
media presented Stalin as a leader of international stature who, with the victory, had won the respect of the world community. However, public representations of Stalin reminded Germans that the nation as a whole remained
guilty of having unleashed World War II. The Soviet press spoke of the "loss
of German honor" and the "mark of the nation's shame." The propaganda of
Stalin became a moral reproach and a demand that the population repent for
war crimes before they could enjoy the forgiveness that only the victor could
give. To encourage the practice of offering apologies, the Soviet leader was
frequently represented in East Germany as the apex of moral authority. In this
guise, Stalin was shown as the only one who could absolve the Germans of
pangs of conscience about their "dark past" and liberate them from an oppressive feeling of guilt toward the Soviets.

On June 22, 1946, *Neues Deutschland*, the SED's main press organ, published an article titled "The Symbol of German Shame." This was the text of a speech Otto Grotewohl gave to commemorate the anniversary of the German invasion of the Soviet Union. Grotewohl told his audience that

> [c]overed with shame, feeling deeply humiliated and ashamed, today we stand before the entire world and the Soviet Union. There is no argument which could explain this most enormous and most monstrous crime of Hitler . . . Each person to whom the fate of Germany is dear is obligated to strive with all his might [so that] Germany henceforth, in every possible way, tries to live in indestructible peace and indissoluble friendship with the Soviet people.[57]

To depict the political death of the German state and nation, Grotewohl did not invoke a universally pilloried Germany. Instead, he employed the rhetoric of repentance to encourage Germans to acknowledge their guilt and take responsibility for the Nazis' crimes; these acts of repentance would pave the way for the rebirth of the German state and nation. Responsibility for unleashing a worldwide military catastrophe that claimed many millions of victims, the sudden attack on the Soviet Union, and the ensuing defeat, with its unconditional surrender, were the fundamental sources of the feelings of shame and guilt toward the USSR that were being constructed. Because the Germans were guilty, they had to acknowledge their guilt and apologize to the Soviet Union, which had lost so much and had suffered so greatly, and they needed to repent.[58]

"A feeling of guilt," Walter Ulbricht told members of the KPD,

> is the prerequisite for our people to finally put an end to the reactionary past and decisively set out on a new path . . . If our people feels profoundly ashamed and is conscious of the crimes of Hitlerism, if our people feels shame and is aware that it committed barbaric crimes, then and only then will it be able to find the internal strength which will allow it to take a new, democratic, progressive path.[59]

The rhetoric of shame was used, especially by German communists, in order to show a German society shattered by defeat how to restore the national honor and the dignity of the state. These political concepts are central to modernity. They arose in tandem with the establishment and legitimation of power during the second half of the nineteenth century, when modern European nations and states took shape. After 1945, friendship with Stalin's Soviet Union was presented as the only possible path the Germans could take to gain forgiveness and restore their damaged national honor. In other words, it was a strategy for social integration and for constructing a collective

identity, but it would only succeed if the entire society engaged in practices
of apology and showed remorse to the victim—who had emerged from the
war as the absolute victor.

During the final period of World War II, the Soviet leadership consciously
employed emotional management in the occupied territories, playing on ideas
about honor and virtue, guilt feelings, and the Germans' sense of culpability
for Nazi crimes. By manipulating these collective feelings, the USSR was
able to successfully enact the politics of the occupied countries' moral subordination, thereby expanding the zone of Soviet influence in Europe. Morally
reeducating the Germans with Soviet propaganda, while simultaneously
appealing to their fear of the Red Army and shame about the Nazi past, was
among the central tasks facing both the Soviet occupiers and German communists returning from Moscow.[60] The Soviets gave the Germans an ultimatum: if they wanted the victor to restore their honor, they must acknowledge
their guilt.[61] As a report on SVAG's political work put it,

> To restore the honor of the German people [and] its prosperity, and to gain the
> trust of the Soviet Union and other nations, the following preconditions must
> be fulfilled: acknowledgement that the German people are responsible for the
> crimes of fascism.[62]

On the level of symbolic politics, guilt was a constant theme in discussions
of Germany's moral debt to the Soviet Union. This moral debt obligated
Germans to undergo a political conversion from being Stalin's "enemies" to
his "friends." In terms of practical interests, constructing a sense of German
guilt initially allowed Moscow to legitimate the Soviet military presence in
East Germany and then enabled it to go on to Sovietize German territory.
Dismantling industry and paying reparations became key components of
the expiation of German guilt toward the USSR. The price of the symbolic
indulgence for restoring the honor of the German people was expressed in its
real monetary equivalent.

Because the price of forgiveness was essentially boundless, constantly
articulating guilt toward the Soviet Union became an ever-present preoccu-
pation. This strengthened the hierarchical model that defined the relationship
between the victor and the vanquished. East Germans' official trips to the
Soviet Union were a unique opportunity for demonstrating a repentance-
driven conversion from "enemies" to "friends." These trips also gave the
Germans a chance to collect evidence that Germany's national honor was
gradually being restored and to document the fact that the USSR was able to
forgive them. For example, on an official visit to the USSR from November
5 to November 18, 1948, a delegation of "cultural and political figures" interpreted Molotov's invitation to an evening reception as a mark of "special

honor." The Germans were pleasantly surprised to see that Molotov shook hands with them as warmly as he did with the representatives of other nations.[63] These gestures were taken as small tokens of forgiveness and acceptance, indications that, step by step, the East Germans were winning the Soviets' trust and were being granted international authority. Therefore, signs of respect and recognition from the Soviets were interpreted as indications that the German people's honor and virtue were gradually being restored.

In doling out German guilt, Moscow tried to maintain a balance between expectations of a public apology and showing that it now recognized the East Germans as "friends" of the USSR. Thus, when working with the representatives from the delegation mentioned above, the Soviet hosts were advised to "draw the attention of the German participants to the damage inflicted on our country by the Hitlerite occupiers and to the efforts made by the Soviet people to heal the wounds inflicted on the Soviet Union by the Nazis."[64] One way to accomplish this was to have the German delegation visit the hero city of Stalingrad and the Museum of the Defense of Leningrad. For the Soviets, these were important *lieux de mémoire* that memorialized their sacrifices, heroism, and victory. On the other hand, for the Germans, these places symbolized their national catastrophe, the loss of family members, and the beginning of a cataclysmic defeat. In the end, the Soviet Foreign Ministry did not include these items as part of the program planned for the delegation, but, in response to "Grotewohl's insistent request," the delegation did visit the Museum of the Defense of Leningrad.

With the entire delegation's approval, Grotewohl wrote the following words of repentance in the visitors' book: "We leave here in shock, here we have seen how the name of Germany was covered in shame and dishonor."[65] However, it is even more noteworthy that, after visiting the museum, members of the delegation described a shift in their emotions, a transition from the depressing feeling of shame to a positive sense of pride:

> Looking at the museum, not only did we experience a burning feeling of shame for the deeds of our compatriots, who tormented this immortal city, but [we also felt] measureless pride in the Soviet people who held high the light of reason and justice in the midst of darkness and grief. Having endured suffering without end at the hands of the Hitlerite occupiers, the Soviet people not only did not preserve a feeling of hatred for the German people but, on the contrary, they have tried, always and in every way, to distinguish the people of Germany from the criminal Nazi clique.[66]

By constructing representations of *friendship* with the Soviet Union, socialist propaganda was able to promise the Germans that their guilt feelings would eventually recede, and they could gain access to the self-affirming feeling of pride. This was a key emotional resource for East German renewal because it let them join the "victor's camp," instead of being stuck as "history's losers."

Guilt, which was constantly being mobilized, imposed a moral debt on the East Germans: they were obligated to repent and make amends, not only to the Soviet people but also to Stalin himself. In these ceaseless invocations of German guilt, the Soviet leader was presented as the one with the ultimate power to pardon the Germans for Nazi crimes against humanity. The mantle of authority that the Soviet leader wore came from representations of Stalin as the guarantor and defender of peace, the spiritual father and mentor of the German people. Propaganda staged the "leader" as the patron of the German people; in his concern for their national and state interests, he was thus a protector who was offering them a path to restore their nation's honor. This image of the Soviet leader—and the fact that ordinary citizens were interested in the victor's plans for the fate of the vanquished—explains the population's keen attention to statements about the "German question" made by Stalin and representatives of the occupying forces.[67] According to one of SVAG's political dispatches, in just two hours the population bought twenty thousand copies of *Tägliche Rundschau* and fifteen thousand copies of the newspaper *Freiheit*, which carried Stalin's responses to questions put to him by journalist Hugh Bailey of the United Press.[68] The population complained about the shortage of newspapers and magazines to local power organs and to SVAG and, indeed, observers noted instances "when one German waits, while another one reads through the paper and then [the person who waited] buys it from him."[69]

The thirst for information came from a lack of clarity about what the future would hold. It also grew out of postwar German society's acute need to trust the authorities and see them as protectors who were able to provide the resources necessary for their survival and, amid the difficult postwar conditions, could offer scenarios for a return to normalcy. The growth of such expectations of Stalin was evident during the Potsdam Conference in August 1945. A university lecturer analyzed the situation this way:

> At the Berlin conference Stalin was first violin, the fate of Germany and the German people depended on him. Truman and Attlee just sat at the conference table and said yes to Stalin, giving the impression that they were also actively participating in discussions about the question of Germany.[70]

In the search for crisis-defeating paths of national development, there was a tendency to idealize the person of Stalin, whose name was connected with hopes that a single German state would eventually be created. Stalin's lofty international stature after the victory was presented to the Germans as the alluring promise that the German question would be resolved quickly and positively.

Exhaustion from the war and an all-consuming need for a predictable daily life helped intensify the sense that Stalin would guarantee and defend peace. The prospect of life without war was very important for East German society, which had been ground down by devastation, hunger, and deprivation. In this complicated postwar scenario, Stalin's image could calm society's strong feelings. The way the image of the "leader" acted as a stabilizing force for the East Germans can be seen in their responses to Stalin's comments about Churchill's Iron Curtain speech, which he delivered at Westminster College (in Fulton, Missouri) on March 5, 1946.[71] On March 14, *Pravda* published an interview with Stalin in which he responded to this speech. The Soviet leader confirmed that there was a real threat of war. However, he assured the Soviet population that the enemy would be defeated. After this statement was reprinted in the East German press, SVAG dispatches documented growing panic and fear of a new war on German territory. But his replies to the interviewer's questions also induced the population to trust Stalin, whose image promised that new military conflicts would be prevented, and peace and prosperity would prevail. Creating representations of Stalin as the guarantor of peace helped the East Germans to become less fearful in a situation in which, according to the words of a cleaning woman who worked at the office of a military commandant, "the smell of gunpowder is in the air again." While people called Churchill "the instigator of war," Stalin was cast as the "defender of peace," the one who was countering the West's aggressive plans.[72] His statements and the interview were reprinted in the East German mass media in order to calm the population and counter anxiety-producing rumors that a new world war was close.[73] Confidence in the Generalissimo's unshakeable authority and his ability to stand firm against the threat of war were reflected in an SVAG report quoting the words of a woman who worked for the city council: "Churchill used to follow Stalin's orders but now, after such a murderous interview, he will be completely silent. Stalin spoke more persuasively than Churchill."[74] Dr. Negach, the president of the Christian Democratic Union (Christlich Demokratische Union) in the small town of Burg, said that "Churchill's politics are well known. They are imperialistic. Generalissimo Stalin was right in saying that Churchill preaches a racial theory and what that theory leads to, we Germans know well. Russia is closer to us than England."[75]

In reports and political dispatches about the populations' sentiments, Stalin was usually depicted as the guarantor of Germany's peaceful postwar development and the upholder of a pledge that a new war would be prevented. These documents present Stalin as the crucial force stabilizing the postwar order: his name was connected with the "peace," "stability," and "safety" that postwar German society so desperately needed. For example, a master shipbuilder commented on the "leader's" talents as a commander-in-chief:

> If the English still [decide to] start a war with Russia, they will remember Russian soldiers and their talented leader Stalin for a long time. Russians have never lost wars but the more so now, when their people are united and ready to go with Stalin for any heroic feats . . . I think that our path is the path of friendship with Russia.[76]

In the Soviet Union, Stalin was represented as the spiritual father of all Soviet citizens. In Germany this was translated into something similar but also different: on the outskirts of the empire, he became the mentor and teacher of the German people, whose guidance would enable them to resolve problems plaguing everyday life and the overarching questions of national life. As Stalin's pupils, the Germans were supposed to obey their wise teacher and meekly follow his recommendations. Even the popular Soviet slogan "To Learn from the Soviet Union Means to Learn to Be Victorious!" was personified in Germany as "To Learn from Stalin Means to Learn to be Victorious!" Representations of Stalin as a fatherly protector were rooted in the propaganda of his pithy saying that "The Hitlers come and go but the German people, the German state, remains." These words, stated in Oder No. 55 of the People's Commissar of Defense of February 23, 1942, made a distinction between active supporters of the Third Reich and the rest of the population, thereby absolving the German people as a whole of guilt for war crimes. This "guilt-free" segment of the population was offered a chance to prove they had broken with the past by demonstrating loyalty to Stalin, whose postwar image was associated with the promise of Germany's unity as a state and a nation. This distinction gave the population a reason to perform acts of repentance which would restore the national honor. Every year on May 8, the Day of Liberation, the population was given the opportunity to repent while simultaneously thanking Stalin for freeing them from the "yoke of fascism."[77] On this day of remembrance, laying flowers and wreathes at memorials to fallen Soviet soldiers and busts of the "leader," sending telegrams and gifts to the Soviet leader, making solemn speeches of repentance, and promising to do better all staged Stalin as the "father confessor" of the German nation, a spiritual patriarch who could exculpate the German people.

German guilt was advantageous for the USSR and East Germany. It became the moral foundation for a cult community which was part of the relationship between the two powers. Constant reminders of Nazi crimes allowed Moscow to construct a rigid hierarchy of power relations and carry out the symbolic politics of the periphery's emotional submission to the center, which helped to spread Soviet influence in Eastern Europe.

In fact, German guilt made it much easier to Sovietize East Germany. As Sovietization proceeded, a complete orientation toward the "Soviet friend" was treated as the only possible path to forgiveness and the remission of sins. The moral code personified in the image of Stalin, with its key elements of shame and guilt, directed the Germans to demonstrate that they felt continual pangs of conscience; but at the same time, it offered a path to salvation— restoration of the nation's honor and initiation into the world of the positive emotions the victors enjoyed. As a result, rituals of apologizing, atoning for wrongdoing, and articulating feelings of shame became inalienable parts of the emotional practices of postwar East Germany. These practices obligated the population to undergo an ideological conversion from "enemies" to "friends" of the Soviet Union. Propaganda created representations of Stalin as the personal patron of East Germany, which showed how much the Soviets greatly trusted the German people and offered a unique opportunity to earn the victorious nation's forgiveness. Thus, the Stalin cult itself became a matter of honor, an East German project that created a way to expiate guilt and, through friendship with the USSR, to be exonerated of the results of a destructive war.

THE STALIN CULT IN THE SED: THE SOVIETIZATION OF EAST GERMAN POLITICAL CULTURE

"After Hitler, we are coming!" (*Nach Hitler kommen Wir!*) During the final phase of the war, German communists in the Soviet Union began to use this slogan with increasing conviction and heightened political awareness.[78] During their Soviet exile, they gave serious thought to what postwar Germany would be like and what would happen if it became a Soviet state.[79] When representatives of the German national committee Freies Deutschland met with the Main Political Administration of the Worker-Peasant Red Army in late 1944, Wilhelm Pieck said "We communists are Marxist-Leninists and we will fight to put the teachings of Marx, Engels, Lenin, and Stalin into practice," (Figure 3.5).[80]

In Moscow, during the final period of the war, Anton Ackermann was already thinking about the ideological foundations of "German-Soviet friendship." He and his fellow German communists planned to mobilize every propaganda resource they had at their disposal, including anything that would allow them to construct traditions of mutual friendship. Speaking at a KPD party school, Ackermann emphasized how important it was to extract the positive experience of the states' cooperation from the lessons of history: "The two countries have not had and do not have opposing interests. History teaches that friendship with the Soviet Union has always been good for Germany while war has always

Figure 3.5   Wilhelm Pieck, the president of the GDR, with a birthday present—a bust of Stalin. January 3, 1950. *Source:* Bildarchiv im Bundesarchiv (Berlin). Signature: Bild 183-S91657.

brought calamity and defeat."[81] German communists saw that taking the USSR as a model was the way to resolve all national problems quickly—and it was the only possible future political scenario for Germany. They knew very well that only cooperation with Moscow and Stalin's personal patronage could guarantee that the KPD's program would be realized after the fall of the Third Reich.

In the scholarly literature, the East German political elites, those who held key leadership positions in the party and state apparatus, have been described as the "generation of patriarchs."[82] Here the term "generation" denotes the socialization and values a particular cohort shared: the internalized rules and norms and the attitudes and sentiments of individuals who were united, in this case by life as émigrés in the Soviet Union in the 1930s and 1940s.[83] For them, the Stalin cult was a fundamental part of Soviet politics and, after the war, German reality. Having lived through the terror of 1937–1938,[84] they were adept at adapting to life under Stalinist rule: they knew how to bow down to hierarchies and show respect for those of higher rank, follow the Kremlin's orders to the nth degree, maintain strict discipline, observe the Soviet moral code, and demonstrate faith in the Soviet Union and unconditional loyalty to Stalin.[85] Raised on the history of the VPK(b) and the classic works of Marxism-Leninism, they learned how to defend and propagandize the Soviet Union, in accordance with the rules of "politically correct behavior."[86] They could impeccably converse, live, and govern Soviet style but their most important skill was that they had learned to be the "friends" of the USSR.[87]

The "myths of the beginning," which formed the core of official discourse in East Germany, reflected the experience and worldview of the "patriarchs' generation." The communists who returned to Germany from the USSR saw themselves as missionaries of Marxism-Leninism, in their Stalinist interpretation of this doctrine. They were the ones who demanded that postwar German society show remorse and repentance for the Nazis' wartime crimes. They called for a cleansing of the national conscience and restoration of the collective honor through rituals of confessing to Stalin. The "generation of patriarchs" could be described as Stalin's high priests. They controlled the transfer, adaptation, and popularization of canonical knowledge about the Soviet leader on the periphery of the Soviet empire. Their image of themselves as missionaries came from the sense of having been chosen and from the feeling that the Soviet authorities trusted them. For example, after receiving special permission to access secret informational bulletins about the political situation in Germany and the population's sentiments, Wolfgang Leonhard remembered that "I was filled with gratitude for being trusted and proud to belong to a group of functionaries who were so politically mature that they could dispassionately become acquainted with different opinions."[88] Leonhard compared this "mark of trust" to such party privileges as being promoted, receiving a decoration, or being given a material incentive. Therefore, the struggle for trust, from the Soviet Union, and Stalin himself, became a major goal of the political work German communists did after returning to their homeland.

There was another, more mundane reason for the German communists' loyalty to the USSR and Stalin personally. In the Soviet Union, many political émigrés already realized that showing loyalty to the "motherland of socialism" and the patronage of a highly placed official would help them to optimize their life strategies, make it possible to get an education, develop a career, and gain access to the luxuries and privileges the Soviet nomenklatura enjoyed while ordinary people struggled with poverty and scarcities of all kinds. After getting used to what Comintern staff members enjoyed in Moscow—living in the comfortable microcosm of the Hotel Lux and being able to patronize special stores and restaurants—they did not want to give up these benefits, even after returning to East Germany. Therefore, living in villas and elegant mansions, having access to hard-to-obtain foods, and vacationing in sanatoria became fundamental parts of the lifestyle of the new governing class amid the ruins of postwar Germany.[89] These privileges were closely linked with the Kremlin's patronage. The German communists' total dependence on Moscow's material, political, and symbolic resources decisively shaped the consolidation of patron-client relationships in Stalin's communications with the East German political elite.

Three "initiative groups," led by Ulbricht, Anton Ackermann, and Gustav Sobottka respectively, arrived in East Germany at the end of April–early

May 1945. They were on a Stalinist mission to "build the antifascist, democratic regime of a parliamentary democratic republic." For them, the June
11, 1945, proclamation that the KPD had been reestablished was the first
concrete result of Stalin's patronage and support from the Soviet side. It
is notable that soon after the end of the war—in the fall of 1945—German
communists had already started to transfer Soviet rituals to East Germany.
The pretext for the ideological transfer was the twenty-eighth anniversary
of the October Revolution. According to one of SVAG's political reports,
there were meetings to commemorate the "red date" on the Soviet calendar
involving 13,600 people in the town of Bernau alone. Speeches given by
members of the KPD presented the Soviet myth about the two "leaders" of
the revolution, Lenin and Stalin. Flower-festooned portraits of Soviet leaders, as well as Ernst Thälmann and Karl Liebknecht, were hung in the rooms
where the meetings were held. From the Soviet point of view, a meeting
in the town of Herzfelde was "particularly positive": the speaker ended his
remarks by saying "Long live the leader of the Soviet people, mighty Stalin,"
and the event itself ended with the laying of wreaths at the tombs of fallen
Soviet soldiers.[90] However, in 1945 these were more likely isolated incidents
that largely reflected initiative and improvisation on the ground rather than
signs that strict control over Soviet rhetoric, rituals, and visual symbols had
emerged in East Germany.

The creation of the SED in April 1946 as a result of the forced merger of
the SPD and the KPD was the next turning point in exporting the Stalin cult
to the Soviet Occupation Zone. In particular, in the middle of 1947 a transition
to accelerated Sovietization meant reorganizing the SED to make it "a new
type of party" on the Bolshevik model.[91] The first milestone in establishing
Soviet rhetoric and symbols was the second SED Congress, which took place
on September 20–24, 1947, in Berlin. The presence of the Soviet delegation,
led by Mikhail A. Suslov and Petr N. Pospelov, signified Soviet control over
political life in the Soviet zone. Otto Grotewohl was ordered to make harsh,
public criticisms of the Social Democrats' policies in the Weimar Republic:
"It would have been better for our people if we had learned more from the
Russians in 1918 instead of putting up with anti-Bolshevik poison."[92] For the
first time, the VKP(b) was openly presented as an example for the Germans
to imitate. Leninism was identified as the new ideological orientation and was
declared the continuation of Marx's teaching: "We recognize the continuation
and application of the teaching of Marx and Engels in the twentieth century
in particular, by Lenin and Stalin and from this we derive something new
and necessary for German conditions."[93] At the end of the congress, foreign
journalists unanimously agreed that "the Russians have switched to a decisive offensive."[94] Certain representations of close friendship with the Soviet
Union were ritualized at later SED congresses: collective singing of the

"Internationale," "continuing and unceasing applause" after every mention of Stalin's name, and electing the Soviet leader to the honorary presidium.[95]

One result of the transition to Sovietization was the renunciation of "a special German path to socialism," which was announced at the Twelfth Plenum of the SED's Central Administrative Board on August 2, 1948. In the Bolshevik tradition of self-criticism, Anton Ackermann tore apart his own theory of the "special path," saying that "there is only one path to socialism, the path [that] Marxist-Leninist doctrine has pointed out."[96] The Thirteenth SED Plenum in September 1948 only reinforced the new party line and significantly strengthened the rhetoric of friendship with the Soviet Union. Wilhelm Pieck called on SED members to study the *History of the All-Union Communist Party (Bolsheviks): Short Course* and the biographies of Lenin and Stalin more deeply. A party resolution of September 20, 1949, called for the creation of fifteen thousand study circles in which more than four thousand party members would study the *Short Course*.[97] The VKP(b) once again became a model for building a "new type of party": the SED charter was explicitly developed in accordance with the charter of the Communist Party of the Soviet Union and approved in the VKP(b) Central Committee before being adopted at the SED's Third Party Congress on July 20–24, 1950.[98] The East German leadership proudly reported to Moscow that the SED was growing by leaps and bounds: on July 1, 1950, there were 1,498,450 party members, but the membership jumped to 1,603,754 as of January 1, 1951.[99]

Changes in visual representations of the classics of Marxism-Leninism in the House of Unity (Haus der Einheit), the building in Berlin's Prenzlauer Berg district housing the SED Central Committee, reflect the gradual process of the SED's Sovietization. As Sergei Tiul'panov, the head of SVAG's Propaganda Department, noted in his memoirs, during the first postwar years only two portraits—of Marx and Engels—hung in the building's vestibule. After some time had passed a bust of Lenin was put up and, finally, one of Stalin.[100] The visible presence of the classics of Marxism-Leninism in the party administration's central building was a public indication that the SED was evolving into a "party of a new type." The cultic artifacts were intended to demonstrate visually who the new leaders' predecessors were and confirm the SED's loyalty to Soviet power.

However, venerating the classics of Marxism-Leninism was only one part of the Sovietization of East German political culture. Both the Social Democratic and Communist traditions of personality cults were honored in the SED. The Social Democrats relied on reverence for Ferdinand Lassalle, Karl Liebknecht, and Rosa Luxemburg, while the Communists bowed down before Ernst Thälmann, Hans Beimler, and Artur Becker. In postwar Germany, honoring antifascist fighters, heroes of the resistance, and socialist martyrs made it easier to transfer their symbolic capital to the leaders of the

SED. This allowed them to propagandize their connection with people who had given their lives in the fight against national socialism—and to present themselves as the successors of these venerated figures. The attempts of party leaders, especially Pieck, to stage themselves as "the people's leaders" and "fathers of the nation" show how badly the new regime needed charisma. Their wartime experience in the Soviet Union taught the German communists how important personifying power was for stabilizing a political order and mobilizing the population to work toward its ideological goals.

Although they were trying to infuse the regime with a sacral character and stage themselves as the nation's leaders, the communists who had been prepared to return to Germany during their stay in the Soviet Union had certainly not been trained to be charismatic rulers. Instead, they had learned how to be ideal apparatchiks—diligent, industrious, loyal bureaucrats who could obediently carry out Soviet directives. Instead of inspiring the masses, they actively used Bolshevik-approved methods of terror and repression to strengthen their own regime and fight against "enemies." In early May 1948, Sergei Tiul'panov developed a new version of SED self-understanding: "The Socialist Unity Party of Germany is situated at the boundary of two worlds—the place where the world of capitalism runs up against the world of socialism. Therefore, tasks of great responsibility are entrusted to it."[101] Intensifying Cold War rhetoric helped to radicalize the struggle with internal "enemies" and to move the Sovietization of East Germany forward. In June 1948, a resolution "On the organized strengthening of the party and its purging of enemy and degenerate elements" was adopted. This resolution made provisions for carrying out "purges": all SED members who did not agree with the pro-Soviet line would be excluded from the party, dismissed from administrative posts, persecuted, and arrested.[102]

Pieck himself insisted that everyone with anti-Soviet views should be dismissed from state and party service.[103] As the Cold War escalated with the Berlin Crisis and the appearance of the Zhdanov doctrine of the systemic conflict's two camps, in August 1949 Pieck called for the stepping up of agitation work among the population:

> People must be shown that there are two camps in the world: the camp of imperialism which the USA heads and the camp of democracy and socialism which the USSR heads. It is necessary to explain to the masses that whoever comes out for the USA is the enemy of the German people.[104]

The party's course led to the use of even more hyperbolic language, especially in characterizing the Cold War as a conflict between "people on *our* side" against "people on *their* side." This culminated in the slogan "The enemies of socialism are the enemies of Stalin, the enemies of the Soviet Union are the enemies of mankind."[105] Thus, Soviet methods of purging, intimidation, and terror, which made ample use of the "friends-enemies" division, became the most important way to reinforce intraparty discipline, along with the demand that rank-and-file members of the party publicly demonstrate their loyalty to Stalin.

The East German leadership's regular consultations with their patron, Stalin, played a key role in establishing the cult of the Soviet leader.[106] Significantly, these encounters took place in Moscow. In the system of Stalinist clientelism, personal meetings with the "leader" were the strongest sign of the Kremlin's goodwill toward the Germans. These were conducted in a strictly hierarchical manner. During the conversation, Stalin listened attentively, smoking his pipe, and he might joke with or even make fun of his interlocutor. The "leader" took charge of the conversation, asked questions, gave advice, promised help in specific matters, and had the right to ask his interlocutor to repeat something and interrupt him; he could also elaborate on something in a way that demanded complete agreement and he might offer harsh commentary. At the same time, as G. Korotkevich (a consultant in the VKP(b) Central Committee's Department of Foreign Policy) noted in March 1948, personal meetings with Stalin—especially his "humanity and warmth"—made a strong impression on the Germans. Thus, Grotewohl "did not expect" that Stalin would ask if they had comfortable living quarters in Moscow and if they needed anything.[107] The Soviet leader's questions about how someone felt, his personal desires and requests, impressed the German guests, creating the feeling of closeness to the "vozhd'." However, the humanity Stalin displayed confirms the traditional, hierarchical model of relationships between a patron and a client: there was an unspoken pact about the Kremlin's patronage in exchange for personal loyalty to the "leader."

As the notes from the protocols of personal meetings and conversations with Stalin show, the East Germans successfully mastered their role, which was to demonstrate loyalty to the "leader." Concrete help from Moscow was the result.[108] As a rule, Pieck, Ulbricht, and Grotewohl asked about economic assistance, wanted to know what the correct political line was, reported on party and state matters, and complained about "the failures and intrigues of enemies." SED delegations learned several things: how to rule in the Stalinist style, the rhetoric of class struggle, and how to play the game "peacefully" during the Cold War. They also learned how to develop the SED as a "new kind of party" and spent hours consulting with Suslov about the VKP(b)'s organization and management, and the principles that guided its work.[109] The SED leadership also saw Stalin as the highest court to which they could appeal. That is, he was the one who could lower reparations payments, curtail the dismantling of industry, help the East Germans obtain foodstuffs and raw materials, and put the GDR on a friendly footing with the countries of the "people's democracies."[110] Their personal communication with Stalin gave East German politicians a unique opportunity to resolve pressing problems, bypassing the numerous bureaucratic levels of authority in SVAG and the VKP(b).[111] The feeling that they had a close relationship with the Soviet leader allowed the East German leadership to ask Stalin directly for help in dealing with problems.[112] The "leader" usually supported requests from the SED elites, which showed that he could exercise absolute power, thereby reinforcing the German functionaries' dependence on the Kremlin.

"Political tourism" to Moscow was not just about getting the center's stamp of approval on policies being implemented in the periphery. It was also a way to learn how to organize life in the Soviet style. For example, the "cultural program" planned for the Germans during their official visit of March 25–April 1, 1948, included a visit to *Pravda*'s offices and a conversation with its editor, P. N. Pospelov.[113] On March 30, the Germans traveled to Bronnitsy, a town in Moscow province, to learn about how rural party organizations worked. A tour of the Borets collective farm was their introduction to life on a collective farm (*kolkhoz*). Otto Grotewohl was especially interested in finding out if peasants living on collective farms had a better life than they did before collectivization. After an inspection of the "exemplary and instructive" farm, the *kolkhoz* president invited the delegation to his home for dinner, surprising the guests with the "picture of abundance" set out on the table. An observant Soviet member of the party noted that after he sat down at the table, Grotewohl whispered to Oelßner, "Yes, now I see how the Russian peasants are starving on the *kolkhozy* and what all this chatter is about."[114] Inspired by what they had seen, Pieck and Grotewohl eagerly demonstrated their mastery of the official Soviet rhetoric, proposing toasts to Stalin's health and to success in setting up collective farms in the GDR.

An obligatory part of the Germans' program was a pilgrimage to communism's sacred sites—especially Lenin's mausoleum on Red Square. By visiting important Soviet *lieux de mémoire*, the Germans learned how to construct a cult commemorating a dead leader and create a socialist culture of memory. Thus, after visiting the mausoleum and looking at the graves at the Kremlin Wall, Grotewohl said "Probably nowhere in the world do people who gave their lives for their people and party receive such honor, nowhere is their memory honored as it is among you, in the Soviet Union." The program for leisure time in the evening reflected the Soviets' task of politically enlightening the SED delegates. Thus, the report said that the Germans watched several Soviet films, including *The Ballad of Siberia* (*Skazanie o zemle sibirskoi*), *Soviet Ukraine* (*Sovetskaia Ukraina*), *The Russian Question* (*Russkii vopros*), *For Those Who Are at Sea* (*Za tekh kto v more*), and *First-Grader* (*Pervoklassnitsa*). An introduction to Soviet culture and art meant going to the Bolshoi Theater, the All-Union Exhibition of the Arts, and the

Red Army Museum. Visiting symbolically highly charged sites that embodied success in constructing socialism was a way to emotionally mobilize the guests and stimulate Soviet cultural transfer to East Germany.

Intensive lessons in Sovietization in Moscow made the East German leaders even more dependent on Stalin. By the time they returned from the Soviet Union, they were certain that the Kremlin's patronage was their only guarantee of remaining in power. Maintaining the strict hierarchy of communication with their patron, they constantly turned to the Soviet leader, becoming hostages to Stalin's will. If necessary, the Kremlin could decide to send the best Soviet doctors to Berlin to monitor Wilhelm Pieck's health and to pay for the GDR president and his wife to have a rest in the prestigious Barvikha sanatorium.[115] The East German elite's total dependence on Stalin's absolute power even extended to resolving "delicate questions" in the personal life of SED members. In his memoirs, Vladimir Semenov, the head of SVAG, gives a telling example. Grotewohl's decision to divorce his wife and marry a member of the secretariat's staff gave rise to a discussion in the SED Politburo. The problem was that this secretary's former husband had been a member of the NSDAP. In the end, Pieck thought it was his duty to ask Stalin himself for advice. Stalin suggested that they stick to the rule that Grotewohl should resolve personal questions, not the party.[116] However, the fact that Pieck turned to Stalin shows that Stalin was seen as a patron, the highest court of appeal, and the arbiter of all sorts of difficult questions, including his clients' personal problems.

Greater ritualization of the party's life and society in general paved the way for further radicalization of the Stalin cult in the Soviet zone. For example, in the second half of 1946, the SED celebrated several Soviet holidays including November 7, the Day of the October Revolution; December 5, the Day of the Soviet Constitution; and December 21, which was the first time the party celebrated Stalin's birthday (his sixty-seventh). Pieck published an article with these words: "The brilliant foresight of the great leader of the Soviet Union is showing the way for the German people."[117] And workers in Leipzig sent a collective gift to the office of the military commandant of Saxony—a portrait of Stalin.[118] These signs of still-latent Sovietization were the first signals of an increasing orientation toward the Soviet Union, reflecting the mentality and wishes of the "generation of patriarchs."

A key aspect of Sovietization was the creation of a shared culture of socialist memory based on practices of commemorating dead "leaders." Thus, in early January 1948 K. V. Martem"ianov, the head of the Soviet Military Administration's Department of Information in Brandenburg, issued a decree about organizing evenings commemorating the twenty-fourth anniversary of Lenin's death.[119] It was recommended that the program include quotations from the works of Stalin, Mayakovsky, and Gorky, and work

by German poets Johannes Becher and Erich Weinert. The musical accompaniment for these evenings was supposed to include pieces by Beethoven
and Tchaikovsky, Shostakovich and Prokofiev. Showing Soviet films such
as *The Vow* (*Kliatva*), *Lenin in October* (*Lenin v Okt"iabre*), and *Lenin in
1918* (*Lenin v 1918 godu*) was also recommended.[120] In late January, people
gathered at factories, in schools, and at houses of culture to listen to the
Berlin Radio Opera's broadcast about Lenin's life and work. A month later,
on February 20, 1948, the SED administration in the town of Brandenburg
held a city-wide meeting devoted to the one-hundredth anniversary of the
Communist Manifesto. Portraits of Marx and Engels decorated the hall
where the "solemn meeting" was held. Addressing those gathered there, Fred
Oelßner emphasized Lenin's and Stalin's special roles in enriching Marxist-
Leninist theory and its practical implementation in the Soviet Union.[121]

Widespread signs of Stalin worship in various parts of the Soviet zone
became increasingly apparent in 1948, showing that the Stalin cult had
expanded beyond the confines of the party into society as a whole. By
synchronizing the political life of the Soviet Union and East Germany, the
leader's birthday became a major media event: reportage about Moscow in
its newly reconstructed state and articles and photographs about Stalin's life
appeared in the December 21 issues of magazines and newspapers, and radio
broadcasts were the first to recount the Soviet leader's biography for their
audience. For example, on December 20 and 21, 1948, an entire broadcast
was devoted to Stalin's "heroic life and titanic achievements."[122] Under the
pseudonym "Michael Storm," Markus Wolf explained the twists and turns of
the life course of the person whom he called the "symbol of a new epoch of
mankind." A reading of excerpts from Henri Barbusse's *Stalin: A New World
Seen Through One Man* punctuated the program, which was accompanied
by music.[123] Hedda Zinner, a radio station staff member who had lived in the
USSR from 1933 to 1945, appeared as an eyewitness of some of the events
that Wolf detailed. She described Stalin as the "incarnation of the will of
the masses" and the "defender of democracy." Stalin's birthday was also
celebrated at an event held at the House of the Culture of the Soviet Union
in Berlin. A. L. Dymshits, the head of the Department of Culture of SVAG's
Information Agency, gave a speech in which he described Stalin as the "liberator of the peoples," the "builder of a better world," and the "supporter of
all oppressed victims."[124]

In December 1948, the SED administration successfully reproduced the
Soviet scenario for celebrating Stalin's birthday in Leipzig. The propaganda
campaign started on December 17 when an exhibition about Stalin's life
opened at the city's police headquarters. On December 20, there were meetings featuring speeches about Stalin in all of the city's social, administrative,
educational, and industrial institutions. More than five hundred congratulatory

telegrams were sent to the central military commandant's office. The height of the celebration was a "solemn meeting" held on December 21 at the Capitol movie theater. After an essay about the Soviet leader's biography was read, by a unanimous vote those present adopted the text of a congratulatory telegram to be sent directly to Stalin:

> On the day of Your sixty-ninth birthday 22,000 workers and white-collar employees of the city administration of the city of Leipzig send You heartfelt wishes for happiness. We are delighted with the successes of Your work and Your unswerving struggle for the workers' just cause. With the Soviet people we take pride in Your mighty life. Together with all progressive forces, the workers and employees of the city administration are obligated to continue the struggle for the victory of socialism in all countries.[125]

On the same day the regional newspaper, the *Leipziger Volkszeitung*, published a front-page article by Anton Ackermann, "Stalin—Leader of the World Proletariat."[126] The SED's gradual transition to open propaganda of Stalin reflected the Sovietization of the political culture of East Germany, a process whereby the rhetoric and rituals of the personality cult became obligatory norms of party life.

In parallel, participation in party rituals and the public use of Stalin cult rhetoric—which symbolized moving from "false" views to the "correct" faith in the Soviet leader—became the criteria for demonstrating political conversion. The Soviets were particularly suspicious of Otto Grotewohl because he had been a Social Democrat. The way Soviet observers scrutinized his words shows how Moscow looked for proof of political conversion. Soviet bureaucrats stated during the East German delegation's visit in February 1947 that after a trip to the Moscow subway, inspired by what he saw, Grotewohl said, "Yes, this is a true civilization!" and after a tour of the Lenin Library exclaimed, "This is wonderful! All Russia learns, all Russia works and creates!"[127] After he met with Stalin on January 31, 1948, the Soviets who had been eavesdropping on their conversation heard Grotewohl tell his East German colleagues that "Comrade Stalin is the most beloved socialist in the world" and "Well, we will return from Moscow and really get down to work."[128] After the Germans' next visit, in March 1948, and the new proof that Grotewohl had been using positive Soviet rhetoric in comments he made to fellow members of the delegation, G. Korotkevich, of the Central Committee's Department of Foreign Policy, drew the satisfactory conclusion that "as a result of this trip to Moscow and especially from his conversations with Comrade Stalin, Grotewohl is even closer to us."[129] Soviet observers assiduously tracked both the Germans' official statements and their private conversations in Moscow. Schooled in the ritual language of praise and veneration for Stalin, they expected a similar style of behavior from the Germans. For example, during a November 1948 visit to the USSR made by an East German delegation of public figures, VOKS staffers noted that many members of the delegation did not know much about the Soviet Union. The VOKS staff complained that they did not mention Stalin's name at all in public speeches. Likewise, at official receptions the absence of toasts to the Soviet Union and to Stalin's heath was recorded. Grotewohl, who had already mastered the rules of Soviet etiquette, came to the rescue in this very "politically incorrect" situation. On November 6, 1948, he ended his first speech with the normative phrase, "Long live your great and wise leader Stalin!" And at the farewell reception at VOKS, Grotewohl conveyed gratitude and greetings to "the great leader of the Soviet people, Joseph Stalin" on behalf of the delegation and the entire German people.[130] In the eyes of Soviet observers, the Germans' use of Stalin cult rhetoric showed their loyalty to Moscow, while for the East German leaders, offering toasts and voicing good wishes in honor of the "leader" was a rhetorical way to win trust and a discursive strategy for becoming closer to the center.[131]

Collecting "dirt or discrediting information" (*kompromat*) on the political leaders of "fraternal countries" was part of the Soviet way of ruling and an effective tool for disciplining the political elites of the "people's democracies." National leaders' negative traits helped the Kremlin to make these men personally dependent on the Soviet leadership. An archival source documents Moscow's disapproval of Walter Ulbricht's behavior. In the Marxist tradition of unmasking internal enemies by using language connected with the "personality cult," it was said that:

> [H]e solves problems on his own, surrounds himself with loyal people and encourages subservience [*podkhalimstvo*]. He allows his wife, Lotte Kühn [who was not an SED member] to interfere in party affairs, criticize and relocate local party workers . . . he is praised as the "German Lenin." He is given the kind of public reception that Pieck and Grotewohl do not enjoy . . . At Politburo meetings, he is the last to present his point of view [calling it] "the opinion of the Soviet friends," which should be accepted without [considering] any other options.[132]

Mikhail Suslov also reported to the Central Committee of the VKP(b) that when Ulbricht was one of his protégés in Karlshorst, he displayed "dictatorial tendencies" and would not take into account the other SED leaders' opinions, which caused tension in the party.[133] Certain features of Ulbricht's cult came in for criticism: an excessive number of his portraits put up at party events and inappropriately prolonged applause after his speeches. However, on the wave of Stalinization, these things could have been compliments from the Soviets since he was trying to copy the Bolshevik style of rule, sought patronage in the Kremlin, and played the Moscow card by emphasizing his close connections with important figures in the Soviet capital to establish his personal monopoly on power in East Germany.

The "generation of patriarchs"—former members of the German Communist Party and the leaders of the SED—initiated the effort to build relationships with Stalin based on the idea that he would be the patron of the German people. This model of political communication with Moscow corresponded to the way other regimes on the periphery of the empire of Stalinism established and legitimized their power. In demonstrating their personal loyalty to the Soviet leader, the SED leadership was fulfilling expectations about a client's behavior enshrined in the code of honor governing patron-client relationships: the Kremlin offered protection to the Germans and promised to defend them in exchange for their unconditional loyalty to Stalin. Thus, for the East German political elite, the Stalin cult was the means of stabilizing their own power; it opened up the possibility that the GDR could be Moscow's protectorate and offered access to the center's resources. The conclusion of a symbolic pact between the patron and his client was the prerequisite for constructing a cult community embracing the entire postwar Soviet empire. With its center in Moscow, the cult offered the periphery—here, East Germany—a scenario for building a new social and political order founded on the ideological postulates of Marxism-Leninism.

It is very important to note that the first signs of the Stalin cult in East Germany—trying out Soviet rituals, engaging in some political improvisations, and taking some initiatives in the localities—had already appeared in the fall of 1945. However, during the early postwar period, veneration of Stalin stayed within the ranks of SVAG and the KPD/SED. As the SED evolved into a "new type of a party," the Stalin cult took root in it. The operation of Stalin's personality cult became an indicator and a key mechanism of the Sovietization of East German political culture. The ritualization of party life and the strengthening of discursive and behavioral norms, as well as the increasingly harsh party discipline and purges, facilitated the SED's internal ideological consolidation. All of these measures helped initiate the policies of importing the Stalin cult from the USSR in a centralized manner and politicizing other areas of East German society. By the time the GDR was founded, the SED had definitively shaped itself by choosing to embed Stalin's image in its ranks, but East German society as a whole had not yet made this contradictory choice.

THE STALIN CULT IN PUBLIC SPACES

During the final months of World War II, the visuality of the Third Reich underwent a dynamic reconfiguration. The mass concealment, destruction, and burning of Nazi symbols showed that many ordinary Germans actively participated in delegitimizing the Third Reich. Purging public space was also a spontaneous, prophylactic measure intended to forestall violence from the Allied armies. Just before the surrender, the national socialist visual order became a security threat. To avoid the rage of the "liberators," portraits of the Führer were covered up with neutral landscapes or pictures of flowers. Everywhere, copies of *Mein Kampf*, portraits of Hitler, and photographs of relatives in military uniform were hidden in attics or basements.[134] In general, hiding artifacts which indicated that the owner once belonged to the "national community" was widespread. Like many other people, for example, one former judge burned his copy of *Mein Kampf* and his party card in the kitchen rather than on the street in front of his house because he did not want to retain evidence of Nazi Party membership but was afraid people would see him destroying these things.[135] Former soldiers put on civilian clothes and hid, buried, or burned their uniforms to get rid of signs of active support for the Third Reich. These acts of spontaneous behavior indicated the Nazi regime's growing loss of visual legitimacy.

Insofar as modern dictatorships of the twentieth century were primarily regimes of visual power, the Third Reich's decreasing visibility in public and private spaces signified the weakening of its dominance.[136] Likewise, the strengths (or weaknesses) of political orders matched the intensity with which they saturated public arenas with the visual artifacts of power. Under the Soviet occupation regime, visuality played an especially important role in proclaiming, justifying, and challenging the legitimacy of Soviet supremacy because the "occupier" and the "occupied" spoke different languages, came from different cultures, and saw each other as sworn enemies. As a result, in practical terms, visuality became the only common mode of communication. Therefore, visuality was central not only to accepting the occupation but also to expressing opposition, resolving conflicts, and mitigating feelings of rage and vengefulness (Figure 3.6).

For Soviet soldiers, the sight of Nazi artifacts justified violence toward individuals and communities. They interpreted Nazi insignia on the flags, badges, official documents, posters, and party cards that they saw when they raided German homes as proof that the inhabitants were Nazis.[137] Categorized as Hitler's accomplices, the owners of these materials were considered "enemy elements" who could be imprisoned in special NKVD-MVD camps or sent to the Soviet Union for compulsory labor.[138] Visual artifacts of the Third Reich often incited Red Army soldiers to vandalism and looting during which they destroyed homes, smashed up furniture, and stole possessions.[139] Sometimes these highly charged objects provoked more extreme violence, which was often expressed by raping women as a way to take vengeance on the enemy.[140] According to numerous memoirs, women crying for help, children shouting, the sight of fire and blood, and the smell of burning and decomposing bodies were the main features of most people's sensory experience during the final months of the war.

Despite the obvious inevitability of defeat, violations of the Third Reich's prevailing visual order were still harshly penalized. Nazi terrorist organizations fought to restore the Third Reich's public symbolism. Distinguished by ideological fanaticism and personal loyalty to Hitler, these groups saw themselves as the last stronghold of the "national community." They defended Nazi visuality as a matter of national honor and were ready to ruthlessly punish fellow citizens for harboring defeatist sentiments. Members of the underground Werwolf organization demanded that people take down white flags and restore Nazi posters to their previously visible positions, threatening to shoot people on the spot for noncompliance.[141] In one such case, a homeowner who had written on his door "We are not Nazis! We welcome the liberators!" was captured by members of the Volkssturm (a national militia organized during the final months of the war) and hanged from a tree.[142] This example demonstrates how individuals who refused to demonstrate loyalty to the "national community" risked severe punishment from the German military police or SS detachments. The bodies of people who had been hanged for disloyalty were left in public places, with placards around their necks bearing derogatory inscriptions which described them as "deserters," "traitors," or "saboteurs" because they had refused to join the Volkssturm or the sanitary service.[143]

The Red Army's offensive and Germany's capitulation on May 8, 1945, led to the practice of putting up white and red flags on buildings, signifying that the inhabitants were reconciled to defeat and recognized the Soviet Union as the victor.[144] "White flags wherever you looked. They were hung from apartment windows in cities and villages, in factories and administrative buildings. Over many days, weeks even, they defined the picture in Germany in the spring of 1945," wrote Stefan Dörnberg (later to become a historian and politician in the GDR) in his memoirs.[145] White became a marker of loyalty. Many Germans thought buildings with white flags would not be set on fire and people wearing white armbands would not be shot.[146] Refugees from East Prussia draped red and white flags over their carts as they made their way to the "homeland," so that they would not anger divisions of Allied soldiers and they wore white armbands to ensure their own safety.[147] In settlements taken by the Red Army, men held out white handkerchiefs as they went to the Soviets to surrender in the hope that they could remain with their families.[148] This very limited palette of colors also helped orient the local population and displaced people. Houses displaying red flags were considered dangerous since people assumed that Red Army soldiers or the Soviet military administration must be quartered there. Many people gave these buildings a wide berth. On the other hand, refugees recognized houses without flags as safe places to rest, seek help, or spend the night.[149]

As soon as Germany signed the "Instrument of Unconditional Surrender," the Allies began removing the symbols of the Third Reich from public spaces.[150] The Allied Control Council decree of May 13, 1946, ordered that, first and foremost, Nazi monuments and emblems should be removed.[151] The Allies' postwar policy of democratization, demilitarization, and de-Nazification made *old* personality cults taboo, which led to a partial paralysis of daily life. Thus, a parcel bearing postage stamps with Hitler's image did not make it to the addressee.[152] On January 23, 1946, the same kind of stamps, which were discovered in a certain Herr Schubert's stationery store, created turmoil in the local administration.[153] This example of the circulation of forbidden postage stamps, which seems insignificant at first glance, only underlines the intensity of the symbolic struggle for the right to design the new political landscape. As a result, SVAG representatives in Zwickau district decided on September 27, 1945, to destroy 2,640,567 marks worth of "fascist stamps, postcards and envelopes."[154]

The establishment of the German Democratic Republic on October 7, 1949, which declared that it was an "antifascist, democratic, peace-loving state," was the final impetus for remaking public space. The task at hand was now the broader effort to remove every symbol with militaristic, fascist, or anti-democratic content. In a resolution issued on January 17, 1950, the Politburo of the SED Central Committee recommended that the Ministry of Internal Affairs carry out a second inspection of place names, memorials, and sites of national memory.[155] The leaders of Imperial Germany were put onto a new list of taboo cult figures since their names had been used as the basis for the Third Reich's historic traditions. As a result, at the Leipzig Trade Fair representatives of the Soviet military administration removed posters with portraits of Fredrick the Great and Bismarck from the Tauber Press's booth, which featured an exhibition on "Paper and Time."[156] In April and May 1951 alone, 159 street signs on streets with "Prussian" names were removed in East Berlin.[157] These streets and squares were now named after socialist and communist leaders.[158]

From the very beginning, it was clear that attempts to reorganize public space in the Soviet zone conflicted with the desire to maintain continuity with the past in honoring royalty as national historical figures. This led to conflicts between the Germans and the occupying forces. Thus, the mayor of the town of Gransee provided funds for upkeep of the monument to Queen Elisabeth of Austria but refused to take part in May First demonstrations featuring portraits of the leaders of the international workers' movement and red flags.[159] Occupying forces responded to similar "political misdeeds" in radical fashion, dismantling or even blowing up monuments with imperial or monarchic content. Memorials were altered or demolished and replaced with monuments honoring fallen Soviet soldiers.[160] In constructing the East Germans' new political topography, attempts were made to export Moscow's cult of World War II to the GDR.[161] Public acts of repentance for unleashing worldwide catastrophe that were carried out at the memorials to fallen Soviet soldiers dramatized a clean break with Prussian militarism and the Nazi past while demonstrating the Germans' political conversion from "enemies" to "friends" of the Soviet Union.

Searching for traditions of German-Soviet friendship became the central task of East German ideologues. However, attempts to track down the sources of this amity and confirm their veracity often led to problems with making the past compatible with the present. The absence of a unified historical master narrative for the entire socialist bloc was keenly felt, especially in the early postwar period. A polyphony of historical narratives from across the region was the result. Thus, a favorable comparison of Bismarck and Lenin as "fighters for peace in Europe," made in a speech at a meeting of the German-Soviet Friendship Society in Saxony, drew harsh criticism from the local party leadership.[162] To avoid such errors and to legitimate German-Soviet friendship, only the names of leaders of workers' movements and the Communist Party could be used. Early on, it became evident that the occupying forces' visual policy would emphasize a pantheon of central figures in order to substantiate longstanding traditions of German-Soviet friendship, highlighting the tendency to centralize received knowledge. Thus, in the autumn of 1945, in connection with celebrations of the twenty-eighth anniversary of the October Revolution, a portrait gallery of the classic figures of Marxism-Leninism (Marx and Engels, Lenin, and Stalin) was introduced and widely circulated. East Germany's new political icons were disseminated to emphasize that the Bolsheviks had borrowed Marxist doctrine. In the aftermath of World War II, this signaled Germany's return to a path of national development that took Soviet experience into account.

In practice, however, the policy of "a special German path to socialism" in force during the early postwar period meant that leaders were assigned to one of two opposing national groups, *ours* (Germans) and *theirs* (Soviets). In November 1946, when hanging portraits of socialist and communist leaders had only recently become a common practice—but one which was still chaotic in the absence of strict regulation—the director of the Labor Exchange in Templin and his deputy had a revealing argument. Notably, this disagreement took place before the first wave of Sovietization of 1947–1948. A portrait of "their head of state" (*chuzhoi gosudarstvennyi deiatel'*)—Stalin—was the source of the conflict. The director demanded that his deputy remove it immediately, conscientiously reproaching him: "As a German you should be ashamed to have such portraits on your wall . . . we don't need foreigners."[163] Soon thereafter, a poster with Stalin's image was found in the wastepaper basket, ripped into shreds. Portraits of *our* German leaders—Ernst Thälmann and Wilhelm Pieck—were given "places of honor" in the office. Higher-ups heard about this and set matters straight. The wrongdoer was disciplined, but he only received administrative punishment, while the commandant's office confined itself to firing the director and evicting him from his home. This example illustrates the symbolic barriers to the transfer of Stalin's cult from the Soviet Union, from "abroad," into the forcibly Sovietized space of East Germany and shows how representations of leaders created conflict-laden tension in public places.

The SED attempted to defuse tension by building up a pantheon of harmoniously coexisting Soviet and German cult figures, synthesizing communist and social democratic traditions of honoring major figures. When the GDR was founded and large-scale preparations to celebrate Stalin's seventieth birthday on December 21, 1949, began, a hierarchical pyramid of cults took shape. Stalin stood at the apex of this pyramid of public symbolism, and propaganda described his role as "teacher and best friend of the German people."[164] The deceased classic figures of Marxism-Leninism—Karl Marx, Friedrich Engels, and Vladimir Lenin—were placed just below Stalin, on the second level (Figure 3.7).

The occupants of the third level, the current leaders of East Germany— Wilhelm Pieck, Otto Grotewohl, and Walter Ulbricht—were building socialism on the work of these predecessors (Figure 3.8).

The leaders of the communist and social democrat workers' movements— Clara Zetkin, Rosa Luxemburg, Karl Liebknecht, August Bebel, and Ernst Thälmann—were on the fourth level. They were central figures in heroic propaganda narratives in which they carried forth the message of antifascism and continued the "struggle for peace."[165] A group of "New People"—real-life activists, heroes of labor, winners of national and Stalin prizes—formed the base of the pantheon.[166] These figures were an idealized political body, the bearers of party and state ideology. As a whole, the pantheon of cults was supposed to produce representations of social consensus among men and women, different age cohorts, and various professional groups, to help stabilize and legitimate the SED regime.

Visualizing the personality cult in public space became a major concern for both SVAG and the SED. Starting in the summer of 1945, window displays of copies of the newspaper *Tägliche Rundschau* were created in shops in the cities, towns, and villages in the Soviet zone. These window displays were intended to give the population a positive image of the Soviet conquerors. In September 1945, a workshop was set up in the small town of Bautzen and the artists who worked there were tasked with making visual propaganda such

Figure 3.6 Anti-Nazi banner in the US sector of Berlin (Neukölln) declaring "That was the reorganization of Europe. 4.5 million antifascists were brutally murdered in Auschwitz alone! Eradicate Nazism, root and branch." Summer 1945. *Source:* Bildarchiv im Bundesarchiv. Signature: Bild 183–2005-0901-517. Photographer: Kurt Ochlich.

as posters and banners for SVAG. Among other assignments, the workshop received orders for portraits of Stalin, General Zhukov, and Ernst Thälmann. Trying to avoid political competition between the Social Democrats and the Liberal Democrats, SVAG deliberately hastened to organize its own visual agitation. It demanded that the local governing organs seize public space by placing visual representations of the new power in every possible public space.[167] At times this visual onslaught provoked fights between SED members and people who belonged to other parties. An incident of this type took place on September 6, 1946, in the Weimar district (*Bezirk*) when SED members who had been sent to put up their posters ran into a group from the Liberal Democratic Party on the same mission who were pasting their posters on top of communist propaganda.[168]

The escalation of the Cold War forced Moscow to put more pressure on SVAG, demanding that it step up political propaganda in East Germany.[169] Although numerous reports noted the "absence of systematic, centralized control over visual agitation" during the early period of the Soviet occupation, the policy of intensified Sovietization in the late 1940s fundamentally changed the situation.[170] From February 1947 on, political posters for visual agitation could be printed only if SVAG issued a special license.[171] To commemorate

Figure 3.7   A column of marchers in a May First parade holding portraits of the classics of Marxism-Leninism. May 1, 1953. *Source:* Bildarchiv im Bundesarchiv (Koblenz). Signature: Bild 183-19400-0029. Photographer: Horst Sturm.

the thirtieth anniversary of the October Revolution in 1947, SVAG adopted a resolution about instituting meticulous oversight of all noticeboards and political information.[172] In 1950, centers for political information were created. These were the "Portrait of the Street" (*Bild der Strasse*) kiosks which were put on the main streets and in squares of cities throughout the GDR. These became centers for political information which preempted posters chaotically hung on the walls of buildings, fences, and bridges. The GDR's Information Service, which was responsible for explaining current domestic and foreign policies to the population, was put in charge of designing the kiosks and monitoring them.[173] For example, in Dresden after a "hidden swastika sign" was detected in the composition of one poster, the Information Service staff consulted with the Stasi and then immediately ordered a copy of the "Activist" poster produced for International Women's Day to be glued on top of the offending visual artifact.[174] Visual agitation was especially important along expressways and major highways in areas bordering West Germany. In these regions, the iconography of the personality cult visualized the border between the two opposing systems and the ideological front line of the Cold War.

Public spaces had to be converted to Sovietized "spaces of jubilation" to stage several essentials: an ideological utopia, a society of social consensus, a positive attitude toward the occupying forces, and nationwide support for German-Soviet friendship.[175] Creating "spaces of jubilation" meant that party-state rituals needed to have a certain performative quality in order to appeal to the public on an emotional level. Groups at various levels of government tried to design such highly charged, propagandized public spaces—and attempted to enlist the population as producers, stage managers, and spectators. For example, on August 16, 1952, the city council of Halle passed a decree requiring everyone in the city to decorate their homes and the adjacent streets with red lanterns and flags in conjunction with a street demonstration of fighters for peace. "Building representatives" (*Hausvertrauensleute*) were in charge of setting up the stage, so to speak. They were ordered to sell a thirty-five-pfennig propaganda packet to each household in the building. The local power organs wanted to make lists of the residents of each building indicating who had bought the packet and who had not; they also wanted a record of the residents' written consent to take part in the action. The organizers' mobilization plan did not work out: the buildings were sparsely decorated, and the planned illumination was barely noticeable. The *Hausvertrauensleute* told the organizers that most people had refused to buy the packet of decorations.[176] As we see, the population once again resisted Sovietization of the private sphere during the first postwar years.

Efforts to visually design political space also ran into a series of organizational complications. This involved, above all, getting rid of old or worn-out posters which "spoil the appearance of cities and villages" instead of being replaced on a regular basis.[177] Reports of party inspectorates noted that the kiosks which were supposed to display official posters were empty, abandoned, or were not used for their intended purpose. Theater groups, cinemas, opera productions, and sports teams used them to put up announcements for their own events.[178] Among the explanations for why visual agitation was not very effective were "not enough posters," "officials were working unsystematically," and "delays in delivering posters on certain dates." For example, most of the posters issued for Stalin's birthday in December 1951 did not arrive at the propaganda department of Saxony until the beginning of January 1952 and they were not put up because they were no longer relevant.[179] At the same time, thousands of copies of posters of the leaders were treated disrespectfully, which denigrated the symbols of power.[180] In one instance, after ceremonial marches and rallies during the Third World Youth and Student Games in August 1951, in East Berlin portraits of the leaders of the Eastern bloc were seen in the personality cult's forbidden zone: "thrown away without a glance in the gutters," "smeared with mud," and "heaped up in a side street."[181]

Posters and other visual materials were so poorly produced that people responded negatively to the symbols of power. As part of the preparations to celebrate Pieck's seventy-fifth birthday, the propaganda organs struggled to centralize the party-state image of the leaders by initiating a campaign to purge political information boards of "poor-quality, kitschy, amateur" portraits of the president of the GDR.[182] But even after these efforts, the propaganda organs still made some blunders. In early January 1951, the public was quite critical of a poster that had been put up to celebrate Pieck's birthday. The president's image was of a very low quality: the Information Bureau reported that in the Zittau area even the people pasting up these posters talked about how he looked "good" from a distance but seen close up he appeared "simply repulsive."[183] To enhance the impact of political posters on the population, the author of a report strongly recommended increasing their verbal content by including headings, slogans, and texts and positioning the text so that every viewer would understand the context of the visual agitation in a unified way.[184]

Public space was politicized by both compressing and expanding the sphere of party-state influence. The Information Service's Agitation Department was responsible for issuing periodic bulletins titled *Advice for Visual Agitation*. These gave practical advice on creating slogans, preparing banners, where to place visual materials, and how to design public spaces such as cafeterias and shops, reading rooms and the vestibules of administrative buildings, train stations and the façades of apartment blocks. From 1949 on, shop windows became an important arena for visual representations of the pantheon of socialist personality cults.[185] In January 1951, the Information Service's Department of Plan and Peace Propaganda in Chemnitz ordered that every public waiting room be supplied with posters, slogans, party newspapers, and the party's literature in order to "appeal to and persuade a large part of the population to engage in progressive, democratic state building," and also to create a "*visual* atmosphere of love for the best friend of the German people, for the great Stalin" [italics mine, A. T.].[186] Places targeted for such appeals included hospital admissions departments and policlinics, the reception rooms of public premises and the bureau of the city administration, kindergartens and schools, that is, the range of public places where men, women, and children from various subsectors of the population were likely to go.[187]

The establishment of a planned socialist economy, which included organized production of the party's cult objects, heightened the intensity with which public space was saturated with the symbols of power. The party put in orders for such items and created a centralized system to sell them. A catalog of objects with political symbolism was published in 1949. It offered consumers an assortment of busts, reliefs, posters, portraits, postcards, and badges with images of the "leaders of the workers movement."[188] As a rule, these objects were churned out on East German soil, using Soviet models,

Figure 3.8 Walter Ulbricht, Wilhelm Pieck, and Otto Grotewohl on the reviewing stand at the SED's Fourth Congress, held April 30–May 6, 1954. *Source:* Bildarchiv im Deutschen Historischen Museum (Berlin). Signature: Bild BA 117028.

and then distributed (with monitoring from above) to mass organizations, party organs, the army, schools, and universities. Attempts to organize retail sales of personality cult objects were not successful. Consumer demand for these things was virtually nil. Thus, the owner of a small store in Leipzig that sold pictures of various types admitted that almost no one was interested in portraits of Stalin, Lenin, Marx, and Pieck. His customers, especially SVAG staff members, were eager to buy "pictures that [were] artistically kitsch" like a picture of a naked woman surrounded by dancing angels.[189]

The policy of intensively saturating public space with the symbols of Soviet power was not without its ups and downs. Thus, during an inspection, staff members of SVAG's Information Bureau themselves compared the buildings of the military commandant's office with exhibition halls at a trade fair and kindergartens. Reports spoke of excessive use of garlands and portraits, flags and banners, which the population saw as "political kitsch," and which gave the impression of being a "farce" and a "circus."[190] Accounts of propaganda work in East Germany recommended struggling with "sectarian ideas," which were responsible for the vast numbers of red flags that were hung out and unauthorized changes in street names to honor the leaders of the German Communist Party.[191] The Soviets themselves were forced to acknowledge the

crude character of agitation work. In July 1946, G. M. Bespalov, the head of
SVAG's Information Bureau, wrote to Moscow that

> Our propaganda is too intrusive, it is served up too openly and hits you right on
> the forehead . . . we must turn away from this style of unassailable statements
> and crude bragging and learn how [to create] more subtle and clever propaganda
> that acquaints the reader with the advantages of our social system in a way that
> escapes his notice.[192]

These "excesses" showed that Soviet propaganda was incompatible with
East German experience and memory. Mayors of cities and small towns indicated that the propaganda posters and slogans did not address German realities.[193] Hoping to improve the situation, Anton Ackermann met with Bespalov
in November 1946. During their conversation, Ackermann complained that
the German power organs had no autonomy because of "SVAG's unceasing
custodial interference in the SED's affairs and constant demands to present
themselves at Karlshorst." "For example," Ackermann said,

> Why do SVAG representatives look over SED leaflets and posters when these
> young and inexperienced officers, although they have the best intentions,
> nonetheless cannot judge these matters with the same competence as old, expe-
> rienced workers from the German Communist Party. Meanwhile, SED leaflets
> and posters are painstakingly examined, corrected everywhere, and, in many
> cases, this makes things worse.[194]

Nonetheless, Soviet control over public space and the arbitrariness of
SVAG's staff continued. For example, a certain Captain Belkin, the SVAG
political commissar in the Dippoldiswalde area in Saxony, demanded that
new photographs of SED candidates running for seats in the local organs of
government be taken on the eve of the elections in 1949 because he thought
headshot of the candidates were inappropriate. He insisted that new posters
with full-length images of the candidates should be distributed because the
original photographs did not fit the "Soviet model."[195]

The SED leadership, including those at the highest level, realized that visual
propaganda had to be adjusted to be meaningful for the German consumer.
While an SED delegation was visiting the All-Union Artistic Exhibition in
Moscow in March 1948, Pieck and Grotewohl discussed a portrait of Russian
military hero Kliment Voroshilov wearing his orders and medals:

> Well we can't do that in Germany. If the ordinary, average German sees a por-
> trait of a Soviet man with a lot of orders, in his mind he will invariably think of
> Goering, who, as is well known, had many orders. One has to say that our Soviet

comrades who are working in Germany don't always understand this. It also happens that reactionary newspapers are happy to publish portraits of Soviet generals and marshals in uniform, with their orders. They do this on purpose, knowing what kind of impression this makes on German readers.[196]

While questions about how to "Germanize" Soviet propaganda in East Germany remained controversial during the first postwar years, there is no doubt that the occupying forces wanted to bring public space under their control and occupy it with symbols of the postwar political order. The extremely high degree of politicization of public space gave birth to an anecdote that reflected the state's control over the individual's behavior in official public spheres. In this anecdote, the simple act of an East Berliner spitting during a walk along the Stalinallee—the main site for staging the building of socialism in East Germany—was interpreted as a political challenge to the regime since an officer of the People's Police soon appeared and sternly reproached the man who had spit: "Comrade, please do not politicize!"[197]

IN A LINE AND AT THE BIERSTUBE: POPULAR OPINIONS ABOUT STALIN IN NONOFFICIAL PUBLIC SPHERES

As a Western tourist put it after visiting the Soviet Occupation Zone in 1949:

Taking a walk along the streets of cities in the Eastern zone is amazing. One has the impression of being in a state with a one hundred percent organized population. Almost everyone is wearing one, two, or more badges from the party and the mass organizations. But if you take a train, go into a restaurant, or chat with old friends, you soon understand that the population's real opinion of the SED is far from favorable. For example, the Day of Liberation begins with laying wreathes on monuments to fallen Soviet soldiers but ends with anti-government conversations in the *Kneipe*.[198]

In fact, primary sources show again and again that behind the façade of a highly ritualized public life, in private niches and the less controlled spaces of interpersonal communication, another life was unfolding, one that was quite different from the official register of narratives, sentiments, and behavioral models.[199]

As a rule, in public spheres organized by the state and party—at party meetings, in the mass organizations, at demonstrations—the population played the prescribed roles. That is, they spoke Soviet and acted accordingly. An incident involving an artist named Ginther reveals some paradoxical but typical behavior. He was a former member of the NSDAP. But because of the high demand for visual products, SVAG ordered Ginther to paint portraits of Stalin, Zhukov, and Thälmann. When a Soviet officer asked him how he felt about depicting VKP(b) leaders and Red Army commanders, the artist gave the expected "correct" answer: "I am doing this with great joy in my heart. I am painting portraits of the great men who freed the German people from Hitlerism, but I was drawn into the Nazi party by deceit and even coercive violence."[200] On the other hand, in informal or anonymous niches of communication, places where one could speak more freely—*Kneipen*, toilet stalls and smoking rooms, at home or at the weekend cottage, among family and friends—people voiced their own opinions about the regime, which were quite different from the official discourse.

Initial reactions to the propaganda of Stalin's image show that the Soviet leader embodied the Germans' feelings about being defeated. Representations of Stalin reminded them of the unconditional capitulation, the loss of loved ones, and the nation's dishonoring. According to SVAG's political dispatches, German audiences rejected the propaganda of the "leader" in *The Fall of Berlin* and another Soviet film, *Stalingrad*, which were both unpopular with German moviegoers.[201] The Minister of Education of the province (*Land*) of Saxony-Anhalt conceded that these films reminded people "of the defeat and Germany's national shame."[202] Reports indicate that the public watched *The Fall of Berlin* in "deathly silence" and audiences left the cinema because they could not stand the emotional stress the film caused. Women wept and asked,

> Why do the Russians open up our wounds, endlessly singing the praises of the war? We can hardly look impassively at the countless battlefields where mountains of corpses of German soldiers lie. My husband, brother, son, or father might be lying among those corpses. We have already been trampled on, why do we have to repeat this every day on the screen like this?[203]

In Bautzen, during a showing of a film about the victory parade in Red Square in 1946, the audience started whistling and began to leave the cinema.[204]

Three factors shaped the popular sentiments about Stalin in postwar Germany: shared experience of life under national socialism, the violence Red Army soldiers unleashed on civilians, and the overwhelming difficulties of daily life after the war—hunger and unemployment, the destruction of family ties and the death of loved ones, deportation and flight, irreparably damaged buildings and infrastructure—and the void created by the absence of any perspective on the future. Above all, people were disappointed because the Soviet occupying forces had failed to speedily establish the postwar order.

Negative comments about Stalin and talk of how much better life had been in the Third Reich grew out of this distress. Memories of the "good old days" conjured up nostalgia for Hitler, their "Führer," who gave them feelings of national greatness, pride, and superiority to other races.[205] In a private conversation, a woman from the town of Neustrelitz said that

> The Red Army is only destroying the German people. I was a National Socialist in body and soul and today I am still true to my beloved leader. It's a pity if the Führer died but if Hitler is alive, that's our salvation.[206]

A man from Ueckermünde nostalgically commented that "However bad the NSDAP was, we were still living better under it than we are now under the current regime and the Communist Party, which can't handle the food supply."[207] People standing in line at a store in Erfurt made similar comments.[208] SVAG's political dispatches described rumors that Hitler was alive and speaking on the radio every night, making appeals to young Germans.[209]

Even after the war ended, East German society perceived Stalin through the prism of national socialist propaganda. Fear of the pan-Slavic threat reappeared. A "young couple who were on their way home from the theater" expressed anxiety about communist ideas being imported. The young man asserted that

> Stalin is a Bolshevik, a communist who wants to take over the entire world with the help of his repulsive communist idea. He sent his people out around the world to organize Communist Parties [and] revolution and to overthrow the existing order.[210]

A leaflet found on the streets of Chemnitz proclaimed that

> Not letting the Russians' plans for annexation come to fruition is what the times demand . . . We must avert the threat of world domination. Stalin is linking his goals with what Ivan the Terrible and Peter the Great wanted to do and with the ideas of pan-Slavism. Peter I wanted to get the Baltic Sea, Stalin the Great wants the Atlantic and the Pacific.[211]

A man from Schwerin tried to persuade a small circle of his acquaintances that "Every German must stay away from communism since communism is Russia and Russia is our ruin."[212] The weight of day-to-day problems—and the fact that these seemed unlikely to end in the foreseeable future—increased the appeal of comforting memories and reinforced the tendency to use racial concepts to interpret reality. This led to the rejection of Stalin as a *foreign* leader and continuing sacralization of Hitler, who was *their own* "Führer."

The violence Red Army soldiers inflicted on civilians had a disastrous impact on Stalin's postwar image in Germany. The wartime desire for vengeance that was such an important motivation for the Soviet troops—the "sons of Stalin" as they were called in Germany—continued to define their relationship with the Germans.[213] There were frequent incidents in which soldiers expropriated clothing, food, farm animals, and machinery without authorization; they stole watches, motorcycles, and bicycles from civilians; they looted homes and took produce from vegetable gardens; and they raped and murdered. Red Army soldiers forced East Germans to chop firewood for them, wash their dishes, and do other household tasks.[214] "Hooligan acts" often took place in public, for all to see: Soviet soldiers were seen to

> Break windows, crudely pester women, swear for no apparent reason, vomit on the train, throw the passengers out of the car, and [then] one drunken soldier would get to the point where he would manage to pull himself together on the platform of the car.[215]

The prosecutor of the Frankfurt garrison thought Soviet soldiers broke the laws mainly because they were not afraid of the mild punishments they would incur and from drunkenness. Efforts to step up educational work with soldiers, which was guided by the slogan "hold high the honor and dignity of the Soviet soldier," failed to produce the desired results.

This kind of arbitrary, destructive behavior created an upsurge in anti-Russian sentiments. Thus, addressing a meeting of the residents of the village of Beek in Brandenburg province, the deputy mayor called for open resistance to the occupying forces: "Stalin's soldiers are thieves and bandits, they need to be physically exterminated since all they do is steal."[216] A leaflet proclaimed that "now not one German woman, not one German man can be found who is safe, 'Stalin's *Kulturträger*' [bearers of culture] are lying in wait for them everywhere."[217] Trying to defend themselves, the population wrote letters to the local administrations, asking for help. Seventeen citizens sent a letter to the commandant of the suburb of Strausberg requesting protection from nighttime raids carried out by Red Army men. One hundred residents of Zeesen sent a letter to the president of Brandenburg province with complaints about the occupying troops' endless looting, murders, and violence.[218] Civilians felt vulnerable and were increasingly afraid to leave their homes, especially after dark. Thus, during celebrations of the twenty-ninth anniversary of the October Revolution, a popular saying made the rounds: "The Russians are celebrating, that means beware."[219] East Germans were so afraid of the Red Army that documents speak of individual and group suicides as the "army of liberators" approached.[220] Rumors that German POWs were being murdered in the USSR and civilians would be banished to Siberia only intensified the general distrust of the Russians and made people skeptical about Soviet propaganda and Stalin's promises of a better future for the Germans.[221]

The Germans documented rapes in areas liberated by the Red Army as acts of deliberate humiliation.[222] In fact, rapes often took place in the presence of husbands, fathers, and sons.[223] Any attempts to defend their women were followed by beatings and shootings.[224] For Red Army soldiers, raping German women—which "de-Aryanized" (*Entarisierung*) them—demonstrated their superiority to German men. Since the Nazi drive to preserve the supposed purity of "Aryan blood" prohibited Germans from having sexual relations with non-Aryans, rapes committed by "Untermenschen" (as Nazi ideology designated the Slavs) were seen as the forcible mixing of blood and an offense against the honor of the entire German people. Edeltraut Woldrich from the town of Oberplan gave voice to the rules governing the sexual behavior of members of the "racial community." As she put it in her memoir: "A German girl does not mess with the enemy."[225] Victory did not turn Soviet soldiers into members of the "Herrenrasse." Germans continued to view them as "impure," describing them as unwashed, wearing dirty uniforms, unshaven, and smelling bad.[226] As a result, Red Army soldiers were seen as a source of pollution. Being raped by them was degrading; it massively destabilized the victims and destroyed their sense of superiority.

Inspecting the mail on July 19, 1948, the Soviet Commandant's Office of the Glauchau district discovered a harshly accusatory letter sent to the Western Zone:

> The Russians have infected us with venereal diseases on an enormous scale. One in two Russian officers has the clap or syphilis. It is ridiculous that these pigs still want to be our liberators. . . . Give us the guns and we'll chase them away. As long as these dirty pigs are here, we won't be happy.[227]

The rapid spread of venereal diseases as a result of rape was interpreted as another humiliation for the Germans: "Untermenschen" were infecting the "clean nation's" healthy body.[228] Venereal diseases reinforced the Germans' sense of being dishonored. They marked the bodies of the victims, condemning them to physical and psychological suffering and pain and traumatic memories that have persisted to the present. Women diagnosed with gonorrhea and syphilis were subject to compulsory treatment in special medical facilities. Being publicly singled out in this way, which could destroy the future of a woman labeled a "Russian whore," was even more traumatic and shameful for many women than the rape itself.[229] In addition, venereal diseases often caused infertility. This added to the burden these women carried, risking condemnation in their own communities, by their families, and especially their husbands. In a patriarchal society, they were not forgiven for defiling the honor of their husbands, who were perceived as "fighting heroically" for the Fatherland at the front under the constant threat of death. Alongside the daily difficulties of the postwar period, this gender conflict created by rape (and other gendered issues) contributed to a high divorce rate, increased domestic violence against women, and a crisis of masculinity in postwar society.[230]

Stalin's presence in Potsdam at the Allies' conference in August 1945 raised hopes that some pressing daily life issues would be resolved but this optimism almost immediately turned into disappointment and a lack of faith in the leader's omnipotence. Making Stalin the "best friend" was not easy under the weight of everyday problems. Above all, the German population expected him to take measures to improve the food supply, "since Stalin was himself in Germany and saw with his own eyes the scale of our destruction."[231] In Frankfurt on the Oder, an SPD member said in a conversation with colleagues,

> My party comrades and I are unhappy that the Russians are taking everything, and nothing is left for the people. The robberies and rapes are continuing. The population is making strenuous efforts to leave for the British and American zones. They say that 80 percent of the Red Army are thieves . . . All of us put our hopes in the Potsdam conference and we thought that Stalin would bring some changes for the better but now disappointment is setting in because everything is going on the way it was before. KPD members assure us that if Stalin knew about what the Russian occupation forces were doing, everything would be different.[232]

On one hand, faith in the "leader's" lack of information about what was happening in Germany removed accusations that Soviet policies were not effective and contributed to the idealization of Stalin and the attribution of mistakes to SVAG and the German authorities. On the other hand, unresolved problems led to more disappointment in the Soviet leader and set up barriers to the transfer of Soviet ideology to East Germany.

Hunger was one of the most acute postwar problems. Because issues involving the food supply were still unresolved, rumors that there were large reserves of food in the Russian military commandants' storerooms abounded. Everywhere people were saying that the Russians were using potatoes to make vodka and then getting drunk and wreaking havoc.[233] In addition, Soviet soldiers were accused of inflating prices and engaging in speculation which, as the population saw it, aggravated an already very complicated economic situation. The food problem was so acute that groups of women, sometimes carrying their babies, frequently went to the offices of the military commandants, insisting that they needed food.[234] In a collective letter to the commandant of the city of Sonnenberg, the residents wrote, "We love the Russian state and Stalin, but we are starving. Help us poor women of Thuringia."[235] On April 24, 1947, thirty women stood in the central square of Aue, a town in Saxony, chanting "Down with the Reds!" and demanded bread and potatoes for their families. A few days earlier, in Heidenau a crowd of a hundred women had called for food. And in yet another town, a similar demonstration began in the morning with one hundred protestors. By evening the number of women grew to over a thousand, forcing the mayor to promise that additional food cards would be distributed.[236] While hunger was an acute concern across postwar Germany, women—but not men—used their right to publicly protest.[237] Reports do not mention men as participants in food riots. In the disrupted gender balance that prevailed after the war, women were the ones who took charge in political space and learned how to engage in dialogue with the occupying forces.

However, the lack of any tangible progress in resolving everyday problems gave the population the impression that the Russians intended to "kill the Germans by starving them." Someone standing in a line was heard to say "The Red Army either doesn't want to establish order, or it can't. It's strong enough to do it. It probably doesn't want to since anarchy is the shortest path to communism."[238] Frau Schulz, who did not belong to a political party, expressed this kind of disappointment when she told her neighbors that "People don't care what kind of a regime they are going to obey. All they want is not to be robbed and raped by the occupiers, to get enough to eat and be able to work."[239] Another report notes that a group of women said "We aren't interested in the conference or its resolutions. Just let them give us enough bread and food so our children don't die of hunger, the rest isn't important."[240] The failure to resolve problems involving the food supply led to the birth of a popular expression: "Stalin is the dictator of famine."[241]

Nationalistic and anti-Russian sentiments continued to circulate in the anonymous leaflets which appeared throughout the Soviet zone. Calling on Germans to take a stand, one flyer vividly pitted the "Herrenrasse" against the "Untermenschen": "Germans, resist! The Bolshevik Stalinist hordes of 'Russians' should leave us our highly developed cultural Fatherland as soon as possible before it is too late! Stalin is pursuing a systematic policy of starvation against us! Stalin is a criminal!"[242] These appeals were one way to express opposition. Iconoclasm was another.

The population's iconoclastic reactions, which focused on damaging the occupying power's official iconography in public places, were expressions of criticism and an attempt to put up symbolic barriers to the transfer of Soviet ideology to East Germany. For example, in August 1945, six posters with excerpts from the Potsdam Conference resolutions to which anti-Soviet slogans had been added were sent to the SVAG administration in the province of Brandenburg. And written in ink, in German, on posters pasted up in the village of Drewitz were these messages:

> 1. He who lied once will no longer be believed; 2. It is all rubbish; 3. You know how to talk; 4. I will teach you culture (Stalin); 5. Why do you steal?; 6. What kind of a woman do you take without asking?

On two propaganda kiosks with posters on which "Marshal Stalin on the Germans and Germany" was printed, the word "Stalin" was crossed out and "Hitler" written in, which pointed out the similarity of the two dictators. On another poster with the message "The Hitlers come and go but the German people, the German state remains," someone wrote "If this continues for a few more years, nothing will remain of the German people."[243]

The attempt to keep Soviet ideology out took several forms. The frightening rumors making the rounds were one form of this. Word on the street had it that during the Potsdam Conference the Allies had secretly agreed to prohibit the creation of a German army for the next seventy-five years; alcohol consumption and marriages would be banned for the next two years; the country would be occupied for twenty years; and prisoners of war would be held in the Soviet Union for thirty-five years.[244] Anti-Soviet sentiments were also voiced in the hostile statements scrawled on the walls of buildings in Brandenburg province during the Nuremburg trials: "Better death than slavery," "Russia is the paradise of murderers, thieves, and criminals," and "Stalin and Molotov should go to Nuremburg, they are the main criminals, scum, and abusers of girls."[245] A letter sent to the editorial board of Radio Berlin in October 1947 spoke of revenge for the dishonoring of Nazi officers:

> Now they are hanging our generals, who have had such a glorious past, in this shameful fashion because they supposedly violated human rights . . . And are the so-called victorious powers guided by law and justice? . . . So, there is going to be a celebration on our street. Germany will stand on its feet again and take its revenge . . . Our spirit does not sleep and one day an avenger will arise again.[246]

The desire for vengeance came from the sense that the nation's honor had been damaged, and injured honor demanded revenge for the abuse inflicted. Similar violations of public order were swiftly reported to the NKVD.

The Soviet policy of demanding reparations and dismantling factories, which the East Germans saw as "robbery and theft in broad daylight," also increased negative feelings about Stalin.[247] Sometimes the dismantling took place in "rough form": office windows were broken, machines were damaged, and furniture was burned in front of Germans, who were beaten up by the dismantling teams.[248] People working in large industrial enterprises were terrified of the all-encompassing nature of the dismantling, fearing that all their equipment, down to the last machine, would be taken away.[249] East Germans rejected the official concept of reparations as a "moral debt" owed to the Russians; in doing so they made a direct connection between reparations payments and hunger, unemployment, their extremely difficult living conditions, and economic stagnation. A typical comment on this situation was,

> The Russians are robbing and destroying Germany. It's the Russians' fault and the Red Army's that the German population is starving now, because the Russians have taken all of our property out of Germany to Russia and they have left nothing for the Germans.[250]

Another typical statement was, "Dismantling factories is leading to mass unemployment and poverty. When the Red Army came, we were hoping for a new life. What can we hope for now?"[251] People in the Soviet zone saw this as a sharp contrast with the fact that the Americans were not dismantling factories in their zone.[252] They blamed Stalin for taking away their personal and national property and for the decline in industrial output, which had been a source of particular pride for Germans. One person in the Soviet zone summed it up this way: "Everything belongs to Stalin. You there, German comrade, you only have the right to look after these assets. Radios, sewing machines and things like that aren't yours anymore, all of it is 'Stalin's.'"[253]

The Soviet political reports informed Moscow about Germans' suffering from the sense that their national dignity had been damaged. Stalin's declaration that the Oder-Neisse line should be Germany's eastern border, and the fact that the border was enshrined in the Potsdam agreements, intensified the shared feeling of a severe blow to their country's dignity, which was an especially acute source of pain for expellees from East Prussia. An expellee lamented that "We will never forget what we were so proud of, what we once possessed."[254] Pomeranian native Bertha Schwartz expressed her distress about the loss of Königsberg by saying

> At the conference it was resolved that Königsberg would henceforth go to the Russians. As a German, this cannot help but disturb me. Königsberg was always considered a truly German city and now it is painful to think that it is no longer ours.[255]

A man working at a brewery said "Our people, who have lived there from generation to generation, have lost our homeland forever. This is very depressing for us."[256] Literature professor Victor Klemperer's diary entry for August 4, 1945, reflects a similar sense of injury:

In the morning the Potsdam communiqué was read out on the wireless. Shattering, quite egotistically shattering. Germany will be so castrated, so poor, such an outcast that we two [Klemperer and his wife] will never get on our feet again. The dry bread, no fat, on which we have been living will accompany us literally for the rest of our lives. Who is going to pay for my demands, my losses? (Nothing in the communiqué suggests that the Allies will want to look after the German Jews.)[257]

Germans from all social strata also criticized the loss of cities and territories, describing Poles and Russians in racial terms, as "backward," "less developed," "stupid," and "dirty" people, "who will only contaminate our land."[258] Germany's losses of land and the rift in the country's territorial integrity called forth the population's most agonized reactions as people inserted their individual traumas into collective ideas about the dishonoring and destruction of the nation.

Feelings about the loss of the eastern territories surfaced with particular intensity at the Leipzig Fair in September 1947. The fair's "New Poland" exhibition was intended to demonstrate the success of socialist construction, including accomplishments in the former eastern territories of the Reich, but Germans reacted with hostility and humiliation. A Soviet report noted that there were so many negative comments in the visitors' book that the exhibition's organizers had to remove it because of "chauvinistic remarks." Some entries praised the German "civilizing mission" in Poland while accusing Poles of an "absence of organizational talent," "vulgarity," and "illiteracy." Numerous comments reveal the ways people asserted the fundamental Germanness of the lost territories: "Silesia was originally a German land and [a land of] German blood. Millions of Germans share this opinion." Other statements reveal how attendees tried to restore their sense of superiority to the Poles and wanted to return to the Nazi racial hierarchy:

The exhibition shows only bad [things about] the Germans and only good [things about] the Poles, which is not true. . . . Around Poznan on the former wastelands there were wonderful buildings and residential houses. Without the Germans, Poland would never have been a civilized state and would have remained without culture.

Other entries explicitly gave voice to the German sense of degradation: "I see no reason to humiliate us with this exhibition. It would be more reasonable to advocate the return of the eastern regions of Germany."[259]

In the early postwar years, the nation's honor was such a burning topic that ordinary citizens sent numerous letters about it to newspaper editors and the editorial staff of radio stations. For example, in February 1947 public discussion of German national honor flared up on radio programs, and SVAG censors intervened. During several broadcasts in succession, the presenter read excerpts from letters attributing the difficulties of the postwar period to the Germans' greatly reduced "national honor." The absence of honor, as one letter writer put it, was the main reason that other nations continued to humiliate the country and hate the Germans.[260] The letters to mass media outlets became a forum in which listeners expressed hopes that the prewar German borders would be restored. Letter writers complained that the unity of "mighty Germany" was not being discussed and refused to bear any blame for the Nazis' crimes.[261] Soviet censors described similar comments as manifestations of "revanchism," "fascism," or "hostility." Official propaganda made expression of such sentiments taboo. On the other hand, a SVAG staff member reported to Moscow with enormous satisfaction about the "appropriate emotions" of a German student who stated that "I am no longer proud of my fatherland, I am ashamed of it."[262]

But the dilemma about whether to feel pride or shame was not the only factor defining the daily life of East Germans. The fear that the Allies might start a new war among themselves was ever present. To some extent, the population thought a next military conflict would save them from their "Soviet liberators" and would allow them to escape from the uncomfortable feeling of having been humiliated.[263] In November 1945, a resident of Rostock was already predicting that an imminent conflict of systems would take place between the West and the East, "A war with England and America against Russia will begin soon . . . Germany won't be the cause of this struggle, it will be the fight of capitalism with communism."[264] In the Brandenburg region a rumor (and the hope) that the Americans would come soon and chase out "Stalin's cadets" was recorded.[265] In another instance, someone hoped that when the Americans and the British arrived, problems with the food supply and reparations would soon be resolved.[266] Rumors that military technology and armed forces were being concentrated in the border regions, weapons were being delivered from England, and former SS divisions were being restored in West Germany led to a general sense that war was inevitable.[267] These signals from below indicated that the population, desperate for a change for the better, even at the price of a new military conflict, had reached the limits of its patience.

In the midst of the prevailing anxiety about a new war, unfulfilled expectations, hopes, and plans for the future were projected onto West Germany and the Western Allies. In censored letters sent from Schwerin in early December 1945, one sees typical postwar expressions of hope for a normalized daily life:

"Dear boys! . . . Judging by the common opinion that complete order already reigns in the west, there is absolute chaos here, thanks to the Russians and the

communists"; "Dear Ilse, I received a letter from my husband who is in Bremen
. . . He doesn't want to come here . . . He won't find a job and there is also the
hunger . . . My husband writes that I should come to him as soon as possible
since life is better under that occupation . . ."; "Dearest Gretchen! . . . After
[Germany] lost the war first we were with the English and then the Russians
and all of a sudden everything changed. Everything is getting worse and worse
here."[268]

In another letter, the author complained that the Red Army brought not
liberation but venereal disease, poverty, and hunger.[269] Many similar reports
made the Soviet occupiers anxious and apprehensive. SVAG tried to calm
the population by using the media to create representations of the poor living
standards in the western zones and in general to depict unemployment, poverty, and misery in the capitalist world.[270] Consequently, socialist newspapers
liked to publish reports about people leaving the western zones. These people
were staged as supposedly enthusiastic about moving to East Germany,
where they found well-paying jobs and a new motherland. Propaganda strove
to present the Soviet zone as an ideal place to live, one that offered many
prospects for a happy future.

In analyzing the world of public opinion in postwar East Germany, it
is noteworthy that statements about Stalin made in official public spheres
usually did not go beyond the concept of Stalin as the "best friend of the
German people," which was securely in place at the end of 1949. However,
in niches that were less politicized and where the regime had less control,
actors' rhetoric and behavior were at odds with the dictatorship's official
discourse. In lines at stores and in train station waiting rooms, in *Kneipen*
and on trains, in circles of friends and family, an alternative discourse about
Stalin took shape. This discourse did not repeat the language of propaganda.
Instead, it expressed experiences, needs, and emotions that were products of
the war and the defeat. The need to reduce the tension between the regime's
claims and the individual's autonomous worldview forced the subject to work
out three key behavioral strategies—to adapt, negotiate with, and resist the
regime, *simultaneously*. The subject had to be flexible and able to change
his/her behavior to correspond to what the situation, the place, and the time
required (or permitted)—or to meet the demands of a given public sphere
and its particular behavioral norms. Based on a set of personal meanings,
these behavioral strategies allowed the individual to maneuver his/her way
through the labyrinths of party and state structures, to cleverly juggle the
rhetorical formulas of the official register of the dictatorship of discourse,
to participate in party rituals, and to help produce—and exercise—power.
The hybrid nature of the East Germans' behavior generated many differing

and seemingly ambivalent evaluations of Stalin. These were not mutually exclusive but rather were the result of a single life strategy of simultaneous adaptation, negotiation, and resistance to life under a socialist dictatorship.

NOTES

1. Thum, *Traumland Osten*; Kienemann, *Der koloniale Blick gen Osten*.
2. Thum, "Ex oriente lux—ex oriente furor."
3. *Vashik*, "Metamorfozy zla."
4. Der Reichsführer-SS, SS-Hauptamt, *Der Untermensch*.
5. See Waddington, "Anti-Komintern."
6. For example, see Pase, *Stalin im Blitzlicht der Presse*; Windecke, *Der rote Zar*; Anti-Komintern, *Der Weltbolschewismus*.
7. On the concept of an emotional community, see Rosenwein, "Worrying about Emotions," 842.
8. Krylova, *Soviet Women in Combat*.
9. Cited in Nitschke, *Vertreibung und Aussiedlung*, 79.
10. Majstorović, "Red Army in Yugoslavia," 402.
11. Over 1,300 newspapers and journals were produced by the Red Army with a total circulation of over 4.38 million across the front line. See Schechter, *Stuff of Soldiers*, 189–90.
12. Schechter, *Stuff of Soldiers*, 190.
13. Budnitskii and Rupp, "Intelligentsia Meets the Enemy," 632.
14. Weiner, "Nature, Nurture, and Memory," 1150.
15. Zaremba, *Die grosse Angst*, 428.
16. Nitschke, *Vertreibung und Aussiedlung*, 92.
17. Szarota, *Warschau unter dem Hakenkreuz*, 285.
18. Scherstjanoi, *Rotarmisten schreiben aus Deutschland*, 114.
19. Senjavskaja, "Deutschland und die Deutschen," 256.
20. Scherstjanoi, *Rotarmisten schreiben aus Deutschland*, 217.
21. Schechter, *Stuff of Soldiers*, 192.
22. On the measures taken by the Red Army from January 1945 onward to tighten discipline, curb senseless destruction and looting, reduce excessive alcohol consumption, and rein in offences against old people and women, see Scherstjanoi, *Rotarmisten schreiben aus Deutschland*, 155–60.
23. Directive No. 11072 of the Headquarters of the Supreme Command of April 20, 1945, to the commanders of the troops of the 1st and 2nd Belarusian and 1st Ukrainian fronts on the need to treat the German population and prisoners of war humanely, in Scherstjanoi, *Rotarmisten schreiben aus Deutschland*, 145.
24. Scherstjanoi, *Rotarmisten schreiben aus Deutschland*, 213. This saying is attributed to Alexander Nevsky, Prince of Novgorod, whose cult flourished across the Soviet Union during the Great Fatherland War. See Schenk, *Aleksandr Nevskij*; the biblical basis is Mt 26: 51–52 ("All who take the sword die by the sword").

25. The soldiers' rhetoric was a response to Stalin's order of May 1, 1944, which called on them to "kill the wounded German beast in its own lair." See Scherstjanoi, *Rotarmisten schreiben aus Deutschland*, 3 as well as soldiers' letters, 26, 44, and 182.

26. Gebhardt, *Als die Soldaten kamen*, 97.

27. Gelfand, *Deutschland-Tagebuch 1945–1946*, 28. For similar attitudes toward the Germans, see Inozemtsev, *Frontovoi dnevnik*, 210.

28. Scherstjanoi, *Rotarmisten schreiben aus Deutschland*, 144.

29. Scherstjanoi, *Rotarmisten schreiben aus Deutschland*, 179, 184.

30. On censorship practices as an integral part of the field post system, see Schechter, *Stuff of Soldiers*, 196–97.

31. Scherstjanoi, *Rotarmisten schreiben aus Deutschland*, 52.

32. Scherstjanoi, *Rotarmisten schreiben aus Deutschland*, 170–71.

33. Schechter, *Stuff of Soldiers*, 199, 202–4.

34. Scherstjanoi, *Rotarmisten schreiben aus Deutschland*, 41. A similar letter from a Red Army soldier can be found in the same volume on page 281.

35. On the topos of hatred toward the Germans in the USSR, see Yekelchyk, "Civic Duty to Hate."

36. During the Third Reich, radio enabled the Führer's speeches to reach millions of listeners and played a key role in symbolic communication between Hitler and the German people. Therefore, Stalin's voice on German radios was a sign that the Third Reich had fallen but it also symbolically heralded the appearance of a new "Führer"—Stalin—in a defeated Germany.

37. In the Soviet Union, the speech was broadcast on May 9 at 20:00 hours (Moscow time) and the text appeared in *Pravda* the next day. See *Pravda*, May 10, 1945.

38. Leonhard, *Die Revolution entlässt ihre Kinder*, 429–30.

39. "Berlinskaia konferentsiia. 17 iiulia–2 avgusta 1945 g. Zapis' vtorogo zasedaniia glav pravitel'stv, 18 iiulia 1945 g., 16 chas. 18 min.," in Gromyko, *Berlinskaia (Potsdamskaia) konferentsiia*," 58. The American rapporteur summarized Stalin's response more succinctly: "Stalin said that Germany was a country with no government and no definite frontier. It had no frontier guards. It did have four occupied zones." See "Rapporteur's Report," 90.

40. "Iz informatsionnoi spravki o politicheskoi rabote sredi naseleniia Germaniia, 5 iiulia 1945 g.," in Bonvech, Bordiugov, and Neimark, *SVAG: Upravlenie propagandy*, 24; see also Stalin, "Ansprache an das Volk," 362–63.

41. "Spravka 7-go Otdeleniia 3-i udarnoi armii o rabote sredi naseleniia, ne pozdnee 21 avgusta 1945 g.," in Timofeeva and Foittsik, *Politika SVAG v oblasti kul'tury*, 329.

42. "Dokladnaia zapiska o politicheskikh nastroeniiakh sredi razlichnykh sloev nemetskogo naseleniia i antifashistskikh partii provintsii Brandenburg i gor. Potsdam, sviazannykh s resheniiami Berlinskoi konferentsii Trekh velikikh derzhav, 30 avgusta 1945 g.," GARF, f. 7077, op. 1, d. 27, l. 43.

43. For an overview of the scholarly literature on the Hitler cult, see Bühmann, "Der Hitlerkult: Ein Forschungsbericht."

44. For example, Vieth, "Die letzte 'Volksgemeinschaft'"; Welch, "Nazi Propaganda and the Volksgemeinschaft."

45. Von Plato and Leh, *Ein Unglaublicher Frühling,*" 208.

46. Gries, "Mythen des Anfangs"; Zimmering, *Mythen in der Politik der DDR*; Hein-Kircher, "'Deutsche Mythen' und ihre Wirkung."

47. Classen, "Vom Anfang im Ende"; Satjukow, *Befreiung?*

48. Zubkova, *Poslevoennoe sovetskoe obshchestvo*, 37, 46–47.

49. Gibas, "'Bonner Ultras,' 'Kriegstreiber' und 'Schlotbarone.'"

50. Faulenbach, "Die DDR als antifaschistischer Staat."

51. Institut Marksizma-Leninizma pri TsK KPSS, *Kommunisticheskaia partiia.*

52. See Mironenko, Niethammer, and von Plato, *Sowjetische Speziallager in Deutschland.*

53. On the Thälmann cult, see Leo, "'Stimme der Faust der Nation': Thälmann-Kult kontra Antifaschismus"; Leo, "'Deutschlands Unsterblicher Sohn . . .'"; Börrnert, *Wie Ernst Thälmann.*

54. Zubkova, *Poslevoennoe sovetskoe obshchestvo*, 137.

55. "O prazdnovanii 30-i godovshchiny Sovetskoi armii v raione Templin, 24 fevralia 1948 g.," GARF, f. R-7077, op. 1, d. 251, l. 51.

56. "Donesenie o politicheskikh nastroeniiakh naseleniia provintsii Brandenburg, 19.02.46 g.," GARF, f. R-7077, op. 1, d. 198, l. 63.

57. Grotewohl, "Simvol nemetskogo pozora."

58. On the psychology and philosophy of shame and guilt, see Izard, *Psikhologiia emotsii*, 342–409; Landweer, *Scham und Macht*; Willams, *Scham, Schuld und Notwendigkeit*; Neckel, *Status und Scham.*

59. Ulbricht, "Das Programm," 19–21.

60. "Protokol No. 5 zasedaniia Biuro propagandy na vrazheskie okkupirovannye vragom strany, 15 fevralia 1945 g.," GARF, f. 8581, op. 2, d. 131, l. 11–12.

61. *Tägliche Rundschau*, June 22, 1945, 1.

62. Bonvech, Bordiugov, and Neimark, *SVAG: Upralenie propagandy*, 22–23.

63. "Iz otcheta VOKS o rabote s delegatsiei obshchestvennykh deiatelei Germanii, 25 noiabria 1948 g.," in Timofeeva and Foittsik, *Politika SVAG v oblasti kul'tury*, 795.

64. Timofeeva and Foittsik, *Politika SVAG v oblasti kul'tury*, 794.

65. "Iz otcheta VOKS o rabote s delegatsiei obshchestvennykh deiatelei Germanii, 25 noiabria 1948 g.," in Timofeeva and Foittsik, *Politika SVAG v oblasti kul'tury*, 795–96.

66. "Pis'mo nachal'nika Upravleniia informatsii SVAG S. I. Tiul'panova Predsedateliu pravleniia VOKS V. S. Kemenovu ob otzyvakh nemetskikh deiatelei kul'tury, posetivshikh SSSR, o zhiznii v Sovetskom Soiuze, 29 maia 1948 g.," in Timofeeva and Foittsik, *Politika SVAG v oblasti kul'tury*, 748.

67. For a detailed analysis of the German question, see Filitov, *Germanskii vopros.*

68. "Vyskazyvaniia nemetskogo naseleniia ob interv'iu tovarishcha Stalina, dannogo prezidentu 'Iunaited Press'gospodinu Kh'iu Beili v provintsii Saksoniia, 14.11.46 g.," GARF, f. R-7133, op. 1, d. 277, l. 226.

69. GARF, f. R-7077, op. 1, d. 18, l. 80.

70. GARF, f. R-7077, op. 1, d. 27, l. 43.

71. Stalin's image had a similar effect in the Soviet Union. See Zubkova, *Poslevoennoe sovetskoe obshchestvo,* 129.

72. "Donesenie o politicheskikh nastroenniakh sredi naseleniia po povodu rechi Cherchillia i interv'iu tovarishcha Stalina, 24.3.46 g.," GARF, f. R-7077, op. 1, d. 198, l. 106.

73. GARF, f. R-7212, op. 1, d. 205, l. 39.

74. "Donesenie o politicheskikh nastroenniakh sredi naseleniia po povodu rechi Cherchillia i interv'iu tovarishcha Stalina, 24.3.46 g.," GARF, f. R-7077, op. 1, d. 198, l. 106.

75. "Dokladnaia zapiska nachal'nika Otdela propagandy USVA provintsii Saksoniia V. M. Demidova nachal'niku Upravleniia Propagandy SVAG S. I. Tiul'panovu i nachal'niku USVA provintsii Saksoniia V. I. Kuznetsovu o nastroeniiakh intelligentsii, 12 aprelia 1946 g.," in Timofeeva and Foittsik, *Politika SVAG v oblasti kul'tury,* 516.

76. "O politicheskikh nastroeniiakh gor. Frankfurta na Odere, 20.5.46 g.," GARF, f. R-7077, op. 1, d. 198, l. 242.

77. See Satjukow, *Besatzer,* 64–67.

78. During the war, there were German political émigrés and German prisoners of war in the USSR. For the latter, on February 9, 1943, the KPSS adopted a resolution on opening antifascist schools which would prepare administrative cadres to carry out a program devoted to postwar Germany's national regeneration. Marxist-Leninist theory and the biographies of Lenin and Stalin would be the main components of the curriculum. See Erler, Laude, and Wilke, *"Nach Hitler Kommen wir,"* 53.

79. "'Was würde sein, wenn Deutschland ein Sowjetstaat würde?' Maschinenschriftliche Ausarbeitung Wilhelm Florins O. D. (1944)," in Erler, Laude, and Wilke, *"Nach Hitler kommen wir,"* 125–30.

80. "Über das Verhältnis von Kommunisten und Kriegsgefangenen im NKFD— Handschriftliche Disposition Wilhelm Piecks für eine Rede auf einer Zusammenkunft mit Vertretern der PURKKA und Mitgliedern des NKFD O. D. (November/Dezember 1944)," in Erler, Laude, and Wilke, *"Nach Hitler kommen wir,"* 304–10, here 309.

81. "'Deutschland und die Sowjetunion'—Handschriftliche Vortragsdisposition Anton Ackermanns für eine Lektion in der Parteischule der KPD, am 15. Oktober 1944 vorgetragen," in Erler, Laude, and Wilke, *"Nach Hitler kommen wir,"* 237–40, here 240.

82. The term "generation of the patriarchs" designates people born between 1893 and 1916 who had a major influence on the political development of the GDR. Walter Ulbricht (1893–1973), Hermann Matern (1893–1971), Friedrich Ebert (1894–1979), and Otto Grotewohl (1894–1964), Alfred Kurella (1895–1975), Alexander Abusch (1902–1982), Herbert Warnke (1902–1975), Erich Mielke (1907–2000), Kurt Hager (1912–1998), and Erich Honecker (1912–1994) belonged to this group of high-level party functionaries. See Ahbe and Gries, "Gesellschaftsgeschichte als Generationengeschichte," 492–502.

83. See, for example, Vatlin, "Nemetskie politemigranty"; Vatlin, "Sovetskii Soiuz v vospriiatii"; Hoppe, "Stalin und die KPD."

84. On repressions in the Communist International, see Lazitch, "Stalin's Massacre"; Chase, *Enemies Within the Gates?*; McDermott, "Stalinist Terror in the Comintern."

85. See Haumann and Studer, *Stalinistische Subjekte*; Wilke, *Die Anatomie der Parteizentrale*; Kaiser, "Sowjetischer Einfluss."

86. For example, Leonhard, *Die Revolution entlässt ihre Kinder*, 255.

87. See Filitov, "Soviet Administrators."

88. Leonhard, *Die Revolution entlässt ihre Kinder*, 256.

89. Leonhard, *Die Revolution entlässt ihre Kinder*, 576, 605–10.

90. "O provodimykh sobraniiakh i mitingakh KPG v Germanii po Berlinskomu okrugu v sviazi s prazdnovaniem 28-i godovshchiny Velikoi Oktiabr'skoi Sotsialisticheskoi revoliutsii, 12 noiabria 1945 g.," GARF, f. R-7077, op. 1, d. 171, l. 6–7.

91. On the internal processes of Sovietization and Stalinization in the SED, see Hurwitz, *Die Stalinisierung der SED*; Schröder, *SED-Staat*; Malycha, *Die SED: Geschichte ihrer Stalinisierung.*

92. "Iz dokladnoi zapiski S. Tiul'panova v TsK VKP(b) M. Suslovu ob itogakh II-go s"ezda SEPG, 28 sentiabria 1947 g.," in Bonvech, Bordiugov, and Neimark, *SVAG: Upravlenie propagandy*, 89.

93. "Iz dokladnoi zapiski S. Tiul'panova v TsK VKP(b) M. Suslovu ob itogakh II-go s"ezda SEPG, 28 sentiabria 1947 g.," in Bonvech, Bordiugov, and Neimark, *SVAG: Upravlenie propagandy*, 90.

94. "Iz dokladnoi zapiski S. Tiul'panova v TsK VKP(b) M. Suslovu ob itogakh II-go s"ezda SEPG, 28 sentiabria 1947 g.," in Bonvech, Bordiugov, and Neimark, *SVAG: Upravlenie propagandy*, 95.

95. RGASPI, f. 17, op. 137, d. 298, l. 72–103.

96. "Iz dokladnoi zapiski Upravleniia informatsii SVAG v TsK VKP(b) L. Baranovu o XII Plenume tsentral'nogo pravleniia SEPG, 2 avgusta 1948 g.," in Bonvech, Bordiugov, and Neimark, *SVAG: Upravlenie propagandy*, 113.

97. Barck, Langermann, and Lokatis, "*Jedes Buch ein Abenteuer*," 31.

98. RGASPI, f. 17, op. 137, d. 298, l. 2, 54–55.

99. RGASPI, f. 82, op. 2, d. 1175, l. 2, 21.

100. Tjulpanow, *Deutschland nach dem Kriege*, 137.

101. "Schriftliche Fassung eines Vortrages von Tulpanow," in R. Badstübner and Loth, *Wilhelm Pieck*, 217.

102. According to Werner Müller's data, in mid-1948, 1.8 million people were SED members and at the beginning of 1950, after "party purges," the SED had approximately 1.55 million members. See W. Müller, "Sozialistische Einheitspartei Deutschlands (SED)," 488.

103. Ulbricht, "Die gegenwärtigen Aufgaben," 137.

104. "Iz informatsionnoi zapiski Upravleniia informatsii SVAG v TsK VKP(b) ob obsuzhdenii itogov vyborov v zapadnogermanskii parlament na chastnom

soveshchanii chlenov politbiuro SEPG, 20 avgusta 1949 g.," in Bonvech, Bordiugov, and Neimark, *SVAG: Upravlenie propagandy*, 130.

105. Eisler, *Freundschaft für immer*, 8–9.

106. The "Moscow consultations" took place on June 4–7, 1945; January 28–February 7, 1948; March 25–April 1, 1948; December 12–24, 1948; September 16–28, 1949; May 3–6, 1950; and March 23–April 10, 1952. See R. Badstübner and Loth, *Wilhelm Pieck*, 15; Scherstjanoi, "Zum Verhältnis zwischen SED- und KPdSU-Führung."

107. "Informatsionnaia zapiska o prebyvanii v Moskve delegatsii SEPG, 10 aprelia 1948 g.," RGASPI, f. 17, op. 128, d. 1166, l. 153–157.

108. See "Za sovetami v Kreml"; "Nuzhno idti k sotsializmu ne priamo"; "'Skostit' polovinu summy reparatsii."

109. "Dokladnaia zapiska o rabote s delegatsiei SEPG s 30 ianvaria po 7 fevralia 1947 g.," RGASPI, f. 17, op. 128, d. 1091, l. 65.

110. See, for example, "Reise nach Moskau vom 16.–28.9.1949 einschl. Vorschläge des Politbüros," in R. Badstübner and Loth, *Wilhelm Pieck*, 296–97.

111. For example, during their stay in the USSR in March 1948, Pieck, Grotewohl, and Fred Oelßner met with Mikhail A. Suslov. The SED leaders asked him for help in resolving the problem of organizing a Gesellschaft für Sport und Technik (Sport and Technology Association) in Berlin since SVAG was not supporting the SED's initiative. In addition, the Germans asked for permission to make it obligatory for all university students and faculty members in the Soviet Zone to take a course on scientific socialism. See "Kratkaia zapis' besedy sekretaria TsK VKP(b) tov. Suslova M. A. s rukovoditeliami i SEPG tov. Pikom, Grotevolem i El'snerom, sostoiavsheisia 29 marta 1948 g.," RGASPI, f. 17, op. 128, d. 1166, l. 148–151.

112. This communication focused on putting together the first five-year plan for the GDR. See "Brief Wilhelm Piecks an Stalin vom 28. Februar 1950," in R. Badstübner and Loth, *Wilhelm Pieck*, 334–35.

113. "Informatsionnaia zapiska o prebyvanii v Moskve delegatsii SEPG, 10 aprelia 1948 g.," RGASPI, f. 17, op. 128, d. 1166, l. 153–157.

114. "Informatsionnaia zapiska o prebyvanii v Moskve delegatsii SEPG, 10 aprelia 1948 g.," RGASPI, f. 17, op. 128, d. 1166, l. 155.

115. RGASPI, f. 82, op. 2, d. 1178, l. 153; d. 1179, l. 97.

116. Semjonow, *Von Stalin bis Gorbatschow*, 271–72.

117. Leonhard, *Die Revolution entlässt ihre Kinder*, 564–65.

118. GARF, f. R-7212, op. 1, d. 186, l. 198.

119. GARF, f. R-7077, op. 1, d. 231, l. 23.

120. "Politdonesenie o provedenii dnia pamiati V. I. Lenina v raione Bel'gits, 23 ianvaria 1948 g.," GARF, f. R-7077, op. 1, d. 231, l. 14, 17, 19.

121. "Donesenie o propagande marksizma-leninizma v sviazi so stoletiem Kommunisticheskogo manifesta v g. Brandenburg, 15 marta 1948 g.," GARF, f. R-7077, op. 1, d. 230, l. 81.

122. Fischer, "Im Zeichen des Personenkults."

123. Fischer, "Im Zeichen des Personenkults," 248.

124. AdsD, Personalia-Sammlung J. W. Stalin: Zeitungsausschnitte, unpag.

125. RGASPI, f. 17, op. 128, d. 1166, l. 234.
126. GARF, f. R-7212, op. 1, d. 235, l. 135.
127. RGASPI, f. 17, op. 128, d. 1091, l. 66–67.
128. "Dokladnaia zapiska o rabote s delegatsiei SEPG s 30 invaria po 7 fevralia 1947 g.," RGASPI, f. 17, op. 128, d. 1091, l. 65–68.
129. RGASPI, f. 17, op. 128, d. 1166, l. 157.
130. "Iz otcheta VOKS o rabote s delegatsiei obshchestvennykh deiatelei Germanii, 25 noiabria 1948," in Timofeeva and Foittsik, *Politika SVAG v oblasti kul'tury*, 793–97, here 796–97.
131. "Informatsionnaia zapiska o prebyvanii v Moskve delegatsii SEPG, 10.04.1948," RGASPI, f. 17, op. 128, d. 1166, l. 153–157, here l. 153.
132. RGASPI, f. 82, op.2, d. 1185, l. 1–2.
133. RGASPI, f. 17, op. 128, d. 960, l. 224.
134. Ronge, *Das Bild des Herrschers*, 335.
135. GARF, f. R-7317, op. 10, d. 29, l. 259.
136. Baberowski, "Was sind Repräsentationen," 8–18, especially 10.
137. *Die Vertreibung der deutschen Bevölkerung*, Bd. 2, 228.
138. Between May 1945 and May 1949, some 41,907 German citizens (35 percent of all Germans in the camps) died in the special NKVD-MVD camps in Germany. See Petrov, *Stalin i organy NKVD-MGB*, 58.
139. GARF, f. R-7317, op. 10, d. 29, l. 259.
140. *Die Vertreibung der deutschen Bevölkerung*, Bd. 1, Teil 1, 396.
141. Keller, *Volksgemeinschaft am Ende*, 187, 408. The death penalty awaited anyone who refused to maintain the ritual order of the "national community": whoever did not want to raise his/her hand in the traditional Nazi salute, saying "Heil Hitler!," was called a traitor and threatened with immediate execution. See *Volksgemeinschaft am Ende*, 411.
142. Keller, *Volksgemeinschaft am Ende*, 143.
143. *Die Vertreibung der deutschen Bevölkerung*, Bd. 1, Teil 1, 285.
144. Leonhard, *Die Revolution entlässt ihre Kinder*, 429–30.
145. Dörnberg, *Befreiung 1945*, 100.
146. *Die Vertreibung der deutschen Bevölkerung*, Bd. 1, Teil 1, 464.
147. On red and white flags on refugees' carts, see *Die Vertreibung der deutschen Bevölkerung*, Bd. 1, Teil 1, 448–49; for their white armbands, see *Die Vertreibung der deutschen Bevölkerung*, Bd. 1 Teil 1, 264–65.
148. *Die Vertreibung der deutschen Bevölkerung*, Bd. 1, Teil 1, 270, 444, 473.
149. *Die Vertreibung der deutschen Bevölkerung*, Bd. 1, Teil 1, 278.
150. Thamer, "Von der Monumentalisierung"; Reichel, "Berlin nach 1945."
151. Sänger, *Heldenkult und Heimatliebe*, 78.
152. GARF, f. R-7077, op. 1, d. 27, l. 57.
153. GARF, f. R-7077, op. 1, d. 192, l. 84.
154. GARF, f. R-7212, op. 1, d. 141, l. 35.
155. Sänger, *Heldenkult und Heimatliebe*, 91.
156. GARF, f. R-7212, op. 1, d. 255, l. 320.
157. Azaryahu, "Zurück zur Vergangenheit?," 142.

158. See Sänger, *Heldenkult und Heimatliebe*, 76–79; Azaryahu, *Von Wilhelmplatz zum Thälmannplatz*, 59–76.

159. Report on May First celebrations in Brandenburg province, May 1947, GARF f. R-7077 (Soviet Military Administration of the state of Brandenburg in Germany), op. 1, d. 213, l. 104.

160. For example, AdsD, SPD-PV-Ostbüro 0362 I, unpag. (Weimar, October 1949); Sächsisches Hauptstaatsarchiv in Dresden (SächsHstAD), 11376 Landesregierung Sachsen (LRS), Ministerium für Volksbildung (MfV), 2374, unpag. (Gutachten über die Herrscherdenkmäler der Stadt Dresden, July 4, 1949). See also Scheer, "Geschützte Leere," in Leo and Reif, *Vielstimmiges Schweigen*.

161. Nina Tumarkin, *Living and the Dead*; Zimmering, *Mythen in der Politik der DDR*.

162. Memorandum on the activity of the German-Soviet Friendship Society in Saxony, July 28, 1950, RGASPI, f. 17, op. 137, d. 307, l. 48.

163. "Bulletin no. 4/88 of international and internal German information," November 23, 1946, RGASPI, f. 17 (Central Committee KPSS), op. 128, d. 159, l. 82–83.

164. On the Stalin cult in East Germany, see Plamper, "'The Hitlers Come and Go...'"; Behrends, *Die erfundene Freundschaft*; Tikhomirov, "Eksport kul'ta Stalina"; Tikhomirov, "Stalin Cult between Center and Periphery."

165. For example, see Leo, "'Deutschlands unsterblicher Sohn...,'" in Gries and Satukow, *Sozialistische Helden*; Börrnert, *Wie Ernst Thälmann treu und kühn!*; Azaryahu, *Von Wilhelmplatz zu Thälmannplatz*, 151–55.

166. See Gries, "Die Heldenbühne der DDR," in Gries and Satjukow, *Sozialistische Helden*, 84–100.

167. "Donesenie o sostoianii nagliadnoi propagandy po Bauttsenskomu raionu, 24 sentiabria 1945 g.," GARF, f. R-7212, op. 1, d. 57, l. 166.

168. "Biulleten' mezhdunarodnoi i vnutrigermanskoi informatsii No. 61/65 ot 13 sentiabria 1946 g.," RGASPI, f. 17, op. 128, d. 157, l. 62.

169. For example, "Proekt postanovleniia TsK VKP(b) 'O rabote Upravleniia propagandy Sovetskoi voennoi administratsii v Germanii" [before December 25, 1946]," in Bonvech, Bordiugov, and Neimark, *SVAG: Upravlenie propagandy*, 198–204.

170. GARF, f. R-7212, op. 1, d. 53, l. 13.

171. "Ukazaniia nachal'nika Upravleniia propagandy SVAG S. I. Tiul'panova nachal'niku otdela propagandy USVA federal'noi zemli Saksoniia A. P. Vatniku i nachal'nikam otdelenii propagandy okrugov ob izmenenii form kontrolia pressy, 27 fevralia 1947 g.," GARF, f. R-7212, op. 1, d. 189, l. 50–54.

172. GARF, f. R-7077, op. 1, d. 213, l. 335.

173. See Klotz, *Das politische Plakat der SBZ/DDR*.

174. "Plakate des DFD vom den 8.03.1951, Dresden, 12.3.1951," SächsHStAD, 11346 LRS, MP, 4574, unpag.

175. Ryklin, *Prostranstva likovaniia*.

176. AdsD, SPD-PV-Ostbüro 0361 I, unpag.

177. "Protokoll über die Sitzung der Werbekommission der erweiterten Abteilung für Aufklärung, Werbung und Schulung des Landesausschusses Sachsen der

Nationalen Front des Demokratischen Deutschland am Mittwoch, den 6. Dezember 1950," SächsHStAD, 11376 LRS, Ministerpräsident (MP), 4576, unpag.

178. "Plakataufstellung 'Bild der Strasse,' Zwickau, den 18.1.1952," SächsHStad, 11376 LRS, MP, 4574, unpag.

179. For example, "Bericht über den Eingang und Aushang von Plakaten, Bautzen, den 3.1.1951," SächsHStAD, 11376 LRS, MP, 4591, unpag.

180. According to documents held in Moscow, for Stalin's seventieth birthday alone, five hundred thousand portraits of the "leader" were printed for distribution in East Germany in 1949. See RGASPI, f. 17, op. 137, d. 100, l. 140; GARF, f. R-7133, op. 1, d. 281, l. 367. In 1951, for the second anniversary of the founding of the GDR, one hundred and forty copies of a poster depicting "J. W. Stalin's Telegram" were issued, and twenty-five thousand copies of the poster "Joseph Vissarionovich Stalin on Germany and the German People" were printed as part of the commemorations of the Day of Liberation on May 8, 1951. See SächsHStAD, 11376 LRS, MP, 4572, 4588, unpag.

181. AdsD, SPD-PV-Ostbüro 0383 A/2 II, unpag.

182. "Bilder des Präsidenten der Republik, Dresden, den 1.12.1950," SächsHStAD, 11376 LRS, MP, 4586, unpag.

183. SächsHStAD, 11376 LRS, MP, 4589, unpag.

184. "Plakate des Amtes für Information Brandenburg, Potsdam, den 4.1.1951," SächsHStAD, 11376 LRS, MP, 4578, unpag.

185. Lokatis, "Berliner Buchschaufenster."

186. "Bericht über eine Aktion zur Erfassung und Ausgestaltung sämtlicher Wartezimmer innerhalb unseres Verwaltungsbereiches. Chemnitz, den 7.2.1951," SächsHStAD, 11376 LRS, MP, 4572, unpag.

187. "Leitsätze für die künstlerische Gestaltung des Parteilebens. Berlin, den 2. Januar 1948," SAPMO-BArch, DY 30/IV 2/9.03/60, Bl. 42.

188. Thüringisches Hauptstaatsarchiv Weimar, Land Thüringen–Ministerium für Wirtschaft und Arbeit Nr. 1006, Bl. 59–60 (Kataloge des Versandhauses für Organisationsbedarf GmbH 1949).

189. AdsD, SPD-PV-Ostbüro 0362 I, unpag.

190. "Biulleten' No. 87/91 mezhdunarodnoi i vnutrigermanskoi informatsii ot 9 dekabria 1946 g.," RGASPI, f. 17, op. 128, d. 159, l. 132–133.

191. "Iz informatsionnoi spravki o politicheskoi rabote sredi naseleniia Germaniia, 5 iiulia 1945 g.," in Bonvech, Bordiugov, and Neimark, *SVAG: Upravlenie propagandy*, 25–27, here 26.

192. RGASPI, f. 17, op. 128, d. 157, l. 72.

193. Staatsarchiv Dresden, F. 11376, D. 4589, unpag.

194. "Zapis' besedy nachal'nika Biuro informatsii SVAG tov. Bespalova s chlenom Tsentral'nogo sekretariata SEPG tov. Akermannom, 20 noiabria 1946 g.," RGASPI, f. 17, op. 128, d. 960, l. 223.

195. AdsD, SPD-PV-Ostbüro, 0413, unpag.

196. "Informatsionnaia zapiska o prebyvanii v Moskve delegatsii SEPG, 10 aprelia 1948 g.," RGASPI, f. 17, op. 128, d. 1166, l. 153–157.

197. Kasper, *100 Kasperiolen*, 8.

198. AdsD, SPD-PV-Ostbüro 0383 A/1 I, unpag.

199. Cf. Rossman, *Worker Resistance under Stalin*, 9.

200. GARF, f. R-7077, op. 1, d. 193, l. 136.

201. GARF, f. R-7077, op. 1, d. 192, l. 269; GARF, f. R-7077, op. 1, d. 247, l. 77.

202. "Biulleten' mezhdunarodnoi i vnutrigermanskoi informatsii No. 92/96 Biuro informatsii SVAG ot 27 dekabria 1946 g.," RGASPI, f. 17, op. 128, d. 158, l. 234.

203. Ibid. Soviet reports mentioned the Germans' astonishment that the Russians had movies at all. See GARF, f. R-7212, op. 1, d. 55, l. 14.

204. GARF, f. R-7212, op. 1, d. 194, l. 154.

205. "Dokladnaia zapiska o nastroenii nemetskogo naseleniia po provintsii Meklenburg i Zapadnoi Pomeranii ot 22 noiabria 1945 g.," GARF, f. R-7103, op. 1, d. 10, l. 95.

206. "Dokladnaia zapiska o nastroenii nemetskogo naseleniia po provintsii Meklenburg i Zapadnoi Pomeranii ot 22 noiabria 1945 g.," GARF, f. R-7103, op. 1, d. 10, l. 95.

207. "Dokladnaia zapiska o nastroenii nemetskogo naseleniia po provintsii Meklenburg i Zapadnoi Pomeranii, 28.11.1945 g.," GARF, f. R-7103, op. 1, d. 10, l. 98.

208. GARF, f. R-7184, op. 1, d. 56, l. 31–32.

209. GARF, f. R-7212, op. 1, d. 57, l. 71.

210. GARF, f. R-7212, op. 1, d. 57, l. 230.

211. AdsD, SPD-PV-Ostbüro, Personalia-Sammlung J. W. Stalin 1, unpag.

212. "Dokladnaia zapiska o politicheskom nastroenii sredi nemetskogo naseleniia provintsii Meklenburg, 9.7.1946 g.," GARF, f. R-7103, op. 1, d. 22, l. 202.

213. For a more detailed discussion of the history of the relationship between Soviet soldiers and civilians in East Germany, see Satjukow, *"Die Russen Kommen!"*; Satjukow, "Der erste Sommer mit den 'Russen'"; C. Müller, "'O Sowjetmensch!'"; Naimark, *Die Russen in Deutschland*.

214. For example, see GARF, f. R-7313, op. 10, d. 31, l. 58–63; f. R-7133, op. 1, d. 277, l. 189; f. R-7077, op. 1, d. 181, l. 43a–43, 79; d. 27, l. 73–74; d. 277, l. 189.

215. "O politicheskikh nastroeniiakh naseleniia gor. Frankfurta na Odere, 19.05.1946 g.," GARF, f. R-7077, op. 1, d. 198, l. 239.

216. GARF, f. R-7077, op. 1, d. 198, l. 24.

217. GARF, f. R-7133, op. 1, d. 277, l. 71.

218. "Dokladnaia zapiska o politicheskikh nastroeniiakh po provintsii Brandenburg, 30 avgusta 1945 g.," GARF, f. R-7077, op. 1, d. 27, l. 25.

219. GARF, f. R-7133, op. 1, d. 274, l. 234.

220. "Iz informatsionnoi spravki o politicheskoi rabote sredi naseleniia Germanii, 5 iiulia 1945 g.," in Bonvech, Bordiugov, and Neimark, *SVAG: Upravlenie propagandy*, 25.

221. GARF, f. R-7212, op. 1, d. 63, l. 2; von Plato and Leh, *"Ein unglaublicher Frühling,"* 231; GARF, f. R-7212, op. 1, d. 63, l. 2.

222. As recent research shows, the perpetrators were not exclusively Red Army soldiers; men serving in other armies and members of the population also raped their

female fellow citizens and the victims were not exclusively German women. See *Petö*, "Memory and the Narrative of Rape"; Majstorović, "Red Army."
223. Burds, "Sexual Violence," 53.
224. *Die Vertreibung der deutschen Bevölkerung*, Bd. 2, 86; DSHI (Dokumentensammlung des Herder-Instituts) 140 OME 001_22, Bl. 20.
225. DSHI 140 OME 001_14, Bl. 11.
226. Satjukow, "Der erste Sommer," 236–37.
227. GARF, f. R-7212, op. 1, d. 205, l. 39–40.
228. Piskorski, *Die Verjagten*, 282–83.
229. Satjukow, "Der erste Sommer," 241.
230. Schneider, *Hausväteridylle*; Goltermann, *Die Gesellschaft der Überlebenden*; Herzog, "Desperately Seeking Normality."
231. GARF, f. R-7212, op.1, d. 57, l. 70.
232. "Dokladnaia zapiska o politicheskikh nastroeniiakh sredi razlichnykh sloev nemetskogo naseleniia i antifashistskikh partii provintsii Brandenburg i gor. Potsdam, sviazannykh s resheniem Berlinskoi konferentsii trekh velikikh derzhav, 30 avgusta 1945 g.," GARF, f. R-7077, op. 1, d. 27, l. 43–44.
233. "Dokladnaia zapiska o nastroenii nemetskogo naseleniia po provintsii Meklenburg i Zapadnoi Pomeranii ot 22 noiabria 1945 g.," GARF, f. R-7103, op. 1, d. 10, l. 96.
234. For example, see GARF, f. R-7184, op. 1, d. 282, l. 86, 87, 91; GARF, f. R-7077, op. 1, d. 27, l. 135; GARF, f. R-7103, op. 1, d. 20, l. 220–221.
235. "Obzor vrazheskikh anonimnykh listovok, obnaruzhennykh v Tiuringii v iiune 1947 g.," GARF, f. R-7184, op. 1, d. 163, l. 154–155.
236. GARF, f. R-7184, op. 1, d. 163, l. 86, 87, 91.
237. Gries, *Die Rationen-Gesellschaft*.
238. "Politdonesenie o nastroeniiakh nemetskogo naseleniia v sviazi s prodovol'stvennym snabzheniem, 18.9.1945 g.," GARF, f. R-7103, op. 1, d. 46, l. 18.
239. Ibid.
240. "Dokladnaia zapiska o politicheskikh nastroeniiakh sredi razlichnykh sloev nemetskogo naseleniia i antifashistskikh partii provintsii Brandenburg i gor. Potsdam, sviazannykh s resheniiami Berlinskoi konferentsii trekh velikikh derzhav, 30.08.1945 g.," GARF, f. R-7077, op. 1, d. 27, l. 54.
241. GARF, f. R-7212, op. 1, d. 187, l. 145.
242. GARF, f. R-7212, op. 1, d. 187, l. 141.
243. GARF, f. R-7212, op. 1, d. 238, l. 260.
244. "Dokladnaia zapiska o politicheskikh nastroeniiakh sredi razlichnykh sloev nemetskogo sloev naseleniia i antifashistskikh partii provintsii Brandenburg i gor. Potsdam," GARF, f. R-7077, op. 1, d. 27, l. 49–50.
245. GARF, f. R-7071, op. 1, d. 212, l. 226; f. R-7077, op. 1, d. 192, l. 236.
246. RGASPI, f. 17, op. 128, d. 359, l. 191.
247. GARF, f. R-7077, op. 1, d. 27, l. 53; GARF, f. R-7212, op. 1, d. 188, l. 6, 20; GARF, f. R-7077, op. 1, d. 271, l. 53. See Boldyrev, "Sovetskaia okkupatsionnaia politika"; Karlsch and Laufer, *Sowjetische Demontagen in Deutschland*.
248. GARF, f. R-7212, op. 1, d. 188, l. 6.

249. For example, in the province of Saxony alone, by mid-1948 approximately one thousand enterprises had been dismantled and 250,000 vehicles had been taken to the USSR. By March 1947, 11,800 kilometers of railroad track had been taken to pieces in the eastern zone. German losses from the dismantling amounted to around $2.6 billion in East Germany, but were only $0.6 billion in the West. See Benz, "Infrastruktur und Gesellschaft," 19–20.

250. "Donesenie o politicheskikh nastroeniiakh naseleniia provintsii Brandenburg, 19.02.1946 g.," GARF, f. R-7077, op. 1, d. 198, l. 64.

251. "Dokladnaia zapiska nachal'nika otdela propagandy USVA provintsii Saksoniia V. M. Demidova nachal'niku Upravleniia propagandy SVAG S. I. Tiul'panovu i nachal'niku USVA provintsii Saksoniia V. I. Kuzentsovu o nastroeniiakh intelligentsii, 12 aprelia 1946 g.," in Timofeeva and Foittsik, *Politika SVAG v oblasti kul'tury*, 515.

252. Ibid.

253. AdsD, SPD-PV-Ostbüro 0361 I, unpag.

254. "Perevod pisem i stikhov revanshistskogo kharaktera, izvlechennykh iz nemetskikh pisem, zaregistrirovannykh tsenzuroi, 8 aprelia 1947 g.," RGASPI, f. 17, op. 128, d. 357, l. 41

255. "Politdonesenie po provintsii Brandenburg, 30 avgusta 1945 g.," GARF, f. R-7077, op. 1, d. 27, l. 53.

256. GARF, f. R-7077, op. 1, d. 199, l. 38.

257. Klemperer, *Lesser Evil*, 34. For the original German, see *So sitze ich*, vol. 1, 64–65.

258. "Dokladnaia zapiska o politicheskikh nastroeniiakh sredi nemetskogo naseleniia po provintsii Brandenburg i gorodu Potsdam, 30 avgusta 1945," GARF, f. R-7077, op. 1, d. 27, l. 42–50.

259. The German population's responses to the "New Poland" exhibition (Otzyvi nemetskogo naseleniia na vystavku "Novaia Pol'sha"), 22.09.1947, GARF, f. R-7212, op.1, d. 202, l. 9–12.

260. "Nazistische Argumente in Rundfunk-Hörerbriefen, 14. Februar 1947," RGASPI, f. 17, op. 128, d. 359, l. 188.

261. Ibid., l. 189.

262. RGASPI, f. 17, op. 128, d. 158, l. 80.

263. "Dokladnaia zapiska o nastroenii nemetskogo naseleniia po provintsii Meklenburg i Zapadnoi Pomeranii ot 22 noiabria 1945 g.," GARF, f. R-7103, op. 1, d. 10, l. 98.

264. Ibid., l. 99.

265. "Donesenie o sostoianii politmassovoi raboty sredi naseleniia v period s 1-go po 28-e fevralia 1946 g. po okrugu Brandenburg, 28.02.1946 g.," GARF, f. R-7077, op. 1, d. 192, l. 211.

266. GARF, f. R-7133, op. 1, d. 277, l. 57.

267. "Dokladnaia zapiska o nastroenii nemetskogo naseleniia po provintsii Meklenburg i Zapadnoi Pomeranii, 9 iiulia 1946 g.," GARF, f. R-7103, op. 1, d. 22, l. 195–199.

268. "Spetssoobshchenie 'Po pis'mam s voskhvaleniiami uslovii zhizni nemetsk-ogo naseleniia v angliiskoi okkupatsionnoi zone Germanii' ot 18.12.1945 g.," GARF, f. R-7103, op. 1, d. 10, l. 291–293.

269. "Politicheskoe polozhenie v Khemnitskom okruge za vtoroi kvartal 1947 g.," GARF, R-7212, d. 205, l. 39–40.

270. For example, "Spetssoobshchenie 'o zhalobakh na tiazhelye material'nye i bytovie usloviia nemtsev, prozhivaiushchikh na territorii, okkuparovannoi angli-chanami' ot 22.12.1945 g.," GARF, f. R-7103, op. 1, d. 10, l. 294–296.

Chapter 4

"The Best Friend of the German People"

The Making of the Cult Community in the GDR

EXPORTING THE STALIN CULT TO EAST GERMANY: LOGISTICS, METHODS, AND AGENTS OF IDEOLOGICAL TRANSFER

Political pressure on the SED increased as SVAG and Moscow continued to force Soviet propaganda on East Germany and demanded that the Stalin cult be moved into the Soviet Occupation Zone. On September 28, 1948, A. G. Russkikh, SVAG's deputy chief political officer, told his staff to step up propaganda of the USSR, the countries of the "people's democracies," and their leaders.[1] Preparations to celebrate Stalin's seventieth birthday are mentioned in SVAG records for the first time in February 1949. Comments that Soviet propaganda materials should be sent to East Germany appeared in the Soviet military administration's documents at around the same time. In the list of Soviet exhibitions planned for the branches of the Society for the Study of the Culture of the USSR (Obshchestvo po izucheniiu kul'tury SSSR), one on "The Life and Activities of Comrade Stalin (for Comrade Stalin's Seventieth Birthday)" had pride of place.[2] From March 1949 on, topics involving Lenin and Stalin regularly figured in the lists of texts sent to the Soviet Occupation Zone every month detailing the talks and lectures to be given at the Society.[3] As early as the summer of 1947, lectures on "The Life and Work of I. V. Stalin" and "The Life and Work of V. I. Lenin" were given in Berlin at the House of Culture of the Soviet Union. It held the first exhibition about Lenin, featuring reproductions devoted to both leaders on loan from the Tret'iakov Gallery.[4] Several separate initiatives taken to popularize the images of Lenin and Stalin in East Germany helped transfer the myth of the two leaders of the revolution without emphasizing the fact that in the USSR the Lenin cult had already been eclipsed by Stalin's cult.

However, preparations for celebrating the Soviet leader's seventieth birthday in December 1949 were the definitive stimulus for exporting normative knowledge about Stalin from the Center to the Periphery. Jürgen Kuczinski (1904–1997), the chair of the Society for Study of the Culture of the Soviet Union, took the first step in importing cultural production about the Soviet leader to East Germany. In June 1949, he wrote to VOKS to learn how to organize the upcoming celebrations and to understand what form the festivities should take. He asked if "you could let us know in general how we should think about the celebrations. Do you think that a wide-ranging committee should be organized in Germany to celebrate Stalin's jubilee or should the SED undertake this?"[5] Here, Kuczynski, who had been a member of the German Communist Party since 1930 and had worked in the Soviet espionage system, was rigidly following the Bolshevik scenario for organizing propaganda campaigns: the first "initiatives" should come from below and only afterward could the central power take them up.

With his excellent command of Bolshevik political methods, Kuczynski knew well that establishing personal relationships with the chiefs of Soviet institutions while lobbying the Center on behalf of German interests was the most effective way to accelerate ideological transfer from Moscow to the GDR. For example, he took advantage of a visit to the USSR made by a delegation of German public figures in April–May 1948 to set up personal contacts with A. I. Denisov, the chair of the VOKS board, and V. S. Kruzhkov, the director of the Marx-Engels-Lenin Institute. After his meetings with high-level Soviet officials, twenty-four volumes of classic Marxist-Leninist works in German were sent directly to Kuczynski. Among other materials sent to Germany were the music and lyrics to the "Song of Stalin" ("Pesnia o Staline") and the Soviet national anthem, 120 Soviet posters, 320 copies of collections of photographs of various subjects related to the Soviet Union, and 700 copies of transcripts of public lectures about Soviet achievements in politics, economics, science, and culture.[6] However, the policy of centralizing the export of Soviet ideology to the Periphery soon replaced personal initiatives. A Central Committee resolution taken on May 10, 1948, made it incumbent on VOKS to keep the Society for the Study of the Culture of the Soviet Union supplied with Soviet cultural production.

From 1948, centralizing the export of ideology was well under way. This is reflected in the role of the Soviet Central Committee's Department of Foreign Policy (OVP). Led by Mikhail Suslov (1902–1982), the Department of Foreign Policy increasingly took the lead in resolving problems involving the export of Stalin's image.[7] There were many questions about issuing materials printed in East Germany because Moscow (i.e., the Central Committee) had to approve every one of these requests. For example, in July 1948, A. G. Russkikh decided to consult with Moscow about a book on Stalin and Lenin after an editorial error in the volume was discovered.[8] This was a collection of Gorky's selected works, which SVAG's publishing house brought out in 1947. In one of the articles, as the report put it, "the image of Lenin has been distorted and praise of the Jew-Trotsky has been permitted." This violation of the official version of history, like other such transgressions, led to numerous inspections of the publishing house and purges of its staff. Inquiries from East Germany and other "people's democracies" indicate that control over the export of knowledge about Stalin was increasingly being concentrated in Moscow. Beginning in October 1949, the Sovinformbiuro began to receive requests from Germany, Poland, Hungary, and Rumania to "send them articles devoted to the seventieth birthday of Joseph Vissarionovich Stalin."[9] Thus, the Central Committee had primacy in controlling the ways in which the official images of Soviet "vozhd'" were distributed across the Eastern bloc. Therefore, the Central Committee now had to consider how sacred knowledge should be transferred *correctly* and what constituted appropriate supervision of the discursive boundaries of the empire of Stalinism.

Exporting the Stalin cult beyond the borders of the Soviet Union meant that state boundaries for printed materials about the "leader" had to be opened up. These were frontiers which the Center alone had the right to establish and control, and consequently to open or close. With closed state borders and limited access to international travel, the problem of exporting propaganda material could not be solved through diplomatic channels alone. From June 1948 to October 1948, all printed entities exported from the USSR were subject to mandatory censorship, which was carried out by Glavlit (Glavnoe upravlenie po delam literatury i izdatel'stv) in Moscow. This rule called for editions of the classics of Marxism-Leninist to be seized at the border if they did not have the appropriate stamp.[10] The "borderline question" was settled when dialogue between VOKS and the Society for the Study of the Culture of the USSR began to intensify: it was decided that the works of Marx, Engels, Lenin, and Stalin, biographies of Stalin, and works written by the members and candidates of the Politburo should be sent to East Germany without hindrance.[11] The decision to open Soviet state borders to export ideological products is yet another indication that the empire's discursive boundaries were expanding. To speed things up, Ulbricht requested over and over that all new publications of the Higher Party School of the Central Committee of the VKP(b) be sent to East Germany on a regular basis so these materials could be used to organize a system of ideological education in the GDR.[12] All other

Russian books, newspapers, and magazines, both those in Russian and those in German translation, were disseminated through the offices of the Soviet state organization for distributing books, Mezhdunarodnaia Kniga (MK; in English, International Book), in Berlin and Leipzig. By taking advantage of the East German postal delivery service, MK was able to send about four million Russian literature titles to the GDR between 1947 and 1950.[13]

Although the first German initiatives in ideological transfer came from *below*, from the mass organizations, after an SED resolution about systematic planning for Stalin's jubilee was taken on July 5, 1949, the Politburo was given responsibility for coordinating the import of Soviet ideological artifacts to East Germany.[14] A few days earlier, the SED's small secretariat had established a commission on preparations for Stalin's seventieth birthday.[15] When the board of the Free German Youth (Freie Deutsche Jugend or FDJ) met on July 12, 1949, it put planning for Stalin's seventieth-birthday celebrations at the top of its agenda.[16] In August, by order of the SED Politburo, an official request for texts, pictures, and busts of Stalin was sent to Moscow. They planned to use these materials as templates in order to reproduce the cult objects in East Germany.[17] Because there was little or no normative knowledge about Stalin, whom the German population knew primarily in national-socialist terms as the enemy of the German people, Moscow sped up the export of Soviet cultural production to the GDR.

In the Soviet Union, VOKS was responsible for exporting Stalin's image to East Germany. It was directly responsible for supplying information to support its dialogue on culture with the German-Soviet Friendship Society (DSF).[18] Materials from the USSR were sent to the House of Culture of the Soviet Union in Berlin, which became the central repository of knowledge about Stalin.[19] So, just before December 21, 1949—the Soviet leader's birthday—in response to urgent requests from the German-Soviet Friendship Society, VOKS hastened to send articles, collections of photographs, portraits, posters, sheet music, and recordings of songs about Stalin.[20] On the wish list it sent to VOKS, the DSF told its Soviet partner organization that the Houses of German-Soviet Friendship needed several copies of Stalin's complete publications as well as Soviet encyclopedias.[21] Exhibitions titled "On the Life and Work of Comrade Stalin," which told the official biography of the "vozhd'" and described the advantages of the Soviet model of development, were in great demand.[22] The Central Committee, in conjunction with the MID, coordinated and approved all lists of materials to be sent out.[23] Moscow continued to control production about Stalin, even after the materials were delivered to Berlin by VOKS's special representative in East Germany.[24] The arrival of the visual and textual templates needed to expand the cult made it possible to replicate canonical versions of Stalin's image in East Germany.

Above all, East Germans had to familiarize themselves with the "leader's" official biography. To make sure that the propaganda narrative was being disseminated properly, in October and November 1949, the DSF set up party schools for political officers; these people would be the mediators in disseminating the Stalin myth to the mass organizations, enterprises, and educational facilities.[25] In order to represent Stalin's biography in public space, special wall newspapers came out. Showing normative epic films about Soviet leaders that introduced the population to the Bolshevik interpretation of the past, films like *Lenin in October, Lenin in 1918,* and *The Oath,* became another important part of the propaganda of the personality cult.

Official statistics on propaganda work in the FDJ show the scale of efforts to mobilize the population: more than twenty thousand meetings featuring talks on Stalin's life and work; at least 7,502 study groups on the biography of the "vozhd'," in which approximately three hundred and fifty thousand FDJ members participated; and 2,023,773 signatures on a letter congratulating Stalin on his jubilee. The German-Soviet Friendship Society reported that it put on more than 650 festive events, which were intended to recognize "Stalin as the best friend of the German people, and friendship with the Soviet Union as the guarantee of the GDR's peaceful development."[26] The SED's statistics were more modest: there were 5,424 study circles devoted to Stalin's biography in which 104,725 people—both party members and candidates for party membership—took part. In addition, 5,300 circles with 119, 544 participants immersed themselves in the history of the VKP(b). In addition, the party trained 57,883 propagandists to carry out its ideological work.[27]

Picking up the baton, the SED began to exert control over the transfer of official knowledge about Stalin. This involved institutionalizing the discourse about the Soviet leader in the East German political system. On March 29, 1949, a resolution of the SED Central Secretariat established the Marx-Engels-Lenin-Institute. One of the Institute's main tasks was to publish Stalin's works.

In 1953, a special Stalin Department was created at the Institute to organize the publication of a complete edition of Stalin's works as well as censorship of all printed production about the "leader."[28] The decisive step toward unification of the discourse about Stalin was the SED Central Committee's resolution of June 5, 1949, which ordered that all texts about the Soviet leader should "be issued in accordance with a single standard, in one format and design."[29] Despite an acute shortage of materials on the eve of the "leader's" seventieth birthday, all the regional publishing houses were forbidden to publish arbitrary materials without the express permission of the special commission at the Marx-Engels-Lenin Institute.[30] There were similar rules for publishing photographs, placing posters, and putting up busts in public places. Thus, the discourse about Stalin would now be subject to oversight from two bodies, the Central Committee in Moscow and the SED Central Committee.

The initiation of a major publishing project—a complete edition of Stalin's works in German—was the next sign that the Soviet leader's cult had been firmly established in East Germany. In September 1949, the SED leadership personally proposed to Stalin that his works be translated into German.[31] Producing German translations of the "leader's" works involved an ongoing process of change on both sides: Berlin gradually gained Moscow's trust and Moscow began to delegate some control over cult production to the East German propaganda organs. At first, the Moscow-based Foreign Languages Publishing House (Izdatel'stvo inostrannoi literatury) was responsible for the translation. In 1949, P. Petrov, the director of the publishing house, reported that the first and second volumes of Stalin's complete works had been translated and sent to Germany to be printed.[32] The first translated volume came out in December 1949, in honor of Stalin's seventieth birthday.[33] But in March 1950, Suslov informed the SED Central Committee (through V. G. Grigor'ian, the head of the Department of Propaganda and Agitation [Otdel propagandy i agitatsii]) that beginning with the fourth volume, the German translation of Stalin's complete works would be published in Berlin, under the auspices of the Marx-Engels-Lenin Institute.[34] However, Moscow only transferred responsibility to Berlin on the condition that the Foreign Languages Publishing House would retain control over the translation. In November 1950, Fred Oelßner, a member of the SED's Politburo, arrived in Moscow to personally deliver the translation of the fourth volume of Stalin's works for verification at the Foreign Literature Publishing House.[35] An obligatory declaration stating, "Published according to decision of the Central Committee of the KPSS and the Marx-Engels-Lenin Institute of the Central Committee of the KPSS," which was stamped on the first three volumes, and which continued to appear on the title page of every subsequent volume, made this clear. All of this meant that Moscow had the final say on images of the Soviet leader and knowledge about him.

Music also played a key role in disseminating the Stalin cult. As Soviet songs and Stalinist lyrics were translated into German, a musical canon for the Stalin cult was exported to East Germany.[36] In 1946, with SVAG's permission, Ernst Busch's music publishing company, which included the record label Song of the Times (Lied der Zeit), made a record featuring compositions devoted to the Soviet leader that came out for Stalin's seventieth birthday.[37] Until 1956, "Stalin, Freund, Genosse" ("Stalin, drug, tovarishch"), "Suliko," "Schwur an Stalin" ("Kliatva Stalinu"), "Lied vom Adler" ("Pesn' orla"), and other songs accompanied "solemn events" and party meetings celebrating the birthday of the "best friend of the German people." They were usually adapted for the needs of the German consumer with the Russian texts translated into German. Music was an important part of radio programing and, starting in December 1952, was also broadcast on television. It was used as an emotion-inducing propaganda instrument to dramatize the Stalin cult in the dictatorship's public spaces. Playing the national anthems of the GDR and the USSR was a mandatory element of the scenario for school events that the German-Soviet Friendship Society sent to educational institutions. Listening to reports about the "leader's" life and reciting poems in Stalin's honor were other required activities.[38] Schools were also encouraged to set up "red corners" featuring portraits of the "leader" and books about him. These were supposed to be places where pupils could reflect on Stalin as the "friend" who made it possible to establish the GDR and provided security during the Cold War.

Importing knowledge about the Soviet leader into East Germany was coordinated at the highest political level. At a November 22, 1949 meeting about preparations for Stalin's seventieth birthday, those present stressed the importance of "working out the key role of Comrade Stalin's personal contribution to the development of German-Soviet relations" in order to produce propaganda materials.[39] Like those in Stalin's inner circle, the members of the SED Politburo decided to publish their own collection of articles about the "leader," thereby underlining their right to formulate knowledge or to adapt what was being transferred from the Soviet Union to East German realities. A list of topics for articles to be written about the Soviet leader was distributed to the highest party functionaries at an SED Politburo meeting. These pieces were published in a book titled *To Our Friend and Teacher: For the Seventieth Birthday of J. W. Stalin* (*Unserem Freund und Lehrer: J. W. Stalin: Zum siebzigsten Geburtstag*). The ways Stalin was depicted in this volume were designed to validate propaganda's main formula, "Stalin, the best friend of the German people," and were intended to show that every German was morally obliged to venerate him.

With the establishment of the GDR on October 7, 1949, Stalin's paternalistic relationship with the new German state began to be publicly proclaimed. The GDR's first propaganda campaign popularized the Soviet leader's telegram of welcome, sent on October 13, 1949, in honor of the creation of the East German state:

> The formation of the German democratic peace-loving republic is a turning point in the history of Europe. There can be no doubt that the existence of a peace-loving democratic Germany, alongside the existence of the peace-loving Soviet Union, precludes the possibility of new wars in Europe and makes it

impossible for European countries to be enslaved by the imperialists of the world.[40]

Socialist propaganda emphasized what this meant for the restoration of the Germans' collective honor. Stalin's words guaranteed that the Soviet Union would protect the GDR's sovereignty and simultaneously indicated that being part of the Soviet-led mission to protect peace in Europe would absolve the East Germans of their guilt for Nazi crimes.

Stalin's telegram was treated as a canonical narrative for the SED regime; it also became a manifesto for German-Soviet friendship and the program for the GDR's national development. The SED presented the establishment of the GDR as evidence of the USSR's profound trust in the East Germans. This confidence consisted of the "leader"—Stalin—delegating power to the Stalinist course's loyal followers—the SED. Newspapers with Stalin's telegram were distributed free of charge on the streets, and leaflets and posters with the text of the telegram were put up in enterprises and educational institutions. Portraits of the Soviet leader that included text with excerpts from the telegram filled squares and buildings housing government offices and the mass organizations. New representations of Stalin as the patron of the East German state made it clear that the Stalin cult had ceased to be an internal SED matter. Now, for the first time, the cult was being presented as a national project that each and every German should join in order to build a socialist state and society. Thus, the Stalin cult became a way to enter the transnational cult community. It offered individuals, subgroups in the population, and the GDR as a whole a path into this larger, all-encompassing entity which was communist in content and national in appearance.

From the moment the GDR was created, its leaders began an unconcealed struggle to bring the "second German state" into the cult community, that is, the bloc of socialist states bound by the Stalin cult's shared myths, rituals, and symbols. The use of Soviet rhetoric or, to put it another way, speaking Soviet in public space, was one of the most basic signs that a state belonged to the postwar empire of Stalinism. Several practices were added to the formal criteria by which the population demonstrated that it had interiorized official knowledge about Stalin: quoting from the classics of Marxism-Leninism, having schoolchildren reproduce the myth of the leader in their compositions and drawings, setting up "red corners," preparing birthday gifts for Stalin, and prolonged applause and cheering when the names of Soviet leaders were mentioned at party meetings. One of SVAG's political reports of November 1949 noted with satisfaction East Germans' "correct use" of Lenin's and Stalin's pronouncements in speeches as well as in academic and political writing.[41] Celebrating the achievements of the education system in 1950, GDR Education Minister Paul Wandel identified a turning point in efforts to raise children "in the spirit of peace and friendship with the USSR": "The pupils write good compositions about Stalin, Pieck [and] German-Soviet friendship."[42] There were additional indications that young Germans were being reeducated and transformed from "enemies" into "friends" of the USSR. SVAG officials observed that members of the FDJ had set up the meeting places for celebrations "correctly," hanging portraits of Stalin, Lenin, Marx, and Engels, noting that they were "neat and orderly at demonstration[s]" and the columns of demonstrators carried red flags and banners.[43]

Censors painstakingly tracked down breaches of the rules governing the party-state discourse about Stalin, and the security organs punished violators. Thus, when an employee of the GDR Information Agency took the liberty of shortening one of Pieck's speeches by removing all the normative expressions of obeisance to Stalin and the Soviet Union at the end of the speech, this act was described as a "crude mistake." The culprit naively considered the fulsome praise unnecessary.[44] As soon as the speech was published, the blunder was discovered, and with the demand that "appropriate measures be taken," an investigation began. A German commentary on an American journalist's interview with Stalin was condemned for transgressing the discursive boundaries of permissible rhetoric: the writer used "measurelessly militaristic" language about the "USSR's transition to peaceful offensive[s]" and spoke of "Marshal" instead of "Generalissimo" Stalin.[45] In another case, a Leipzig district court sentenced Hugo Polkehn, the editor of the trade union newspaper *Tribune*, to five years in prison because he failed to notice a misprint in Stalin's obituary. The obituary, which appeared on March 7, 1953, included a sentence stating that "with him died a superlative fighter for the preservation and fortification of war throughout the world."[46] "War" instead of "peace" was clearly a typographical error; in the GDR this was interpreted as "anti-state, criminal act." These examples illustrate the single-minded drive to preserve the boundaries of the "dictatorship of discourse" and the state's stringent control over the purity of informational space in East Germany. While the party and the state considered correct public use of personality cult rhetoric a way to demonstrate socialist consciousness (and thus a down payment on raising one's social status), attempts to defile ritual language meant wrongdoers would be excluded from the cult community.[47] In other words, the Stalin cult began to determine the norms of public behavior and rhetoric, enjoining the Periphery to speak Soviet and to act in accordance with the rules shared across the Eastern bloc.

Long before the formation of the GDR, Stalin's name was well known in Germany. Information about Stalin came from many sources, not just Nazi propaganda. As noted earlier, German communists played a significant role in popularizing the Soviet leader in the West. One of the first German publications on Stalin, titled simply *J. W. Stalin*, appeared in 1930. This was a collection of essays by members of the Comintern's executive committee, among them leading figures such as Kalinin, Kaganovich, Voroshilov, and Ordzhonikidze, translated from the Russian with a foreword by Heinz Neumann.[48] In the foreword, Neumann, a member of the KPD and the Comintern and the editor of the KPD's newspaper, *Die Rote Fahne*, noted that "In this book for the first time the political persona of Comrade J. W. Stalin is presented to the broad working masses in German."[49] He described Stalin as the "vozhd'" of the Soviet people and the worldwide proletarian movement, using the term in the Marxist sense. Echoing Plekhanov's ideas, he presented the leader as "the concentrated expression of the collective will of the proletarian masses" and "the leader of the party and the revolution," the one who, "in thoughts, feelings and actions, in their suffering, life and struggle . . . supports the entire working class, the mass of many millions of workers."[50]

Timed to coincide with Stalin's fiftieth birthday, the publication of the Russian-language volume, *Stalin: Sbornik statei k piatidesiatiletiiu so dnia rozhdeniia*, and *J. W. Stalin* showed that the Stalin cult was gradually taking root in the USSR—and in the framework of the Communist International. Looking at the jubilee volume for Stalin's sixtieth birthday in 1939, we see that during the decade following the publication of Neumann's book, printed materials about the Soviet leader changed radically. The German-language jubilee volume for his sixtieth birthday was fundamentally different from the one marking his fiftieth birthday. The Foreign Languages Publishing House brought out *Stalin: Der große Fortsetzer des Werkes Lenins* in a print run of eight thousand copies. There was no foreword, no preface, and no commentary authored by Germans; all the articles were written by members of the Politburo.[51] These absences were conspicuous indications of centralization in the production and distribution of knowledge about Stalin, the position of whose cult had been decisively consolidated in the Soviet Union by 1939.[52]

Western journalists and other well-informed observers who had spent time in the Soviet Union also wrote books about political life in Soviet Russia. Addressed to a broad Western public, these books were written from a different perspective than the Soviet narratives disseminated by German communists. For example, Artur W. Just, the Moscow correspondent for German newspapers (*Kölnische Zeitung* and later *Frankfurter Zeitung*), published a book about Stalin as part of a Lübeck publisher's series of biographies of "great men," among them, Hindenburg, Mussolini, and Hitler.[53] Just, who had spent several years in the USSR, described how Stalin's personality cult began to take hold in the USSR around 1929 as a result of vigorous efforts to spread propaganda of the ideal image of the "leader," falsification of the facts of his biography, and the terroristic destruction of all intra-party opposition. He noted that for the broad masses of the population, Stalin was not a flesh and blood person but rather an idea and the embodiment of power: the "vozhd'" drew people to himself with the magnetic pull of charismatic leadership but his striking ability to promote social integration through violence was also fundamental to his power.

Just also gave the Western reader some details about the dictator's private life: his appearance and the state of his health, the kinds of things he enjoyed, and what he did when he was at work in the Kremlin, at his dacha at Odintsovo, and on vacation in the Caucasus. To help his readers understand the Soviet leader's lifestyle, he compared Stalin to the "general director of a mid-sized company," noting that "He often smokes a pipe. He drinks large quantities of wine and vodka. He does not go to the theater often although he loves music and understands acting."[54] Just pointed out that Soviet citizens saw Stalin as a guarantee that they would enjoy stability and security after a long period of revolutionary upheaval. However, he issued a warning to his Western readers. He depicted Stalin as the incarnation of absolute violence and a military threat to European civilization. In postwar East Germany, publications like this vanished from the shelves of bookstores and libraries.

Exhibitions were an important way to represent the Stalin cult to the East Germans (Figure 4.1).[55]

Figure 4.1   An exhibit about Stalin at a conference of SED state delegates held in the House of Workers in Halle/Saale. December 1949. *Source:* Bildarchiv im Bundesarchiv (Koblenz). Signature: Bild 183-2004-0603-500. Photographer: Günther Paalzow.

A series of exhibitions was prepared for Stalin's seventieth birthday in 1949. The first one, which was held in the House of the Press Union in Berlin, was devoted to the Soviet leader's biography.[56] An exhibition in Potsdam focused on popularizing Stalin's role in the Potsdam Agreement, highlighting both the ways "American imperialists" violated the agreement, and the GDR's special role in the "struggle for peace" under the leadership of the "best friend of the German people."[57] Propaganda made a direct connection between prospects for German unification and Stalin worship. Another exhibition about him was held at the House of the SED's National Association, in November 1949.[58] Here, booths displaying portraits and quotations from the "leader's" works and photomontages showing the great construction sites of communism, the giants of industry, and peasant-heroes gathering the harvest were supposed to show Germans how effective the Soviet model of a communist society was. Representations of the "leader's" publications were the heart of the exposition. These formed a collection of the sacred knowledge that enabled the Soviet people to enthusiastically build communism and look toward the future with confidence. Representatives of VOKS and the Soviet embassy regularly visited such exhibitions. They monitored how the "ideological and political content" was presented and what people wrote in the visitor's book.[59] For example, in 1952, reviewing an agricultural exhibition held in the GDR, the Soviet side was critical of the central pavilion. Representatives from the embassy noted that the portraits of Stalin had been placed at the end of the hall, in an area that was poorly lighted, and Soviet tractors and combines were dirty and disfigured by oil stains while German machines were well kept.[60] Needless to say, the pavilion was reorganized to highlight the USSR's leading role in transforming nature.

The annual Leipzig Trade Fair was a key venue for staging the official image of Stalin as the "best friend." Moscow and the GDR worked together on the fair, with a focus on promoting the Soviet Union's impressive achievements under Stalin's leadership, but the Soviet side had the final word on all arrangements. The Soviet pavilion at the 1950 Spring Fair was designed to impress visitors with the magnificence of its décor, an abundance of quotations from Stalin, and many visual depictions of him.[61] For example, an enormous panel depicting Red Square with the Lenin Mausoleum was placed above the entrance to the central exhibition hall. In front of the panel, on a pedestal, a five-meter-high sculpture of Stalin towered over the crowd.[62] The exhibits showcased the USSR's vigorous, progressive economic development and advances in technology, agriculture and industry, the arts and literature. These displays implicitly promised that Stalin, as the "best friend and patron of the German people," would guarantee that East Germany could achieve similar successes. The exhibits turned socialism into virtual reality. They invited visitors to enjoy aesthetically staged Soviet accomplishments and project positive emotions onto their own national future.

German responses were just what Soviet officials wanted to hear. "With a feeling of deep satisfaction," they reported to Moscow on comments about the USSR and Stalin recorded in the visitor's book such as, "If you need a compass in life, look at the great Stalin!" and "The Soviet [pavilion] is the best proof of the validity of the teachings of Marx-Engels-Lenin-Stalin that the socialist order alone gives people a prosperous life." Thoroughly impressed, one visitor wrote, "Stalin shows the world facts, not bluff." Someone else was inspired to write that

> Workers around the world cannot choose a better leader, a better example than the great Soviet Union. A great commitment for us Germans after watching the exhibition: to learn more, more intensively from the great Soviet people. The victory of the world peace movement, the victory of the teachings of Marx-Engels-Lenin-Stalin, is ensured. The goal of my life is an old dream—to stand just once at the tomb of great Lenin, just once to see our great teacher, Generalissimo Stalin.[63]

Propagandizing Stalin was also an important function of Soviet film festivals. These began in the Soviet Zone of Occupation in 1947 and continued after the GDR was founded. Sovexportfilm was responsible for delivering Soviet movies to German audiences. Films about Soviet leaders were an obligatory part of every festival program.[64] For example, films like *Lenin in October*, *Lenin in 1918*, and *The Vow* set out the official history of the USSR and presented Stalin as Lenin's true successor.[65] For Stalin's seventy-second birthday, *May Day Parade 1951* was shown in movie theaters throughout the GDR. This film gave viewers the rare opportunity to see documentary footage of the Soviet leader on Red Square, greeting columns of demonstrators from the rostrum of the Lenin Mausoleum. Movies were supposed to demonstrate the advantages of life under socialism and develop the socialist worldview of East German viewers.[66] However, reports often noted that moviegoers wanted to see how ordinary people lived; East Germans were hoping to look beyond the facades of monumental edifices to find out what daily life was like in the USSR's provincial cities. Unsurprisingly, the population tried to avoid watching Soviet propaganda films, and their reactions ranged from disappointment to occasional protests.[67]

In comparison with the USSR, a relatively unchanging image of Stalin was typical of representations of the Soviet "leader" in the GDR.[68] Ready-made cultural production about Stalin was exported to East Germany, copied according to Soviet standards, and adapted slightly or translated into German. There were several reasons why the development of Stalin's image, and negotiations around it, were more dynamic in the USSR than in East Germany. The German political establishment distanced themselves from active work on the Stalin cult since the Hitler cult was still a vivid living memory and helping to create a new cult threatened to discredit them yet again. In addition, rigid control over knowledge about the leader hindered improvisation and creativity in producing the personality cult's artifacts. Only an extremely limited group of East German political, intellectual, and creative elites made contributions to the creation of the Stalin cult in the GDR. Most of their work was directed toward replacing both Nazi-era representations of Stalin as the "enemy" and portrayals of the "triumphant victor," which were associated with the bitterness of defeat, with a softer, more positive image of the GDR's patron as the "teacher and best friend of the German people." Not least, there was just not enough time for East Germans to create cultural production about Stalin. In the presence of Soviet colleagues, a staff member at the GDR Academy of the Arts (Akademie der Künste der DDR) complained that she was under such intense time pressure that she could not do meticulous work on personality cult materials such as busts, monuments, and portraits of the "leader." She noted regretfully that in contrast to the more measured approach taken in the Soviet Union, the SED was putting in "rush orders" and expected "immediate results" when "work on creating the image of the leader should have time to mature and be carefully considered."[69]

The question of who initiated transfer of the Stalin cult to East Germany and gave the signal that set it in motion is still open. In neither the German nor the Russian archives did I uncover documents with ready-made answers for historians. Certainly, East Germany and the Soviet Union were both deeply interested in Sovietization. Both sides used the Stalin cult to remake the Periphery in the way Center imagined the postwar Soviet empire and to unify it ideologically with Moscow. To create a new political reality, East Germany needed Soviet representations of power, that is, a register of official narratives, images, and symbols that would legitimize and stabilize the SED regime. For the USSR, exporting the Stalin cult meant expanding the boundaries of the Soviet empire and the zone of Moscow's influence in Central Europe. The mechanisms of export involved the formation of complex communication networks linking various levels of institutional authority in the SED, SVAG, and the VKP(b) as well as personal contacts and bureaucratic procedures, communicative channels, and administrative pressure, and the introduction of censorship practices and terror. Random initiatives and organized propaganda campaigns alike aimed to achieve a unique goal: replacing the "old" ways of representing Stalin as an "enemy" and staging the Soviet leader as the "teacher, patron and best friend of the German people."

RESPECT, GRATITUDE, AND LOVE FOR STALIN: EMOTIONS AND FEELINGS IN THE EMPIRE OF STALINISM

The "emotional regime" of the empire of Stalinism took shape in the course of preparations to celebrate Stalin's seventieth birthday. William Reddy, who coined the term "emotional regime," defines it as "sets of normative emotions and the official rituals, practices, and emotives which express and inculcate them."[70] The SED regime constructed normative discourses about respect, gratitude, friendship, and love for the Soviet leader. These feelings were used to promote social integration by creating a new sense of "we" for the German nation and establishing the population's emotional ties with the Soviet leader. In the following section, I analyze the role of the Stalin cult in constructing an official register of emotions and the significance of these feelings in Sovietizing the East German state. Which feelings did the propaganda state assemble to represent Stalin as a "friend" and to justify the GDR's very obvious dependence on the Soviet Union?

A positive model of the Periphery's emotional connection with the Center was designed to facilitate East Germany's integration into the cult community. One key element of this model was the discourse of the German people's gratitude to the Soviet leader, which initiated the legitimization of Stalin's image. As socialist propaganda put it, the Germans owed him gratitude because he freed them from the national-socialist menace; made it possible for them to construct a "peace-loving, anti-fascist, democratic state"; and was working to preserve the political and economic unity of Germany. Speaking about the formation of the GDR at the SED Central Committee plenum, Otto Grotewohl proclaimed the statewide and national character of the discourse of gratitude:

> The Soviet Union is the leader of the camp of democracy and peace, it stands up for the interests of the German people everywhere. This noble and magnanimous struggle of the Soviet Union deserves the deep gratitude of all honorable Germans.[71]

Grotewohl argued that the German people should be grateful to Stalin for concluding the Treaty of Rapallo in 1922, which removed the humiliating sanctions of the Treaty of Versailles from Germany.[72]

The discourse of gratitude showed itself in public space throughout the GDR. For example, when the East Berlin city council passed a resolution in December 1949 calling for the Frankfurter Allee to be renamed the Stalinallee, this symbolic act was described as an "expression of deep gratitude and unbreakable friendship."[73] At the unveiling of a monument to the

Soviet leader on August 1, 1951, in East Berlin, Ulbricht characterized the monument as a "sign of gratitude to Stalin and a symbol of the struggle for peace."[74] Frieda Hartung, a pensioner who attended the unveiling, expressed joy and pride: "We are proud that from now on our liberator will be with us."[75] Stalinstadt, which was founded in May 1953, was hailed as a "city of gratitude."[76] The feeling of gratitude staged in public space could be called a spatial "moral memory" that imposed the duty of friendship with the Soviet Union on East Germans. More specifically, this obligation was presented as the only way to earn the victor's forgiveness for Nazi crimes and to establish a normal relationship between the two parties.[77] The SED planned to involve former NSDAP members in the postwar reconstruction. Their intention was to present this work not as a penalty but as a way to atone for actively supporting the Hitler state. To attract such people to the new regime, the SED did not rule out an "individual approach" which aimed to emotionally reeducate former Nazis.[78]

The language of emotions changed as the Stalin cult became more radical in 1949: in addition to being grateful to Stalin, the population was now expected to love the "best friend of the German people." The official discourse declared that, like gratitude, love was the population's moral obligation and proof of being a "true" German patriot. The party demanded that East Germans show sincerity in friendship with the Soviet Union and express personal intimacy with the Soviet leader. Leonid Gozman and Alexander Etkind have compared the totalitarian state to a "ministry of love" and, in fact, the discursive production of love was a crucial resource for mobilizing society and legitimizing the leader's absolute power.[79] The East German leadership first ordered the population to love Stalin in the December 1949 holiday issue of *Neues Deutschland*, which was published in honor of the leader's seventieth birthday:

> Everyone who comes out against the Soviet Union's peaceful initiatives, is a criminal and the enemy of peace-loving mankind. The contemporary world situation demands each patriot's disciplined devotion to the camp of peace under the leadership of the USSR. Everyone who does not want to be included in the ranks of criminals must in practice demonstrate his love for the Soviet Union, love for Joseph Vissarionovich Stalin.[80]

The public rhetoric of the highest party leaders shows with particular clarity how the propagandized register of feelings for Stalin was integrated into the discourse of the Cold War. Calls to love the "leader" went hand in hand with demands to hate the West because being grateful to Stalin implied actively fighting against the "enemies" of the socialist order. In one of his articles, Grotewohl noted that "If today the majority of German people knows on what side its true friends are found and where its enemies stand, then it follows that we should thank our great friend Joseph Vissarionovich Stalin for explaining this."[81] Propaganda worked hard to create negative representations of West Germany as a "colony of American imperialists" and a "clique of the revived fascist regime."[82] The myth of the leader and a declaration that West Germany had been colonized by world imperialists allowed the GDR leadership to appear as the only legal representatives of the German people and the German state. Under their guidance, they promised that there would be a new rebirth of the nation: East Germans were not Nazis, not warmongers, but the "morally better" representatives of the nation.

From the official point of view, national pride, patriotism, and support for the GDR as the East Germans' new homeland were key components of the love for Stalin enjoined on the population. As part of the celebrations of the thirty-fourth anniversary of the October Revolution, each adult resident of the GDR received a personal letter from Gerhard Eisler, the head of the Office for Information (Amt für Information), setting out five reasons to trust Stalin and to be proud of belonging to the socialist world. These reasons were inextricably intertwined with what ordinary people longed for: a speedy end to the schism of the German state and nation, the conclusion of a peace treaty, the departure of the occupying forces, maintaining and strengthening the peace, and a steady improvement in living standards and prosperity.[83] An orientation toward Moscow allowed the East Germans to bring the rhetoric of national pride—an unspoken taboo after the fall of the Third Reich—into public discourse once again. The discourse of pride argued that the young East German state needed to assert itself because, under the leadership of the all-powerful leader-victor, it belonged to the "camp of history's victors."

East Germans were not only required to articulate the feelings generated by propaganda, they were also supposed to give proof of these in concrete acts and gestures. The practice of accepting collective obligations was one frequently used method for emotional mobilization. For example, apropos of Stalin's interview with a correspondent for *Pravda* in 1951, workers at the Kirchberg-Berk textile factory signed a letter stating that

> We promise to fulfill the five-year economic plan ahead of schedule. This commitment is meant to express our gratitude to Generalissimo Joseph Vissarionovich Stalin for his untiring efforts to preserve peace throughout the world and for the magnanimous help and support which he gave to the German people in its struggle for national independence.[84]

Likewise, practices of gathering and presenting gifts to the Soviet leader had connotations of showing respect, gratitude, and love for Stalin (Figure 4.2).[85]

Figure 4.2   An FDJ member looks at an item in an exhibition of gifts for Stalin held in the House of German-Soviet Friendship. December 1950. *Source:* Bildarchiv im Bundesarchiv (Koblenz). Signature: Bild 183-09104-0001. Photographer: Kümpfel.

It was not a coincidence that in Moscow, after an excursion to see an exhibition of gifts to Stalin, the members of East German delegation made a cautious but quite critical comment to their tour guide. The Germans recommended that in the future the guide should not talk so much about the exhibits as valuable material objects but ought to concentrate on the symbolic significance of the items presented, which they described as repositories for the "great emotions of the giver's love for the Soviet leader."[86]

The popularization of the Stalin Note was a large-scale effort to mobilize emotions during propaganda of the Soviet leader as the "best friend of the German people." On March 10, 1952, the Soviet press published the proposal the Soviets made to the Western powers about the peaceful unification of Germany. Researchers are still discussing the motives and reasons behind this initiative of Soviet diplomacy. However, the focus here is the propaganda campaign in connection with the published document, which embraced all of East German society.[87] The text of the Stalin Note could be found in all kinds of public spaces, in "peace corners" and the reading rooms in libraries, in cafes and cloakrooms, on public transport and in bookstore windows.

The regional newspaper *Volkstimme* published a special supplement about the Stalin Note. The Free German Trade Union developed plans to distribute it among workers in the GDR and the FRG. It became the main topic of discussion at innumerable meetings across the country. Workers and the intelligentsia alike accepted the obligation to express love and gratitude by studying Stalin's works, and a commission on children's literature in Saxony promised to redouble efforts to bring children up with "feelings of love for the USSR."[88] Official reports unanimously documented the "universal agreement with and approval of the USSR's note by the population of the eastern zone."[89]

Grotewohl was clearly being crafty when he announced that the Stalin Note set out a programmatic guide for Germany's political development:

> Only Stalin's path [will] lead to peace, restoration of the unification of Germany and the conclusion of a peace treaty. If the German people choose a peaceful path to a happy future, then they are obliged to choose the path outlined by Stalin.[90]

The official discourse of German-Soviet friendship called for people to make a similar declaration. In reality though, as Alexei M. Filitov has noted, positive agreements between the USSR and the West about German unification would have meant the collapse of the SED regime. The note was based on the rational course of Soviet diplomacy, which was counting on bringing the East German leadership to heel and reinforcing the status quo of bloc discipline in Europe.[91] This propaganda campaign had two important results: the definitive confirmation of Stalin as the guarantor and preserver of peace in Germany and throughout the world and fortification of the official emotional language for describing East Germans' connection to the Soviet leader.

Propaganda activities were imbued with emotion to politically mobilize and ideologically indoctrinate postwar society. The feelings staged were responsible, as German sociologist Georg Simmel claimed, for forming social relationships and ensuring social solidarity.[92] In constructing feelings of gratitude, friendship, and love for Stalin, trust—the basic integrating emotion of twentieth-century dictatorships—was the common denominator. In sociology and psychology, trust is treated as a central connecting force that operates in all societies and cultures: it stabilizes social ties, reduces the feeling of complexity, and makes the surrounding world less complicated and more understandable. Trust ensures stability and cooperation, creates the feeling that daily life is predictable and reliable, and is a resource for reducing risks and strengthening confidence in the future.[93]

These characteristics of trust are evident in the propaganda of Stalin's image as the "best friend, protector and teacher of the German people." Addressed to postwar feelings of anxiety, representations of Stalin as the "guarantor of a peaceful future" promised that belonging to the socialist bloc would make the future more predictable and positive. However, in this symbolic system of trust, an essential feature is missing: the mutual, voluntary communication of equal partners. Under the conditions of a dictatorship, we are clearly dealing with a type of trust that is different from trust in democratic societies. Modern dictatorships were *regimes of forced trust* in which trust was organized and programmed, managed and directed, hierarchized and doled out.[94]

A regime of forced trust in Stalin was manufactured in the GDR. Defeat in World War II, the loss of a homeland during forced removals, the destruction of familial and kinship ties, the death of relatives at the front, the collapse of the national-socialist worldview, along with the limited effectiveness of the occupying forces, led to a sharp rise in generalized distrust.[95] A situation where complete distrust flourished gave rise to the need for sources of trust to serve as one of the most basic resources for organizing individual life and establishing a new social order. With the help of the rhetoric of trust and distrust, the state and party defined the "enemies" and "friends" of the socialist society. In this system of coordinates, Stalin was staged as the source of absolute trust, the one who had to be loved and venerated. The positive emotions that were so strongly linked with Stalin's image made it possible for the regime to make postwar society a tempting offer: by accepting the SED regime, the population could gain access to the source of absolute trust and thus enjoy everything that the propaganda of the Soviet leader promised. That is, the East Germans would see a speedy improvement in their drab daily lives as they put their energies into building socialism; the Nazi past would be consigned to oblivion and they could start over without any guilt or shame; and they would be delivered from fear and anxiety by going over to the "winning side of history" and helping to build the communist future. Thus, in postwar Germany an acute need for sources of trust—but also an escalating distrust—was an important precondition for establishing the Stalin cult and constructing emotional bonds linking the East Germans and the Soviet leader. Under these conditions, the register of emotions put together by the state and the party was transformed into the central means of legitimating the Stalin cult in the GDR and it became an important channel for transferring the official ideology into the body and soul of the East German subject.

THE RITUALS OF THE STALIN CULT: MODELS AND ALGORITHMS FOR SYMBOLIC COMMUNICATION

The rituals of the Stalin cult were crucial in legitimating the SED regime. With their help, the regime designed and constructed the political order, filled public space with the symbols of power, and transmitted knowledge about how the world was organized and how it should be seen and interpreted. Stalin cult rituals could be called the "translation of the myth of the leader into action": propaganda texts were staged—brought to life—in public space and people carried out collective acts intended to create intense emotional experiences of gratitude, respect, and love for the "leader."[96] By sharing the emotional experience and the physical participation in ritual actions, each attendee was able to identify personally with the regime's political mission. Because the regime and society met in the space of symbolic face-to-face communication, ritual can not only be seen as a way to manipulate the masses but, to a much greater extent, can be understood as a method for mobilizing the population to join the project of building socialism in East Germany.[97]

In the empire of Stalinism, personality cult rituals were a central technology for gathering diverse states, nations, and territories into a united political body. They promoted Sovietization, helped bring the Periphery closer to the Center, and enabled its symbolic inclusion in the cult community.[98] Drawing on Émile Durkheim's work, one could describe personality cult rituals as the regime's instrument for creating, reproducing, and renewing the collective ideas which helped people understand and interpret social reality.[99] The annual cycle of official rituals ensured the cult community's regeneration. These rituals built up the main type of symbolic communication between the Center and the Periphery: they reinforced the imperial hierarchy, confirmed representations of power, catalyzed cultural transfer from the Soviet Union, and legitimated totalitarian structures and institutions in the East German political system. The Soviet scenario of power played out in the rituals of the Stalin cult, which took place in public spheres organized and controlled by the state and the party. By following the prescribed roles and scenarios, the individual learned to speak Soviet, used the norms and rules of public behavior to normalize daily life, practiced recognizing "friends" and "enemies," trying on masks that expressed various social roles, languages, and models of behavior that were acceptable in this rigidly hierarchical "classless socialist society."[100]

In what follows I examine the three levels of the "ritual order" (as Henri Bergson called it) of the cult community in East Germany.[101] The first, the micro level, generated the personal identification with the regime which developed when individuals interiorized the ritual language of the dictatorship. This language offered people a path to self-realization, self-improvement, and participation in political projects. In doing so, it became part of the search for the meaning of one's existence as a private individual. The middle level involved the cultic rituals of everyday communication. Here I will look at how class, gender, social, and professional identities were established and adopted as a result of the Stalin cult in two mass organizations, the FDJ and the DSF. Finally, I will examine the third, or macro, level of the ritual order, the party and state personality cult rites in which society, region, and nation, the state, and the empire experienced themselves as a whole and collectively staged this unity in public events.

From "Darkness" to "Light": Subjectivity and Self-Improvement in the Micro-Rituals of the Stalin Cult

The rituals of the Stalin cult offered a space for individual transformation, political self-activation, and self-perfection, in short, a way to achieve the socialist personality. The ideal product of the state-sponsored politics of social engineering was envisioned as the "new man," the socialist subject in a Sovietized Germany, who was characterized by loyalty and an "active life attitude" toward the "dictatorship of the proletariat" led by the SED. The ambitious ideological project of modern dictatorships to remake humans into citizens of the dictatorship and to mobilize them for political goals was a distinguishing feature of both the national socialist and the Bolshevik regimes. Life in the Third Reich was given over to the task of reproducing the "new man." This person was a member of "national community" of Nazi Germany and a representative of the "highest race, the Aryans," a group that was utterly different from "subhumans" (*Untermenschen*) or Slavs, Jews, and Roma, who embodied the "Jewish-Bolshevik threat" to the existence of the German nation and Western civilization as a whole. In contrast to the hierarchical, racially based ideology of Hitler's Reich, in the Soviet Union the ideal personality to be propagated was imbued with a revolutionary spirit and an openness to the outside world. He and she were endowed with strength of will, enthusiasm, and a deeply held belief that every member of a socialist society should enjoy equal rights.[102]

After 1945, the Soviet occupying forces set about implementing the Bolshevik project of constructing the new socialist personality beyond the borders of the USSR, in postwar East Germany. To break with the Nazi past, SVAG renounced almost completely the propaganda of the perfected body, which had been the object of a widespread cult in the Third Reich.[103] Under early postwar conditions, the Soviet control authorities' efforts were focused primarily on reshaping the Germans' consciousness. They concentrated on offering them the opportunity to alleviate the burden of Nazi crimes by showing loyalty to the SED and expressing respect and love for the new Führer, Stalin. The racial worldview of the Nazi past was replaced by the new outlook of the self-proclaimed "anti-fascist state" and reinforced with the Marxist idea of a "classless society." German writer Bernhard Kellermann, a founder of the Kulturbund who also served as the chairman of the German-Soviet Friendship Society, defined the distinctive features of socialist subjectivity during an official visit to the USSR made by a delegation of East German writers and cultural figures:

> Your country [the USSR] is undoubtedly the first where new scales for evaluating humans have been created. For you, a man's value is determined not by his origin, wealth, or race, but exclusively by his political consciousness and what he has created. Your country is undoubtedly the first and only country in the world where people can live without fear: they are not threatened with unemployment, they are not afraid of disease or old age. Your country is home to people who are free from fear, full of true human dignity.[104]

German politicians' and intellectuals' dreams of creating a socialist personality in Germany were yet to be realized. The question of the recent—Nazi—past became a fundamental issue for people as they strove to create postwar "social selves." As building a socialist state and society got underway, everyone was preoccupied with questions about how they had lived through Nazism. In personal narratives and everyday practices, people invented stories in their biographies supporting claims of little or no contact with Nazism: they described behaviors ranging from distancing and passivity all the way up to opposition and outright resistance against the Hitler state. Terrified by the Nuremberg Tribunal and other trials of war criminals, no one wanted to be tagged as an "active Nazi." What kinds of strategies for adaptation, integration, and accommodation did former members of the NSDAP, the Hitler Youth, and the SS, bystanders, or completely "ordinary citizens" use to fill their own lives with new meanings? Which memories, traditions, and experiences did they turn to in order to cover up the "black mark" of life in Hitler's Germany and legitimate their fight for a *normal* life in a Sovietized East Germany? How did they adapt, use, and manipulate official discourses to construct a "self" and advance private goals?

To address these questions, Stephen Kotkin's concept of "speaking Bolshevik," especially his discussion of the Soviet subject's rational "identification games," which aimed to instrumentalize communist ideology and the official language, is helpful.[105] At the same time, Igal Halfin's work and Jochen Hellbeck's, with its emphasis on the importance of ideology in deciphering the "communist hermeneutics of the soul," is pivotal for delving into the daily-life practices of self-empowerment, self-improvement, and self-politicization employed by ordinary people, and for examining their ability to create spaces of agency and invent practices for participation in mass dictatorships.[106] Hellbeck's argument that the ideology could be successfully reproduced because of ways it could be personalized in the lives of millions of Soviet citizens is especially relevant in looking at how East Germans strove to adapt to postwar political realities.[107] Anyone, they argued, could become a communist if they were willing to work on their own consciousness and the politicization of the self in accordance with party ideals.

The (self-)remaking of German selves into Sovietized selves was a burning issue after the fall of the Third Reich. To demonstrate the emergence of socialist consciousness under greatly changed circumstances, people were forced to demonstrate a critical distance from their involvement in the Third Reich, and they had to invent alibis—arguments which were (self-)justifying and defended support, collaboration, and participation in the Nazi project. Millions of life stories had to be rewritten and integrated with the Soviet discourse of power. Consequently, ego-documents usually contain few if any references to German guilt for World War II and Nazi crimes against humanity. On the contrary, people presented themselves as *not* Nazis, not members of the SS or Wehrmacht, and in general as non-supporters of the Nazi system. Three claims were the core of a common, exculpatory narrative: "we knew nothing and saw nothing," "we did not actively support the regime," and "if we participated, it was because we were forced to, and we just followed orders from above." As a result, Germans conceptualized themselves as victims twice over, as people who suffered first under Hitler and then under Stalin.[108] Because *they* were "innocent victims," Hitler and his inner circle were blamed for the NSDAP dictatorship and the destructive war.

Sovietization was applied as an imperial project and as the opportunity for East European national states to undergo a vital renewal. On the personal level, Sovietization was an individual endeavor. The Stalin cult offered East Germans a unique opportunity to self-construct a forward-looking personal identity: an individual with a socialist consciousness and will who was free of responsibility for Nazi crimes and hence guilt-free. By portraying themselves as "victims" of the Nazi regime, ordinary people renounced the role of "executioner" and rebalanced the scales so that pride in belonging to the "red" present outweighed shame about the "brown" past. Soviet-style narratives penned or spoken by ordinary Germans were public signs of participation in the new political order. Such narratives reflected the need to compensate for the day-to-day struggles of a precarious postwar existence with positive, life-affirming visions. As a result, the official language made its way into individual use in public rhetoric and behavior.[109] Ritualistic use of the language of the Stalin cult opened up the possibility that Germans could rewrite their life histories and thus insert individual fates into the discourse of antifascism and resistance, liberation, and the Soviet victory. In other words, people could give public proof of their political conversion from an "enemy" to a "friend" of the Soviet Union by presenting their life stories in the new language. While the majority were not able to demonstrate an antifascist and communist background, some people showed that they had been "friends" of the Soviet Union all along. As postwar selves were being reimagined, corrected, and redefined, the Sovietized subject began to take shape. Its central feature was expressing loyalty to the SED, the USSR, and Stalin personally.

Let's look at an example. In November 1949, schools and tertiary education institutions in Saxony began their preparations to celebrate Stalin's seventieth birthday. As part of the mobilization campaign, each student was given the opportunity to write a personal letter to the Soviet leader, describing his or her own fate in the maelstrom of postwar transformations. I found some of these letters in Dresden, in the regional archive for Saxony.[110] One letter writer was a student at the Leipzig University faculty of social sciences. Describing life in the Third Reich in purely negative terms while reproducing the myth of the Soviet leader and describing postwar Sovietization in glowing language, his letter exemplifies the ideal self-formation of a socialist personality in postwar East Germany. The letter was preserved in the archives because of its "impeccable" antifascist rhetoric and the author's "correct" class background as a member of a family of workers and communists.[111] An unknown bureaucrat probably chose this letter out of hundreds of others and decided to send it to the archive because he wanted to show higher, (possibly) supervisory bodies how successfully the socialist consciousness of East German youth was being developed.

At the beginning of his letter, the author states his goals: he wants to show Stalin how his own personality is changing; how German youth and society in general are being transformed politically; how German perceptions of the Soviet Union are changing; and how the foundations of German-Soviet friendship are becoming stronger. This confessional letter, which the author sees as an "account of [my] personal contribution to building a new social order," is a singularly lucid example of how an individual biography could be woven by using the postwar discourse of power, but it also reveals a search for personal meanings of life during Sovietization. The author begins to reconstruct his personal history by identifying himself as a member of the German proletariat: "I was born in 1929 [and] grew up in a family of Communist workers." Recounting childhood memories and speaking of himself as a victim of the Third Reich, he describes his parents' active opposition to the national-socialist regime: his family took part in protest demonstrations, and the Gestapo arrested his father in 1935 and sent him to Buchenwald. He also mentions that his uncle was murdered by the Gestapo in the final months of the war. Although the majority of the "generation of builders of a new life" or *Aufbaugeneration* (identified by historians as men and women born in the late 1920s and early 1930s) was socialized within the educational and institutional framework of the "racial community" on the basis of anti-Jewish, anti-Bolshevik, and anti-Slavic sentiments, by experiencing the war's end as a traumatic defeat, the author claims that there were instances of active resistance and even communist attitudes in his extended family.

The year 1945 was shown as a crucial historical divide and a major turning point in many German lives. In personal narratives, it was presented as a break with the Nazi past by showing a general transformation from "being a Nazi" to "becoming a Communist" and more metaphorically, by describing a political conversion from "darkness" to the "light" on the way to the "true faith." While "darkness" was equated with the recent past and personal sins connected with involvement in the Nazi state, the socialist way of life—the "light"—offered a new perspective enabling self-realization, participation in the cult community built around Stalin, and belonging to the postwar Soviet empire. Consequently, 1945 marked a "new beginning" or a "zero hour" in individual lives by offering a way to consign membership in the "national community" to oblivion by taking an active part in building socialism and venerating the Soviet leader. In our example letter, the author treats May 1945 as a turning point in his biography: the moment of "long-awaited liberation from fascism through the blows of the Red Army."[112]

For the overwhelming majority of the *Aufbaugeneration*, defeat meant the traumatic collapse of the national-socialist worldview. It was just this "Hitler Youth" generation that the young GDR state targeted, offering them opportunities to receive an education, employment, and upward social mobility, even though so many of them had been actively involved in the political life of the Third Reich, were members of the Nazi mass organizations, served in the military, and followed their own Führer—Hitler. The creation of the GDR also allowed members of this generation to break with the "dark past" and turn over a new leaf. The new German state needed young, engaged, politically educated citizens who would support the regime and transmit its ideology to future generations. Grateful for being liberated from the need to show guilt feelings, this generation adapted itself and integrated into the new order: they spoke the party's language and participated in official rituals. They supported Sovietization and accepted the Stalin cult since they had an acute need for ready-made models of behavior and simple answers to complicated questions about the past. They were counting on the "victors" to put an end to hunger, scarcity, and violence.

Although the author's self-representations contrasted with those of most young people, his narrative was also typical of the "generation of builders of the new life." He demonstrates his transformation from a persecuted, passive victim of the Nazi regime into an active builder of socialism in his own country and creator of the new world, narrating the symbolic rebirth of a politically conscious subject. Using Marxist language, this Leipzig University student described the period between 1945 and 1949 as a time when the proletariat's class consciousness was increasing. He saw the new policy of German-Soviet friendship and the acknowledgment of Stalin as the "best friend of the German people" as signs of increasing class consciousness. Stalin's works gave detailed explanations of the "right" way to learn how to build the future:

> You Comrade Stalin were someone who gave us a clear answer to thousands of things that were obscure, through your simple works with deep scientific content. During the last year you became a dear friend to the working class, [a friend] who, thanks to your accomplishments, showed us the path to life, the path to socialism and gave us an ideological orientation for accomplishing our goals.

For the author, the different ways the Soviet leader's birthday was honored in 1948 and 1949 reveal the rise in Stalin's popularity. While more than five hundred people came to the birthday celebrations at the university in 1948, the following year there was a sharp contrast: "The whole city and the whole university got involved in celebrating Comrade Joseph Stalin's jubilee." In this brief period of time, the author did a great deal of emotional work to develop his personality, moving from his confusion about the sparse attendance at the 1948 celebrations to personal pride in his own work and what society had accomplished by December 1949. At this point, the author justifies his political immaturity in 1948: "At that time I already was conscious of the worth of [your] human potential and even wrote you a letter that I did not send because I was ashamed of my low level of political education." The decisive moment, the proof of his "mature communist consciousness," was when he joined the SED and began to study the classics of Marxism-Leninism. His transformation into a party member was a rite of passage that divided the individual's life into a dark "before" and a bright "after" and filled it with zeal for the political struggle to build socialism in the GDR.

The letter reproduces the narratives and metaphors of East German propaganda: because German resistance forces emerged from the underground and antifascists returned from prisons and emigration, efforts to restore postwar life were only beginning. The creation of the GDR with Stalin's personal support reinforces the author's hopes that the German state and nation will be unified. He describes Red Army soldiers in Germany as "exemplary representatives of the Soviet people" and "teachers and helpers in the development of democratic institutions," identifying their presence as part of successfully constructing a socialist society. The author told Stalin that millions of Germans venerate the leader and have adopted German-Soviet friendship as a "matter of the heart." Calling for vengeance, which was typical of the communist movement, the author asserted that party purges in the Soviet Union were legitimate and demanded that "enemies" in the SED be unmasked to strengthen party discipline. The letter ended with a ritualistic expression of gratitude to the leader:

> Allow me to congratulate you on your seventieth birthday and, in your person, [to congratulate] the entire Soviet people for liberation from fascism thanks to your brilliant leadership and because you showed our people the path that portends a happy existence for people. Thanks to your example millions of people's hearts will light up, people for whom you became a dear friend, especially amongst the youth. In your name, in the name of Stalin, lies an entire epoch, showing the way for mankind. You—who continue the work of Lenin and Marx—will lead us to communism.

Similar propaganda campaigns, which mobilized people to write to Stalin, gave the SED regime control over how the myth of the leader was articulated and showed how effective state propaganda was. Letters to Stalin usually assessed SED politics positively and expressed support for land reforms and changes in the financial system and educational institutions. The authors praised the effectiveness of the Stakhanovite movement in German industry and conveyed appreciation for the Red Army's stabilizing presence as guarantors of peace and security. Following the logic of Cold War confrontation, letter writers also spoke of their fear of nuclear war. They linked the United States with anxiety about a possible nuclear war, calling it a worldwide source of instability, uncertainty, and military threats. This example of a letter to Stalin shows how an individual, by taking pen in hand, transformed himself into a political subject, inscribed his private life into the discourse of power, and thereby helped stabilize the SED political order. Working on one's personality by writing to the "leader" as the highest moral authority to whom one could appeal had some additional results: through the act of writing a correspondent constructed his/her "social self" and made sense of life in the "second German state." By articulating propaganda narratives, individuals were able to overcome the limitations of their own resources, infuse their personal life with the all-national meanings of building a socialist future, and identify themselves with the macro processes of state transformation and global politics.

Competitions in which children produced drawings or compositions about the "best friend of the German people" were analogous to Stalin cult microrituals. Thus, on the eve of Stalin's birthday in 1949, the German-Soviet Friendship Society organized a contest for the best composition about the "leader." The Berlin schoolchildren who entered the contest could choose any topic and genre for expressing their creativity but there was one obligatory condition: the text had to include "words and deeds showing clearly that Stalin is your friend."[113] First-place winners could choose between a camera or an accordion, second prize was a wristwatch or a violin, and third was a microscope or binoculars. The other four hundred prizes were footballs, athletic clothing, books, and theater tickets. The five most active schools were promised books, including the classics of Marxism-Leninism.

The prizes were handed out on February 2, 1950, the Day of Remembrance of the Battle of Stalingrad, which was a new holiday in East Germany. In order to consolidate the GDR's understanding of itself as an antifascist state, the SED Central Committee's Politburo adopted a resolution to hold an annual celebration marking the Wehrmacht's surrender at Stalingrad. Former German soldiers who had returned from Soviet captivity played a key role in marking this day. Since they were usually members of the German-Soviet Friendship Society, they were assigned to speak at public events and share propagandistic, affirmative accounts of their experience of socialist construction in the USSR.[114] In the East German official remembrance culture, this commemoration was a milestone in the semantic shift away from treating Stalingrad as a symbol of national catastrophe and the beginning of the German defeat and toward using a state-sponsored event to simultaneously remind the population about the Nazis' crimes and offer them the life-giving project of building communism in the present. Thus, the Stalin cult created a symbolic place of memory where the past could be surmounted and the struggle for the future could unfold.

A children's art contest for the best drawing about German-Soviet friendship was held alongside the composition contest. The entries show clearly that the official ideology, values, and imaginations were making their way into children's worlds. For example, a schoolboy from Zittau drew a "peace bridge" along which oil, cotton, trucks, and tractors were delivered to Berlin from Moscow. Another drawing compared Hitler's Germany with Stalin's Russia. War, tanks, and weapons with fascist symbols and ruined houses next to burial mounds were drawn on one side of the paper. Life in peacetime was depicted on the other side: houses, industry, and agriculture were being restored, and a line of tractors and machines that the USSR sent to the GDR was traveling along a broad street. In a greeting card written by schoolchildren, visual images of gratitude to the "leader" were conveyed in words:

> We thank the protector of the German Democratic Republic, the proponent of German unity, the guarantor of the preservation of the peace, the friend of all peacefully living peoples—Generalissimo Stalin—and we send him greetings for his seventieth jubilee.[115]

The propaganda organs organized mobilization and indoctrination campaigns to popularize positive connotations of Stalin's image among the generation of "war children" (*Kriegskinder*).[116] They were born in the Third Reich

but were too young to be educated in the Nazi mass organizations and socialized as members of Nazi Germany's "racial community." Consequently, the
SED state saw this social cohort as a potential reservoir of the GDR's most
important supporters and understood that educating them politically was a
strategic investment in the future.

The common socialist practice of accepting individual obligations was
another ritualistic way to express gratitude, love, and trust in the Soviet
leader. As a rule, on Stalin's birthday individuals accepted the obligations
propaganda presented by making a personal vow to the "leader" that he/she
would go beyond targets set by the plan for education, party activities, and
industry, and would reach new heights in terms of personal achievements.
Making such a pledge was intended to spur individuals on to personal victories and to mobilize the population emotionally and physically to meet the
goals set by the party and the state. Propaganda treated the act of accepting
obligations as each individual's own commitment to the common cause of
building socialism, as a chance to provide self-evidence of socialist consciousness, and as a way the state gave citizens opportunities to infuse the
regime with life-sustaining energy.

The practice of taking on obligations brought together people from different social groups, classes, and cohorts: workers and white-collar employees,
peasants and members of the intelligentsia, schoolchildren and university
students, athletes and activists, German men who were former POWs, veterans, and disabled soldiers, mothers and widows.[117] Propaganda called on
each citizen, regardless of his or her past and social status, to make a personal
contribution to building socialism. Individual resources (professional, material, and symbolic) were central to promises made to the Soviet leader. Some
people promised to diligently study the Stalin Constitution and the leader's
literature; others pledged to keep increasing their productivity in order to
introduce Stalin's methods of production at their workplaces, while a third
group vowed to set aside part of their wages for the national program of
restoring Berlin and they committed themselves to actively participating in
the actual construction work. A fourth group simply undertook to "struggle
for truth" and "expose enemies."[118] This practice allowed individuals to
experience the feeling that they belonged to a great chain of people who were
purposefully rebuilding the world under Stalin's guidance.

The examples discussed above show how Stalin cult micro-rituals operated
as practices of self-Sovietization carried out by individuals: these micro-
rituals stimulated people to transform themselves into political subjects who
inserted their personal life and biography into socialist language and behavior patterns. The state counted on rituals of personal mobilization to trigger
political self-activation on the individual level. The propaganda state also

encouraged people to invest emotional energy in the power structures and in stabilizing the SED regime as a whole. At the same time, the language and practices analyzed above present a variety of micro-rituals that gave individuals tools for understanding and interpreting their Sovietized reality as they adapted and made sense of life in the second German dictatorship. As more and more subjects interiorized the Stalin cult's rhetoric and practices, this became a significant source of cult regeneration. Opportunities to participate in myth-making by creating compositions and drawings, participating in campaigns to collect gifts and signatures on congratulatory letters, or joining a lottery to restore the Stalinallee reinforced the Soviet leader's sacrality, but, most importantly, these possibilities created "spaces of agency" within which Sovietized "selves" were formed.[119]

Between the Factory and the Mass Organization: Political Classes and Hierarchies in the Cult Community

In a society that the state heralded as a "classless socialist society," the Stalin cult reinforced class, gender, social, and professional identities and, as such, social hierarchies. A network of mass organizations helped to reimagine the structure of postwar East German society. These organizations became a key feature of the country's political system.[120] The regime used them to split the masses into generational cohorts, assign a particular political mission to each social group, and mobilize people to carry out specific political tasks. The mass organizations also gave the SED a way to manage social mobility and control participation in public life.[121] Virtually the entire population, with the exception of people in prison, the mentally ill, and a few subcultures, were involved in these organizations. They were a space established by the state, which used it not only to control public spheres themselves but to indoctrinate, mobilize, and discipline its citizens inside them.

Walter Ulbricht described the mass organizations' main job at a conference of officials of the Free German Youth (FDJ) in November 1950:

> Every person who wants to do conscious work must know which path to take to go forward. Otherwise, he will be like a cane for a blind man, looking for the road. Therefore, each progressive person must acquaint himself with Marxism-Leninism. The teachings of Marx, Engels, Lenin, and Stalin should be taught in each mass organization.[122]

Ulbricht gave the mass organizations a clear directive: start turning the individual into a political subject who uses the party's language and who acts to strengthen the regime. Thus, the mass organizations were tasked with forging cadres and creating significant social support for the SED political order.[123]

The FDJ, which was created in March 1946, was one of the first mass organizations in East Germany. Its members were young people between fourteen and twenty-five years old. The FDJ's political mission was to mobilize youth to undertake three main tasks: rebuild the country after the war, maintain German unity, and, above all, create a socialist society on the Soviet model. SED leaders expected that, freed from guilt for Nazi crimes because they supported the new political order, young Germans would become the active builders of socialism in East Germany.[124] Indeed, from the FDJ's earliest days, the SED authorities repeatedly stated that young people were not guilty of the crimes of the Third Reich. On those grounds, SVAG joined the program of ideologically reeducating young people. In November 1946, P. B. Bannik, one of the leaders of SVAG's political division, sent the heads of political departments in the provinces a list of appropriate topics for lectures directed to young people. Seminars on the biographies of Lenin and Stalin were essential as were lectures on "Comrade Stalin, the organizer and inspirer of the victories of the Soviet people."[125] This knowledge was declared a critical component of the social engineering which would strengthen a socialist consciousness and grow the socialist personality.

From the end of the 1940s through the early 1950s, the FDJ underwent intensive Stalinization (Figure 4.3).[126] This is clear from reports on the 1949 and 1952 youth parliaments. Whenever Stalin's name was mentioned, rituals of worshiping the "leader" ensued: "wild ovations," "long, unbroken cries of 'bravo' and 'hurrah,'" and "'Pieck, Stalin' chanted in unison." The rhetoric and rituals of the Stalin cult permeated the protocols of the sessions of the fourth FDJ parliament (held in Leipzig in May 1952). For example, the Soviet delegation to the parliament handed over the red Komsomol flag to Erich Honecker, the chairman of the FDJ, and an "honor guard" was appointed for it. These acts were "the expression of the deep love young German fighters for peace [feel] toward the peoples of the Soviet Union and [our] wise leader, Stalin."[127] In this context, Honecker stated that

> With deep trust in the true path of our people and our own strengths, with trust in the indomitable strength of the peace-loving camp of peace, led by the mighty Soviet Union we wish as never before to fulfill the great and binding task set by wise Stalin—to be active builders of one, democratic, peace-loving Germany.[128]

The FDJ's "political school" began its "academic year" in January 1950. The course it offered (as a supplement to compulsory political education in schools) became, in essence, systematic propaganda of Stalin's image among young people. FDJ members studied the Soviet leader's biography in study circles especially created for this purpose. The mass organizations held training sessions for agitators, especially on promoting the "leader's" biography.[129] Propagandists assumed that studying the classic works of Marxism-Leninism would give young people the sense of joining a community of the "most progressive people on Earth": "This should become our great pride, when we can tell the youth of the entire world that we have studied the work of Marx, Engels, Lenin, and Stalin in order to use this knowledge in the struggle for peace."[130] Students were also advised to read Soviet literature and watch Soviet films, which taught young people how to speak, see the world, and feel Soviet.[131] After finishing the course, the pupils had to take an exam. Only students who "regularly attended the political school, participated in a circle for studying the leader's biography and those who attained the requisite level of knowledge through independent study" would receive the certificate of completion.[132] In the oral part of the exam, students were asked to demonstrate their proficiency in knowledge of the Soviet leader's achievements, the life of Wilhelm Pieck, German history, and the current international situation. For the written part, exam-takers could write an essay on German history or "the life and struggle of I. V. Stalin." Demonstrating "social activism" was a mandatory condition for obtaining a certificate. This usually meant submitting articles about the FDJ's forward-looking work to school, university, or factory wall newspapers.[133] Those who passed the exam received the "For Good Knowledge!" (*Für gutes Wissen*) badge. FDJ members who displayed the greatest mastery of the official rhetoric of the "dictatorship of discourse" were awarded gold badges while those who passed the exams but were less proficient were given the silver or bronze badge.

The Stalin cult's rituals were an essential part of propaganda campaigns to mobilize young people. For example, just before Stalin's seventieth birthday, an FDJ initiative to collect signatures on a congratulatory letter to Stalin began. The text of this telegram dramatized a symbolic solidarity between East German youth and the Soviet leader using emotionally saturated language:

> Deeply respected Generalissimo! Please accept our heartfelt greetings and congratulations on your seventieth birthday. We thank you for the telegram you sent for the founding of the GDR. We want to justify the trust shown to us. All young German men and women will work to achieve peace and the unity of Germany. We promise that we will use all our strength to build our republic, for the constitution, to honor our president, Wilhelm Pieck. We promise to build a peacetime economy and strengthen friendship with both the Soviet Union and all peace-loving peoples.[134]

On December 20, 1949, the official results of the campaign were announced: 2,022,308 young Germans had signed a message congratulating Stalin.

The Stalin cult's potential to mobilize youth was dramatized in an exchange of telegrams between representatives of the FDJ and Stalin himself. This act of charismatic communication was staged to mark the first all-German meeting of teenagers and young adults, which was held on May 27–29, 1950, in East Berlin. The high point of the gathering was the collective acceptance of the text of a message for Stalin, which was accompanied by a demonstration of 700,000 young people on May 29. Columns of demonstrators carried portraits of the Soviet leader and shouted his name, promising never to fight against the USSR again. For the Soviet authorities, this state-organized meeting in East Berlin was an "indicator of increased political consciousness among German youth."[135] That same day, V. G. Grigor'ian, the chairman of the VKP(b) Central Committee's Foreign Policy Commission, reported to Stalin on the East German leadership's request, made through the Soviet Embassy in Berlin, to send a telegram in response.[136] Stalin's brief answer, expressing his wishes for "new successes in building a united, democratic, peace-loving Germany," was the impetus for radicalizing the propaganda of "the best friend of the German people" in the GDR. The FDJ newspaper *Junge Welt* shined a spotlight on Stalin's telegram by putting out a special issue with a print run of 800,000 copies. On the first page

Figure 4.3   Erich Honecker surrounded by FDJ members at a regional conference in Chemnitz. July 6, 1951. *Source:* Bildarchiv im Bundesarchiv (Koblenz). Signature: Bild 183-11076-0006. Photographer: Seidel.

was a portrait of Stalin and the text of his message. Three hundred thousand posters and 100,000 wall newspapers with the portrait and Stalin's message were printed with the FDJ's support.[137] This medial production was designed to make this act of successful communication with the "leader" highly visible in the dictatorship's public space.

To demonstrate that German-Soviet friendship was growing stronger, during the first all-German youth meeting, the USSR State Folk Dance Ensemble was sent to East Germany. From May to July, the ensemble gave concerts across the country, featuring the songs and dances of the multinational Soviet empire. According to Soviet observers, the concerts succeeded in inspiring their East German audiences; one report emphasized that the GDR citizens saw the ensemble as "ambassadors of Great Stalin." Each performance included activities representing German-Soviet friendship: the mandatory scenario included playing the national anthems of the USSR and the GDR, reading out telegrams welcoming the ensemble in honor of Stalin, and exchanging gifts. During its concert in Berlin, the ensemble was presented with the city's coat of arms, made of fresh flowers. However, the next morning it was found thrown away in a crowded street, causing doubts about the sincerity of the friendship that had been performed. Despite such incidents, portraits of the leaders and the flags of the "countries of the people's democracies" were placed on the stage to represent the socialist bloc's solidarity. Every concert ended with the audience ritually chanting "friendship" (*druzhba*), "Komsomol," and "Stalin." While on tour in East Germany, the ensemble gave twenty-seven concerts, attended by 1,200,00 spectators and an additional eleven performances exclusively for Soviet troops. The performers also laid wreaths at the graves of fallen Soviet soldiers as representatives of SVAG, the SED, and the mass organizations looked on, a ritual designed to strengthen the cult of World War II outside the USSR.[138]

Staging charismatic communication with Soviet leaders had several important functions in the East German propaganda state. Above all, Stalin's telegram gave German youth a key role in creating the new postwar political order.[139] Propaganda actively used the rhetoric of trust, and Stalin's words were interpreted as "a gesture showing great trust and great honor on Stalin's part," which obligated the younger generation to build socialism under the aegis of the SED.[140] In this respect, the telegram helped to bring to heel, encourage, and, at the same time, discipline yesterday's "Hitler Youth generation" while educating young people in Soviet rhetoric, practices, and emotions. The feeling of trust in Stalin being constructed was also inextricably linked with teaching young people to distrust the West as dangerous and the source of a new military threat. For example, the youth division of the People's Police put out a brochure calling on young people to rally around Stalin against the backdrop of a supposedly increasing threat of Western aggression.[141] It alleged that the former allies were planning to blow up the Lorelei, a 433-foot-high slate cliff in the Rhine Gorge (the Middle Rhine region), which was one of Germany's most important cultural sites and a traditional symbol of German national identity. Staging this communication with East German youth also reinforced propaganda representations of the Soviet leader's charismatic qualities and roles; from 1949, in all the socialist countries, the most important ones were "a fighter for peace" and "the guarantor of the peaceful coexistence of the peoples."

Stalin's role as a "fighter for peace" was vividly presented during Third World Youth and Student Games, which took place in East Berlin on August 5–19, 1951 (Figure 4.4).

The festival's slogan was "For Peace and Friendship—Against Atomic Weapons." Approximately 26,000 athletes from 104 countries and more than two million Germans, from both East and West Germany, took part in the games. For the SED regime, the event was a propaganda spectacle intended to consolidate the GDR's legitimacy in the "cohort of the countries of the people's democracy," and the international arena as a whole.[142] But how did the SED get young people in East Germany to participate in the Youth Games and other events organized by the party and state? And what motivated young Germans to express loyalty and support for the socialist state?

Figure 4.4   A demonstration in East Berlin during the Third World Youth and Student Games. August 9, 1951. *Source:* Bildarchiv im Bundesarchiv (Koblenz). Signature: Bild 183-11500-0994. Photographer: Martin Schmidt.

A more detailed look at the algorithm used to mobilize young people in conjunction with the Third World Youth and Student Games will help answer these questions. On May 30, 1951, the SED Politburo adopted a resolution to carry out a propaganda campaign named "For Stalin!" The goal of the campaign was the complete mobilization of young people to organize the games.[143] Regional FDJ offices competed to win the so-called Stalin banner: the contestants were given points for the number of new members joining each regional FDJ, the number of meetings held, and the number of new subscriptions to *Junge Welt*. They also received points for the number of people who promised to study Stalin's *On the Foundations of Leninism*. The official results of the campaign surpassed the FDJ leadership's expectations. In June 1951 alone, 58,955 people joined, and by mid-July of that year, the number of new members had risen to 83,223. By the end of July 1951, more than 700,000 FDJ members had promised to study *On the Foundations of Leninism*, whereas in June 1951 the number of such commitments was just over one million.[144] In order to motivate young people to join the FDJ, the mass organization prepared 1,767 specially trained political workers to become the new leaders of Pioneer groups. More than eight thousand new groups of agitators began to implement educational programs. A similar mobilization spurred more than two thousand representatives of Berlin youth to make a commitment stimulating productivity in order to fulfill economic plans more quickly than had previously been expected.[145]

However, hasty efforts focused on quantity did not produce mobilization of the desired quality. Shortly after the campaign began, party authorities uncovered a series of "organizational mistakes." For example, in compiling lists of people to receive admission tickets to the games, and striving to over-fulfill the plan, the leadership of the Erfurt district added all the young people twice, listing them both by workplace (or educational institution) and by residence.[146] Reports noted that the actual results of promises to study *On the Foundations of Leninism* left a great deal to be desired. At the end of the first week of the mobilization campaign, it became known that out of six thousand FDJ members who had committed themselves to study Stalin's text, only 186 people had actually kept their promise. Difficulties involving payment of membership dues were ubiquitous.[147] In their frustration, GDR leaders at the highest level demanded that the shortcomings be dealt with immediately.[148]

The next call to mobilize young people was the Central Committee's July 3, 1951, resolution on collecting signatures for a telegram of greetings to be sent to Stalin.[149] This action took place from August 5 to August 11. The expectation was that every German between the ages of twelve and twenty-five would be involved. Collection points for signatures—marked by a portrait of the "leader" above the slogan "German youth greet the great Stalin!"—were set up throughout East Berlin.[150] The FDJ organized daily meetings and collective processions to publicly express support for the Soviet leader's "peaceful initiatives." A contest for the best "song about peace" sponsored by President Pieck himself was held on the city's squares.[151] The results of the "For Stalin" campaign, especially the number of young people's signatures collected, would be reported directly to the "best friend of the German people" in a special letter.[152] To do this, the GDR government asked the VKP(b) Central Committee to allow FDJ delegates to travel to Moscow for an in-person meeting with Stalin.[153] For the Germans, this was something to boast about to Moscow, and the socialist press reported with pride that 4,145,839 young Germans signed the letter to the leader of the USSR.[154]

On August 12, 1951, the final results of the "For Stalin!" campaign were unveiled. The celebrations of the Day of Young Fighters for Peace were staged as a symbolic report to the Soviet leader "about the scale of efforts made by German youth to defend the peace."[155] At nine o'clock in the evening, a fanfare and then a song about Stalin opened the festivities on Marx-Engels Square (Marx-Engels-Platz), in the very heart of Berlin. Six powerful floodlights lit up a portrait of the "leader" which was hovering in the air. Erich Honecker and Walter Ulbricht gave the first prize to the winner of the campaign, the regional division of the FDJ from Saxony-Anhalt. This was the "Stalin banner," a red flag with a portrait of the "vozhd'." The most active FDJ members were given volumes of Stalin's publications. Outstanding FDJ divisions received portraits and busts of the Soviet leader to thank them for what they had accomplished.[156] Collective singing of the "Internationale" was the finale.[157]

Although it goes without saying that the number of people mobilized during propaganda campaigns was inflated, many young people did participate in them. Why did they take part in these campaigns? I would argue that East German young people's engagement in the regime's political initiatives was not driven by fanatical faith in the SED. Their involvement was instead the result of rational thinking and the desire to enjoy certain practical advantages. Publicly demonstrating one's loyalty to the regime made it possible to enjoy material resources and leisure-time activities that were inaccessible in other everyday spheres as well as various privileges and "small pleasures" which were hard if not impossible to come by otherwise. FDJ membership opened the door to more (and better) opportunities to find a job, get an education, advance at work or simply pass exams, participate in recreational activities, and receive the best food at a factory or university dining hall.[158] One pragmatic reason for joining the mass organization was the chance to engage in a special hobby, for example, studying astronomy at the observatory or mastering photography or making movies. An FDJ membership card gave teenagers a chance to meet members of the opposite sex at dances and on co-ed trips. As an FDJ member said, acknowledging that a certain, rational meeting of minds brought the state and young people together, "The government helps us—and we help the government."[159]

Despite so much evidence of FDJ members' enthusiasm, doubts about the sincerity of their political attitudes did arise from time to time. A spontaneous test of "political strength" that showed how weak the regime's popular support really was confirmed these suspicions. An officer of the Soviet Ministry of State Security (MGB) serving in Germany reported to the VKP(b) Central Committee on an incident that began on July 14, 1950, when some adult FDJ mentors allegedly spread "provocative rumors" in a youth recreation camp in the province of Saxony to demonstrate the strength of their members' convictions, more specifically, their "persistence . . . in case of war." The adults let it be known that US troops had occupied the eastern sector of Berlin, while the SED and GDR leaders—Ulbricht, Pieck, and Grotewohl—were out of the country. This information circulated through the camp. During the panic that ensued, 114 of the 120 members in the camp removed their uniforms and destroyed their membership cards and badges. And six members of the People's Police on duty in the camp ripped off their shoulder straps, declaring that they were not going to resist the US army. The MGB launched an investigation that determined that the FDJ members' "shameful behavior" showed signs of being "criminal anti-state acts."[160]

Like the FDJ, other mass organizations offered powerful incentives for becoming a member. Although the population was generally unwilling to "pay for friendship with the Soviet Union," that is, to pay dues to the German-Soviet Friendship Society, its membership reached more than three million in the early 1950s.[161] The DSF offered its members some attractive benefits, including its literary and musical evenings, film screenings, and dances, which were especially well attended.[162] Among other reasons for participating in the Society's activities were that "the organization had at its disposal heated buildings, which was especially important for frequent meetings of elderly people"; "students received good conditions for work and had access to a library"; "cheap and tasty food was served"; and "after the official part of the meeting was over, dances were organized."[163] To attract the public, by the mid-1950s the DSF had organized literary, opera, chess, and language clubs. Later, events like "A Samovar Hour with Georgian Tea" and "How Do People Cook in the Soviet Union?" were popular. These reasons for demonstrating loyalty to the regime through membership in a mass organization reveal an important mechanism for producing conformism and stabilizing the dictatorship: the population was looking out for its *Eigen-Sinn* or "personal interests" in the process of normalizing postwar daily life.[164]

Workers were another social stratum that the regime sought to mobilize and shape into a state-approved working class, hence factories were key sites for mobilization and indoctrination. The factory, as Louis Althusser pointed out, was the central institution for both ideological indoctrination and the production of ideology itself. Factories were places where "subordination to the state ideology or mastery of the practice of such subordination" took place.[165] The ritual of establishing the state's patronage of an enterprise by naming it after Stalin confirms this thesis. For example, on the eve of International Workers' Day in 1953, the SED Politburo adopted a resolution to name the Treptow Electrical Appliance Factory after the Soviet leader, who, at that point, had already died. The "solemn act" of renaming the factory was part of the conclusion of a social contract. In this case, a group of workers handed a folder over to party representatives and the enterprise's management, who then signed off on a promise to increase production norms and improve the quality of the work being done.[166] The factory's management and its workers participated in the state's staging of social support for the SED regime *from below*. But, by naming the factory after Stalin, the enterprise gained several advantages, many of which improved the workers' daily life: additional state subsidies and investment had a positive impact on the fulfillment of production plans and helped pay for improvements in working and living conditions, raises in wages, and the expansion of social services like kindergartens, medical care, and even possibilities for travel abroad.

The Treptow factory became an exhibition hall of sorts, one that showcased successes in building socialism in East Germany. The press described the benefits of being a member of the class of workers with access to the system of party-state profits and privileges: a rest cure at a sanatorium, vacations organized for children, better medical services, additional payments, and the like. Propaganda pointed out that daily life at the factory was improving because the proletariat's political consciousness was growing stronger and because of the care the state bestowed on its citizens. On the Soviet leader's seventy-fourth birthday, the press reported that the enterprise had filled its production plan ahead of schedule and had opened a "Stalin study room" with propagandistic materials and images about the life of the "best friend of the German people."[167] This is how the Stalin cult generated interactions that empowered both workers and the state. On one hand, the regime deployed the Stalin cult to strengthen and promote acceptance of the political order. On the other hand, the enterprise's management and workers used the cult in a rational way to improve working conditions in the factory and daily life for its employees.

The practice of sending collective greetings and taking on social obligations in honor of the Soviet leader's birthday was another method of constructing group identity that was imposed from above. For example, in a telegram congratulating Stalin on his seventy-first birthday sent by the machine-building enterprises in Erfurt, the workers expressed their hope that the Soviet leader would eternally lead the Germans on the path of the construction of socialism.

In this telegram, which made it all the way to Moscow, the rhetoric of clientelism is easy to spot:

> Deeply respected Generalissimo Stalin! . . . On this day we workers and white-collar employees of the mechanical engineering works in Erfurt celebrate the great contributions of the leader of all workers in the struggle to preserve peace. The great socialist October Revolution of 1917, victorious under the leadership of the great Lenin and Stalin, showed humanity the path to a better future. We workers are guided by the experience of Lenin, [the experience] of the brilliant Stalin, not to retreat in the struggle to preserve peace and to increase our production. We Germans are especially grateful to Stalin for his help, which he gave us from 1945 on. In the person of Stalin, we honor the entire Soviet people who, paying the price with many sacrifices, also won freedom for us.

After the basic elements of the myth of the Soviet leader were set out, a normative statement about accepting collective obligations followed. The promise that the vow would be fulfilled anchored the communication with the leader:

> We pledge: 1. Not to waste a single day and hour in order to use these to preserve the peace and to keep the Soviet Union from being slandered; 2. To use all the resources we have to support the initiatives of the Soviet Union on the question of German unification. . . .; 3. The collective pledges to fulfill the five-year plan ahead of schedule . . . At our enterprise reinforcing and further developing German-Soviet friendship should be considered our very highest goal. We want to develop this friendship so that, together with the Soviet peoples, under the leadership of brilliant Stalin, we can preserve peace throughout the world.[168]

These examples illustrate the Stalin cult's prodigious capacity to politically mobilize the population. At the same time, they indicate the extraordinary attention to detail with which the state and the party organized public spheres in Soviet-style societies: the meticulously elaborated scenarios for mass events imposed from above, the careful calculations of individual and group actions, and the variety of practices through which people could belong to the project of building socialism. By taking part in the cult rituals, citizens divided themselves into different social strata; they could confirm a certain class identity and claim membership in social hierarchies by including the symbolic Soviet order in many aspects of their life and sense of self. In the "classless society" proclaimed by propaganda, the state and the party were the arbiters. They assessed how social hierarchies were being maintained and the correctness (or incorrectness) of group behavior in the framework in which prescribed identities were defined.

The Stalin Cult in the Macro-Rituals of Constructing the State, the Nation, and the Empire: Producing Shared Meanings and Securing Hierarchies

The "red calendar" of holidays created in East Germany and other Eastern bloc countries after 1945 shows that Sovietization was well underway in Central and Eastern Europe in the late 1940s and early 1950s.[169] Between 1949 and 1954, Stalinist rituals became essential components of the GDR's official culture of celebrations. Celebrated on December 21, Stalin's birthday became the central ritual for constructing the imagined cult community. During preparations to celebrate the leader's seventieth birthday in 1949, the political rituals of the postwar Soviet empire were synchronized across the Eastern bloc and the Soviet Union for the first time. By publishing the congratulatory telegrams which had been sent to the "leader of the world proletariat" from all corners of the earth, print media depicted the Stalin cult as a transnational, indeed global, phenomenon that extended from the Pacific to the Atlantic, from the Arctic to the Antarctic, from West to East.[170]

Despite the cult's apparently global reach, some parts of the world were more important than others: Stalin's birthday united the key players, the "countries of the people's democracy," with the Center or Moscow. Thus, the Soviet ambassador to Czechoslovakia reported to Soviet capital about plans for a monument to Stalin in Prague that reflected the state's internal consolidation: stones would be brought from all over the country for the foundation.[171] In Hungary, workers at an agricultural cooperative planted four rows of walnut trees in lines running from East to West, as a "symbol of the truth that the star of the world, rising in the Soviet Union, is shedding its light over the entire world."[172] In a village in Bulgaria, the project of gathering signatures on a greeting card for Stalin began with a celebration—an ox was slaughtered, and the villagers shared a festive meal with many toasts to the Soviet leader's health.[173] Reports from Romania described the opening of 2,500 exhibits about the life and deeds of the "leader," which were "expressions of the love of the Romanian people for Comrade Stalin."[174] The entire Periphery used the "leader's" birthday for two types of centralization: the birthday celebrations helped to promote social integration around national communist regimes, while producing representations of the localities' symbolic subordination to their patron, Stalin, connected them with the Center.

To consolidate Stalin's global significance as the "protector and guarantor of world peace," a 1949 decree of the Presidium of the Supreme Soviet of the USSR established the International Stalin Prize for Peace and Progress.[175] Awarded from 1950 for contributions to strengthening peace between peoples, it became the Soviet alternative to the Nobel Peace Prize. The prize gained international prestige not only for its symbolic recognition of "outstanding writers, scientists, and political figures" but also because of the substantial award that came with it: in addition to a gold medal with Stalin's profile, each winner received the dollar equivalent of 100,000 rubles. The awards ceremony took place in the Kremlin, in the presence of international delegations from around the world, on the eve of the leader's birthday. Three GDR citizens were among the first laureates: writer and cofounder of the GDR Academy of the Arts Anna Seghers (1951); novelist, poet, and politician Johannes Becher (1952); and playwright, novelist, and poet Bertolt Brecht (1954). Honoring citizens of the "second German state" in this way emphasized the GDR's special role in the postwar Soviet empire during the Cold War. Broad media coverage of the award helped promote Soviet-style construction of socialism in the GDR around the world.[176]

The campaign to prepare for Stalin's jubilee was in full swing in the USSR in 1949. The fanaticism of Soviet initiatives *from below* was undoubtedly quite different from the Periphery's more restrained efforts. A few examples drawn from letters written by Soviet citizens to the Central Committee illustrate that. A disabled World War II veteran from Molotov asked that the Order of the Genius of Mankind be created in honor of the leader, and someone from the village of Fastovtsy in the Chernigov region (in today's Ukraine) suggested making Stalin's birthday a national holiday.[177] Initiatives to put up a golden bust and a crystal monument were far from exceptions in an upsurge of suggestions about how to monumentalize Stalin's image in public space. A resident of Kaunas (in the Lithuanian SSR) suggested giving Stalin the title Hero of Peace and a Muscovite suggested Scholar of Peace (*Uchenyi mira*). However, there were even more grandiose projects. Thus, a member of the Novyi Mir kolkhoz (collective farm) in Kursk *oblast'* suggested that a 250-meter-high tower topped with a 25-meter guiding star bearing portraits of Stalin and Lenin should be built in Moscow on Red Square. Lights would be attached to the points of the star, and the letter writer thought these should burn around the clock and for eternity.[178]

Suggestions about how to glorify the "leader" abounded in the USSR, but Soviet citizens also used the practice of writing to the Central Committee on the occasion of Stalin's birthday to talk about day-to-day problems. Letter writers frequently asked for supplements to their pensions and increases in state benefits. Thus, a correspondent from Svatovo asked that people with category I or category II disabilities (*invalidy I i II gruppy*) be given a personal pension or the yearly Stalin benefit. Some people suggested lowering the price of bread and essential goods to coincide with the jubilee; others suggested giving schoolchildren free meals and declaring an amnesty for people convicted of misdemeanors. A veteran of the Great Fatherland War who had lost both his legs requested cars with manual controls for disabled people.[179]

The Soviet population actively participated in creating the myth of the leader since they saw him as their "last hope," the "highest authority of appeal," or simply as the "most important person in the country" for resolving personal problems and defending the interests of individuals, groups, and entire generations.[180] The leader's person became a public figure onto which every ordinary citizen could project something of his or her own, ascribe personal meanings to it, or use the leader cult to optimize everyday life and accept Stalinism as a way of life.[181] It seems that the Kremlin responded, at least to some extent, to citizens' inquiries. Thus, from December 21, 1949 onward, pensions for those too old to work were increased and in major industrial cities there were plans to build twenty-six homes for the disabled.[182] In short, like East Germans, ordinary Soviet people also used and manipulated the Stalin cult for their personal benefit.

In East Germany, Stalin's birthday was used to stage a nationwide, statewide, and empire-wide holiday. With the founding of the GDR on October 7, 1949, East Germany began to assert itself as a valued member of the socialist bloc. The German delegation's participation in Stalin's seventieth birthday celebrations in Moscow was a public initiation ritual that brought the GDR into the cult community.[183] The first public journey to Moscow made by leading figures in the GDR was the ritual demarcation of the country's new status: it had moved from the liminal condition of the "Soviet-occupied zone of Germany" to being a new, recognized state within the Soviet bloc—the German Democratic Republic. At the celebratory meeting at the Bolshoi Theater, in the presence of the other leaders of the world proletariat, Walter Ulbricht, the head of the German delegation, affirmed the paternalistic relations between the Soviet Union and East Germany in the following words: "Beloved friend Joseph Vissarionovich! Millions of workers, toiling peasants, the progressive intelligentsia, and two million young German men and women greet You, beloved Joseph Vissarionovich, as the best friend of the German people."[184] Official photographs of the celebration event showed Ulbricht next to Stalin, thus proclaiming the two leaders' intimacy and the two countries' exclusive friendship.

The East Germans' first public trip to Moscow was a symbolic gesture that proclaimed Germany's dependence on and subordination to the Center.[185] In its semantics, the act of raising the status of East Germany is reminiscent of the medieval ritual establishing a vassal's dependence on his lord. This ritual was based on the principle of mutual obligations: the patron gave his protection, and the client pledged his loyalty.[186] The USSR covered all the expenses of the foreign delegations that came to Moscow to celebrate Stalin's seventieth birthday. Delegates from the "people's democracies" were given luxury hotel suites equipped with TV sets, fresh fruits, and expensive cigarettes and they were provided with a translator and a car to travel around Moscow. In exchange for such generous hospitality, the Soviet authorities expected their Soviet bloc guests to ensure their countries' political loyalty to the "fatherland of socialism."[187]

Swearing an oath of fealty to the Center became part of the dramaturgy of the cult community since this and other rituals created the sacral meaning of the connection between the Center and the Periphery.[188] In this case, the semantics of the oath assigned Stalin the role of the highest arbiter, who takes it upon himself to carry out his part of the symbolic contract. The East Germans staged the leader in this role on an intercontinental scale in the "oath of peace," the text of which was published in 104 languages and read out (in German) at the August 19, 1951, closing ceremony of the Third International Youth and Student Games in East Berlin.[189] To fulfill the oath was understood as an act of honor and failure to do so was shameful. For that reason, announcing a course for the systematic construction of socialism in June 1952, the SED regime demanded total mobilization of the population to accomplish the project of building socialism.[190]

In its telegram congratulating the Soviet leader on his seventieth birthday, the executive board of the German Communist Party (Kommunistische Partei Deutschland or KPD) of West Germany used the rhetoric of taking an oath to Stalin to express loyalty to the Center and as a rhetorical demonstration that the cult not only existed in the GDR but in the FRG as well. The text proclaimed:

> We swear to you Comrade Stalin that we will tirelessly strive to ensure that in the West[ern part] of our homeland our brothers and sisters will put their trust in the Soviet Union in matters of peace, democracy and freedom . . . We swear to you that we will tirelessly work to make the KPD ideologically and politically conscious and an organizationally stronger party under the banner of Marxism-Leninism. Armed with your doctrine, we swear that we will struggle without compromise with all the hostile influences in our party in order to win the trust of the entire working class.[191]

Swearing an oath of loyalty to Stalin would secure the Soviet leader's patronage on the "German question," the problem of the unity of state and nation, by linking the Germans and Moscow on the basis of their mutual moral obligations to observe the symbolic pact of "friendship."

Gift-giving is a traditional way to establish closeness and create reciprocity.[192] The East Germans did not go empty-handed to Moscow for Stalin's birthday celebrations; they came bearing gifts. The practice of presenting gifts to the leader was an important part of rituals of gratitude which were intended to cement the imperial hierarchy and demonstrate deference to the sacral center, that is, to the figure of the leader. For example, the government of the GDR planned to give Stalin a copy of a rare seventeenth-century book, scholar and diplomat Adam Olearius's *Description of a Journey to the Muscovite and Persian Kingdoms* (*Vermehrte newe Beschreibung der Muscowitischen und Persischen Reyse*, sixth edition, 1696).[193] The gift was supposed to emphasize centuries-long traditions of a mutual relationship, reflecting the concept of German-Soviet friendship proclaimed in propaganda.

The SED Central Committee announced plans to build a planetarium in Stalingrad as a gift from the entire German people.[194] In his congratulatory telegram, Pieck explained that the East Germans' choice of this gift reflected their eagerness to be reconciled with their former enemies:

> Stalingrad is not only a city that bears your name, but it is simultaneously a worldwide symbol of your genius as a commander, your courage, your steadfastness and political acumen. Your global-historical victory at Stalingrad put an end to a dark chapter of German history. Therefore, allow us to describe this gift—a gift of friendship and love—as the beginning of an eternal, close friendship between our peoples.[195]

Voluntary donations from the German population would pay for the construction of the planetarium, and more than three and a half million marks were donated to a "Stalin account" set up for this purpose. Propaganda called this sum the direct equivalent of "the German people's deep respect and love for Stalin."[196] One report to Moscow indicated that thousands of workers, teachers, and engineers worked overtime to finance the construction of the planetarium in Stalingrad.[197] The Karl Zeiss optical instruments firm, which was located in Jena, one of Germany's oldest industrial centers, would make the telescopes and other precision instruments for the planetarium. For the East Germans, the state's commission to Zeiss symbolized the beginning of the rebirth of East German industry and was intended to draw the USSR's attention to the peaceful nature of postwar German industry.[198]

In addition to the nation's gift, Eastern Germans also joined a campaign to gather individual and collective gifts from mass organizations and enterprises, kindergartens and educational institutions. The SPD's Eastern Bureau estimated that the total value of gifts from East Germany might be as high as million Eastern marks.[199] The Germans were not alone in their generosity. All of Eastern Europe collected gifts for the Soviet leader. In the GDR, gifts were collected under the auspices of the DSF and the Free German Trade Union (Freier Deutscher Gewerkschaftsbund or FDGB) during the German-Soviet Friendship Month in the autumn of 1949. The presents themselves were announced as clear proof of respect, love, and trust in the "friend." The best and most valuable of these were exhibited in regional centers, competing to be dispatched to Moscow. Pieck was informed through the Soviet embassy that the USSR would accept gifts from East Germans. In December 1949, the

Ministry of Railways of the USSR provided the necessary number of wagons and locomotives to deliver the gifts to Moscow.[200] The festive ceremony of sending off the gift-laden train to Moscow was held on December 16, 1949.[201] Such trains with presents for the leader sped to the capital of the USSR from all the countries of the "people's democracies" to be displayed in an exhibition set to open on December 22, 1949.

In late December 1949, dozens of carriages stuffed with gifts for Stalin stood on the Moscow railway lines. The organizers had to work day and night to open the exhibition on December 22. Rooms in the Pushkin State Museum of Fine Arts and the State Museum of Revolution of the USSR were allocated to the exhibition. The results of the global campaign to collect gifts undoubtedly attracted the interest of Soviet and foreign citizens. In the first half of the year alone, more than 820,000 people visited the exhibition: the rooms devoted to the exhibition at the Pushkin Museum had 516,939 visitors and 303,750 people came to see it at the Museum of the Revolution. By the end of June 1950, more than one million people had seen it. As of August 1950, 480 foreign delegations and groups had visited the exhibition. By the time it closed in August 1953 the collection of gifts received over four million visitors.[202]

However, from the moment the exhibition opened, its director, A. Tolstikhina, began sending complains to the Central Committee's Department of Propaganda and Agitation: there was not enough space for the exhibition, the inventory process left much to be desired, and artifacts were stolen on a regular basis.[203] As of January 1, 1953, 14,200 items were recorded in the inventory books, which was only 35–40 percent of the total number of gifts received. By early 1953, the total number of gifts was 31,752. The museum also received more than a million congratulatory letters and postcards. Although tour guides told visitors about Stalin's role in constructing socialism around the world in the halls of the museum, in the basement rooms there were no traces of the triumph of communism: gifts were heaped up in piles, vases and dishes were broken, and food rotted and was left for the mice to demolish.[204] In January 1952, D. M. Gusev, the VOKS representative in Berlin, reported to Moscow that a huge number of gifts with no material or artistic value, which should in fact be destroyed, had been collected.[205]

The GDR sent its first shipment of gifts to Moscow in December 1949. Among the 550 items were paintings, busts, and reliefs bearing the image of the "best friend" as well as tobacco pipes, and models of houses, cars, and ships. But there were also all kinds of other things: five boxes of stone salt (from the producer in Erfurt); a knitting machine (from the workers of the "Elite-Diamant" factory in Siegmar-Schönau); five cactuses (from gardeners in Weimar); a metal canister (from the workers at a car repair shop in Erfurt); three metal powders (from an unknown donor); and toys, including a teddy

bear and an elephant wearing a crown (from the Thuringian Democratic
Women's Union). The train also carried 4,599 pieces of children's clothing
and 440 toys given by women and children. As a rule, the gifts came with
letters. A letter from women in the Chemnitz Democratic Women's Union,
who presented Stalin with twelve dolls from the local children's theater, was
typical:

> Honorable Generalissimo Stalin! Women think about you with great gratitude
> . . . You are a great example for us of a man who devoted his life to the benefit
> of mankind, to the peace and happiness of children of all countries. We are par-
> ticularly touched by your generous help to the German people and thus to our
> women, mothers and children in the establishment of the GDR . . . For us, you
> represent peace and we wish you many fruitful years.[206]

The rituals of the Stalin cult had an important temporal dimension. In East
Germany celebrations of the Soviet leader's birthday and other cult rituals
reflected efforts to combine the Stalin cult's secular rituals with religious
practices connected with Christianity.[207] For example, the tradition of saying
a prayer before a meal was maintained in the Stalin cult. "Bow your heads
and think about our beloved Stalin for a moment," a teacher instructed her
young charges as part of the daily before-dinner ritual in a children's group.[208]
The Christian liturgical year's Christmas season overlapped with the cult's
secular holidays: Stalin's birthday on December 21 was, in essence, the
beginning of the cycle of birthday celebrations that continued until January 3,
the birthday of Wilhelm Pieck, the "father of the nation."[209] Unlike the Soviet
regime, the SED did not attempt to make Bolshevik rituals take the place of
Christmas but instead tried to integrate socialist symbols and cult imagery
into traditional Christian holidays to popularize the regime. The scenarios for
the Christmas holidays (especially in propaganda for children) included identifying Stalin with St. Nicholas by showing the "leader" bringing symbolic
gifts like "peace," "security," and "a happy future," which were so important
for postwar German society.[210]

While the Stalin cult was being established in the GDR, "small" cults of
communist leaders were also being introduced. Their central element was
celebrating the cult figure's birthday. The celebrations usually followed more
or less the same scenario, but the festive events differed in scale, depending
on the particular leader's status in the hierarchy of personality cults. Thus,
on January 3, 1951, the celebration of Wilhelm Pieck's seventy-fifth birthday was celebrated on January 3, 1951, as "an important political event in
the country." The list of activities approved by the SED Central Committee
included several publications: anthologies of his speeches and articles, a special supplement to daily newspapers, and a special issue of *Einheit*, a journal

devoted to the theory and practice of scientific socialism. An illustrated biography of Pieck would be distributed through the mass organizations, educational institutions, the army, and bookshops. Preliminary plans also called for a "good portrait" of the president to be released in order to take the usual poor-quality images out of circulation. In addition, one hundred "Pieck scholarships" enabling outstanding graduates of workers' and peasants' faculties to study Marxism-Leninism were established. Pieck was awarded the title "Hero of Labor" (*Held der Arbeit*) against the backdrop of a campaign of collective and individual commitments to fulfill the economic plan ahead of schedule.[211] Similar large-scale celebrations of Ulbricht's sixtieth birthday were in the works, but these plans were shelved after the June 17, 1953 protests that erupted across East Germany.

The personality cult's mass rituals also had a spatial dimension. Only certain sites could become the cult's sacred spaces. Among these were the main streets and squares named after "leaders of the world proletariat," memorials to fallen Soviet soldiers, and monuments to Stalin. It is revealing that initially monuments to the Soviet leader were the ones the SED asked Moscow for after they were showcased at an exhibition of Soviet fine arts in East Berlin in the summer of 1951. The very first monument, erected in August 1951 on the Stalinallee in East Berlin, was a result of a request made by Ulbricht himself to the Central Committee of the VKP(b), and Stalin gave it his personal approval (Figure 4.5).[212]

A pointed sign of the Center's trust was a resolution about the immediate transfer of monuments designed by renowned sculptors Nikolai Tomsky and Grigorii Postnikov as gifts to the German people.[213] Despite the official version of the "Soviet gift," Walter Ulbricht was in charge of making the payments: Postnikov's work cost 25,000 rubles, while Tomsky's was estimated at 10,000 rubles.[214]

However, the GDR also wanted to produce its own monuments, and the first German-made statue of the Soviet leader was unveiled in the Saxon town of Riesa in March 1954, just before the first anniversary of Stalin's death (Figure 4.6).

The unveiling ceremony was filled with gestures demonstrating the GDR's symbolic rapprochement with Moscow. Wilhelm Koenen, a member of the SED Central Committee, concluded his speech by saying, "We are fighting for German unification and for peace in Europe on the side of the glorious Soviet Union, on behalf of the German people, for the glory and in honor of Stalin."[215] The eternal flame was lit, and as the drapery was removed from the statue, a cantata glorifying Stalin was sung while delegations of the People's Police and the Soviet army stood at attention. Afterward, to the solemn strains of "Immortal Victims" ("Bessmertnye Zhertvy"), representatives of the Young Pioneers, factories, the party, the mass organizations, the Soviet armed forces, and the Soviet diplomatic mission in Germany laid wreaths at

Figure 4.5   GDR leaders at the unveiling of a monument to the Soviet leader on the Stalinallee in East Berlin. August 3, 1951. *Source:* Bildarchiv im Bundesarchiv (Koblenz). Signature: Bild 183-11500-0375. Photographer: Walter Heilig.

the base of the monument. Right up to the beginning of de-Stalinization in 1956, the area around the monument became a center for organizing mass political rituals.

A wave of toponymic revolution was part of the rituals of centralizing socialist space.[216] Renaming cities, streets, and squares with the leader's name created a topographic cult of personality—places saturated with honor and obedience to Stalin. In other words, the Stalin cult was used to gather together the territories of the socialist empire and it facilitated the socialist nations' symbolic gravitational attraction to the Center. Thus, cities bearing Stalin's name appeared on the political maps of East Germany, Poland, Rumania, Hungary, Bulgaria, Czechoslovakia, and Albania.[217] A measure of the Center's closeness to the Periphery could be seen in the ubiquitous practice of listing the Soviet leader as an honorary citizen of towns and communes. To commemorate the thirtieth anniversary of the October Revolution, Stalin was designated an honorary citizen of the Hungarian capital, Budapest. On January 6, 1947, Stalin was proclaimed an honorary citizen of Sofia.[218] The choices of the date and place of the ceremony were linked to the anniversary of the capital's 1878 liberation from Turkish rule by Russian troops. Integrating the Stalin cult into national models of memory became an

Figure 4.6   Unveiling a monument to Stalin in Riesa. March 4, 1954. *Source:* Bildarchiv im Bundesarchiv (Koblenz). Signature: Bild 183-23647-0005. Photographer: Siegert.

important method of creating historically verified ties between Moscow and the regions of the empire.

To strengthen such ties, the SED made efforts to rewrite German national history in several different ways. Bolstered by the fact that Marx and Engels were German by nationality, these initiatives were designed to give the GDR a more "communist" history and memory culture. At its Seventh Plenum, on October 18–21, 1951, the SED Central Committee took the first steps toward adding days honoring the leaders of the international communist movement to the calendar of East German holidays. Likewise, the KPD's cult of Lenin found expression in annual commemorations of the anniversary of the death of "the first Soviet leader" as well as the anniversaries of the deaths of Rosa Luxemburg and Karl Liebknecht, the leaders of the German social democratic movement and the founders of the KPD. In addition, an order went out to identify German "sites of memory" associated with the activities of Marx, Engels, Lenin, and Stalin and to place commemorative plaques in appropriate places. Another step toward giving the GDR a truly communist history was the SED Politburo's decision to rename the Lustgarten's Schlossplatz (formerly the site of the Berlin Palace, the residence of the House of Hohenzollern) as Marx-Engels-Square and to erect a monument to "great German philosophers" on the square.[219] In addition, a Museum of German

History slated to open in 1953 was created in East Berlin.[220] At around the same time, the SED decided to speed up the publication of Stalin's works and begin publishing Lenin's complete oeuvre in German. With Moscow's agreement, the Secretariat of the SED Central Committee decided in November 1950 to turn Leipzig's Imperial Court (*Reichsgericht*) building into a museum honoring Georgi Dimitrov, a member of the Bulgarian Communist Party and general secretary of the Comintern from 1935 to 1944. They also planned to rename the square on which the museum was located and a thermal power station after him.[221] Official statistics showed Moscow that thousands of study groups were immersing themselves in Marxist-Leninist texts and underlined the endless events honoring the leaders. One SED member admitted that he was tired of the excessive celebrations and wished he could just spend an evening alone with a bottle of vodka.[222]

Socialist rituals used the Stalin cult in the dramaturgy of the Cold War. On one hand, Stalin personified the unity of the cult community, including visually dramatizing local leaders' brotherhood with the leader in Moscow. On the other hand, the Stalin cult drew the symbolic borders of the socialist world, which was placed in opposition to the capitalist West.[223] To personify the negative image of the West, anti-cults were used, featuring such heroes of negative identity as Konrad Adenauer, Ludwig Erhardt, Harry Truman, George Marshall, and Dwight Eisenhower. Their images appeared as caricatures on effigies carried by columns of demonstrators and in other political events (Figure 4.7). A well-known symbolic code of swastikas, dollar signs, and weapons was used to denote the "enemies of socialism" (Figure 4.8).

Western politicians were publicly mocked to demonstrate where the borders of empire lay and to set up a contrast between socialist and capitalist morality via the symbolic opposition of two social orders and by ritually excluding all that was other from the cult community. Under Cold War conditions, the window dressing of its loyalty to the Center allowed East Germany to act as the main boundary of the cult community—"the European outpost and showcase of socialism"—and to fight to have its own special status in the cohort of socialist states acknowledged.

The use of national flags and coats of arms, portraits, and posters of leaders, and banners with the words of the Soviet leader created the visual effect of blending the Center into the Periphery. In the words of a Western tourist in the GDR who noted the homogenization of the Soviet empire's public space: "If you stand on the Alexanderplatz in Berlin today, it seems that you are in Moscow, Leningrad, or Kiev. The enormous posters with their images of Stalin and Lenin, and the backdrops of Russian landmarks create the impression of identicalness" (Figure 4.9).[224]

In fact, the backdrop of Red Square and the Kremlin became the traditional setting for the personality cult's rituals. Thus, for Stalin's seventieth birthday,

Figure 4.7 Contrasting socialist leaders with their Western counterparts: a column marching in a May First demonstration in East Berlin, 1951. *Source:* Bildarchiv im Deutsches Historischen Museum (Berlin). Signature: BA 99/100.

the management of the Bukau-Wolf-Fabrik decided it was important to drape one of its factory buildings with an image of the Kremlin tower. During the period of state mourning after Stalin's death, a monument to the leader was set up on the central square in Leipzig. This monument had an enormous panel depicting a panorama of Moscow seen from the vantage point of the Kremlin's Spassky Tower and the Mausoleum (Figure 4.10). With the help of these decorations, the visual unity of Center and Periphery was dramatized, creating a feeling of synchronicity as the cult members seemed to experience grief at the same time and in one place.

Figuring out how to add the cult community's visual symbols to its rituals was extremely important for the Periphery. In fact, efforts to create appropriate visual symbolism were so highly charged that the satellite states used these while fiercely competing to win Moscow's trust and approval. For example, after visiting the KPD congress in Weimar in March 1951, the general secretary of the Central Committee of the Hungarian Labor Party Mátyás Rákosi, who called himself "Stalin's best Hungarian pupil," wrote to Mikhail Suslov, a member of the Presidium of the Supreme Soviet, detailing a series of critical observations that surprised him. Rákosi

Figure 4.8 Stigmatizing, deriding, and disgracing the enemies of socialism: a demonstration of Young Fighters for Peace during the Third Youth and Student World Games in East Berlin. August 12, 1951. *Source:* Bildarchiv im Bundesarchiv (Koblenz). Signature: Bild 183-11500-1414. Photographer: Martin Schmidt.

complained about an insufficient number of portraits of Lenin and Stalin in the congress's decorations. The inadequate dimensions of a large Party emblem depicting Marx, Engels, Lenin, and Stalin, which was only one square meter in size and "did not reflect the grandeur of the classics of Marxism-Leninism," was striking to him.[225] This example vividly demonstrates the extent to which the politics of symbolism and the ritual order of the cult community actually were a way to draw closer to Moscow and to struggle for the Center's trust.

Provincializing the Cult: Stalin's Birthday in Saxony

Let's look at a local example of Stalin's seventieth birthday to understand how regional identity was constructed and how the regions were situated in the nationwide and global contexts of the cult community. The Saxon Landtag (state parliament) approved a detailed program for the festivities

Figure 4.9 The subjection of public space to the Stalin cult: preparations for the Third Youth and Student World Games on the Alexanderplatz, East Berlin. July 1951. *Source:* Bildarchiv im Bundesarchiv (Koblenz). Signature: Bild 183-11433-0003. Photographer: Schmidtke.

on December 3, 1949. The height of the celebrations would be a "solemn meeting" like the one planned for Berlin, which was to be held in Dresden's Great House on December 20, 1949. A special speaker was invited, Hermann Matern, who was a member of the Central Secretariat of the SED executive. Electing an honorary presidium, collective singing of the GDR's national anthem, playing the Soviet anthem, congratulatory speeches, and politicians' speeches to the musical accompaniment of the Staatskapelle were all on the program. The grand finale would be the acceptance of the text of a telegram to Stalin that had been prepared beforehand:

> Along with millions of citizens of the USSR, along with millions of people around the world, the people of the province of Saxony are thinking about you today with heartfelt joy and a feeling of close unity with you. Our sincere and ardent wishes are for you, the great leader of the Soviet people, a fighter for the freedom of peoples and for socialism. The entire Saxon population's only desire is for you to continue to work for long years and in full bloom of strength for the good of all mankind.[226]

Figure 4.10   The dramaturgy of the Stalin cult: mourning Stalin's death with a funeral march in Leipzig. March 9, 1953. *Source:* Bildarchiv im Bundesarchiv (Koblenz). Signature: Bild 183-18688-0004. Photographer: Illner.

The open, unanimous acceptance of the congratulatory message to Stalin and the strategic planning about who should be invited to the meeting show how carefully and with what deliberation the regional elite organized the public sphere of the holiday. Nothing was left to chance, and all the participants were supposed to adhere to the rhetorical and behavioral norms of the "dictatorship of discourse." Thus, those given the "high honor" of being present at the meeting were representatives of the Landtag and the regional government, the mass organizations and the party, people who had won national prizes, heroes of labor, and activists. The procedure for distributing the tickets made it possible to compile lists of names, which gave the organizers a record of which professional groups and age cohorts were represented. Journalists and photographers were also invited to the event since the celebration of Stalin's birthday was supposed to be a carefully choreographed media event that would be reported in the local press and on the radio. Likewise, the minister-president of Saxony's administration tried hard to stage a society of consensus on the local and national levels and thereby show the public how the region was helping to confirm the GDR's membership in the cult community of the postwar Soviet empire.[227]

Young people had an important role to play in Saxony's painstaking preparations to celebrate Stalin's birthday. In October 1949, all of the province's educational institutions received a directive from the Ministry of National Education with a special plan enjoining them to carry out the appropriate celebrations.[228] At schools, lessons were canceled on December 21, but every pupil was required to take part in the afternoon festivities. Propagandists saw the holiday as a way to help children develop the "correct [*richtig*] ideas" about the Soviet leader, especially in his role as the "great friend of the German people and the preserver of peace throughout the world." It was especially important to include lessons about the leader's biography, his role in developing science and culture, and the Soviet Union's contribution to the social progress of mankind in the curriculum. Students were supposed to devote special attention to "the study of the multifaceted quotation from Stalin," which proclaimed that "the Hitlers come and go, but the German people, the German state remains."[229] A contest for compositions and drawings about the "best friend of the German people" was organized. The contest would be a window into how well children were assimilating the rhetoric and imagery of the Soviet leader. Schoolchildren were expected to reproduce official narratives about the positive experience of the German people when Red Army soldiers arrived on German territory. That is, East German propagandists expected children to express "children's love of the Soviet army" by showing how the Red Army helped people obtain food, repaired bridges, and rebuilt cities while ensuring peace around the world. The best compositions and drawings would be made into a special volume to be sent to the leader as a present from all the young people in Saxony.

The regional government used the practice of giving gifts to Stalin to introduce Saxony to the national and worldwide holiday marking the leader's seventieth birthday. Otto Buchwitz, the president of the Saxon Landtag, insisted that the Landtag adopt a resolution about how much money Saxony would contribute to the nation's gift to Stalin, the planetarium for Stalingrad. In addition, a volume of letters written by Thomas Müntzer, the leader of the 1525 German peasants' revolt, would be a special gift from the Saxons. This gift allowed them to incorporate traditions of regional memory into the gift-giving and establish a positive identification with Moscow. Despite some difficulties in getting the gift to Stalin, East German propagandists explained that it was "a sign of Stalin's farsighted policy, which acquainted the peasantry with the working class's revolutionary struggle and guaranteed the victory of socialism."[230] As this example shows, the political elite in Saxony tried to include the traditions of revolutionary struggle and popular protest in the official holiday culture while simultaneously integrating regional memory culture into the narrative and rituals of the Stalin cult.

As always, the press reported on innumerable rallies and meetings, which were described as evidence of the population's loyalty to the Soviet Union and the GDR government.[231] Every administrative building had to be decorated with flags and portraits of the "leader," and stores were supposed to put posters and books about Stalin in their shop windows.[232] Regional events showed much greater creativity and initiative than the corresponding ones in East Berlin. For example, in 1951 an employee of a library in Dresden collaborated with the photography workshop at the School of Vocational Education to prepare 225 slides of photographs and paintings with Stalin's image. These visual materials illustrated the life and accomplishments of the "leader." They were shown in libraries and schools to accompany a lecture titled "The Road of Life."[233] In December 1949, the initiative group of Dresden University's Faculty of Philosophy organized a conference on Stalin's intellectual contribution to the development of world science and invited Soviet experts to participate.[234]

Stalin's Death and Funeral: Mourning Ceremonies and Representations of Social Consensus

Medial homogenization of the ideological landscape and the synchronization of political life in the socialist bloc countries with Moscow were key endeavors driving the Sovietization of Eastern Europe. The use of the Stalin cult to create an imagined community was one of the most overarching projects in the realm of symbolic politics carried out to integrate the Periphery's disparate elements—ethnic groups, nationalities, and states—into a unified political body. Stalin's death in March 1953 was the high point in dramatizing the solidarity of the cult community, especially in the mass media. Radio broadcasts of the funeral rites from Moscow, the publication of photographs of the leader accompanied by bulletins about the state of his health (and later, the condolences that poured in from every corner of the empire), the pilgrimages to Stalin monuments, and the visits to Soviet embassies organized to express sympathy with the Soviet people all created an impression of total synchronicity between the Center and the Periphery. This was the sense of life in a single rhetorical, ritual, emotional, spatial, and temporal dimension. As a result, in the media the Stalin cult was presented as a binding force aspiring to generate uniformity and homogeneity across the Soviet bloc.

In East Germany, Stalin's death called forth a carefully choreographed scenario. The SED Politburo, which had two emergency meetings on March 6, 1951, was the chief producer of the propaganda spectacle of "state mourning." The Politburo discussed a telegram from the Soviet Central Committee bearing news of the leader's death and adopted the text of the telegram of condolence to be sent to the Soviet government.[235] Both texts and a message about the creation of a state commission to organize mourning for the "leader" were published in *Neues Deutschland*. A German delegation led by Ulbricht flew to Moscow to take part in the central event, the burial.[236] In

East Germany, a general plan for activities expressing grief was approved by the SED Politburo and reprinted in newspapers along with an appeal to the population to take an active part in ceremonies of bidding farewell to the "best friend."[237] This is how the propaganda state used the "leader's" death to reinforce a Stalinist public sphere within which individual and group identities were shaped and beliefs, emotions, and behavior were prescribed.

"State mourning" in the GDR went on from March 6, when Stalin's death was publicly announced, until March 11, 1953, when the official East German delegation returned from Moscow.[238] For six days, life did not run in its usual course. Entertainment of all kinds, including dances, movies, plays, and concerts were banned. Busts and portraits of Stalin were supposed to be put up at every workplace and square, placed in shop windows, and added to "red corners" dedicated to the "leader's" life.

In addition, orders came down that delegations from the regions should travel to the Soviet Embassy in Berlin, the regional offices of the Soviet Control Commission in Germany, and places where divisions of Soviet troops were deployed to "express condolences and show unity with the Soviet Union."[239] The Ministry of Internal Affairs gave instructions that all flags on state and public buildings should be lowered and wreaths should be laid on monuments and memorials to Soviet soldiers.[240] The columns of the mourning processions were to be decorated with red banners and the GDR flag. But creating a column adorned exclusively with portraits of Stalin and images of the classics of Marxism-Leninism received widespread approval. Marchers were instructed to maintain silence as they moved past party and state representatives standing on tribunes decorated with portraits of Stalin. The dramatic nature of the event had to be emphasized with somber music.[241]

At ten o'clock on the morning of March 9, 1953, the day Stalin was buried in Moscow, a siren sounded at industrial enterprises across the GDR. At that moment, factories, public transportation, and educational and administrative institutions were instructed to stop work and honor the memory of the Soviet leader with a "minute of silence." A red flag on the Brandenburg Gate was lowered as a sign of mourning. A "solemn meeting" of the SED Central Committee and the government of the GDR opened at the exact same time at the State Opera House in East Berlin. Members of the party and state establishment stood to honor Stalin's memory. The decorations on the stage—a portrait of the leader draped with red flags with black mourning ribbons—dramatized the nation's grief at the loss of the "best friend of the German people." A red armband with a black ribbon placed in the midst of all those present in the hall symbolized the feeling of collective sadness. After the meeting, a delegation of members of the Politburo and the SED Central Committee went to Treptower Park to lay wreaths at the monument to the Unknown Soviet Soldier.

The East German leadership staged a "crisis situation" and simultaneously offered a solution: under the guidance of the SED as the "leader's" successor, the country should continue the Stalinist course of building socialism. These kinds of "self-legitimation" tactics were evident in media reports. It was equally clear that the regime aspired to create a society where discipline, subordination, and uniformity prevailed. Stalin's death became the starting point for a propaganda campaign designed to educate the population ideologically and mobilize them in the regime's interests. The SED state also saw official mourning as a way to stage the utopian idea of a "society of consensus"—the harmonious coexistence of the state and society without any conflicts.[242] Stressing its urgency, a party report described the agitation work to be done among the masses to ensure "full participation" in this imagined society:

> 1) expand the campaign to nominate party members; 2) conduct an advertising campaign to popularize the People's Police; 3) create an advertisement for the German-Soviet Friendship Society; 4) encourage the introduction of Soviet methods of work in production; 5) develop socialist competitions.[243]

Various authorities asserted "the German people's solidarity with Soviet people" and reported about different kinds of active participation in official events.[244] For example, on the central squares in Dresden, Suhl, Chemnitz, Rostock, and Leipzig distinctive altars were set up. These were gigantic portraits of the "leader." An "honor guard" composed of representatives of the mass organizations, educational institutions, factories, and the People's Police stood by.[245]

East Berlin's Stalinallee was the main site where the media enacted mourning on a nationwide scale. This was by no means a randomly chosen site. In official discourse, this, the most important street in the GDR, represented the "construction of a new, peaceful life," the "rebirth of the economy and industry," and "the first successes in building socialism under Stalin's aegis." A monument to Stalin stood in the center of this street. The official mourning procession began there at midday on March 9. Delegations from all the *Länder* came to East Berlin to take part in it. A brigade of construction workers who had helped to build the Stalinallee led the procession. The men in the first row carried a portrait of the Soviet leader and people carrying a picture of the four classics of Marxism-Leninism followed directly behind. The press emphasized that divisions of the People's Police, women, children, workers, and old people were all part of the procession—in other words, people from every social class and all the generations.[246] The mass media presented the wreaths and bouquets laid at the Stalin monument, which came from every segment of society, including enterprises, the mass organizations, housing communities, and private individuals, as communicative acts expressing the people's love for and gratitude to the "best friend," but it also emphasized symbolic gestures, promises "to fulfill all the leader's behests with all [our] strength in the struggle for unification of the German capital, for German unity, and the wellbeing of the German nation."[247]

The regional centers of East Germany were actively involved in organizing and carrying out "state mourning." The long-drawn-out sound of a siren on March 6, 1953, informed people in the Bitterfeld region that Stalin had died.[248] On the same day, the leadership of the Guben administrative division called on all enterprises to stop work and prepare brief essays on the leader's life and his significance for the GDR's political development. Five minutes of silence were recommended for schools and other educational institutions.[249] In schools in Dessau, "honor guards" of Pioneers took up their positions near busts and portraits of the "friend."[250] At factories, schools, and administrative offices, mourning meetings took place. Speeches made by the leaders of the Soviet Union and the GDR were read out, either by factory directors or party secretaries. Workplaces everywhere were decorated with posters, slogans, and portraits of "leader." In Potsdam, a ceremony was held to unveil a plaque marking a building where the Soviet leader stayed during the Berlin Conference.[251]

In the GDR, "state mourning" for Stalin ended on March 11, 1953. On their return from Moscow, the GDR leadership, representatives of the SED, and the Soviet ambassador met the German delegation on the tarmac at Schönefeld airport. Once again, the media's presentation revealed this event as a "self-legitimation" tactic which the "second German state" was deploying to overcome the "crisis situation." The anthems of the GDR and the USSR, played by an orchestra composed of members of the German People's Police, underlined the significance of the "historical moment." According to the official press, the returning delegates were not ordinary leaders but "strong men" who embodied communist power's new energy in East Germany. They were represented as the heirs of Stalin's cause, filled with enthusiasm and resolutely continuing the "Stalinist course of building socialism" in East Germany.[252] Questions about what would happen and what should be done after the "leader's" death were reflected in work produced by the GDR's intellectual elite. In an essay titled "The Portrait of Hope" ("Das Abbild der Hoffnung"), the well-known writer Stephan Hermlin pointed out that

> Without Stalin we have to keep on living. Without him we will go forward, constantly asking ourselves, what would Stalin say about this? To the greatness we inherited belong his best pupils, that is, the leaders of East Germany. We are obligated to unite even more strongly around them.[253]

Propaganda legitimized the continuity of the Stalinist course in narratives recounting the masses' trust in the SED regime and affirming this trust as a precondition of national unity, pride, and well-being.[254]

All the state-sponsored media helped make Stalin's funeral in Moscow a major media event in East Germany. Radio audiences learned of Stalin's death early on the morning of March 6, 1953. With a portrait of Stalin placed next to the radio, people gathered around the radio to listen to mourning speeches by Soviet and East German leaders. Photos of the "leader" filled the pages of newspapers. Texts of condolence telegrams sent to Moscow were reprinted in the press.[255] Motifs of solidarity and synchronicity were displayed in photographs of the entire population—young and old, men, women, and children, members of mass organizations and the party, workers and intelligentsia—bidding farewell to Stalin.[256] Photomontages of masses walking past the Stalin monument in Berlin and the one in Leipzig presented grief as a collective trauma.[257] Images of individuals looking at the Stalin monument with tears in their eyes or streaming down their faces depicted grief as personal pain.[258] Media created representations of nationwide mourning that united East and West Germany. Newspapers reported about West Germans laying wreaths in the Tiergarten, which was in the British sector of Berlin.[259] The press also helped to construct the transnational character of the grieving by publishing condolence telegrams from France, Italy, Great Britain, the United States, Argentina, and China. Stalin's funeral was described hyperbolically as a worldwide event shared by "the entire peace-loving population of the planet": "When Marx died his loyal friends, his supporters, and a few progressive workers in Europe wept for him. When Lenin died, the Soviet people and workers of the party of peace wept. All of peace-loving mankind is mourning Stalin."[260]

Immediately after Stalin's death, two special newsreels produced by the DEFA film studio were distributed to East German movie theaters.[261] One film told the myth of the "leader" visually, presenting official images and narratives about Stalin's life path on his way to becoming the "most beloved human in the world." The other documented, and thus affirmed, the nation's sorrow during the period of "official mourning."[262] Television, which began regular broadcasting in the GDR on December 21, 1952—Stalin's seventy-third birthday—did not play a major role in the propaganda of the Stalin cult in East Germany. However, the news of Stalin's illness and death rippled through the entire broadcast network. As soon as the leader's illness was officially announced, *Aktuelle Kamera*, the main news program in the GDR, began regular reporting on the state of Stalin's health. Entertainment programs ceased to be shown and classic Soviet dramas were broadcast in their place.[263]

A year later, the day of the "leader's" death became an official event for remembrance in the East German calendar of political rituals, and a cult of commemoration was being constructed.[264] In terms of the state's symbolic politics, this memorial cult did several important things to preserve the Eastern bloc's political cohesion.[265] It kept alive the message that the population had a moral obligation to continue Stalin's course of building socialism in the "second German state" and wholeheartedly support the SED. It also mobilized people and reinforced social expectations which Stalin had promised to fulfill. By shoring up the dead "leader's" "political immortality," the memory cult became a key component of East German national memory. The SED Politburo worked out the scenario for the first time that Stalin's death would be commemorated, at a meeting on February 19, 1954. There were plans to publish articles and photographs; and public lectures, conferences, and meetings at every party and administrative level were to be organized.[266] A list of printed materials recommended for propaganda of the Stalin myth was drawn up.[267] There were calls to perpetuate Stalin's memory by putting up monuments and busts of the "best friend," naming streets and cities after him, and immortalizing him on posters and in other kinds of visual art. The response *from below* was affirmative and eager. Thus, just before the one-year anniversary of the "leader's" death, a four-meter high bronze statue of Stalin was unveiled on Alexander Pushkin Square in Riesa, paid for by contributions from the population.[268] The central council of the German-Soviet Friendship Society adopted a resolution to put up monuments to the Soviet leader in each of the GDR's fourteen regional centers.[269] According to one report, not long after that, monuments and busts of Stalin were put up in Bad Doberan, Gera, Freiberg, Weimar, and Hettstedt.[270]

And there was an announcement on August 3, 1955, that the Babelsberg villa where the "leader" stayed during the Potsdam Conference would be designated a site of national memory and listed as "Stalin House" in the register of Germany's most important landmarks.[271] Thus, after March 5, 1953, the Stalin cult lived on in the GDR. Despite his physical death, the "leader's" political life continued. But while the Periphery was sticking to the policy of the Stalin cult to preserve the existing political order, Moscow was distancing itself ever more resolutely from manifestations of the personality cult as the power struggle in the Kremlin escalated.[272]

"THE 'ENEMIES OF THE PEOPLE' ARE THE ENEMIES OF STALIN": VIGILANCE IN UNCERTAIN TIMES

"Enemy of the people" was a basic ideological concept in Stalinist civilization and one of the central categories used, not least after uprising of June 17, 1953, to criminalize oppositional individuals or groups. In Stalinist Russia, this formulation legitimized the destruction of the opposition, which is why,

at the so-called Thaw Party Congress in 1956, Nikita S. Khrushchev emphasized the political dimension of the imagined enemy:

> This term immediately freed you from the need to argue that the opinion of the
> person you are discussing with is incorrect. This term opened up the possibility
> of taking harsh action to suppress those who were against Stalin or those who
> were simply slandered. In order to justify the physical extermination of such
> people, the formula "enemy of the people" was inserted.[273]

As Sovietization unfolded, the Soviet Union exported the image of the
internal enemy to East Germany. From the time the GDR was founded, ubiquitous "enemies of the people" were a constant presence in the propaganda
of the "workers' and peasants' state" (Figure 4.11).

Biological imagery was a prominent feature of the language of both Nazi
racial ideology and socialist propaganda in the GDR, where an "enemy"
was compared to an active pathogen and a bacillus in the healthy body of
the state which threatened to cause considerable harm to the "newborn GDR
baby."[274] Party and state authorities therefore took on the role of rescuers,
skilled physicians who declared themselves responsible for this pure and
innocent infant. The party was the antidote to the enemy's creeping poison.
It could heal and rehabilitate the afflicted body of the nation and was vigilant
in taking "precautionary measures" against all hidden enemies. Agitators
and propagandists used these and similar canonical images to justify the
harsh measures deployed by the regime for its pervasive disciplining and
mobilizing of East German subjects. Under attack, the GDR had to defend
itself. Propaganda presented the fight against "enemies" as an indispensable
act of self-preservation: the ideology of the "inner enemy" paved the way
for manifold political, propagandistic initiatives but it was also used for
practical administrative purposes. The imperative to defend against enemy
assaults not only legitimized the establishment of the national armed forces
and the People's Police but also spurred the SED's transformation into a
"new type of party."[275] The principle that "an ounce of prevention is worth a
pound of cure" was put into practice, and the struggle against the "enemies
of the people" became the linchpin of "workers' and peasants' power."[276]
As a result, party and state organs, namely the party, the People's Police,
the State Security Service, and the judiciary, instrumentalized images of the
"enemy."

Stalin's death on March 5, 1953, created uncertainty, and this threatening
situation demanded vigilance. Bereft of the "leader" as the highest authority,
the wise "oracle in the Kremlin," the GDR leadership and the population
alike feared a new war and were acutely aware that they were facing an

Figure 4.11 GDR poster: "Workers! Be vigilant, seize your enemies!" April 1949.
Source: Bildarchiv im Bundesarchiv (Koblenz). Signature: Plak 100-024-023. Artist: Helmut Seifert.

unpredictable future.[277] The party's district bosses also reported on a growing sense of insecurity as a result of "the enemy's extensive and varied work" in response to the government's New Course.[278] To keep things under control, the party began an offensive against the "consistent and dangerous enemy of the German Democratic Republic" in cooperation with the police, the state security organs, and the judiciary.[279] With Order 16/53, the People's Police became involved in this campaign:

> There is no doubt that after the death of Comrade Stalin, the reactionary forces will try to create unrest and confusion through increased agitation, provocations, espionage and sabotage of all kinds, thereby shattering confidence in the invincible power of the camp of peace and the successful construction of the foundations of socialism in the GDR.[280]

Across the country in 1953, the security organs helped develop strategies for combatting the enemy on the spot and "the appropriate measures were discussed and initiated with the security services."[281] At the same time, various meetings under the rubric of "strengthening vigilance and security measures against the attacks of the enemies of the people" were held in the mass organizations and educational institutions.[282] The call for extreme vigilance and iron discipline demanded that employees of the security organs expose, arrest, and bring the alleged "enemies" to judgment. And all "conscious citizens" were required to maintain the highest level of vigilance. Anyone who did not take part in the state-sponsored program of struggle with "dangerous elements" was in constant danger of being declared an "enemy" himself or herself. This was made unmistakably clear, not least by the chief of the German People's Police when he ordered that "Every case of carelessness and indifference towards criminal acts and attacks by class enemies must be personally examined."[283] Naturally, the unofficial agents of the Stasi were also mobilized to guarantee the success of the ongoing action through denunciations.[284]

Numerous Stasi documents give detailed insight into how the image of the "enemy" circulating in the state apparatus operated and they shed light on the effect of this image on administrative routines. Each official proceeding against a defendant had a "political part." This is where the Zhdanovian theory of two "world camps," the "new democratic state's" great need for German-Soviet friendship, and Stalin's significance for Germany and the German people were usually set out. Placed in such a scientifically irrefutable context, every reason for the arrests seemed legitimate. The investigations and repressions were all aimed at protecting the foundations of the socialist state and social system. This was clearly the most important part of the documents: without this ideological justification, the harsh sentences would have been in vain. As a result, the majority of the delinquents were sentenced "in the name of the people," even though the court hearings were not public trials.[285]

According to the investigative documents, there were hardly any individual perpetrators. Instead, the "enemy" was exposed as a collective criminal whose actions were organized, directed, and controlled by far more dangerous powers in the West. The convictions usually followed certain pattern: those who were arrested were accused of "having carried out inflammatory work against the GDR and fascist propaganda and thus endangered the peace of the German people."[286] Their main aim was to "create confusion and insecurity and in that way to interfere with initiatives to build socialism."[287] The "enemies'" approach was explained in detail in the highly formalized trials. They started by spreading rumors, repeating arguments hostile to the regime, sending out inflammatory letters or distributing leaflets, and damaging "peace corners" and the leaders' portraits. "Hostile activities" included tearing down a flag "in a fascist manner," making "inflammatory statements," "ripping up pictures of Stalin," destroying busts of him, and damaging telephone and power lines. Most "enemy" activity took place in factories and pubs, but some of the abovementioned acts were also carried out at schools and other institutions. Other enemy actions were closer to deeds of omission. For example, in the Anton S. Makarenko Primary School in Halle, a teacher ignored the "passing of Comrade Stalin" and made the class sing funny songs; not even the objections of a particularly politically conscious pupil could stop her. In Wolgast, six young people were imprisoned because they had organized a dance party the day after Stalin's death. In Leipzig, high school students made derisive remarks as they marched past the tribune filled with party and state representatives. In Wismar, the funeral procession was pelted with rotten apples.[288] Whoever had "unpleasant discussions" during those March days could be turned into the "enemy" at the drop of a hat. These and other acts were quickly judged to be "crimes against the socialist order" and were severely punished. The defendant usually admitted his or her guilt at the end of an interrogation lasting several hours, often an entire night.[289]

In order to personalize and remove "hidden enemies" from the community, the criminal justice system was put at the party's service. The ultimate aim of party and legal disciplinary measures was not merely to punish but also to contribute to the accused's personal development by changing his/her ideological views. These measures were intended to motivate the defendant to undergo a political conversion from being an "enemy" to becoming a "useful member" of socialist society.[290] Such a conversion could take a long time and, in the meantime, society had to be protected. Therefore, it was necessary to "isolate the respective accused person from human society for an appropriate period of time until the foundations of socialism in the GDR were consolidated and he could no longer cause damage to the new social order by his attitude."[291] In addition to imprisonment, exclusion from the socialist community included "atonement measures" which deprived the accused of his/her civil rights:

1. He shall hold no public office, including notary and barrister.
2. He loses all legal rights to a pension or allowance payable from public funds.
3. He loses the right to vote and to stand for election, the right to engage in any political activity or to be a member of a political party.
4. He is forbidden to work as a teacher, preacher, editor, writer, or radio commentator for a period of five years after the end of his sentence.
5. He is subject to housing and residency restrictions.[292]

Who was this imaginary "enemy within"? Who were the people behind this label? What were the enemy's distinctive features? State security documents show that invariably, under the rubric of "enemy" there were people in very concrete situations. The enemy's key attributes were projected onto them almost automatically. The ideal "enemy" was often identified as the offspring of the "bourgeois classes," and there was an emphasis on his background as a member of a long-established, prosperous family of landholders, which meant that he advocated "Prussian militarism." After completing his schooling and vocational training, he voluntarily joined the Wehrmacht and soon distinguished himself by his bravery. Even before 1941, the Hitler state promulgated hostile attitudes toward the Soviet Union. In the postwar period and later, as a citizen of the GDR, the potential "enemy" proved not to be a "new man in a new life" but remained demonstratively inactive. He avoided political training, and the classical works of Marxism-Leninism remained unknown to him. He was only a passive member of one of the mass organizations, if he joined at all; he did not want to develop a socialist consciousness and participate in the socialist way of life. He also maintained numerous connections to the West, receiving letters and parcels from abroad. In addition, his "poor attitude" was frequently reflected in an immoral lifestyle marked by excessive alcohol consumption or unstable relationships with female partners. Such an "enemy" spread RIAS's lies, prepared "boycott rushes," and made "propaganda for fascism."

Was there a real chance for an "enemy" to return to socialist society as a normal citizen? A typical answer to this question from the criminal records is ambiguous:

> It will be up to the accused himself whether he has to serve this punishment in full or whether he will prove in prison that he honestly regrets his actions and shows through good work that he is worthy to be accepted into society again.[293]

While exclusion from society followed clearly defined criteria, paths to possible rehabilitation and re-inclusion usually remained obscure. Therefore, a citizen was marked as an "enemy of the people" for his/her whole life, and until 1989, the GDR anthem promised that "When we unite as brothers, we strike the enemy of the people!" (*Wenn wir brüderlich uns einen, schlagen wir des Volkes Feind!*)

LIFE AND WORK STALINIST-STYLE: THE STALINALLEE AND STALINSTADT

An important element of the making of the Stalin cult in the GDR was the regime's efforts to stage a shared understanding of socialist modernity. This was closely connected with the ways in which the ideas about the "right" lifestyle for the "new man" were turned into lived experience. Propaganda represented the "new man" as an idealized bearer of socialist consciousness and morality—and a faithful follower of the Stalin cult. The "new man's" key characteristics were his/her political loyalty and publicly displayed devotion to the regime, which was the central source of the SED dictatorship's legitimation. In return for their trust in the regime, the state and the party gave a chosen circle of people access to a set of benefits and privileges which were not available to the population as a whole. These individuals were given the ideological mission of living and working in a socialist way and they received the corresponding advantages: they could enjoy living in new buildings on the Stalinallee, having a rest in special sanatoriums and going to specialized polyclinics, making purchases in exclusive shops, or working at a metallurgical plant named after the Soviet leader in the eponymous city, Stalinstadt. By inviting people to join the project of building socialism in one city or on one street, the regime attempted to politicize the spaces of daily life: home and family, working and leisure time, gender relationships and consumption, which were the most difficult realms for the state and party to control. In the GDR, precisely these spaces of everyday life became targets for ideological interventions and a terrain for social engineering. This shows how closely linked the political and the sphere of day-to-day routines were in the drive to produce everyday legitimacy for communist rule in East Germany.

Scholars of the history of propaganda in totalitarian regimes agree that advertising strategies paved the way for popular acceptance of modern dictatorships.[294] In her study of the Hitler cult, Sabine Behrenbeck describes how the "Führer" became a brand that stood for the style and quality of life under national socialism.[295] Similar marketing strategies were used to establish the Stalin cult in the GDR. Propaganda created representations of the ideal living space on the Stalinallee and in Stalinstadt, locations which signified progress and success, happiness and confidence in future postwar renewal and increasing material prosperity, all connected with building socialism. In this material microcosm, Stalin was presented as a new brand and the guarantor of the *socialist way of life*. The figure of the "leader" was used to advertise the idea of socialism, which was packaged as a narrative, an image, and a feeling about building the future in East Germany. Thus, as imaginations of the "vozhd'" penetrated the structures of daily life, the Stalin cult politicized both private and public spaces in the life of the individual.

The mediatization of the dictatorship's public sphere was essential in making Stalin's figure the sacral center of society.[296] On one hand, the capacity to systematically transmit official representations over the radio and through the press, television, and posters—in other words, to communicate in ways that reached the entire population more or less at the same time—made it easier to automatically subordinate, discipline, and ideologically indoctrinate the population. The representations of the regime thus instructed people to immerse themselves in the socialist order, which consisted of a set of norms and rules, emotions, and taboos. By observing these, they were given a chance to access exclusive resources for organizing daily life without deficits, violence, and fear. On the other hand, the narratives and images of success, prosperity, and a happy future replicated in the media were the regime's proposal to society: support the SED regime, accept Stalin as the "best friend," participate in building socialism, and then, as a reward, you will receive the honored title of "new man" and, as a consequence, the necessary resources for living socialism as a way of life.

The large-scale mobilization of the population to take part in the "great construction projects of socialism" showed that a symbolic pact could be effective, at least to some extent. By promising to quickly resolve such pressing postwar problems as insufficient housing, unemployment, a shortage of goods, and the absence of municipal services, the propaganda state appealed to a significant part of the population. Representations of the regime also took into account what society expected after the destructive war: a peaceful life, one's own hearth and home, and the feeling that the course of daily life was predictable and reliable. Consequently, propaganda presented Stalin as the guarantor that these promises would be fulfilled. The Soviet dictator's image was also connected with access to an elegant, and even luxurious, life. Thus, the Soviet automobile industry's latest models were exhibited in a pavilion at the Leipzig Fair in 1950 under gigantic bas-reliefs of the Soviet leader's profile. A journalist from the Western magazine *Der Spiegel* noted with surprise that Soviet automobiles were very similar to American Packards, Chevrolets, and Oldsmobiles, and observed that the Soviet cars reminded him more of the capitalist way of life than socialist realities.[297]

The first step in integrating the Stalin cult into the structures of daily life was building the Stalinallee, which was presented in official media as the "first socialist street in Germany." In honor of the leader's seventieth birthday, on December 21, 1949, the East Berlin city council adopted a resolution to give the Frankfurter Allee the Soviet leader's name. Renaming the street was symbolically very significant for several reasons. In official narratives, Soviet soldiers entered Berlin on this very avenue to free the German people from Nazism. Constructing Stalin's street was a constituent element of both the National Program for the Restoration of Berlin and the first five-year economic plan in the GDR, which was supposed to solve the acute housing problem and generally raise the population's standard of living.[298] The Stalinallee was also inserted into Cold War discourse: restoring the bombed-out street under the rubric of building socialism contrasted with narratives about the American bombardment of Germany in the final months of the war. All of these prescribed meanings represented the Stalinallee as a central symbol of East German identity and built up a key narrative of national renewal under Stalin's supervision. This meaning-laden site demonstrated the move from German aggression and expansionism to peaceful postwar construction under the Soviet Union's guidance and highlighted the transition from total defeat to the nation's political and economic rebirth. Of equal importance, by celebrating socialism's superiority to capitalism, the Stalinallee was a manifestation of the Cold War competition of two diametrically opposed systems.

After the GDR was established, East German propaganda began active media support of postwar reconstruction on the Stalinallee by creating representations of socialism as a way of life. On January 18, 1952, a film called *Story of a Young Couple* (*Roman einer jungen Ehe*) opened in East Berlin. It was a love story but also a manifesto about building a socialist life on the "first socialist street" in East Germany.[299] Directed by Kurt Maetzig, the film is the story of Agnes (Yvonne Merin) and Jochen (Hans-Peter Thielen), a recently married couple who struggle when the Cold War and the division of Germany into two parts intrude on their love for each other. Agnes is an actress in East Berlin. Jochen is also an actor but he performs in West Berlin. Under the pressure of the Cold War divide, they are forced to divorce because of their increasing ideological differences. However, Jochen soon loses his job and his friends in the "pitiless" world of capitalism fade away, and he starts to rethink his attitude toward socialism. When they meet at the divorce court, love wins out: they reconcile and move to East Berlin to an apartment on the Stalinallee. The film uses Agnes's and Jochen's lives to present the victory of socialism over capitalism as the triumph of "good" over "evil." It established a new gender order that was very different from the one enshrined in the Third Reich and also contrasted with the gender order prevailing in the "capitalist West." Since German men were more likely to be implicated in the Nazi past, women in the GDR were given an active political role. According to socialist propaganda, communist ideology was transmitted by emancipated women who were growing increasingly politically aware, but men were politically weak and ideologically vulnerable, hence tending to betray and deceive. The gender-specific binaries constructed in postwar East German society consisted of a number of negative traits gendered male which were the opposites of positive qualities which were gendered female. The film's audiences saw male backwardness versus female progress; male passivity versus female consciousness; and male ideological weakness versus female loyalty to the SED state.

In the film's closing scene, Agnes reads a "solemn ode" in honor of Stalin at the *Richtfest* (the roof-raising ceremony), the traditional German celebration marking the placement of the beam that completes the construction of a

new house or other building. The day after the premier, the virtual became
real: the film's final scene was reproduced with almost uncanny precision
during the *Richtfest* on Weberwiese, the street adjacent to the Stalinallee. As
Agnes, Yvonne Merin recited lines from the poem "Stalinallee," written by
KuBa (the pseudonym of writer and politician Kurt Barthel) for the Soviet
leader's seventieth birthday:

> On this street peace came to the city / The city was dust / We were dust and bro-
> ken pieces / And dead tired. / But tell me, how should one die? / Stalin himself
> took us by the hand / And bid us / Proudly raise our heads /And as we cleared
> away the rubble and made our plans / Greensward and housing blocks contrived
> / We became the victors / And the city began to live. / Straight to Stalin runs
> the road along which the friends came. / Never in these windows new and shiny
> may the fire blaze! / Tell me, how should we thank Stalin? / We gave this street
> his name.[300]

After Merin read the final words, "Stalin, Friend, Comrade," a hymn honoring
the Soviet leader rang out.[301] Like the celebration in the film, the Soviet leader
took center stage at the celebration held in honor of the completion of the first
apartment buildings on Weberwiese. The newly constructed buildings were not
only described as "proof of Stalin's peace-loving policy" but were also called an
expression of East German trust in the leader and gratitude to him. These buildings were a visible example of the first successes in building socialism Stalinist
style in East Germany with Stalin's patronage (Figure 4.12).[302]

A few weeks later, the East German mass media once again focused on the
Stalinallee. On February 3, 1952, the foundation for another apartment block
was laid. This action had great symbolic significance for Berlin's postwar
reconstruction. February 3 was the seventh anniversary of the Americans'
devastating bombing of the city. As Friedrich Ebert, the mayor of Berlin,
stood by, Otto Grotewohl put down a copper suitcase filled with propagandistic materials as the symbolic foundation stone of the building on Weberwiese.
The contents of the suitcase included the text of "A National Program of
Restoration," newspaper articles, architectural plans, deeds, and banknotes.[303]
At the end of the ceremony, the prime minister of the GDR made the traditional toast in honor of the completion of the building and struck the foundation stone three times with a hammer to celebrate the bedding of the last
brick. The first blow was for "the peace-loving German people's friendship
with the peoples of the Soviet Union," the second "for the restoration of
Germany's capital, Berlin, and a happy future for its inhabitants," and the
third was for the "unity of Germany in freedom and peace."[304]

The first *Richtfest* on the Stalinallee itself took place on June 12, 1952. The
completion of the new apartment block was timed to coincide with the SED's

Figure 4.12 *Richtfest* at the new high-rise building on Weberwiese. January 19, 1952. *Source:* Bildarchiv im Bundesarchiv (Koblenz). Signature: Bild 183-13318-0008. Photographer: Schack.

Second Party Conference, which announced the policy of building socialism in East Germany. Headed by Ulbricht, a delegation from the conference went directly to the celebration, which was being held on the street. The culmination of the ceremony was the raising of a celebratory wreath over the roof of the new building on whose facade a gigantic image of Stalin hung. Radio reports informed listeners that the celebration ended with "happy people" enjoying beer and singing and dancing.[305] The *Richtfest* reflected the integration of socialist symbols into folk traditions—and the way these traditions were politicized during the ongoing process of Sovietization. The newly finished building showcased the regime's resources for stabilizing daily life and mobilizing the population to meet the state's goals: all of German society, and indeed the entire world, could see how successful the government of the GDR was and could sense its potential for creating an impressive new civilization that would surpass what had gone before. More than eighty meetings and demonstrations took place on the Stalinallee in 1954, a clear sign that this street had been transformed into the central political space of the capital and the country as a whole.[306]

On December 21, 1952, during a meeting at the State Opera House in East Berlin, the mayor announced that 1,148 apartments would be transferred into "the hands of deserving activists," "deserving inventors," "leading workers of production," members of the brigades of "heroes of labor," "laureates of the national prize," and "deserving people's teachers." Six hundred and seventy-seven workers, 322 white-collar employees, and 149 representatives of the intelligentsia were among the fortunate ones.[307] These figures show that only a small group of carefully vetted people gained access to the high living standards befitting the "new man." They were handpicked to advertise socialism as the way to individual happiness but a path that was inseparable from social usefulness and service to the state and party. Media representations of how they lived, socialist-style, sent the masses a clear ideological message: this is how people who show loyalty and devotion to the SED regime will soon be living.

On January 7, 1953, the first tenants of the apartments on the Stalinallee entered the newly constructed, modern buildings. "The most beautiful homes in Germany," as the newspapers and radio put it, were equipped with elevators, central heating, modern plumbing, hot and cold water, bathrooms, and kitchens with gas stoves and refuse chutes.[308] These high-rise buildings had rooftop gardens where the residents could relax, read the newspaper, or just sit, soaking in the sunshine. Along with spacious apartments, the housing complex on the Stalinallee was equipped with infrastructure that made domestic life something most of the population could only dream about: laundry rooms, state and private shops, a library and a kindergarten, playing fields, and playgrounds for children.[309] In short, the Stalinallee was "prosperity's visiting card." The mass media reported on "streets filled with people who made purchases in the stores."[310]

A radio report from the Stalinallee that aired on May 5, 1952 described a genuine "oasis of plenty in the midst of shortages."[311] A fortunate woman who lived on "Germany's first socialist street" boasted about the impressive selection of products on sale: shoppers could patronize state stores such as flower kiosks, milk bars, and stores selling vegetables and fruit, meat, fish, cheese, and other dairy foods while tobacco stores, liquor stores, and delicatessens were among the private cooperatives. Photojournalism about the Stalinallee gives the impression that in this ideal space for life socialist-style everything had been thought out, down to the smallest details. Store windows with neon signs and smiling salesclerks behind the counters offered customers a wide assortment of goods, from Brazilian cigars for adults to every imaginable kind of candy for children.[312] "Everything the heart desires" was available in new stores designed to display an exemplary socialist "culture of trade and consumption."[313]

The Stalinallee was supposed to showcase socialism for visitors from the FRG, surprising them and making them envy the GDR's political achievements. The dreams of millions of Germans—a private home and a happy family life, stores with full shelves, and a satisfying supper—came true in the photographs on the pages of illustrated magazines and in radio broadcasts from "Germany's first socialist street." After a tiring night shift, an activist said, "Now I'm going to sleep as if I were in seventh heaven and [so] work makes me doubly happy. The very best thing I earn from my work is the fact that I can live on a street named after Stalin."[314] Photographs of the housing complex showing every convenience were complemented by shots of cozy living conditions and smiling children, images which contrasted sharply with the photographs of ruined buildings in West Berlin placed alongside them.[315] Faced with the ubiquitous postwar shortages of housing and basic necessities, Germans from East and West Germany alike were impressed with how comfortable, even luxurious, the new homes on the Stalinallee were.

Constructing the Stalinallee was not just an aesthetic propaganda project. It was above all a way to mobilize and attract East Germans to the project of building socialism.[316] "We are talking about the creation of an entire people," Otto Grotewohl said when he laid the foundation stone for another building on the Stalinallee in February 1952.[317] These words reflected the state's desire to stage a potent image of social consensus and, at the same time, they were an appeal intended to mobilize the entire population for political goals. On the Stalinallee, propaganda represented the new collective feeling of "we" that the entire nation experienced as collective pride and happiness about the nation's postwar rebirth on the street named after the Soviet leader. Buying tickets in the lottery set up to fund national regeneration, visiting the building sites as a leisure-time activity, doing voluntary construction work, and taking regular deductions from one's pay to help fund the construction were all ways that people participated in the nationwide and statewide project of building a new social order.[318] Propaganda presented the chance to live on the Stalinallee—in other words, being able to live socialist-style—as the citizen's biggest reward for supporting the project of socially transforming the country into the "better Germany." "The day is coming," propaganda proclaimed,

> When everyone in our republic will live in homes like these! . . . The homes we are building are one of the foundations of socialism. With each stone [we add] we are strengthening love for our republic, pride in being its citizens, readiness to defend our homeland.[319]

Stalinstadt was another vivid example of how socialism emerged as a way of life. Magnitogorsk in the USSR was the model for Stalinstadt and other exemplary cities in the "people's democracies" like Nowa Huta in Poland and Sztálinváros in Hungary.[320] The giant steel towns in East Germany,

Poland, and Hungary were microcosms of "Stalinist civilization," declaring the triumph of industrialization and technological progress, and trumpeting the fact that individuals could attain happiness as part of a collective social body. They were "new cities" for "new men," places where gender hierarchies were reconsidered, and material well-being was redefined. Stalinstadt created an alternative—socialist—modernity. It was imagined as a "socialist island" where landscapes could be reshaped, society remolded, and beliefs, values, and behavior could be reprogrammed on an individual level. In short, its designers envisioned it as a site where a new, meticulously planned type of human society could be brought to fruition.

At the SED's Third Congress of July 20–24, 1950, a resolution was approved to build a metallurgical plant near the historic town of Fürstenberg am Oder and a new town on the German-Polish border. Soon after, on August 18, 1950, Fritz Selbstmann, the minister of industrial development, laid the foundation stone for the Eisenhüttenkombinat steelworks. These political decisions laid the foundations for organizing a modern living space that could boast high living standards and would enjoy public representations of technological progress. The planners also envisioned that the new city would have the power to generate feelings of shared happiness because it would offer every inhabitant many different possibilities for fulfilling his/her potential as a "socialist personality." The next step was the SED Central Committee's March 17, 1953 resolution to rename Fürstenberg (Oder) as Stalinstadt and give the metallurgical combine Stalin's name. The renaming ceremony took place on May 7, 1953 the day before the Day of Liberation.[321] Propaganda created colorful images of the "first socialist city in Germany," a municipality that was supposed to demonstrate the successful, concrete results of the policy of putting socialism into practice.[322] A radio broadcast described how the city would be organized:

> The town hall, the House of the Mass Organizations, and the Palace of Culture will make up the city center. Housing complexes which will be residences for five to six thousand people will radiate out from the center. To enhance cultural life, a stadium, a swimming pool, and a stage will be built in the summer park. These will be a cultural center for the whole city. An ultra-modern, six-hundred-bed hospital with cutting-edge equipment will be built in the leafy park. To create the most favorable living conditions for workers, laundries, bakeries, and a meat-processing plant will be built.[323]

"A new city for a new man" was the leitmotif of the construction and propaganda of the town named after the Soviet leader. The high salaries workers at the J. W. Stalin Metallurgical Combine earned and their low living costs were staples of radio reports. Photographs published in the popular magazine *Neue Berliner Illustrierte* showed that the dreams of millions of East

Germans were a reality. The first photographs were visual propaganda narratives that let readers see the new school, the new apartments, and the new stores being built in honor of Stalin's birthday on December 21, 1953. The nationwide propaganda of Stalinstadt was addressed to society as a whole, and the regime expected to hear supportive statements from most Germans echoing the sentiments of one of the city's residents: "I am proud and happy to be able live and work in the city with Stalin's name."[324] In fact, the population of the city grew rapidly from 2,400 residents in 1952 to 15,150 in 1955. Job creation, along with the high living standards guaranteed, triggered labor migration. In addition, a significant number of unemployed refugees from what had been East Prussia were already living in the city. After the factory was constructed, they had opportunities for employment and housing, but most importantly, they regained a previously lost homeland and affirmative meanings of their lives.

At the same time, representations in the media taught the public what the standards of socialist life were, instilled a sense of what socialist aesthetics, taste, and design were like, and introduced the socialist culture of consumption and recreational activities.[325] The upper echelon of GDR officials monitored efforts to create a socialist way of life. After visiting the city's first residential buildings in January 1952, Ulbricht was disappointed with defects in planning the apartments, demanding that they be constructed with higher-quality building materials and have more space. In the same year, Prime Minister Grotewohl was shocked by the apartments' "primitive furnishings," which looked like leftovers from peasant cottages. He ordered that the citizens should learn about modern design to improve the appearance of their new living space. New people, he said, had to get rid of old habits and acquire the necessary skills for organizing urban—modern—life. There were also calls to improve the supply of products and goods to the city. After meeting with the workers at the steelworks, on August 16, 1952, Minister of Trade Kurt Gregor wrote an angry letter to the city administration, informing them that the population was complaining about the poor supply of vegetables, fruits, and other goods. To address this situation, it was decided to hold regular fairs (*Einkaufsmessen*) and to allocate 740 bicycles, 5,000 buckets, 2,400 pairs of shoes, and 10,000 sets of bed linen to the residents. According to the regime, in order to banish discontent from socialist daily life, the "new man" had to be fed, satisfied, and happy. Therefore, as a representative object of propaganda for socialist construction in the GDR (but also in the international arena) Stalinstadt had a special status. It received more and better supplies than those available to most East Germans.[326]

For women, living and working in the first "socialist city" promised gender equality, emancipation, and spaces for self-realization. With its opportunities for women to engage in (self-)fashioning as a new kind of wife, worker, and

comrade, Stalinstadt offered its female inhabitants liberation from the constraints of the patriarchal family and integration into a masculinized working
environment, in short, life as modern citizens. The new roles for women met
the actual needs of the labor force and the ideological mission of state- and
nation-building and an opening to participate in the postwar Soviet imperial
project.[327] In contrast to Nazi propaganda, which depicted women predomi-
nantly as housewives and mothers who were economically dependent on the
family patriarch, the socialist project promoted an image of women who were
emancipated, economically independent, socially engaged, and politically
aware.[328]

Needless to say, the postwar society sought the normalization of family
life, and propaganda promoted images of the happy nuclear families most
people desired. In a radio report broadcast from a young family's kitchen, the
husband and wife discussed the city's ideal living conditions, which made it
possible to harmoniously combine work and childrearing.[329] The journalist
spoke with the couple while the husband prepared a dinner of filets of fish
with fried potatoes for his wife, who had just come home from her morning work shift at the metallurgical combine. They proudly explained that
while their two daughters were at kindergarten they helped each other do the
housework and they praised the factory's flexible system of work shifts. This
was how women were able to combine the officially promoted female roles
of mother, worker, and party member. The young couple also spoke about
the low rent they paid for their apartment, thirty-six marks, which included
all the utilities. Reportage like this let the nation see, hear, smell, and feel
ideology's living presence in the most intimate sphere of modern life—the
nuclear family. Images of the welfare and the material and emotional support
the state provided for socialist women and the happy family life which this
assistance gave them were distributed across the country. But the truth behind
this propagandistic facade was that husbands and wives often lived separately
in barracks. And they did not always live happily ever after: domestic violence against women and children might be excluded from any given account.
Although poorly documented in the sources, there is reason to believe that
abuse in the family was not infrequently fueled by the experience of forced
removal from Eastern Europe and traumatic disorders among men.

The myth of the Soviet leader was so attractive to postwar East German
society because it offered its consumers ready-made scenarios of belonging, well-being, and self-realization. The media created the story of a young
worker who was supposed to be a role model for various kinds of GDR citizens, including many male German refugees from Eastern Europe. The tale of
a young worker named Klaus Kleinert, the hero of an article in the *Sächsische
Zeitung*, shows how ideology and the individual merged. He was supposed to
be a role model who would inspire youth to help build socialism and attract

new workers to the city. By joining the FDJ, he heard about opportunities to get an education, learned how to become ideologically enlightened, and was able to perform patriotic service for his new homeland, the GDR. Being active in the mass organization was the decisive factor in his efforts to go to the university and upgrade his professional qualifications, while the promise of a monthly student stipend was the material stimulus for turning himself into a "new man" with no connections to the recent Nazi past. At this point in telling Kleinert's story, the negative national-socialist past was mentioned briefly, as a time when workers' children had no access to higher education and political enlightenment.

Right after the war, independent study of texts written by the classics of Marxism-Leninism and regular attendance at the party school guaranteed Klaus Kleinert's success and was a down payment on career advancement:

> We are studying Stalin's writings and we draw new strength from them for our work and struggle. Thanks to a friend like Stalin, whom we trust completely, victory in the struggle for the unity of our homeland can be considered certain.[330]

The short newspaper article ended with an explicit call to the reader to choose this young man's strategy for improving his life by himself:

> Today thousands of workers' children can live the same way. Today they are looking with trust and love at Stalin and the Soviet army, both of which helped open the doors of the universities to them. They are looking with complete trust at the best friend of German youth, whose teaching will help us to preserve and protect the peace.[331]

The city and the Eisenhüttenkombinat needed newcomers. They were invited to start life on a "clean page," regardless of their past or national or racial origin. Indeed, the new city seemed like an ideal place to make a new career, new friends, a new family—in short, to build a new identity.

The myth of the leader was also used to draw in people from different generations and a wide range of social strata. Stalin's official image promised something for everyone: athletes would achieve their personal bests; women would have equal rights, a peaceful childhood for their children, and social help from the state; young people would have opportunities for education and fulfilling careers; and activists and heroes of labor could obtain the conditions necessary for creating a pleasant home for their family as well as financial and material security.[332] By appealing broadly across the population, those who created the image of the "leader" were trying to persuade every single East German to put their trust in the SED regime. Propaganda presented an ideal version of the socialist way of life that included attractive promises of highly paid work and improved social status; it also told East Germans they could expect social guarantees and care from the state, high-quality consumer goods, and modern, comfortable homes.

However, the picture presented in the official mass media did not correspond to reality. Propaganda proclaimed that socialism was being successfully constructed on the Stalinallee or in Stalinstadt at the "best friend's" behest, but on the ground, day in and day out, the Stalin myth went to pieces under the weight of everyday problems. That is why the editorial office of *Neues Deutschland*, the main party newspaper, received numerous complaints from residents of the "first socialist street" describing their experience of life on the Stalinallee—which was quite different from what propaganda reported. The "happiest people in Germany" wrote about the high cost of living, not enough streetlights, and intersections "covered with construction debris, metal scrap, wire, and wood," which caused many accidents, especially after dark.[333] For the most part, the "new people" in Stalinstadt were young, male, uneducated workers. Instead of acquiring *kul'turnost'* through self-education and reading literary classics, seeing appropriate movies and going to the theater, they spent their time in bars, drank too much, and got into fights. The difficulties of daily life in the workers' barracks, where ten people often shared one room, had something to do with this "immoral behavior." Some people were given their own apartments, but others were not, which increased the sense of social inequality and injustice in the community. As a result, workers were reluctant to help decorate "red corners" and participate in study circles devoted to works by the "classics of Marxism-Leninism."

Increasing prostitution and, as a result, more cases of venereal disease among workers sparked moral panic in Stalinstadt. There was an emergency meeting for the residents of the Helmut Just apartment complex in November 1953. The discussion centered on the rise in "chaotic sexual relationships" in the town. The contrast in what workers said and the rhetoric of party representatives shows how propaganda narratives foundered when faced with the actual problems of daily life. Thus, a man who was a "hero of labor" and a party member called for a struggle against "amoral" behavior, which he described as "antisocialist." He insisted that the workers should adhere to the rules of hygiene, discipline, and order, identified the source of venereal disease as Western agents who were trying to undermine socialist production, and demanded that they be unmasked. A shop manager named Herr Tuxweiler saw the problem differently. He pointed out that more than seventy married couples were unable to live together. They were housed in separate barracks for men and women and could only visit each other. Describing other difficulties, he pointed out that "people are forced to live seven in one small, dirty room in some barracks. There is one private and one state store for five thousand people. After hard physical work, people have to spend hours standing in line." The management responded to the workers' criticism with platitudes about how people had to be patient during difficult times, trust the combine's leadership to unmask the Western agents, and not give in to the enemy's provocations. The inhabitants of Stalinstadt typically reacted to such meetings with SED officials by whistling and hissing—or by getting sick notes and staying home from work.[334]

The most important element of the Stalinallee and Stalinstadt was ideology.[335] It gave individuals the language, values, and behavioral patterns necessary for developing a socialist personality and participating—as modern citizens—in the rebirth of the nation. Official representations explicitly contrasted the deficiencies of the Western world with East Germany's socialist supremacy. These representations promised the public a much better life in the future but made it clear that this depended on subordination and loyalty to the SED regime in the present. The state chose two central objects of propaganda, the Stalinallee in Berlin and Stalinstadt, the city with the leader's name, to mobilize and to indoctrinate the population politically. Media images depicted these spaces as ideal places for staging the successes of SED politics, socialist everyday life, and individual well-being. As this chapter has shown, the Stalin cult became a significant component of the propaganda of these places as a way of creating an attractive facade for socialism. Indeed, alluring representations of building socialism and a set of heartening promises reached millions of citizens through the official mass media. By reading official newspapers, looking at photographs in illustrated magazines, and listening to the radio, and from their daily exposure to posters and slogans in public spaces, millions of East Germans had a chance to develop identical ideas about the socialist lifestyle and the idealized spaces in which the cult community was constructed, staged, and, in the end, fell apart.

Media representations of socialist spaces were supposed to produce a new feeling of "we" within which the (self-)creation of the "new man" could take place. Thus, the regime used the media to connect ideological values with personal meanings. It did so by presenting social solidarity around the SED regime as the way to build a "bright future" for the entire German people in accordance with Stalin's directives. On the Stalinallee above all, the new national identity elaborated in propaganda became a reality and played an important part in the symbolic struggle for a single German capital, in Berlin not Bonn. However, while the rhetoric of nationalism and national revival contributed to the power of the Stalinallee and Stalinstadt to mobilize the masses, improving the East German subject's everyday life became the Stalin cult's key ideological promise. The stories of happy, successful, and prosperous individuals designed to appeal to the popular imagination demonstrate the regime's efforts to add daily life to its discourse and fill private spheres of life with ideological content. The leader cult made an offer to the East Germans: you too can join the project of building socialist modernity—a peaceful, rational, urbanized, scientific, and highly technologically developed "Stalinist civilization" where a fully realized, politically conscious, happy socialist personality can develop.

Imaginations of time, as historians recently have argued, are key cultural determinants in legitimating modern dictatorships and designing modern states.[336] Representations of the Stalinallee and Stalinstadt defined the SED regime's temporal style, its focus on renouncing the "brown past," overcoming the difficulties of the postwar present, and looking toward the "bright future" that shimmered on the horizon. Representations of the socialist lifestyle embodied the spirit of the time: they showed the rapid pace and the dynamics of rebirth from the ruins. Faith in progress and confidence in forward movement on the path to achieving communism and going toward the best possible life in the foreseeable future were the characteristic traits of the socialist culture of time. As the dynamic construction of socialism unfolded, the capitalist West lurked in the background. Depicted as the land of "Nazi reaction" and the home of "vestiges of imperialism and militarism," the West was the world of the past, a place where people had no chance of achieving a successful future. A starkly contrasting temporal scenario gave the Stalin cult its power to mobilize. Its propaganda of the future could already be seen, heard, tasted, and touched in the present: the Stalinallee and Stalinstadt were celebrated as actually existing places for really existing people. These propaganda objects were a tangible promise that similar successes in building socialism would be achieved soon and every East German would enjoy them. With its focus on the future, the chronotope of socialism was the polar opposite of the Third Reich's temporality. The Nazis used the past to legitimize the Hitler state, maintaining social consensus until the end of the Third Reich by emphasizing that if Germany were to capitulate, the nation would have no future.[337] Against this contrasting background, the propaganda of the Soviet leader, calibrated to give people confidence in what tomorrow would bring, made an especially highly charged symbolic promise: "Stalin—this is life in happiness and prosperity! Stalin—this is peace! Stalin—this is our victory! Stalin is our confidence! Stalin is our future!"[338]

NOTES

1. "Ukazanie zamestitelia Glavnonachal'stvuiushchego SVAG po politicheskim voprosam A. G. Russkikh nachal'nikam USVA zemel', upravlenii i otdelov SVAG ob usilenii propagandy SSSR na stranitsakh nauchnykh zhurnalov, 28 sentiabria

1948 g.," in Timofeeva and Foittsik, *Politika SVAG v oblasti kul'tury*, 782–87, here 784–85.

2. "Dokladnaia zapiska zamestitelia Glavnonachal'stvuiushchego SVAG po politicheskim voprosam A. G. Russkikh sekretariu TsK VKP(b) M. A. Suslovu o meropriiatiiakh po uluchsheniiu deiatel'nosti Doma Kul'tury SSSR v Berline i Obshchestva po izucheniiu kul'tury SSSR, 12 fevralia 1949 g.," in Timofeeva and Foittsik, *Politika SVAG v oblasti kul'tury*, 820–25, here 824. The Society for the Study of the Culture of the Soviet Union was founded in 1947 and became the German-Soviet Friendship Society in 1949.

3. "Perechen' tem lektsii, dokladov Obshchestva po izucheniiu kul'tury SSSR i voprosov slushatelei, ne pozdnee 16 marta 1949 g.," in Timofeeva and Foittsik, *Politika SVAG v oblasti kul'tury*, 828.

4. "Pis'mo nachal'nika Upravleniia informatsii SVAG S. I. Tiul'panova predsedateliu Pravleniia VOKS V. S. Kemenovu o deiatel'nosti Doma Kul'tury Sovetskogo Soiuza v Berline, 27 iiunia 1947 g.," in Timofeeva and Foittsik, *Politika SVAG v oblasti kul'tury*, 691–94.

5. GARF, f. 5283, op. 16, d. 146, l. 74.

6. "Spravka Tsentral'no-Evropeiskogo otdela VOKS o khode vypolneniia postanovleniia TsK VKP(b) ot 10 maia 1948 g. o rabote VOKS v Germanii, noiabr' 1948 g.," in Timofeeva and Foittsik, *Politika SVAG v oblasti kul'tury*, 797–800.

7. On Suslov's role in Sovietizing Eastern Europe, conducting the Cold War, and amassing power on the Central Committee, see R. A. Medvedev and Ermakov, *Seryi cardinal*; Zh. A. Medvedev, *Neizvestnyi Stalin*, 70–76.

8. The error was found six months after the book was published and being sold in retail establishments. See RGASPI, f. 17, op. 132, d. 140, l. 104.

9. RGASPI, f. 17, op. 132, d. 108, l. 116–117.

10. Dokladnaia zapiska upolnomochennogo Soveta ministrov SSSR po okhrane voennykh i gosudarstvennikh tain v pechati K. Omel'chenko zamestiteliu nachal'nika Otdela propaganda i agitatsii TsK VKP(b) L. F. Il'ichevu o vnesenii popravok v ustanovlennyi poriadok prosmotra organimi Glavlita provozimoi cherez granitsu literatury, 20 oktiabria 1948 g.," in Timofeev and Foittsik, *Politika SVAG v oblasti kul'tury*, 788–90.

11. RGASPI, f. 17, op. 128, d. 574, l. 25.

12. RGASPI, f. 17, op. 137, d. 307, l. 75.

13. RGASPI, f. 17, op. 137, d. 483, l. 34–38.

14. "Protokoll Nr. 31 der Sitzung des Politbüros am 5. Juli 1949. Vorbereitung des 70. Geburtstages J. W. Stalins," SAPMO-BArch, DY 30/IV 2/2/31, Bl. 13.

15. Behrends, *Die erfundene Freundschaft*, 225–26.

16. Mählert, "Die gesamte junge Generation," 81. In Russian, this mass organization was known as the Soiuz svobodnoi nemetskoi molodezhi (Union of Free German Youth). The FDJ will be discussed in more detail later in this chapter.

17. "Protokoll Nr. 37 der Sitzung des Politbüros am 9. August 1949," SAPMO-BArch, DY 30/IV 2/2/37.

18. See Hartmann and Eggeling, *Sowjetische Präsenz*, 176–81, 259–62.

19. For example, see GARF, f. 5283, op. 16, d. 133, l. 60–61.

20. See "Spisok portretov i plakatov dlia obshchestva germano-sovetskoi druzhby, 1949 g.," AVP RF, f. 742, op. 32, p. 1115, d. 800, l. 76–81. A detailed list of materials about Stalin can be found in the correspondence of VOKS with the German-Soviet Friendship Society. See GARF, f. 5283, op. 16, d. 147, l. 5–8.

21. GARF, f. 5283, op. 16, d. 139, l. 8–9.

22. "Tematika vystavok, kotorye zhelatel'no poluchit' ot VOKS'a dlia klubov Obshchestva po izucheniiu kul'tury SSSR," RGASPI, f. 17, op. 132, d. 108, l. 12.

23. For example, AVP RF, f. 742, op. 32, p. 1115, d. 800, l. 76.

24. Hartmann and Eggeling, *Sowjetische Präsenz*, 261.

25. SAPMO-BArch, DY 32/10072; RGASPI, f. 17, op. 137, d. 637, l. 12–13.

26. SAPMO-BArch, DY 32/10072, Bl. 4.

27. Spravka o sostoianii partiinogo prosveshcheniia v SEPG, RGASPI, f. 17, op. 137, d. 637, l. 13–14, 112.

28. "Protokoll Nr. 6/53 der Sitzung des Politbüros des Zentralkomitees am 3. Februar 1953," SAPMO-BArch, DY 30 J IV 2/2/260, Bl. 103–104.

29. "Protokoll Nr. 31 der Sitzung des Politbüros am 5. Juli 1949. Vorbereitung des 70. Geburtstages J.W. Stalins," SAPMO-BArch, DY 30/IV 2/2/31, Bl. 13.

30. Protokoll Nr. 37 der Sitzung des Politbüros am 9. August 1949. Herausgabe von Werken Stalin," SAPMO-BArch, DY 30/IV 2/2/37, Bl. 11.

31. "Brief der SED-Führung an J. W. Stalin, den 19. September 1949," quoted in Dietrich Staritz, "Die SED, Stalin und die Gründung der DDR," *Aus Politik und Zeitgeschichte*, January 25, 1991, 10–12.

32. "Spravka ob izdanii proizvedenii klassikov marksizma-leninizma na nemetskom iazyke v 1948–1950 gg., 14 marta 1950 g.," RGASPI, f. 17, op. 132, d. 361, l. 39.

33. Fred Oelßner, "Der erste Band der Werke J. W. Stalins in deutscher Sprache," *Neues Deutschland*, December 15, 1949, 4.

34. "Anlage Nr. 1 zum Protokoll Nr. 79 vom 24. März 1950," SAPMO-BArch, DY 30/IV 2/2/79, Bl. 5. According to the SED's data, between 1945 and 1954 the party's publishing house, Dietz Verlag, put out 9,587 thousand copies of Stalin's works, including 920,000 copies of the *Short Course* (*Kratkii kurs istorii VKP(b)*). See "Die Werke J. W. Stalins in der DDR," *Tägliche Rundschau*, March 5, 1954. It is interesting to note that Dietz Verlag published the German translation of the first volume of Lenin's complete works on a wave of latent de-Stalinization in April 1955 under the auspices of the SED Central Committee's Institute of Marxism-Leninism. After 1956, the institute prioritized publication of the works of Marx and Engels.

35. RGASPI, f. 17, op. 137, d. 307, l. 69.

36. For example, Otto, *Mutter von Gori*; *Begegnungen mit Stalin*; Caspar, *Du Welt im Licht*.

37. I would like to thank Jochen Voit for the reference about exporting music from the USSR to East Germany. See www.erinnerungsort.de.

38. SAPMO-BArch, DY 32/10072.

39. "Anlage Nr. 1 zum Protokoll Nr. 57 der Sitzung des Politbüros vom 22. November 1949," SAPMO-BArch, DY 30/IV 2/2/57, Bl. 12.

40. *Pravda*, October 14, 1949, 1. As Stefan Dörnberg recalls, the GDR government actually did not receive a telegram from Stalin about the creation of the GDR on October 13, 1949. It was only the next day that the German press figured it out: "Perhaps Stalin simply forgot to give the order, because without him no one felt entitled to do so." See Dörnberg, *Fronteinsatz*, 154.

41. GARF, f. R-7184, op. 1, d. 262, l. 135.

42. RGASPI, f. 17, op. 137, d. 637, l. 4.

43. "Iz dokladnoi zapiski nachal'nika ONO UVK g. Berlina A. N. Sudakova nachal'niku ONO SVAG A. D. Danilovu o demokraticheskikh organizatsiiakh v shkolakh sovetskogo sektora g. Berlina, 29 oktiabria 1949 g.," in Timofeeva and Foittsik, *Politika SVAG v oblasti kul'tury*, 501–2.

44. GARF, f. R-7133, op. 1, d. 282, l. 74.

45. GARF, f. R-7133, op. 1, d. 282, l. 102–103.

46. AdsD, SPD-PV-Ostbüro 0349 A/B, unpag.

47. Tikhomirov, "Feinde des Volkes," in Satjukow and Gries, *Unsere Feinde*.

48. In addition to translating the essays, Neumann is credited with editing the German edition. See Buckmiller and Meschkat, *Biographisches Handbuch*, 424n26. For the Russian-language volume, see *Stalin: Sbornik statei*.

49. Neumann, "Vorwort," 3.

50. Neumann, "Vorwort," 3.

51. The book consisted of articles by Molotov, Voroshilov, Kaganovich, Mikoian, Kalinin, Khrushchev, Beria, Malenkov, Shvernik, and other members of the Politburo. See *Stalin: Der große Fortsetzer*. The Foreign Languages Publishing House also brought out Jemelyan Jaroslawski's *Aus dem Leben und Wirken des Genossen Stalin* in 1940.

52. See Khlevniuk, *Stalin i utverzhdenie*.

53. Just, *Joseph Wissarionowitsch Dshugaschwili-Stalin*.

54. Just, *Joseph Wissarionowitsch Dshugaschwili-Stalin*, 37.

55. See Kivelitz, *Die Propagandaausstellung*.

56. "Besprechung im Sitzungssaal der SED, 2.11.1949," SAPMO-BArch, DY 34/24029, Bl. 114.

57. "Protokoll Nr. 152 der Sitzung des Politbüros des Zentralkomitees vom 10. Juni 1951," SAPMO-BArch, DY 30 J IV 2/2/260.

58. For more information, see "J. W. Stalin, der große Staatsmann und Lehrer: Eine Stalin-Ausstellung im Hause des Landesverbandes der SED," *Neues Deutschland*, November 29, 1949, 3.

59. For an example, see RGASPI, f. 17, op. 137, d. 772, l. 108.

60. RGASPI, f. 17, op. 137, d. 772, l. 109–111.

61. The facade of the USSR's pavilion was a stone portico with five entrances to the building. In the center of the facade were three-dimensional neon letters spelling out "USSR" (in Cyrillic "SSSR") and a large inscription in German reading "Union der Sozialistischen Sowjetrepubliken." To the right and left of the Cyrillic letters, illuminated openwork emblems of each of the USSR's sixteen republics that were two meters across adorned the frieze. In the frieze's central part was the emblem of the USSR, illuminated, five meters high, and made of aluminum.

Above it a twenty-meter-long bas-relief inscription welcomed visitors with Stalin's words: "Long live one, independent, peace-loving Germany!" Sixteen red flags fluttered on flagpoles placed above the emblem. The building's tower was crowned with a spire which was topped with a five-pointed, bright red Duralumin star. See "Ekspozitsionnyi plan sovetskogo pavil'ona na vesennei tekhnicheskoi iarmarke v Leiptsige 1950," RGASPI, f. 17, op. 132, d. 310, l. 2.

62. Ibid., l. 4.

63. Kniga otzyvov posetitelei sovetskogo pavil'ona na Mezhdunarodnoi vystavke v Leiptsige (GDR), March 5–19, 1950, RGASPI, f. 17, op. 137, d. 181, l. 39, 48, 213, 226.

64. See Hülbusch, "Dschugaschwili der Zweite."

65. For example, see "Spisok fil'mov, rekomendovannykh Predstavitel'stvu 'Soveksportfil'm' v Germanii dlia vkliucheniia v repertuar festivalia, posviashchennogo 30-letiiu Sovetskoi kinematografii, 26 noiabria 1949," RGASPI, f. 17, op. 132, d. 250, l. 102–103.

66. "Der Weg des sowjetischen Films," *Neues Deutschland*, December 2, 1949, 3.

67. See Karl, "Von Helden und Menschen . . ."

68. On the people who produced the Stalin cult in the USSR, see Plamper, *Stalin Cult*; Devlin, *Visualizing Political Language*.

69. "Erfahrungsaustausch der Sektion Bildende Kunst der Akademie der Künste mit einer Delegation sowjetischer bildender Künstler. Berlin, den 17.03.1953," Archiv der Akademie der Künste der DDR. AdK-O 49. Bl. 58–59.

70. Reddy, *Navigation of Feeling*, 129.

71. *Pravda*, October 10, 1949, 3.

72. Grotewohl, "Stalin und das deutsche Volk," in *J. W. Stalin zum Gedenken*, 352.

73. *Neues Deutschland*, December 18, 1949, 1.

74. "Protokoll Nr. 57 der Sitzung des Politbüros am 17. Juli 1951," SAPMO-Barch. DY 30/IV 2/2/157.

75. "Stalin-Denkmal in Berlin enthüllt," *Neues Deutschland*, August 4, 1951, 1.

76. *Neue Berliner Illustrierte*, no. 11 (March 1953).

77. Flam, *Soziologie der Emotionen*, 20.

78. See *Biulleten' mezhdunarodnoi informatsii po Germanii*, no. 35/39 ot 31 maia 1946 g., RGASPI, f. 17, op.128, d. 155, l. 192.

79. Gozman and Etkind, "Kul't vlasti," in Kobo, *Osmyslit' kul't Stalina*, 358.

80. *Neues Deutschland*, December 20, 1949, 4.

81. Grotewohl, "Stalin und das deutsche Volk," 357.

82. For more detail, see Gibas, "'Bonner Ultras,' 'Kriegstreiber,' und 'Schlotbarone.'"

83. "Freundschaft für immer. Brief an alle Bürger der DDR anlässlich des 34. Jahrestages der Großen Sozialistischen Oktoberrevolution," Amt für Information der DDR, Berlin, 1951.

84. RGASPI, f. 17, op. 137, d. 639, l. 61.

85. "Spiski podarkov iz GDR," RGASPI, f. 558, op. 11, d. 1420, l. 113–123; f. 17, op. 132, d. 444, l. 45–61.

86. "Otchet o prebyvanii v SSSR delegatsii nemetskikh pisatelei i deiatelei kul'tury s 7 aprelia po 4 maia 1948 g.," RGASPI, f. 17, op. 128, d. 574, l. 18.

87. See Stoecker, "Stalin, das ist der Frieden!"

88. "Resolution der Mitglieder der Sächsischen Kinderbuchkommission zur Note der Sowjetunion an die drei Grossmächte, Dresden, 14.03.1952," Staatsarchiv Dresden, LRS, Ministerium für Volksbildung Nr. 1840, unpag.

89. "Vorschlag der Sowjetunion für einen Friedensvertrag mit Deutschland, Glauchau, den 15 März 1952," Staatsarchiv Dresden, LRS, Ministerium für Volksbildung Nr. 1840, unpag.

90. Grotewohl, "Stalin und das deutsche Volk," 357.

91. Filitov, "SSSR i germanskii vopros."

92. Flam, *Soziologie der Emotionen*, 16–43.

93. For example, see Fukuyama, *Trust*; Misztal, *Trust in Modern Societies*; Govier, *Social Trust*; Sztompka, *Trust: A Sociological Theory*; Frevert, *Vertrauen: Historische Annäherungen*.

94. See also Tikhomirov, "Regime of Forced Trust."

95. See Hosking, "Trust and Distrust in the USSR." See also Luhmann, *Vertrauen*.

96. Hein, *Der Pilsudski-Kult*, 11.

97. Dörner, *Politischer Mythos*, 54.

98. Danyel, "Politische Rituale als Sowjetimporte."

99. Durkheim, *Die elementaren Formen des religiösen Lebens*, 498.

100. See Siegelbaum and Sokolov, *Stalinism as a Way of Life*; Fitzpatrick, *Tear Off the Masks!*

101. Bergesen, "Die rituelle Ordnung," in Belliger and Krieger, *Ritualtheorien*.

102. Fritzsche and Hellbeck, "New Man in Stalinist Russia," in Geyer and Fitzpatrick, *Beyond Totalitarianism*.

103. The Soviet proscription of the Nazi cult of the body is evident in SVAG's decrees, which were aimed at banning (or at least controlling) sporting events, athletic groups, and sports clubs. For example, see "Prikazanie nachal'nika USVA federal'noi zemli Saksoniia D. G. Dubrovskogo No. 0153 voennym komendantam okrugov i gorodov o zapreshchenii fashistskikh sportivnykh organizatsii," in Timofeeva and Foittsik, *Politika SVAG v oblasti kul'tury*, 94, and "Prikazanie nachal'nika shtaba USVA federal'noi zemli Tiuringii No. 0102 o narushenii nemetskimi organami upravleniia direktivy Kontrol'nogo soveta 23 ot 17 dekabria 1945 g. 'Ob ogranichenii i demilitarizatsii sporta v Germanii,' 21 iiunia 1946 g.," cited in N. V. Petrov, "Formirovanie organov nemetskogo samoupravleniia i sovetizatsiia Vostochnoi Germanii," in Petrov, *SVAG i nemetskie organy samoupravleniia*, 332.

104. Otchet o prebyvanii v SSSR delegatsii nemetskikh pisatelei i deiateli kul'tury, 7 aprelia–4 maia 1948g., RGASPI, f. 17, op. 128, d. 574, l. 20.

105. Kotkin, *Magnetic Mountain*.

106. Halfin, *From Darkness to Light*; Hellbeck, *Revolution on My Mind*.

107. Hellbeck, "Alltag in der Ideologie."

108. On Germans' perception of themselves as victims, during both the Nazi and Soviet regimes, see Fulbrook, *Dissonant Lives*; Kessel, *Gewalt und Gelächter*.

109. See Halfin, *From Darkness to Light*; Halfin, *Stalinist Confessions*; Hellbeck, *Revolution on My Mind*.

110. Staatsarchiv Dresden, Landesregierung Sachsen, Ministerium für Volksbildung, Nr. 1245, Bl. 89–94.

111. According to Bernhard H. Bayerlein, during the Nazi dictatorship out of some 300,000 KPD members (in 1932), around 150,000 were in prison and approximately 20,000 were murdered. See his "Stalin und die Kommunistische Partei Deutschlands," in Engwert and Knabe, *Der rote Gott*, 13–17.

112. For a detailed discussion of the features of the generation of the "builders of the new life," see Ahbe and Gries, *Gesellschaftsgeschichte als Generationengeschichte*, 502–18.

113. "Wir rufen die Berliner Jugend zum Wettbewerb," SAPMO-BArch, DY 32/10072.

114. Of two million German prisoners of war in the USSR, about 700,000 returned to the Soviet Occupation Zone in Germany between 1945 and 1949. Morina, *Legacies of Stalingrad*, 76–77, 149.

115. SAPMO-BArch, DY 32/12562.

116. Fulbrook, *Dissonant Lives*, 15–16.

117. For example, see *Freiheit*, December 21, 1951, 5.

118. For example, *Lausitzer Rundschau*, December 21, 1951, 3, in SAPMO-BArch, DY 132/10277.

119. On mental illnesses and suicides in postwar Germany as responses to Sovietization, see Grossmann, *Jews, Germans and Allies*.

120. Rittersporn, Behrends, and Rolf, "Öffentliche Räume und Öffentlichkeit," 13; Fitzpatrick, "Ascribing Class."

121. The main East German mass organizations were the Free German Trade Union Federation (Freier Deutscher Gewerkschaftsbund), which was created in 1945, the Free German Youth (Freie Deutsche Jugend or FDJ), which was also known as the Union of Free German Youth, the Democratic Women's League of Germans (Demokratischer Frauenbund Deutschlands), which was founded in 1947, and the German-Soviet Friendship Society (Gesellschaft für Deutsche-Sowjetische Freundschaft).

122. Quoted in Mählert, *Blaue Hemden—Rote Fahnen*, 78–79.

123. In June 1950, the FDJ had 1,200,856 members or 38.5 percent of all fourteen- to twenty-five-year-olds. See Mählert, "Zur Geschichte der Freien Deutschen Jugend," in Weber and Ammer, *Der SED-Staat*.

124. See, for example, Ulbricht, *An die Jugend*.

125. GARF, f. R-7313, op. 11, d. 11, l. 92–93.

126. Mählert, *Die Freie Deutsche Jugend*.

127. Mählert, *"Blaue Hemden—Rote Fahnen,"* 9–10.

128. AdsD, SPD-PV-Ostbüro 0383 G, unpag.

129. SAPMO-BArch, DY 32/10072.

130. "Anlage Nr. 6: Plan für zusätzliche Literatur zum Schuljahr der FDJ. Zum Protokoll 141/III/51," SAPMO-BArch, DY 24/2408.

131. Konstantin Simonov's novella *Days and Nights* (*Dni i nochi*), Ilya Ehrenburg's *The Storm* (*Shturm*), *The Young Guard* (*Molodaia gvardiia*) by Alexander Fadeev, and Boris Polevoi's novel *The Story of a Real Man* (*Povest' o nastoiashchem cheloveke*), based on the life of World War II fighter pilot Aleksei Mares'ev, were on the list of recommended literature. *The Battle of Stalingrad* (*Stalingradskaia bitva*), *The Fall of Berlin* (*Padenie Berlina*), *Burning Hearts* (*Goriashchie serdtsa*), and *Encounter at the Elbe* (*Vstrecha na El'be*) were on the list of films to be watched. See *Stalin, der große Feldherr*, 63.

132. *Unter dem Banner*, 45; Stalin, *Stalin und die Jugend*.

133. "Prüfungsbedingungen für das Abzeichen "Für gutes Wissen" in Gold. Zum Protokoll 141/III/51," SAPMO-BArch DY 24/2480.

134. SAPMO-BArch, DY 24/3430.

135. RGASPI, f. 17, op. 137, d. 311, l. 120–122.

136. RGASPI, f. 82, op. 2, d. 1168, l. 60.

137. See Mählert, *"Blaue Hemden—Rote Fahnen,"* 79–80.

138. O prebyvanii Gosudarstvennogo ansamblia narodnogo tantsa SSSR v GDR s 26 maia po 16 iiulia 1950 g., RGASPI, f. 17, op. 137, d. 297, l. 26–38.

139. RGASPI, f. 588, op. 11, d. 1406, l. 20–22.

140. Hauptverwaltung für Ausbildung der FDJ, *Vorwärts junge Friedenskämpfer*, 6–7.

141. Hauptverwaltung für Ausbildung der FDJ, *Vorwärts junge Friedenskämpfer*, 4.

142. The ceremony of greeting the delegation from the USSR at Schönefeld airport was staged as a demonstration of German-Soviet friendship. In the breaks between speeches given by leaders of the state and party and representatives of the Soviet diplomatic corps, people could be heard vigorously chanting in unison, "Glory to Generalissimo Stalin, the mentor of Soviet and German youth!" and "Stalin—Pieck, Pieck—Stalin." See "Berlin begrüßt ruhmreiche Sowjetjugend," *Neues Deutschland*, August 4, 1951, 1; "In der Wuhlheide begannen glückliche Tage," *Neues Deutschland*, August 5, 1951, 1.

143. "Aufgebot zu Ehren des großen Stalin vom 6.6.1951. Protokoll Nr. 49/51 der Sitzung des Politbüros des Zentralkomitees am 30.05.51," SAPMO-BArch, DY 30 J IV 2/2/149.

144. Cf. "Anlage Nr. 1: Mecklenburg führt im Stalin-Aufgebot! Kommuniqué der außerordentlichen Sitzung des Sekretariats des Zentralrats der FDJ," SAPMO-BArch, DY 24/2410; "Anlage Nr. 1: Sachsen-Anhalt und Thüringen an der Spitze. Protokoll Nr. 179 der Sitzung des Sekretariats des Zentralrats der FDJ," SAPMO-BArch, DY 24/2412.

145. "Berlins FDJ noch aktiver im Stalin-Aufgebot," *Neues Deutschland*, July 1, 1951, 4.

146. "Sinnlose Jagd nach Prozentzahlen," *Neues Deutschland*, July 24, 1951, 4.

147. "Anlage Nr. 1: Mecklenburg und Sachsen führen im Stalinaufgebot. Protokoll vom 5.7.51," SAPMO-BArch, DY 24/241.

148. "Der FDJ im Stalin-Aufgebot helfen!" *Neues Deutschland*, July 15, 1951, 4.

149. "Protokoll Nr. 55 der Sitzung des Politbüros am 3. Juli 1951," SAPMO-BArch, DY 30/IV 2/2/155.

150. "Anlage Nr. 1: Plan für die Unterzeichnungsaktion der Grußbotschafter an J. W. Stalin anlässlich des großen Friedensmarsches der deutschen Jugend gegen die Remilitarisierung für den Abschluss eines Friedensvertrages am 12.8.1951. Protokoll Nr. 183 vom 20. Juli 1951," SAPMO-BArch, DY 24/1013.

151. "Präsident Pieck stiftete wertvolle Ehrenpreise," *Neues Deutschland*, August 4, 1951, 1.

152. "Anlage Nr. 1: Entwurf 'Unser Gruß dem großen Stalin!'" Protokoll Nr. 187 vom 28. Juli 1951," SAPMO-BArch, DY 24/1013.

153. "Protokoll Nr. 84 der Sitzung des Politbüros am 1. August 1951," SAPMO-BArch, DY 30/IV/2/2/159.

154. "Festival des Friedens," special issue of *Neue Berliner Illustrierte*, August 1951, 3.

155. "Das Programm des großen Festivals junger Friedenskämpfer," *Neues Deutschland*, August 2, 1951, 4.

156. "Anlage Nr. 2: Zur Auszeichnung der Sieger im Aufgebot zu Ehren Stalins. Protokoll Nr. 183 vom 20. Juli 1951," SAPMO-BArch, DY 24/1013.

157. "Anlage Nr. 1 zum Protokoll Nr. 189: Plan zur Kundgebung anlässlich des Abschlusses des Aufgebotes zu Ehren des großen Stalin am 12. August 1951 auf dem Marx-Engels-Platz," SAPMO-BArch, DY 24/1013.

158. AdsD, SPD-PV-Ostbüro 0351 A I Allgemein, unpag.

159. AdsD, SPD-PV-Ostbüro 0383 H-K, unpag.

160. RGASPI, f. 82, op. 2, d. 1181, l. 42.

161. Foittsik, *Sovetskaia politika v otnoshenii Germanii*, 95.

162. "Kratkaia spravka ob obshchestve germano-sovetskoi druzhby v okruge Rostok," AVP RF, f. 742, op. 8, d. 12, l. 15, 21.

163. Hartmann and Eggeling, *Sowjetische Präsenz*, 67.

164. Hartmann, *Die Gesellschaft für Deutsch-Sowjetische Freundschaft*, 68.

165. Al'tiusser, "Ideologiia i ideologicheskie apparaty gosudarstva."

166. "Feierliche Verleihung des Namens "J. W. Stalin" an die Elektro-Apparate-Werke Treptow," *Neues Deutschland*, May 1, 1953, 2.

167. "EAW 'J. W. Stalin' erfüllte den Jahresplan: Übergabe eines Stalin-Kabinetts anlässlich des Geburtstages J. W. Stalins," *Neues Deutschland*, December 22, 1953, 6.

168. RGASPI, f. 558, op. 11, d. 140, l. 51–53.

169. For example, von Klimo, "'Runde' Jahrestage." On the culture of holidays and celebrations in Stalin's Russia, see Petrone, *Life Has Become More Joyous*; Rolf, "Constructing a Soviet Time"; Chatterjee, *Celebrating Women*; Rolf, *Das sowjetische Massenfest*.

170. For example, see "Heimat des siegreichen Sozialismus: Vorbereitungen in aller Welt zum 70. Geburtstag von Generalissimus Stalin," *Neues Deutschland*, December 4, 1949, 1.

171. Volokitina, *Sovetskii faktor*, vol. 2, 214–16.

172. RGASPI, f. 17, op. 128, d. 1186, l. 348–49.

173. RGASPI, f. 17, op. 128, d. 1186, l. 360–64.

174. *Sovetskii faktor*, vol. 2, 225–30.

175. RGASPI, f. 558, op. 11, d. 1378, l. 14.

176. Nagornaia, "Esli druz'ia sochtut tselesoobraznym."

177. The city of Perm was renamed to honor Vyacheslav Molotov in 1940 but reverted to its original name in 1957.

178. See "Predlozheniia grazhdan SSSR v sviazi s semidesiatiletiem Iosifa Vissarionovicha Stalina," RGASPI, f. 558, op. 11, 1377, l. 105–42. For examples of Soviet citizens congratulating Stalin on his seventieth birthday, see RGASPI, f. 558, d. 878–83.

179. RGASPI, f. 558, d. 878–83.

180. See "Svodki na pis'ma i zaiavleniia na imia Stalina I. V.," RGASPI, f. 558, op. 11, d. 865–882.

181. Fitspatrik, *Povsednevnyi stalinizm*, 10.

182. "Ukaz Prezidiuma Verkhovnogo Soveta SSSR o meropriiatiiakh po uluche-niiu material'nogo obespecheniia po starosti i invalidnosti v oznamenovanie semide-siatiletiia so dnia rozhdeniia I. V. Stalina," RGASPI, f. 558, op. 11, d. 1378, l. 26.

183. Van Gennep, *Rites of Passage*; Turner, *Ritual Process*.

184. *Pravda*, December 22, 1949, 3.

185. When asked if the USSR would receive a German delegation, the International Department of the Central Committee (at that time called the Vneshnepoliticheskaia komissiia or Commission on External Politics) told SVAG to send an affirmative response to Pieck. The German side assumed responsibility for all the costs connected with its stay in the capital and delivering gifts to Stalin. Perhaps it is not surprising that luxurious rooms in Moscow's best hotels were booked for the Germans. See "Vypiska iz protokola No. 72 Politbiuro TsK VKP(b) 'O priezde inostrannykh delegatsii v sviazi s 70-letiem I. V Stalina'," RGASPI, f. 558, op. 11, d. 1377, l. 59, 66, 70.

186. Muir, *Ritual in Early Modern Europe*, 29–31.

187. RGASPI, f. 558, op. 11, d. 1377, l. 59.

188. Prodi, *Il sacramento del potere*.

189. Naumann, "Die III. Weltfestspiele der Jugend," 217.

190. Schroeder, *Der SED-Staat*, 119.

191. AdsD, Personalia-Sammlung J. W. Stalin, Zeitungsausschnitte, unpag.

192. Mauss, *Die Gabe*; Ssorin-Chaikov and Sosnina, "Faculty of Useless Things."

193. SAPMO-BArch, DY 30/IV 2/2/62, Bl. 26.

194. RGASPI, f. 17, op. 137, d. 311, l. 44–46; *Tägliche Rundschau*, November 29, 1949, 1.

195. *Neues Deutschland*, December 16, 1949, 1.

196. AdsD, Personalia-Sammlung Stalin J.W. 2968, Zeitungsausschnitte.

197. RGASPI, f. 17, op. 317, d. 307, l. 3.

198. See an article that appeared in a special edition of *Neues Deutschland* published for Stalin's birthday, "Zeiß, Jena-demontiert? Zeiß, Jena-schöner und stärker als je!" *Neues Deutschland*, December 21, 1949.

199. AdsD, Personalia-Sammlung "Stalin J. W." 2970, Zeitungsausschnitte.

200. RGASPI, f. 558, op. 11, d. 1377, l. 59.

201. *Neues Deutschland*, December 17, 1949, 1.

202. RGASPI, f. 17, op. 132, d. 442, l. 51.

203. RGASPI, f. 17, op. 132, d. 442, l. 1, 4, 51.

204. RGASPI, f. 17, op. 81, d. 13, l. 1–2.

205. RGASPI, f. 17, op. 81, d. 13, l. 1–2.

206. RGASPI, f. 17, op. 132, d. 444, l. 45–61.

207. Gries, "Dramaturgie der Utopie."

208. AdsD, SPD-PV-Ostbüro 0362 I, unpag.

209. Wierling, "Über die Liebe."

210. Tikhomirov, "Stalin-Bild(er) in der SBZ/DDR," 493–94.

211. Podgotovka k prazdnovaniiu 75-letiia so dnia rozhdeniia tovarishcha V. Pika, dekabr' 1949, RGASPI, f. 17, op. 137, d.297, l. 87–89.

212. RGASPI, f. 82, op. 2, d. 1169, l. 70–72; RGASPI, f. 17, op. 137, d. 495, l. 33.

213. RGASPI, f. 17, op. 137, d. 495, l. 31–33.

214. RGASPI, f. 17, op. 137, d. 495, l. 31. See also Engwert, "Ikonografie des Stalin-Kultes."

215. *Tägliche Rundschau*, March 5, 1954, 1.

216. See Guseinov, *Karta nashei rodiny*; Sänger, *Heldenkult und Heimatliebe*; Azaryahu, *Von Wilhelmplatz zu Thälmannplatz*.

217. *Neues Deutschland*, December 21, 1952, 4.

218. *Tägliche Rundschau*, November 7, 1947, 1.

219. RGASPI, f. 17, op. 317, d. 637, l. 1–2.

220. RGASPI, f. 17, op. 317, d. 638, l. 52.

221. RGASPI, f. 17, op. 137, d. 307, l. 93.

222. GARF, f. R-7212, op. 1, d. 229, l. 249.

223. Gibas, "'Bonner Ultras,' 'Kriegstreiber' und 'Schlotbarone.'"

224. Sozialdemokratischer Pressedienst, August 13, 1951, 6.

225. RGASPI, f. 17, op. 137, d. 639, l. 46–49.

226. "Generalissimus Stalin J. W. Stalin, dem genialen Führer der Sozialistischen Sowjetunion," Staatsarchiv Dresden, LRS, Ministerium für Volksbildung Nr. 215, unpag.

227. "Feier zu Ehren des 70. Geburtstages des Generalissimus Stalin am 20.12.49, 11 Uhr im Großen Haus (undated)," Staatsarchiv Dresden, LRS, Ministerium für Volksbildung Nr. 215, unpag.

228. "Richtlinien für die Durchführung von Feiern zum 70. Geburtstag J.W. Stalins. Berlin, Oktober 1949," Staatsarchiv Dresden, LRS, Ministerium für Volksbildung Nr. 1840, unpag.

229. Ibid.

230. "Generalissimus Stalin J. W. Stalin, dem genialen Führer der Sozialistischen Sowjetunion," Staatsarchiv Dresden, LRS, Ministerium für Volksbildung Nr. 215, unpag.

231. For example, *Neues Deutschland*, December 22, 1951, 1.

232. On decorations, see "Zeitausschnitte anlässlich des 72. Jahrestages J. W. Stalin am 21.12.1951 in der DDR," SAPMO-BArch, DY 32/10277. For store window displays, see "Vorbereitung und Durchführung des Monats der deutsch-sowjetischen Freundschaft," SAPMO-BArch, 32/6153. See also Pence, "Schaufenster des sozialistischen Konsums."

233. "Geburtstag des Generalissimus Stalin am 21.12.1951. Dresden, den 28.12.1951," Staatsarchiv Dresden, LRS, Ministerium für Volksbildung Nr. 1840, unpag.

234. Informatsionnaia svodka o podgotovke k prazdovaniiu 70-letiia IV Stalina v GDR, November 24, 1949 г., RGASPI, f. 17, op. 137, d. 100, l. 136–144.

235. "Stenographische Niederschrift der Trauersitzung des Zentralkomitees der Sozialistischen Einheitspartei Deutschlands am 6. März 1953, 18.00 Uhr, im Haus der Einheit," SAPMO-BArch, DY 30/IV 2/1/113. Bl. 2–8; see also Schmidt, "Als Stalin starb."

236. See "Protokoll Nr. 15/53 der außerordentlichen Sitzung des Politbüros des Zentralkomitees am 7. März 1953," SAPMO-BArch, DY 30 J IV 2/2/269.

237. For example, Ulbricht was responsible for an article titled "The Testament of J. W. Stalin," Pieck authored "Stalin, the Creator of an Invincible Camp of Peace," Friedrich Ebert wrote "Stalin's Care for His People," Grotewohl wrote "Stalin Laid Down and Pointed Out the Path of Development for All of Peace-Loving Mankind," and Fred Oelßner wrote "Stalin, the Builder of Communism." See "Anlage Nr. 2 zum Protokoll Nr. 14/53 v. 6. März 1953. Plan der Leitartikel," SAPMO-BArch, DY 30/J IV 2/2/268. Bl. 5.

238. German scholar Volker Ackermann argues that the length of official mourning is symbolically significant and indicates the value of the deceased in the eyes of the state and society. While mourning for Stalin lasted for six days, Pieck was mourned for four days, Otto Grotewohl for three, and Ulbricht for a single day. See Ackermann, *Nationale Totenfeiern in Deutschland*, 52.

239. "Die Tätigkeit der leitenden Parteiorgane und ihre Führung im Kampf um die Erhaltung des Friedens und die Einheit Deutschlands," SAPMO-BArch, DY 30/V/2/5/269. Bl. 102.

240. "Bekanntmachung des Ministeriums des Innern," *Neues Deutschland*, March 7, 1953, 2.

241. See "Anlage Nr. 1 zum Protokoll Nr. 14/53 vom 6. März 1953, SAPMO-BArch," DY 30/J IV 2/2/268. Bl. 2–3.

242. Karl-Heinz Schmidt estimates that on March 9, 1953, approximately 3,600,000 people took part in mourning events in the GDR. For more detailed information, see "Als Stalin starb," 91–95.

243. "Informationsbericht Nr. 3 (7.3.1953, 8 Uhr früh)," SAPMO-BArch, DY 30/IV/2/5/268. Bl. 309.

244. SAPMO-BArch, DY 30/IV/2/5/268. Bl. 295–340.

245. For example, see *Der Spiegel*, April 1, 1953, 8; "Trauerfeiern in Städten und Dörfern der Republik," *Junge Welt*, March 10, 1953, 3.

246. "Der große Trauermarsch der Berliner Werktätigen," *Neues Deutschland*, March 10, 1953, 1.

247. Ibid.

248. "Informationsbericht Nr. 2 über Maßnahmen der Parteileitungen und Stimmung der Bevölkerung anlässlich des Ablebens des Genosse Stalin. Berlin, den 06.03.1953 von 15–18 Uhr," SAPMO-BArch, DY IV/2/5/268, Bl. 304.

249. "Information über die von den Bezirks- und Kreisleitung aufgrund des Todes des Genossen Stalin ergriffenen Maßnahmen und die Anteilnahme der Bevölkerung. Berlin, den 6.3.53," SAPMO-BArch, DY IV/2/5/268, Bl. 300.

250. "Informationsbericht Nr. 2. (6.3.1953)," SAPMO-BArch, DY IV/2/5/268, Bl. 305.

251. "Unsere Republik trauerte um ihren besten Freund," *Neues Deutschland*, March 10, 1953, 2.

252. "Deutsche Delegation aus Moskau zurückgekehrt," *Neues Deutschland*, March 12, 1953, 1.

253. Hermlin, "Das Abbild der Hoffnung," 141.

254. The construction of the people's trust in the SED regime can be traced in the following propaganda narrative: "Mama, why are you crying?" "Stalin is dead." The child's eyes fill with tears. "But who will do his work now?" The mother confidently answers her son: "All of us. We will struggle on his side and continue what he began." The woman looks toward the tribune, at the leaders of the party. The solemn promise can be read on their faces: "You can count on us completely, under the banners of Lenin and Stalin we will go forward to communism." See Margot Pfannstiel, "Zu neuen Siegen im Stalinschen Geist," *Neues Deutschland*, March 10, 1953, 2.

255. *Neues Deutschland*, March 6, 1953, 1; *Neues Deutschland*, March 7, 1953, 1.

256. It is important to note that under national socialism women did not participate in official funeral ceremonies, with the exception of funerals for those in state service. Thus, official mourning for Stalin in East Germany was the first time that women were able to take part in funeral rituals without any restrictions. Ackermann, *Nationale Totenfeiern in Deutschland*, 57.

257. For example, see *Neue Berliner Illustrierte*, no. 12 (March 1953), 3.

258. Analyzing a photograph taken by well-known East German photographer Gerhard Kiesling that appeared on the cover of the March 3, 1953, issue of the weekly magazine *Neue Berliner Illustrierte*, Jörg-Uwe Fischer shows the key role that photographs played in visualizing private grief. He notes that the photograph shows "a family, father, mother, and young child, standing in front of a monument to Stalin. The image conveys deep mourning and genuine gratitude to the dead dictator. At the same time, one sees pride, pride in belonging to Stalin. The viewer learns much more about these people's feelings from looking at the photograph than the text alone can tell." Light emanating from the "stone leader" falls on the open, upraised faces, their eyes focused on a single point. In this way, the technical possibilities inherent in the play of light and shadow, highlighting facial expressions, and staging a shared background, made it possible to vividly convey people's emotional states and show the individual dimension of the ritual of state mourning. Fischer, "Illustrierte Trauer," 40–41. See also D. Mühlberg, "Alltag in der Medienöffentlichkeit."

259. "Ganz Berlin nahm Abschied von J. W. Stalin," *Neues Deutschland*," March 10, 1953, 2; "In Trauer und Entschlossenheit: Berlin am Tage der schmerzlichen Nachricht vom Hinscheiden J. W. Stalin," *Neues Deutschland*, March 7, 1953.

260. "Abschied von Stalin," *Neues Deutschland*, March 10, 1953, 2; "Die Länder der Volksdemokratie gedenken ihres großen Lehrmeisters," *Neues Deutschland*, March 10, 1953, 3.

261. The *Wochenschau* (weekly newsreel) was a short documentary film about current news stories, sensational events, and entertainment. Before television, the newsreel was the public's only audiovisual source of information. For more detail, see the liner notes for *Der Augenzeuge-Die DEFA-Wochenschau*. See also Turovskaja, "Das Kino der totalitären Epoche."

262. During the newsreel about the mourning, the drama gradually increases. The film begins by showing people of all ages and from all social groups listening to the radio and reading about Stalin's death in newspapers. Their initial reactions of shock, fear, and distress compel the viewer to ask, "What will happen now?" Later in the film, the range of intense emotions expressed to a portrait of the "leader" and other representations of Stalin convey the emotional essence of mourning: there is a moment of silence as schoolchildren stand in front of the portrait; a group decorates the portrait with a black ribbon and flowers; we see someone carefully leafing through the pages of Stalin's works. And then we see a line of children led by their teacher approach the monument to the "father." Cadres of softly crying women, distress on children's faces, and a few masculine tears were meant to demonstrate the collapse of hopes, which Stalin's person promised to fulfill during his life. The special newsreels produced in conjunction with Stalin's death can be viewed at the German Federal Archives. See "DEFA-Wochenschau 'Augenzeuge': Stalins Werk ist unsterblich" (11/1953); "Dem großen Stalin ewiges Gedenken" (1953), Filmarchiv-Bundesarchiv in Berlin.

263. On the beginnings and the development of East German television, see Hickethier, *Geschichte des deutschen Fernsehens*.

264. "Protokoll Nr. 10/54 der außerordentlichen Sitzung des Zentralkomitees des Politbüros am 19. Februar 1954," SAPMO-BArch, DY 30 J IV 2/2/348, Bl. 1.

265. On cults commemorating Soviet and other communist leaders, see Tumarkin, *Lenin Lives!*; Ledderose, "Die Gedenkhalle für Mao Zedong"; Ennker, *Die Anfänge des Lenin-Kults*; Todorova, "Mausoleum of Georgi Dimitrov."

266. "Maßnahmen zum Gedenken J. W. Stalins. Anlage Nr. 2 zum Protokoll 10/54," SAPMO-BArch, DY 30/J IV 2/2A/333, Bl. 8–9.

267. In March 1953, the SED Politburo was still planning to ask Soviet institutions for permission to replicate Stalin cult materials: Merkurov's busts and statues, pictures depicting Stalin and members of the Presidium of the Central Committee, and brochures with biographies of Malenkov, Beria, and Molotov. See "Anlage Nr. 5a zum Protokoll Nr. 16/53 vom 17. März 1953," 212–13.

268. "Stalin-Denkmal in Riesa feierlich enthüllt," *Neues Deutschland*, March 5, 1954, 1. See also Koselleck, "Einleitung," in Koselleck and Jeismann, *Der politische Totenkult*, 9–20.

269. Azaryahu, *Von Wilhelmplatz zu Thälmannplatz*, 166.

270. Azaryahu, *Von Wilhelmplatz zu Thälmannplatz*, 167–68.

271. "Fotosammlung 'J. W. Stalin,'" Bildarchiv im Bundesarchiv-Koblenz.

272. For example, Zubkova, "Malenkov i Khrushchev."

273. See Aimermakher, *Doklad Khrushcheva*. 58. The expression "enemies of the people" was introduced during the French Revolution in the June 1, 1794 decree on the persecution of enemies of the people. The term was incorporated

into the Russian political lexicon after the 1917 February Revolution. The quotation from Khrushchev's speech can be found in Russian in Aimermakher, *Doklad Khrushcheva*, 151.

274. On the metaphor of the "newborn state," see Gries and Gibas, "Die Inszenierung des sozialistischen Deutschlands," in Gibas et al., *Wiedergeburten*, 32.

275. Staritz, *Geschichte der DDR*, 36 and 80ff. Party members were especially likely to become "enemies." During the party purge in 1951, the SED expelled 100,000 members, of whom no less than 37,000 were explicitly declared "party enemies."

276. Investigation Procedure (UV) No. U. 56/53, Der Bundesbeauftrage für die Unterlagen des ehemaligen Staatssicherheitsdienstes der DDR (BStU), AST Chemnitz, Bezirksverwaltung (BV) Karl-Marx-Stadt AU 160/53, Bl. 156.

277. Neubert, *Stalin wollte ein anderes Europa*, 163.

278. Stiftung Archiv der Parteien und Massenorganisationen (SAPMO)—Federal Archive (BArch), DY 30N/2/51269, Bl. 300, 306, 326.

279. UV No. U. 56/53; BStU, AST Chemnitz, BV Karl-Marx-Stadt AU 160/53 (UV), Bl. 153.

280. Order No. 16/53 to the German People's Police of March 17, 1953; BStU, ZA MfS-BdL, Doc. No. 050823, Bl. 1.

281. SAPMO-BArch, DY 30/V/2/5/269, Bl. 301, 311.

282. BStU, ZA MfS-BdL No. 050823, Bl. 1f.

283. BStU, ZA MfS-BdL No. 050827, Bl. 2.

284. BStU, BV Gera AGI 9/55 T. II. BI. 68–69; BStU, ZA MfS-BdL No. 002709, Bl. 1ff.

285. According to Article 6 of the Constitution of the GDR and Kontrollrat Directive No. 38, Art. III A.

286. SAPMO-BArch DY 30/V/2/5/269, Bl. 317.

287. BStU, AS BV Suhl AU 9/53, Bl. 66.

288. SAPMO-BArch DY 30/V/2/5/269, Bl. 131, 315, 317.

289. BStU, BV Suhl AU 11/53 (UV), Bl. 6.

290. UV No. U. 56/53; BStU, AST Chemnitz, BV Karl-Marx-Stadt AU 160/53, Bl. 184.

291. UV No. U. 18/53; BStU, AST Suhl, BV Suhl AU 39/53, Bl. 22.

292. BStU, AST Suhl, BV Suhl AU 9/53, Bl. 86.

293. BStU, AST Suhl, BV Suhl AU 9/53, Bl. 89.

294. Groys, *Gesamtkunstwerk Stalin*; Ehalt, *Inszenierung der Gewalt*; Sennebogen, "Propaganda als Populärkultur?"; Reichel, *Der schöne Schein*; Czech and Doll, *Kunst und Propaganda*.

295. Behrenbeck, "Der Führer."

296. On the mediatization of the public sphere and public spaces in modern dictatorships, see Giunter and Khensgen, *Sovetskaia vlast' i media*; Bösch and Borutta, *Die Massen bewegen*; Lindenberger, *Massenmedien im Kalten Krieg*; Daniel and Schildt, *Massenmedien im Europa*.

297. *Der Spiegel*, March 16, 1950, 23.

298. On the National Program for the Restoration of Berlin, see Peters, "Nationale, klassizistische und fortschrittliche Bautradition." The Third SED Congress adopted a resolution to restore Berlin's destroyed city center on July 20–27, 1950; they accepted a five-year plan for 1951–1955 at the same congress.

299. *Roman einer jungen Ehe* was produced by the DEFA-Studie für Spielfilme. Kurt Maetzig and Bodo Uhse wrote the screenplay.

300. KuBa, "Stalinallee," 242 (translation by J. F.).

301. See "Stalin, Freund, Genosse," in Bloch, *Lieder der UdSSR*, 86–88. Alexei Surkov wrote the text of the original Russian song ("Pesnia o Staline," 1938) and Alexander Ott [Georg Schmidt] wrote the German lyrics (1949); Soviet composer Matvei Blanter wrote the music to which both the Russian text and the German translation are set.

302. "Richtfest am Hochhaus der Weberwiese," January 19, 1952, on Deutsches Historisches Museum and Deutsches Rundfunkarchiv, *Stalinallee—Stalinstadt*, track no. 1.

303. See D. Müller, "Wir bauen," 385.

304. D. Müller, "Wir bauen."

305. "Richtfest an ersten drei Wohnblöcken in der Stalinallee," July 14, 1952, on Deutsches Historisches Museum and Deutsches Rundfunkarchiv, *Stalinallee— Stalinstadt*, track no. 4.

306. Azaryahu, *Von Wilhelmplatz zu Thälmannplatz*, 165.

307. See D. Müller, "Wir bauen," 386.

308. *Neue Berliner Illustrierte*, January 5, 1953, 7.

309. "Deutschlands erster großer Neubau beginnt," *Neues Deutschland*, December 21, 1949, 8; *Neue Berliner Illustrierte*, no. 52 (December 1951), 6–7.

310. For example, *Neue Berliner Illustrierte*, no. 5 (January 1953), 7.

311. "Der Aufbau der Stalinallee schreitet voran, 5. Mai 1952," on Deutsches Historisches Museum and Deutsches Rundfunkarchiv, *Stalinallee—Stalinstadt*, track no. 3.

312. *Neue Berliner Illustrierte*, no. 5 (January 1953), 7.

313. "Visitenkarte des Wohlstandes: Bummeln durch die neuen Läden in der Stalinallee," *Neue Berliner Illustrierte*, no. 5 (January 1953), 7.

314. "Die glücklichsten Menschen Deutschlands," *Neue Berliner Illustrierte*, no. 4 (1953), 4–5.

315. *Neue Berliner Illustrierte*, no. 4 (1953), 4–5.

316. In 1952 alone, approximately 45,000 workers volunteered about four million hours of work to construct the Stalinallee. See D. Müller, "Wir bauen."

317. Grotewohl, "Stalinallee—Straße der unverbindlichen Freundschaft," in *Im Kampf*, vol. 3, 35.

318. In February 1953, *Neues Deutschland* published a series of articles titled "What Happiness Looks Like" (*Wie Glück aussieht*) describing the winners of the lottery raising funds to construct the Stalinallee. The articles presented receiving an apartment on East Germany's "first socialist street" as the moment when the recipient became a "new man," rewarded for his/her success in work, study, or

postwar reconstruction, regardless whatever he/she had done before 1945. See *Neues Deutschland*, February 3, 1953, 6; February 5, 1953, 6; February 7, 1953.

319. *Neue Berliner Illustrierte*, no. 4 (1953), 4–5.

320. Kotkin, *Magnetic Mountain*; Lebow, *Unfinished Utopia*; Horváth, *Stalinism Reloaded*; Jaješniak-Quast, *Stahlgiganten*. Architecturally, these cities, like others in the "people's democracies," made a similar impression. The socialist classicism marking postwar reconstruction across Eastern Europe was an additional sign of the Soviet bloc's ideological homogenization.

321. In June 1960, the SED Third Congress passed a resolution to establish a metallurgical center close to Fürstenberg am Oder. Construction of the metallurgical combine began in August 1950, and in the autumn of 1951, work began on creating a city with twenty-five thousand residents. From 1953 to 1961, the city was called Stalinstadt, but in 1961 as a result of a wave of de-Stalinization, the name was changed to Eisenhüttenstadt. See Ludwig, *Eisenhüttenstadt*; Richter, Förster, and Lakemann, *Stalinstadt—Eisenhüttenstadt*.

322. "Stadt der Dankbarkeit," *Neue Berliner Illustrierte*, no. 11 (1953).

323. "'Das neue Leben': Funkbericht über den Aufbau der Stalinstadt, Mai 1953," on Deutsches Historisches Museum and Deutsches Rundfunkarchiv, *Stalinallee— Stalinstadt*, track 10.

324. "'Ich bin stolz und glücklich, in dieser Stadt leben und arbeiten zu können': Produktionsverpflichtungen der Werktätigen an den Baustätten des Eisenhüttenkombinats," *Neues Deutschland*, May 9, 1953, 4.

325. See Reid and Crowley, *Style and Socialism*; Reid, "Cold War in the Kitchen"; Reid, "Khrushchev Modern."

326. Applebaum, *Iron Curtain*, 391–94.

327. Under state socialism, as Katherine Lebow states, "the new woman extended her traditionally nurturing role beyond the sphere of the nuclear family to embrace not only the nation but also the wider family of international progress and peace." See *Unfinished Utopia*, 100.

328. Mohrmann, "Male Heroes and Female Comrades."

329. "Sendung anlässlich des zweijährigen Bestehens der Stalinstadt," May 1955, on Deutsches Historisches Museum and Deutsches Rundfunkarchiv *Stalinallee— Stalinstadt*, track 11.

330. W. Berkner, "Stalin ist unser Lehrmeister," *Sächsische Zeitung*, December 21, 1951

331. "Wie Klaus Arbeiterstudent wurde," *Sächsische Zeitung*, December 21, 1951.

332. On athletes, see, for example, "Neue Schwimmrekorde zu Ehren Stalin," *Bauern Echo*, December 21, 1951, and Rossbach, "Täve." For things which would attract women, see E. Schmidt, "Die Lehre von Marx, Engels, Lenin und Stalin— Programm zur Befreiung der Frau," *Neues Deutschland*, March 8, 1953, 6 and "Gelöbnis einer Arbeiterin," *Lausitzer Rundschau*, December 21, 1951, 3. On benefits for young people, see, for example, "Stalins Leben ein Beispiel für Jugend," *Neues Deutschland*, December 18, 1951, 1; for activists, see "Stalin—Vorbild des Aktivisten Josef Walljasper," *Volksstimme*," December 21, 1951, 3.

333. "Analyse der Leserbriefe. Neues Deutschland an das Zentralkomitee der SED," SAPMO-BArch, DY IV/2/5/254. Bl. 13.

334. AdsD, SPD-PV-Ostbüro 0257, unpag.

335. In *Seeing Like a State*, James Scott has also analyzed the emergence of new towns as examples of "authoritarian high modernism" by showing where ideology, science, and practice intersected in creating a "new society" and a "new man."

336. Sabrow, "Time and Legitimacy." For analogous observations, see Jessen, "Semantic Strategies," especially 277–80.

337. Sabrow, "Time and Legitimacy," 365.

338. Caspar, "Zum Geleit," 15.

Chapter 5

"The Fierce Enemy of the German People"

The Personality Cult and Iconoclasm in East Germany

THE POTENTIAL FOR CONFLICT IN OFFICIAL PUBLIC SPHERES

It all turned into a movement on the city streets. In a short time, all the banners and posters on the public buildings and peoples' enterprises were removed. As each poster bearing a slogan proclaiming honor to the Soviet Union and German-Polish friendship was torn off, the crowd cheered wildly. This is also just how all the buildings housing state institutions and schools were cleansed of the portraits of Stalin, Lenin, Pieck, Grotewohl, and Ulbricht. The busts of the leaders were smashed to pieces on the street-bridge and ground into the dirt. In the schools, Russian-language textbooks were ripped up and set on fire. Finally, the SED's regional House of Correction was stormed and taken. The windows and doors were forced open and, in a matter of a few minutes, the rebels threw portraits, the busts of Stalin, the flags, and volumes of Marxist-Leninist classics onto the street and then they set them on fire on the squares.

> SPD Eastern Bureau report on events taking place in Görlitz on June 17, 1953

The uprising of June 17, 1953 was the first widespread protest on the outskirts of the Soviet Empire. It unfolded throughout the country as a ritual of overt popular violence against the East German dictatorship. The symbols of the personality cult—monuments, busts, portraits, posters, and works written by the leaders—were the main targets of the social aggression that had been unleashed. Storming the East German "Bastilles"—the party houses and buildings belonging to the mass organizations, the jails and houses of preliminary detention that were the dictatorship's bastions of discipline and repression—also became a component of the scenario for overthrowing the regime's icons.[1] Engaging in the ritual acts of setting on fire, damaging, and destroying the objects of the personality cult, the population demonstrated its distance from the ideology of the "worker-peasant state" and its desire to free itself from the chains of dictatorship. However, this type of overt struggle in Soviet-style societies was the exception, not the rule. More often the harsh rules governing rhetoric and behavior imposed by the dictatorship forced the population to look for indirect methods, by using the means that daily life offered, to articulate their needs and expectations, criticisms and disappointments.

In East Germany, the ideology of the "workers' and peasants' state" ruled out the possibility of any conflict between the regime and the population. According to Marxist-Leninist theory, the regime was based on the postulates that the state-dominated society and individual interests should be subordinated to the goals of the party and the state—that is, to building socialism.[2] A key dramatization of the society of social consensus depicted in propaganda took place during demonstrations. This was the ritual procession of the masses moving past a reviewing stand (*Tribüne*) where representatives of the regime stood.[3] This ritual was intended to demonstrate that the regime had made a social pact with the population and was supposed to represent the people's support for the regime's politics. When the regime and society came together, however, open conflict often threatened to break out. For example, during a 1951 May First demonstration in Potsdam, the toasts the speaker offered in honor of the Soviet Union and Stalin provoked a reaction from the population that the authorities had not anticipated: the participants pointedly averted their faces from the reviewing stand and, at the point when they should have responded to the toasts by shouting "Hurrah!" they chose to remain silent.[4] Stalin's death prompted further incidents. In Leipzig, "caustic comments" about Stalin made by secondary school students as they moved past a grandstand decorated with a huge picture of the Soviet leader, and their teachers' pointed refusal to remove their hats as they walked by the reviewing stand, disrupted official mourning for the Soviet leader.[5] Similar gestures became telling signs of the population's distance from the regime. They indicate that in official spheres the public not only assimilated and followed the prescribed models of behavior but also reinterpreted the Soviet symbols handed down from above.

How iconoclastic acts were woven into the rituals of violence can be seen during the June 1953 uprising in the village of Zodel in the Görlitz region. To enact overthrowing the SED regime, the rebels used the normative model of the ritual procession of the masses moving past a reviewing stand on which representatives of the regime stood. Unnerved by the uprising, the party functionaries had made themselves scarce. During the procession around the village, however, the crowd hunted them down and forced them to form a "column of shame" consisting of the mayor, a representative of the agricultural produce cooperative, the school director, a representative of the German-Soviet Friendship Society, and the leader of the Pioneers. Treating the captured SED members like prisoners intensified the ritual shaming. Tied up with red flags around their necks, the "captives" were chased through the village to the inhabitants' mocking laughter.[6] During the proceedings, the representative of the German-Soviet Friendship Society was forced to carry Stalin's portrait in front of him. People cursed it as it passed by. This incident, with its elements of carnivalesque behavior, recalls the iconoclastic ritual of the "defamed image" (*Schandbild*), in which scorning and damaging the picture dishonored the depicted person.[7]

Another important carnivalesque aspect of the events of June 1953 in Zodel was the people's impulse to "turn the world upside down" by enacting role changes and the seizure of power.[8] After political demands for "a free government, liquidation of the SED, free elections, the return of Silesia, abolition of obligatory production norms, equal rights for all peasants, and elimination of the requirement to study Russian and compulsory instruction on world current events in the schools" were voiced, a "reviewing stand" was set up.[9] The mayor was brought to the table and the crowd demanded that he publicly renounce the regime and his own authority. When he refused to bend to the will of the people, he was pushed off the table onto the ground.[10] Forcing the mayor to relinquish his authority was the work of a court of the people and a celebration of popular justice. The way this was carried out is reminiscent of the tradition of toppling a statue from its pedestal as an iconoclastic gesture. A statue overturned and damaged by a crowd demonstrates that the people stripped the regime of honor, value, and trust—fundamental categories that confirm the legitimacy of political regimes. The ritual of violence enacted in Zodel was simultaneously both a spontaneous legal process intended to deprive party functionaries of their status and an act of physical harm done to the bodies of the authorities which symbolically defiled representations of the party and the state. In these acts, we see elements of a "ritual of shaming and expelling" detested representatives of the regime.[11] It is also clear that mockery, physical violence, and folk justice were key methods for dishonoring the SED and seeking deliverance from it.

The population used another of the personality cult's rituals—collecting gifts for the leaders' birthdays—to damage representations of the regime.[12] For example, in 1951, just before Stalin's birthday, a "congratulatory postcard" was circulating in the population. This card visually deconstructed the myth of the friendship of the peoples flourishing under the Soviet leader's aegis. It depicted workers in chains, presenting Stalin with a coffin as a gift. The image's impact was intensified by the accompanying text, which urged the viewer, "Don't forget to celebrate the birthday of the best friend of the German people since this might be his last."[13] Sometimes people simply refused to participate in propaganda campaigns. For example, the students at Dresden's Higher School declined to collect money for a gift for Stalin.[14] Proximity to the West and, as a result, the illegal presence of Western mass media in the GDR meant that there was an alternative source of information that hindered efforts to propagandize the Soviet cults. For example, for Stalin's birthday in 1950, the West Berlin Fighting Group against Inhumanity (Kampfgruppe gegen Unmenschlichkeit) sent the SED's Central Committee an eight-kilogram barbed-wire wreath, asking the committee to give it to the Soviet leader.[15] The way this gesture was staged in the Western press resonated throughout East Germany and helped strengthen the population's negative image of Stalin.

Although the regime mobilized its resources of propaganda and terror, tense incidents and sometimes open conflict between representatives of the regime and the population inside official public spheres were constantly being recorded. A decided lack of trust in the cults that had been proclaimed was expressed during auto races in Dessau on October 1, 1950. The president's visit gave the sporting event a political overtone. The public reaction to Pieck's tour of the car rally route showed how ineffective the "father of the nation's" propaganda-generated charisma was. When the president appeared, the representatives of the regime, the party, and the mass organizations reacted in a highly ritualized manner—with "wild applause" and "friendly cries of 'Hurrah!'" from their grandstand. In the public stands, by contrast, there were signs of displeasure—silence, hissing, and whistling.[16]

The feeling of group solidarity and the sense that it was possible to collectively avoid participation in personality cult rituals expanded opportunities for demonstrating distance from rhetorical and behavioral norms in the dictatorship's official public spheres. In November 1951, the workers at the Karl Liebknecht Electrical Power Substation in Berlin, one and all, ignored Ulbricht's evening visit to the substation as they hurried from the official to the private realm, that is, the nonpolitical, and therefore more comfortable, niches of private life—home, the weekend cottage, the pub, one's circle of family and friends.[17] That same year, in many schools the upperclassmen chose not to watch a film about the president of the GDR, refusing to pay 20 cents to enter the theater.[18] In Cottbus, workers refused to participate in the ritual mourning for Stalin. At a party gathering, the SED secretary called for a moment of silence in memory of the Soviet leader, but none of those in the hall rose from their chairs (except the presidium), pointedly remaining seated.[19]

Silence is one of the practices bordering on iconoclasm. It is tolerated—to some degree—by repressive regimes. Silence could indicate anxiety about crossing the line separating what could or could not be said aloud or done in public. Or silence might well be connected with fear of persecution and the loss of accumulated symbolic capital. Silence could also reflect rational conformism and the loyalty to the regime given by an individual who was well-schooled in adapting and integrating him- or herself and capable of speaking the party's language.[20] Finally, silence could be interpreted as an act of passive enmity toward the regime. Thus, at one holiday celebration in the city of Halle, before the fireworks started, toasts were made in honor of Stalin, Pieck, and the party. Functionaries waited for the population to respond by shouting "Hurrah" in unison, but the propaganda slogans dissolved into the stillness of the silent crowd.[21]

To get people to participate in party and state rituals and to make sure that citizens were active in the official public sphere, at least to some extent, the regime was forced to resort to various kinds of manipulations. For example, in 1951 an effort to assemble workers at the Buna Works in Merseburg to celebrate Stalin's birthday only succeeded because each "active participant" was promised two mugs of beer and ten cigarettes.[22] In some cases, wages were paid only after celebrations of the Soviet leader's birthday were over. Propagandistic events frequently took place during working hours since it was obvious to everyone that workers had no desire to waste their free time on political activities. Materials collected by the Eastern Bureau of the SPD indicate that the population rejected the SED regime and tried hard to avoid participating in party and state rituals by withdrawing into private and anonymous spaces of personal life—the realm of the family and friends.

The state went after iconoclasm in official public spheres ever more vehemently, criminalizing it and creating "enemies" of the regime. For example, on January 3, 1951, a celebration of Pieck's birthday was cut short soon after it started because plumes of smoke from smoke bombs began to appear in what was apparently an act of arson.[23] Fifty-three people, ranging in age from fifteen to twenty-three years old, most of whom were students in their final years of secondary school, were arrested by the People's Police and the Stasi (Ministry for State Security) on suspicion of conspiracy. The arrestees were presumed guilty. They were criminalized by being branded "enemies of the people," an ideological construction often deployed in the corridors of power.[24] After interrogation, the accused were convicted of conspiring against the state and belonging to a fascist youth organization with headquarters in West Berlin. The trial—intended for public edification—ended with sentences being handed down, the most severe of which was twenty-five years in jail. Under the dictatorship's repressive policies, the judicial apparatus and the courts instrumentalized the personality cult to create an atmosphere of fear, to legitimate the policy of excluding people who displeased the regime, and to establish the boundaries of which activities were allowed and how much individual activity was permissible.

The politicization of criminal acts of vandalism shows that the state and party had acquired a monopoly on control of public space: If anything associated with a personality cult was among the objects damaged, the regime automatically attributed this vandalism to the "enemy activity of reactionary elements." In other words, it equated such acts with iconoclastic practices. For example, during the night of August 12–13, 1946, a meeting hall in Leschnitz that had been set up for a ceremony commemorating the Day of Victims of Fascism was turned upside down. Flags and portraits of the leaders were ripped to shreds and the cloths that had draped the tables were stolen.[25] In September 1948, bricks and stones were hurled at the windows of the SED building in Potsdam, shattering a bust of Marx.[26] Near the West German border, in the village of Legenfeld unter Stein, there was a nighttime raid on a party agitation office (*agitpunkt*) in which the windows were broken, all the posters torn up, and vases and furniture destroyed.[27]

In these instances, it is difficult to draw a precise line demarcating the practices of vandalism from those of iconoclasm, especially if one takes into account the fact that at times the regime itself resorted to staging acts of vandalism and iconoclasm in order to get even with "enemies of the regime." One of the SPD Eastern Bureau's reports describes a political raid in Eichwald, where representatives of the People's Police entered the train station and hid some banners there so that they could then discover "two newly prepared banners with a sketch of Hitler and a caption declaring that he would return soon." This "discovery" was the pretext for the arrest and subsequent criminalization of the station's director and staff, with whom the local leadership of the SED "had old scores to settle."[28]

Thus, the personality cult's symbols—portraits, posters, and busts of the leaders—were personified targets for expressing social aggression in official public spheres, that is, those organized and controlled by the regime. If party-state rituals were called upon to legitimate and stabilize the regime, the complex of anti-rituals—or rituals of violence—that received the population's approbation aimed to achieve the exact opposite. As tactics for distancing from and opposing the official order, these rituals of violence were used to delegitimize, destabilize, and cast doubt on the order decreed by the dictatorship. Attempts to discipline and exclude people with alternative views by criminalizing those who displeased the regime are evidence of the regime's weakness and unpopularity. The many and varied possibilities for schism that party-state public spheres offered point to the personality cult's limited resources for producing social consensus.

THE TIMES AND SPACES OF ICONOCLASM

According to political reports and summaries of the population's moods, acts of iconoclasm took place primarily "during the evening hours," and "after twilight falls," or "in the dark of the night." Every day at sunset a political revolution of sorts took place. With the onset of darkness, the occupying powers let go of their monopoly on vigorous surveillance of public space. Sensing that the fetters on its autonomy had been loosened, society took the initiative and committed political acts in those zones of social life which, during the day, demanded strictly regulated behavior. Thus, the night was a transitional zone, a borderland where actors could leave the public spheres of party and state and enter an anonymous sphere of political activity. At dawn, the regime took the reins of government back into its hands, removing all traces of popular violence from the streets and squares.

The competition between day and night, a reflection of the political conflict between the regime and society, showed itself in the Saxon town of Strehla, where the Thälmann cult was proclaimed with posters bearing his image. These were put up during the day and torn down at night.[29] In Glauchau, anti-Stalin and anti-Soviet graffiti were scrawled on the walls of the town's main factory during the night before the May First demonstration. At dawn, police patrols had to hurry to wipe away all traces of social indignation in a space which, a few hours later, would become an arena for staging a society of collective consensus.[30] At dawn, the decorations that had been put up on the eve of May First in Wernigerode were nowhere to be found. Unknown persons tore down all the posters and defaced them. Instead of officially approved decorations, paper swastikas were strewn about the town center.[31] Likewise, we see how dusk was used to change propaganda's official messages after the Day of Liberation in Friedersdorf. Wreaths that had been laid at Soviet obelisks were discovered the following morning on the graves of German soldiers.[32] On the night of September 12, 1948, the Day of Commemoration of the Victims of Fascism, a poster was put up on the town of Lübbenau's memorial to heroic Soviet soldiers. It proclaimed that "Instead of honoring scoundrels, we want to honor the memory of those who fell in the war and the victims of the current terror."[33]

Iconoclastic practices took place in different locales during daylight hours and at night. By day it was possible to voice opinions freely, without risk of persecution, inside certain intimate niches of public space. Thus, during a Soviet inspection of the Lindner rolling stock factory in Ammendorf in October 1948, antigovernment graffiti was discovered in the toilets. The head of the Inspection Commission ordered that all seditious graffiti in the toilets be wiped off and recommended increased surveillance.[34] In 1953, just after Stalin's death, at another enterprise in Thuringia, a campaign of spontaneous iconoclasm unfolded on the walls of the toilet stalls. Portraits of the leaders were removed from high-status locations in the building and taken into the toilet stalls, where they were adorned with drawings of gallows and animal body parts as well as crude anti-Soviet and antigovernment graffiti.[35]

To reduce the communicative potential of the toilets, the management had to issue numerous orders about repainting them every week. Such displacements of the symbols of power from "sacral zones" to "dirty places" disrupted the official system of public symbolism, which revealed the regime's unpopularity and demeaned its legitimacy.[36]

At times, those in authority and social actors negotiated openly about the reception of personality cults. In the name of legitimizing the status quo under the dictatorship, all concerned were prepared to look for compromises, to work out a resolution tolerable to both sides, and to take action together. Thus, on May 1, 1954, at the Georgi Dimitrov Factory in Magdeburg, an argument between the party leadership and the workers flared up. The workers refused to carry portraits of socialist bloc leaders as they marched in the columns of demonstrators. Unfortunately, the document to which I had access does not reveal what took place during the process of resolving this quarrel but only gives a summary of what happened. After a great deal of back-and-forth, a certain compromise was reached: images of Ulbricht and Mao Zedong would be excluded from the list of portraits already drawn up.[37] Significantly, this symbolic bargaining took place a year after Stalin's death and on the eve of the anniversary of the June 1953 uprising. This indicates a bolder rejection of propagandized cults as a result of weakened party-state control over representations of leaders in public spheres as still-latent de-Stalinization began to develop.

Like the times chosen for iconoclastic acts, such as party-state holidays, propaganda campaigns, and leaders' birthdays, the places where such acts took place intensified their political tone. Defacing portraits and damaging busts of the leaders in "peace corners" and the rooms dedicated to the leaders in factories, schools, buildings housing the mass organizations, the pavilions at the Leipzig trade fair, and party and state institutions were automatically considered political acts carried out by "internal and foreign enemies." Thus, one night, in the peace corner of a factory in Teltow, a deerstalker cap was placed on a bust of Stalin.[38] The regime called on the population not to delay in reporting instances of "destruction of the social order" to the People's Police. Another incident took place in Leuna, on the eve of the Day of the October Revolution. During the night of November 2–3, 1951, a bust of Stalin was abducted from the peace corner at the Walter Ulbricht Factory. On the following day, smeared with dirt, the bust was put near the factory directors' offices by unknown persons. A sign had been hung around its neck that said, "You are as worthless as W. Pieck."[39]

The official regime's shakiness during the nighttime hours spurred the politicization of night and the expansion of the dictatorship's daytime order to the conditions of darkness. Sovietization had to proceed in full swing—by night as well as by day. One of the first attempts to subjugate the night was the introduction of a curfew from 11:00 p.m. to 8:00 a.m. by order of Military Commandant no. 1 of Berlin.[40] On May 13, 1945, SVAG issued Order No. 5 on electric lighting for the streets of Berlin, which was a new step toward establishing control over the night hours.[41] The practice of illuminating portraits of the leaders as a form of nighttime propaganda was introduced on central streets and squares across the country and was used in train stations, offices of the military commandants, and government buildings.

The expansion of public spheres such as holidays and other celebrations staged by the state during the hours of darkness further politicized nighttime space. One of the first night events with overarching state significance took place in conjunction with Pieck's election as president of the GDR. On the night of October 11, 1949, 200,000 members of the Union of Free German Youth marched through Berlin at night, carrying posters of Stalin and Pieck and "peace torches" to honor the creation of "a new, antifascist, democratic state."[42] Late in the evening of October 12, Pieck inspected an honor guard of the People's Police, an event that was staged in one of the photo documentaries about the SED's night patrol.[43] In December 1949, the grand finale of the birthday celebrations was a fireworks display. As twilight fell, the bright flames of the fireworks lit up Stalin's profile along with a propaganda slogan, *Proletarier aller Länder vereinigt euch!* (Workers of the World Unite!) (Figure 5.1).

Use of the personality cult to conquer nighttime space was in evidence during the Third International Youth and Student Games, held in East Berlin in August 1951 (Figure 5.2). At one of the evening events, a summary of the results of the competition, dedicated "To peace and for Stalin!" (*Za mir i za Stalina!*), was read out. The dramaturgy for the games' closing ceremony followed Moscow's scenario for Stalin's seventieth-birthday celebrations on Red Square. A fanfare gave the signal for six powerful floodlights to illuminate the image of the leader soaring in the air.[44]

Despite the regime's attempts to control the hours of darkness, the screen that night offered for iconoclastic acts meant that, in most cases, the security organs were unable to identify those who performed rituals of violence. Official party-state documents establish the regime's impotence in the fight against those who wreaked havoc on its order by night. Patrols, ambushes, raids, and the 1952 creation of a "brigade of volunteer assistants to the People's Police," who were on duty at night, did not produce noticeable results.[45] Only rarely could individuals on the other side of the ideological front be identified by name. Thus, one of SVAG's political dispatches from Gera reported that "reactionaries are winning over twelve- to fifteen-year-olds, who scrawl fascist slogans on the walls after night falls."[46] In Soviet-style societies, night remained more anonymous and, therefore, a more autonomous niche in social life, despite the regime's ubiquitous efforts to subordinate it to the daytime order of the dictatorship.

Figure 5.1 The grande finale of a demonstration celebrating the Soviet leader's birthday and the renaming of the Frankfurter Allee as the Stalinallee. **December 21, 1949.** *Source:* Bildarchiv im Bundesarchiv (Koblenz). Signature: Bild 183-S91408. Photographer: Eva Kemlein.

Figure 5.2 Closing ceremonies of the World Youth and Student Games in East Berlin. **August 19, 1951.** *Source:* Bildarchiv im Bundesarchiv (Koblenz), Signature: Bild 183-19000-102.

DISHONORING THE REGIME AND THE
EMOTIONAL WORK OF EAST GERMAN SOCIETY

The most widespread forms of covert or anonymous iconoclasm ranged from taking down and ripping up the posters, banners, and emblems put up by the state to breaking shop windows that displayed leaders' portraits.[47] Yet it was the damage inflicted on visual images—specifically, on the facial features of political leaders—that constituted the most serious insults to the regime. These were the first depredations to come to the attention of the security organs. Thus, the SPD's Eastern Bureau reported that on the eve of Stalin's birthday, portraits of the Soviet leader were smeared with mud and ink, and the eyes and mouth were gouged out.[48] Portraits of Thälmann taken down in Lugau were discovered the next day with the eyes gouged out, and the nose and mouth ripped off.[49] The semantics of iconoclastic violence inflicted on portrait images bears the symbolic burden of a "loss of face," a form of defiling propagandized figures by gravely injuring representations of power.

The goal when adding drawings or text was analogous to intentions expressed in crossing text out on images bearing the iconography of the personality cult: these alterations demonstrated the regime's loss of authority in the eyes of the population. These practices were intended to show publicly that it was possible to change propaganda's official meanings. For example, on January 7, 1946, a copy of an issue of the *Thüringer Volkszeitung* with a portrait of Pieck was put in the editorial staff's mailbox. Pieck's nose had been colored red and immediately after the slogan published with the portrait, "W. Pieck—son of the people," a question mark had been added.[50] An inscription followed: "The same kind of lies the Nazis told."[51] This inscription thematized the problem of trusting the East German leadership, whose methods of doing ideological work evoked the population's associations with Goebbels's Ministry of Propaganda. In Brandenburg, someone used the text of a poster proclaiming one of Stalin's key slogans—"The Hitlers come and go, but the German people, the German state remains"— to sum up the results of the Soviet occupation regime in East Germany.[52] An appeal to the civilian population was added to the poster's official text:

> To the German people of the Eastern zone! Stalin said, 'The Hitlers come and go, but the German people remain!' But what has really happened? Three years of robbery and theft! Three years of famine and death! Three years of assaults on our girls and women! Three years of lies about the people's democracy! Let's drive out the ones who besmirch culture![53]

Similar reinterpretations of propaganda included adding drawings of the gallows or a guillotine to portraits of the leaders. Such images articulated the motif of punishing the leaders, which was regularly thematized in iconoclastic acts.[54] A call to exercise popular justice vis-à-vis the East German leadership was recorded on the eve of celebrations of the one-hundredth anniversary of the 1848 Revolution. These celebrations were one of the SED's first attempts to present a new picture of the past, one linked to the traditions of a democratic popular movement.[55] On a notice board in the city of Bernau in the district of Zwickau, someone scrawled the following in chalk: "In honor of the holiday hang the slaves of the Russians—Pieck, Seidewitz [the prime minister of Saxony—*A. T.*] and Grotewohl by their feet. Heil Hitler!"[56] The semantics of deprivation of honor included symbolically bringing leaders down to the level of animals. This was done by adding text making offensive comparisons of the leaders with animals or drawing animal body parts on their images. Thus, in October 1950, in the border town of Faulungen insulting words were written on an SED election campaign poster: "W. Pieck is a fat pig."[57] A swastika was discovered on a building in Potsdam. Underneath it was a message signed by the Werewolf organization: "We are back again. If the Americans come, we will hang the red dogs."[58] Thus, official representations of the personality cult were transformed; "sacred" images became "profane" and "dirty" in the widespread practice of dishonoring and insulting the SED regime.

Overt symbolic violence in iconoclastic rituals was often expressed verbally by hooting or cursing, insulting, mocking, catcalling, and directing hostile comments at the images of leaders but ignoring them in public places was another type of explicit symbolic violence.[59] For the first time after the war, East Germans showed their capacity for collective emotional work in response to Sovietization. Hence, in 1947–1948, they began once again to express shared feelings in places where crowds gathered. In large groups, people were able to articulate political sympathies and antipathies, trust and distrust of propaganda figures.[60] Social actors registered their opposition to the regime in movie theaters and in stadiums, and at public celebrations of various kinds. In other words, in places where people could act anonymously and therefore avoid punishment for violating the established political order. Thus, in movie theaters during showings of the weekly newsreel (the state-owned DEFA film studio's *Augenzeuge*) whenever Stalin, Ulbricht, or Pieck appeared on the screen, loud laughter and derisive shouting were heard.[61] During a football match in Dresden in July 1948, the spectators whistled, trying to drown out a speaker uttering slogans in honor of German-Soviet friendship.[62] At another match, this one in Halle on March 31, 1952, the fans in the stands booed Hero of Socialist Labor Adolf Hennecke and at halftime they pelted him with snowballs.[63] As these examples of iconoclastic behavior indicate, in the first years of the GDR the population had already ceased to distinguish between German and Soviet leaders instead of seeing them as a single entity. This shows a gradual interpenetration of "our" (German) political spaces and "theirs" (Soviet) during the intensive phase of Sovietization in East Germany, which took place between 1947–1948 and 1953.

Overt forms of iconoclasm were distinguished by including a broad swath of the public in the rituals and adopting a more aggressive scenario for communicating with the regime. The June 1953 uprising was the high point of public violence directed against symbols of the dictatorship. Inspired by Natalie Zemon Davis's work on confessional conflicts in Early Modern France, I read the events of June 17 from a perspective within the protests, looking at prewar and postwar German sensibilities and the performance of protest. Natalie Zemon Davis taught us to understand the social and cultural meanings of the rituals of religious violence by showing how these acts were rooted in a common understanding of community and how the borders between the "sacred" and the "profane" and the participants' perceptions of threats to their faith were defined. Davis set out an innovative way for historians to understand the inner life of communities and a new way to explain the radicalization of violence by arguing that in the minds of perpetrators and in their confidence in a sacred struggle with the "devil" that presented a mortal danger to the wholeness of the imagined community, violence was justified and even legitimized.[64] In postwar East Germany, the Russians were such "devils" as were representatives of the SED regime who destroyed the former "people's community" (*Volksgemeinschaft*), which was united by a shared sense of national honor, a desire for racial purity, and desire for the "Führer."

In fact, June 17, 1953, was the first public action of redefining the community, which had been Sovietized by force. Echoes of national-socialist propaganda were quite evident—invocations of stereotypes of Russian savagery and backwardness that were still prevalent and expressions of fear of the dangers of pan-Slavism. On June 18, at the sight of Soviet troops, shipyard workers in Wismar shouted: "Under these Asiatics, under this cudgel, we will not work: they should go back home."[65] The rebels often shouted out anti-Russian slogans such as "Ivan go home," "No 1945," and "No rapes."[66] Rumors of another wave of rapes like those of the early postwar period circulated among women. In Fürstenberg, insurgents shouted "Iwan, geh' heim!" at the sight of Soviet tanks.[67] A man who was photographed throwing a stone at a Soviet tank (the photograph became one of the visual icons of the uprising) remembered that at that moment he did not feel fear, "only rage, a lot of anger at the Russians."[68]

Rebels' actions were often driven by nationalistic feelings. Anti-Polish hostilities were observed in the borderland region between the GDR and Poland.

In Görlitz rebels demanded the abolition of the Oder-Neisse line, chanting "Long live Greater Germany."[69] In Fürstenberg, insurgents shouted, "Throw the Polacks out of Germany." Similar voices calling for the return of German territory given to Poland by the Potsdam Agreement were heard in Berlin, Halle, and Leipzig, especially from refugees from the eastern territories.[70] Another manifestation of collective "revanchist" sentiments and a nationalistic mood was the singing of the *Deutschlandlied* and the *Schlesierlied*. People who witnessed the events describe weeping and seeing tears in people's eyes during collective singing and processions of demonstrators marching in columns.[71] Written sources mention a feeling of intoxication, a euphoria that eyewitnesses confessed they had not felt since the prewar period.

A key element of rituals of violence, as Natalie Zemon Davis stresses, was the dehumanizing of victims as "'vermin' to be stamped out, 'devils' to be destroyed."[72] The crowd objectified the "devil" in several different ways. First, the rebels applied the semantics of deprivation of honor by bringing officials down to the level of animals in their slogans and practices. Suspecting that members of the Red Army were somewhere in the town hall building, the rebels shouted, "Hang the red swine!" (*Hängt das rote Schwein auf!*), "Beat the red dog [until he is] dead" (*Schlagt den roten Hund tot*).[73] In Niesky, the following scenario unfolded: after taking over the Stasi building, the rebels shut up three employees in the dog kennel where they were abused and forced to eat a red flag first and then dog food while the prisoners were freed from their cells.[74] Likewise, in Leipzig, party functionaries who refused to go over to the rebels' side when they stormed the "people's house" (*Volkshaus*) were insulted with cries of "Traitors to the working class, swine, dogs" (*Arbeiterverräter, Schweine, Hunde*).[75]

In rituals of violence, the crowd also violated the official order of dress and social status. Rebels tore official uniforms off the wearers or ripped off the shoulder straps.[76] They tore badges designating various organizations and the SED emblem off the clothes worn by state and party representatives. They pulled off the light blue ties worn by members of the FDJ.[77] In a notorious case, a young functionary dressed in the uniform of the organization Dienst für Deutschland (the voluntary service branch of the Free German Youth [FDJ]) was stripped naked and publicly ridiculed.[78] The crowd deprived such people of their official status and political capital, dehumanizing, abusing, and shaming their victims.

Moreover, the crowd destroyed the artifacts of power in order to disrupt official public symbolism. Portraits and busts of state and party leaders, propaganda images and books written by the communist leaders were the first objects to be destroyed.[79] In the insurgents' hands, personality cult artifacts lost their status as symbols of power: they were converted into objects for meting out physical violence to SED supporters. For example, in the town of

Eisleben, a portrait of Stalin was jammed onto the head of a Soviet soldier who attempted to defend the "leader's" image.[80] Something similar happened to the mayor of Ludwigsdorf when he refused to give up his authority: a portrait of Pieck was placed on his head.[81] Public rituals of violence upended people's usual roles and positions, transforming representatives of the regime into victims while simultaneously turning the population into judges and executioners.

Examining the escalation of violence in France during the religious wars of the sixteenth century, Barbara B. Diefendorf makes a point that is very relevant to my analysis. She notes that acts of violence included two key elements: the intention "to restore community and hostility toward those who did not share their views."[82] Diefendorf concludes that "rituals of repair" aimed to restore imagined community by excluding, humiliating, and expressing hatred of the other. During the events of June 17, the population strove—by using the practices of violence—to restore shared positive emotions of national purity and unity. In forming local communities of violence, the insurgents experienced tabooed feelings of national pride and tried to effect healing after the trauma of national and state schism resulting from defeat in World War II by taking vengeance on representatives of SVAG, the Red Army, and the SED regime.[83] By demythologizing these events, which appear in an official "culture of remembrance" (*Erinnerungskultur*) in today's Germany as "a nationwide uprising for democracy and the rule of law," the arguments detailed above suggest the value of rethinking June 17, 1953 as a nationalistic movement.[84]

A damaged community could be restored through the ritual of publicly burning symbols of the regime. The population in the GDR indicated that they approved of this ritual in 1951.[85] Only during the June days of 1953, however, did reports about burning any and all personality cult objects multiply rapidly. The ritual usually followed a certain sequence of events. After seizing party and administrative buildings and wreaking havoc in them, the insurgents carried things bearing the regime's insignia—banners, flags, posters, portraits of leaders—to nearby central squares, heaped these things up, and set them on fire.[86] Images of the leaders were put on top of the pyramid.

The moment the fire was lit was the emotional high point of the rite of purging public spaces of the dictatorship's symbols. It was accompanied by the crowd's shrieks and wild applause, which turned into collective contemplation of the flames (Figure 5.3, Figure 5.4).

The meaning of this act, a "ritual of purification," as Robert Scribner put it, is evident: for the crowd, burning the symbols of power was cathartic. They were able to discharge their emotions and distance themselves from the norms and rules of life under the SED dictatorship.[87]

Figure 5.3   An incident taking place during the uprising of June 17, 1953 on Brunnenstrasse in East Berlin. *Source:* AdsD. Signature: Bild 6/FOTB037506.

The appearance of such overt, conflict-laden tension in official public spheres forced the regime to resort to prophylactic measures, clearing these spaces of the symbols of power. This was especially true during crises. Faced with the threat of popular unrest, the state was forced to temporarily remove portraits, posters, and banners from places where large crowds gathered, train stations, stores, main streets, and central squares. Thus, during the uprising in 1953, the administration took down images of Pieck, Ulbricht, and Grotewohl in train-station waiting rooms in Bitterfeld and Dessau to avoid provoking unrest.[88] After the uprising of June 17, 1953, the regime began to think more carefully about saturating public places with symbols of power and, at the same time, it started to work on crisis management in public space. The regime's representatives finally realized that although the symbols of power were a way to proclaim a political order, these symbols also concealed within themselves the threat that the regime could be overturned. They could become targets of popular iconoclasm in an instant, sparking rituals of violence. This is why, in the fall of 1956, after the first reports of disturbances in Hungary, the border guard in Eichwald hastily took down red flags, portraits of the leaders, and party-state posters, fearing the population's aggressive reactions to these objects.[89]

Figure 5.4   An incident taking place during the uprising of June 17, 1953 on Brunnenstrasse in East Berlin. *Source:* AdsD. Signature: Bild 6/FOTB044693.

Thus, anonymous iconoclastic practices—especially overt ones—articulated aggression and anger, distrust and disappointment, resentment and vengefulness. Iconoclasm reflected the emotional work of East German society and gave the population a distinctive escape valve for its negative feelings. In rituals of violence, a shattered postwar society experienced itself as a united emotional community, showing solidarity in order to abuse and defile the central figures of socialist propaganda. The result was surprisingly paradoxical. On one hand, these iconoclastic gestures became an indicator of the regime's unpopularity, a sign of the population's resistance to the regime and alienation from it. On the other hand, having an outlet for negative emotions strengthened conformism, helped to produce submission, and made it easier to work out ways in which the regime could be tolerated. The result was a therapeutic effect that influenced the political system and society alike, allowing the East German dictatorship to maintain its stability.

Terror, repression, and show trials—the classic tools for intimidating and subjugating the population—clearly helped to ensure this stability, but these were not the only methods. My analysis of the sources shows that the state devised public "rituals of repentance" to restore its damaged honor. For example, after the June 1953 uprising, to avoid arrest, students and teachers in Jena who were found guilty of "crimes against the state" were ordered to apologize publicly by making reparations for the personality cult objects that had been damaged: They were required to restore, or repair, placards, portraits, and posters of the leaders and return them to high-status places thereby restoring the official order of public symbolism.[90] By staging acts of self-criticism, confessions of guilt, and repentance, the state struggled to return the leader cult's symbols to the center of public space. Similarly, it fought to make the regime's legitimacy visible, at the very least in the dictatorship's official public spheres, that is, those sites organized and controlled by the state and party.

The examples of iconoclasm analyzed here reflect the Germans' emotional need to insult and humiliate symbols of Soviet power in order to avenge their damaged national honor. Defeat in World War II and the establishment of a Soviet protectorate on German soil were extremely strong blows to the Germans' self-esteem and their sense of national dignity. Under national socialism, "German honor" was a fundamental part of the state's ideology. It symbolized pride, exclusivity, and the Germans' superiority to other races and peoples.[91] The loss of state sovereignty and a nation split in two, unconditional surrender and territorial losses, the rapes carried out by the liberating forces, and the mass deportations were all evidence of damage done to the state's and the nation's honor. Iconoclastic acts were the population's way of defending their country's honor, restoring it, or at least avenging its injuries. Iconoclasm was East Germans' attempt to free themselves from the remorse and guilt about war crimes imposed on them by the victors. At the same time, iconoclasm expressed the population's need to work through the trauma of the Soviet occupation and their desire to restore national honor as an integrated model of collective identity.

SYMBOLIC COMPETITION BETWEEN THE STALIN CULT AND THE HITLER CULT

Propaganda of the image of Stalin in East Germany impeded, and indeed attempted vigorously to displace continued attachment to the Hitler cult of the Third Reich. In 1948–1949 the Society for the Study of the Culture of the USSR issued a series of pamphlets titled *The Soviet Union through German Eyes* (Deutsche sehen die Sowjetunion). These contained the reminiscences of well-known cultural figures about their sojourns in the "homeland of socialism." In his contribution, writer and diplomat Eduard Claudius remembered watching columns of May First demonstrators pass by Stalin in the grandstand in Moscow, and asked:

> For what is the person who leads the people valued? What relationship do the people have to him? It is a mystery of the time. To make an analogy with our recent past is blasphemy. Those who gleefully supported Hitler, who wanted to

conquer the world with him and here . . . here where there is no thought about conquering the world, about oppressing other peoples. Here is a country building its own future, the life of each individual person. Therein lies all the difference. Is this a large difference? How can its extent be measured?[92]

As historian Simone Barck points out, in the "atmosphere of communist-antifascist thought" raising the issue, even unintentionally, of a structural feature shared by totalitarian regimes—leader cults—was already enough to quickly cut off readers' access to such a critical publication.

Nonetheless, symbolic competition between the Hitler and Stalin cults became a central theme in iconoclastic acts. With the Sovietization of East Germany, Hitler's name and image were turned into rhetorical and visual taboos. The only place where drawing parallels between the two dictators or making an unwitting comparison was permissible was in SVAG's internal political dispatches. Public comparisons of Stalin and Hitler infuriated the occupying powers, and the security organs immediately began looking for provocateurs. For example, the fall 1945 dispatch from the village of Drewitz in Brandenburg province reported an extraordinary incident. The word "Stalin" was crossed out and replaced with "Hitler" on posters with text reading "Stalin's remarks about Germany and the German people" and "Generalissimo of the Soviet Union I. V. Stalin."[93] In a public space in Erfurt, someone compared the Bolshevik and Nazi dictators by rearranging a propaganda slogan honoring Stalin to glorify Hitler. On the wall of a store, unknown persons altered the text on a SED banner hung the night before. The original text read "According to Stalin's model!" (*Nach STALINS Vorbild!*), but after some of the letters were removed the remaining part of the slogan indicated that the SED regime and the Third Reich were identical. It now read "national-socialist model" (*NS Vorbild!*).[94] Clearly, experience with the Hitler cult allowed the population to distance itself from the Stalin cult, looking at it with a critical eye and noting the similarity of the two dictators and the two political orders, each based on the leader's personal power.

Most often, however, Hitler's and Stalin's names were used to indicate a binary opposition. The words "German Führer" connoted the characteristics of *ours* and meant something good and understandable, but the term "Soviet leader" meant *theirs* and indicated an incomprehensible, hidden, potent threat. Evaluating the two leaders in black-and-white terms provoked distrust of *their* Stalin, resulting, somewhat automatically one might say, in the need to trust *our* Hitler. This dichotomy shows up in the record of a private conversation in the community of Krölpa in the Saalfeld district:

At least then [during the Third Reich—A. T.] we trusted a German, even though he was an Austrian. But now they [the SED—A. T.] show their trust in a man

who led a gang in the Caucasus and attacked merchants . . . This was the great
leader of the camp of peace—Stalin.[95]

In Schwerin, a Soviet observer recorded nationalistic sentiments, which
he characterized as "evil statements" about the Soviet leader, expressed by
members of a crowd of women: "We are Germans, so why are they organizing such pompous ceremonies in honor of a foreign statesman? Now there's
more hype than there was before, on Hitler's birthday."[96] And in the mailbox
at the SED office in the Stendal district a box with an insulting inscription
was discovered: "Who cares about the birth of your Ivan? Get out of here,
we're Germans!"[97]

Nostalgia for the Third Reich as the "good" past of the Germans in contrast to the "bad"—Sovietized—present is another example of this binary
evaluation of Hitler and Stalin. Thus, a leaflet suggesting that Stalin should be
exchanged for Hitler with a surcharge was discovered in an apartment building in Leipzig.[98] In another instance, an unknown person used the wall of an
administrative building to write out an ultimatum addressed to the occupying
forces: "If you won't let us eat, we won't be able to forget our Führer."[99]
A leaflet commemorating Hitler's birthday, posted in the community of
Lüdersdorf in the Angermünde region during the night of April 19–20, 1948,
was tinged with nostalgia: "Hitler—our pride!" and "We congratulate Hitler
on his 59th birthday."[100] Despite his physical death, the German dictator's
political life continued in the population's positive memories of the Third
Reich. These iconoclastic acts reflected the collective emotional work being
done in a society that longed for the positive feeling of national pride, which
became taboo after the country's defeat in World War II.

To articulate an alternative collective identity the population used public
space as a platform for unofficial opinions about current political events.[101] If
open reflection on the population's traumatic experience of the violence, robbery, and looting carried out by Red Army soldiers was taboo until discussion
"about the Russians and about us" began in 1948, practices of iconoclasm
allowed people to bypass official taboos and thematize forbidden questions.
Thus, the Nuremburg trials inspired a wave of popular iconoclasm. A SVAG
report to the Central Committee of the KPSS indicates that former German
prisoners of war ripped down propaganda posters about the international
tribunals prosecuting the Nazis. In another incident, while watching a sketch
about "Hitler's soldiers" during a comedy show, as a sign of protest former
German POWs defiantly walked out of the theater.[102] During one of the trials,
people wrote insulting statements on the walls of administrative buildings:
for example, "Russia—a country of murders, thieves, and criminals" and
"Stalin and Molotov should be sitting in the dock in Nuremberg. They are the
chief culprits, bastards, rapists of young girls."[103] One leaflet suggested that

Molotov should join the defendants since in 1939 he negotiated with Nazi foreign minister Ribbentrop about dividing Europe into German and Soviet spheres of influence.[104] Another leaflet wove together the motifs of abusing women and the national honor: "No German woman, no German man can live in peace, Stalin's culture-bearers lie in wait for them everywhere."[105] The personified motif of taking revenge on the Russian occupying forces for sullying female honor during the postwar rapes was intensified by the use of national-socialist stereotypes of an Asiatic lack of culture, backwardness, and wildness as arguments for engaging in political struggle with the SVAG regime.[106] In avenging the degradation of German women, the population saw the possibility of an overarching restoration of national honor. On a postcard with a photograph from the 1933 NSDAP congress sent to Colonel Kirsanov, the editor of the newspaper *Tägliche Rundschau*, the anonymous sender had written, "We will take revenge on you Bolshevik swine for defiling our women!"[107]

On one hand, gestures of iconoclasm in public places were automatically addressed to the representatives of SVAG. Yet these gestures were also an appeal to a broad swath of society, calling for solidarity and national unity in the struggle with the Soviet occupying forces and the SED authorities. In both cases, iconoclastic acts showed how to affirmatively reinterpret Sovietized reality. Thus, in Leipzig, anti-Soviet leaflets signed by the "Brown Shirts" were affixed to lamp posts on Karl Marx Square. They pointed out that the Nazis and Bolsheviks had a great deal in common and that both turned into dead-end regimes.[108] In May 1949, just before elections to choose delegates to the Third People's Congress, the security organs discovered leaflets pasted up in many villages and small towns. These said: "I'm voting for Hitler! Down with Stalin! Death to the Russians!" and "Our leader is Hitler and we won't allow anyone else to lead us."[109] During the elections, there were cases of damaged ballots. In villages in the Zeitz region, the people pasted postage stamps depicting Hitler in the circle indicating "yes." Swastikas were also drawn on ballots and "Heil Hitler!" was written on them.[110] "Heil Hitler" often appeared in a coded form as the number eighty-eight. This number was chosen to stand for "H[eil] H[itler]" since "h" is the eighth letter of the German alphabet. "Eighty-eight" could be seen, especially on the "Führer's" birthday, scrawled on the walls of buildings, sidewalks, and posts and poles.[111] The continuous invocations of the name of the German "Führer" attest to the fact that the figure of Hitler still occupied symbolic space and they show that the very idea of a "Führer" (*vozhd'*) was attached to the figure of the German dictator, whose memory became a cultural barrier to Soviet efforts to transfer the Stalin cult to East Germany.

The motif of a competition between "old" personality cults and "new" ones was so popular in the postwar period that the population used it in iconoclastic actions to draw attention to the everyday problems. In June 1946, the military commandant of the city of Mannheim received an old postcard with a picture of Hitler giving a little girl a copy of *Mein Kampf.*[112] On it was written, "You are swine. We will never forget Hitler, he gave us more to eat. Stalin, give us the fifth empire, the fourth one is a lot like the third one."[113] The occupying forces were accused of failing to use material resources to help the starving, using them instead for Bolshevik propaganda, to print portraits of leaders, and publish Marxist-Leninist classics. As a result, a note offering to exchange portraits of Lenin for food was found on a notice board in Lössnitz. Anyone interested in such an exchange was advised to apply directly to the mayor.[114] A leaflet urged workers in Bitterfeld not to subscribe to party newspapers so as not to finance the printing of "gigantic portraits of Stalin."[115] At a kiosk, the salesperson offered customers a pack of old party newspapers at a low price, pointing out that this worthless stuff would be useful for kindling the stove during a cold winter.[116] A complaint circulated among women that paper, which was in short supply, was being used for "empty propaganda" instead of notebooks for schoolchildren or notepaper for writing to POWs.[117] Suggestions about buying clothes, shoes, and products for children, and building houses, hospitals, and schools instead of spending money on gifts to the Soviet leader were voiced everywhere. "If we give Stalin so much money," a resident of Halle commented, "he will be a capitalist millionaire."[118] These examples make it clear that among the German population the bitter experience of defeat and Sovietization did not correspond to the utopias of Soviet propaganda. This explains the tendency to idealize life in the Third Reich and nostalgia for the mighty national past, while the population distanced itself and became alienated from the socialist experiment proclaimed in the slogans of the *other*—Soviet—Führer.

NOTES

1. The events in Görlitz described in the epigraph were repeated throughout the GDR. For the report quoted above, see Archive der sozialen Demokratie der Friedrich Ebert Stiftung (AdsD), Bonn (Germany), SPD-PV-Ostbüro, 0434b, 17.6.1953 (Situationsbericht vom 17. Juni 1953 in Görlitz, Sachsen), II Berichte, unpag.

2. Gibas, "Die 'einheitliche öffentliche Meinung,'" 540–49.

3. See Gibas and Gries, "'Vorschlag für den Ersten Mai'"; Rolf, *Das sowjetische Massenfest*, 162.

4. "Ergänzungsbericht zu Bericht 1–327," May 9, 1951, AdsD, SPD-PV-Ostbüro 0361 II, unpag.

5. Stiftung Archiv der Parteien und Massenorganisationen der ehemaligen DDR im Bundesarchiv, Berlin (SAPMO-BArch), DY 30/V/2/5/269, Bl. 315, 317

(Stimmung der Bevölkerung anlässlich des Ablebens I. W. Stalins. Berlin, March 21, 1953). On the iconoclastic responses to Stalin's death, see also Allinson, *Politics and Popular Opinion*, 52–54.

6. "Bericht über die Demonstration am 17.6.1953 in Zodel Kr. Görlitz," AdsD, SPD-PV-Ostbüro 0434 b, 17.6.1953 II Berichte, unpag.

7. Scribner, *For the Sake of Simple Folk*, 78–81.

8. See Bakhtin, *Rabelais and His World*; Scribner, *Popular Culture*, 71–102.

9. Roth, *Der 17. Juni 1953*, 112.

10. Roth, *Der 17. Juni 1953*, 111–12.

11. See Scribner, "Ritual and Reformation," in Hsia, *German People*, 138–41.

12. In research on the semantics of gifts to leaders, discussion of the iconoclastic aspect of gift-giving practices is nowhere to be found. See Sosnina and Ssorin-Chaikov, *Dary vozhdiam*; Ssorin-Chaikov and Sosnina, "Faculty of Useless Things"; Brooks, *Thank You Comrade Stalin*, chap. 4; Gries, ". . . deckt alle mit den Tisch," in Gibas, *Wiedergeburten*.

13. "Allgemeiner Stimmungsbericht: Berlin," May 22, 1951, AdsD, SPD-PV-Ostbüro 0350, unpag.

14. Staatsarchiv Dresden, LRS, Ministerium für Volksbildung Nr. 1840, unpag.

15. "Stalingeschenk aus Westberlin," *Berliner Stadtblatt*, December 22, 1951, 1.

16. "Ergänzungsbericht zu Bericht 1-327/15," May 9, 1951, AdsD, SPD-PV-Ostbüro 0361 II, unpag.

17. "Ulbricht unerwünscht: Berlin," November 15, 1951, AdsD, SPD-PV-Ostbüro 0257 I, unpag.

18. AdsD, SPD-PV-Ostbüro 0361 II, unpag., Berlin, January 1951.

19. "Bericht 9/53 an das Sekretariat des Zentralkomitees über die Stimmung der Bevölkerung und die Tätigkeit der Parteiorgane anlässlich des Ablebens des Genossen Stalin: Berlin," March 11, 1953, SAPMO-BArch, DY 30/IV 2/5/268, Bl. 340.

20. On the semantics of silence in totalitarian regimes, see Noel'-Noiman, *Obshchestvennoe mnenie*; Humphrey, "Dangerous Words"; Stark, *"Wenn Du willst."*

21. AdsD, SPD-PV-Ostbüro 0361 I, unpag., Halle an der Saale, undated.

22. AdsD, SPD-PV-Ostbüro 0257 I, unpag. (Merseburg, 3.01.1952.)

23. "Verhaftungen in Jena, Berlin," January 1951, AdsD, SPD-PV-Ostbüro 0362 I, unpag.

24. Tikhomirov, "Feinde des Volkes."

25. "Report on the political condition of the federal state of Saxony for August–September 1947," GARF, f. R-7212, op. 1, d. 218, l. 49.

26. "Report of the Head of the Information Department of the UVK in Potsdam, I. S. Stroilov, to the Head of the Information Department of USVA of the state of Brandenburg on Anglo-American propaganda in Potsdam," September 1948, GARF, f. R-7077, op. 1, d. 230, l. 247.

27. AdsD, SPD-PV-Ostbüro 0383 O, unpag., Berlin, 1948.

28. "Provokation mit Hitlerbildern, Berlin," February 18, 1954, AdsD, SPD-PV-Ostbüro 0407, unpag.

29. "Political report on the moods of the German population of the federal state of Saxony," September 21, 1945, GARF, f. R-7212, op. 1, d. 51, l. 90.

30. "Report on May First celebrations in the Chemnitz region," May 7, 1947, GARF, f. R-7212, op. 1, d. 203, l. 158.

31. "Bulletin No. 50/54 of international and intra-German information," SVAG Information Bureau, July 27, 1946, RGASPI, f. 17, op. 128, d. 157, l. 101. As a symbol of the "Aryan race" and the emblem of the Third Reich, the swastika was one of SVAG's most frequent sources of irritation. It was forbidden to display the swastika in public spaces, which is why the occupying forces' dispatches contain so many reports about swastikas in public spaces. See, for example, "Bulletin No. 41 of international and intra-German information," SVAG Information Bureau, September 23, 1948, RGASPI, f. 17, op. 128, d. 581, l. 34, 37.

32. AdsD, SPD-PV-Ostbüro 0361 I, unpag., Berlin, May 25, 1950.

33. "Bulletin No. 41 of international and intra-German information," SVAG Information Bureau September 23, 1948, RGASPI, f. 17, op. 128, d. 581, l. 34.

34. "On hostile graffiti in the toilets and shops of the Soviet rolling stock factory 'Lindner' in Ammendorf," October 7, 1948, GARF, f. R-7133, op. 1, d. 280, l. 34.

35. "Bericht aus Sömmerda-Thüringen," April 25, 1953, AdsD, SPD-PV-Ostbüro 0257 I, unpag.

36. See the important observations in Scribner, "Ritual and Reformation," 133–34.

37. "Vorbereitungen und Stimmung der Arbeiter im Georgij-Dimitroff-Werk (Magdeburg) zum 1. Mai 1954," AdsD, SPD-PV-Ostbüro 0257 I, unpag.

38. *Nacht-Depesche*, January 13, 1953, 2.

39. "Sachsen-Anhalt, SAG-Leunawerke 'Walter Ulbricht,'" November 7, 1951, AdsD, SPD-PV-Ostbüro 0257/I, unpag.

40. "Prikaz nachal'nika garnizona i voennogo komendanta g. Berlina No. 1 o regulirovanii politicheskoi i sotsial'no-ekonomicheskoi zhizni goroda. 30.04.1945 g.," in Timofeeva and Foittsik, *Politika SVAG v oblasti kul'tury*, 85–87.

41. Liman, *Mehr Licht*, 38.

42. "Jubeln und Begeisterung in der Hauptstadt: Über 800,000 Berliner begrüßen den Präsidenten," *Neues Deutschland*, October 12, 1949, 1.

43. See the photograph taken by Walter Heilig, "Berlin, DDR-Gründung, Ehrenformation der VP," October 12, 1949, Bild 183–S88877, Bildarchiv im Bundesarchiv (Berlin), 183–S88877, https://www.bild.bundesarchiv.de/dba/en/.

44. "Anlage Nr. 1 zum Protokoll Nr. 189: Plan zur Kundgebung anlässlich des Abschlusses des Aufgebotes zu Ehren des großen Stalins am 12. August 1951 auf dem Marx-Engels-Platz," SAPMO-BArch, DY 24/1013, unpag.

45. Lindenberger, *Volkspolizei*, 271–82.

46. "Hostile rumors and the activity of reactionary elements during the last days of May in Thuringia," June 11, 1947, GARF, f. R-7184, op. 1, d. 163, l. 142–144.

47. For example, "On making a monthly assessment of German-Soviet friendship in Germany," December 28, 1951, AVP RF, f. 742, op. 38, p. 239, d. 112, l. 21; "On the political mood of the German population of the state of Thuringia in January 1946," GARF, f. R-7184, op. 1, d. 56, l. 19.

48. "Results of the celebration of the seventieth birthday of Comrade I. V. Stalin," RGASPI, f. 17, op. 137, d. 3071, l. 13; AdsD, SPD-PV-Ostbüro 0349 A/B, unpag., Cottbus, November 8, 1952.

49. "Political report about incidents in the federal state of Saxony for September 1945," GARF, f. R-7212, op. 1, d. 55, l. 18. The European tradition of injuring the face, and especially the nose, has its roots in the Middle Ages and the early modern period. This ritual practice continued into the modern period, evolving into a symbolic form of social protest in which its fundamental meaning—harming someone's honor and dignity—has been preserved. See Groebner, "Losing Face, Saving Face"; Niccoli, *Rinascimento anticlericale*, 131–36. On injuring the nose as a form of judicial punishment, see Zorzi, "Rituali e cerimoniali penali."

50. In iconoclastic acts the population used the color red as a negative symbol of the Soviet occupation regime. Red had connotations of Bolshevism, the Red Terror, and the apocalypse. For example, when members of the SED entered the hall for a meeting of the Union of Free German Youth, a cry rang out: "The Reds are coming." A case involving the symbolic dimension of the color red was recorded in the village of Waldkirchen in the Zschopau district of Saxony: a certain Herr Schmidt showed a fake ID at the office of the military command, declared that he was the mayor, and ordered all the windowsills to be painted red. In a sermon at a meeting of Jehovah's Witnesses, the color red was characterized in apocalyptic terms as a red flag, which was called the "scarlet cloth which causes mankind unhappiness and discord" and the SVAG regime was compared to the Devil "come to the earth in the form of something large and red like flames from a dragon." See "Report on measures taken on the occasion of the thirtieth anniversary of VLKSM," November 2, 1948, GARF, f. R-7212, op. 1, d. 233, l. 327; "Political report on the moods of the German population of the federal state of Saxony," September 21, 1945, GARF, f. R-7212, op. 1, d. 51, l. 66; "Memorandum of the Deputy Supreme Commander on Political Questions A. G. Russkikh to the TsK VKP(b) about anti-democratic statements made by members of the religious sect Jehovah's Witnesses," August 26, 1949, GARF, f. R-7317, op. 3, d. 4, l. 136–138.

51. "On the political mood of the German population in the state of Thuringia in January 1946," GARF, f. R-7184, op. 1, d. 56, l. 19.

52. In the state of Saxony alone, 500,000 posters with quotations from Stalin were put up in September 1945. See GARF, f. R-7212, op. 1, d. 55, l. 17.

53. "Report of the Head of the Information Department of the Military Command in the city of Brandenburg A. E. Karetnikov to the Head of the Information Department of USVA of the state of Brandenburg K. Martem"ianov on the appearance of anti-Soviet leaflets in the city of Brandenburg, July 12, 1948," GARF, f. R-7077, op. 1, d. 233, l. 69.

54. The iconoclastic tradition of "punishing the image" took shape in the late Middle Ages and during the Reformation. It belonged to both popular culture and the juridical practice of judicial punishment. The ritual of publicly burning or hanging an image of the guilty one was equated with an individual's corporeal death. This punishment was applied when a criminal's body could not be punished directly and

personally. See Schnitzler, "Geschmähte Symbole," in Schreiner and Schwerhoff, *Verletzte Ehre*, 296–301.

55. See Assmann and Frevert, *Geschichts-Vergessenheit—Geschichts-Versessenheit*, 151–57.

56. "Report of the Head of the Information Department of the UVK in the city of Potsdam I. S. Stroilov to the Head of the Department of Information of the USVA of the state of Brandenburg about Anglo-American propaganda in Potsdam," GARF, f. R-7077, op. 1, d. 230, l. 274.

57. AdsD, SPD-PV-Ostbüro 0383 O, unpag.

58. "Report of the Head of the Information Department of the UVK in the city of Potsdam I. S. Stroilov to the Head of the Information Department of the USVA of the state of Brandenburg about Anglo-American propaganda in Potsdam," GARF, f. R-7077, op. 1, d. 230, l. 274.

59. Cf. Imbusch, *Moderne und Gewalt*, 24; Montagu, *Anatomy of Swearing*; S. Smith, "Social Meanings of Swearing."

60. See Koller, "'Es ist zum Heulen.'"

61. "Bericht aus Ostberlin," 30.7.1952, AdsD, SPD-PV-Ostbüro 0361 I, unpag. For similar examples, see Wolle, "Die Welt der verlorenen Bilder," 340.

62. Stimmungsbilder, Berlin, 3.08.1948, AdsD, SPD-PV-Ostbüro 0361 I, unpag. On sport as an alternative public sphere, see Dunning, *Sport Matters*; Ganzenmüller, "Bruderzwist im Kalten Krieg," in Malz, Rohdewald, and Wiederkehr, *Sport zwischen Ost und West*.

63. AdsD, SPD-PV-Ostbüro 0361 I, upag. (Berlin, n.d.). On the cult of Adolf Hennecke in East Germany, see Satjukow, "Propaganda mit dem menschlichen Antlitz," in Gries, Schmale, and Ahbe, *Kultur der Propaganda*.

64. N. Z. Davis, "Rites of Violence."

65. Sperber, "17 June 1953," 636.

66. Sperber, "17 June 1953," 636.

67. AdsD, SPD-PV-Ostbüro 0434 b II Berichte, unpag.

68. Julia Brömse and Dieter Schlüter, "17 Juni 1953: BILD fand den berühmtesten Fotografen des Tages . . . und den Steinewerfer," *Bild* website, June 16, 2013, http://www.bild.de/politik/inland/ddr/17-juni-1953-das-foto-der-fotograf-30835104 .bild.html .

69. Sperber, "17 June 1953," 636.

70. Sperber, "17 June 1953," 636.

71. Roth, *Der 17. Juni 1953*, 212.

72. N. Z. Davis, "Writing 'The Rites of Violence,'" 16.

73. Seybold, "Ländlicher," in Rupieper, Bohse, and Grebe, ". . . und das Wichtigste ist doch die Einheit," 153.

74. "Kurzbericht über Streik Ereignisse vom 17. Juni 1953 in Görlitz und Niesky," July 29, 1953, AdsD, SPD-PV-Ostbüro 0434 b II Berichte, unpag.

75. Roth, *Der 17. Juni*, 130.

76. For example, Witkowski, "Peasants Revolt?"

77. AdsD, SPD-PV-Ostbüro 0434 b II Berichte, unpag.

78. Niethammer, von Plato, and Wierling, *Die Volkseigene Erfahrung*, 57.

79. Roth, *Der 17. Juni 1953*, 73. See also Behrends, *Die Erfundene Freundschaft*, 313–20.

80. "Bericht über die Streikbewegungen in Eisleben am 17. Juni 1953," AdsD, SPD-PV-Ostbüro 0434 b, unpag.

81. Roth, *Der 17. Juni 1953*, 109.

82. Diefendorf, "Rites of Repair," 34.

83. See Witkowski, "Peasants Revolt?"; Tilly, *Contentious French*, 391–92; Scott, *Weapons of the Weak*.

84. "Bundespräsident Joachim Gauck bei der Gedenkstunde des Deutschen Bundestags zum 60. Jahrestag des Volksaufstands vom 17. Juni 1953," website of Der Bundespräsident, June 14, 2013, http://www.bundespraesident.de/SharedDocs/Reden /DE/Joachim-Gauck/Reden/2013/06/130614-17-Juni-BT.html, accessed March 10, 2016. See also Tikhomirov, "Beyond 'Fascist Sortie.'"

85. See Port, "Der erste Arbeiteraufstand in der DDR," 608.

86. For example, "Bericht über die Vorgänge in Gotha, Berlin," June 18, 1953, AdsD, SPD-PV-Ostbüro 0434 b, unpag.; Roth, *Der 17. Juni 1953*, 119.

87. Scribner, "Ritual and Reformation," in Hsia, *German People*, 142–43.

88. "Situationsbericht aus Wolfen b. Bitterfeld (Sachsen)," June 23, 1953, AdsD, SPD-PV-Ostbüro 0434 b, 17.6.1953 II, unpag.

89. AdsD, SPD-PV-Ostbüro 0257/II, unpag., Berlin, October 1956.

90. "Bericht über die Vorgänge am 17. Juni 1953 in Jena," June 27, 1953, Stadtarchiv Jena, E 217, unpag.

91. Frevert, *Emotions in History*, 37–38. See for example the Law for the Protection of German Blood and German Honor (Gesetz zum Schutze des deutschen Blutes und der deutschen Ehre) of September 15, 1935, http://www.documentarchiv .de/ns/nbgesetze01.html .

92. Claudius, *Notizen nebenbei*, 67.

93. The first campaign of visual Stalin propaganda addressed to the East German population popularized the resolutions of the Potsdam conference. In the state of Thuringia alone, more than 320,000 of the posters mentioned above were distributed. See "Report for August 1945 on the work done by the Soviet Military Administration of Thuringia with the population," GARF, f. R-7184, op. 1, d. 46, l. 25.

94. *Der Spiegel*, January 10, 1951, 2.

95. Informationsnotiz Nr. 96 52. Erfurt, den 14.05.1952, Thüringisches Hauptstaatsarchiv Weimar, Land Thüringen—SED, Landesleitung Thüringen, Abteilung Parteiorgane, A IV/2/5-228. Bl. 24–25.

96. RGASPI, f. 17, op. 317, d. 307, l. 14.

97. RGASPI, f. 17, op. 317, d. 307, l. 13.

98. "Report on fundamental stages of the social-political life of Leipzig in the third quarter of 1947," GARF, f. R-7212, op. 1, d. 202, l. 45.

99. "On anti-Soviet propaganda during the May First celebrations," May 14, 1948, GARF, f. R-7133, op. 1, d. 279, l. 1–2.

100. "Report of the Head of the Information Department of the Military Commandant of the Angermünde region, S. V. Titulenko, to the Head of the

Information Department of USVA for the state of Brandenburg, K. Martem"ianov on distribution of sheets of anti-Soviet material," GARF, f. R-7077, op. 1, d. 233, l. 47.

101. Warneken, "'Die Straße ist die Tribüne des Volkes.'"

102. RGASPI, f. 17, op. 128, d. 357, l. 85.

103. GARF, f. R-7071, op. 1, d. 212, l. 226.

104. "Bulletin No. 52/56 of international and intra-German information," SVAG Information Bureau, August 6, 1946, RGASPI, f. 17, op. 128, d. 157, l. 157.

105. GARF, f. R-7133, op. 1, d. 277, l. 71.

106. Tikhomirov, "Stalin-Bild(er) in der SBZ/DDR," in Timmermann, *Historische Erinnerung im Wandel*, 477–78.

107. "Bulletin No. 49/53 of international and intra-German information: SVAG Information Bureau," July 26, 1946, RGASPI, f. 17, op. 128, d. 157, l. 89. On rapes of German women by Allied soldiers, see Naimark, *Russians in Germany*, 69–140; Gebhardt, *Als die Soldaten kamen*.

108. "Report on manifestations of pro-Nazi sentiments in the German population of the state of Saxony," April 12, 1946, GARF, f. R-7133, op. 1, d. 187, l. 16.

109. "Report on the results of elections of delegates to the Third German People's Congress that took place May 15 and 16, 1949 in the state of Saxony-Anhalt," June 2, 1949, GARF, f. R-7133, op. 1, d. 282, l. 318.

110. Ibid.

111. "Bulletin No. 26/30 of international and intra-German information," SVAG Information Bureau, April 30, 1946, RGASPI, f. 17, op. 128, d. 155, l. 5.

112. "Bulletin No. 39/43 of international and intra-German information," SVAG Information Bureau, June 17, 1946, RGASPI, f. 17, op. 128, d. 156, l. 81.

113. Ibid.

114. "Report on the political state of affairs in the federal state of Saxony for August–September 1947," GARF, f. R-7212, op. 1, d. 218, l. 49.

115. "Sachsen-Anhalt/Wolfen, Kreis Bitterfeld," January 14, 1952, AdsD, SPD-PV-Ostbüro 0257/I, unpag.

116. GARF, f. R-7212, op. 1, d. 230, l. 204.

117. "Report on propaganda in the Soviet Zone of Occupation," February 1946, RGASPI, f. 17, op. 128, d. 149, l. 57.

118. RGASPI, f. 17, op. 317, d. 307, l. 11.

Chapter 6

"We Wanted to Make a God but He Turned Out to Be the Devil"

The Politics and Practices of De-Stalinization in the GDR

WALTER ULBRICHT AND REACTIONS TO HIM INSIDE THE SED

Khrushchev gave his Secret Speech on February 25, 1956, during a closed session of the Communist Party's Twentieth Congress.[1] Information about an event of such magnitude could not remain unpublicized in the Soviet Union or beyond its borders. In early March, while the Central Committee was dealing with leaks and trying to figure out how to manage public opinion and handle the population's participation in de-Stalinization in the USSR itself, some socialist bloc leaders took initiatives that aggravated an already tense international situation.[2] Without consulting Moscow, Walter Ulbricht, the first secretary of the SED Central Committee, published an account of the Twentieth Communist Party Congress in *Neues Deutschland* on March 4, 1956. The article did not say anything explicitly about Khrushchev's speech but Ulbricht's statement that "Stalin is not one of the classics of Marxism" was like a bursting bombshell.[3] This pronouncement quite clearly conveyed information about the new political course in the Soviet Union. His initiative took the rhetoric of de-Stalinization across the USSR's discursive borders to launch a discussion about Stalin and Stalinism in the West.

Before turning to how de-Stalinization unfolded in the GDR, let's look at what happened in the days after the Secret Speech and before the publication of Ulbricht's article in *Neues Deutschland*. Representatives of the socialist states were not invited to the closed session on February 25, 1956. However, as the head of the German delegation, Ulbricht was one of the first foreign guests to be given information about Khrushchev's revelations. The most widespread version of what happened is that Ulbricht and the other heads of delegations from the "people's democracies" became acquainted with the contents of Khrushchev's report two days later. Copies of the text of the speech (in Russian) were given to a select group of foreign delegates through the Central Committee's Department for Relations with Foreign Communist Parties with strict instructions to return them "before these comrades leave Moscow."[4] Ulbricht was the only German delegate entrusted with a copy. At the same time, there were rumors that, during the night of February 25–26, after the congress had ended, an envoy from the Soviet party's apparatus read a German translation of Khrushchev's speech privately to SED representatives. Someone from the delegation allegedly took notes and these made their way back to Berlin.[5]

It is telling that Ulbricht was the first leader of a socialist country to distance himself from Stalin. What caused such a drastic shift in his views? Which factors influenced changes in the rhetoric and behavior of the "Stalin of the Soviet zone," as Ulbricht was called in popular parlance? Ulbricht's real motives, the ones that impelled him to publish the article, remain unknown. However, one can assume that with his sensitive nose for the dynamics of Soviet politics—and because he was acutely aware that continuing as Moscow's protectorate was essential for the stability of the East German state—Ulbricht did not hesitate. Taking on the rhetoric of de-Stalinization, almost automatically as it were, he tried to adapt to the new situation and secure Khrushchev's patronage as the new Soviet leader. Fear of another uprising like the one in June 1953 undoubtedly also played a role in this about-face. Thus, Ulbricht began the "prophylactic" discourse of desacralizing Stalin. He decided to prepare East German society for the changes in public discourse about Stalin, because it was expected from day to day that West Germany would disseminate this information. And finally, Ulbricht's words, the first public critique of Stalin voiced in the socialist bloc, were an attempt to distance himself from the political style of Stalinism, as he ascribed all the mistakes, blunders, and excesses in Stalinizing East Germany to external Soviet pressure and, more specifically, to the "best friend of the German people." Ulbricht was extremely worried about drawing obvious parallels between the Soviet and East German politics of the personality cult because such a comparison would completely discredit the SED regime. He was afraid there would be an upsurge in popular vengeance for radical Sovietization in the GDR, which would be exacted on the local party and state leaders. This is, in fact, what happened in subsequent practices of de-Stalinization.

Ulbricht's account of the Twentieth Congress was the first eruption of de-Stalinization in East Germany, marking the beginning of the official revision of Stalin's image outside the Soviet Union. Initial reactions soon followed. KPD members in West Germany and SED comrades in the GDR were "shocked," "stupefied," and "resistant to de-Stalinization." For example, in the KPD's Rhineland-Palatinate office, after Ulbricht's report was published, as a sign of protest, a portrait of Stalin, adorned with ribbons and flowers, was put up.[6] A participant in the Third Conference of SED regional delegates in Halle (on March 9–11, 1956) remembered being angry about the way objects belonging to the Soviet leader's cult were being treated:

> When we arrived at the conference we saw that the bust of Comrade Stalin was standing in a half-open cupboard next to three dirty cups of tea and coffee. That isn't right . . . I am of the opinion that the position of the comrades at the Twentieth Congress was one of healthy criticism of the Central Committee of the KPSS in terms of ignoring Leninist principles of collective administration. But this should not lead to the bust of Comrade Stalin sitting next to dirty china.[7]

Similar incidents were observed everywhere in early March because there was no centralized management of the discourse of de-Stalinization. As German historian Angelika Klein notes, knowledge of Khrushchev's speech "was still not authorized" since "during these weeks the Politburo of the SED itself was making efforts to get the text of the speech from Moscow."[8]

When Ulbricht's article was reprinted in the Western press, rumors began to multiply. The country was also rife with speculation about developments in Moscow that might have powered Ulbricht's overnight transition from Stalinist to anti-Stalinist rhetoric. The abrupt change in Ulbricht's public statements became clearer after publicity in the GDR about Khrushchev's "secret" speech.[9] On March 17, 1956, news about criticism of Stalin's personality cult at the Twentieth Congress appeared in the West Berlin press. This information immediately spilled over to East Berlin. On the same day, Ulbricht found himself in a "delicate situation" at a party conference of district delegates. The participants pelted him with questions about what happened in Moscow, why there were changes in the official language, and what the new norms for assessing Stalin were. Trying to get control of the discourse on de-Stalinization and to stop the spread of rumors, on March 18 Ulbricht published a new article in *Neues Deutschland* in which he discussed the "Stalin question" more extensively.[10]

Here Ulbricht dwelt in more detail on Stalin's "mistakes": one-man rule, promotion of the personality cult, and an arbitrariness which his failure to convene party congresses and the extremely rare meetings of the Politburo and the Central Committee so clearly demonstrated. He told readers that Stalin was not the author of the *History of the Communist Party of the Soviet Union (Bolsheviks) (Istoriia Vsesoiuznoi Kommunisticheskoi Partii [Bol'shevikov]: Kratkii kurs)*. He also deconstructed and refuted the myth of the "vozhd'" (including Stalin's sacred roles as "Lenin's true pupil and successor"), and the notions that "leader" was "one of the classics of Marxism-Leninism," and a "military genius and the organizer of the victory over fascism."[11] Ulbricht also made an initial attempt to soften his tone while establishing the boundaries for what could and could not be discussed about de-Stalinzation. Therefore, the first secretary explained that SED members were not released from their obligation to study the "leader's" pronouncements:

> Criticism of Stalin does not mean that everything that he wrote is false and his work is not worth using. No one said that. At present Stalin occupies a place corresponding to his role and deeds but not the place that the personality cult gave him. This is the actual state of affairs.[12]

Neither SED members nor the rest of the population of the GDR found the article reassuring. The increasing number of rumors and a new flurry of questions for the SED Central Committee created the impression that the situation had spiraled out of control and effective anti-crisis measures were sorely needed. Under this kind of pressure, Ulbricht sent a personal telegram to Khrushchev, asking for permission to take "independent action" in order to explain the situation to the population without waiting for instructions from Moscow.[13] The GDR leadership could not delay resolving the "Stalin question" since the population was being drawn into Western discourses of de-Stalinization with increasing eagerness. Popular rhetoric and practices of de-Stalinization outstripped official versions of new ways of looking at the Soviet leader.

Before carrying out propaganda work among the population, the SED Central Committee had to develop a unified assessment of Stalin's personality and figure out how to revise the "personality cult" for the population. This was the focus of the SED Central Committee's Twenty-sixth Congress, which took place on March 22, 1956, just before the Third Party Conference. On one hand, receiving the text of Khrushchev's speech and Moscow's official permission to acquaint party members with it were reasons for calling the meeting. On the other hand, the impetus for gathering the Central Committee was the broad public response to de-Stalinization. The uncontrolled nature of this response forced the political elite to think seriously about how to establish new boundaries for interpreting Stalin's crimes. The protocols of the meeting reveal how shocked the political elites of the GDR were on becoming acquainted with the material from Moscow. They were bewildered, had clearly lost their orientation, and feared for the future: "[U]ntil now I still cannot understand what happened"; "[F]or all of us this is stunning news"; "[R]eally, it is very complicated to define my relationship to what has happened"; "[W]hat will the future bring?"[14]

Doing away with the aura of sacrality around Stalin's person plunged the SED leadership into an ideological crisis. Central Committee member Paul Wandel acknowledged to his colleagues that the party was in the midst of a dramatic situation, noting that

[I]t is extremely difficult for every party member to see the destruction of what took decades to forge. The deep shock, the deplorable and intensely painful shock amongst us, cannot even be compared with what is happening now with the youth.[15]

As Kurt Hager put it,

Who among us has not been affected by what has happened? In the end, we have already been in the Party for several decades [and] many of us grew up on Stalin's works. We worshipped Stalin.. . . Without doubt, this is a heavy shock for both young and old.[16]

For members of the SED's Central Committee, men who genuinely believed in the ideals of Stalinism, recasting the image of the "vozhd'" precipitated a crisis of personal identity. Their shock, sorrow, and anger meant that neither the KPSS Central Committee nor the SED Politburo was able to put out any centralized information about Khrushchev's speech at this crucial juncture. The SED Central Committee's pride was hurt because even party apparatchiks at the highest level had to resort to reading the Western press to learn about Moscow's critique of the Stalin cult.[17] Kurt Hager confessed that he had read about it in the *Daily Worker* and the *Neue Züricher Zeitung*.[18]

Although the SED leadership was struggling with their distress, the party elite was trying to figure out how to manage the discourse of de-Stalinization and control public opinion. Ulbricht hastened to reassure his colleagues that, "[m]embers of the Party will be informed and everything will be in order," while also trying to reduce the range of issues under discussion.[19] They insisted on clarifying some questions: "How should what happened be explained to others and in what framework should Stalin's personality be criticized? Is it worthwhile to continue studying Stalin's works and the *Short Course*?" Those discussing these issues unanimously agreed that a select group of party members could become familiar with part of the text of Khrushchev's speech, but they were doubtful about the expediency of allowing the masses to be exposed to it. Thus, Otto Buchwitz argued for a complete information blackout, saying that, "There are things which we must keep shut up in ourselves and pass over in silence in the interests of the party and further work."[20] However, most members of the SED Central Committee understood that the GDR was teeming with rumors and therefore acknowledged that "sometimes a bit of the truth is better than gossip."[21]

The predictable result of the party conference was the decision to orient intra-party discussion toward officially published material and to selectively familiarize party members with the Secret Speech. Thus, like what happened in Moscow, "On the Cult of Personality and its Consequences" was read in closed sessions of the SED's Third Party Conference on March 30, 1956. A resolution about struggling with manifestations of the personality cult and the necessity of reinforcing the principles of "collective government" (*kollektivnoe upravlenie*) in the SED's ranks was another outcome of the Central Committee meeting. In the best traditions of self-criticism, members of the Central Committee confessed that they had participated in the Stalin cult in East Germany. Facing his colleagues, Paul Wandel expressed contrition, saying that

[T]here was a personality cult in our country too. We must frankly acknowledge that similar tendencies were observed amongst us. It is not that individual people were lauded [or] that too many portraits were put up. It is that the Soviet Union and the entire international workers movement suffered considerable harm because the principle of collective governance was violated, downgraded and ignored.[22]

He proposed that in drawing up and adopting resolutions they "give serious thought" to reducing the role of the Politburo and strengthening the Central Committee's voice. Kurt Hager also openly acknowledged that

Manifestations of the personality cult in the past were also disseminated among us. The same kinds of literary production and art about Stalin as those in the USSR were spread in our country. We ourselves had a hand in replicating them.[23]

However, the Central Committee conference did not come up with a well-defined party line for managing the discourse and practices of de-Stalinization. The cacophony of opinions expressed in the ranks of the highest party functionaries has a parallel in an incident that took place at the regional conference of party activists in the region of Halle in April 1956. On the first day of the meeting, Kurt Hager gave a speech about the personality cult. There was no discussion. The session ended with the ritual expression of complete trust in SED policy, which included a reference to the fact that there were no signs of the personality cult in East Germany. On the following day, another Central Committee member, Fred Oelßner, expressed an opposing viewpoint. He attacked the idea that the personality cult was absent in East Germany, citing evidence of the personality cult in the SED and in the East German mass organizations.[24] His remarks were received with disapproval and found little support. However, exchanges of directly opposed viewpoints of this kind left rank-and-file party members with "no idea of what to say and what to think."[25]

During this period, ordinary party members struggled with a dilemma: should they trust or distrust the SED Central Committee? The party leadership's silence and the fact that they were intentionally withholding facts gave rise to suspicions that were fueled by the lack of enough (even internal) information to interpret what had happened.[26] Many people said they felt disappointed and humiliated because they had to resort to reading the Western press and listening to Western radio and were upset because the Politburo's silence contrasted drastically with the openness of other (Western) sources of information. The leaders of regional party cells turned to the center, asking for official denials of all false rumors about Stalin. Questions from party members demanding explanations from Central Committee speakers show how bewildered they were: "Why doesn't Stalin belong to the classics of Marxism-Leninism and what did he do that was wrong"?[27] "It's not clear why Stalin doesn't belong to the classics anymore since he wrote numerous works on Marxism, he took an oath of loyalty to Comrade Lenin and carried on his work." [28]

SED veterans, especially former KPD members, were anxious to defend the "leader": "I cannot reconcile myself to the idea that Stalin made such mistakes"; "It's incredible that at present Stalin's policy is being slandered in this way"; "Stalin didn't make mistakes, everything was staged by his followers"; "Comrade Stalin has such high merits that he should not be reproached for anything."[29] After finishing his speech at the meeting in Halle, a party veteran defiantly shouted "Long live Stalin!"[30] These examples show discursive resistance to de-Stalinization. The absence of a clear-cut party line and new rules of rhetoric and behavior for rank-and-file party members amplified the flabbiness of the regime's discourse about the Stalin era.

At the same time, some active involvement in the process of de-Stalinization could be detected in the SED. Gestures indicating participation in de-Stalinization ranged from refusing to study Stalin's works to leaving the party and the mass organizations.[31] The discourse of de-Stalinization allowed party members to feel so free that they broke the long-standing taboo of publicly comparing Stalin with Hitler. Thus, an instructor in the SED regional administration in Greifswald noted parallels in the two dictators' politics: "Stalin used exactly the same kind of model for setting up a dictatorship as Hitler in the Third Reich. Like Hitler, Stalin appointed his friends to the highest offices."[32] In Stasi reports, similar instances were described as "especially negative occurrences." However, given the prevailing discursive paralysis, the Stasi did not know how to react to these ways of deconstructing and demolishing the sacred narrative about Stalin. The state's repressive machinery temporarily stopped persecuting those who expressed seditious sentiments.

Such radical breaches of party-state rhetoric were graphic indications that the discursive order of the official public sphere was malfunctioning in some ways. Mass reactions to obvious deviation from ritualistic rules and norms of behavior were, as many party members admitted, confusion about how to act and what to say in discussions with comrades. For most people, the new rhetoric, in particular the concept of "collective leadership," was merely an empty phrase. No one knew what this term meant or how to use and interpret it. This explains the large collection of requests for an explanation of the situation with Stalin the Central Committee received as well as an increase in demands to postpone discussion and refusals to participate in it. In this situation, the party secretary at Erfurt's electrical engineering works spoke with satisfaction about the decision to stop all discussion until the German delegation returned from Moscow with actual documents. He pointed out that conversations were meaningless since there was no unified party line on how to evaluate Stalin's work and personality.[33] Statements of this kind attest to the key role played by the party and the state's official language, which was used to preserve political homogeneity in the GDR by constructing political identity and disciplining "other-speaking" individuals.

Forced to remain silent, party members became irritated and downright angry. The process of de-Stalinization deprived the apparatchiks of the ritual language—which was a major resource supporting their political power and activities. Using this language, they took action in the political field and participated in social networks, organized everyday life, and set up hierarchies. Because the official discourse was paralyzed, they were forced to remain silent in public and to be inactive while there was growing protest among the rest of the population. As a result, a palpable longing for Stalin's style of putting things in order permeated a report ending with the following words:

> This is an inexplicable and unhealthy position, that any political events can be discussed before orders come from above. If anyone before the XX Congress cast doubt in any way on Stalinist theory, those moods would be reduced to zero.[34]

Fear of being punished for an extra word was another dominant emotion in the discourse of de-Stalinization. As a rule, ordinary party members absorbed and reacted to the flood of information about Stalin with anxiety. Not knowing how the regime would respond to seditious statements they were afraid of persecution and preferred to remain silent. This kind of apprehension shows up in the words of a white-collar worker from Rostock who admitted in conversation with colleagues that

> It's necessary to wait and see what sorts of additional things will follow in the question of the personality cult so as not to get stung in the discussion. Better to be silent. Others can be the ones to blurt out some excess.[35]

Fear permeated a session at a conference of party functionaries in Zeulenroda in the Gera region. Afraid to utter an unnecessary word, all who were present decided not to participate in a discussion about the personality cult, preferring silence to taking a risk.[36] Thus, reactions to de-Stalinization in the ranks of the SED show that it was not seen simply as a signal of freedom from the "discursive prison" of Stalinism (as Martin Sabrow put it).[37] Ordinary party members responded very cautiously to changes in the official language for describing Stalin because memories of the wave of purges and repressions at the beginning of the 1950s were still fresh. As a result, passive reactions dominated the party as its members played a waiting game and used the strategy of silence in official public spheres of the dictatorship, which was still quite capable of exerting control over minds and feelings, especially among SED followers.

Nonetheless, at the party, people soon began to ask questions about the nature of the personality cult and how it manifested itself not just in East Germany but across German political culture as a whole. Thus, one party member examined sources of leadership in the organizational philosophy of a "Bolshevik party of a new type" as follows: "After the death of Lenin, whom the people loved greatly, there arose the need to set over the state and party a new leader who could accumulate the people's love. This was Stalin."[38] In another instance, a "German predisposition" to "Führer"-cults was noted. In the Academy of Science, SED members discussed the connection of the leader cult with the German national character:

> Germans are very susceptible to personality cults. The SED too furthered establishment of the personality cult [although] it knew about various manifestations of illegality and furthered injustice against its will. The time came when our first secretary, Walter Ulbricht, was able to learn lessons from the Twentieth Congress.[39]

Ulbricht eventually became the target of intra-party dissatisfaction, and all the political mistakes of the past were ascribed to him. Party members complained that they were ashamed of having *that kind* of SED leader, since they were the ones who, day in and day out, had to deal with all the nasty things people said about Ulbricht—the numerous expressions of distaste, hateful comments, rumors, and insults directed at the head of the party.[40] As a result, there were calls in the party to get rid of Ulbricht and find someone new for the top position.[41] Criticism quickly spread to other members of the GDR political elite. During meetings, rank-and-file party members accused the members of the Central Committee and the Politburo of responsibility for the transfer and propaganda of the Stalin cult, asking

> Who stuck us with Stalin as an intelligent leader? This was the Politburo, all the members came back from the Soviet Union. In all their speeches Ulbricht and Grotewohl painted him as a great man. And now our Politburo isn't capable of self-criticism.[42]

Party members in the Leipzig region pointed out the shared roots of the Soviet and East German political regimes and GDR leadership's involvement in the crimes of the Stalin era: "Wilhelm Pieck, Walter Ulbricht and many others were in emigration in the USSR when Stalin made his mistakes. They should have noticed these shortcomings earlier. Criticizing Stalin is simultaneously criticizing our comrades."[43] In the Halle region, party members saw the Politburo's and the Central Committee's actions as an attempt to excuse themselves, find a "scapegoat," and write off all mistakes as the deeds of the "dead man."[44]

Freed from constraints, the discourse on de-Stalinization shocked East Germany's political elite. Although Ulbricht had adapted to Moscow's new rhetoric with singular skill, ordinary party members were more conflicted. Seeing that the regime's discourse had come to a halt, they did not know what to say or how to act in the turbulent field of de-Stalinization. The sudden revision of Stalin deprived them of their usual mechanisms for constructing identity, developing meanings, and interpreting reality. Two mutually exclusive proposals made at the same party meeting show the ambivalence pervading attempts to evaluate Stalin: there was a call to erect another monument to the "leader" but also a motion to discuss taking down and destroying portraits of Stalin.[45]

Opinion in the SED was quite polarized. Proponents of de-Stalinization, mostly former Social Democrats, were on one end of the spectrum of reactions. They used the discourse of unmasking Stalin to distance themselves from former KPD members, blaming them for the forced merger of the SPD and the KPD, the radical Sovietization of East Germany, and the use of repressive measures to strengthen communist rule. Former members of the German Social Democratic Party, who had pointed out the dangers inherent in the Soviet leader's one-man rule, even before 1933, strongly advocated for revising the narrative about the "best friend of the German people" and were perplexed by the question "Do the Stalins come and go but socialism rises in spite of this?"[46]

At the other end of the spectrum were apologists for the Soviet leader, largely former KPD members. They responded to criticism of the personality cult by defending the "leader" on the grounds of his "infallibility," "great authority," and "boundless trust."[47] These SED followers held fast to the earlier presentation of Stalin despite clear signals from Moscow that the image of the "vozhd'" was being revised. In assessing Stalin, most SED members were forced to tack between these two extreme positions. Thus, de-Stalinization turned out to be an acute political crisis for the "second German state." This forced ordinary party members to play a waiting game that called for resourcefulness and silence in rapidly changing political circumstances.

POPULAR RESPONSES TO DE-STALINIZATION IN EAST GERMAN SOCIETY

Ulbricht's March 4 article threw all of East German society into confusion. The distinctive feature of the East German case of de-Stalinization is what *Pravda* correspondent M. V. Podkliuchnikov described as the failure to "psychologically prepare the East Germans for the resolutions of the Twentieth Congress of the KPSS."[48] Although revision of the Stalinist political course in the Soviet Union was observed in the immediate aftermath of the "leader's" death, during the same period in the GDR the Stalin cult was flourishing.[49] On May 8, 1953, the village of Fürstenberg-on-the-Oder was renamed Stalinstadt. In 1955, a museum opened in the villa in Babelsberg where the Soviet leader spent the night during the Potsdam Conference. This building, now called the Stalin-Villa, was added to the list of the most important sights in the GDR. In addition, the policy of Stalinizing public space was ongoing: new monuments and busts of the Soviet leader were put up and streets, squares, enterprises, and schools were named after the "leader." Until Khrushchev's Secret Speech, it was impossible to publicly cast doubt on Stalin's authority. In February 1956, on the eve of the Twentieth Congress, the socialist press in the GDR was still singing the "leader's" praises, using the usual rhetoric of the personality cult.[50] Therefore, it is not surprising that for many contemporaries the revision of official knowledge about Stalin that was being initiated in Moscow caused, at the very least, distress and confusion.

One of the first results of Ulbricht's article was a malfunction in the public production of official narratives of the Stalin cult. A telling incident took place in Greifswald during a lecture at the university's medical faculty. On March 5, 1956, the students asked their teacher if Stalin could be considered a classic of Marxism-Leninism. Still unaware of Ulbricht's March 4 revisionist article, the faculty member answered in the affirmative, and applause rang out across the auditorium. Only after this, was he shown the first secretary's article, which shocked and amazed him.[51] This was not the only case of this kind. Teachers and students everywhere admitted that they wanted to keep quiet; they avoided even saying the word "vozhd'" for fear of being punished and seeing their party trajectories and academic careers ruined.[52] Fear, and the sense that one had to be on guard, fed rumors that the authorities intended to "put everyone who disobeys the regime under lock and key."[53]

According to official reports on the moods of the population, some young people reacted extremely harshly and negatively to Ulbricht's announcement. Yesterday's "Hitler Youth generation" saw a new betrayal in the unexpected abandonment of the Stalin cult since the SED regime was now demanding that they renounce the myths and rituals of the "Soviet Führer," which echoed the postwar command to give up the Hitler cult. Therefore, Ulbricht's words provoked a wave of protest in the mass youth organizations and educational institutions. As a rule, defense of the Soviet leader turned into an angry critique of the East German leadership. For example, a group of upper-grade pupils in Saalfeld expressed confusion about groundless blackening of the "best friend of the German people," saying that, "It is simply swinish that now they only show Stalin as very bad in order to represent other party members in the best light." In Erfurt, senior students wrote a letter to the regional administration of the SED in which they condemned the removal of portraits of the "leader." Students from Golzow in the Seelow/Frankfurt region even justified Stalin's repressive policies by arguing that it was only possible to make a revolution by using weapons and violence, that is, by sacrificing victims on the altar of communism. They demanded that the school director give a detailed explanation of the resolutions of the Twentieth Congress and rehabilitate Stalin.[54]

Similar expressions of resistance came from people who were integrated into the party's structures and state institutions. Representatives of organs of power, state institutions, political parties, and the mass organizations used the previously approved language of state propaganda to defend the former image of the "vozhd'." For example, in response to Ulbricht's words, a teacher in Berlin-Lichtenberg said,

> In my opinion, Stalin did much that was useful and here I only wanted to remember the Second World War. I consider it absolutely fair that people revered him for his merits and this should not be called a personality cult. If it is asserted today that Stalin put himself above the party, this is not his fault. It is the fault of the whole party leadership.[55]

White-collar workers from Zwickau continued to call Stalin a "very clever military leader."[56] In the same vein, a doctor from Torgau defended the "leader" as a classic of Marxism-Leninism, calling it incorrect to renounce the scientific theories of the "vozhd'."[57]

Unsurprisingly, Ulbricht's March article became a central focus of discussion at meetings of workers' collectives. For example, the teaching staff of the Higher School of Economics and Planning in Dresden unanimously adopted a resolution refuting Ulbricht's article. They resolved to continue to consider Stalin a classic of Marxism-Leninism since all of his works had gone through a process of approval in the KPSS Central Committee. They also decided to deny indiscriminate accusations, oppose the wholesale dismissal of all the Soviet leader's merits, and wait until "the situation normalizes" to hold discussions.[58] The mass organizations also came out with an appeal to suspend examination of a question that was so sensitive for the political culture of East Germany. Thus, the leadership of the German-Soviet Friendship Society spoke of the senselessness of public talk about Stalin's mistakes, which "only turns into violations of public order."[59]

Malfunctions in the dictatorship's discursive order led to questions about what kind of language and which categories should be used to characterize Stalin: "Can Stalin be called a classic? Is it permissible to consider him a great commander and a faithful pupil of Lenin"?[60] People were bewildered by the sharp turn in official rhetoric. As a photographer from Grevesmühlen put it, "For all these years Stalin was the savior of humanity, the brilliant follower of Lenin's ideas, our ideal. And all at once all this is erased. This is inexplicable for me. What is happening?"[61]

This was in fact the very question agitating East German society. Without a clear party line for managing the discourse of de-Stalinization, members of the mass organizations tried to interpret what was happening on their own initiative. After discussing the results of the Twentieth Congress, FDJ members in the Königs Wusterhausen district resolved that "Marxism is not dogma and Comrade Stalin was mistaken about the characteristics of world development."[62] At a meeting in Magdeburg, FDJ representatives asked whether Stalin should be considered an "enemy of the people" like Beria, who put himself above the principles of collective leadership.[63] At another youth meeting, people drew direct parallels between the Stalin and the Ulbricht cults. As a result, there were calls for Ulbricht to resign from his post as first secretary of the SED Central Committee since he was the main conduit for disseminating Stalinist politics in the GDR.[64]

Reports on the population's moods document discord and clashing opinions, but they also divulge much more. The documents I analyzed reveal the qualitatively new nature of public rhetoric: discussions became more "heated," "open," and "free." These sources tell us about what men and women, party members and non-members, people in various professions and of different religions had to say. Their rhetoric and behavior were free of

any fear of violating previously established discursive taboos. Thus, it was
noted that young people openly debated issues on the street, talking about
the advantages of life in the West, and deriding the anti-Stalin campaign.[65]
Everywhere people were asking if political prisoners should be freed and
discussing the issue.[66] An official from the Potsdam region who had been
expelled from the SED during a period of purges claimed that "For the first
time it's possible to openly criticize Stalin's work and at the same time show
that Stalin was a dictator."[67]

There were more open violations of the dictatorship's rhetorical norms
in major industrial centers than in the countryside. Workers at the factories in Wildau did not hesitate to call the Soviet leader a "dictator" and the
"Soviet Hitler," asking each other if they had seen any Western newspapers
with revealing materials.[68] Talking with a friend, a housewife from Königs
Wusterhausen district called Stalin a criminal who should be punished as
severely as possible.[69] Public use of the terms "dictator," "enemy," and "criminal" to stigmatize Stalin became an indicator of serious shifts in the East
German discursive order. As new rhetoric for describing the "leader" began
to compete with the normative language of propaganda, there was a dichoto-
mous split in the image of Stalin. The reactivation of negative stereotypes of
the Soviet leader from the Weimar period and the Third Reich contributed to
this schism. For example, a woman in Berlin-Pankow affirmed that Germans
had had a "low opinion" of Stalin for a long time, but it had been forbidden
to articulate this obvious fact so publicly in the GDR.[70]

As soon as the discourse of de-Stalinization began to make its way into
East Germany, society was gripped by an epidemic of rumors. In fact,
rumors became the motor of de-Stalinization in the GDR. Hearsay allowed
the population to find out why the SED had distanced itself so suddenly from
the Stalin cult. The word on the street also helped people compensate for the
shortage of information and offered material to use as they tried to envision
what the future might bring. For example, a popular rumor conveyed false
information about an alleged official ban on having Stalin's works in one's
possession and reading them. These conjectures were based on gossip about
an order, supposedly given by Bulganin, that Stalin's books should be pulped
and all portraits of him destroyed.[71] The consequence of such rumors was a
crisis in the sale of Stalin's works in the retail and wholesale sectors, which
brought publishing houses to the brink of bankruptcy.[72] Booksellers saw a
sharp drop in an already low demand for Stalin's works and felt they should
be removed completely from circulation.[73] In addition, instances in which
books by the "leader" were handed over to be pulped and even burned were
recorded throughout the country.[74] The word on the street about de-Stalinization forecast changes in the East German cultural-symbolic landscape. Thus,
talk of the city's imminent renaming and removal of the plaques with the

Soviet leader's name made the rounds in Stalinstadt.[75] Likewise, people conversing in a restaurant in Berlin-Lichtenberg analyzed the change in political course by predicting that the Stalinallee would be renamed in honor of Ulbricht or Khrushchev.[76]

The Stasi's reports anxiously described the topography through which "hostile rumors were spread": railway stations, trains and public transport, hotels and restaurants, stores and lines, in other words, places where there were large, anonymous crowds of people. The authorities thought housewives, cleaning ladies, and pensioners were the main sources of rumors which sowed panic and distrust of the regime. A pensioner from Lauscha (in the Neuhaus region) summarized the word on street about the far-reaching consequences of de-Stalinization. After hearing rumors in a shop, he told neighbors that political prisoners would soon be released and images of the "vozhd'" would be taken down in Leipzig.[77] Housewives living in the Brandenburg, Nauen, and Pritzwalk districts were gossiping about the widespread practice of removing portraits of Stalin and getting rid of days of memory in honor of the "leader" in the USSR; they also passed on the possibility that he would be posthumously given the death penalty for setting up a personality cult.[78] The rumors grew out of semantic changes the population observed taking place in public space. At first there was little explanation of the sudden disappearance of portraits of Stalin from administrative buildings, city streets, and squares.

The population responded to the ubiquitous political anxiety with iconoclastic gestures and discussions preliminary to carrying out acts of iconoclasm. Thus, conversations about how portraits of Stalin, Ulbricht, Pieck, and Grotewohl should be removed were widespread.[79] During meetings, the population tried to find out whatever they could about changes in the norms for dealing with portraits, posters, and busts of the "leader," which, to the surprise of many, had been turned into disgraced symbols of power. For example, the staff of the Sondershausen statistical service asked their director about issues like the following:

> What should we do with the posters of Stalin that we had to buy and put up in our homes? On this question it's necessary to have centralized direction so that they don't look askance at us when we take down the portraits of Stalin and put up other ones.[80]

At a meeting, an engineer asked the presidium how long the "plaster head of the criminal" would be in the dining hall.[81] And in Karl-Marx-Stadt, employees in the office of the magistrate were talking about how absurd the public use of "images of four heads—Marx, Engels, Lenin and Stalin" was.[82] A technical employee in Rostock called hanging portraits of state

leaders a manifestation of the personality cult. He suggested there should
be a resolute struggle against this practice, and it should be ended once and
for all.[83]

The population moved quickly from talking to taking action. Throughout
the GDR people destroyed busts of the Soviet dictator.[84] When a woman who
worked in Suhl in the Sonnenberg regional administration district called for
all portraits of Stalin to be destroyed, her colleagues responded by removing portraits of Pieck, Grotewohl, and Ulbricht.[85] A report from the Potsdam
region described how someone working in the regional administrative offices
took a portrait of Stalin off the wall, remarking that "[T]here is nothing more
for him to do here."[86] In the central school of the town of Sternberg, in the
Schwerin region, in many textbooks for teaching Russian, Stalin's image
was cut out, or sometimes it was crisscrossed.[87] In other cases, teachers and
students reacted even more boldly. After a teachers' meeting in a school in
Rüdersdorf, in the Fürstenwald region, a portrait of the "vozhd'" was found in
the rubbish bin.[88] At the steelworks in Maxhütte, a picture of Stalin was torn
to pieces, and the remnants of the portrait were nailed to the speakers' podium
in the factory meeting hall.[89] At enterprises in Gera, quarrels about the personality cult became so heated that the FDJ leadership was told to transfer
wreaths that had been placed on the bust of the Soviet leader in Stalin Park
to other memorials.[90] The escalation of iconoclastic practices very clearly
revealed the regime's crisis of representations. Intended to visualize, legitimize, and reinforce the regime before 1956, the artifacts of the personality
cult became the central target of popular aggression and the political system's
most vulnerable spot.

It is also notable that Lenin and Stalin were treated as two distinct entities
in the popular discourse of de-Stalinization. Positive qualities were attributed
to Lenin as an "authentic" leader while Stalin alone was blamed for creating his personality cult. A domestic servant who worked for a Berlin doctor
severely criticized Stalin, arguing in defense of the true "leader" that

> Stalin was a big swine. During Lenin's illness he deprived him of the possibility
> of taking part in the life of the party, he banned many [of Lenin's] works, which
> have remained unpublished even now. It was only because of this that he rose
> to the height of the state apparatus and became the first secretary of the party.[91]

Rumors that Stalin's body would be removed from communism's sacred
space—Lenin's Mausoleum—show the symbolic destruction of the propaganda narrative about the two leaders of the October Revolution.[92] In the
German context of de-Stalinization, the population also tended to reject
Soviet leaders and return to the German theoretical foundations of building
socialism based on the works of Marx and Engels.[93] Many similar ideas are

expressed in my sources. For example, in conversation with his classmates, a student named Klaus Priebe argued that

> Lenin was the same kind of dictator as Stalin, who falsified the doctrine of Marx and Engels about building socialism in exactly the same way Stalin did. Lenin was the one who prepared Stalin's ascent . . . If we really care about building socialism, then we have to go back and start where Marx left off.[94]

The SPD's Eastern Bureau and the Western mass media played an active role in de-Stalinization, encouraging the population to participate in reevaluating Stalin's image. While the SED did nothing, waiting for directives from Moscow about how to handle de-Stalinization, the Western press attacked Stalin cult propaganda in the GDR and the SED's cult of Ulbricht. They concentrated on broadly publicizing how much the SED's first secretary depended on the Kremlin. The RIAS radio and television station condemned the SED in general: "Ulbricht is the Stalin of the GDR"; "Walter Ulbricht doesn't have his own opinion and his own will, he always orients himself solely toward Moscow"; "Ulbricht made a 180-degree turnaround"; "It is unlikely that Walter Ulbricht, who always spoke positively about Stalin will now voice a directly contradictory opinion."[95] And Radio London predicted that the SED first secretary's career would end with "Stalin's political death."[96]

After Ulbricht's article came out, the Western newspaper *Der Tag* made it its mission to discredit the East German leadership by publishing a series of questions that it suggested people in the GDR should ask at meetings:

> From which point did Ulbricht think Stalin was a saboteur and for what reasons did he not publicly state this important opinion earlier? One can also ask why he judged Stalin so harshly if not long before this he had extolled Stalin as a brilliant, great and wise leader of the peoples? Or is a similar question about the sudden change in Ulbricht's political convictions dangerous?[97]

In articles and broadcasts, Ulbricht was accused of using Bolshevik methods to hold onto his one-man rule: eliminating political competitors by repressing them, introducing censorship, and weakening the collective bodies of power. Western radio discussed the possibility of organizing a public trial at which Ulbricht could answer for all his crimes before the entire nation.[98] *Der Tag* also pointed out that

> None of the world's communist parties was as strongly and dogmatically built on Stalin's doctrine as the SED . . . In no country except the USSR did the Stalin cult exist on the same scale as it did in the GDR.[99]

The Western discourse of de-Stalinization urged East Germans to over-throw the Soviet protectorate and the SED regime; the media argued that these were the fundamental prerequisites for building a strong, independent, and prosperous Germany. More specifically, the Western mass media called on the population of the GDR to organize a new popular uprising like the mass unrest in June 1953. Radio broadcasts from the Federal Republic addressed the leaders of the GDR with political, economic, and social demands. For example, on the eve of the SED's Third Party Conference, there were appeals for the "removal of Ulbricht and the entire Stalinist government," and exhortations to establish the fundamental institutions of Western democracies—free elections and free speech—as well as calls for complete rehabilitation of members of the workers' opposition who were arrested during the June days in 1953. There were also demands that the terrorist apparatus be replaced by the regular police force and pressure to abolish collective farms and to adopt labor and social legislation.[100] Economic ultimatums included the introduction of a seven-hour workday, improvement of working conditions, and changes in the social welfare system.

In the countryside, the idea of doing away with collective farms was extremely mobilizing. Collective farms were the result of agricultural reforms that began in 1948 and were very unpopular in the GDR. Therefore, this sector of the population used criticism of Stalin as a "legitimate" way to leave collective farms and promote the development of individual farming.[101] However, speaking out against collective farms was not how these East Germans participated in the discourse of de-Stalinization. Accusing the regime of complicity in Stalinist crimes, agricultural workers formulated a series of political demands addressed to the GDR leadership. One farmer drew a simple, logical conclusion: Stalin was guilty and so were his SED comrades.[102] What followed from this conclusion went far beyond hostility to collective farms. As a farmer from the Frankfurt-on-Oder region put it at a meeting of collective farmers, calling for the end of the SED dictatorship and the introduction of free elections:

> What has the party done for us? They only want us to earn money for them. But soon we will deal with them differently. We are free farmers and we don't want to live under a dictatorship. You want to see all of us on collective farms but we aren't on the same road as you. We demand free elections which will show who is coming to power.[103]

The uprisings in Poland and Hungary in the fall of 1956 were a turning point that changed the dynamics of de-Stalinization in the Eastern bloc. In the GDR, the population responded to these events with a new wave of oppositional activity, but the state reacted by "putting the screws on"—limiting freedom of speech and repressing nonconformists. The Western mass media once again kept East Germans informed about popular protests on the Periphery of the Soviet empire. For example, RIAS explained to its listeners that under the pressure of the Polish uprising there was a general amnesty of Polish communists and thirty thousand arrestees had been released.[104] Citing an example in which the opposite situation prevailed in East Germany, the radio station asserted that there were "twenty thousand innocent victims of Stalin's justice in the GDR who have been imprisoned until now."[105] In this case, Minister of Justice Hilde Benjamin, often dubbed the "red guillotine," was harshly criticized. She publicly refused to admit that the judicial system had made mistakes in unmasking "enemies of the people" and rejected de-Stalinization as a reason to liberalize the political order in East Germany.[106]

The uprising in Hungary radicalized anti-Russian sentiments. Above all, the bloody reprisals against the insurgents stirred memories of Soviet tanks on the streets of East Berlin in June 1953. Thus, in the Grimm region, rumors that Soviet troops were coming to Germany began to circulate. People were saying that it was dangerous to leave home in the evening because of more cases of Soviet soldiers harassing and robbing women.[107] Similar rumors, along with talk of disruptions in food imports from Eastern Europe, caused panic and led to deserted streets in the evening hours.[108] Not surprisingly, there was a rise in anger, and even hatred toward Russians. Thus, university students demanded an end to the requirement that they study Russian.[109] And slogans like "Freedom for Hungary" and "Ivan Go Home" were scrawled on trains carrying German goods to the Soviet Union.[110]

Germans showed their solidarity with the Hungarian people in numerous indirect or symbolic ways rather than through open protest. Thus, dropping one's membership in the German-Soviet Friendship Society and refusing to pay dues in other mass organizations were interpreted as gestures of support for the Hungarian insurgents that were covert, but unequivocally understood by everyone. At a factory in Ludwigsfelde, workers unanimously chose not to participate in a lottery to win a trip to the Soviet Union.[111] At public meetings everywhere, people asked the moderators if the Soviet Union had the right to invade Hungary.[112] Echoes of the Hungarian protest led to new talk of dismissing the government, especially Ulbricht.[113] The first secretary was accused of silence about Stalin's politics of terror, which he could not fail to be aware of while he was in emigration in Moscow, living with other exiled communists in the Hotel Lux.

The Hungarian uprising clearly put an end to the liberalizing trend that had emerged in the GDR with the first public signs of de-Stalinization. The SED regime began to control public discourse more harshly, and it turned once again to the repressive policy of excluding nonconformists. Thus, in October 1956, a wave of arrests of intellectuals and students, who were victims of fabricated charges, swept East Germany.[114] At the same time, the powers of the police and the Stasi were broadened. A series of demonstrative trials of "violators of the social order" and "enemies of the people" once again drummed the ritualistic use of state and party-sanctioned language into the population. On November 20, 1956, the SED Politburo adopted a resolution about suppressing all hostile attacks and groups of agents provocateurs in universities: arrests of students in Leipzig, Jena, Dresden, and Berlin followed.

Although de-Stalinization ended with more radical repression in East Germany, it had an important therapeutic effect on postwar German society. The chaos reigning in the dictatorship's discursive order allowed the population to break the state-imposed silence and speak openly about painful issues. Thus, when revision of Stalin's image was put on the agenda, the distressing territorial question of the Oder-Neisse line as the GDR's eastern border surfaced. For people living in the border regions, the establishment of a German-Polish border after World War II, and the resultant expulsion of the German population from Silesia, remained deeply traumatic. However, until 1956, this issue, although raised only occasionally—and timidly—was still a rhetorical taboo. In regions near the Polish frontier, only after the Twentieth Party Congress were there open calls to redraw the border. Under the new conditions, people described the creation of the frontier as "one of the mistakes in Stalinist nationality policy."[115] The idea that "establishing the Oder-Neisse line was intended to set the Poles and the Germans against each other and create a hotbed of constant strife in Eastern Europe" came up over and over again in conversations in the Cottbus and Frankfurt am Oder districts.[116]

East Germans used de-Stalinization to help come to terms with the Nazi past. Criticism of the Stalin cult allowed East Germans to take a fresh look at their own experience with the Hitler cult and refuse to be characterized in terms of a "German predisposition" to leader cults. Thinking logically, a student pointed out to his classmates that "They berate us for belonging to the Hitler cult, but really, the Soviet people did the same thing themselves with Stalin."[117] Moreover, the growth of anti-Russian sentiment enabled former German POWs, who had returned to East Germany from Soviet captivity labeled as "war criminals," to break the silence decreed by state policy for the first time and openly share traumatic memories of their imprisonment in the USSR.[118] Thus, the official revision of Stalin's image opened the way for collective emotional work on postwar experiences of a society that was marked by the expulsion, violence, and the loss of the eastern territories.

Almost every stratum of East German society was caught up in the discourse of de-Stalinization and contributed to the reappraisal of Stalin's image. Taking note of the regime's silence and its inability to shape the discourse of de-Stalinization, the population used Moscow's revision of the image of the "leader" to expand the boundaries of permissible rhetoric and behavior: citizens now felt they could articulate their personal grievances to the regime, and there was an unprecedented upsurge in the expression of previously tabooed collective feelings and experiences. The Western mass media and the SPD's Eastern Bureau saw de-Stalinization as an opportunity to mold the East Germans' outlook. As alternative information sources in the "second German state," they presented knowledge that led people to formulate demands for political, economic, and social change—and to openly insist that the GDR government respond. In essence, these were calls for Ulbricht to go and for liberalizing reforms. As a result, the most important outcome of the desacralization of Stalin was, as a housewife from Schmalkalden aptly put it, the "SED's political bankruptcy."[119] The scale and nature of discussion about Stalin revealed a significant degree of popular distrust of the regime: the massive loss of trust extended not just to the political elite but to the East German state as a whole. This distrust was expressed in ways that ranged from leaving the party and the mass organizations to skipping party meetings, from burning Stalin's works to fleeing to West Germany.[120]

The removal of Stalin's halo made people anxious about the predictability of their days, weeks, and months, and the years to come, since propaganda had cast the "leader" in the role of the patron of the German people and, in terms of imagining the future, he had been designated as the guarantor of peace, stability, and prosperity. The disappearance of the sacral center of East German symbolic politics sparked a crisis of confidence with an ensuing collapse of the expectations and hopes the population had invested in the SED regime. In private conversations among family members, with friends and colleagues, or standing in line waiting to go into a shop, people discussed troubling questions: Would the German question actually be resolved, and would a single state be created? Would their living standards improve? When would the "bright future" arrive? In earlier GDR propaganda, these questions had been bound up with expectations and promises linked to the Soviet leader. In one fell swoop, de-Stalinization not only nullified all of the propaganda's power but also negated the population's expectations. Therefore, society began to look for new leaders to carry the collective hopes, political figures who could win the population's trust. The fact that portraits of Stalin were replaced by images of Bulganin and Khrushchev in the town of Binz might have reflected a basic, collective need for a feeling of security and powerful patrons in the process of identifying a new, strong leader.[121]

THE CRISIS IN PUBLIC SYMBOLISM AND
THE SEARCH FOR REPRESENTATIONS
OF POWER AFTER STALIN

De-Stalinization provoked a profound crisis and an all-encompassing reconstruction of the entire East German landscape of public symbolism. The
May First celebrations in 1956 were a clear sign of this transition. For the
first time after the end of the war, Moscow chose not to insist on centralizing power representations in the "people's democracies." Instead, it gave
the socialist countries the right to self-determination in the matter of how
leaders were visualized in columns during the demonstrations—and they
were allowed to decide whether or not Stalin's portrait should be carried.[122]
As a result, across the Soviet bloc there were no manifestations of symbolic
homogeneity and the synchronicity of the cult community was absent. In
the GDR, no special decree was issued about how to stage the procession of
columns of demonstrators. In China, images of the "leader of all the peoples"
were still part of the publicly displayed visual trappings of the holiday. And
in Poland, demonstrators carried portraits of the current leaders as well as
Polish communists repressed by Stalin in the 1930s.[123] Thus, for the first
time, Moscow allowed the Periphery a certain amount of independence in
implementing its symbolic politics. The "people's democracies" used this
modest degree of autonomy to begin what was initially a spontaneous and
later a much more organized process of de-Stalinization in the realm of
public symbolism.

In the summer of 1956, after its initial shock and dismay, the SED regime
began to implement a more coherent policy of consigning the Soviet leader
to oblivion. Removal of every representation of the Stalin cult in public
space was a key element of this course. Thus, in July 1956, the Stalinallee in
Leipzig became the Friedrich-Ludwig-Jahn-Allee. A month later, a statue of
the Soviet leader in Karl Marx Square vanished. Preparations to build a new
sports complex were the official reason given for its disappearance. In East
Berlin, the portrait of the "leader" was removed from the exit of the S-Bahn's
Stalinallee station in August 1956. While all the visible signs of the Stalin cult
were being removed from public areas, the SED Central Committee received
a flood of letters asking that industrial enterprises and educational facilities
that had previously been named in honor of Stalin now be spared the shameful name of *their* "leader." The population responded positively to the SED
regime's initial efforts to cleanse public space. For example, officers in the
People's Police were glad to be rid of the representations of an "absolutely
alien state," and they called for a return to honoring Thälmann, saying that
"at least this leader was German."[124] Thus, from the summer of 1956 onward,
one sees something new: the population began to show that it rejected

the Sovietization of public space. Once again, people were differentiating between the cults of *our* (German) leaders and *theirs* (Soviet).

Little by little, the regime began to deal with the all-encompassing taboo of memories about Stalin. First, some revisions to the official discourse were necessary. Thus, the name of the Central Committee's Marx-Engels-Lenin-Stalin Institute was changed to the Institute of Marxism-Leninism.[125] The plan to publish the Soviet leader's complete works was canceled. In September 1956, the renamed institute handed the party authorities a document with a selection of little-known citations drawn from the works of Marx, Engels, and other leading Marxist theorists on the principles of "collective leadership." Included in this compilation was a critique of the personality cult as it was practiced by Stalin.[126] The fact that such a document was created shows that the official discourse of power was in dire straits. It also demonstrates how acutely the SED needed a new rhetoric of "collective government" drawn from the work of *German* leaders of the revolutionary workers' movement.

Revising the official discourse of power included removing various other familiar features of daily life. For example, excursions to Cecilienhof, the site of the August 1945 Potsdam Conference, with the guide's traditional expatiation on the "role of mighty Stalin in German history," were canceled. The book *Stalin Brought Us Up* vanished from bookstores and library shelves after the publisher informed booksellers and librarians that it was forbidden to read, sell, or lend this book. Sales of all of Stalin's works were suspended, and the books themselves were taken to the publishers' warehouses. Traditional cinematic epics propagandizing the leader cult, films such as *The Vow*, *The Fall of Berlin*, and *Meeting on the Elbe*, were removed from distribution in the GDR. And, at the beginning of the academic year, schools were told to take down portraits of Stalin and to go through textbooks, cutting, tearing out, or gluing together pages devoted to Soviet leader.[127]

Personality cult objects, which had been symbols of power until February 1956, were moved out of the center into the shadowy zones of public space. Removed from highly visible places, they were shoved into cupboards and storage areas, piled up in warehouses as unclaimed discards, covered with drop cloths, and concealed in out-of-the-way places—under staircases, in basements, corners, and dark alleys; in other words, they were hidden from public view.[128] Leader cult representations vanished from reviewing stands at party congresses and rallies. Demonstrations were now devoid of the leaders' images, red corners were dismantled, the rooms dedicated to the "vozhd'" were closed, and portraits and quotations from the leaders' works were taken down. This sudden disappearance created a void. Initially, the regime tried to cover up the empty places with more neutral, impersonal national and imperial symbols. In place of portraits, a collection of East German and Soviet flags appeared in public places. Bouquets of flowers and the emblems of the party and the mass organizations rounded out the design. Images of the collective—workers, peasants, and the intelligentsia—now became the mainstays of the visual culture of socialism, which corresponded to the propagandized principle of "collective government" (Figure 6.1).

While public space was neglected because the regime had "lost face," the propaganda apparatus was preoccupied with searching for new representations to defuse the crisis and developing a new iconography of power after Stalin was banished from public symbolism. Essentially, this involved reforming the traditions of the personality cult. To fill the voids created by de-Stalinization, the deities in the pantheon of leaders were rearranged. After a trip to Moscow, the director of the newly renamed Institute of Marxism-Leninism presented the first secretary of the Soviet embassy, A. E. Karetnikov, with a plan that came to occupy a central place in propagandizing Marxism-Leninism. The proposal focused on popularizing German propaganda figures, who were now called on to strengthen German national identity. In July 1957, the centennial of Clara Zetkin's birth, the idea of opening a museum devoted to her life and work in Birkenwerder (in the Potsdam region), came up. The SED Central Committee's Department of Agitation and Propaganda directed all the district and regional party committees to schedule a lecture

Figure 6.1   Reviewing stand at the SED's Fifth Congress, held in East Berlin, July 10–16, 1958. *Source:* Bildarchiv im Deutschen Historischen Museum (Berlin). Signature: Bild F58/1620.

on July 5, 1957, describing Zetkin's role in the struggle for women's rights in the GDR.[129] There was also a plan to create an Ernst Thälmann museum in Berlin.[130] In May and again in July 1960, Ludwig Einicke, the director of the Institute of Marxism-Leninism, urged the director of the Department of Agitation and Propaganda to speed up the publication of Rosa Luxemburg's works.[131] In July 1961, the party began preparations to celebrate the ninetieth anniversary of Karl Liebknecht's birth, which would culminate in opening a museum devoted to his life and thought.[132] The inauguration of national personality cults was supposed to compensate for Stalin's disappearance from the pantheon of leaders and to appeal to German national sentiments.

To preserve the imperial hierarchy and the personified motif of German-Soviet friendship, a return to "Leninist norms" was proclaimed in Moscow and then taken up in Berlin. This developed into affirmation of the Lenin cult in the GDR. In February 1956, even before de-Stalinization began, the SED announced that it was important, indeed necessary, to produce a German translation of the complete edition of Lenin's works.[133] After the revelations of the Soviet dictator's crimes, the Stalin Prize became the International Lenin Prize for Strengthening Peace among Peoples. Efforts to promote the Lenin cult peaked in 1960 with events marking the ninetieth anniversary of his birth. Lenin was celebrated along traditional lines: statues and busts were put up; a complete edition of his works was published; portraits and posters were printed; exhibitions were organized; memorial plaques were installed; a series of postage stamps came out; and museums devoted to his life and work opened in Leipzig and Berlin.[134] The SED Central Committee's Department of Agitation and Propaganda efficiently issued detailed recommendations for celebrations, and it produced materials speakers could use for lectures and to address meetings and ceremonial gatherings.[135] These materials presented Lenin as the "leader and teacher of the international proletarian movement."

Aiming to replace the Stalin cult, the KPSS Central Committee coordinated measures to revitalize "Leninist principles" in ideological work and to establish the cult of the October Revolution. The first step was to disband the exhibition of gifts to Stalin to create more exposition space for displays that would "reflect the role of the revolution in history."[136] Then, in the summer of 1956, Aleksandr N. Shelepin, the secretary of the Komsomol Central Committee, proposed that, in conjunction with the upcoming publication of a memory book about important sites related to Lenin in Moscow and the Moscow region, tours of the sites highlighted in the book should be organized for young people. To displace the Stalin cult, the head of the Komsomol offered to install monuments, busts, and memorial plaques honoring heroes of the revolutionary movement and to organize excursions and commemorative visits to *lieux de mémoire* about the October Revolution, the civil war, and the Great Patriotic War.[137] The preparations to celebrate the fortieth anniversary of the October Revolution in 1957 included plans to release an album about Lenin's life in a print run of 100,000 copies and to schedule lectures, film festivals, and exhibitions across the USSR.[138] At the same time, Stalin's works became write-offs and were destroyed. The KPSS Central Committee reported that more than five million copies, worth 2,280,000 rubles, had been pulped. The total value of "outdated literature" glorifying Stalin, which was written off as wastepaper on the wave of de-Stalinization, was estimated at 110,000,000 rubles.[139] Stigmatization of Stalin took place against the backdrop of proclamations of the communist system's legitimacy in the USSR and the "people's democracies" and other efforts to maintain the authority of the KPSS and other communist parties. The cults of the revolution and World War II were designed to become new integrative structures for the entire communist space, transforming the cult community into a community of memory with a shared sense of pride in the glorious—imperial and national—past.

Moscow was anxiously looking at how de-Stalinization was unfolding outside the Soviet Union. As it observed the multitude of interpretations in play, the KPSS understood how hard it would be to control the discourse of de-Stalinization in the USSR and beyond its borders. Therefore, the new Soviet leadership adopted several measures intended to discipline the population and reduce the broad range of ideas, opinions, and feelings about Stalin to a single, party-state controlled version of the "vozhd'." On June 30, 1956, the Presidium of the KPSS Central Committee approved the "Draft Resolution of the KPSS on Overcoming the Personality Cult and Its Consequences."[140] This document was one of the Soviets' first attempts to control the discourse of de-Stalinization outside the USSR. It was translated and published in *Neues Deutschland* in early July. Here the KPSS Central Committee described the initial manifestations of the personality cult and passed judgment on the repressions connected with it, but most importantly, the "Draft Resolution" emphasized that the bond between the state and the people was crucial in order to avoid similar mistakes.[141] It declared that a return to Marxism-Leninism was the best way to prevail over the personality cult and affirm the principles of "collective government." This document also asserted that the personality cult warped the Soviet political system and it condemned efforts to locate the personality cult's sources in the nature of Bolshevik rule as "gross mistake[s]" and "absolutely wrong."[142] The regime attributed every opinion falling outside the framework of this text to "enemies of the Soviet order," accusing them of exacerbating the class struggle and the Cold War. The "Draft Resolution" concluded by calling on citizens to adhere to the rhetorical norms established by the state and the party, to join forces to build socialism, and to strengthen the unity of the "people's democracies."

From that point on, Moscow's text became the basis for all discussion of the "Stalin question" in the GDR. Ulbricht was accused of setting up his own personality cult, and within the ranks of the SED there were immediate demands that this be officially acknowledged. At a meeting of the Politburo on July 3, 1956, Fred Oelßner attacked the first secretary:

> Until now we still have not begun to correctly summarize the results of the Twentieth Congress . . . In connection with this, an important question for us has arisen: Is there a personality cult in the SED? Yes, it certainly exists, and it is based on the regime of one-man rule established by Walter Ulbricht.[143]

The Soviet ambassador also shared his observations on the negative manifestations of the Ulbricht cult in the SED: there were too many quotations of his works, and he quoted himself too much, not to mention the ubiquitous portraits and posters bearing his image. However, Ulbricht's position and status remained firmly in place, criticism in the party notwithstanding.

Consequently, at the SED Central Committee's thirtieth conference, in February 1957, Ulbricht personally began to limit the discourse of de-Stalinization and came out in favor of partially rehabilitating the late leader, saying that

> An enemy deliberately criticized specific mistakes made by Comrade Stalin in order to condemn all of his actions ... The speech at the closed meeting of the Twentieth Congress of the KPSS dealt exclusively with questions of the personality cult and its consequences, in particular violations of Soviet law. The purpose of the speech was not to assess the past, the merits and certain mistakes made by Comrade Stalin . . . It was correct that the Soviet government and Comrade Stalin took the necessary security measures after Hitler seized power. In doing so, Comrade Stalin misused Soviet laws during a specific period of time.[144]

Ulbricht's remarks reflected the spirit of the time. In other words, they were in tune with a gradual curtailment of de-Stalinization, which opened the way to persecuting political apostasy and made it easier to establish the first secretary's cult.

Ulbricht's cult was publicly confirmed in 1958. He finally managed to celebrate his sixty-fifth birthday on the grand scale, as a state event of national importance. As was noted earlier, the June uprising cut short preparations to celebrate his sixtieth birthday in 1953. But this time around, the celebrations were marked by an outpouring of enthusiasm. Newspapers published many pledges of fealty to the German leader and assertions of respect, trust, and love for him. Leading East German party functionaries sang his praises:

Johannes Becher wrote a biography of the "son of the working class," calling Ulbricht the model of the new person; Alexander Abusch described him
as the "embodiment of the vital spirit of the party, consistently struggling
against German imperialism"; and Paul Verner characterized the leader of the
GDR as "an example and a model for all worker youth and the entire younger
generation."[145] Ulbricht received the title of Hero of Labor (Held der Arbeit)
for the second time, adding it to his collection of state honors and titles. These
included the Patriotic Order of Merit (Vaterländischer Verdienstorden), the
Karl Marx Order (Karl-Marx-Orden), and the title of honored citizen of
Berlin. A worker from the Aue region summed up the situation as follows:

> The policy of the personality cult is still in effect for us. I haven't seen Soviet
> postage stamps with a picture of Khrushchev and there aren't any factories and
> stadiums with his name. In contrast, in the GDR you find Walter Ulbricht's
> name everywhere and his image is even found on postage stamps.[146]

A year later, socialist propaganda of leader cults showed yet another sign
of a comeback as the country prepared to celebrate the tenth anniversary of
the founding of the "second German state." The propaganda organs focused
on popularizing Pieck, Ulbricht, and Grotewohl as the key representatives of
the East German state. As the first significant anniversary of the GDR was
approaching, their images were given a central place in public spaces, and
their names were heard everywhere: in slogans, in the press, on the radio,
and on television.[147] The following year was taken up with celebrations of
the ninetieth anniversary of Lenin's birth and commemorations of Pieck's
life and legacy, following his death in September 1960. The efforts to mark
these major events made it clear that by 1960 the personality cult had returned
to symbolic politics as a crucial way to legitimate communist regimes.[148] In
April 1960, the SED Central Committee's Department of Propaganda and
Agitation asked the editors of regional newspapers to send in articles, texts
of speeches, and minutes of meetings containing statements made by the
leaders of the GDR. They also requested photographs and portraits of Pieck,
Ulbricht, and Grotewohl, as well as other pictures with the leaders. These
materials were being gathered to bolster a planned history of the German
proletarian movement after 1945.[149] The documents collected were archived
in the Institute of Marxism-Leninism as a repository of national memory for
future generations. The party strictly controlled the use of this collection, and
it was an important indicator of the rise in the symbolic meaning of these
artifacts for upholding the East German state's legitimacy.

The restoration of cults of state leaders in East Germany is somewhat unexpected given the resolutions taken at the KPSS's Twenty-Second Congress,
which breathed new life into de-Stalinization. During the night of October

31–November 1, 1961, Stalin's body was taken out of the Lenin Mausoleum and buried in the Kremlin Wall. This deeply symbolic gesture was a sign of the Soviet dictator's "political death." The GDR signaled the definitive removal of representations of the Stalin cult from public space. During the night of November 13–14, a Stalin monument was dismantled in East Berlin. In Weimar and Wittenburg, streets named after Stalin were renamed.[150] A worker at the Elektro-Apparate-Werke J. W. Stalin in Berlin-Treptow noted that all the portraits and busts of Stalin were taken away, never to return, and stored in a shed near the factory's stadium. Stalin's name vanished from the plates and labels affixed to products intended for export, without any explanation from the factory's director.[151]

The crisis of trust in the regime, which the second wave of de-Stalinization intensified, led to a loss of faith in the regime's viability, and even its future. Thus, the very idea of communism appeared as something abstract and incomprehensible in the reasoning of a woman from Plaue (in the district of Flen). Commenting on a resolution on the program for decisively building communism by 1980 taken at the KPSS Twenty-Second Congress, she pessimistically commented that

> I can't imagine what it will be like when communism and the era of abundance come. Will people have to work then? Will the factories close? What will happen to the work force? How will society develop further or will the world end?[152]

Instead of having a sense of safety and stability, the population was more likely to be wary of the regime's new initiatives. Most East Germans were just not interested in what would happen in the far-off and fateful year of 1980. By the fall of 1961, the Berlin Wall had become an unremarkable part of the landscape of everyday preoccupations. According to Stasi reports, people were worried about "the question of the potato supply, making sure they have soap and laundry detergent, meat products and light bulbs."[153] Daily life pushed people to struggle to survive and normalize life, which gave rise to a new aperçu: "Khrushchev hurt us more than Stalin, because he built a wall."[154]

Only in February 1956, after Moscow's first intra-party dispatch about revising the image of Stalin, did the SED regime consign the Soviet leader to oblivion and make all memories of him taboo. This process reached its height in 1961, after the removal of Stalin's body from the Lenin Mausoleum and its reburial in the Kremlin Wall signaled the "leader's" political death. The entire Periphery responded to the Center in unison, ridding public space of all representations of Stalin. His name vanished from the imperial discourse. Portraits, busts, and statues of the "leader" were demolished. The rituals of the Stalin cult were abolished. A wave of iconoclasm led to a burst of popular anti-Soviet uprisings, most notably in Poland and Hungary. In East Germany, the crisis in the system of public symbolism brought on by de-Stalinization forced the SED to seek out new, anti-crisis representations of power. As a result, small national cults burgeoned, and the Lenin cult was reinvigorated. However, attempts to conserve, seek out, and strengthen such cults failed to boost their popularity among the people, and even the regime was not very interested in them. After the second signal of de-Stalinization from Moscow was sounded at the Twenty-Second Party Congress in November 1961, the Stalin monument in East Berlin vanished overnight. One might say that, after it got rid of the Soviet dictator's statue, East Germany was left with a "bare pedestal," having ended up in a cul-de-sac of party-state representations. The twofold desacralization of Stalin, in 1956 and again in 1961, put an end to the project of constructing the sacral center of the postwar Soviet empire. Summing up the failure of this transnational project of the symbolic politics of Stalinism, the secretary of the KPSS Central Committee, Averkii Aristov, acknowledged that "[w]e wanted to make a god, but he turned out to be the devil."[155]

NOTES

1. Khrushchev's speech was not announced in the invitation to foreign communist parties and did not appear on the agenda of the Twentieth Party Congress. See RGANI, f. 1, op. 2, d. 2, l. 3.

2. On de-Stalinization in the USSR, see Aksiutin, *Khrushchevskaia "ottepel'"*; Filtzer, *Khrushchev Era*; Zubkova, *Russia after the War*, 178–90; Jones, "From Stalinism to Post-Stalinism"; Jones, *Dilemmas of De-Stalinization*; Loewenstein, "Re-Emergence of Public Opinion."

3. Walter Ulbricht, "Über den XX. Parteitag der Kommunistischen Partei der Sowjetunion," *Neues Deutschland*, March 4, 1956, 3–4, here 4.

4. "Spisok rukovoditelei zarubezhnykh kommunisticheskikh partii, oznakomlennykh s postanovleniem XX s"ezda KPSS i dokladom t. Khrushcheva o kul'te lichnosti i ego posledstviiakh [27 fevralia 1956 g.]," in Aimermakher, *Doklad N. S. Khrushcheva*, 252–53.

5. See Foitzik, "Die parteiinterne Behandlung," in Kircheisen, *Tauwetter ohne Frühling*, 68.

6. "Iz zapisi besedy sovetnika posol'stva SSSR v GDR V. I. Kochemasova s 1-m sekretarem TsK KP Germanii M. Reimanom 14 marta 1956 g. ob otklikakh v Zapadnoi Germanii na XX s"ezd KPSS," in Aimermakher et al., *Doklad N. S. Khrushcheva*, 634.

7. Quoted in Klein, "Zwischen Entstalinisierung und neostalinistischer Erstarrung," in Kircheisen, *Tauwetter*, 115.

8. Ibid., 114.

9. On the ways in which information about Khrushchev's Secret Speech made its way to the West, see Prozumenshchikov, "'Sekretnyi' doklad N. S. Khrushcheva."

10. "Antwort auf Fragen auf der Berliner Bezirksdelegiertenkonferenz der SED," *Neues Deutschland*, March 18, 1956, 3.

11. See "O kul'te lichnosti i ego posledstviiakh: Doklad Pervogo sekretaria TsK KPSS tov. Khrushcheva N. S. XX s"ezdu Kommunisticheskoi partii Sovetskogo Soiuza 25 fevralia 1956 goda," in Aimermakher *Doklad N. S. Khrushcheva*, 57, 89, 103.

12. "Antwort auf Fragen."

13. "Telegramm Walter Ulbrichts an das Präsidium des ZK der KPdSU—N. S. Chruschtschow vom 19. März 1956," in Gabert and Prieß, *SED und Stalinismus*, 91.

14. "Protokoll 26. ZK-Tagung vom 1956.03.22," SAPMO-BArch, DY 30/IV 2/1/156, Bl. 64, 70, 78.

15. "Protokoll 26. ZK-Tagung vom 1956.03.22," SAPMO-BArch, DY 30/IV 2/1/156, Bl. 78.

16. "Protokoll 26. ZK-Tagung vom 1956.03.22," SAPMO-BArch, DY 30/IV 2/1/156, Bl. 96. Hager (1912–1998) was a leading Party ideologue (*Chefideologe*) who occupied a series of positions involving propaganda and culture in the GDR.

17. Although materials from the congress were classified as secret, the complete text of Khrushchev's talk was published in the United States in early June 1956. The Western radio stations Radio Free Liberty and Voice of America played a major role in disseminating the contents of the Secret Speech. See Foitzik, "Die parteiinterne Behandlung," in Kircheisen, *Tauwetter*, 68.

18. "Protokoll 26. ZK-Tagung vom 1956.03.22," SAPMO-BArch, DY 30/IV 2/1/156, Bl. 95.

19. "Protokoll 26. ZK-Tagung vom 1956.03.22," SAPMO-BArch, DY 30/IV 2/1/156, Bl. 137. "Protokoll 26. ZK-Tagung vom 1956.03.22," SAPMO-BArch, DY 30/IV 2/1/156, Bl. 70.

20. "Protokoll 26. ZK-Tagung vom 1956.03.22," SAPMO-BArch, DY 30/IV 2/1/156, Bl. 70.

21. "Protokoll 26. ZK-Tagung vom 1956.03.22," SAPMO-BArch, DY 30/IV 2/1/156, Bl. 70.

22. "III. Parteikonferenz der SED (2. Bericht), Berlin, den 24.3.1956," BStU, ZS MfS-AS Nr. 89/59, Bl. 78.

23. "III. Parteikonferenz der SED (2. Bericht), Berlin, den 24.3.1956," BStU, ZS MfS-AS Nr. 89/59, Bl. 64.

24. Klein, "Zwischen Entstalinisierung und neostalinistischer Erstarrung," in Kircheisen, *Tauwetter*, 115–16.

25. Klein, "Zwischen Entstalinisierung und neostalinistischer Erstarrung," in Kircheisen, *Tauwetter*, 115–16.

26. In April 1956, a delegate to a regional party conference in Magdeburg who was dissatisfied with official explanations expressed his indignation to his colleagues during a break in the meeting: "Comrade Otto Schön's remarks didn't clarify anything for us. What we really want is an explanation for the criticism of Stalin at the

Twentieth Congress." See "Neue Argumente zum XX. Parteitag der KPdSU (5. Bericht), Berlin, den 14.03.1956," BStU, ZS MfS-AS, Nr. 216/56, Bl. 41.

27. "Stimmung zur Veröffentlichung des Genossen Walter Ulbricht über den XX. Parteitag der KPdSU (2. Bericht), Berlin, den 8.3.1956," BStU, ZS MfS-AS, Nr. 216/56, Bl. 24.

28. "Stimmung zur Veröffentlichung des Genossen Walter Ulbricht über den XX. Parteitag (1. Bericht), Berlin, den 7.03.56," BStU, ZS MfS-AS, Nr. 216/56, Bl. 21.

29. "Information Nr. 90/56," BStU, ZS MfS-AS Nr. 216/56, Bl. 21.

30. "Information Nr. 90/56," BStU, ZS MfS-AS Nr. 216/56, Bl. 21.

31. "Neue Argumente zum XX. Parteitag der KPdSU (5. Bericht)," Bl. 41.

32. BStU, ZS MfS-AS Nr. 216/56, Bl. 159.

33. "Neue Argumente zum XX. Parteitag der KPdSU (5. Bericht)," Bl. 40–41.

34. "Stimmung zur Veröffentlichung des Genossen Walter Ulbricht über den XX. Parteitag d. KPdSU (2. Bericht)," Bl. 25.

35. "Stimmung zur Veröffentlichung des Genossen Walter Ulbricht über den XX. Parteitag d. KPdSU (2. Bericht)," Bl. 41.

36. "Stimmung zum XX. Parteitag der KPdSU (6. Bericht), Berlin, den 23.03.1956," BStU, ZS MfS-AS, Nr. 216/56, Bl. 60.

37. Sabrow, *Verwaltete Vergangenheit*.

38. BStU, ZS MfS-AS Nr. 216/56, Bl. 67.

39. "Hetze gegen den Genossen W. Ulbricht und andere, Berlin, den 25.4.1956," BStU, ZS MfS-AS Nr. 89/59, Bl. 102.

40. "Feindpropaganda zum XX. Parteitag der KPdSU," BStU, AS BVfS Leipzig 815/01, Bl. 67–70.

41. "Feindpropaganda zum XX. Parteitag der KPdSU," BStU, AS BVfS Leipzig 815/01, Bl. 67–70.

42. "Hetze gegen den Genossen Walter Ulbricht und andere," Bl. 103.

43. "Hetze gegen den Genossen Walter Ulbricht und andere," Bl. 104.

44. BStU, ZS MfS-AS Nr. 216/56, Bl. 79.

45. BStU, ZS MfS-AS Nr. 216/56, Bl. 67.

46. Kettner, "Die Fragen und die Freiheit," in Hilse and Winkler, *Die Fragen und die Freiheit*, 22. In the 1950s–1960s, philosophy professor and journalist Wolfgang Harich developed some of the most widely discussed ideas about reforming socialism and liberalizing the GDR. See Harich, *Keine Schwierigkeiten*, 123.

47. See "Neue Argumente zum XX. Parteitag der KPdSU (5. Bericht)," Bl. 42.

48. "Informatsionnoe pis'mo korrespondenta gazety 'Pravda' v GDR M. V. Podkliuchnikova v redaktsiiu gazety o reaktsii v GDR na soobshcheniia o rabote XX s"ezda KPSS," in Aimermakher, *Doklad N. S. Khrushcheva*, 629.

49. The KPSS's new policy was an early signal that local cults of party leaders on the periphery of the Soviet empire would be subject to criticism. Moscow censured Valko Chervenkov, the general secretary of the Communist Party of Bulgaria for setting up his own personality cult, which was evident in the fulsome praise heaped on him by the press and at meetings, and in the ubiquity of his image. In Poland, Bolesław Beirut was the president of the Council of Ministers and the party leader.

However, in response to an initiative of the Central Committee of the KPSS, party members began to ask if two different people should hold these positions. Likewise, Hungarian leader Mátyás Rákosi's policies were criticized harshly during his visit to Moscow in March 1953. Attuned to signals from Moscow, the SED Politburo halted preparations for Ulbricht's birthday and began to check materials about the German leader that had already been prepared for dissemination. See Volokitina, *Sovetskii faktor*, vol. 2, 853–54, 876; Hegedüs and Wilke, *Satelliten nach Stalins Tod*, 48.

50. "Iz soprovoditel'nogo pis'ma zamestitelia nachal'nika 1-go upravleniia KGB pri SM SSSR A. M. Sakharovskogo sekretariu TsK KPSS B. N. Ponomarevu o napravlenii v TsK KPSS dokumentov SDPG," in Aimermakher, *Doklad N. S. Khrushcheva*, 705–9, especially 706.

51. "Neue Argumente zum XX. Parteitag der KPdSU (5. Bericht)," Bl. 43.

52. BStU, ZS MfS-AS Nr. 216/56, Bl. 66.

53. "Stimmung zum XX. Parteitag der KPdSU (6. Bericht)," Bl. 61.

54. "Neue Argumente zum XX. Parteitag der KPdSU (5. Bericht)," Bl. 43.

55. BStU, ZS MfS-AS Nr. 216/56, Bl. 80.

56. BStU, ZS MfS-AS Nr. 216/56, Bl. 129.

57. BStU, ZS MfS-AS Nr. 216/56, Bl. 56.

58. "Stimmung zum XX. Parteitag der KPdSU (6. Bericht)," Bl. 60.

59. BStU, ZS MfS-AS Nr. 89/59, Bl. 117.

60. "Neue Argumente zum XX. Parteitag der KPdSU. Berlin, den 14.3.1956," BStU, ZS MfS-AS Nr. 216/56, Bl. 37; "Stimmung zur Veröffentlichung des Genossen Walter Ulbricht über den XX. Parteitag (1. Bericht)," Bl. 22.

61. BStU, MfS-AS, Nr. 216/56, Bl. 152.

62. BStU, MfS-AS, Nr. 216/56, Bl. 70.

63. "Stimmung zur Veröffentlichung des Genossen Walter Ulbricht über den XX. Parteitag (1. Bericht)," Bl. 23.

64. BStU, ZS MfS-AS Nr. 216/56, Bl. 21.

65. "Anti-Stalin-Kurs," Berlin, May 2, 1956, AdsD, SPD-PV-Ostbüro 0257 II, unpag.

66. "Anti-Stalin-Kurs," Berlin, May 2, 1956, AdsD, SPD-PV-Ostbüro 0257 II, unpag.

67. BStU, ZS MfS-AS Nr. 216/56, Bl. 43.

68. Informationsbericht "Die Lage und Stimmung in den Industrie- und Verkehrsbetrieben in Potsdam," February 27, 1956, BStU, ZS MfS-AS Nr. 216/56, Bl. 73.

69. BStU, ZS MfS-AS Nr. 216/56, Bl. 70.

70. "Stimmung zur Veröffentlichung des Genossen Walter Ulbricht über den XX. Parteitag der KPdSU (2. Bericht)," Bl. 25.

71. "Stimmung zur Veröffentlichung des Genossen Walter Ulbricht über den XX. Parteitag der KPdSU (2. Bericht)," Bl. 24, 125.

72. "Neue Argumente zum XX. Parteitag der KPdSU (5. Bericht)," Bl. 42.

73. "Stimmung zur Veröffentlichung des Genossen Walter Ulbricht über den XX. Parteitag (1. Bericht)," Bl. 23.

74. BStU, MfS-AS, Nr. 216/56, Bl. 156.

75. BStU, MfS-AS, Nr. 216/56, Bl. 140.
76. BStU, MfS-AS, Nr. 216/56, Bl. 81.
77. BStU, MfS-AS, Nr. 216/56, Bl. 155.
78. BStU, MfS-AS, Nr. 216/56, Bl. 95.
79. "Neue Argumente zum XX. Parteitag der KPdSU (5. Bericht)," Bl. 39–40.
80. "Stimmung zur Veröffentlichung des Genossen Walter Ulbricht über den XX. Parteitag (1. Bericht)," Bl. 23.
81. AdsD, SPD-PV-Ostbüro 0322 II, unpag.
82. BStU, ZS MfS-AS Nr. 216/56, Bl. 129.
83. "Neue Argumente zum XX. Parteitag der KPdSU (5. Bericht)," Bl. 39.
84. "Die Stimmung der Bevölkerung zum XX. Parteitag der KPdSU," 26. Mai 1956, BStU, ZS MfS-AS Nr. 216/56, Bl. 75–76.
85. "Hetze gegen den Genossen Walter Ulbricht, Berlin, den 7.5.1956," BStU, ZS MfS-AS Nr. 89/59, Bl. 104.
86. "Neue Argumente zum XX. Parteitag der KPdSU (5. Bericht)," Bl. 39–40.
87. "Stimmung zum XX. Parteitag der KPdSU (6. Bericht)," Bl. 61.
88. BStU, ZS MfS-AS Nr. 216/56, Bl. 156.
89. "Stimmung zum XX. Parteitag der KPdSU (6. Bericht)," Bl. 61.
90. "Stimmung zum XX. Parteitag der KPdSU (6. Bericht)," Bl. 85.
91. BStU, ZS MfS-AS Nr. 216/56, Bl. 74.
92. "Stimmung zur Veröffentlichung des Genossen Walter Ulbricht über den XX. Parteitag (1. Bericht)," Bl. 23; See also "Iz spravki konsul'stva SSSR vo Frankfurtena-Odere 'Otkliki naseleniia okrugov Frankfurt-na-Odere i Kottbus na itogi XX s"ezda KPSS,' 26 marta 1956 g.," in Aimermakher, *Doklad N. S. Khrushcheva*, 650–53.
93. BStU, ZS MfS-AS Nr. 216/56, Bl. 142.
94. AdsD, SPD-PV-Ostbüro 0383 O, Veterinär-Medizinische Fakultät der Humboldt-Universität, Berlin, den 8.4.1956, unpag.
95. "Hetze gegen den Genossen W. Ulbricht und andere. Berlin, den 25.4.1956," BStU, Archiv der Zentralstelle, MfS-AS Nr. 89/59, Bl. 105; "Stimmung zur Veröffentlichung des Genossen Walter Ulbricht über den XX. Parteitag der KPdSU (2. Bericht)," Bl. 25–26.
96. "Feindpropaganda zum XX. Parteitag der KPdSU, Berlin, den 9.3.1956," BStU, ZS MfS-AS Nr. 216/56, Bl. 27–28.
97. "Feindpropaganda zum XX. Parteitag der KPdSU, Berlin, den 9.3.1956," BStU, ZS MfS-AS Nr. 216/56, Bl. 31.
98. "Feindpropaganda zum XX. Parteitag der KPdSU (5. Bericht)," Bl. 54.
99. "Feindpropaganda zum XX. Parteitag der KPdSU, Berlin, den 5.3.56," BStU, ZS MfS-AS Nr. 216/56, Bl. 17.
100. "Feindpropaganda zum XX. Parteitag der KPdSU, Berlin, den 5.3.56," BStU, ZS MfS-AS Nr. 216/56, Bl. 48–49.
101. "Neue Argumente zum XX. Parteitag der KPdSU (5. Bericht)," Bl. 39–40.
102. "Der Widerstand der ländlichen Bevölkerung. Berlin, 23.05.1956," AdsD, SPD-V-Ostbüro 0257 II, unpag.
103. "Hetze gegen den Genossen W. Ulbricht und andere," Bl. 106.

104. "Feindpropaganda zu den Problemen des XX. Parteitages der KPdSU und der III. Parteikonferenz der SED, Berlin, den 22.5.1956," BStU, ZS MfS-AS Nr. 89/59, Bl. 84.

105. "Feindpropaganda zu den Problemen des XX. Parteitages der KPdSU und der III. Parteikonferenz der SED, Berlin, den 22.5.1956," BStU, ZS MfS-AS Nr. 89/59, Bl. 86.

106. Nonetheless, in the fall of 1956, around 21,000 political prisoners were released, and hundreds of victims of the SED regime were rehabilitated. See Kowalczuk, "Zwischen Hoffnungen und Krisen," 25.

107. SAPMO-BArch, DY 30/IV 2/5/282. Bl. 439.

108. "Situationsbericht aus Leipzig, Berlin, 15.11.1956," AdsD, SPD-PV-Ostbüro 0361 IV, unpag.

109. "Stimmungsbericht aus Berlin-Leipzig-Böhlen, den 5.11.56," AdsD, SPD-PV-Ostbüro 0361 IV, unpag.

110. AdsD, SPD-PV-Ostbüro, 0361 IV, unpag.

111. "Stimmung im Industrie-Werk Ludwigsfelde, 18.11.1956," AdsD, SPD-PV-Ostbüro 0257/II, unpag.

112. SAPMO-BArch, DY 30/IV 2/5/282, Bl. 366.

113. On reactions to the Hungarian uprising in the GDR, see Granville, "Ulbricht in October 1956," 478–80.

114. Ansorg, *Kinder im Klassenkampf*, 152–53; Kowalczuk, "Zwischen Hoffnungen und Krisen," 28–29.

115. "Neue Argumente zum XX. Parteitag der KPdSU (5. Bericht)," Bl. 38.

116. "Iz spravki konsul'stva," in Aimermakher, *Doklad N. S. Khrushcheva*, 650.

117. "Stimmung zur Veröffentlichung des Genossen Walter Ulbricht über den XX. Parteitag der KPdSU (2. Bericht)," Bl. 24.

118. "Stimmungsbericht aus Brikettfabrik Senftenberg. Berlin, den 12.11. 1956," AdsD, SPD-PV-Ostbüro 0361 IV, unpag. See also Morina, "Instructed Silence, Constructed Memory."

119. "Hetze gegen den Genossen Walter Ulbricht," Bl. 104.

120. De-Stalinization triggered an exodus of East Germans to West Germany. In the first quarter of 1956 alone, the number of arrivals from the GDR reached 75,200. Approximately 40 percent of those who left the GDR were between fifteen and thirty-five years old. About 14 percent of them were members of political parties and the mass organizations. Almost 25,000 members of the FDJ and more than 8,000 SED members sought a new homeland in the FRG. See Staritz, *Geschichte der DDR: 1949–1985*, 149.

121. BStU, ZS MfS-AS Nr. 216/56, Bl. 160.

122. "Postanovlenie Prezidiuma TsK KPSS 'Proekt soobshcheniia dlia TsK kommunisticheskikh i rabochikh partii stran narodnoi demokratii o poriadke oformleniia pervomaiskikh demonstratsii,' 18 aprelia 1956 g.," in Aimermakher, *Doklad N. S. Khrushcheva*, 295–96.

123. Prozumenshchikov, "Sekretnyi doklad N. S. Khrushcheva," in Aimermakher, *Doklad N. S. Khrushcheva*, 23.

124. "Nachrichten aus Torgelow, 3.9.1956," AdsD, SPD-PV-Ostbüro 0043 L, unpag.

125. In Moscow too, the Marx-Engels-Lenin-Stalin Institute was renamed as the Institute of Marxism-Leninism of the KPSS Central Committee. See RGANI, f. 5, op. 33, d. 4, l. 2.

126. "Angaben und Auszüge zu Fragen des innerpolitischen Lebens der Partei, von Marx, Engels, Bebel, Luxemburg, Liebknecht, Zetkin. Zusammengestellt von der Marx-Engels-Abteilung des Instituts für Marxismus-Leninismus, Berlin, den 19.09.1956," SAPMO-BArch, DY 30/V 2/9.03/35, Bl. 63–65.

127. AdsD, SPD-PV-Ostbüro 0322 II, unpag.

128. Not long after de-Stalinization began in East Germany, this became evident in the work of publishing houses, which were all under state control. In the period when Stalin was the subject of public criticism, enough portraits of the "leader" had been produced to satisfy the anticipated demand for several years. The disappearance of this demand meant that 16,000 portraits of Stalin and 13,000 portraits of Malenkov piled up in Die Kunst publishing house's warehouses. Despite pulping the "leader's" works, "491,000 copies of Stalin's collected works expected [to satisfy demand] during the best times" moldered in the Dietz publishing house's warehouses. See Barck, Langermann, and Lokatis, *"Jedes Buch ein Abenteuer,"* 67–68.

129. "Geburtstag von Clara Zetkin. Berlin, den 24.06.1957," SAPMO-BArch, DY 30/IV 2/9.02/48, Bl. 85, 100.

130. "From the diary of the First Secretary of the USSR Embassy in the GDR A. E. Karetnikov: Note on a conversation with Director of the Institute of Marxism-Leninism of the ZK SED Ludwig Einicke," RGANI, f. 5 (Apparat of the Central Committee KPSS), op. 33, d. 27, l. 62.

131. "Neuauflage von R. Luxemburg, Ausgewählte Reden und Schriften. Berlin, den 14.07.1960," SAPMO-BArch, DY 30/IV 2/9.02/32, Bl. 27.

132. SAPMO-BArch, DY 30/IV 2/9.02/55, Bl. 15–16 (Dresden, den 25. Juli 1961); "Konzeption zur Neugestaltung der August-Bebel-Wilhelm-Liebknecht-Ged enkstätte im Schloss Hubertusburg in Wermsdorf. Oschatz, den 4.05.1963," SAPMO-BArch, DY 30/IV A2/9.03/71, unpag.

133. "Werke W. I. Lenins vollständig herausgeben," *Neues Deutschland*, February 24, 1956, 4.

134. "Vorbereitungen zum 60. Geburtstag von W. I. Lenin am 22. April 1960," SAPMO-BArch, DY 30/IV 2/9.02/32, Bl. 17–18. For similarities to the revival of the Lenin cult in the USSR, see RGANI, f. 5, op. 55, d. 6–7, l. 66. In November 1956, the SED Politburo asked the KPSS Central Committee for Soviet materials for the Lenin Museum in Leipzig. See RGANI, f. 5, op. 33, d. 4, l. 111.

135. "Vorbereitung und Durchführung des 90. Geburtstages von W. I. Lenin am 22. April 1960. Berlin, den 21.12.1959," SAPMO-BArch, DY 30/IV 2/9.02/16, Bl. 160–164.

136. Report on the restructuring of the Museum of the Revolution in Moscow, March 1, 1956, RGANI, f. 5, op. 33, d. 4, l. 1.

137. RGANI, f. 5, op. 33, d. 4, l. 2, 44–46.

138. RGANI, f. 5, op. 33, d. 8, l. 66.

139. RGANI, f. 5, op. 33, d. 16, l. 70–72.

140. "Postanovlenie Prezidiuma TsK KPSS 'Proekt postanovleniia TsK KPSS o preodolenii kul'ta lichnosti i ego posledstvii,' 30 iiunia 1956 g.," in Aimermakher, *Doklad N. S. Khrushcheva*, 352–68.

141. Ibid., 355.

142. Ibid., 361.

143. Cited in Ansorg, *Kinder*, 150.

144. Walter Ulbricht, "Grundfragen der Politik der SED," *Neues Deutschland*, February 5, 1957, 1.

145. Alexander Abusch, "Über die revolutionären Methoden des Genossen Walter Ulbricht," *Einheit*, no. 6 (1958); Paul Verner, "Leben und Kampf des Genossen Walter Ulbricht, Vorbild für jedes Parteimitglied," *Neuer Weg*, no. 12 (1958).

146. "Stimmung der Bevölkerung zum XXII. Parteitag der KPdSU. Karl-Marx-Stadt, den 5.11.1961," BStU, AS Chemnitz, CAKG-24, PI 266/61, Bl. 298.

147. For example, "Losungen des ZK der SED, des Ministerrates der DDR und des Nationalrates der Nationalen Front des Demokratischen Deutschlands zum 10. Jahrestag der Gründung der DDR," SAPMO-BArch, DY 30/IV 2/9.02/16, Bl. 99.

148. "Anlage Nr. 3 zum Protokoll Nr. 41 vom 9.9.1960," SAPMO-BArch, DY 30 J IV 2/2/722, Bl. 10–11. See also Behrends, "Nach dem Führerkult," in Münkel and Seegers, *Medien und Imagepolitik*.

149. "An alle Chefredaktionen der Bezirkszeitungen. Berlin, den 19.04.1960," SAPMO-BArch, DY 30/IV 2/9.02/32, Bl. 22.

150. *Telegraf*, November 26, 1961.

151. "Stimmungsbericht aus VEB-EAW-'J. W. Stalin' in Berlin Treptow. Berlin, den 9.11.1956," AdsD, SPD-PV-Ostbüro 0361 IV, unpag.

152. "Stimmung der Bevölkerung zum XXII. Parteitag der KPdSU. Karl-Marx-Stadt, den 2.11.1961," BStU, Außenstelle Chemnitz, Informationen an den 1. Sekretär der SED-Bezirksleitung, CAKG-26, PI 265/61, Bl. 302.

153. "Stimmung der Bevölkerung zum XXII. Parteitag der KPdSU. Karl-Marx-Stadt, den 15.11.1961," BStU, Außenstelle Chemnitz, Informationen an den 1. Sekretär der SED-Bezirksleitung, CAKG-26, PI 282/61, Bl. 251. See also SAPMO-BArch, DY 30/IV 2/9.02/6, Bl. 39–42.

154. "Otchet o poezdke v GDR B. Brainina s 17 noiabria po 16 dekabria 1964 g.," RGANI, f. 5, op. 55, d. 131, l. 79.

155. Fursenko, *Prezidium TsK KPSS, 1954–1964*, vol. 1,102.

Conclusion

In the summer of 1952, an official delegation of East German farmers went to the Soviet Union to see the "homeland of socialism" with their own eyes. The narratives and pictures from their stay in the USSR featured in a brochure about the trip described how excited they were to watch communism being constructed.[1] The members of the delegation presented themselves as eyewitnesses to impressive technical achievements, Stalin's wonderful new buildings, and progressive collective farms. They were enthusiastic about everything they saw but had special praise for the Soviet people as the most important creators of socialist reality. The delegates emphasized the educational aspects (the "illustrative teachings") of their trip to the Soviet Union. They praised the new knowledge they received and the striking evidence of positive developments in a country that they had previously known from national socialist propaganda as the embodiment of the "Jewish-Bolshevik threat to Western civilization." By eradicating old images of the enemy from popular attitudes, representations of a harmonious socialist world with no incompatible features or mutually exclusive contradictions could take root. The principle of racial inequality became irrelevant, and ideological unification with Moscow offered the East Germans some significant benefits: they could join the bloc of socialist countries, declare that they had established an "anti-fascist democratic state," and join the global Soviet mission of "protecting world peace," an especially attractive possibility in the light of the Cold War conflict, which had been intensifying since the spring of 1946.[2]

While looking out the window as he sat on a train, watching landscapes and cities rush by, Erich Knorr (1912–2012) reflected on what he was seeing:

A train trip gives the opportunity for a variety of observations. Our delegates stand at the window and never tire of recording everything that can be seen outside. After the great impressions in Moscow, stone by stone the contours of a large mosaic emerge. Gradually, the monumental picture of the Soviet Union emerges and organizes itself.[3]

Knorr presented the train journey as an active process that turned him into a spectator who became convinced that the "great building of communism" was indubitably successful, and that the Germans had indeed undergone a transformation from "enemies" into "friends" of the USSR. At the same time, he recorded a critical distance from his own national past. In the postwar conditions of defeat, destruction, and a lack of clear perspectives, opportunities to observe what was going on in the USSR enabled the East Germans to develop a scenario for solving current problems which also promised peace and security, progress and prosperity, happiness and a stable, predictable future. At the same time, Stalin was presented as the embodiment of the highest moral authority, the one who could forgive the German nation and deliver its citizenry from remorse for Nazi war crimes. Thus, journeys to the USSR were also called "journeys into the future." They shaped East Germans' moral duty to develop a post-Nazi Germany by following the Soviet path. Following the logic that "to learn from the Soviet Union is to learn from Stalin what it finally meant to learn to win" offered a cosmological sense of salvation: they could make a transition from being "war losers" to becoming "history's winners."

As recent scholarship in visual and cultural studies has made clear, an observer-position with a precisely focused way of seeing reality is a historical construct for realizing power over the subject.[4] It is a way to form subjectivities by visually determining the ideological prism through which the world is interpreted. Of equal importance, it also ensures that the borders separating the visible and the hidden are strictly defined. The public proclamations of German-Soviet friendship helped to create positive representations of the Soviet Union. These affirmative images in turn enabled the citizens of a defeated nation to see their country afresh, no longer viewing it as the aggressor state of the recent past. After their return from Moscow, numerous publications, films, photo exhibitions, and posters about their trip turned the agriculturalists into ambassadors of socialist modernity in their own country. These media representations built up shared knowledge and a common visual space where the individual Sovietization of subjects could take place through forming a united *way of seeing*. The delegates' political task was to focus their fellow citizens' ideological line of sight on the USSR's achievements.

The regime was able to mobilize the population to (re)produce the Soviet symbolic order by creating situations of subjectivation in which East Germans could not only learn to "speak Bolshevik" but could also become skilled in recognizing, seeing, and looking at the world Soviet-style. In postwar Germany, the populace was the object of observation by the Soviet authorities, but they were also subjects observing socialist reality. Taking this perspective, I have made two crucial points. I have shown that the East Germans engaged with official representations and ideological discourses not so much by internalizing them as by creating "spaces of agency." These spaces of agency enabled people to develop positive modes of self-identification and self-optimization and allowed individuals to generate their private meanings of life under state socialism beyond the binary of belief and cynicism.

The other crucial point is that the link between visuality and state-, nation-, and empire-building was particularly evident in the propaganda of the Stalin cult. In this context, understanding iconoclastic actions as a reflection of multiple ways of perceiving, using, manipulating, and negotiating Stalin's image in public spaces is important. In contrast to authoritative research on iconoclastic phenomena, which has examined these acts exclusively as markers of revolutionary eras, I analyze iconoclasm as a normal feature of actors' everyday behavior in authoritarian societies.[5] Iconoclastic acts helped ordinary people to interpret the world and generate meanings for their lives in dramatically changing postwar circumstances. At the same time, this book presents a model for studying the influence of personality cults and the modalities of their reception in Soviet-style societies. While most research on leader cults does not go beyond questions about how the cults were constructed, their creators, and the production of official representations from above, I am suggesting a very different way of looking at the significance of personality cults and iconoclasm by situating them in relation to the mechanism for stabilizing and negotiating the political order of the East German dictatorship.

This book has examined iconoclastic acts directed at symbols of power *from above* in terms of policies created and implemented by the state and the party and *from below* as a social practice in which the population engaged. Combining these levels of analysis reveals that in authoritarian systems iconoclasm was a communicative process operating through visuality, a kind of communication that the state and society carried on with each other and used to negotiate the foundations of their coexistence. In this "dialogue" actors found resources for changing propaganda's meanings, revising official discursive boundaries, and raising barriers to Soviet cultural transfer to East Germany. Unlike research on how dictatorships use domination and repression to organize public and private life, I show that even the common places and public spheres created and controlled by the regime contained realms where the population could search for independent meanings (*Eigen-Sinn*). These were limited spheres of relative autonomy for a subject capable of both acting rationally and articulating emotions. Such a subject was able to adapt the ideology propagated from above to his or her own needs and s/he could both struggle for the right to change the official semantics of the regime's symbols and put limits on the power of these symbols.[6]

I have highlighted several stages in the dynamics of iconoclastic acts which show how the relationship of the state and society changed between 1945 and 1961. In the first postwar years, iconoclasm was a constituent element in the process of reexamining the past, for both the new regime and defeated German society. The Soviet occupying forces purged public space of the symbols of the Third Reich and imperial Germany while simultaneously saturating it with the visible signs of their victory. As a result, East Germans' iconoclastic gestures in 1945–1946 were reactions to their first visual contact with Soviet symbols, which spoke to the population of defeat, occupation, and the apocalypse of the German state and nation. They demonstrated the population's desire for reconciliation with the occupiers, its distancing from or complete rejection of the Nazi past, and, in some cases, nostalgia for that past.

Between 1947–1948 and 1953, iconoclasm was a (re)interpretation of the present: it was intertwined with reflection and understanding, adaptation and life in a Sovietized reality. One important result of Sovietization was the creation of a system of public symbolism. The new symbols of power organized public spheres in which the regime not only proclaimed its legitimacy but also made itself visible; they also created a space where an individual could experience and assimilate personality cults into his or her daily life. But many people had trouble getting used to communist symbols and leader cults. It was no coincidence that this period is known for the intensity with which the regime and society opposed each other. Most of the sources I used that mention iconoclastic practices come from the years 1947–1948 and 1953. At this stage, the characteristic feature of iconoclastic practices was the collective emotional work they did: these practices were the beginnings of public demonstrations of emotional solidarity through distancing from Soviet symbols, discourses, and rituals. This collective emotional work indicates the population's gradual rehabilitation from the burden of defeat and its need for an emotionally experienced national identity.

The year 1953 marked a turning point in how the population and the state understood iconoclasm. Stalin's death in March 1953, the first signals of de-Stalinization from Moscow, and the June uprising, which took place throughout East Germany, forced the regime to rethink its strategies for reacting to antistate acts and pushed it into implementing a gentler policy of public symbolism. As a result of this policy, efforts to saturate public space with symbols of power now took popular opinions and emotions into account. At the same time, the population began to use iconoclastic acts in more deliberate, bolder, and more focused way to pressure the regime and to articulate collective interests and demands. Thus, after 1953, iconoclasm became an important instrument for stabilizing the dictatorship, because the population and the state negotiated and came to an agreement about the foundations of their coexistence. In the GDR, this mechanism for reinforcing the regime's legitimacy was demonstrated during the double de-Stalinization of 1956 and 1961: the state's policy of iconoclasm vis-à-vis the Stalin cult corresponded to the population's mood. This legitimized the SED regime by strengthening national feelings at home, thanks to the propaganda of German national cults, while reviving the Lenin cult helped preserve the imperial hierarchy and maintain good relations with Moscow.

The history of generations has much to offer in explaining the East German ruling class's strong connections with the Kremlin *and* the ongoing tumult within society about accepting Stalin as the "best friend." The transfer of the Stalin cult to East Germany was initiated by the "generation of the patriarchs." These were members of the East German political elite who were between forty and sixty years old in 1949. Many of this cohort, who were born roughly between 1893 and 1916, had strong prewar connections with Moscow and had spent the war years in exile in the Soviet Union. Establishing the cult allowed them to put their political plans into action and guaranteed that their claim to rule was legitimate. The Stalin cult also gave them a way to strengthen patron-client relationships with Stalin himself. Because of the complete postwar break with Germany's past, they saw the cult as a conduit for ideological transfer from the Soviet Union to the GDR, which would create a new political order. This generation worked hard to present Stalin as the "best friend, teacher, and patron of the German people" while also calling on the population to fulfill the moral obligation to expiate German guilt for complicity in the Nazis' wartime crimes.

Scholars have singled out two generations that played a key role in creating the social basis of the SED regime, the "generation of postwar renewal" and the "generation of GDR children." Could these cohorts trust propaganda's claim that the Soviet leader was the "best friend of the German people"? Representatives of the generation of renewal, that is, people born between the late 1920s and the mid-1930s, found themselves in a very delicate situation. They had believed in Hitler. They had belonged to the Third Reich's mass organizations. They had actively served on the Eastern front during the war. By 1945, their plans for the future, which had been based on what the Nazi regime offered them, had vanished. Nonetheless, the SED regime targeted this generation to power Germany's economic and political rebirth. As a result, propaganda offering opportunities for rapid upward mobility was addressed specifically to this sector of the population. They could turn defeat into victory, disappointment into the joy of building socialism, nostalgia for the "good old days" into faith in the bright future, and they could transform their "enemy"—Stalin—into a "friend." Stalin-worship opened up opportunities for them to get an education and find a job. As loyal citizens, the state offered them access to resources for material well-being and the promise of a happy life in a communist homeland.

At the least publicly, representatives of the "generation of postwar renewal" staged themselves as supporters of the SED regime. As historians Thomas Ahbe and Rainer Gries put it, "They adapted themselves, integrated, spoke the party's language but at the same time they maintained an internal distance from the norms proclaimed."[7] Their experience of life under national socialism and their desire not just to survive but to lead a "normal" life under another oppressive regime meant they had to support the SED regime in public. They engaged in the discourses and practices of the Stalin cult while distancing themselves from the state in private, in the anonymous niches everyday life provided. At home and at the weekend cottage, at the *Bierstube* and among friends, relatives, or members of one's nuclear family, the lived experience of Sovietized reality belonged to the subject: s/he interpreted and reacted to the image of the Soviet leader, stood up for his/her own rights and interests, sought reconciliation with the past and meanings for life in the present, and fought to restore individual and collective honor as a counterweight to the feelings of guilt and shame imposed from above.

The SED regime put a great deal of effort into propaganda directed toward the "generation of GDR children" because, taking a long-term perspective, it expected that this social cohort would be the future builders of socialism.[8] This generation was made up of young people born between the mid-1930s and the late 1940s. They were supposed to become loyal citizens, "new people" for a "new Germany" that was "an antifascist, democratic, peace-loving state in the community of socialist states." The "generation of GDR children" was the first cohort of GDR citizens to grow up and be socialized exclusively in the "second German state." They were the first to thoroughly assimilate the language of the party and state and they carried participation in official public spheres and rituals to the point of automatism. They played an important role in mobilizing the generation of postwar renewal, urging their parents to accept the moral obligation to build a socialist homeland and lay the foundations for socialist construction in East Germany for the sake of future generations, above all for their children. In this way, with the support of the generation of GDR children, the regime demanded that the renewal generation do all it could in the present to build a peace-loving Germany with Stalin as its protector.

The generation of the patriarchs offered the generation of postwar renewal and the generation of GDR children the opportunity to conclude a symbolic pact that would ensure social consensus: the elders demanded fidelity, submission, and loyalty. In return, the younger generations would receive opportunities for social and political mobility and access to the dictatorship's material and symbolic resources. For these cohorts, the Stalin cult held out a way to resolve current problems. It promised an exit from the crisis of personal and national identity and a way to enjoy a positive, life-affirming outlook: by joining the postwar Soviet empire's cult community. However, former prisoners of war and members of the NSDAP who remained unrepentant were largely excluded from this pact. Socialist propaganda made hardly any political appeals to them. These actors were granted fewer chances for successful integration into a socialist society. This group was a reservoir that the regime drew on to create "enemies of the people" and "enemies of Stalin." Other groups were also excluded from the Stalin cult. These were, as a rule, housewives, old people or pensioners, and everyone who did not try to accumulate political capital and was therefore not considered a useful member of society in the process of building a socialist Germany. After the KPSS's Twentieth Congress, the attempt to conclude a generational pact about social consensus ended when the generation of patriarchs was forced to imitate Moscow's rhetoric of de-Stalinization and begin to deconstruct the image of the "best friend of the German people."

The most important factor for my interpretation of how the Stalin cult was established in the GDR, and more generally for my analysis of the consolidation of the Soviet empire after World War II, is the designing of a single system of public symbolism on the Soviet model in the GDR and across the socialist bloc. After 1945 the cult of the "leader" became the most important transnational project of symbolic politics, which aimed to merge the empire's various nations, ethnic groups, and states into a single political body, that is, to create a unified cult community with the image of Stalin at its center. The postwar Soviet empire itself was in fact an imagined cult community whose territorial and symbolic boundaries enclosed a commonwealth of socialist countries that stood apart from the Western capitalist world. The myth of the "leader" was an integrating narrative that offered those who participated in the project innovative ways to make sense of postwar construction, organize daily life, and conceptualize "new men" for "new times." The creation of a single discursive and ritual, spatial, and temporal expanse secured the cult community's homogeneity, which in turn helped to synchronize political life across the countries of Central and Eastern Europe. The Stalin cult was a powerful instrument of symbolic politics, especially in 1949–1953, the years of high Stalinism. It was singularly effective at subordinating the peripheral regimes to the center, proclaiming the imperial hierarchy, and consolidating this inequality through both visual-discursive representations and the expansion of ideology into daily life practices. By compelling the population to speak and act, feel and see Soviet, the Stalin cult was a significant element in the Sovietization of East Germany and the entire Eastern bloc.

The formation of a unified medial space across the Eastern bloc transformed the cult community into an affective empire: all of its members were
prescribed a set of normative feelings of trust, respect, and love for the Soviet
leader. The party-state-sponsored control of the press, radio, cinema, and
later television, along with surveillance practices, empowered communist
states to develop emotional regimes by offering avenues of affective management of the population and navigating remembrance and forgetting through
propagated feelings. Instead of memories of a disgraceful defeat and the
German nation's shameful loss of honor, the cult of the Soviet leader offered
the vanquished a more positive way forward: traditions of German-Soviet
friendship could be established and the rhetoric of membership in the antifascist resistance could be taken up. The new metanarrative was designed to
break with the national socialist past and turn the Germans into "friends" of
the Soviet Union. Not least, it was also intended to show them how to reach
the "bright future." With the founding of the "second German state," the
German Democratic Republic, membership in the Stalin cult was declared a
matter of honor for every German patriot and maintaining the cult's vitality
became a nationwide project. Propaganda presented it as a central, integrating
force: it would legitimate the East German state and generate solidarity, while
membership in the cult community—the bloc of socialist states—would compensate for a profoundly disrupted sense of national identity. Worshipping
Stalin, as we have seen, meant that the concepts of national pride, honor,
and patriotism had to be reinvented. The fall of the Third Reich made them
taboo but in postwar conditions they could be rehabilitated and could take
on redefined national meanings by expressing the GDR's full accord with
the Soviet Union. From this point of view, my analytical focus has primarily
been on the power of symbolic politics and on reconstructing the mechanisms
of subordination which ensured the population's loyalty to the party and the
state in Soviet-style societies.

An examination of the possibilities and limits of the Stalin cult in the
dynamics of imperial consolidation reveals the strengths and weaknesses
of Soviet power in postwar Europe. Searching for answers to questions
about how the Stalin cult on the periphery of the postwar Soviet empire
managed to produce a certain amount of tolerance for an unpopular regime
and why the East Germans participated in party-state cult rituals although
they clearly did not trust the "best friend" opens a window onto the ways
that Soviet civilization functioned beyond the boundaries of the USSR.
Political scientist Lisa Wedeen has asked similar questions in her analysis
of the cult of Syrian president Hafiz al-Assad. Wedeen explains the vitality
and effectiveness of the Syrian cult in terms of the ability of authoritarian
regimes to mobilize their citizens by forcing them to participate in symbolic politics; she also focuses on the way the Assad cult became a form

of social control, indoctrination, and mobilization as a result of the state's "disciplining-symbolic politics."[9] On the basis of Wedeen's analysis of the cult of the Syrian president, I believe that the Stalin cult in East Germany was also the result of forced participation, here participation in producing the Soviet symbolic order, which depended to a much greater degree on mobilizing and indoctrinating the population than on the concept of the regime's legitimacy.[10] Like the Assad cult, in the GDR worship of Stalin took place against a backdrop of hypocrisy that was obvious to everyone. Despite the public farce, a similar politics of cynicism turned out to be effective enough since it allowed the regime to attain the illusion of social consensus. That is, the population was drawn into cult practices although everyone could also experience indifference and articulate distance from the propagandized leader in many ways.[11] Conforming to the ritual order of the cult community did not require sincere political convictions. For "weak" power regimes, forcing their citizens to participate formally and play by the prescribed rules of the game was much more important. Therefore, the Stalin cult rituals do not tell us a great deal about the Soviet leader's actual popularity in East Germany. They have much more information to deliver about the techniques used in Soviet-style societies for mobilizing the population to stage social consensus and to proclaim the regime's legitimacy in the dictatorship's public spaces.

In conclusion, it is important to note that participation in the personality cult was defined in a rather narrow, limited way: it meant using public cult rhetoric and carrying out the prescribed ritual acts in official spheres. Compliance in these areas enabled the state and party to exert control over public language, performative behavior, and staged emotions. For individuals living under a dictatorship, mastering normative public behavior and rhetoric triggered an internal self-empowerment: one had to speak the party's and the state's language and participate in official rituals—in other words, publicly demonstrate submission to the regime—in order to preserve a certain amount of autonomy and to avoid provoking the state's repressive interference in one's private sphere. The subject intentionally staged him/herself as an object of big politics in order to hold onto a private, autonomous space where s/he could have her/his own interests and opinions, needs and hopes, individual experience and memory. In other words, in East Germany, we see the paradox of the subject's public self-politicization for the sake of preserving her/his private space and the concomitant depoliticization of the private niches of people's lives. This fact is proof of the hybrid behavior of a subject who, living under the constraints of a dictatorship, adapted, reached an agreement with the state, and resisted, *simultaneously*. This mental resourcefulness helped stabilize the dictatorship, while preserving spaces and niches of limited autonomy. An exemplary anecdote from the first years of the GDR's existence conveys this harmony of ambivalence, which is a crucial analytic key to explaining how Soviet-style societies function:

> A Soviet school inspection delegation came to Berlin. The head of the delegation was very satisfied with the results of his examination of the school, concluding that the ideological enlightenment and political education of young Germans was proceeding on a high level. At the end of the inspection, he stopped one of the boys as he was running by and said "Well, tell me, who is your father?" The pupil fired off an answer: "Our beloved leader Joseph Vissarionovich Stalin!"
>
> "Good. And who is your mother?"
>
> Once again, the pupil answered without thinking, "The great and unconquerable Soviet Union."
>
> "Very good. But tell me please, what do you dream of becoming?"
>
> This time the boy took a while to answer and, looking down, he said, "An orphan!"[12]

NOTES

1. *Werktätige Bauern, Traktoristen und Landarbeiter besuchen die Sowjetunion.*

2. Behrends, "Vom Panslavismus zum 'Friedenskampf.'"

3. *Werktätige Bauern, Traktoristen und Landarbeiter*, 20.

4. Crary, *Suspensions of Perception*, Orlova, "'Karty dlia slepykh,'" in Iarskaia-Smirnova and Romanov, *Vizual'naia antropologiia*; Golubev, "Zapadnyi nabliudatel' i zapadnyi vzgliad," in Pinskii, *Posle Stalina.*

5. For example, see Gleason, Kenez, and Stites, *Bolshevik Culture*; Kelly and Shepherd, *Constructing Russian Culture*; Figes and Kolonitskii, *Interpreting the Russian Revolution*; Boldrick and Clay, *Iconoclasm.*

6. Lüdtke, "Geschichte und Eigensinn," in Berliner Geschichtswerkstatt, *Alltagskultur, Subjektivität und Geschichte*; Lindenberger, *Die Diktatur der Grenzen*; Sabrow, *Herrschaft und Alltag in der DDR.*

7. Ahbe and Gries, "Gesellschaftsgeschichte als Generationengeschichte," in Schüle, Ahbe, and Gries, *Die DDR aus generationengeschichtlicher Perspektive*, 502–18.

8. Ibid., 518–31.

9. Wedeen, *Ambiguities of Domination*, 145–52. Analogous observations appear in Plamper, "The Hitlers Come and Go . . .," in Heller and Plamper, *Personality Cults*, 326–27 and Leese, *Mao Cult*, 18–19.

10. Wedeen, *Ambiguities of Domination*, 6.

11. On the connections between cynicism and daily life in the late Soviet Union, see Yurchak, *Everything Was Forever.*

12. AdsD, SPD-PV-Ostbüro 0350, unpag.

Bibliography

ARCHIVAL SOURCES

State Archive of the Russian Federation (Gosudarstvennyi arkhiv Rossiiskoi Federatsii, GARF)

Fond 5283. VOKS (Vsesoiuznoe obshchestvo kul'turnoi sviazi s zagranitsei/All-Union Society for Cultural Ties with Foreign Countries).

Fond R-7077. Directorate of the Soviet Military Administration in Brandenburg Province (Upravlenie Sovetskoi voennoi administratsii provintsii Brandenburg).

Fond R-7103. Directorate of the Soviet Military Administration in Mecklenburg Province (Upravlenie Sovetskoi voennoi administratsii provintsii Meklenburg).

Fond R-7133. Directorate of the Soviet Military Administration of *Land* Saxony-Anhalt (Upravlenie Sovetskoi voennoi administratsii zemli Saksoniia-Angal't).

Fond R-7212. Directorate of the Soviet Military Administration of the *Land* of Saxony (Upravlenie Sovetskoi voennoi administratsii zemli Saksoniia).

Fond R-7184. Directorate of the Soviet Military Administration the *Land* of Thuringia (Upravlenie Sovetskoi voennoi administratsii zemli Tiuringiia).

Fond R-7317. Soviet Military Administration in Germany (Sovetskaia voennaia administratsiia v Germanii).

Fond R-9401sr. Special Folder of Comrade Stalin (Osobaia papka tovarishcha Stalina).

Russian State Archive of Socio-Political History (Rossiiskii gosudarstvennyi arkhiv sotsial'no-politicheskoi istorii, RGASPI)

Fond 17. TsK VKP(b), Department of Propaganda and Agitation (Otdel propagandy i agitatsii).

Fond 17. Ts KPSS, Department of Propaganda and Agitation (Otdel propagandy i agitatsii).

Fond 558. Inventory list of the personal fond of Stalin, I. V. 21.XII.1879–5.III.1953 (Opis' lichnogo fonda Stalina I. V. 21.XII.1879–5.III.1953).

Russian State Archive of Contemporary History (Rossiiskii gosudarstvennyi arkhiv noveishei istorii, RGANI)

Fond 1. KPSS Congresses (1955–1986) (S"ezdy KPSS [1955–1986]).
Fond 5. Executive Office of the Central Committee of the Communist Party of the Soviet Union (1952–1984) (Apparat TsK KPSS [1952–1984]).

Foreign Policy Archive of the Russian Federation (Arkhiv vneshnei politiki Rossiiskoi Federatsii, AVP RF)

Fond 7. Secretariat of Comrade Vyshinskii (Sekretariat tov. Vyshinskogo).
Fond 742. (082) Executive Office for Germany of the Ministry of Foreign Affairs of the USSR (Referentura po Germanii MID SSSR).
Fond 166. Embassy of the USSR in the GDR (Posol'stvo SSSR v GDR).

Archiv der sozialen Demokratie der Friedrich-Ebert-Stiftung (AdsD)

SPD-PV-Ostbüro

Archiv der Akademie der Künste
Bildarchiv des Bundesarchivs Deutschlands (Koblenz)
Bildarchiv im Deutschen Historischen Museum (DHM)
Stiftung Archiv der Parteien und Massenorganisationen der ehemaligen DDR im Bundesarchiv (SAPMO-BArch)

Abteilung Agitation des ZK der SED, 1946–1962
Bildarchiv (Berlin und Koblenz)
Demokratischer Frauenbund Deutschlands (DFD)
Erinnerungen, Personalien
Freie Deutsche Jugend (FDJ)
Freier deutscher Gewerkschaftsbund (FDGB)
Gesellschaft für deutsch-sowjetische Freundschaft (GDSF)
Kulturbund der DDR
Politbüro des ZK der SED (Protokolle), 1949–1960
Tagungen des Parteivorstandes bzw. des ZK der SED, 1946–1989
Zentralvorstand, Unterricht und Erziehung, Abt. Kader
ZK der SED, Parteiorgane

Der Bundesbeauftragte für die Unterlagen des Staatssicherheitsdienstes der ehemaligen Deutschen Demokratischen Republik (BStU)

Ministerium für Staatssicherheit, Zentralstelle
Aussenstelle Gera
Aussenstelle Leipzig
Aussenstelle Karl-Marx Stadt
Aussenstelle Suhl
Aussenstelle Chemnitz

Deutsches Rundfunkarchiv (Babelsberg, Potsdam)
Filmarchiv im Bundesarchiv (Berlin)
Das Sächsische Hauptstaatsarchiv Dresden
Thüringisches Hauptstaatsarchiv, Weimar (ThHStAW)

Land Thüringen 1945–1952: Amt für Information; Büro des Ministerpräsidenten; Ministerium des Innern

PUBLISHED PRIMARY SOURCES

Abusch, Alexander. *Stalin und die Schicksalsfragen der deutschen Nation.* Berlin: Aufbau Verlag, 1952.

"Anlage Nr. 5a zum Protokoll Nr. 16/53 vom 17. März 1953." In "Dokumentation: Der Tod des Diktators—ein Circulus vitiosus für die SED." Edited by Wilfriede Otto. Special issue, *UTOPIE kreativ,* Heft 149 (March 2003): 212–13.

Anti-Komintern, ed. *Der Weltbolschewismus: Ein internationales Gemeinschaftswerk über die bolschewistische Wühlarbeit und die Umsturzversuche der Komintern in allen Ländern, herausgegeben von der Anti-Komintern, mit 400 Bilddokumenten, Karten und Anschauungstafeln.* Berlin: Nibelungen Verlag, 1936.

Barbius, Anri [Henri Barbusse]. *Stalin: Chelovek, cherez kotorogo raskryvaetsia novyi mir.* Translated by A. I. Stetskii. Moscow: Khudozhestvennaia literatura, 1936.

Begegnungen mit Stalin: Aussagen sowjetischer und deutscher Autoren. 2nd ed. Berlin: Verlag Kultur und Fortschritt, 1953.

Caspar, Günter, ed. *Du Welt im Licht: J. W. Stalin im Werk deutscher Schriftsteller.* Berlin: Aufbau, 1954.

———. "Zum Geleit." In *Du Welt im Licht: J. W. Stalin im Werk deutscher Schriftsteller,* edited by Günter Caspar, 15. Berlin: Kultur und Fortschritt, 1954.

Claudius, Eduard. *Notizen nebenbei.* Berlin: Kultur und Fortschritt, 1948.

"'Das neue Leben': Funkbericht über den Aufbau der Stalinstadt," May 1953. On *Stalinallee—Stalinstadt: Die "erste sozialistische Straße" und die "erste sozialistische Stadt" in Tonodokumenten, 1952–1955,* edited by Deutsches Historisches Museum and Deutsches Rundfunk Archiv, track no. 10.

"Der Aufbau der Stalinallee schreitet voran, 5. Mai 1952." On *Stalinallee—Stalinstadt: Die "erste sozialistische Straße" und die "erste sozialistische Stadt" in Tonodokumenten, 1952–1955*, edited by Deutsches Historisches Museum and Deutsches Rundfunk Archiv, track no. 3.

Der Augenzeuge—Die DEFA-Wochenschau. Berlin: ICESTORM Entertainment GmbH/DEFA-Stiftung, 2001.

Der Reichsführer-SS and SS-Hauptamt, eds. *Der Untermensch.* Berlin: Nordland-Verlag, 1942.

Deutsches Historisches Museum and Deutsches Rundfunkarchiv, eds. *Stalinallee—Stalinstadt: Die erste sozialistische Strasse und die erste sozialistische Stadt in Tondokumenten, 1952–1955.* Compact disc. Liner notes by Claudia Freytag. Frankfurt am Main and Potsdam-Babelsberg: DHM/DRA, 1997.

Dörnberg, Stefan. *Befreiung 1945: Ein Augenzeugenbericht.* Berlin: Dietz, 1985.

———. *Fronteinsatz: Erinnerungen eines Rotarmisten, Historikers und Botschafters.* Berlin: Edition Ost, 2004.

Eisler, Gerhart. *Freundschaft für immer: Brief an alle Bürger der DDR anlässlich des 34. Jahrestages der Grossen Sozialistischen Oktoberrevolution.* Berlin: Amt für Informationen, 1952.

Gelfand, Wladimir. *Deutschland-Tagebuch 1945–1946: Aufzeichnungen eines Rotarmisten.* Translated by Anja Lutter and Hartmut Schröder. Berlin: Aufbau, 2005.

Goebbels, Joseph. "People, Rise Up, and Storm, Break Loose!" In *Landmark Speeches of National Socialism.* Edited and translated by Randall L. Bytwerk. College Station: Texas A&M University Press, 2008.

Grotewohl, Otto. "Simvol nemetskogo pozora: K piatoi godovshchine fashistskogo napadeniia na Sovetskii Soiuz 22 iiunia 1941 goda." In *Izbrannye stat'i i rechi (1945–1959 gody),* 15–19. Moscow: Gospolitizdat, 1961.

———. "Stalinallee—Straße der unverbindlichen Freundschaft: Rede zur Grundsteinlegung in der Stalinallee. 3. Februar 1952." In *Im Kampf um die einige Deutsche Demokratische Republik, Reden und Aufsätze,* edited by Otto Grotewohl, 31–40. Vol. 3, *1952–1953.* Berlin: Dietz, 1954.

———. "Stalin und das deutsche Volk." In *I. W. Stalin zum Gedenken,* 352. Vienna: Sowjetischer Informationsdienst, 1953.

Harich, Wolfgang. *Keine Schwierigkeiten mit der Wahrheit.* Berlin: Dietz, 1993.

Hauptverwaltung für Ausbildung der FDJ, ed. *Vorwärts junge Friedenskämpfer der VP: Schulen/Bereitschaften im Friedensaufgebot der deutschen Jugend!* Berlin: FDJ Verlag, 1950.

Hermlin, Stephan. "Das Abbild der Hoffnung." In *Begegnungen mit Stalin: Aussagen sowjetischer und deutscher Autoren,* 141. Berlin: Kultur und Fortschritt, 1953.

Inozemtsev, N. N. *Frontovoi dnevnik.* Moscow: Nauka, 2005.

Institut Marksizma-Leninizma pri TsK KPSS. *Kommunisticheskaia partiia Germaniia v bor'be protiv fashizma: Rechi Vil'gema Pika, Florina, Val'tera, Akkermana, Frantsa, Funka, Karla—delegatov Germanskoi kompartii: VII Vsemirnyi kongress Kommunisticheskogo internatsionala.* Moscow: Partizdat, 1935.

Just, A. W. *Joseph Wissarionowitsch Dshugaschwili-Stalin.* Lübeck: Coleman, 1932.

Kaprinskij, W. A. *Die Gesellschafts-und Staatsordnung der UdSSR.* Vol. 3 of *Das Sowjetland, 1917–1947.* Berlin: SWA-Verlag, 1947.

Kasper, Hans, ed. *100 Kasperiolen.* Berlin-Grunewald: Arani, no date.

Klemperer, Viktor. *LTI: Iazyk Tret"ego reikha: Zapisnaia knizhka filologa.* Translated by A. Grigor'ev. Moscow: Progress-traditsiia, 1998.

———. *So sitze ich denn zwischen allen Stühlen: Tagebücher 1945–1949.* Vol. 1. Edited by Walter Nowojski. Berlin: Aufbau Verlag, 1999.

———. *The Lesser Evil: The Diaries of Victor Klemperer 1945–59.* Abridged and translated by Martin Chalmers. Phoenix: London, 2004.

Kolesnichenko, I. S. *Bitva posle voiny.* Moscow: Voennoe izdatel'stvo, 1987.

KuBa [Kurt Barthel]. "Stalinallee." In *Gedichte*, 242. Rostock: VEB Hinstorff Verlag, 1961.

Leonhard, Wolfgang. *Die Revolution entlässt ihre Kinder.* 23rd edition. Cologne: Kiepenheuer und Witsch, 2006.

Michajlow, N. N. *Die Weiten und Reichtümer des Sowjetlandes.* Vol. 5 of *Das Sowjetland, 1917–1974.* Berlin: SWA-Verlag, 1947.

Minz, I. I., I. M. Rasgon, and A. L. Sidorov. *Der große vaterländische Krieg der Sowjetunion.* Vol. 4 of *Das Sowjetland, 1917–1947.* Berlin: SWA-Verlag, 1947.

Neumann, Heinz. "Vorwort." In *J. W. Stalin*, edited by Heinz Neumann. Hamburg and Berlin: Carl Hoym, 1930.

"'Nuzhno idti k sotsializmu ne priamo, a zigzagami': Zapis' besedy I. V. Stalina s rukovoditeliami SEPG, Dekabr 1948 g." *Istoricheskii arkhiv*, no. 5 (2002): 3–26.

Otto, Herbert. *Mutter von Gori wie gross ist dein Sohn: Deutsche Dichter singen von Stalin.* Berlin: Verlag Kultur und Fortschritt, 1952.

Pase, Martin. *Stalin im Blitzlicht der Presse und Karikatur.* Dresden: Müller, 1941.

Plekhanov, George [G. V. Plekhanov]. "On the Role of the Individual in History." In *Essays in Historical Materialism: The Materialist Conception of History; The Role of the Individual in History.* New York: International Publishers, 1940.

"Rapporteur's Report of the Meeting of the Foreign Ministers, July 18, 1945." (Unnumbered Document Following Document 710 (#12) [#13]). In *Foreign Relations of the United States, Diplomatic Papers: The Conference of Berlin (the Potsdam Conference), 1945*, edited by Richardson Dougall. Vol. 2. Washington, DC: U.S. Government Printing Office, 1960.

"Richtfest am ersten drei Wohnblöcken in der Stalinallee zu Ehren zu II. Parteikonferenz der SED," July 14, 1952. On *Stalinallee—Stalinstadt: Die "erste sozialistische Straße" und die "erste sozialistische Stadt" in Tonodokumenten, 1952–1955*, edited by Deutsches Historisches Museum and Deutsches Rundfunk Archiv, track no. 11.

"Richtfest am Hochhaus der Weberwiese," January 15, 1952. On *Stalinallee—Stalinstadt: Die "erste sozialistische Straße" und die "erste sozialistische Stadt" in Tonodokumenten, 1952–1955*, edited by Deutsches Historisches Museum and Deutsches Rundfunk Archiv, track no. 1.

"Sendung anlässlich des zweijährigen Bestehens der Stalinstadt," May 1955. On *Stalinallee—Stalinstadt: Die "erste sozialistische Straße" und die "erste sozialistische Stadt"* in *Tonodokumenten, 1952–1955*, edited by Deutsches Historisches Museum and Deutsches Rundfunk Archiv, track no. 11.

"'Skostit' polovinu summy reparatsii ... my mozhem': Vstrechi Stalina s rukovodst-vom SEPG." *Istochnik*, no. 3 (2002): 100–28.

"Stalin, der große Feldherr und Organisator des Sieges über den Faschismus." In *Leseheft für den Zirkel zum Studium der Biographie J. W. Stalins*. Berlin: Junge Welt, 1952.

Stalin: Der große Fortsetzer des Werkes Lenins. Moscow: Verlag für fremdsprachige Literatur, 1940.

"Stalin, Freund, Genosse." In *Lieder der UdSSR: Lieder um Stalin*, edited by Ernst Busch, 86–88. Berlin: Lied der Zeit, 1949.

Stalin, J. W. "Ansprache an das Volk." In *Zur Geschichte der neuesten Zeit*, edited by Walter Ulbricht, 362–63. Berlin: Dietz, 1955.

———. "Stalin und die Jugend." In *Leseheft für den Zirkel zum Studium der Biographie J. W. Stalins*, edited by the FDJ Central Council, Propaganda Department. Berlin: Junge Welt, 1953.

Stalin: Sbornik statei k piatidesiatiletiiu so dnia rozhdeniia. Moscow: Gosudarstvennoe izdatel'stvo, 1929.

Tjulpanow, Sergej. *Deutschland nach dem Kriege (1945–1949): Erinnerungen eines Offiziers der Sowjetarmee.* Edited by Stefan Dörnberg. 2nd edition. Berlin: Dietz, 1987.

Ulbricht, Walter. *An die Jugend.* Berlin: Neues Leben, 1954.

———. "Das Programm der antifaschistisch-demokratischen Ordnung: Rede auf der ersten Funktionärkonferenz der KPD Gross-Berlins am 25. Juni 1945." In *Die Entwicklung des Deutschen Volksdemokratischen Staates 1945–1958*, 19–21. Berlin: Dietz, 1959.

———. "Die gegenwärtigen Aufgaben der demokratischen Verwaltung: Aus dem Referat auf der ersten Staatspolitischen Konferenz der SED in Werder 23. und 24. Juli 1948." In *Die Entwicklung des deutschen Volksdemokratischen Staates 1945–1958.* Berlin: Dietz, 1959.

Unserem Freund und Lehrer: J. W. Stalin: Zum siebzigsten Geburtstag. Berlin: Dietz, 1949.

"Unter dem Banner Lenins und Stalins schreitet das Sowjetvolk zum Kommunismus." In *Lehrheft für den Zirkel zum Studium der Biographie J. W. Stalins, 2 Schuljahr der Freien Deutschen Jugend.* Berlin: Verlag Junge Welt, ca. 1951.

"'V spokoinom tone dat' stat'iu': Lidery partii ob otsenke Stalina." *Istochnik*, no. 4 (1996): 145–51.

Werktätige Bauern, Traktoristen und Landarbeiter besuchen die Sowjetunion: Bericht der ersten Delegation der werktätigen Bauern, Traktoristen und Landarbeitern der Deutschen Demokratischen Republik über ihre Reise in die Sowjetunion. Berlin: Deutsche Bauernverlag, 1952.

Windecke, Christian. *Der rote Zar: Genosse Stalins Weg zur Macht.* Leipzig: Quelle und Meyer, 1932.

"Za sovetami v Kreml': Zapis' besedy I. V. Stalina s rukovoditeliami SEPG, Mart 1948 g." *Istoricheskii arkhiv*, no. 2 (2002): 3–27.

DOCUMENT COLLECTIONS

Aimermakher, K. [Karl Eimermacher], ed. *Doklad N. S. Khrushcheva o kul'te lichnosti Stalina na XX s"ezde KPSS: Dokumenty.* Moscow: ROSSPEN, 2002.

Badstübner, Rolf, and Winfried Loth, eds. *Wilhelm Pieck: Aufzeichnungen zur Deutschlandpolitik, 1945–1953.* Berlin: Akademie, 1994.

Bonvech, B. [Bernd Bonwetsch], G. Bordiugov, and N. Neimark [Norman Naimark], eds. *SVAG: Upravlenie propagandy (informatsii) i S. I. Tiul'panov, 1945–1949; Sbornik dokumentov.* Moscow: Rossiia molodaia, 1994.

Bonwetsch, Bernd, Gennadij Bordjugov, and Norman Naimark, eds. *Sowjetische Politik in der SBZ, 1945–1949: Dokumente zur Tätigkeit der Propagandaverwaltung (Informationsverwaltung) der SMAD unter Sergej Tjulpanow.* Bonn: Dietz, 1998.

Erler, Peter, Horst Laude, and Manfred Wilke, eds. *"Nach Hitler Kommen wir": Dokumente zur Programmatik der Moskauer KPD-Führung 1944/45 für Nachkriegsdeutschland.* Berlin: Akademie, 1994.

Fursenko, A. A., ed. *Prezidium TsK KPSS, 1954–1964: Chernovye protokol'nye zapisi zasedanii; Stenogramm; Postanovleniia.* Vol. 1. Moscow: ROSSPEN, 2004.

Gabert, Josef, and Lutz Prieß, eds. *SED und Stalinismus: Dokumente aus dem Jahre 1956.* Berlin: Dietz, 1990.

Gromyko, A. A., ed. *Berlinskaia (Potsdamskaia) konferentsiia rukovoditelei trekh soiuznykh derzhav—SSSR, SShA i Velikobritanii (17 iiulia–2 avgusta 1945 g.)* Vol. 6 of *Sovetskii Soiuz na mezhdunarodnykh konferentsiiakh perioda Velikoi Otechestvennoi voiny 1941–1945 gg.: Sbornik dokumentov.* Edited by A. A. Gromyko. Moscow: Izdatel'stvo politicheskoi literatury, 1984. http://www.hist.msu.ru/ER/Etext/War_Conf/berlin03.htm.

Kynin, G. P., and I. Laufer, comps. *9 maia 1945 g.—3 oktiabria 1946 g.* Vol. 2 of *SSSR i germanskii vopros, 1941–1949: Dokumenty iz Arkhiva vneshnei politiki Rossiiskoi Federatsii.* Moscow: Mezhdunarodnye otnosheniia, 2000.

Petrov, N. V., O. V. Lavrinskaia, and D. N. Nokhotovich, eds. *SVAG i nemetskie organi samoupravleniia: Sbornik dokumentov.* Moscow: ROSSPEN, 2006.

Timofeeva, N. P., and I. A. Foittsik [Jan Foitzik], eds. *Politika SVAG v oblasti kul'tury, nauki i obrazovaniia: Tseli, metody, rezul'taty, 1945–1949; Sbornik dokumentov.* Moscow: ROSSPEN, 2006.

Volokitina, T. V., ed., *Sovetskii faktor v Vostochnoi Evrope, 1944–1953gg.: V dvukh tomakh; Dokumenty.* Vol. 2, *1949–1953gg.* Moscow: ROSSPEN, 2002.

SECONDARY SOURCES

Ackermann, Volker. *Nationale Totenfeiern in Deutschland: Von Wilhelm I. bis Franz Josef Strauss; Eine Studie zur politischen Semiotik.* Stuttgart: Klett-Cotta, 1990.

Afanas'ev, M. N. *Klientelizm i rossiiskaia gosudarstvennost'*. Moscow: Tsentr kon-stitutsionnykh issledovanii, 1997.

Ahbe, Thomas, and Rainer Gries. "Gesellschaftsgeschichte als Generationengeschichte: Theoretische und Methodologische Überlegungen am Beispiel der DDR." In *Die DDR aus Generationengeschichtlicher Perspektive: Eine Inventur*, edited by Annegret Schüle, Thomas Ahbe, and Rainer Gries, 475–572. Leipzig: Leipziger Universitätsverlag, 2006.

Aksiutin, Iurii. *Khrushchevskaia "ottepel'" i obshchestvennye nastroeniia v USSR v 1953–1964 gg.* Moscow: ROSSPEN, 2004.

Alföldi, Andreas. *Der Vater des Vaterlandes im römischen Denken*. Darmstadt: Wissenschaftliche Buchgesellschaft, 1971.

Algazi, Gadi, Valentin Groebner, and Bernhard Jussen. *Negotiating the Gift: Premodern Figurations of Exchange*. Göttingen: Vandenhoeck & Ruprecht, 2003.

Allinson, Mark. *Politics and Popular Opinion in East Germany, 1945–1968*. Manchester: Manchester University Press, 2000.

Altendorf, Gabriele. "Denunziation im Hochschulbereich der ehemaligen DDR." In *Denunziation: Historische, juristische und psychologische Aspekte*, edited by Günter Jerouschek, Inge Marßolek, and Hedwig Röckelein, 183–206. Tübingen: Edition Diskord, 1997.

Al'tiusser, Lui [Louis Althusser]. "Ideologiia i ideologicheskie apparaty gosu-darstva." *Neprikosnovennyi zapas*, no. 3 (77) (2011): 14–58.

Anderson, Benedict. *Imagined Communities: Reflections on the Origin and Spread of Nationalism*. London: Verso, 1983.

Ansorg, Leonore. *Kinder im Klassenkampf: Die Geschichte der Pionierorganisation von 1948 bis Ende der fünfziger Jahre*. Berlin: Akademie, 1997.

Antonov-Ovseenko, A. V. *Stalin bez maski*. Moscow: Vsia Moskva, 1990.

———. *Teatr Iosifa Stalina*. Moscow: Greigori-Peidzh, 1995.

Apor, Balázs. "Communist Leader Cults in Eastern Europe: Concepts and Debates." In "Cultic Revelations: Studies in Modern Historical Cult Personalities and Phenomena." Edited by Anssi Halmesvirta. Special issue, *Spectrum Hungarologicum* 4 (2010): 37–62 .

———. *The Invisible Shining: The Cult of Mátyás Rákosi in Stalinist Hungary, 1945–1956*. Budapest: Central European University Press, 2017.

Apor, Balázs, Jan C. Behrends, Polly Jones, and E. A. Rees, eds. *The Leader Cult in Communist Dictatorships: Stalin and the Eastern Bloc*. Basingstoke: Palgrave Macmillan, 2004.

Apor, Balázs, Peter Apor, and E. A. Rees, eds. *The Sovietization of Eastern Europe: New Perspectives on the Postwar Period*. Washington, DC: New Academia Publishing, 2008.

Applebaum, Anne. *Iron Curtain: The Crushing of Eastern Europe, 1944–1956*. London: Allen Lane, 2012.

Arendt, Hannah. *The Origins of Totalitarianism*. New York: Harcourt Brace & World, 1966.

Armstrong, Charles K. *The North Korean Revolution, 1945–1950*. Ithaca, NY: Cornell University Press, 2003.

Arthurs, Joshua, Michael Ebner, and Kate Ferris, eds. *The Politics of Everyday Life in Fascist Italy: Outside the State?* New York: Palgrave Macmillan, 2017.

Asch, Ronald G., and Dagmar Freist, eds. *Staatsbildung als kultureller Prozess: Strukturwandel und Legitimation von Herrschaft in der Frühen Neuzeit.* Cologne: Böhlau, 2005.

Ashirova, Aygul. *Stalinismus und Stalin-Kult in Zentralasien: Turkmenistan 1924– 1953.* Stuttgart: Ibidem-Verlag, 2009.

Assmann, Aleida, and Ute Frevert. *Geschichtsvergessenheit—Geschichtsversessenheit: Vom Umgang mit deutschen Vergangenheiten nach 1945.* Stuttgart: Deutsche Verlags-Anhalt, 1999.

Azaryahu, Maoz. *Von Wilhelmplatz zu Thälmannplatz: Politische Symbole im öffentlichen Leben der DDR.* Translated by Kerstin Amrani and Alma Mandelbaum. Gerlingen: Bleicher, 1991.

———. "Zurück zur Vergangenheit? Die Straßennamen Ost-Berlins 1990–1994." In *Denkmalsturz: Zur Konfliktgeschichte politischer Symbolik,* edited by Winfried Speitkamp, 137–54. Göttingen: Vandenhoeck & Ruprecht, 1997.

Baberowski, Jörg. *Der rote Terror: Die Geschichte des Stalinismus.* Munich: Deutsche Verlags-Anstalt, 2003.

———. *Scorched Earth: Stalin's Reign of Terror.* Translated by Steven Gilbert, Ivo Komljen, and Samantha Jeanne Taber. New Haven, CT: Yale University Press, 2016.

———. "Selbstbilder und Fremdbilder: Repräsentation sozialer Ordnung im Wandel." In *Selbstbilder und Fremdbilder: Repräsentationen sozialer Ordnung im Wandel,* edited by Jörg Baberowski, Hartmut Kaelble, and Jürgen Schriewer, 9–13. Frankfurt am Main: Campus, 2008.

———. *Verbrannte Erde: Stalins Herrschaft der Gewalt.* Munich: C. H. Beck, 2012.

———. "Was sind Repräsentationen sozialer Ordnungen im Wandel? Anmerkungen zu einer Geschichte interkultureller Begegnungen." In *Arbeit an der Geschichte: Wie viel Theorie braucht die Geschichtswissenschaft,* edited by Jörg Baberowski, 7–18. Frankfurt am Main: Campus, 2009.

———. "Zivilisation der Gewalt." *Historische Zeitschrift,* no. 281 (2005): 59–102.

Bachmann-Medick, Doris. *Cultural Turns: Neuorientierungen in den Kulturwissenschaften.* Hamburg: Rowohlt, 2006.

Badstübner, Evemarie. *Befremdlich anders: Leben in der DDR.* Berlin: Dietrich Mühlberg, 2000.

Badstübner, Rolf, and Winfried Loth, eds. *Wilhelm Pieck: Aufzeichnungen zur Deutschlandpolitik, 1945–1953.* Berlin: Akademie, 1994.

Bairau, Ditrikh [Dietrich Beyrau]. "Vykhodtsy iz sovetskogo inkubatora: Sovetskaia gegemoniia i sotsialisticheskii stroi v Tsentral'no-Vostochnoi Evrope." *Ab Imperio,* no. 4 (2011): 203–35.

Bakhtin, Mikhail. *Rabelais and His World.* Translated by Hélène Iswolsky. Cambridge, MA: MIT Press, 1968.

Barck, Simone. "The Fettered Media: Controlling Public Debate." In *Dictatorship as Experience: Towards a Socio-Cultural History of the GDR*, edited by Konrad H. Jarausch, 213–40. New York: Berghahn, 1999.

Barck, Simone, Martina Langermann, and Siegfried Lokatis. *"Jedes Buch ein Abenteuer": Zensur-System und literarische Öffentlichkeit in der DDR bis Ende der sechziger Jahre*. Berlin: Akademie, 1997.

Barclay, David E. "Ritual, Ceremonial, and the 'Invention' of a Monarchical Tradition in Nineteenth-Century Prussia." In *European Monarchy: Its Evolution and Practice from Roman Antiquity to Modern Times*, edited by Heinz Duchhardt, Richard A. Jackson, and David Sturdy, 207–20. Wiesbaden: F. Steiner Verlag, 1992.

Barkey, Karen. *Empire of Difference: The Ottomans in Comparative Perspective*. New York: Cambridge University Press, 2008.

Barlova, Iu. "'Novaia politicheskaia istoriia' v sovremennoi istoriografii." In *Aktual'nye problemy vseobshchei istorii: Diplomatiia i bezopasnost', kommunikatsiia i politicheskaia kul'tura, gender*, edited by A. S. Khodnev, 51–58. Iaroslavl': Izdatel'stvo Iarosl. GPU im. K. D. Ushinskogo, 2003.

Barmé, Geremie. *Shades of Mao: The Posthumous Cult of the Great Leader*. Armonk, NY: M. E. Sharpe, 1996.

Bärwald, Helmut. *Das Ostbüro der SPD, 1946–1971: Kampf und Niedergang*. Krefeld: Sinus-Verlag, 1991.

Batkin, L. "Son razuma: O sotsiokul'turnykh masshtabakh lichnosti Stalina." In *Osmyslit' kul't Stalina*, edited by Kh. Kobo, 9–53.

Bauer, Martin, Stephanie Kappacher, Baran Korkmaz, Karsten Malowitz, and Stefan Mörchen, eds. "Antun und Erleiden: Über Gewalt." Special issue, *Mittelweg 36*, Heft 3 (June/July 2017).

Bauman, Zygmunt. *Moderne und Ambivalenz: Das Ende der Eindeutigkeit*. Hamburg: Junius, 1992.

Bayerlein, Bernhard H. "Stalin und die Kommunistische Partei Deutschlands in der Weimarer Republik." In *Der rote Gott: Stalin und die Deutschen; Katalog zur Sonderausstellung*, edited by Andreas Engwert and Hubertus Knabe, 13–17. Berlin: Lukas, 2018.

Behrenbeck, Sabine. "'Der Führer': Die Einführung eines politischen Markenartikels." In *Propaganda in Deutschland: Zur Geschichte der politischen Massenbeeinflussung im 20. Jahrhundert*, edited by Gerald Diesener and Rainer Gries, 51–78. Darmstadt: Primus, 1996.

Behrends, Jan C. *Die erfundene Freundschaft: Propaganda für die Sowjetunion in Polen und in der DDR*. Cologne: Böhlau, 2006.

———. "Exporting the Leader: The Stalin Cult in Poland and East Germany (1944/45–1956)." In *Leader Cult in Communist Dictatorships*, edited by B. Apor et al., 161–78.

———. "Freundschaft zur Sowjetunion, Liebe zu Stalin: Zur Anthropomorphisierung des Politischen im Stalinismus." In *Die Massen bewegen: Medien und Emotionen in der Moderne*, edited by Frank Bösch and Manuel Borutta, 172–92. Frankfurt am Main: Campus, 2006.

————. "Nach dem Führerkult: Repräsentationen des Generalsekretärs im kommunistischen Polen und in der DDR (1956–1989)." In *Medien und Imagepolitik im 20. Jahrhundert: Deutschland, Europa, USA*, edited by Daniela Münkel and Lu Seegers, 57–83. Frankfurt am Main: Campus, 2008.

————. "Vom Panslavismus zum 'Friedenskampf': Außenpolitik, Herrschaftslegitimation und Massenmobilisierung im sowjetischen Nachkriegsimperium (1944–1953)." *Jahrbücher für Geschichte Osteuropas* 56, Heft 1 (2008): 27–53.

Belaj, Marijana. "'I'm Not Religious, But Tito is a God': Tito, Kumrovec, and the New Pilgrims." In *Shrines and Pilgrimage in the Modern World: New Itineraries into the Sacred*, edited by Peter Jan Margry, 71–93. Amsterdam: Amsterdam University Press, 2008.

Benz, Wolfgang. "Infrastruktur und Gesellschaft im zerstörten Deutschland." In *Deutschland 1945–1949: Besatzungszeit und Staatengründung*, edited by Bundeszentrale für Politische Bildung, 13–20. Munich: Franzis, 1998.

Berenson, Edward, and Eva Giloi, eds. *Constructing Charisma: Celebrity, Fame, and Power in Nineteenth-Century Europe*. New York: Berghahn Books, 2010.

Berger, Peter L., and Thomas Luckmann. *Die gesellschaftliche Konstruktion der Wirklichkeit*. 20th edition. Frankfurt am Main: Fischer-Taschenbuch-Verlag, 2004.

Bergesen, Albert. "Die rituelle Ordnung." In *Ritualtheorien: Ein einführendes Handbuch*, edited by Andréa Belliger and David J. Krieger, 49–96. Wiesbaden: VS, 2006.

Bernhard, Patrick. "Metropolen auf Achse: Städtebau und Großstadtgesellschaften Roms und Berlins im faschistischen Bündnis, 1936–1943." In *Berlin im Nationalsozialismus: Politik und Gesellschaft, 1933–1945*, edited by Rüdiger Hachtmann, Thomas Schaarschmidt, and Winfried Süss, 132–57. Göttingen: Wallstein, 2011.

Bernstein, Richard B. *The Founding Fathers Reconsidered*. Oxford: Oxford University Press, 2009.

Bessmertnyi, I. L. "Nekotorye soobrazheniia ob izuchenii fenomena vlasti i o kontseptsiiakh postmodernizma i mikroistorii." *Odissei: Chelovek v istorii; Predstavleniia o vlasti*, no. 7 (1995): 5–19.

Beyrau, Dietrich. "Mortal Embrace: Germans and (Soviet) Russians in the First Half of the 20th Century." *Kritika: Explorations in Russian and Eurasian History* 10, no. 3 (Summer 2009): 423–39.

Bim-Bad, B. M. *Stalin: Issledovanie zhiznennogo stilia*. Moscow: Izd-vo URAO, 2002.

Bizeul, Yves, ed. *Politische Mythen und Rituale in Deutschland, Frankreich und Polen*. Berlin: Duncker & Humblot, 2000.

Black, Monica. *A Demon-Haunted Land: Witches, Wonder Doctors, and the Ghosts of the Past in Post-WWII Germany*. New York: Metropolitan Books, 2021.

Blockmans, Wim, André Holenstein, and Jon Mathieu, eds. *Empowering Interactions: Political Cultures and the Emergence of the State in Europe, 1300–1900*. Burlington, VT: Ashgate, 2009.

Bodenschatz, Harald, ed. *Städtebau für Mussolini: Auf der Suche nach der neuen Stadt im faschistischen Italien*. Berlin: DOM Publishers, 2011.

Boldrick, Stacy, and Richard Clay, eds. *Iconoclasm: Contested Objects, Contested Terms*. Burlington, VT: Ashgate, 2007.

Boldyrev, R. Iu. "Sovetskaia okkupatsionnaia politika v Vostochnoi Germanii 1945–1949: Ekonomicheskii aspect." Kand. nauk diss., Pomorskii gosudarstvennyi universitet imeni M. V. Lomonosova, 2004.

Bonwetsch, Bernd. "Die Sowjetisierung Osteuropas: Moskaus Politik im Interpretationswandel." In *Kommunismus und Osteuropa: Konzepte, Perspektiven und Interpretationen im Wandel*, edited by Eva Schmidt-Hartmann, 85–100. Munich: Oldenbourg, 1994.

Borev, Iu. B. *Staliniada*. Moscow: KRPA Olimp, 2003.

Börrnert, René. *Wie Ernst Thälmann treu und kühn! Das Thälmann-Bild der SED im Erziehungsalltag der DDR*. Bad Heilbrunn: Julius Klinkhardt, 2004.

Bösch, Frank, and Manuel Borutta, eds. *Die Massen bewegen: Medien und Emotionen in der Moderne*. Frankfurt am Main: Campus, 2006.

Bourdieu, Pierre. *Die männliche Herrschaft*. Translated by Jürgen Bolder. Frankfurt am Main: Suhrkamp, 2005.

Boym, Svetlana. *The Future of Nostalgia*. New York: Basic Books, 2010.

Boytsov, Mikhail A. "Ghostly Knights: Kings' Funerals in 14th Century Europe and the Emergence of an International Style." In *Death in Medieval Europe: Death Scripted and Death Choreographed*, edited by Joelle Rollo-Koster, 149–63. London: Routledge, 2016.

Brandenberger, D. L., and A. M. Dubrovsky. "'The People Need a Tsar': The Emergence of National Bolshevism as Stalinist Ideology, 1931–1941." *Europe-Asia Studies* 50, no. 5 (July 1998): 873–92.

Brooks, Jeffrey. *Thank You, Comrade Stalin! Soviet Public Culture from Revolution to Cold War*. Princeton, NJ: Princeton University Press, 2000.

Broszat, Martin, and Hermann Weber, eds. *SBZ-Handbuch: Staatliche Verwaltungen, Parteien, gesellschaftliche Organisationen, und ihre Führungskräfte in der Sowjetischen Besatzungszone Deutschlands 1945–1949*. Munich: Oldenbourg, 1990.

Brückweh, Kerstin, Dirk Schumann, Richard F. Wetzell, and Benjamin Ziemann, eds. *Engineering Society: The Role of the Human and Social Sciences in Modern Societies, 1880–1980*. New York: Palgrave Macmillan, 2012.

Buckmiller, Michael, and Klaus Meschkat, eds. *Biographisches Handbuch zur Geschichte Kommunistischen Internationale: Ein deutsch-russisches Forschungsprojekt*. Berlin: Akademie, 2007.

Budnitskii, Oleg, and Susan Rupp. "The Intelligentsia Meets the Enemy: Educated Soviet Officers in Defeated Germany, 1945." *Kritika: Explorations in Russian and Eurasian History* 10, no. 3 (Summer 2009): 629–82.

Bühmann, Henning. "Der Hitlerkult: Ein Forschungsbericht." In *Personality Cults in Stalinism*, edited by K. Heller and J. Plamper, 109–57.

Bulgakowa, Oksana. "Der Mann mit der Pfeife oder das Leben ist ein Traum: Studien zum Stalinbild im Film." In *Führerbilder: Hitler, Mussolini, Roosevelt, Stalin in Fotografie und Film*, edited by Martin Loiperdinger, Rudolf Herz, and Ulrich Pohlmann, 210–31. Munich: Piper, 1995.

———. "Herr der Bilder—Stalin und der Film, Stalin im Film." In *Agitation zum Glück: Sowjetische Kunst der Stalinzeit*, edited by Hubertus Gassner, 65–96. Bremen: Edition Temmen, 1993.

Burds, Jeffrey. "Sexual Violence in Europe in World War II, 1939–1945." *Politics and Society* 37, no. 1 (March 2009): 35–73.

Büschel, Hubertus. *Untertanenliebe: Der Kult um deutsche Monarchen.* Göttingen: Vandenhoeck & Ruprecht, 2006.

Butzer, Günter, and Manuela Günter, eds. *Kulturelles Vergessen: Medien—Rituale— Orte.* Göttingen: Vandenhoeck & Ruprecht, 2004.

Cassiday, Julie A., and Emily D. Johnson. "Putin, Putiniana and the Question of a Post-Soviet Cult of Personality." *Slavonic and East European Review* 88, no. 4 (October 2010): 681–707.

Cassirer, Ernst. *Der Mythos des Staates: Philosophische Grundlagen politischen Verhaltens.* Frankfurt am Main: Fischer-Taschenbuch-Verlag, 1985.

Chartier, Roger. "Die Welt als Repräsentation." In *Alles Gewordene hat Geschichte: Die Schule der Annales in Ihren Texten*, edited by Matthias Middel, 320–47. Leipzig: Reclam, 1994.

Chase, William J. *Enemies Within the Gates? The Comintern and Stalinist Repression, 1934–1939.* New Haven, CT: Yale University Press, 2001.

Chatterjee, Choi. *Celebrating Women: Gender, Festival Culture, and Bolshevik Ideology, 1910–1939.* Pittsburgh, PA: University of Pittsburgh Press, 2002.

Clark, Katerina. *Moscow, the Fourth Rome: Stalinism, Cosmopolitanism, and the Evolution of Soviet Culture, 1931–1941.* Cambridge, MA: Harvard University Press, 2011.

———. *The Soviet Novel: History as Ritual.* 3rd edition. Bloomington: Indiana University Press, 2000.

Classen, Christoph. "Vom Anfang im Ende: 'Befreiung' im Rundfunk." In *Geschichte als Herrschaftsdiskurs*, edited by M. Sabrow, 87–118.

Cohen, Yves. "The Cult of Number One in an Age of Leaders." *Kritika: Explorations in Russian and Eurasian History* 8, no. 3. (Summer 2007): 597–634.

Connelly, John. *Captive University: The Sovietization of East German, Czech, and Polish Higher Education, 1945–1956.* Chapel Hill: University of North Carolina Press, 2000.

Corner, Paul, ed. *Popular Opinion in Totalitarian Regimes: Fascism, Nazism, Communism.* Oxford: Oxford University Press, 2009.

Courtois, Stéphane, Nicolas Werth, Jean-Louis Panné, Andrzej Paczkowski, Karel Bartošek, and Jean-Louis Margolin. *The Black Book of Communism: Crimes, Terror, Repression.* Translated by Jonathan Murphy and Mark Kramer. Cambridge, MA: Harvard University Press, 2009.

Crary, Jonathan. *Suspensions of Perception: Attention, Spectacle and Modern Culture.* Cambridge, MA: Harvard University Press, 2001.

Creuzberger, Stefan. *Gleichschaltung unter Stalin? Die Entwicklung der Parteien im östlichen Europa 1944–1949.* Paderborn: Schöningh, 2002.

Crowley, David, and Susan E. Reid, eds. *Pleasures in Socialism: Leisure and Luxury in the Eastern Bloc.* Evanston, IL: Northwestern University Press, 2010.

———, eds. *Socialist Spaces: Sites of Everyday Life in the Eastern Bloc.* Oxford: Berg, 2002.

Cummings, Sally N. "Leaving Lenin: Elites, Official Ideology and Monuments in the Kyrgyz Republic." *Nationalities Papers* 41, no. 4 (July 2013): 606–21.

Czech, Hans-Jörg, and Nikola Doll, eds. *Kunst und Propaganda im Streit der Nationen 1930–1945: Katalog der Ausstellung im Deutschen Historischen Museum.* Dresden: Sandstein, 2007.

Daniel, Ute, and Axel Schildt, eds. *Massenmedien im Europa des 20. Jahrhunderts.* Cologne: Böhlau, 2010.

Danyel, Jürgen. "Politische Rituale als Sowjetimporte." In *Amerikanisierung und Sowjetisierung*, edited by Konrad Jarausch and Hannes Siegrist, 67–88.

"Das Politische als Kommunikationsraum in der Geschichte." SFB Antrag auf den Sonderforschungsbereich 584. Bielefeld, 2000.

Daunton, Martin, and Matthew Hilton, eds. *The Politics of Consumption: Material Culture and Citizenship in Europe and America.* Oxford: Berg, 2001.

David-Fox, Michael, Peter Holquist, and Alexander M. Martin, eds. *Fascination and Enmity: Russia and Germany as Entangled Histories, 1914–1945.* Pittsburgh, PA: University of Pittsburgh Press, 2012.

Davies, Sarah. *Popular Opinion in Stalin's Russia: Terror, Propaganda and Dissent, 1934–1941.* Cambridge: Cambridge University Press, 1997.

Davis, Belinda, Thomas Lindenberger, and Michael Wildt, eds. *Alltag, Erfahrung, Eigensinn: Historisch-anthropologische Erkundungen.* Frankfurt am Main: Campus, 2008.

Davis, Natalie Zemon. *Fiction in the Archives: Pardon Tales and Their Tellers in Sixteenth-Century France.* Stanford, CA: Stanford University Press, 1987.

———. *The Gift in Sixteenth-Century France.* Chicago: University of Chicago Press, 2001.

———. "The Rites of Violence: Religious Riot in Sixteenth-Century France." *Past and Present*, no. 59 (May 1973): 51–91.

———. "Writing 'The Rites of Violence' and Afterward." In *Ritual and Violence: Natalie Zemon Davis and Early Modern France*, edited by Graeme Murdock, Penny Roberts, and Andrew Spicer. Supplement 7, *Past and Present*, no. 214 (2012): S8–S29.

De Certeau, Michel. *The Practice of Everyday Life.* Translated by Steven F. Rendall. Berkeley: University of California Press, 1984.

Denison, Michael. "The Art of the Impossible: Political Symbolism, and the Creation of National Identity and Collective Memory in Post-Soviet Turkmenistan." *Europe-Asia Studies* 61, no. 1 (September 2009): 1167–87.

Derix, Simone. *Bebilderte Politik: Staatsbesuche in der Bundesrepublik Deutschland, 1949–1990.* Göttingen: Vandenhoeck & Ruprecht, 2009.

Devlin, Judith. "Visualizing Political Language in the Stalin Cult: The Georgian Art Exhibition in the Tretyakov Gallery." In *Political Languages*, edited by W. Steinmetz, 83–104.

Diefendorf, Barbara B. "Rites of Repair: Restoring Community in the French Religious War." In *Ritual and Violence: Natalie Zemon Davis and Early Modern France*, edited by Graeme Murdock, Penny Roberts, and Andrew Spicer. Supplement 7, *Past and Present*, no. 214 (2012): 30–51.

Die Vertreibung der deutschen Bevölkerung aus den Gebieten östlich der Oder-Neisse. Band 1, Teil 1. Bonn: Bundesministerium für Vertriebene, Flüchtlinge und Kriegsgeschädigte, 1954.

Die Vertreibung der deutschen Bevölkerung aus den Gebieten östlich der Oder-Neiße. Band 2. Munich: Deutscher Taschenbuch Verlag, 1984.

Dikötter, Frank. *How to Be a Dictator: The Cult of Personality in the Twentieth Century*. London: Bloomsbury, 2019.

Directorate-General for Communication (European Commission). *The Founding Fathers of the EU*. Luxembourg: Publications Office of the European Union, 2013.

Dobrenko, E. A. *Metafora vlasti: Literatura stalinskoi epokhi v istoricheskom osveshchenii*. Munich: O. Sagner, 1993.

———. "Mezhdu istoriei i proshlim: Pisatel' Stalin i literaturnye istoki sovetskogo istoricheskogo diskursa." In *Sotsrealisticheskii kanon: Sbornik statei*, edited by Kh. Giunter and E. A. Dobrenko, 639–72. St. Petersburg: Akademicheskii Prospekt, 2000.

———. *The Political Economy of Socialist Realism*. New Haven, CT: Yale University Press, 2007.

Dobrenko, Evgeny, and Eric Naiman, eds. *The Landscape of Stalinism: The Art and Ideology of Soviet Space*. Seattle: University of Washington Press, 2003.

Dobson, Miriam. "'Show the Bandit-Enemies No Mercy!': Amnesty, Criminality, and Public Response in 1953." In *Dilemmas of De-Stalinization*, edited by P. Jones, 21–40.

Dörner, Andreas. *Politischer Mythos und symbolische Politik: Sinnstiftung durch symbolische Formen am Beispiel des Herrmannmythos*. Opladen: Westdeutscher Verlag, 1995.

Doyle, Michael W. *Empires*. Ithaca, NY: Cornell University Press, 1986.

Dror, Olga. "Establishing Ho Chi Minh's Cult: Vietnamese Traditions and Their Transformations." *Journal of Asian Studies* 76, no. 2 (May 2016): 433–66.

Duggan, Christopher. *Fascist Voices: An Intimate History of Mussolini's Italy*. Oxford: Oxford University Press, 2013.

Dunning, Eric. *Sport Matters: Sociological Studies of Sport, Violence and Civilization*. London: Psychology Press, 1999.

Durkheim, Émile. *Die elementaren Formen des religiösen Lebens*. Translated by Ludwig Schmidts. Frankfurt am Main: Suhrkamp, [1912] 1994.

Easter, Gerald M. *Reconstructing the State: Personal Networks and Elite Identity in Soviet Russia*. Cambridge: Cambridge University Press, 2000.

Edelman, Murray J. *Politik als Ritual: Die symbolische Funktion staatlicher Institutionen und politischen Handelns*. Frankfurt am Main: Campus, 1976.

Eghigian, Greg. "Der Kalte Krieg im Kopf: Ein Fall von Schizophrenie und die Geschichte des Selbst in der sowjetischen Besatzungszone." *Historische Anthropologie* 11, Heft 1 (April 2003): 101–22.

Ehalt, Hubert Christian, ed. *Inszenierung der Gewalt: Kunst und Alltagskultur im Nationalsozialismus*. Frankfurt am Main: Lang, 1996.

Eisenstadt, S. N. *The Political System of Empires*. New Brunswick, NJ: Transaction Publishers, 1992.

Eliade, Mircea. *Myth and Reality*. New York: Harper & Row, 1963.

Elias, Norbert. *The Civilizing Process: The History of Manners and State Formation and Civilization*. Oxford: Blackwell, 1994.

Engwert, Andreas. "Ikonografie des Stalin-Kultes in der DDR." In *Der rote Gott: Stalin und die Deutschen*, edited by Andreas Engwert and Hubertus Knabe, 129–41. Berlin: Lukas, 2018.

Ennker, Benno. "Der Führer im Europa des 20. Jahrhunderts—eine Synthese." In *Der Führer im Europa*, edited by B. Hein-Kircher and H. Ennker, 347–78.

———. *Die Anfänge des Leninkults in der Sowjetunion*. Cologne: Böhlau, 1997.

———. "Führerdiktatur—Sozialdynamik und Ideologie: Stalinistische Herrschaft in vergleichender Perspektive." In *Terroristische Diktaturen im 20. Jahrhundert: Strukturelemente der nationalsozialistischen und stalinistischen Herrschaft*, edited by Matthias Vetter, 85–117. Opladen: Westdeutscher Verlag, 1996.

———. "Leninkult und mythisches Denken in der sowjetischen Öffentlichkeit 1924." *Jahrbücher für Geschichte Osteuropas* 44, Heft 3 (1996): 431–55.

———. "Politische Herrschaft und Stalinkult 1929–1939." In *Stalinismus: Neue Forschungen und Konzepte*, edited by Stefan Plaggenborg, 151–84. Berlin: A. Spitz, 1998.

———. "The Stalin Cult, Bolshevik Rule and Kremlin Interaction in the 1930s." In *Leader Cult in Communist Dictatorships*, edited by B. Apor, et al., 83–101.

Ennker, Benno, and Heidi Hein-Kircher, eds. *Der Führer im Europa des 20. Jahrhunderts*. Marburg: Herder-Institut, 2010.

Eriksonas, Linas. *National Heroes and National Identities: Scotland, Norway and Lithuania*. Brussels: Lang, 2004.

Esposito, Elena. *Soziales Vergessen: Formen und Medien des Gedächtnisses der Gesellschaft*. Frankfurt am Main: Suhrkamp, 2006.

Fainsod, Merle. *How Russia is Ruled*. Cambridge, MA: Harvard University Press, 1967.

Fait, Barbara. "Landesregierungen und Verwaltungen: Einleitung." In *SBZ Handbuch: Staatliche Verwaltungen, Parteien, gesellschaftliche Organisationen, und ihre Führungskräfte in der Sowjetischen Besatzungszone Deutschlands, 1945–1949*, edited by Martin Broszat and Hermann Weber, 73–79. Munich: Oldenbourg, 1990.

Falasca-Zamponi, Simonetta. *Fascist Spectacle: The Aesthetics of Power in Mussolini's Italy*. Berkeley: University of California Press, 1997.

————. "The 'Culture' of Personality: Mussolini and the Cinematic Imagination." In *Personality Cults in Stalinism*, edited by K. Heller and J. Plamper, 83–108.

Faulenbach, Bernd. "Die DDR als antifaschistischer Staat." In *Halbherziger Revisionismus: Zum postkommunistischen Geschichtsbild*, edited by Rainer Eckert and Bernd Faulenbach, 47–68. Munich: Olzog, 1996.

Feinstein, Margarete Myers. *State Symbols: The Quest for Legitimacy in the Federal Republic of Germany and the German Democratic Republic, 1949–1959*. Boston: Brill, 2001.

Figes, Orlando, and Boris Kolonitskii. *Interpreting the Russian Revolution: The Language and Symbols of 1917*. New Haven, CT: Yale University Press, 1999.

Filitov, A. M. *Germanskii vopros: Ot raskola k ob"edineniiu; Novoe prochtenie*. Moscow: Mezhdunarodnye otnosheniia, 1993.

————. "SSSR i germanskii vopros: Povorotnye punkty (1941–1961 gg.)." In *Kholodnaia voina, 1945–1963: Istoricheskaia retrospektiva; Sbornik statei*, edited by N. I. Egorov and A. O. Chubar'ian, 223–56. Moscow: Olma, 2003.

————. "The Soviet Administrators and their German 'Friends.'" In *Establishment of Communist Regimes*, edited by N. M. Naimark and L. Gibianski, 111–22.

Filtzer, Donald. *The Khrushchev Era: De-Stalinisation and the Limits of Reform in the USSR, 1953–1964*. Basingstoke: Macmillan, 1993.

Fischer, Jörg-Uwe. "Illustrierte Trauer—staatliche Totenfeiern: Symbolische Inszenierung der Trauer in der DDR-Illustrierten." In *DDR-Bilder: Staat-Stadt-Heimat*, edited by Alf Lüdtke, 35–44. Seelze: Friedrich, 2004.

————. "Im Zeichen des Personenkults: Stalins Geburtstag im ostdeutschen Rundfunk (1945–1956)." *Rundfunk und Geschichte* 21, no. 4 (1995): 247–53.

Fitspatrik, Sheila [Sheila Fitzpatrick]. *Povsednevnyi stalinizm: Sotsial'naia istoriia Sovetskoi Rossii v 30-e gody; Gorod*. Translated by L. Iu. Lantina. Moscow: ROSSPEN, 2001.

Fitzpatrick, Sheila. "Ascribing Class: The Construction of Social Identity in Soviet Russia." In *Stalinism: New Directions*, edited by Sheila Fitzpatrick, 20–46. London: Routledge, 2000.

————. "Politics as Practice: Thoughts on a New Soviet Political History." *Kritika: Explorations in Russian and Eurasian History* 5, no. 1 (Winter 2004): 27–54.

————. *Tear Off the Masks! Identity and Imposture in Twentieth-Century Russia*. Princeton, NJ: Princeton University Press, 2005.

Fitzpatrick, Sheila, and Robert Gellately. "Introduction to the Practices of Denunciation in Modern European History." In "Practices of Denunciation in Modern European History, 1789–1989." Edited by Sheila Fitzpatrick and Robert Gellately. Special issue, *Journal of Modern History* 68, no. 4 (December 1996): 746–67.

Flam, Helena. *Soziologie der Emotionen: Eine Einführung*. Konstanz: UVK, 2002.

Foittsik, Ian [Jan Foitzik], ed. *Sovetskaia politika v otnoshenii Germanii, 1944–1954: Dokumenty*. Moscow: ROSSPEN, 2011.

Foitzik, Jan. "Die parteiinterne Behandlung der Geheimrede Chruschtschows auf dem XX. Parteitag der KPdSU durch die SED, die PVAP und die KPTsch." In *Tauwetter ohne Frühling*, edited by I. Kircheisen, 60–83.

————. *Inventar der Befehle des obersten Chefs der Sowjetischen Militäradministration in Deutschland (SMAD) 1945–1949.* Munich: K. G. Saur, 1995.

Foucault, Michel. *Die Ordnung der Dinge.* 12th edition. Translated by Ulrich Köppen. Frankfurt am Main: Suhrkamp, 1994.

Fowkes, Reuben. "The Role of Monumental Sculpture in the Construction of Socialist Space in Stalinist Hungary." In *Socialist Spaces: Sites of Everyday Life in the Eastern Bloc*, edited by David Crowley and Susan E. Reid, 65–84. Oxford: Berg, 2002.

Frevert, Ute. *Emotions in History: Lost and Found.* Budapest: Central European University Press, 2011.

————. *Gefühlspolitik: Friedrich II. als Herr über die Herzen?* Göttingen: Wallstein Verlag, 2011.

————. "Neue Politikgeschichte." In *Kompass der Geschichtswissenschaft*, edited by Joachim Eibach and Günther Lottes, 152–64. Göttingen: Vandenhoeck & Ruprecht, 2006.

————. *Vertrauen: Historische Annäherungen.* Göttingen: Vandenhoeck & Ruprecht, 2003.

Friedrich, Carl J. *The Pathology of Politics: Violence, Betrayal, Corruption, Secrecy and Propaganda.* New York: Harper and Row, 1972.

Friedrich, Carl J., and Zbigniew K. Brzezinski. *Totalitarian Dictatorship and Autocracy.* Cambridge, MA: Harvard University Press, 1965.

Fritzsche, Peter, and Jochen Hellbeck. "The New Man in Stalinist Russia and Nazi Germany." In *Beyond Totalitarianism: Stalinism and Nazism Compared*, edited by Michael Geyer and Sheila Fitzpatrick, 302–42. Cambridge: Cambridge University Press, 2008.

Führer, Karl Christian, and Corey Ross, eds. *Mass Media, Culture and Society in Twentieth-Century Germany.* Basingstoke: Palgrave Macmillan, 2006.

Fukuyama, Francis. *Trust: The Social Virtues and the Creation of Prosperity.* New York: Penguin Books, 1995.

Fulbrook, Mary. *Dissonant Lives: Generations and Violence through the German Dictatorships.* Oxford: Oxford University Press, 2011.

————. *The People's State: East German Society from Hitler to Honecker.* New Haven, CT: Yale University Press, 2005.

Gaßner, Hubertus, Irmgard Schleier, and Karin Stengel, eds. *Agitation zum Glück: Sowjetische Kunst der Stalinzeit.* Bremen: Ed. Temmen, 1994.

Ganzenmüller, Jörg. "Bruderzwist im Kalten Krieg: Sowjetisch-tschechoslowakische Länderspiele im Umfeld des 'Prager Frühlings.'" In *Sport zwischen Ost und West: Beiträge zur Sportgeschichte Osteuropas im 19. und 20. Jahrhundert*, edited by Arié Malz, Stefan Rohdewald, and Stefan Wiederkehr, 113–30. Osnabrück: Fibre, 2007.

Gaudenzi, Bianca. "Dictators for Sale: The Commercialisation of the Duce and the Führer in Fascist Italy and Nazi Germany." In *Rewriting German History: New Perspectives on Modern Germany*, edited by Jan Rüger and Nikolaus Wachsmann, 267–87. London: Palgrave Macmillan, 2015.

Gebhardt, Miriam. *Als die Soldaten kamen: Die Vergewaltigung deutscher Frauen am Ende des Zweiten Weltkriegs*. Munich: Deutsche Verlags-Anstalt, 2015.

Geertz, Clifford. "Centers, Kings, and Charisma: Reflections on the Symbolics of Power." In *Rites of Power: Symbolism, Ritual, and Politics since the Middle Ages*, edited by Sean Wilentz, 13–38. Philadelphia: University of Pennsylvania Press, 1985.

Gentile, Emilio. *Politics as Religion*. Translated by George Staunton. Princeton, NJ: Princeton University Press, 2006.

Gerasimov, Ilya, Sergey Glebov, Jan Kusber, Marina Mogilner, and Alexander Semyonov. "New Imperial History and the Challenges of Empire." In *Empire Speaks Out: Languages of Rationalization and Self-Description in the Russian Empire*, edited by Ilya Gerasimov, Jan Kusber, and Alexander Semyonov, 3–32. Boston: Brill, 2009.

Gerwarth, Robert. *The Bismarck Myth: Weimar Germany and the Legacy of the Iron Chancellor*. Oxford: Oxford University Press, 2005.

Gerwarth, Robert, and Lucy Riall. "Fathers of the Nation? Bismarck, Garibaldi and the Cult of Memory in Germany and Italy." *European History Quarterly* 39, no. 3 (July 2009): 388–413.

Getty, J. Arch. *Practicing Stalinism: Bolsheviks, Boyars, and the Persistence of Tradition*. New Haven, CT: Yale University Press, 2013.

Geyer, Michael, and Sheila Fitzpatrick, eds. *Beyond Totalitarianism: Stalinism and Nazism Compared*. Cambridge: Cambridge University Press, 2009.

Gibas, Monika. "'Bonner Ultras,' 'Kriegstreiber' und 'Schlotbarone': Die Bundesrepublik als Feindbild der DDR in den fünfziger Jahren." In *Unsere Feinde: Konstruktionen des Anderen im Sozialismus*, edited by Silke Satjukow and Rainer Gries, 75–106. Leipzig: Universitätsverlag, 2004.

———. "Die 'einheitliche öffentliche Meinung': Zur Kampagnenpolitik und Kommunikationspraxis." In *Zwischen "Mosaik" und "Einheit": Zeitschriften in der DDR*, edited by Simone Barck, Martina Langermann, and Siegfried Lokatis, 540–49. Berlin: Links, 1999.

Gibas, Monika, and Rainer Gries. "'Vorschlag für den Ersten Mai: Die Führung zieht am Volk vorbei!'; Überlegungen zur Geschichte der Tribüne in der DDR." *Deutschland Archiv* 28, Heft 5 (1995): 481–94.

Gieseke, Jens. *Der Mielke-Konzern: Die Geschichte der Stasi 1945–1990*. Munich: Deutsche Verlags-Anstalt, 2006.

Gill, Graeme. "Personality Cult, Political Culture and Party Structure." *Studies in Comparative Communism* 17, no. 2 (Summer 1984): 111–21.

———. *Symbols and Legitimacy in Soviet Politics*. Cambridge: Cambridge University Press, 2011.

Giloi, Eva. *Monarchy, Myth and Material Culture in Germany, 1750–1950*. Cambridge: Cambridge University Press, 2011.

———. "'So Writes the Hand that Swings the Sword': Autograph Hunting and Royal Charisma in the German Empire, 1861–1888." In *Constructing Charisma: Celebrity, Fame, and Power in Nineteenth-Century Europe*, edited by Edward Berenson and Eva Giloi, 41–51. New York: Berghahn Books, 2010.

Giunter, Khans [Hans Günter]. "Arkhetipy sovetskoi kul'tury." In *Sotsrealisticheskii kanon*, edited by Kh. Giunter and E. A. Dobrenko, 743–84.

———. "Totalitarnoe gosudarstvo kak sintez iskusstv." In *Sotsrealisticheskii kanon*, edited by Kh. Giunter and E. Dobrenko, 7–15.

Giunter, Khans, and Evgenii Dobrenko, eds. *Sotsrealisticheskii kanon*. St. Petersburg: Akademicheskii Proekt, 2000.

Giunter, Khans, and S. Khensgen [Sabine Hänsgen], eds. *Sovetskaia vlast' i media: Sbornik statei*. St. Petersburg: Akademicheskii proekt, 2006.

Giustino, Cathleen M., Catherine J. Plum, and Alexander Vari, eds. *Socialist Escapes: Breaking Away from Ideology and Everyday Routine in Eastern Europe, 1945–1989*. New York: Berghahn, 2013.

Gleason, Abbott, Peter Kenez, and Richard Stites, eds. *Bolshevik Culture: Experiment and Order in the Russian Revolution*. Bloomington: Indiana University Press, 1985.

Glebkin, V. V. *Ritual v sovetskoi kul'ture*. Moscow: Ianus-K, 1998.

Glyptis, Leda. "Living Up to the Father: The National Identity Prescriptions of Remembering Atatürk; His Homes, His Grave, His Temple." *National Identities* 10, no. 4 (December 2008): 353–72.

Goltermann, Svenja. *Die Gesellschaft der Überlebenden: Kriegsheimkehrer und ihre Gewalterfahrungen im Zweiten Weltkrieg*. Munich: Deutsche Verlags-Anstalt, 2009.

Golubev, Aleksei. "Zapadnyi nabliudatel' i zapadnyi vzgliad v affektivnom menedzhmente sovetskoi sub"ektivnosti." In *Posle Stalina: Pozdnesovetskaia sub"ektivnost' (1953–1985 gg.)*, edited by Anatolii Pinskii, 219–54. St. Petersburg: EUSPB, 2018.

Gonzalez, Servando. *The Secret Fidel Castro: Deconstructing the Symbol*. Oakland, CA: Spooks Books, 2001.

Gorsuch, Anne E., and Diane P. Koenker, eds. *Turizm: The Russian and East European Tourist under Capitalism and Socialism*. Ithaca, NY: Cornell University Press, 2006.

Goscilo, Helena. *Putin as Celebrity and Cultural Icon*. London: Routledge, 2012.

Govier, Trude. *Social Trust and Human Communities*. Montreal: McGill-Queen's University Press, 1997.

Gozman, Leonid, and Alexander Etkind. "Kul't vlasti: Struktura totalitarnogo soznaniia." In *Osmyslit' kul't Stalina*, edited by Kh. Kobo, 337–71.

Gradel, Ittai. *Emperor Worship and Roman Religion*. Oxford: Clarendon Press, 2002.

Granville, Johanna. "Ulbricht in October 1956: Survival of the Spitzbart during Destalinization." *Journal of Contemporary History* 41, no. 3 (July 2006): 477–502.

Gries, Rainer."'… deckt alle mit den Tisch der Republik!': Kleine Geschichte der Geburtstagsgeschenke." In *Wiedergeburten: Zur Geschichte der runden Jahrestage der DDR*, edited by Monika Gibas, Rainer Gries, Barbara Jakoby, and Doris Müller, 86–90. Leipzig: Leipziger Universitätsverlag, 1999.

———. "Die Heldenbühne der DDR: Zur Einführung." In *Sozialistische Helden*, edited by S. Satjukow and R. Gries, 84–100.

————. *Die Rationen-Gesellschaft: Versorgungskampf und Vergleichsmentalität; Leipzig, München und Köln nach dem Kriege.* Münster: Westfälisches Dampfboot, 1991.

————. "Dramaturgie der Utopie: Kulturgeschichte der Rituale der Arbeiter-und-Bauern-Macht." In *Arbeiter im Staatssozialismus: Ideologischer Anspruch und soziale Wirklichkeit,* edited by Peter Hübner, Christoph Kleßmann, and Klaus Tenfelde, 191–214. Cologne: Böhlau, 2005.

————. "Mythen des Anfangs." *Aus Politik und Zeitgeschichte: Beilage zur Zeitung Das Parlament,* nos. 18–19 (2005): 12–18. http://www.bpb.de/apuz/29070/mythen -des-anfangs.

————. "Propagandageschichte als Kulturgeschichte: Methodische Erwartungen und Erfahrungen." *Deutschland Archiv* 33, Heft 4 (2000): 558–70.

————. "Zur Ästhetik und Architektur von Propagemen: Überlegungen zu einer Propagandageschichte als Kulturgeschichte." In *Kultur der Propaganda,* edited by Rainer Gries and Wolfgang Schmale, 9–35. Bochum: Verlag Dr. Dieter Winkler, 2005.

Gries, Rainer, and Monika Gibas. "Die Inszenierung des sozialistischen Deutschlands: Geschichte und Dramaturgie der Dezennienfeiern in der DDR." In *Wiedergeburten: Zur Geschichte der runden Jahrestage der DDR,* edited by Monika Gibas, Rainer Gries, Barbara Jakoby, and Doris Müller, 11–40. Leipzig: Leipziger Universitätsverlag, 1999.

Grigorov, Dimitar. "Could a Communist Leader be a Godfather?" In *Bridging the Gap: Sources, Methodology and Approaches to Religion in History,* edited by Joaquim Carvalho, 211–54. Pisa: Pisa University Press, 2008.

Groebner, Valentin. "Losing Face, Saving Face: Noses and Honour in the Late Medieval Town." *History Workshop Journal,* no. 40 (1995): 1–15.

Gromov, E. S. *Stalin: Vlast' i iskusstvo.* Moscow: Respublika, 1998.

Großbölting, Thomas. *Der Tod des Diktators: Ereignis und Erinnerung im 20. Jahrhundert.* Göttingen: Vandenhoeck & Ruprecht, 2011.

Grossmann, Atina. *Jews, Germans, and Allies: Close Encounters in Occupied Germany.* Princeton, NJ: Princeton University Press, 2007.

Groys, Boris. *Gesamtkunstwerk Stalin: Die gespaltene Kultur der Sowjetunion.* Munich: Hanser, 1988.

Guseinov, G. Ch. *Karta nashei rodiny: Ideologema mezhdu slovom i telom.* Moscow: OGI, 2005.

Halfin, Igal. *From Darkness to Light: Class, Consciousness, and Salvation in Revolutionary Russia.* Pittsburgh, PA: University of Pittsburgh Press, 2000.

————. *Stalinist Confessions: Messianism and Terror at the Leningrad Communist University.* Pittsburgh, PA: University of Pittsburgh Press, 2009.

Hanioğlu, M. Şükrü. *Atatürk: An Intellectual Biography.* Princeton, NJ: Princeton University Press, 2017.

Härter, Karl, and Cecilia Nubola, eds. *Grazia e giustizia: Figure della clemenza fra tardo Medioevo ed età contemporanea.* Bologna: Società editrice il Mulino, 2011.

Hartmann, Anne, and Wolfram Eggeling. *Sowjetische Präsenz im kulturellen Leben der SBZ und frühen DDR, 1945–1953*. Berlin: Akademie, 1998.

Hartmann, Annelie [Anne Hartmann]. *Die Gesellschaft für Deutsch-Sowjetische Freundschaft: Zum Aufbau einer Institution in der SBZ/DDR zwischen deutschen Politzwängen und sowjetischer; Analysen (Aus Deutschlands Mitte)*. Berlin: Akademie, 1993.

Harvey, Elizabeth, Johannes Hürter, Maiken Umbach, and Andreas Wirsching, eds. *Private Life and Privacy in Nazi Germany*. Cambridge: Cambridge University Press, 2020.

Haumann, Heiko, and Brigitte Studer, eds. *Stalinistische Subjekte: Individuum und System in der Sowjetunion und der Komintern, 1925–1953*. Zürich: Chronos, 2005.

Häusermann, Jürg, ed. *Inszeniertes Charisma: Medien und Persönlichkeit*. Tübingen: Niemeyer, 2001.

Heal, Felicity. *The Power of Gifts: Gift-Exchange in Early Modern England*. Oxford: Oxford University Press, 2014.

Hegedüs, András B., and Manfred Wilke, eds. *Satelliten nach Stalins Tod: Der "Neue Kurs," 17. Juni 1953 in der DDR, Ungarische Revolution 1956*. Berlin: Akademie, 2000.

Hein, Heidi. *Der Pilsudski-Kult und seine Bedeutung für den polnischen Staat, 1926–1939*. Marburg: Herder-Institut, 2001.

Hein-Kircher, Heidi. "'Deutsche Mythen' und ihre Wirkung." *Aus Politik und Zeitgeschichte: Beilage zur Zeitung Das Parlament*, nos. 13–14 (2013). http://www.bpb.de/apuz/156772/deutsche-mythen-und-ihre-wirkung?p=all.

———. "Führerkult und Führermythos: Theoretische Reflexionen zur Einführung." In *Der Führer im Europa des 20. Jahrhunderts*, edited by Heidi Hein Kircher and Benno Ennker, 3–23. Marburg: Herder-Institut, 2010.

Hein-Kircher, Heidi, and Hans Henning Hahn, eds. *Politische Mythen im 19. und 20. Jahrhundert in Mittel- und Osteuropa*. Marburg: Herder-Institut, 2006.

Hellbeck, Jochen. "Alltag in der Ideologie: Leben im Stalinismus." *Mittelweg 36: Zeitschrift des Hamburger Instituts für Sozialforschung* 19, Heft 1 (2010): 19–32.

———. *Revolution on My Mind: Writing a Diary under Stalin*. Cambridge, MA: Harvard University Press, 2006.

Heller, Klaus, and Jan Plamper, eds. *Personality Cults in Stalinism—Personenkulte im Stalinismus*. Göttingen: V & R Unipress, 2004.

Herzfeld, Michael. *The Social Production of Indifference: Exploring the Symbolic Roots of Western Bureaucracy*. New York: Berg, 1991.

Herzog, Dagmar. "Desperately Seeking Normality: Sex and Marriage in the Wake of the War." In *Life After Death: Approaches to a Cultural and Social History during the 1940s and 1950s*, edited by Richard Bessel, 161–92. Cambridge: Cambridge University Press, 2003.

Hickethier, Knut. *Geschichte des deutschen Fernsehens*. Weimar: J. B. Metzler, 1998.

Hirsch, Francine. *Empire of Nations: Ethnographic Knowledge and the Making of the Soviet Union*. Ithaca, NY: Cornell University Press, 2005.

Hobsbawm, Eric. "Introduction: Inventing Traditions." In *The Invention of Tradition*, edited by Eric Hobsbawm and Terence Ranger, 1–14. Cambridge: Cambridge University Press, 2013.

———. *The Age of Extremes: The Short Twentieth Century, 1914–1991*. London: Michael Joseph, 1994.

Hobsbawm, Eric, and Terence Ranger, eds. *The Invention of Tradition*. Cambridge: Cambridge University Press, 1983.

Hollander, Paul. *From Benito to Hugo Chavez: Intellectuals and a Century of Political Hero Worship*. Cambridge: Cambridge University Press, 2017.

Holquist, Peter. "'Information is the Alpha and Omega of Our Work': Bolshevik Surveillance in its Pan-European Context." *Journal of Modern History* 69, no. 3 (September 1997): 415–50.

Holzweißig, Gunter. *"Die schärfste Waffe der Partei": Eine Mediengeschichte der DDR*. Cologne: Böhlau, 2002.

———. *Zensur ohne Zensor: Die SED-Informationsdiktatur*. Bonn: Bouvier, 1997.

Hoppe, Bert. "Stalin und die KPD in der Weimarer Republik." In *Stalin und die Deutschen: Neue Beiträge der Forschung*, edited by Jürgen Zarusky, 19–42. Munich: Oldenbourg, 2006.

Horváth, Sándor. *Stalinism Reloaded: Everyday Life in Stalin-City, Hungary*. Bloomington: Indiana University Press, 2017.

Hosking, Geoffrey. "Patronage and the Russian State." *Slavonic and East European Review* 78, no. 2 (April 2000): 301–20.

———. "Trust and Distrust in the USSR: An Overview." In "Trust and Distrust in the USSR." Edited by Geoffrey Hosking. Special issue, *Slavonic and East European Review* 91, no. 1 (January 2013): 1–25.

Hülbusch, Nikolas. "Dzugasvili der Zweite: Das Stalin-Bild im sowjetischen Spielfilm (1934–1953)." In *Personality Cults in Stalinism—Personenkulte im Stalinismus*, edited by K. Heller and J. Plamper, 207–38.

———. *Im Spiegelkabinett des Diktators: Stalin als Filmheld im sowjetischen Spielfilm (1937–1953)*. Alfeld: Coppi-Verlag, 2001.

Humphrey, Caroline. "Dangerous Words: Taboos, Evasions, and Silence in Soviet Russia." *Forum for Anthropology and Culture*, no. 2 (2005): 374–96.

Hung, Chang-tai. "The Cult of the Red Martyr: Politics of Commemoration in China." *Journal of Contemporary History* 43, no. 2 (April 2008): 279–304.

Hunt, Lynn. *The Family Romance of the French Revolution*. London: University of California Press, 1992.

Hurwitz, Harald. *Die Stalinisierung der SED: Zum Verlust von Freiräumen und sozialdemokratischen Identität in den Vorständen, 1946–1949*. Opladen: Westdeutscher Verlag, 1997.

Imbusch, Peter. *Moderne und Gewalt: Zivilisationstheoretische Perspektiven auf das 20.Jahrhundert*. Wiesbaden: VS Verlag für Sozialwissenschaften, 2005.

Inkeles, Alex, and Raymond A. Bauer. *The Soviet Citizen: Daily Life in a Totalitarian Society*. Cambridge, MA: Harvard University Press, 1961.

Ironside, Kristy. "'I Beg You Not to Reject My Plea': The Late Stalinist Welfare State and the Politics of One-Time Monetary Aid, 1946–1953." *Journal of Social History* 51, no. 4 (Summer 2018): 1045–68.

Izard, K. E. [Carroll E. Izard]. *Psikhologiia emotsii.* Translated by A. Tatlibaeva. St. Petersburg: Piter, 2006.

Izmozik, V. S. *Glaza i ushi rezhima: Gosudarstvennyi politicheskii kontrol' za naseleniem Sovetskoi Rossii v 1918–1928 godakh.* St. Petersburg: Izdatel'stvo Sankt-Peterburgskogo universiteta ekonomiki i finansov, 1995.

———. "Perliustratsiia v pervye gody sovetskoi vlasti." *Voprosy istorii,* no. 8 (1995): 26–35.

Jajeśniak-Quast, Dagmara. *Stahlgiganten in der sozialistischen Transformation: Nowa Huta in Krakau, EKO in Eisenhüttenstade und Kunčice in Ostrava.* Wiesbaden: Harrassowitz, 2010.

Jarausch, Konrad H., and Hannes Siegrist, eds. *Amerikanisierung und Sowjetisierung in Deutschland, 1945–1970.* Frankfurt am Main: Campus, 1997.

Jensen, Uffa, and Daniel Morat, eds. *Rationalisierungen des Gefühls: Zum Verhältnis von Wissenschaft und Emotionen, 1880–1930.* Munich: Fink, 2008.

Jessen, Ralph. "Diktatorische Herrschaft als kommunikative Praxis: Überlegungen zum Zusammenhang von 'Bürokratie' und Sprachnormierung in der DDR-Geschichte." In *Akten. Eingaben. Schaufenster: Die DDR und ihre Texte,* edited by Alf Lüdtke and Peter Becker, 57–78. Berlin: Akademie, 1997.

———. "Semantic Strategies of Inclusion and Exclusion in the German Democratic Republic (1949–1989)." In *Political Languages,* edited by W. Steinmetz, 275–91.

Jones, Polly. "From Stalinism to Post-Stalinism: De-Mythologising Stalin, 1953–1956." In *Redefining Stalinism,* edited by Harold Shukman, 127–45. London: Frank Cass, 2003.

———. *Myth, Memory, Trauma: Rethinking the Stalinist Past in the Soviet Union, 1953–1970.* New Haven, CT: Yale University Press, 2013.

———. *The Dilemmas of De-Stalinization: Negotiating Cultural and Social Change in the Khrushchev Era.* London: Routledge, 2009.

Jütte, Robert. *Geschichte der Sinne: Von der Antike bis zum Cyberspace.* Munich: C. H. Beck, 2000.

Kaiser, Monika. "Sowjetischer Einfluss auf die ostdeutsche Politik und Verwaltung 1945–1970." In *Amerikanisierung und Sowjetisierung,* edited by K. Jarausch and H. Siegrist, 111–33.

Kämper, Heidrun. "Telling the Truth: Counter-Discourses in Diaries Under Totalitarian Regimes (Nazi Germany and Early GDR)." In *Political Languages,* edited by W. Steinmetz, 215–41.

Kantorowicz, Ernst H. *Die zwei Körper des Königs: Eine Studie zur politischen Theologie des Mittelalters.* Munich: Deutscher Taschenbuch Verlag, 1994.

———. *The King's Two Bodies: A Study in Medieval Political Theology.* 7th edition. Princeton, NJ: Princeton University Press, 1997.

Karl, Lars. "'Von Helden und Menschen...': Der zweite Weltkrieg im sowjetischen Spielfilm und dessen Rezeption in der DDR, 1945–1965." PhD diss., University of Tübingen, 2002.

Karlsch, Rainer, and Jochen Laufer, eds. *Sowjetische Demontagen in Deutschland, 1944–1949: Hintergründe, Ziele und Wirkungen.* Berlin: Duncker & Humblot, 2002.

Keller, Sven. *Volksgemeinschaft am Ende: Gesellschaft und Gewalt, 1944/45.* Munich: Oldenbourg Verlag, 2013.

Kelly, Catriona, and David Shepherd, eds. *Constructing Russian Culture in the Age of Revolution, 1881–1940.* New York: Oxford University Press, 1998.

Kenez, Peter. *The Birth of the Propaganda State: Soviet Methods of Mass Mobilization, 1917–1929.* Cambridge: Cambridge University Press, 1986.

Kershaw, Ian. *Hitler: 1889–1936.* Stuttgart: Deutsche Verlags-Anstalt, 1998.

———. *The 'Hitler Myth': Image and Reality in the Third Reich.* Oxford: Oxford University Press, 1987.

———. "'Working Towards the Führer': Reflections on the Nature of the Hitler Dictatorship." *Contemporary European History* 2, no. 2 (July 1993): 103–18.

Kershaw, Ian, and Moshe Lewin, eds. *Stalinism and Nazism: Dictatorships in Comparison.* Cambridge: Cambridge University Press, 1997.

Kessel, Martina. *Gewalt und Gelächter: "Deutschsein," 1914–1945.* Stuttgart: Steiner Verlag, 2019.

Kettner, P. "Die Fragen und die Freiheit." In *Die Fragen und die Freiheit: Schubladentexte aus der DDR*, edited by Torsten Hilse and Dieter Winkler, 17–52. Berlin: Verbum, 1999.

Khlevniuk, O. V. *Khoziain: Stalin i utverzhdenie stalinskoi diktatury.* Moscow: ROSSPEN, 2010.

Kienemann, Christoph. *Der koloniale Blick gen Osten: Osteuropa im Diskurs des Deutschen.* Paderborn: Schöningh, 2018.

Kircheisen, Inge, ed. *Tauwetter ohne Frühling: Das Jahr 1956 im Spiegel blockinterner Wandlungen und internationaler Krisen.* Berlin: Bugrim Berlin, 1995.

Kivelitz, Christoph. *Die Propagandaausstellung in europäischen Diktaturen: Konfrontation und Vergleich; Nationalismus in Deutschland, Faschismus in Italien und die UdSSR der Stalinzeit.* Bochum: Winkler, 1999.

Klaniczay, Gábor. *Holy Rulers and Blessed Princesses: Dynastic Cults in Medieval Central Europe.* Cambridge: Cambridge University Press, 2002.

Klark, K. [Katerina Clark]. "Polozhitel'nyi geroi kak verbal'naia ikona." In *Sotsrealisticheskii kanon*, edited by H. Giunter and E. Dobrenko, 569–84.

Klein, Angelika. "Zwischen Entstalinisierung und neostalinistischer Erstarrung: Die SED—Parteiorganisation Halle nach dem XX. Parteitag der KPdSU (eine Fallstudie)." In *Tauwetter ohne Frühling*, edited by I. Kircheisen, 113–25.

Klotz, Katharina. *Das politische Plakat der SBZ/DDR, 1945–1963: Zur politischen Ikonographie der sozialistischen Sichtagitation.* Aachen: Shaker Verlag, 2006.

———. "Führerfiguren und Vorbilder: Personenkult in der Ära Ulbricht." In *Parteiauftrag*, edited by D. Vorsteher, 322–36.

Kobo, Kh. [Juan Cobo], ed. *Osmyslit' kul't Stalina.* Moscow: Progress, 1989.

Koenen, Gerd. *Der Russland-Komplex: Die Deutschen und der Osten, 1900–1945.* Munich: C. H. Beck, 2005.

Kolesov, D. V. *I. V. Stalin: Pravo na vlast'.* Moscow: Moskovskii psikhologo-sotsial'nyi institut: Flinta, 2000.

———. *I. V. Stalin: Zagadki lichnosti.* Moscow: Moskovskii psikhologo-sotsial'nyi institut: Flinta, 2000.

Koleva, Daniela, ed. *Negotiating Normality: Everyday Lives in Socialist Institutions.* New Brunswick, NJ: Transaction, 2012.

Koller, Christian. "'Es ist zum Heulen': Emotionshistorische Zugänge zur Kulturgeschichte des Streikens." *Geschichte und Gesellschaft,* no. 1 (2010): 66–92.

Kolonitskii, B. I. *Simvoly vlasti i bor'ba za vlast': K izucheniiu politicheskoi kul'tury Rossiiskoi revoliutsii 1917 goda.* St. Petersburg: D. Bulanin, 2001.

Koselleck, Reinhart. "Einleitung." In *Die politische Totenkult: Kriegerdenkmäler in der Moderne,* edited by Reinhart Koselleck and Michael Jeismann, 9–20. Munich: Wilhelm Fink, 1994.

Koselleck, Reinhart, and Michael Jeismann, eds. *Der politische Totenkult: Kriegerdenkmäler in der Moderne.* Munich: Fink, 1994.

Kotkin, Stephen. *Magnetic Mountain: Stalinism as a Civilization.* Berkeley: University of California Press, 1995.

Kowalczuk, Ilko-Sascha. "Zwischen Hoffnungen und Krisen: Das Jahr 1956 und seine Rückwirkungen auf die DDR." In *Jahrbuch für Historische Kommunismusforschung,* 15–33. Berlin: Aufbau-Verlag, 2006.

Kraa, Detlev, and Ralf Rytlewski. "Politische Rituale in der UdSSR und der DDR." *Aus Politik und Zeitgeschichte* 87, no. 3 (1987): 33–48.

Kramer, Mark. "The Soviet Union and the Founding of the German Democratic Republic: 50 Years Later—A Review Article." *Europe-Asia Studies* 51, no. 6 (September 1999): 1093–116.

Krom, M. M. "Novaia politicheskaia istoriia: Temy, podkhody, problemy." In *Novaia politicheskaia istoriia: Sbornik nauchnykh rabot,* edited by B. I. Kolonitskii, M. M. Krom, and N. D. Potapov, 7–17. St. Petersburg: Aleteiia, 2004.

Krylova, Anna. *Soviet Women in Combat: A History of Violence on the Eastern Front.* Cambridge: Cambridge University Press, 2010.

———. "The Tenacious Liberal Subject in Soviet Studies." *Kritika: Explorations in Russian and Eurasian History* 1, no. 1 (Winter 2000): 119–46.

Lamla, Jörn, and Sighard Neckel, eds. *Politisierter Konsum, konsumierte Politik.* Wiesbaden: VS Verlag für Sozialwissenschaft, 2006.

Landweer, Hilge. *Scham und Macht: Phänomenologische Untersuchungen zur Sozialität eines Gefühls.* Tübingen: Mohr Siebeck, 1999.

Landwehr, Achim. "Diskurs-Macht-Wissen: Perspektiven einer Kulturgeschichte des Politischen." *Archiv für Kulturgeschichte* 85, Heft 1 (2003): 71–117.

Lazitch, Branko M. "Stalin's Massacre of the Foreign Communist Leaders." In *The Comintern: Historical Highlights, Essays, Recollections, Documents,* edited by Milorad M. Drachkovitch and Branko M. Lazitch, 139–83. New York: Praeger, 1966.

Leach Neil, ed. *Architecture and Revolution: Contemporary Perspectives on Central and Eastern Europe*. London: Routledge, 1999.

Lebow, Katherina. *Unfinished Utopia: Nowa Huta, Stalinism, and Polish Society, 1949–1956*. Ithaca, NY: Cornell University Press, 2013.

Ledderose, Lothar. "Die Gedenkhalle für Mao Zedong: Ein Beispiel von Gedächtnisarchitektur." In *Kultur und Gedächtnis*, edited by Jan Assmann and Tonio Hölscher, 311–39. Frankfurt am Main: Suhrkamp, 1988.

Leese, Daniel. *Mao Cult: Rhetoric and Ritual in China's Cultural Revolution*. Cambridge: Cambridge University Press, 2011.

———. "The Cult of Personality and Symbolic Politics." In *The Oxford Handbook of the History of Communism*, edited by Stephen A. Smith. Oxford: Oxford University Press, 2017.

Le Gof, Zh. [Jacques Le Goff]. "Iavliaetsia li vse zhe politicheskaia istoriia stanovym khrebtom istorii?" *Thesis*, no. 4 (1994): 177–92.

Lemke, Michael, ed. *Sowjetisierung und Eigenständigkeit in der SBZ/DDR (1945–1953)*. Cologne: Böhlau, 1999.

Lenoe, Matthew E. *Closer to the Masses: Culture, Social Revolution, and Soviet Newspapers*. Cambridge, MA: Harvard University Press, 2004.

Leo, Annette. "'Deutschlands unsterblicher Sohn…': Der Held des Widerstandes Ernst Thälmann." In *Sozialistische Helden*, edited by S. Satjukow and R. Gries, 101–14.

———. "'Stimme der Faust der Nation': Thälmann-Kult kontra Antifaschismus." In *Die geteilte Vergangenheit: Zum Umgang mit Nationalsozialismus und Widerstand in beiden deutschen Staaten*, edited by Jürgen Danyel, 205–11. Berlin: Akademie, 1995.

Lepsius, Rainer. "Das Modell der charismatischen Herrschaft und seine Anwendbarkeit auf den 'Führerstaat' Adolf Hitlers." In *Demokratie in Deutschland: Soziologisch-historische Konstellationsanalysen; Ausgewählte Aufsätze*, edited by Rainer Lepsius, 95–132. Göttingen: Vandenhoeck & Ruprecht, 1993.

Lieven, Dominic. *Empire: The Russian Empire and its Rivals*. London: John Murray, 2000.

Lim, Jie-Hyun, and Karen Petrone, eds. *Gender Politics and Mass Dictatorship: Global Perspectives*. Basingstoke: Palgrave, 2011.

Liman, Herbert. *Mehr Licht: Geschichte der Berliner Straßenbeleuchtung*. Berlin: Haude und Spener, 2000.

Lindenberger, Thomas. "Alltagsgeschichte und ihr möglicher Beitrag zu einer Gesellschaftsgeschichte der DDR." In *Die Grenzen der Diktatur: Staat und Gesellschaft in der DDR*, edited by Richard Bessel and Ralph Jessen, 298–325. Göttingen: Vandenhoeck & Ruprecht, 1996.

———. "Die Diktatur der Grenzen: Zur Einleitung." In *Herrschaft und Eigen-Sinn in der Diktatur: Studien zur Gesellschaftsgeschichte der DDR*, edited by Thomas Lindenberger, 13–44. Cologne: Böhlau, 1999.

———, ed. *Massenmedien im Kalten Krieg: Akteure, Bilder, Resonanzen*. Cologne: Böhlau, 2006.

————. *Volkspolizei: Herrschaftspraxis und öffentliche Ordnung im SED-Staat.* Cologne: Böhlau, 2003.

Livschiz, Ann. "De-Stalinizing Soviet Childhood: The Quest for Moral Rebirth, 1953–58." In *Dilemmas of De-Stalinization,* edited by P. Jones, 117–34.

Lobacheva, G. V. *Samoderzhets i Rossiia: Obraz tsaria v massovom soznanii rossiian (konets XIX—nachalo XX veka).* Saratov: Saratov gos. tekhn. u-nt, 1999.

Loewenstein, Karl E. "Re-Emergence of Public Opinion in the Soviet Union: Khrushchev and Responses to the Secret Speech." *Europe-Asia Studies* 58, no. 8 (December 2006): 1329–45.

Löhmann, Reinhard. *Der Stalinmythos: Studien zur Sozialgeschichte des Personenkultes in der Sowjetunion (1929–1935).* Münster: Lit, 1990.

Loiperdinger, Martin, Rudolf Herz, and Ulrich Pohlmann, eds. *Führerbilder: Hitler, Mussolini, Roosevelt, Stalin in Fotografie und Film.* Munich: Piper, 1995.

Lokatis, Siegfried. "Berliner Buchschaufenster im Kalten Krieg." In *Schaufenster der Systemkonkurrenz: Die Region Berlin-Brandenburg im Kalten Krieg,* edited by Michael Lemke, 297–316. Cologne: Böhlau, 2006.

Luckey, Heiko. *Personifizierte Ideologie: Zur Konstruktion, Funktion und Rezeption von Identifikationsfiguren im Nationalsozialismus und im Stalinismus.* Göttingen: V & R unipress, 2008.

Lüdtke, Alf. "Einleitung: Herrschaft als soziale Praxis." In *Herrschaft als soziale Praxis: Historische und sozialanthropologische Studien,* edited by Alf Lüdtke, 9–63. Göttingen: Vandenhoeck & Ruprecht, 1991.

————, ed. *Everyday Life in Mass Dictatorships: Collusion and Evasion.* New York: Palgrave, 2016.

————. "Geschichte und Eigensinn." In *Alltagskultur, Subjektivität und Geschichte: Zur Theorie und Praxis von Alltagsgeschichte,* edited by Berliner Geschichtswerkstatt, 139–53. Münster: Westfälisches Dampfboot, 1994.

Lüdtke, Alf, and Gerhard Fürmetz. "Denunziation und Denunzianten: Politische Teilnahme oder Selbstüberwachung?" *Sozialwissenschaftliche Informationen* 27, Heft 2 (1998): 80–86.

Ludwig, Andreas. *Eisenhüttenstadt: Wandel einer industriellen Gründungsstadt in fünfzig Jahren.* Potsdam: Brandenburgische Landeszentrale für politische Bildung, 2000.

Luhmann, Niklas. *Vertrauen: Ein Mechanismus der Reduktion sozialer Komplexität.* Stuttgart: Lucius & Lucius, 1968.

Lukin, P. V. *Narodnie predstavleniia o gosudarstvennoi vlasti v Rossii XVII veka.* Moscow: Nauka, 2000.

Maertz, Gregory. *Nostalgia for the Future: Modernism and Heterogeneity in the Visual Arts of Nazi Germany.* Stuttgart: Ibidem-Verlag, 2019.

Mählert, Ulrich. *Blaue Hemden—Rote Fahnen: Die Geschichte der Freien Deutschen Jugend.* Opladen: Leske + Budrich, 1996.

————. *Die Freie Deutsche Jugend: Von den "antifaschistischen Jugendausschüssen" zur SED-Massenorganisation; Die Erfassung der Jugend in der sowjetischen Besatzungszone.* Paderborn: Schöningh, 1995.

———. "'Die gesamte junge Generation für den Sozialismus begeistern': Zur Geschichte der Freien Deutschen Jugend." In *Der SED-Staat: Neues über eine vergangene Diktatur*, edited by Jürgen Weber and Thomas Ammer, 73–98. Munich: Olzog, 1994.

Majstorović, Vojin. "The Red Army in Yugoslavia, 1944–1945." *Slavic Review* 75, no. 2 (Summer 2016): 396–421.

Malycha, Andreas. *Die SED: Geschichte ihrer Stalinisierung*. Paderborn: Schöningh, 2000.

Mannheim, Karl. "Das Problem der Generationen." In *Wissenssoziologie*, edited by Karl Mannheim and Kurt H. Wolff, 509–65. Berlin: Luchterhand, 1970.

Martin, Terry. *The Affirmative Action Empire: Nations and Nationalism in the Soviet Union, 1923–1939*. Ithaca, NY: Cornell University Press, 2001.

Mauss, Marcel. *Die Gabe: Form und Funktion des Austausches in archaischen Gesellschaften*. Translated by Eva Moldenhauer. Frankfurt am Main: Suhrkamp, 1968.

McDermott, Kevin. "Stalinist Terror in the Comintern." *Journal of Contemporary History* 30, no. 1 (January 1995): 111–30.

Medvedev, R. A. *O Staline i stalinizme*. Moscow: Progress, 1990.

Medvedov, R. A., and D. Ermakov. *Seryi kardinal: M. A. Suslov; Politicheskii portret*. Moscow: Respublika, 1992.

Medvedev, Zh. A. *Neizvestnyi Stalin*. Moscow: AST, 2004.

Mergel, Thomas. "Überlegungen zu einer Kulturgeschichte der Politik." *Geschichte und Gesellschaft* 28, Heft 4 (2002): 574–606.

Merkel, Ina, *Utopie und Bedürfnis: Die Geschichte der Konsumkultur in der DDR*. Cologne: Böhlau, 1999.

Merl, Stephan. *Politische Kommunikation in der Diktatur: Deutschland und die Sowjetunion im Vergleich*. Göttingen: Wallstein, 2012.

Mertsalov, A. N., comp. *Istoriia i stalinizm*. Moscow: Politizdat, 1991.

Meuschel, Sigrid. *Legitimation und Parteiherrschaft: Zum Paradox von Stabilität und Revolution in der DDR, 1945–1989*. Frankfurt am Main: Suhrkamp, 1992.

Miller, Frank J. *Folklore for Stalin: Russian Folklore and Pseudofolklore of the Stalin Era*. Armonk, NY: M. E. Sharp, 1990.

Mironenko, Sergei, Lutz Niethammer, and Alexander von Plato, eds. *Sowjetische Speziallager in Deutschland 1945 bis 1950*. 2 vols. Berlin: Akademie, 1998.

Misztal, Barbara. *Trust in Modern Societies: The Search for the Bases of Social Order*. Cambridge: Polity Press, 1996.

Mohrmann, Sibylle. "Male Heroes and Female Comrades: The Image of the Russians in Soviet Films in Post-War Berlin." In *Sovietization of Eastern Europe*, edited by B. Apor, P. Apor, and E. A. Rees, 115–32.

Möller, Frank, ed. *Charismatische Führer der deutschen Nation*. Munich: Oldenbourg, 2004.

Montagu, Ashley. *The Anatomy of Swearing*. New York: Macmillan, 1967.

Moor, Robert Laurence. *Selling God: American Religion in the Marketplace of Culture*. Oxford: Oxford University Press, 1994.

Morgan, Kevin, ed. "Communism and the Leader Cult." Special issue, *Twentieth Century Communism*, no. 1 (May 2009).

———. *International Communism and the Cult of the Individual: Leaders, Tribunes and Martyrs under Lenin and Stalin*. London: Palgrave, 2017.

Morina, Christina. "Instructed Silence, Constructed Memory: The SED and the Return of German Prisoners of War as 'War Criminals' from the Soviet Union to East Germany, 1950–1956." *Contemporary European History* 13, no. 3 (August 2004): 323–43.

———. *Legacies of Stalingrad: Remembering the Eastern Front in Germany since 1945*. Cambridge: Cambridge University Press, 2011.

Mosse, George L. *The Nationalization of the Masses: Political Symbolism and Mass Movements in Germany from the Napoleonic Wars through the Third Reich*. New York: Howard Fertig, 1975.

Mudragei, V. I., and V. I. Usanov, comps. *Kvintessentsiia: Filosofskii al'manakh*. Moscow: Politizdat, 1990.

Mühlberg, Dietrich. "Alltag in der Medienöffentlichkeit: Illustrierte Zeitschriften und Magazine als Quellen kulturhistorischer Forschung." In *Zwischen "Mosaik" und "Einheit": Zeitschriften in der DDR*, edited by Simone Barck, Martina Langermann, and Siegfried Lokatis, 32–47. Berlin: Links, 1999.

Mühlberg, Felix. *Bürger, Bitten und Behörden: Geschichte der Eingabe in der DDR*. Berlin: Dietz, 2004.

Muir, Edward. *Ritual in Early Modern Europe*. Cambridge: Cambridge University Press, 1997.

Müller, Christian Th. "'O Sowjetmensch!': Beziehungen von sowjetischen Streitkräften und DDR-Gesellschaft zwischen Ritual und Alltag." In *Ankunft-Alltag-Ausreise: Migration und interkulturelle Begegnung in der DDR-Gesellschaft*, edited by Christian Th. Müller and Patrice G. Poutrus, 17–134. Cologne: Böhlau, 2005.

Müller, Doris. "'Wir bauen die erste sozialistische Straße Berlins': Die Stalinallee in der politischen Propaganda im ersten Jahr des Nationalen Aufbauprogramms Berlin 1952." In *Parteiauftrag*, edited by D. Vorsteher, 369–88.

Müller, Werner. "Sozialistische Einheitspartei Deutschlands (SED)." In *SBZ-Handbuch*, edited by M. Broszat and H. Weber, 481–514.

Müller-Enbergs, Helmut. "Zum Verhältnis von Norm und Praxis in der Arbeit mit Inoffiziellen Mitarbeitern des Ministeriums für Staatssicherheit." In *Staatspartei und Staatssicherheit: Zum Verhältnis von SED und MfS*, edited by Siegfried Suckut and Walter Süß, 57–76. Berlin: Links, 1997.

Münkel, Daniela, and Lu Seegers, eds. *Medien und Imagepolitik im 20. Jahrhundert. Deutschland, Europa, USA*. Frankfurt am Main: Campus, 2008.

Nagornaia, O. S. "Esli druz'ia sochtut tselesoobraznym … my podderzhim: Mezhdunarodnye Leninskie premii mira v sisteme sovetskoi kul'turnoi diplomatii." *Noveishaia istoriia Rossii* 8, no. 3 (2018): 737–53.

Naimark, Norman M. *Die Russen in Deutschland: Die sowjetische Besatzungszone 1945 bis 1949*. Berlin: Propyläen, 1997.

————. *The Russians in Germany: A History of the Soviet Zone of Occupation, 1945–1949*. Cambridge, MA: Harvard University Press, 1995.

Naimark, Norman M., and Leonid Gibianskii, eds. *The Establishment of Communist Regimes in Eastern Europe, 1944–1949*. Boulder, CO: Westview, 1997.

Naumann, Gerhard. "Die III. Weltfestspiele der Jugend und Studenten 1951 in Berlin: Vorgeschichte—Verlauf—Ergebnisse." *Zeitschrift für Geschichtswissenschaft* 35, Heft 3 (1987): 209–17.

Navaro-Yashin, Yael. *Faces of the State: Secularism and Public Life in Turkey*. Princeton, NJ: Princeton University Press, 2002.

Neckel, Sighard. *Status und Scham: Zur symbolischen Reproduktion sozialer Ungleichheit*. Frankfurt am Main: Campus, 1991.

Neubert, Harald, ed. *Stalin wollte ein anderes Europa: Moskaus Außenpolitik 1940 bis 1968 und die Folgen; Eine Dokumentation*. Berlin: Ed. Ost, 2003.

Niccoli, Ottavia. *Rinascimento anticlericale: Infamia, propaganda e satira in Italia tra Quattro e Cinquecento*. Rome: Laterza, 2005.

Nicklas, Thomas. "Macht-Politik-Diskurs: Möglichkeiten und Grenzen einer politischen Kulturgeschichte." *Archiv für Kulturgeschichte* 86, Heft 1 (2004): 1–25.

Niethammer, Lutz, Alexander von Plato, and Dorothee Wierling. *Die Volkseigene Erfahrung: Eine Archäologie des Lebens in der Industrieprovinz der DDR*. Berlin: Rowohlt, 1991.

Nitschke, Bernadetta. *Vertreibung und Aussiedlung der deutschen Bevölkerung aus Polen 1945 bis 1949*. Munich: Oldenbourg. 2003.

Noel'-Noiman, Elizabet [Elisabeth Noelle-Neumann]. *Obshchestvennoe mnenie: Otkrytie spirali molchaniia*. Moscow: Progress, 1996.

Odesskii, M. P., and D. M. Fel'dman. "Poetika 'ottepeli': Materialy k izucheniiu propagandistkoi modeli XX s"ezda KPSS: Ideologema 'kul't lichnosti.'" *Nestor*, no. 7 (2005): 374–402.

Orlova, Galina. "'Karty dlia slepykh': Politika i politizatsiia zreniia v stalinskuiu epokhu." In *Vizual'naia antropologiia: Rezhimy vidimosti pri sotsializme*, edited by Elena R. Iarskaia-Smirnova and Pavel V. Romanov, 57–104. Moscow: Variant, 2009.

Orlovsky, Daniel T. "Political Clientelism in Russia: The Historical Perspective." In *Leadership Selection and Patron-Client Relations in the USSR and Yugoslavia*, edited by T. H. Rigby and Bohdan Harasymiw, 174–99. London: Allen & Unwin, 1983.

Paczkowski, Andrzej. "Polish-Soviet Relations 1944–1989: The Limits of Autonomy." *InterMarium* 3, no. 3 (1999). https://ece.columbia.edu/files/ece/images/paczkowski -1.pdf.

Palmowski, Jan, and Geoff Eley, eds. *Citizenship and National Identity in Twentieth-Century Germany*. Stanford, CA: Stanford University Press, 2008.

Paperno, Irina. "Intimacy with Power: Soviet Memoirists Remember Stalin." In *Personality Cults in Stalinism*, edited by K. Heller and J. Plamper, 331–61.

Passeron, Jean-Claude, and Jacques Revel. "Penser par cas: Raisonner à partir de singularités." In *Penser par cas*, edited by Jean-Claude Passeron and Jacques

Revel, 9–44. Paris: Éditions de l'École des hautes études en sciences sociales, 2005.

Paulmann, Johannes. *Pomp und Politik: Monarchenbegegnungen in Europa zwischen Ancien Régime und Erstem Weltkrieg*. Paderborn: Schöningh, 2000.

Pence, Katherine. "Schaufenster des sozialistischen Konsums: Texte der ostdeutschen 'consumer culture.'" In *Akten: Eingaben: Schaufenster: Die DDR und ihr Texte; Erkundungen zu Herrschaft und Alltag*, edited by Alf Lüdtke and Peter Becker, 91–118. Berlin: Akademie, 1997.

Pence, Katherine, and Paul Betts, eds. *Socialist Modern: East German Everyday Culture and Politics*. Ann Arbor: University of Michigan Press, 2008.

Perrie, Maureen. "Nationalism and History: The Cult of the Ivan the Terrible in Stalin's Russia." In *Russian Nationalism: Past and Present*, edited by Geoffrey A. Hosking and Robert Service, 107–27. London: Palgrave Macmillan, 1998.

Peters, Günther. "'Nationale, klassizistische und fortschrittliche Bautradition': Zur Baugeschichte der Berliner Stalinallee 1949–1955." In *Berlinische Monatsschrift*, Berlin von A bis Z, Website, March 2001. https://berlingeschichte.de/bms/bmstxt01/0103prof.htm. Last accessed January 23, 2021.

Petö, Andrea. "Memory and the Narrative of Rape in Budapest and Vienna in 1945." In *Life After Death: Approaches to a Social and Cultural History of Europe During the 1940s and 1950s*, edited by Richard Bessel and Dirk Schumann, 129–48. Cambridge: Cambridge University Press, 2003.

Petrone, Karen. *Life Has Become More Joyous Comrades: Celebrations in the Time of Stalin*. Bloomington: Indiana University Press, 2000.

Petrov, N. V. "Formirovanie organov nemetskogo samoupravleniia i sovetizatsiia Vostochnoi Germanii." In *SVAG i nemetskie organy samoupravleniia, 1945–1949*, edited by N. V. Petrov, 15–56. Moscow: ROSSPEN, 2006.

———. *Po stsenariiu Stalina: Rol' organy NKVD-MGB SSSR v sovetizatsii stran Tsentral'noi i Vostochnoi Evropy, 1945–1953 gg*. Moscow: ROSSPEN, 2011.

———. *Stalin i organy NKVD-MGB v sovetizatsii stran Tsentral'noi i Vostochnoi Evropy*. Moscow: ROSSPEN, 2011.

Pike, David. "Censorship in Soviet-Occupied Germany." In *Establishment of Communist Regimes*, edited by N. M. Naimark and L. Gibianskii, 217–41.

Piskorski, Jan M. *Die Verjagten: Flucht und Vertreibung im Europa des 20. Jahrhunderts*. Munich: Siedler, 2013.

Plaggenborg, Stefan. *Experiment Moderne: Der sowjetische Weg*. Frankfurt am Main: Campus, 2006.

Plamper, Jan. "Beyond Binaries: Popular Opinion in Stalinism." In *Popular Opinion in Totalitarian Regimes: Fascism, Nazism, Communism*, edited by Paul Corner, 64–80. Oxford: Oxford University Press, 2009.

———. "'Die Hitler kommen und gehen…,' der Führerkult aber bleibt bestehen: Der Stalinkult in der SBZ/DDR." *Zeitschrift für Geschichtswissenschaft*, Heft 5 (2007): 435–56.

———. "Georgian Koba or Soviet 'Father of Peoples'? The Stalin Cult and Ethnicity." In *Leader Cult*, edited by B. Apor, et al., 123–40.

———. *Geschichte und Gefühl: Grundlagen der Emotionsgeschichte.* Munich: Siedler, 2012.

———. "'The Hitlers Come and Go...,' the Führer Stays: The Stalin Cult in East Germany." In *Personality Cults in Stalinism*, edited by K. Heller and J. Plamper, 301–29.

———. *The Stalin Cult: A Study in the Alchemy of Power.* New Haven, CT: Yale University Press, 2012.

Plunkett, John. *Queen Victoria: First Media Monarch.* Oxford: Oxford University Press, 2003.

Polese, Abel, and Slavomir Horák. "A Tale of Two Presidents: Personality Cult and Symbolic Nation-building in Turkmenistan." *Nationalities Papers* 43, no. 3 (March 2014): 457–78.

Port, Andrew I. "Der erste Arbeiteraufstand in der DDR: Die Proteste der Wismut-Arbeiter im thüringischen Saalfeld 1951." *Deutschland Archiv* 4, Heft 4 (2007): 605–13.

Postoutenko, Kirill. "Stalin's Two Bodies? A Socio-Political Dimension." In *Words, Bodies, Memory: A Festschrift in Honor of Irina Sandomirskaja*, edited by Lars Kleberg, Tora Lane, and Marcia Sá Cavalcante Schuback, 379–98. Huddinge: Södertörns Högskola, 2019.

———, ed. *Totalitarian Communication: Hierarchies, Codes and Messages.* Bielefeld: Transcript, 2010.

Postoutenko, Kirill, and Darin Stephanov, eds. *Ruler Personality Cults from Empires to Nation-States and Beyond: Symbolic Patterns and Interactional Dynamics.* London: Routledge, 2020.

Prodi, Paolo. *Il sacramento del potere: Il giuramento politico nella storia costituzionale dell'Occidente.* Bologna: Il Mulino, 1992.

Prosperi, Adriano. *Justice Blindfolded: The Historical Course of an Image.* Leiden: Brill Academic, 2018.

Prozumenshchikov, M. Iu. "'Sekretnyi' doklad N. S. Khrushcheva na XX s"ezde KPSS i mezhdunarodnoe kommunisticheskoe dvizhenie." In *Doklad N. S. Khrushcheva o kul'te lichnosti*, edited by K. Aimermakher, 17–40.

Quinn Judge, Sophie. "Ho Chi Minh: Creator or Victim of Vietnamese Communism?" *Twentieth Century Communism*, no. 1 (Summer 2009): 72–90.

Ransel, David L. "Character and Style of Patron-Client Relations in Russia." In *Klientelsysteme im Europa der Frühen Neuzeit*, edited by Antoni Mączak, 211–31. Munich: Oldenbourg, 1988.

Rausch, Helke. *Kultfigur und Nation: Öffentliche Denkmäler in Paris, Berlin und London, 1848–1914.* Munich: Oldenbourg, 2006.

Razumikhin, A. M., comp. *Vozhd': Khozian; Diktator.* Moscow: Patriot, 1990.

Reddy, William M. *The Navigation of Feeling: A Framework for the History of Emotions.* Cambridge: Cambridge University Press, 2001.

Rees, E. A. "The Sovietization of Eastern Europe: Introduction." In *Sovietization of Eastern Europe*, edited by B. Apor, P. Apor, and E. A. Rees, 1–27.

Reichel, Peter. "Berlin nach 1945—eine Erinnerungslandschaft zwischen Gedächtnis-Verlust und Gedächtnis-Inszenierung." In *Architektur als politische Kultur:*

Philosophia Practica, edited by Hermann Hipp and Ernst Seidl, 273–96. Berlin: Reimer, 1996.

———. *Der schöne Schein des Dritten Reiches: Gewalt und Faszination des deutschen Faschismus.* Hamburg: Ellert & Richter, 2006.

Reid, Susan E. "Cold War in the Kitchen: Gender and the De-Stalinization of Consumer Taste in the Soviet Union under Khrushchev." *Slavic Review* 61, no. 2 (Summer 2002): 211–52.

———. "Khrushchev Modern: Agency and Modernization in the Soviet Home." *Cahiers du Monde russe* 47, no. 1 (2006): 227–68.

Reid, Susan E., and David Crowley, eds. *Style and Socialism: Modernity and Material Culture in Post-War Eastern Europe.* Oxford: Berg, 2000.

Riall, Lucy. *Garibaldi: Invention of a Hero.* New Haven, CT: Yale University Press, 2008.

Richter, Jenny, Heike Förster, and Ulrich Lakemann. *Stalinstadt—Eisenhüttenstadt: Von der Utopie zur Gegenwart.* Marburg: Schüren, 1997.

Rittersporn, Gábor T., Jan C. Behrends, and Malte Rolf. "Öffentliche Räume und Öffentlichkeit in Gesellschaften sowjetischen Typs: Einleitung." In *Sphären von Öffentlichkeit in Gesellschaften sowjetischen Typs,* edited by Gábor T. Rittersporn, Jan C. Behrends, and Malte Rolf, 7–22. Frankfurt am Main: Lang, 2003.

Rolf, Malte. "Constructing a Soviet Time: Bolshevik Festivals and Their Rivals during the First Five-Year Plan; A Study of the Central Black Earth Region." *Kritika: Explorations in Russian and Eurasian History* 1, no. 3 (Summer 2000): 447–73.

———. *Das sowjetische Massenfest.* Hamburg: Hamburger Edition, 2006.

———. "The Leader's Many Bodies: Leader Cults and Mass Festivals in Voronezh, Novosibirsk and Kemerovo in the 1930s." In *Personality Cults in Stalinism,* edited by K. Heller and J. Plamper, 197–206.

———. *Sovetskii massovyi prazdnik v Voronezhe i Tsentral'no-Chernozemnoi oblasti Rossii (1927–1932).* Voronezh: Izd-vo Voronezh. gos. un-ta., 2000.

———. "Working Towards the Centre: Leader Cults and Spatial Politics in Pre-war Stalinism." In *Leader Cult,* edited by B. Apor, et al., 141–57.

Ronge, Tobias. *Das Bild des Herrschers in Malerei und Grafik des Nationalsozialismus: Eine Untersuchung zur Ikonografie von Führer- und Funktionärsbildern im Dritten Reich.* Münster: Lit, 2010.

Rosenwein, Barbara H. "Worrying about Emotions in History." *American Historical Review* 107, no. 3 (June 2002): 821–45.

Ross, Corey. "Zwischen politischer Gestaltung und sozialer Komplexität— Überlegungen zur Debatte über die Sozialgeschichte der DDR." In *Jahrbuch für Historische Kommunismusforschung,* edited by Hermann Weber, Egbert Jahn, and Bernhard H. Bayerlein, 140–64. Berlin: Metropol, 2003.

Rossbach, Norbert. "'Täve': Der Radsportler Gustav-Adolf Schur." In *Sozialistische Helden,* edited by S. Satjukow and R. Gries, 133–46.

Rossman, Jeffrey J. *Worker Resistance under Stalin: Class and Revolution on the Shop Floor.* Cambridge, MA: Harvard University Press, 2005.

Roth, Heidi. *Der 17. Juni 1953 in Görlitz: Dokumentation zum Volksaufstand.* Bautzen: Lusatia, 2003.

Russo, Henry, ed. *Stalinism and Nazism: History and Memory Compared.* London: University of Nebraska Press, 2004.

Rybakow, Alexei. "'Es wird ganz Deutschland einstmals Stalin danken': Johannes R. Bechers 'Stalin-Oden' und die Strukturen der totalitären 'Kultur.'" *Forum für osteuropäische Ideen- und Zeitgeschichte* 8, no. 1 (2004). https://www1.ku-eichstaett.de/ZIMOS/Netwerk/Dateien/RybakovBecher.pdf.

Ryklin, M. K. *Prostranstva likovaniia: Totalitarizm i razlichie.* Moscow: Logos, 2002.

Sabrow, Martin. "Einleitung: Geschichtsdiskurs und Doktringesellschaft." In *Geschichte als Herrschaftsdiskurs*, edied by M. Sabrow, 9–35.

——, ed. *Geschichte als Herrschaftsdiskurs: Der Umgang mit der Vergangenheit in der DDR.* Cologne: Böhlau, 2000.

——. "Herrschaft und Alltag in der DDR." In *Parteidiktatur und Alltag in der DDR: Aus den Sammlungen des Deutschen Historischen Museums*, edited by Regine Falkenberg, 10–19. Berlin: Deutsches Historisches Museum, 2007.

——. "Time and Legitimacy: Comparative Reflections on the Sense of Time in the Two German Dictatorships." *Totalitarian Movements and Political Religions* 6, no. 3 (December 2005): 351–69.

——, ed. *Verwaltete Vergangenheit: Geschichtskultur und Herrschaftslegitimation in der DDR.* Leipzig: Akademische Verlagsanstalt, 1997.

Sänger, Johanna. *Heldenkult und Heimatliebe: Strassen- und Ehrennamen im offiziellen Gedächtnis der DDR.* Berlin: Links, 2006.

Santana, Marco Aurélio, "Re-Imagining the Cavalier of Hope: The Brazilian Communist Party and the Images of Luiz Carlos Prestes." *Twentieth Century Communism* 1, no. 1 (June 2009): 110–27.

Satjukow, Silke. *Befreiung? Die Ostdeutschen und 1945.* Leipzig: Leipziger Universitätsverlag, 2009.

——. *Besatzer: "Die Russen" in Deutschland 1945 bis 1994.* Göttingen: Vandenhoeck & Ruprecht, 2008.

——. "Der erste Sommer mit den 'Russen': Momentaufnahmen zwischen Erwartung und Erfahrung." *Deutschland Archiv* 38, Heft 2 (2005): 236–44.

——. "Propaganda mit dem menschlichen Antlitz im Sozialismus: Über die Konstruktion einer Propagandafigur: Der 'Held der Arbeit' Adolf Hennecke." In *Kultur der Propaganda*, edited by Rainer Gries, Wolfgang Schmale, and Thomas Ahbe, 167–91. Bochum: Winkler, 2005.

——, ed. *"Die Russen kommen!" Erinnerungen an sowjetische Soldaten von 1945 bis 1992.* Erfurt: Landeszentrale für politische Bildung, 2005.

Satjukow, Silke, and Rainer Gries. "Zur Konstruktion des 'sozialistischen Helden': Geschichte und Bedeutung." In *Sozialistische Helden*, edited by S. Satjukow and R. Gries, 15–34.

——, eds. *Sozialistische Helden: Eine Kulturgeschichte von Propagandafiguren in Osteuropa und der DDR.* Berlin: Links, 2002.

Scarpellini, Emanuela. *Material Nation: A Consumer's History of Modern Italy.* Oxford: Oxford University Press, 2011.

Schechter, Brandon M. *The Stuff of Soldiers: A History of the Red Army in World War II Through Objects.* Ithaca, NY: Cornell University Press, 2019.

Scheer, Regina. "Geschützte Leere: Ein Rechercherbericht über politische Denkmäler in Brandenburg." In *Vielstimmiges Schweigen: Neue Studien zum DDR-Antifaschismus,* edited by Annette Leo and Peter Reif-Spirek, 127–51. Berlin: Metropol, 2001.

Schenk, Frithjof Benjamin. *Aleksandr Nevskij: Heiliger—Fürst—Nationalheld; Eine Erinnerungsfigur im russischen kulturellen Gedächtnis (1263–2000).* Cologne: Böhlau Verlag, 2004.

Scherstjanoi, Elke, ed. *Rotarmisten schreiben aus Deutschland: Briefe von der Front (1945) und historische Analysen.* Munich: Saur, 2004.

———. "Zum Verhältnis zwischen SED- und KPdSU-Führung." In *SED: Geschichte—Organisation—Politik; Ein Handbuch,* edited by Andreas Herbst, Gerd-Rüdiger Stephan, and Jürgen Winkler, 177–96. Berlin: Dietz, 1997.

Schieder, Wolfgang. *Mythos Mussolini: Deutsche in Audienz beim Duce.* Munich: Oldenbourg Verlag, 2013.

Schlumbohm, Jürgen. "Mikrogeschichte—Makrogeschichte: Zur Eröffnung einer Debatte." In *Mikrogeschichte—Makrogeschichte: Komplementär oder inkommensurabel?,* edited by Jürgen Schlumbohm, 7–32. Göttingen: Wallstein, 1998.

Schmeitzner, Mike, Andreas Weigelt, Klaus-Dieter Müller, and Thomas Schaarschmidt, eds. *Todesurteile sowjetischer Militärtribunale gegen Deutsche (1944–1947): Eine historisch-biographische Studie.* Göttingen: Vandenhoeck & Ruprecht, 2015.

Schmidt, Karl-Heinz. "Als Stalin starb: Die Reaktion des SED-Regimes in die Bevölkerung im Spiegel interner Berichte." In *Geschichte und Transformation des SED-Staates: Beiträge und Analysen,* edited by Klaus Schroeder, 85–111. Berlin: Akademie, 1994.

Schmidt-Glintzer, Helwig. "Mao Zedong die Inkarnation Chinas." In *Virtuosen der Macht,* edited by Wilfried Nippel, 260–77. Munich: C. H. Beck, 2000.

Schneider, Ute. *Hausväteridylle oder sozialistische Utopie? Die Familie im Recht der DDR.* Cologne: Böhlau, 2004.

Schnitzler, Norbert. "Geschmähte Symbole." In *Verletzte Ehre: Ehrkonflikte in Gesellschaften des Mittelalters und der Frühen Neuzeit,* edited by Klaus Schreiner and Gerd Schwerhoff, 279–302. Cologne: Böhlau, 1995.

Schrift, Melissa. *Biography of a Chairman Mao Badge: The Creation and Mass Consumption of a Personality Cult.* New Brunswick, NJ: Rutgers University Press, 2001.

Schröder, Klaus. *SED-Staat: Geschichte und Strukturen der DDR.* Munich: Bayerische Landeszentrale für politische Bildungsarbeit, 1999.

Schüle, Annegret, Thomas Ahbe, and Rainer Gries, eds. *Die DDR aus generationengeschichtlicher Perspektive: Eine Inventur.* Leipzig: Leipziger Universitätsverlag, 2006.

Schwab, Dieter. "Familie." In *Geschichtliche Grundbegriffe*. Vol. 2, edited by Otto Brunner, Werner Conze, and Reinhart Koselleck, 253–301. Stuttgart: Klett-Cotta, 1979.

Scott, James. *Weapons of the Weak*. New Haven, CT: Yale University Press, 1985.

Scribner, Robert. *For the Sake of Simple Folk: Popular Propaganda for the German Reformation*. Cambridge: Cambridge University Press, 1981.

———. *Popular Culture and Popular Movements in Reformation Germany*. London: Hambledon Press, 1987.

———. "Ritual and Reformation." In *The German People and the Reformation*, edited by Ronnie Po-chia Hsia, 122–44. Ithaca, NY: Cornell University Press, 1988.

Seidel Menchi, Silvana. "Storia alta, storia sommessa: Dicotomia della ricerca e storia della famiglia." In *Famiglie e poteri in Italia tra medioevo ed età moderna*, edited by Anna Bellavitis and Isabelle Chabot, 17–31. Rome: École française de Rome, 2009.

Semjonow, Wladimir S. *Von Stalin bis Gorbatschow: Ein halbes Jahrhundert in diplomatischer Mission 1939–1991*. Berlin: Nicolai, 1995.

Senjavskaja, Elena. "Deutschland und die Deutschen in den Augen sowjetischer Soldaten und Offiziere des Großen Vaterländischen Krieges" In *Rotarmisten schreiben aus Deutschland: Briefe von der Front (1945) und historischen Analysen*, edited by Elke Scherstjanoi, 247–66. Munich: Saur, 2004.

Sennebogen, Waltraut. "Propaganda als Populärkultur? Werbestrategien und Werbepraxis im faschistischen Italien und in NS-Deutschland." In *Faschismus in Italien und Deutschland: Studien zu Transfer und Vergleich*, edited by Sven Reichardt and Armin Nozin, 119–47. Göttingen: Wallstein, 2005.

Seybold, Katja. "Ländlicher Protest—Der 17. Juni 1953 in Jessen und Umgebung." In *"... und das Wichtigste ist doch die Einheit": Der 17. Juni 1953 in den Bezirken Halle und Magdeburg*, edited by Hermann-Josef Rupieper, Daniel Bohse, and Inga Grebe, 140–61. Münster: Lit, 2003.

Sherlock, Thomas D. *Historical Narratives in the Soviet Union and Post-Soviet Russia: Destroying the Settled Past, Creating an Uncertain Future*. Basingstoke: Palgrave Macmillan, 2007.

Siegelbaum, Lewis, and Andrei Sokolov, eds. *Stalinism as a Way of Life: A Narrative in Documents*. New Haven, CT: Yale University Press, 2000.

Simmel, Georg. *Untersuchungen über die Formen der Vergesellschaftung*. Edited by Otthein Rammstedt. Frankfurt am Main: Suhrkamp, 1992.

Slezkine, Yuri. "The USSR as a Communal Apartment, or How a Socialist State Promoted Ethnic Particularism." *Slavic Review* 53, no. 2 (Summer 1994): 414–52.

Smith, Steve. "The Social Meanings of Swearing: Workers and Bad Language in Late Imperial and Early Soviet Russia." *Past and Present*, no. 160 (August 1998): 167–202.

Snyder, Timothy. *Bloodlands: Europe Between Hitler and Stalin*. New York: Basic Books, 2010.

Sosnina, Olga, and Nikolai Ssorin-Chaikov. "The Archaeology of Power/The Anatomy of Love." In *Dary vozhdiam—Gifts to Soviet Leaders*, edited by Olga Sosnina and Nikolai Ssorin-Chaikov, 12–37. Moscow: Pinakoteka, 2006.

————, eds. *Dary vozhdiam—Gifts to Soviet Leaders: Katalog vystavki, sostoiavshei-,sia v "Novom manezhe" 26 oktiabria–26 noiabria 2006 g.* Moscow: Pinakoteka, 2006.

Sperber, Jonathan. "17 June 1953: Revisiting a German Revolution." *German History* 22, no. 4 (October 2004): 619–43.

Ssorin-Chaikov, Nikolai, and Olga Sosnina. "The Faculty of Useless Things: Gifts to Soviet Leaders." In *Personality Cults in Stalinism*, edited by K. Heller and J. Plamper, 277–300.

Staritz, Dietrich. *Geschichte der DDR: 1949–1985*. Frankfurt am Main: Suhrkamp, 1996.

Stark, Meinhard. *"Wenn Du willst Deine Ruhe haben, schweige": Deutsche Frauenbiographien des Stalinismus*. Essen: Klartext, 1991.

Steinberg, Mark D., and Valeria Sobol, eds. *Interpreting Emotions in Russia and Eastern Europe*. DeKalb: Northern Illinois University Press, 2011.

Steinmetz, Willibald. "Neue Wege einer historischen Semantik des Politischen." In *"Politik": Situationen eines Wortgebrauchs im Europa der Neuzeit*, edited by Willibald Steinmetz, 9–40. Frankfurt am Main: Campus, 2007.

————, ed. *Political Languages in the Age of Extremes*. Oxford: Oxford University Press, 2011.

Stephanov, Darin. "Publichnye chestvovaniia imperatora Nikolaia I (1825–1855) v Velikom kniazhestve Finliandskom: Tipologiia, dinamika, vozdeistvie." In *400-letie Doma Romanovykh, 1613–2013: Politika pamiati i monarkhicheskaia ideia; Sbornik statei*, edited by V. V. Lapin and Iu. A. Safronova, 89–103. St. Petersburg: EUSPB, 2016.

————. *Ruler Visibility and Popular Belonging in the Ottoman Empire*. Edinburgh: Edinburgh University Press, 2018.

Stieglitz, Olaf, and Christoph Thonfeld. "Denunziation als Medium des kultural-istisch erweiterten Diktaturvergleichs: Thüringen im Nationalsozialismus, unter sowjetischer Besatzung und in der frühen DDR." *Werkstatt Geschichte*, no. 38 (December 2004): 77–89.

Stites, Richard. "Utopian or Antiutopian? An Indirect Look at the Cult of Personality." In *The Cult of Power: Dictators in the Twentieth Century*, edited by Joseph Held, 77–94. Boulder, CO: East European Monographs, 1983.

Stoecker, Holger. "'Stalin, das ist der Frieden!': Die Stalin-Note vom 10. März 1952 und die friedenspolitische Propaganda in der DDR." In *Parteiauftrag*, edited by D. Vorsteher, 395–405.

Stoun, L. [Lawrence Stone]. "Budushchee istorii." *Teoriia i istoriia ekonomicheskikh i sotsial'nykh institutov i sistem*, no. 4 (1994): 158–74.

Strunk, Peter. *Zensur und Zensoren: Medienkontrolle und Propagandapolitik unter sowjetischer Besatzungsherrschaft in Deutschland*. Berlin: Akademie, 1996.

Stykalin, Aleksandr S. "Ideologiia i kul'turnaia ekspansiia stalinizma v Vengrii (vtoraia polovina 1940-kh–nachalo 1950-kh godov)." *Slavianovedenie*, no. 6 (1992): 15–26.

————. "Politika SSSR po formirovaniiu obshchestvennogo mneniia v stranakh Tsentral'noi Evropy i nastroeniia intelligentsii (vtoraia polovina 1940-kh godov)." *Slavianovedenie*, no. 3 (1997): 50–62.

Swett, Pamela. *Selling Under the Swastika: Advertising and Commercial Culture in Nazi Germany*. Stanford, CA: Stanford University Press, 2014.

Szarota, Tomasz. *Warschau unter dem Hakenkreuz: Leben und Alltag im besetzten Warschau; 1.10.1939 bis 31.7.1944*. Paderborn: Schöningh, 1985.

Sztompka, Piotr. *Trust: A Sociological Theory*. Cambridge: Cambridge University Press, 1999.

Tacke, Charlotte. *Denkmal im sozialen Raum: Nationale Symbole in Deutschland und Frankreich im 19. Jahrhundert*. Göttingen: Vandenhoeck & Ruprecht, 1995.

Thamer, Hans-Ulrich. "Von der Monumentalisierung zur Verdrängung der Geschichte: Nationalsozialistische Denkmalpolitik und die Entnazifizierung von Denkmäler nach 1945." In *Denkmalsturz: Zur Konfliktgeschichte politischer Symbolik*, edited by Winfried Speitkamp, 109–36. Berlin: Vandenhoeck & Ruprecht, 1997.

Thompson, Robert J. "Reassessing Personality Cults: The Case of Stalin and Mao." *Studies in Comparative Communism* 21, no. 1 (Spring 1988): 99–128.

Thum, Gregor. "Ex oriente lux—ex oriente furor: Einführung." In *Traumland Osten: Deutsche Bilder vom östlichen Europa im 20. Jahrhundert*, edited by Gregor Thum, 7–15. Göttingen: Vandenhoeck & Ruprecht, 2006.

————, ed. *Traumland Osten: Deutsche Bilder vom östlichen Europa im 20. Jahrhundert*. Göttingen: Vandenhoeck & Ruprecht, 2006.

Tikhomirov, Alexey. "Beyond 'Fascist Sortie' and 'Popular Uprising for Democracy and Rights': Rethinking the 17 June 1953 Unrest in East Germany." (in preparation).

————. "Eksport kul'ta Stalina v Vostochnuiu Germaniiu s 1945 po 1956 gg." In *Poslevoennaia istoriia Germanii: Rossiisko-nemetskii opyt i perspektivy*, edited by B. Bonvech and A. Iu. Vatlin, 83–96. Moscow: Direktmedia Pablishing, 2007.

————. "'Feinde des Volkes': Zur (Re-)Konstruktion des inneren Feinds in der stalinistischen Phase der DDR (1949–1953)." In *Unsere Feinde: Konstruktionen der Andere im Sozialismus*, edited by Silke Satjukow and Rainer Gries, 167–78. Leipzig: Leipziger-Univ.-Verlag, 2004.

————. "Prisposablivat'sia, dogovarivat'sia, soprotivliat'sia: K voprosu o strate-giiakh zhizni cheloveka sovetskogo tipa." In *Vlast' i obshchestvo v usloviiakh diktatury: Istoricheskii opyt SSSR i GDR, 1945–1965*, edited by R. Iu. Boldyrev, 259–74. Arkhangel'sk: Pomorskii gosudarstvennyi universitet imeni M. V. Lomonosova, 2009.

————. "The Regime of Forced Trust: Making and Breaking Emotional Bonds Between People and State in Soviet Russia, 1917–1941." In "Trust and Distrust in the USSR." Edited by Geoffrey Hosking. Special issue, *Slavonic and East European Review* 91, no. 1 (January 2013): 78–118.

————. "Stalin-Bild(er) in der SBZ/DDR: Die deutsche Nachkriegsgesellschaft im Spannungsfeld zwischen Propaganda und Erfahrung." In *Historische Erinnerung im Wandel: Neuere Forschungen zur deutschen Zeitgeschichte unter besonderer*

Berücksichtigung der DDR-Forschung, edited by Heiner Timmermann, 467–509. Münster: Lit, 2007.

———. "The Stalin Cult between Center and Periphery: The Structures of the Cult Community in the Empire of Socialism, 1949–1956—The Case of GDR." In *Der Führer im Europa des 20. Jahrhunderts*, edited by Benno Ennker and Heidi Hein-Kircher, 297–321. Marburg: Herder-Institut, 2010.

———. "The State as a Family: Speaking Kinship, Being Soviet and Reinventing Tradition in the USSR." *Journal of Modern European History* 15, no. 3 (January 2017): 395–418.

———. "Symbols of Power in Rituals of Violence: The Personality Cult and Iconoclasm on the Soviet Empire's Periphery (East Germany, 1945–61)." *Kritika: Explorations in Russian and Eurasian History* 13, no. 1 (Winter 2012): 47–88.

Tilly, Charles. *The Contentious French*. Cambridge, MA: Harvard University Press, 1986.

Todorova, Maria. *Bones of Contention: The Living Archive of Vasil Levski and the Making of Bulgaria's National Hero*. Budapest and New York: Central European University Press, 2008.

———. "The Mausoleum of Georgi Dimitrov as *Lieu de Mémoire*." *Journal of Modern History* 78, no. 2 (June 2006): 377–411.

Todorova, Maria, and Zsuzsa Gille, eds. *Post-Communist Nostalgia*. New York: Berghahn, 2010.

Truesdell, Matthew N. *Spectacular Politics: Louis-Napoleon Bonaparte and the Fête Impérial, 1849–1870*. New York: Oxford University Press, 1997.

Tumarkin, Nina. *Lenin Lives! The Lenin Cult in Soviet Russia*. Enlarged edition. Cambridge, MA: Harvard University Press, 1997.

———. *The Living and the Dead: The Rise and Fall of the Cult of World War II in Russia*. New York: Basic Books, 1994.

Turkmenbashi, Saparmurat. *Ruhnama*. Ashgabat: Turkmenskaia gosudarstvennaia izdatel'skaia sluzhba, 2001.

Turner, Victor. *The Ritual Process: Structure and Anti-Structure*. Chicago: University of Chicago Press, 1969.

Turovskaja, Maja. "Das Kino der totalitären Epoche." In *Politische Inszenierung im 20. Jahrhundert: Zur Sinnlichkeit der Macht*, edited by Sabine R. Arnold, Christian Fuhrmeister, and Dietmar Schiller, 75–82. Vienna: Böhlau, 1998.

Uhl, Matthias. "Repressionen als Instrument stalinistischer Herrschaft in Ostdeutschland." In *Der rote Gott: Stalin und die Deutschen; Katalog zur Sonderausstellung*, edited by Andreas Engwert and Hubertus Knabe, 75–81. Berlin: Lucas Verlag, 2018.

Uortman, R. [Richard Wortman]. *Stsenarii vlasti: Mify i tseremonii russkoi monarkhii*. Vol. 1, *Ot Petra Velikogo do smerti Nikolaia I*. Moscow: OGI, 2002.

Vaiskop, M. *Pisatel' Stalin*. Moscow: NLO, 2001.

Van Gennep, Arnold. *The Rites of Passage*. Translated by Monika B. Vizedom and Gabrielle L. Caffee. Chicago: University of Chicago Press, 1960.

Bibliography 357

Vashik, Klaus [Klaus Waschik]. "Metamorfozy zla: Nemetsko-russkie obrazy vraga v plakatnoi propagande 30–50-kh godov." In *Obraz vraga*, edited by Lev Gudkov, 191–229. Moscow: OGI, 2005.

Vatlin, Aleksandr. "Nemetskie politemigranty v Sovetskom Soize: Zhizn' pod kontrolem." In *Forum noveishei vostochnoevropeiskoi istorii i kul'tury*, no. 2 (2007). http://www1.ku-eichstaett.de/Zimos/Forum/Docs/4vatlin07.pdf.

———. "Sovetskii Soiuz v vospriatii nemetskikh politemigrantov 30-kh gg." *Forum noveishei vostochnoevropeiskoi istorii i kul'tury*, no. 2 (2008). http://www1.ku -eichstaett.de/Zimos/Forum/Docs/Forumruss10/1vatlinfr10.pdf.

Velikanova, O. V. "Berichte zur Stimmungslage: Zu den Quellen politischer Beobachtung der Bevölkerung in der Sowjetunion." *Jahrbücher für Geschichte Osteuropas* 47, Heft 2 (1999): 227–43.

———. "Obraz Lenina v massovom soznanii." *Otechestvennaia istoriia*, no. 2 (1994): 177–85.

———. *Popular Perceptions of Soviet Politics in the 1920s: Disenchantment of the Dreamers*. Basingstoke: Palgrave Macmillan, 2013.

———. *The Public Perception of the Cult of Lenin Based on Archival Materials*. Lewiston, NY: Edwin Mellen, 2001.

Vieth, Eva. "Die letzte 'Volksgemeinschaft'—Das Kriegsende in den Bildern einer deutschen Illustrierten." In *Kriegsende 1945 in Deutschland*, edited by Jörg Hillmann and John Zimmermann, 265–86. Munich: Oldenbourg, 2002.

Vihavainen, Timo, ed. *Sovetskaia vlast'—narodnaia vlast'? Ocherki istorii narodnogo vospriiatiia sovetskoi vlasti v SSSR*. St. Petersburg: Evropeiskii dom, 2003.

Voigt, Rüdiger, ed. *Des Staates neue Kleider: Entwicklungslinien moderner Staatlichkeit*. Baden-Baden: Nomos-Verlag, 1996.

Volkogonov, D. A. *Triumf i tragediia: Politicheskii portret I. V. Stalina*. 2 vols. Moscow: Novosti, 1990.

Volkov, F. D. *Vslet i padenie Stalina*. Moscow: Spektr, 1992.

Volokitina, T. V., G. P. Murashko, A. F. Noskova, and T. A. Pokivailova. *Moskva i Vostochnaia Evropa: Stanovlenie polititicheskikh rezhimov sovetskogo tipa (1949–1953); Ocherki istorii*. Moscow: ROSSPEN, 2002.

Von Busse, Mark-Christian. *Faszination und Desillusionierung: Stalinismusbilder von sympatisierenden und abtrünnigen Intellektuellen*. Pfaffenweiler: Centaurus, 2000.

Von Hagen, Mark. "Stalinism and the Politics of Post-Soviet History." In *Stalinism and Nazism: Dictatorships in Comparison*, edited by Ian Kershaw and Moshe Lewin, 285–310. Cambridge: Cambridge University Press, 1997.

Von Klimo, Árpád. "'Runde' Jahrestage in der DDR und Ungarn: Überlegungen zu einem Vergleich staatssozialistischer Gründungsfeier." *Comparativ: Zeitschrift für Globalgeschichte und vergleichende Gesellschaftsforschung* 10, Heft 2 (2000): 108–18.

Von Klimó, Árpád, and Malte Rolf, eds. *Rausch und Diktatur: Inszenierung, Mobilisierung und Kontrolle in totalitären Systemen*. Frankfurt am Main: Campus, 2006.

Von Plato, Alexander, and Almut Leh, eds. *"Ein Unglaublicher Frühling"*: *Erfahrene Geschichte im Nachkriegsdeutschland, 1945–1948*. Bonn: Bundeszentrale für politische Bildung, 1997.

Vorsteher, Dieter, ed. *Parteiauftrag: Ein neues Deutschland; Bilder, Rituale und Symbole der frühen DDR*. Munich: Koehler und Amelang, 1997.

Waddington, Lorna L. "The Anti-Komintern and Nazi Anti-Bolshevik Propaganda in the 1930s." *Journal of Contemporary History* 42, no. 4 (October 2007): 573–94.

Walzer, Michael. "On the Role of Symbolism in Political Thought." *Political Science Quarterly* 82, no. 2 (June 1967): 191–204.

Warneken, Bernd Jürgen. "'Die Straße ist die Tribüne des Volkes': Ein Vorwort." In *Massenmedium Straße: Zur Kulturgeschichte der Demonstration*, edited by Bernd Jürgen Warneken, 7–16. Frankfurt am Main: Campus, 1991.

Waylen, Georgina, Karen Celis, Johanna Kantola, and S. Laurel Weldon, eds. *The Oxford Handbook of Gender and Politics*. Oxford: Oxford University Press, 2013.

Wedeen, Lisa. *Ambiguities of Domination: Politics, Rhetoric, and Symbols in Contemporary Syria*. Chicago: University of Chicago Press, 1999.

Weiner, Amir. "Nature, Nurture, and Memory in a Socialist Utopia: Delineating the Soviet Socio-Ethnic Body in the Age of Socialism." *American Historical Review* 104, no. 4 (October 1999): 1114–55.

Welch, David. "Nazi Propaganda and the Volksgemeinschaft: Constructing a People's Community." *Journal of Contemporary History* 39, no. 2 (April 2004): 213–38.

Werner, Michael, and Benedicte Zimmermann. "Vergleich, Transfer, Verflechtung: Der Ansatz der *histoire croisée* und die Herausforderung des Transnationalen." *Geschichte und Gesellschaft*, no. 28 (2002): 607–36.

Wierling, Dorothee. "Über die Liebe zum Staat—der Fall der DDR." *Historische Anthropologie*, 8, Heft 2 (2000): 236–63.

Wilke, Manfred, ed. *Die Anatomie der Parteizentrale: Die KPD/SED auf dem Weg zur Macht*. Berlin: Akademie, 1998.

Willams, Bernard. *Scham, Schuld und Notwendigkeit: Eine Wiederbelebung antiker Begriffe von der Moral*. Translated by Martin Hartmann. Berlin: Akademie, 2000.

Witkowski, Gregory R. "Peasants Revolt? Re-evaluating the 17 June Uprising." *German History* 24, no. 2 (April 2006): 243–66.

Wolf, Christiane. "Monarchen als religiöse Repräsentanten der Nation um 1900? Kaiser Wilhelm II., Königin Viktoria und Kaiser Franz Joseph im Vergleich." In *Nation und Religion in Europa: Mehrkonfessionelle Gesellschaften im 19. und 20. Jahrhundert*, edited by Heinz-Gerhard Haupt and Dieter Langewiesche, 153–72. Frankfurt am Main: Campus, 2004.

Wolle, Stefan. "Die Welt der verlorenen Bilder: Die DDR im visuellen Gedächtnis." In *Visual History: Ein Studienbuch*, edited by Gerhard Paul, 333–52. Göttingen: Vandenhoeck & Ruprecht, 2006.

Wortman, Richard. "Moscow and Petersburg: The Problem of the Political Center in Tsarist Russia, 1881–1914." In *Rites of Power: Symbolism, Ritual, and Politics Since the Middle Ages*, edited by Sean Wilentz, 244–71. Philadelphia: University of Pennsylvania Press, 1985.

Yekelchyk, Serhy. "The Civic Duty to Hate: Stalinist Citizenship as Political Practice and Civic Emotion (Kiev, 1943–53)." *Kritika: Explorations in Russian and Eurasian History* 7, no. 3 (Summer 2006): 529–56.

Yurchak, Alexei. *Everything Was Forever, Until It Was No More: The Last Soviet Generation.* Princeton, NJ: Princeton University Press, 2005.

Zagatta, Martin. *Informationspolitik und Öffentlichkeit: Zur Theorie der politischen Kommunikation in der DDR.* Cologne: Wissenschaft und Politik, 1984.

Zakharov, V. V., D. N. Filippovykh, and M. Khainemann [Manfred Heinemann], eds. *Politicheskie struktury SVAG.* Vyp. 1 of *Materialy po istorii sovetskoi voennoi administratsii v Germanii v 1945–1949 gg.: Naucho-spravochnoe izdanie.* Moscow: Izdatel'stvo Dzhangar, 1998.

Zaremba, Marcin. *Die grosse Angst: Polen 1944–1947; Leben im Ausnahmezustand.* Paderborn: Schöningh, 2016.

Zarusky, Jürgen, ed. *Stalin und die Deutschen: Neue Beiträge der Forschung.* Munich: Oldenbourg, 2006.

Zezina, M. R. "Iz istorii obshchestvennogo soznaniia perioda 'otteplei.'" *Vestnik Moskovskogo universiteta.* Series 8. Istoriia, no. 6 (1992): 17–28.

———. "Shokvaia terapiia: Ot 1953-ogo k 1956 godu." *Otechestvennaia istoriia*, no. 2 (1995): 121–35.

Zimmering, Raina. *Mythen in der Politik der DDR: Ein Beitrag zur Erforschung politischer Mythen.* Opladen: Leske und Budrich, 2000.

Zorzi, Andrea. "Rituali e cerimoniali penali nelle città italiane (secc. XIII–XVI)." In *Riti e rituali nelle società medievali*, edited by Jacques Chiffoleau, Lauro Martines, and Agostino Paravicini Bagliani, 141–57. Spoleto: Centro Italiano di Studi sull'Alto Medioevo, 1994.

Zubkova, E. Iu. "'Dvulikii Ianus': Obshchestvennoe mnenie v usloviiakh diktatury (1945–1953)." In *Rossiia v XX veke: Problemy izucheniia i prepodavaniia; Materialy nauchnoi konferentsii, Moskva 2 dek. 1998*, 127–29. Moscow: Ros. gos. gumanitar. un-t, 1999.

———. "Malenkov i Khrushchev: Lichnyi faktor v politike poslestalinskogo rukovodstva." *Otechestvennaia istoriia*, no. 4 (1995): 103–15.

———. "Mir mnenii sovetskogo cheloveka, 1945–1948 gody: Po materialam TsK VKP(b)." *Otechestvennaia istoriia*, no. 3 (1998): 25–39; no. 4 (1998): 99–108.

———. *Obshchestvo i reformy, 1945–1964.* Moscow: Rossiia molodaia, 1993.

———. "Obshchestvo, vyshedshee iz voiny: Russkie i nemtsy v 1945 godu." *Otechestvennaia istoriia*, no. 3 (1995): 90–100.

———. "Öffentliche Meinung und Macht im Nachkriegsrussland, 1945–1953." *FORUM für osteuropäische Ideen- und Zeitgeschichte*, no. 2 (1998): 227–52.

———. *Poslevoennoe sovetskoe obshchestvo: Politika i povsednevnost'.* Moscow: ROSSPEN, 1999.

———. *Russia after the War: Hopes, Illusions, and Disappointments, 1945–1957.* Translated by Hugh Ragsdale. Armonk, NY: M. E. Sharpe, 1998.

———. "Stalin i obshchestvennoe mnenie v SSSR, 1945–1953." In *Stalinskoe desiatiletie kholodnoi voiny: Fakty i gipotezi*, edited by A. O. Chubar'ian, 151–70. Moscow: Nauka, 1999.

Index

Ackermann, Anton, 91, 93, 95, 101,
114, 130n81
Adenauer, Konrad, 192
Alexander III, 39
Allgemeine Deutsche Nachrichtendienst
(General German News Service), 55
Allied Control Council, 106
Alltagsgeschichte, 13, 24n31
Althusser, Louis, 180
anti-Polish hostilities, 253
Arendt, Hannah, 13
Aristov, Averkii, 298
authoritarianism/authoritarian, 13–15,
30, 239n335, 309, 314

Barbusse, Henri, 47, 100
Becher, Johannes, 50, 66n18, 100, 193,
296
Becker, Artur, 95
Beimler, Hans, 95
Benjamin, Hilde, 287
Beria, Lavrenty, 225n51, 235n267, 281
Berlin Wall, 65, 297
Bespalov, Georgii M., 52, 67n29, 114,
135n194
Brandenburg, 67n24, 69n57, 70n81, 83,
99–100, 118–25, 128n42, 129n56,
132n121, 134n159, 135n184, 136n218,
137n232, 137n240, 137n244, 138n250,

138n255, 138nn256–65, 199, 251,
259, 263n26, 265n53, 266n56, 266n58,
267–68n100, 283
Brecht, Bertolt, 183
Brzezinski, Zbigniew, 13, 24n34
Buchwitz, Otto, 197, 273
Busch, Ernst, 146

capitalism/capitalist, 5, 13, 55–56,
60–61, 80, 96, 125–26, 192, 210–11,
222, 262, 313
Castro, Fidel, 14, 25n37
charisma, 12, 24n21, 30, 35, 43n2,
44n28, 96, 244
charismatic leadership, 151
Christlich Demokratische Union
(Christian Democratic Union), xiii,
89
Churchill, Winston, 89
class struggle, 8, 48, 59, 97, 294
Claudius, Eduard, 258, 267n92
Cold War, 5–6, 13–17, 96–97, 109–10,
147, 156, 168, 183, 192, 210–11,
223n7, 238n325, 294, 307
collective government (*kollektivnoe
upravlenie*), 274, 291–94
communism/communist, 3, 10, 14,
18, 23n4, 25n36, 30, 31, 36, 41,
43n5, 43n20, 46n82, 47–49, 59, 62,

65n3, 74, 81–82, 85–86, 91–96, 98,
100–109, 113–17, 121–26, 131n84,
148–52, 160–69, 182, 187–92, 201,
209–11, 222, 233n237, 234n254,
235n265, 254, 259, 269–78, 280,
284–85, 287, 290, 294–95, 297,
298n1, 300n49, 307–14
Communist International (Comintern),
81, 93, 131n84, 150, 192
Communist Party of Germany (KPD),
8, 23n9, 57–59, 85, 91–94, 103, 120,
130n81, 131n83, 150, 185, 191–93,
228n111, 270–79. *See also* German
Communist Party
cult of personality, 11, 24n16, 29,
44n39, 44n46, 46n80, 190, 274. *See
also* personality cult
cults, 12, 14–17, 21–22, 24nn14–33,
29–38, 40–43, 43nn5–6, 48, 95, 106,
108, 112, 188, 192, 235n265, 244,
248, 259–61, 277, 281, 288, 291–98,
300n49, 309–11, 316n9

de-Nazification, 81, 106
Denisov, Andrei I., 142
dictatorship, 3, 8–11, 13–16, 19–21,
24n12, 24n24, 24n30, 24n32, 24n34,
25n40, 31, 42, 43n5, 45–46n77,
50–50, 64–65, 65n3, 67n25, 104,
126–27, 147–49, 159–64, 171, 173,
175, 179, 196, 209, 222, 228n111,
236n296, 241–42, 244–49, 253–55,
257–58, 275–77, 281–82, 286–88,
309–12, 315
Dimitrov, Georgi, 192, 235n265, 248

Eastern bloc, 5, 12, 16, 33, 38, 47–48,
111, 143, 149, 182, 203, 286, 313–14
Ebert, Friedrich, 23n9, 68n47, 130n82,
212, 233n237, 262n1
Ehrenburg, Ilya, 74, 229n131
Einicke, Ludwig, 293, 304n130
Eisenhower, Dwight, 192
Eisenhüttenkombinat, 216, 219,
238n324

Eisler, Gerhart, 132n105, 157
Elisabeth, queen of Austria, 44n29,
106
Elizabeth I, 35
enemies of the people, 8, 11, 54, 63,
203–4, 206, 235–36n273, 245,
287–88, 313
Ennker, Benno, 25n35, 26n52, 43n2,
44n46, 65n3, 235n265
Erhardt, Ludwig, 192
Etkind, Alexander, 156, 226n79

fascist Italy, 14, 25n35
father of the nation, 25n38, 31–33,
40–41, 45n65, 96, 188, 244
Filitov, Alexei M., 129n67, 131n87,
159, 227n91
five-year economic plan (five-year
plan), 132n112, 157, 181, 210,
237n298
Free German Trade Union, 159, 186,
228n121
Freie Deutsche Jugend (Union of
Free German Youth, FDJ), 10,
55, 72n121, 144–145, 149, 158,
171–78, 219, 223n16, 228nn121–27,
228n130, 254, 281, 284, 303n120
Freies Deutschland (German National
Committee), 91
Friedrich, Carl J., 13

Gelfand, Vladimir, 75, 128n27
German Communist Party, 103, 113–14,
142, 185
German fighters for peace, 111, 172,
178, 194
German question (debate pertaining to
the division of Germany), 50, 88–89,
129n67, 185, 289
German-Soviet friendship, 6, 17–18,
81–82, 91, 107, 111, 148–49, 165–
67, 169, 175, 181 186, 206, 229n142,
252, 264n47, 293, 308, 314
German-Soviet Friendship Society,
10, 57, 107, 134n162, 144–45, 147,

163, 168–69, 179, 200, 203, 223n2, 224n20, 228n121, 243, 281, 287

Glavlit (the USSR's General Directorate of Literature and Publishing), 143, 223n10

Goebbels, Joseph, 1, 23n1, 52, 251

Gorky, Maxim, 99, 143

Görlitz, 241–42, 254, 262n1, 263n6, 266n74

Gozman, Leonid, 156, 226n79

Gregor, Kurt, 217

Grigor'ian, V. G., 146, 174

Grotewohl, Otto, 85–87, 94–114, 129n57, 130n82, 132n111, 155–59, 179, 212–17, 226n72, 226n81, 227n90, 233nn237–38, 237n317, 241, 252, 256, 278, 283–84, 296

Hager, Kurt, 63, 72n107, 130n82, 273–74, 299n16

Hennecke, Adolf, 252, 266n63

Hermlin, Stephan, 201, 234n253

Herzfeld, Michael, 33, 43n17

Hitler, Adolf, 3, 6, 14, 25n35, 26n64, 44n35, 45–46n77, 62, 68n35, 71n85, 77–91, 104–22, 128nn26–36, 128n43, 130nn78–81, 133n141, 134n164, 150, 154, 156, 162–69, 175, 197, 208–9, 222, 246, 251–52, 258–62, 263n28, 275, 280, 282, 288, 295, 311, 316n9

Ho Chi Minh, 14, 25n37, 37, 44n46

Honecker, Erich, 130n82, 172–78

House of German-Soviet Friendship, 55, 144, 158, 159

Hungarian and Polish uprisings of 1956, 286, 287, 298, 303n113

Hunt, Lynn, 31, 43n8

iconoclasm, 44n27, 60, 121, 241–61, 283, 297, 309–11, 316n5

identity, 7, 12, 19, 24n28, 30, 42, 50, 60, 86, 164, 176, 180–81, 192–94, 211, 219–21, 258–60, 273–78, 292, 310–14

Iron Curtain, 15, 23n4, 66n10, 89, 238n326

Jewish-Bolshevik threat, 1, 3, 73, 162, 307

June 17, 1953 uprising (East German uprising), 189, 203, 241–42, 248, 253, 255–57, 262n1, 264n46, 266nn67–78, 267nn80–90, 270, 286–87, 295, 310

Just, Artur W., 150

Kampfgruppe gegen Unmenschlichkeit (Fighting Group against Inhumanity), 244

Karetnikov, A. E., 265n53, 292, 304n130

Karlshorst, 57, 67n24, 102, 114

Kellermann, Bernhard, 162

Khrushchev, Nikita S., 11, 15, 30, 204, 225n51, 235–36nn272–73, 238n325, 269–73, 279–89, 296–97, 298nn1–6, 299nn9–17, 300n48, 301n50, 302n92, 303n116, 303nn122–23, 304n140

Knorr, Erich, 307–8

Koenen, Wilhelm, 27n72, 189

Kolesnichenko, Ivan S., 53, 68n39, 68n42, 69n69

Kommunistische Partei Deutschlands (KPD), 8, 23n9, 57, 94, 103, 120, 150, 185, 191, 193, 228n111, 270–71, 275, 278–79

Kruzhkov, Vladimir S., 142

Kuczynski, Jürgen, 52, 142

Leipzig, 64, 99–101, 106, 113, 144, 149, 165–66, 172, 192–93, 196, 200, 202, 207, 242, 248, 254, 260–61, 267n98, 278, 283, 288, 290, 293, 300nn40–41, 303nn108–9, 304n134

Leipzig Fair (Leipzig Trade Fair), 106, 124, 152, 210

Lenin [Ul'ianov], Vladimir Il'ich, 14, 16, 25n35, 26n57, 37, 44n26, 44n46,

81–82, 94–95, 98–100, 102, 107,
    113, 130n78, 132n120, 141, 143,
    148–49, 153, 168, 172–73, 181,
    183, 191–94, 202, 224n34, 234n254,
    235n265, 238n332, 241, 262, 271,
    275, 277, 281, 283–85, 293–96, 298,
    304nn125–26, 304nn133–35, 311
Leonhard, Wolfgang, 93, 128n38,
    131n86, 131nn88–89, 132n117,
    133n144
Liberal Democratic Party (LDP),
    109
Liebknecht, Karl, 94–95, 108, 191, 244,
    293, 304n126, 304n132
Lüdtke, Alf, 24nn30–31, 27n81
Luxemburg, Rosa, 95, 108, 191, 293,
    304n131

Magnitogorsk, 215
Malenkov, Georgii M., 225n51,
    235n267, 235n272, 304n128
Mao Zedong, 14, 24n23, 25n37, 36–37,
    40, 43n23, 44n35, 44n39, 44n46,
    45n51, 45n61, 45n69, 235n265, 248,
    316n9
Marshall, George, 192
Marshall Plan, 61
Martem"ianov, K. V., 99, 265n53,
    267–68n100
Marx-Engels-Lenin-Institute (Marx-
    Engels-Lenin-Stalin-Institute,
    Institute of Marxism-Leninism),
    142, 145–46, 224n34, 291, 292, 296,
    304n125
Marxism-Leninism, 48, 59, 91–95, 101,
    103, 107–8, 130n78, 132n121, 142,
    148, 167, 169, 171, 173, 185, 189,
    194, 199–200, 208, 219–20, 241–42,
    262, 272, 275, 279, 281, 291–96,
    303n125
Matern, Hermann, 130n82, 195
Mauss, Marcel, 39, 45n56, 231n192
Mayakovsky, Vladimir V., 99
May First demonstration (May First
    celebrations), 106, 110, 134n159,

193, 242, 247, 258, 264n30, 267n99,
    290
Mecklenburg, 54–56, 58, 67n24,
    229n144, 229n147
memory, 6, 10, 12, 18, 21, 24n24,
    25n45, 36, 37, 40, 48, 73, 75, 82, 98–
    99, 106, 114, 127n14, 136–37n222,
    154, 156, 169, 190–91, 197, 199,
    203, 244, 247, 261, 283, 293–94,
    296, 303n118, 315
MGB (Soviet Ministry of State
    Security), 62, 64, 133n138, 179
MID (Soviet Ministry of Foreign
    Affairs), 10, 144
MK (Mezhdunarodnaia Kniga, the
    Soviet state book-distribution
    organization), 144
modernity, 14, 30, 40, 45n75, 49, 85,
    208, 216, 222, 308
Molotov, Vyacheslav M., 86–87, 122,
    123, 225n51, 231n177, 235n267,
    260–61
Mussolini, Benito, 14, 36, 44n24, 150

Napoleon III, 35
Nazi Germany, 14, 30, 74, 162, 170, 308
Neues Deutschland (newspaper), 2,
    23n3, 63, 66n4, 72n107, 85, 156,
    198, 220, 224n33, 225n58, 226n66,
    226n73, 226n75, 226n80, 229n142,
    229nn145–46, 229n148, 230n151,
    230n155, 230nn166–67, 230n170,
    231n195, 231n198, 231n201,
    232n217, 232n231, 233n240,
    233n46, 234nn251–52, 234nn254–
    55, 234nn259–60, 235n268,
    237n209, 237–38n218, 238n324,
    238nn332–33, 264n42, 269, 285,
    294, 298n3, 299n10, 304n133,
    305n144
Neumann, Heinz, 150, 225nn48–50
Nevsky, Alexander, 40, 127n24
NKVD (People's Commissariat for
    Internal Affairs), 57, 61, 62–64, 69–
    70n70, 71n95, 104, 122, 133n138

NSDAP (National Socialist German Workers' Party), 23n1, 60, 99, 116, 117, 156, 163–64, 261, 313
Nuremberg Trials, 163, 260

October Revolution, 94, 99, 107, 110, 118, 157, 181, 190, 226n83, 248, 284, 293–94
Oelßner, Fred, 98, 100, 132n11, 146, 224n33, 233n237, 274, 295
OVP (Otdel vneshnei politiki, the Soviet Central Committee's Department of Foreign Policy), 142

"people's community"/"national community" (*Volksgemeinschaft*), 73, 78, 104, 105, 129n44, 133nn141–42, 162, 166, 253
personality cult, 7, 11–12, 14, 17–19, 21–22, 24n14, 24n17, 24n33, 30–31, 36, 38, 41, 43nn5–6, 48, 95, 101–103, 106, 108, 110–13, 145, 149, 150, 154, 161–62, 188–89, 192, 203, 241–246, 248, 249, 251–52, 254–55, 257, 261, 270–72, 274–75, 277, 279–80, 283–84, 291, 292–94, 295–96, 300–301n49, 309–10, 315, 316n9
Petrov, Nikita, 23n4, 64, 68n42, 69–70n70, 70n81, 71n95, 71nn100–103, 72n109, 72nn115–16, 72n121, 133n138, 227n103
Pieck, Wilhelm, 81, 91–92, 59–96, 97–99, 114, 130n80, 131n101, 132n106, 132nn110–12, 149, 172–79, 186, 188–89, 229n142, 230n151, 231n185, 233nn237–38, 241, 244–45, 248, 249, 251–52, 255–56, 278, 283–84, 296
Pilsudski, Jozef, 27n85, 40, 45n49, 227n96
Plamper, Jan, 16, 18, 24n14, 25n35, 26n53, 26n62, 26n64, 30, 43n6, 44n33, 45n75, 65n3, 66n8, 66n16, 70n74, 71n85, 134n164, 226n68, 316n9

Plekhanov, Georgii, 24n14, 29–30, 43n1, 150
Polkehn, Hugo, 149
Ponomarev, Boris N., 16, 68n39, 301n50
popular justice, 243, 252
Pospelov, Petr N., 94, 98
Potsdam Conference in 1945/Potsdam Agreement, 49, 51, 71, 78, 88, 120–23, 152, 203, 254, 267n93, 279, 291
Pravda (official newspaper of the Communist Party of the Soviet Union), 71n88, 84, 89, 98, 128n37, 157, 225n40, 226n71, 231n184, 279, 300n48
prisoners of war (POWs), 54, 72, 118, 122, 127n23, 130n78, 170, 228n114, 260, 262, 288, 313
Prokofiev, Sergei S., 100
propaganda, 1–10, 16–18, 22, 23n2, 26n68, 27n90, 48–57, 61–65, 67n28, 67n30, 67n33, 70n81, 73–75, 80, 84, 86–88, 90–91, 95, 100–101, 108–17, 122, 125–26, 129n44, 141–62, 168–88, 198–222, 223n10, 225n55, 234n254, 236n294, 244–62, 263n26, 266n56, 266,58, 266n63, 267n93, 268n117, 272, 278–96, 299n16, 300nn40–41, 302nn96–100, 303nn104–105, 307–14
public symbolism, 6–7, 18, 21–22, 41, 105, 108, 248, 254, 258, 290, 292, 298, 310, 313
purges, 74, 96, 103, 131n102, 143, 167, 277, 282

Rákosi, Mátyás, 41, 193, 300–301n49
Red Army, 3, 16, 50–51, 54, 59, 62, 74–82, 86, 91, 99, 104–5, 116–21, 123, 126, 127nn10–11, 127n22, 128n34, 136–37n222, 166–68, 197, 254–55, 260
Reddy, William, 155, 226n70
revolution, 1, 24n26, 25n41, 27n71, 34, 36, 40, 41, 45n70, 48–49, 73, 94,

117, 128n38, 131n86, 131nn88–89,
132n117, 133n144, 142, 150–51,
187, 190, 227n106, 228n109, 247,
280, 284, 291, 293–94, 304n136,
316n5
RIAS (Rundfunk im amerikanischen
Sektor, Radio in the American
Sector), 65, 208, 285, 287
rituals of violence, 241, 243, 246, 249,
254–57
Russkikh, A. G., 69n63, 141, 143,
222n1, 223n2, 265n50

Sabrow, Martin, 24n29, 67n25,
239nn336–37, 277, 300n37, 316n6
Saxony, 61, 67n24, 99, 107, 111, 114,
121, 134n162, 138n249, 159, 165,
179, 194–97, 252, 263n25, 264n29,
265nn49–50, 265n52, 268n108,
268n114
Saxony-Anhalt, 67n24, 116, 178,
229n144, 268n109, 268n115
Scribner, Robert, 255, 263nn7–8,
263n11, 264n36, 267n87
Secret Speech, 11, 15, 30, 269, 271,
274, 279, 299n9, 299n17
Seghers, Anna, 183
Selbstmann, Fritz, 216
Semenov, Vladimir, 99
Serov, Ivan Aleksandrovich, 62
Shelepin, Aleksandr N., 293
Shostakovich, Dmitrii, 100
SKK (Soviet Control Commission), 57,
199
Sobottka, Gustav, 93
Soviet Military Administration in
Germany (SMAD/SVAG), 8–10, 51–
52, 53–56, 57–62, 64, 67nn23–24,
67nn31–33, 68nn36–37, 68nn41–42,
68nn44–45, 68n48, 69nn53–55,
69n57, 69nn61–63, 69–70nn70–71,
70n81, 71n90, 71n95, 82–82, 84,
86, 88–89, 94–95, 98–100, 103,
106, 108–110, 113–14, 116–17,
120, 121, 125–26, 128nn40–41,

129nn62–66, 130n75, 131nn92–94,
131n96, 131–32n104, 132n111,
133n130, 134n159, 134n169,
134n171, 135n191, 135n194,
136n202, 136n220, 138n251, 141,
143,146, 148–49, 154, 162, 172,
175, 222–23nn1–4, 223n6, 223n10,
225n43, 227n103, 231n185, 249,
255, 259–61, 264n31, 264n33,
264n40, 265n50, 268n104, 268n107,
268nn111–12
Soviet Occupation Zone (SBZ), 3, 5,
17, 22, 23n9, 51, 67n23, 69n67,
73, 78, 94, 115, 134n173, 141,
153, 228n114, 232n210, 268n106,
268n117
Soviet Union, 1–2, 25n35, 30, 33, 37,
40, 43n18, 47–55, 58–64, 66n8,
69n53, 72n113, 77, 80–82, 84–87,
90–100, 102, 104, 107–8, 122,
127n24, 128n37, 130n71, 130nn78–
81, 141–56, 161–85, 189, 197–212,
223n2, 227nn88–89, 241–42, 258–
59, 269–87, 294, 298n3, 307–8, 311,
314, 316, 316n1, 316n3, 316n11
Sovinformbiuro (Soviet Information
Bureau), 143
Sozialdemokratische Partei
Deutschlands (German Social
Democratic Party, SPD), 9–10,
23n9, 68n47, 69n58, 69nn64–65,
71nn85–86, 71n91, 71n95, 71n98,
72n105, 72n108, 72nn111–12,
72n117, 94, 120, 134n160, 135n181,
135n189, 135n195, 136n198,
136n211, 138n253, 186, 225n46,
228n128, 230nn158–59, 232n208,
238n334, 241, 245–46, 251, 262n1,
262n4, 263n6, 263n13, 263nn16–
17, 263nn21–22, 263nn27–28,
264n32, 264n35, 264n37, 264n39,
264n48, 266n57 266nn61–63,
266n67, 266n72, 266n80, 267n86,
267nn88–89, 268n115, 278, 285,
289, 301nn65–66, 302n81, 302n94,

302n102, 303nn108–111, 303n118,
303n124, 304n127, 305n151, 316n12
Sozialistische Einheitspartei
Deutschland (Socialist Unity
Party, SED), 2, 6–11, 57–58,
60–65, 72n117, 72n121, 80–85,
91–115, 131n91, 131n102, 132n106,
132nn111–12, 141–80, 185–204,
209–22, 224n31, 224n34, 225n56,
225n58, 228n123, 231n190,
233n235, 234n254, 235n267,
236n275, 237n298, 238n321,
239n333, 241–55, 259–61, 265n50,
267n95, 269–98, 299n9, 299n13,
299nn22–23, 300–301n49, 302n104,
303nn104–106, 303n120, 304n130,
304n134, 305n144, 305n147,
305nn152–53, 311–12
SPD's Eastern Bureau, 9–10, 23n9, 186,
245–46, 251, 285, 289
Stalinallee, 115, 155, 171, 189–90, 200,
208–15, 220–22, 237n300, 237n302,
237n305, 237n311, 237n313,
237nn316–17, 237–38n218,
238n323, 238n329, 250, 283, 290
Stalingrad, 1, 87, 116, 169, 186, 197,
228n114, 229n131
Stalin Note, 158–59
Stalinstadt, 156, 208–9, 215–22,
237n302,237n305, 237n311,
238n321, 328n323, 238n329, 279,
283
Stasi (East German Ministry of State
Security), 10, 63–64, 72n110, 110,
206, 245, 254, 275–76, 283, 288,
297
Stassen, Harold, 61
subjectivity, 19, 31, 162–63
Suslov, Mikhail A., 69n63, 94, 97, 102,
131nn92–94, 132n111, 142, 146,
193, 223n2, 223n7

Tägliche Rundschau (newspaper),
54–55, 84, 88, 108, 129n61, 224n34,
231n194, 232n215, 232n218, 261

TASS (Telegraph Agency of the Soviet
Union), 52, 55
Tchaikovsky, Pyotr I., 100
Thälmann, Ernst, 26n63, 44n25,
82–83, 94–95, 108–9, 116, 129n53,
134n158, 134n165, 232n216,
235nn269–70, 237n306, 247, 251,
290, 293
Third Reich, 2, 6–8, 22, 73, 78, 80,
90–92, 103–6, 117, 128n36, 157,
162–72, 211, 222, 258–62, 264n31,
275, 282, 310–14
Thüringer Volkszeitung (newspaper),
251
Thuringia, 53, 67n24, 121, 188, 247,
264nn46–47, 265n51, 267n93
Tito, Josip Broz, 36–38, 43n20, 43n22,
44n35, 44n38, 44n40, 45n51
Tiul'panov, Sergei I., 52–57, 68n48,
69n57, 69n61, 71n90, 95–96,
129n66, 130n75, 131nn92–94,
134n171, 138n251, 223n4
totalitarianism/totalitarian, 9, 13–14, 17,
24nn24–25, 24n32, 24n34, 30–31,
41, 45–46n77, 50, 156, 161, 209,
227n102, 259, 263n20
Truman, Harry, 77, 88, 192

Ulbricht, Walter, 26n63, 85, 93, 97,
102, 108, 113, 129n59, 130n82,
131n103, 143, 156, 171, 178–79,
184, 189, 198, 213, 217, 228n124,
233nn237–38, 241, 244, 248, 252,
256, 263n17, 264n39, 269–73,
277–89, 295–96, 298n3, 299n13,
300nn27–28, 300nn34–35, 300nn39–
44, 300n48, 300–301n49, 301n50,
301nn54–55, 301nn58–60, 301nn63–
64, 301nn70–71, 301n73, 302n85,
302nn95–99, 302nn102, 303n113,
303n119, 305nn144–45

VKP(b) (All-Union Communist Party of
Bolsheviks), 52–53, 67n32, 68n39,
69n63, 94–102, 116, 131nn92–96,

131–32n104, 132n111, 134n169,
143–45, 154, 174, 178–79, 189,
223n2, 223n6, 223n10, 224n34,
231n185, 265n50
VOKS (All-Union Society for Cultural
Relations with Foreign Countries), 9,
52, 67n34, 102, 129n63, 129nn65–
66, 133n130, 142–44, 152, 187,
223n4, 223n6, 224n20, 224n22

Wandel, Paul, 148, 273–74
Weber, Max, 30
Werewolf organization, 62

World War II/Second World War, 2, 5, 7,
15–16, 40, 62, 84, 86, 103, 107, 160,
183, 229n131, 255, 258, 280, 288
World Youth and Student Games, 111,
176–77, 250

Zemon Davis, Natalie, 253–54
Zetkin, Clara, 108, 292–93, 304nn126–
29
Zhdanov, Andrei A., 96, 206
Zhukov, Georgy K., 48, 51, 62, 68n36,
109, 116

About the Author

Alexey Tikhomirov is assistant professor of East European history at Bielefeld University in Germany.